DIVINATION AND INTERPRETATION OF SIGNS IN THE ANCIENT WORLD

DIVINATION AND INTERPRETATION OF SIGNS IN THE ANCIENT WORLD

edited by

AMAR ANNUS

with contributions by

Amar Annus, Francesca Rochberg, James Allen, Ulla Susanne Koch, Edward L. Shaughnessy, Niek Veldhuis, Eckart Frahm, Scott B. Noegel, Nils Heeßel, Abraham Winitzer, Barbara Böck, Seth Richardson, Cynthia Jean, JoAnn Scurlock, John Jacobs, and Martti Nissinen

THE ORIENTAL INSTITUTE OF THE UNIVERSITY OF CHICAGO
ORIENTAL INSTITUTE SEMINARS • NUMBER 6
CHICAGO • ILLINOIS

Library of Congress Control Number: 2009943156
ISBN-13: 978-1-885923-68-4
ISBN-10: 1-885923-68-6
ISSN: 1559-2944

The Oriental Institute, Chicago

THE UNIVERSITY OF CHICAGO

ORIENTAL INSTITUTE SEMINARS • NUMBER 6

Series Editors

Leslie Schramer

and

Thomas G. Urban

with the assistance of

Felicia Whitcomb

Publication of this volume was made possible through generous funding from the Arthur and Lee Herbst Research and Education Fund

Cover Illustration: Bronze model of a sheep's liver indicating the seats of the deities. From Decima di Gossolengo, Piacenza. Etruscan, late 2nd–early 1st c. B.C. Photo credit: Scala / Art Resource, NY

Printed by Edwards Brothers, Ann Arbor, Michigan

The paper used in this publication meets the minimum requirements of American National Standard for Information Services — Permanence of Paper for Printed Library Materials, ANSI Z39.48-1984.

TABLE OF CONTENTS

PREFACE

This book makes available the revised versions of the papers read at the fifth annual University of Chicago Oriental Institute Seminar *Science and Superstition: Interpretation of Signs in the Ancient World*, which took place at March 6–7, 2009. The printed volume has a slightly different title, and it includes two papers from scholars who were invited to the seminar, but could not come — from Barbara Böck and Niek Veldhuis, while two participants, Clifford Ando and Ann Guinan, have decided to publish their papers elsewhere. I remain thankful to all the contributors for a very smooth and efficient collaboration that gave birth to this sizable volume.

I am grateful to Gil Stein, who initiated this remarkable post-doctoral symposium program, and to the Oriental Institute for giving me the opportunity to organize this event, so making one of my dreams a reality. I would like to extend my warmest thanks to Mariana Perlinac, Kaye Oberhausen, and Christopher Woods for all that they have done to help me organize this event. I also thank Thomas Urban and Leslie Schramer for their help with the printing and editing of this book. I am also thankful to Cathy Dueñas for her help in everyday matters.

Finally, I should mention my family — my wife Merili, and children Kaspar and Kreeta, who patiently shared half of my time here in Chicago. I am happy that they were willing to come with me to a far-away city, where Kaspar could satisfy his ever-increasing curiosity, and where Kreeta literally made her first steps in life.

Amar Annus

Seminar participants, from left to right: Front row: John Jacobs, Amar Annus, JoAnn Scurlock, Ulla Koch, Martti Nissinen, Ann Guinan, Francesca Rochberg, James Allen. Back row: Edward Shaughnessy, Nils Heeßel, Eckart Frahm, Seth Richardson, Scott Noegel, Clifford Ando, Abraham Winitzer, Robert Biggs. Photo by Kaye Oberhausen

1
ON THE BEGINNINGS AND CONTINUITIES OF OMEN SCIENCES IN THE ANCIENT WORLD

AMAR ANNUS, UNIVERSITY OF CHICAGO

INTRODUCTION

The study of signs, portents observed in the physical and social worlds indicating the will of supernatural agents and the course of future events, was undoubtedly important in all ancient cultures. The first written evidence for a concept of sign, however, comes from cuneiform texts of ancient Mesopotamia. The study of signs from gods was vitally important for ancient Mesopotamians throughout their history. The first references to diviners and divination are already found in the written sources of the third millennium B.C., which indicate a number of professional titles (see Falkenstein 1966). Among the early examples of celestial divination one can point to the cylinders of King Gudea, who needed an auspicious sign (ĝiškim in Sumerian) from his divine master Ningirsu, confirming his consent for building a new temple in Lagaš. This evidence from the twenty-second century B.C. is the earliest that clearly attests to the idea of signs in heaven and that omens conveyed divine decisions (Rochberg 2006: 337–38, 346–47). Subsequently, consulting the will of the gods is a well-attested practice in ancient Mesopotamia, accompanying every significant political or private action or undertaking.

The omen lore of the third millennium B.C. must have been of oral nature, because texts recording omens do not appear in Mesopotamia until more than a millennium after the invention of writing.[1] The first written samples of omen collections using the list format are attested in the texts from the Old Babylonian period onward. According to N. Veldhuis, the list as a traditional text type in Mesopotamia was put to a much wider use in that period than previously. Word lists had existed from the very beginning of cuneiform writing, but in the Old Babylonian period

> ... an entirely new set of lexical texts was invented and put to use in the scribal schools.... Lists are used to explain writing, Sumerian vocabulary, grammar, and mathematics. List-like texts are used to record laws, medicine, and omens. The list becomes the privileged format for recording knowledge. The list-like format of the omen compendium, therefore, indicated that this is scholarly knowledge. It connects to the conventional format of a knowledge text, a format that was expanded and explored in particular in the Old Babylonian period (Veldhuis 2006: 493–94).

By establishing the format of knowledge text, the systematic omen recording into lists could begin. Under long processes of adding and editing, these collections grew into

[1] For a discussion of this situation in regard to liver divination, see Richardson, this volume.

compendia of ominous phenomena, where segments of original observations were expanded into very comprehensive omen series, found in the archives and libraries of first-millennium B.C. Mesopotamia (see Maul 2003). These omen compendia were given both practical and theoretical value, which explains comprehensiveness of the phenomena recorded in the collections, as practically everything observable in the universe could have an ominous import to mortals.[2] The holistic worldview of the ancient Mesopotamians assigned a firm place to every object and event in the universe according to divine will. Thus the incipit of the celestial omen series *Enūma Anu Enlil* suggests that the gods Anu, Enlil, and Ea themselves designed the constellations and measured the year in primeval times, thereby establishing the heavenly signs. Accordingly, Mesopotamian divination was an all-embracing semantic system designed to interpret the whole universe.[3] The belief that the entire universe is causally connected is an Ionian Greek invention (Scurlock 2003: 397), but a forerunner of it is already found in the Babylonian Diviner's Manual (ll. 38–42):

> The signs on earth just as those in the sky give us signals. Sky and earth both produce portents though appearing separately. They are not separate (because) sky and earth are related. A sign that portends evil in the sky is (also) evil in the earth, one that portends evil on earth is evil in the sky (Oppenheim 1974: 204).

As the divinatory texts testify, not all omens occurring in the cuneiform series were observed in the real world, because many examples describe phenomena that are impossible and could never occur.[4] This indicates that simple observation and recording was complemented by theorization and systematization. The original practical purpose of omen collections was later expanded, and even superseded, by theoretical aspirations (Oppenheim 1964: 212). When every single phenomenon in the world could be considered as a possible object for recording in the spirit of examination and divinatory deduction, one can see in this attitude an early example of the encyclopaedic curiosity, which is the basis for all scientific endeavor (Bottéro 1992: 127). Once an element of ominous import was uncovered, Mesopotamian scholars were able to record it extensively in hypothetically varying circumstances, sometimes creating attenuated and increasingly arcane sequences (Guinan 2002: 19). The format of the knowledge text endorses speculation in its own right, which comfortably steps over the boundary of the observable.[5]

The worldview represented by the omen series is not irrevocable determinism, in the sense that every event is causally determined by an unbroken chain of prior occurrences. The

---

[2] The standardized omen compendia cover, in J. Bottéro's words, "almost the entire material universe: stars and meteorites; the weather and the calendar; the configuration of the earth, of waterways, and of inhabited areas; the outlook of inanimate and vegetal elements; the birth and the conformation of animals and their behaviour, especially of man himself — his physical aspects, his behaviour, his conscious and sleeping life, and so on. In addition to these phenomena which present themselves to observation, a number of others were latent and had to be revealed, such as the internal anatomy of sacrificed animals. Or they could be virtual and needed to be provoked, such as the shape taken by oil or flour thrown in water" (Bottéro 1992: 127).

[3] Koch-Westenholz 1995: 13–19; see also Winitzer, this volume.

[4] See Brown 2000: 109; and Rochberg, this volume.

[5] As N. Veldhuis points out, "... the speculative or scholarly side of divination is a context and use of its own, with its own relevance.... Speculation does not stop at the border of the possible; the systematic character of compendia actually encourages crossing this border, exploring the observed, the likely, the unlikely, and the impossible on an equal footing" (Veldhuis 2006: 494).

omens revealed a conditional future, best described as a judicial decision of the gods, who gave "a verdict against the interested parties on the basis of the elements in the omen, just as each sentence by a tribunal established the future of the guilty person based upon the dossier submitted to its judgement" (Bottéro 1992: 142). It is best described as an assembly of gods making decisions concerning the course of world's affairs and the fate of human beings. In the Mesopotamian system of sign interpretation, the portent which predicted, for example, the king's death, was not the cause of the king's death, but only the sign for it. The prediction was considered solely a warning that could be diverted by ritual measures provided by the series *Namburbi*.[6] The heart and core of these release rituals is an appeal from the part of the person affected by an evil omen to the divine judicial court, in order to effect a revision of the individual's fate, announced by a sinister omen (Maul 1999: 124–26). The metaphor of the court of law promotes the presentation of the omen as a communicative sign sent by an angry god whom the ritual serves to appease (Koch, this volume). The Mesopotamian omen texts had diverse origins, and among several of their functions was to represent the god-given "laws" of divination (Fincke 2006–2007).

It seems reasonable to insist that for ancient Mesopotamian societies the omens recorded in compendia enjoyed the status of the "laws" of the divine world order. As a consequence, the process of interpretation of a sign was understood as a performative act that empowered the interpreter, while simultaneously promoting the cosmological system upon which mantic exegesis was based (Noegel, this volume). The unique window into how everyday divination worked in a framework of royal power is provided by numerous letters and reports sent by the Neo-Assyrian scholars to the kings Esarhaddon and Assurbanipal. The omens and other lore of the Mesopotamian scholars represented divine wisdom that ideologically originated in primeval times of the antediluvian period, but which was being continuously updated and outlined by the scientific methods of the day (Veldhuis, this volume). The omen compendia and their commentaries represented both speculative sciences and the most valuable practical means for predicting what was about to happen.[7] The speculative and practical aspects are also present side-by-side in Mesopotamian law codes, and similar cyclic processes of omen collecting and law collecting may have applied to the creation of both kinds of compendia (see Westbrook 1985).

THE FORM AND USE OF AN OMEN

The sentences in the Mesopotamian knowledge texts or scientific handbooks almost always occur in the specific format of conditionals (see Rochberg, this volume). The first part of a sentence is called a "protasis" in modern scholarship, and is introduced by the indication of an observation or a hypothesis — "if (something happens)." The second part, the "then" clause, is called the "apodosis," which shows the part of the future that can be derived from

[6] For an edition of these texts, see Maul 1994. In addition to *Namburbi*s, some omens derived from human voluntary acts with favorable outcome may also reflect their deliberate use for revoking ill omens, for example, *Šumma ālu* 10.161: "If somebody renovates (the figure) of Gilgamesh, the anger of his god will be re[leased]" (Freedman 1998: 168).

[7] For an analysis of the full support divination enjoyed in the Neo-Assyrian society, that is, political, social, and psychological validation, see Jean, this volume.

the omen, the prognosis, or the prediction. It is the universal form for many Mesopotamian scientific treatises, where concrete circumstances are always described as leading to a specific outcome. Like Mesopotamian law codes and medical treatises, Babylonian omen texts never outline the principles behind the concrete "if ... then" sentences and observations. The nature of principles behind the concrete statements should be reconstructed on the basis of written examples contained in the law codes and omen texts, assumed that these texts reveal only some parts of the oral lore they are based on. The oral background of the ancient Mesopotamian celestial omen literature is emphasized by D. Brown as follows:

> ... not only the categorisation of celestial phenomena, but the establishment of a simple code and a series of rules, which enabled them to be interpreted, had taken place before the writing down of the first celestial omens took place. Some of these *premises* must, to a large extent, be understood to be *given* — or in other words recognised that they derive from an oral background, or are "traditional" (Brown 2000: 112).

When celestial omens first appear in writing, some already demonstrate the effects of their literate production (Brown 2000: 112). The Babylonian omen compendia represent parts of the ancient Mesopotamian worldview and are by no means separated from other genres of literature. Thus, the observation of Anzu's footprints in a house or in a city is an ill omen according to terrestrial omen series *Šumma ālu* 1.155 and 19.38′, reminding us of Anzu's sinister role in the Akkadian Epic of Anzu (Freedman 1998: 38, 278). Also, the city making noise is prone to dispersal, while the quiet city "will go on normally" (*Šumma ālu* 1.8–13), reminding us of the Babylonian Epic of Atrahasis, where the disturbed gods attempt to destroy mankind on account of the noise they make. Accordingly, studies in intertextuality indicate that there is no sea change in terms of content between the omens and other Mesopotamian texts:

> As for subject matter and style, the apodoses of the omen literature are closely linked to literary texts of the late periods that describe the blessings of peace and prosperity or the horrors of war, famine, and rebellion as well as elaborate blessings and curses similar to those found in certain Mesopotamian royal inscriptions and public legal documents (Oppenheim 1964: 211).

There are some historical texts that extensively record omens or ominous happenings — the Chronicle of Early Kings and the Religious Chronicle. The material contained in the first gathers the apodoses of historical omens about the kings Naram-Sin and Sargon. The second chronicle collects bizarre events observed during New Year festivals in Babylon, such as wild animals appearing in the city, statues moving, and astronomical phenomena. This recording of bizarre phenomena, which have some similarity to omens, was a major concern for the author of the Religious Chronicle (Grayson 1975: 37). The content of the Chronicle of Early Kings finds its origin in prognostic literature, as it consists of omen apodoses, while the content of the Religious Chronicle is similar to omen protases. However, the Religious Chronicle does not mention any events which could be construed as results of the protases, and these protases seem not to occur in omen collections. On the other hand, the Chronicle of Early Kings used the so-called historical omens as source material (Grayson 1975: 37, 45). The historical omens often summarize anecdotal stories or legends about kings, and therefore they are of very dubious historical value (see Cooper 1980). A lesson to learn from these historical omens is that certain omens were written down to record legends about eminent historical personages. It finds a parallel in the Hebrew Bible, where certain historical events were presented as highly ominous on a literary level (Scurlock, this volume).

It seems that the "if ... then" scientific format is only a pragmatic characteristic of omen sentences, which does not prescribe any special type of content. One could easily transcribe different types of traditional oral lore and teachings into this handbook format of conditional sentences for its use by the omen interpreters. For example, the tablets pertaining to human behavior in the series of physiognomic omens *Alandimmû* were called by its first modern editor F. Kraus as "ein Sittenkanon in Omenform," a canon of good manners in the form of omens (Kraus 1937). This circumstance indicates that omen compendia occasionally collect and contain some items of oral lore, especially of wisdom literature. The inevitable conclusion is that the material included in the omen texts is of diverse origin, including proverbs, parables, fables, and perhaps also other types of learned folklore. Accordingly, it is of heterogeneous origins, culled from the accumulated oral wisdom, from an "inherited conglomerate" of a community (Böck, this volume).

Fables

Erica Reiner has pointed out that apodoses of some omens "read as if they were the summary or the moral of a story" (1998: 651). Her observation can be complemented because some protases, especially in human behavioral omens, also look like abbreviated stories.[8] In the Babylonian Diviner's Manual there are many incipits of the omen series for which we lack textual evidence in cuneiform texts. Some of the protases give an impression of an underlying fairy tale or a popular story, for example "If bundles of reeds walk about in the countryside," or "If a wildcat opens its mouth and talks like a man," or "If a great beast that has two legs like a bird...," etc. (Oppenheim 1974: 203, lines 11–12, 20). Such omens probably summarize certain popular stories with a pedagogical import belonging to the repertoire of Babylonian wise men, and to the teaching example is given the scientific form of an omen.

Parables and Logia

Reiner also demonstrates that some Babylonian omens remind the hearers of traditional stories, some of which are present in the New Testament. Sometimes an omen apodosis corresponds to a saying that we find in the New Testament logia, like "He who exalts himself will be humbled, and he who humbles himself will be exalted" (Reiner 1998: 652). The introductory statement of the parable of the rich fool (Luke 12:16ff.), who does not know where to store his crops, finds a forerunner in a Babylonian omen. In both instances the rich man needs to find storage place for his harvest, but only the New Testament relates the full story about his death before he could enjoy his riches. Both the canonical and apocryphal gospels contain sayings that are comparable to parts of wisdom recorded in the Mesopotamian omen compendia (see Reiner 1998: 653–54). It is intriguing to compare, for example, the beginning of the first line in the Babylonian compendium *Šumma ālu* "If a city is set on high..." to a logion found in the Gospel of Thomas (no. 32), "A city built on a high mountain and fortified, it cannot fall, nor can it be hidden" (cf. Matthew 5:14). The image of a city situated on a high

[8] For example, the following omen may have been based on a well-known story or a popular "Decameronian" novella: "If a man talks with a woman on a bed and then he rises from the bed and makes manhood (= masturbates?), that man will have happiness and jubilation bestowed upon him; wherever he goes all will be agreeable; he will always achieve goal" (see Guinan 1998: 43).

place was probably used as a metaphor for several thousand years before the gospels, being an image used in wisdom sayings. Moreover, the first omen of the compendium *Šumma ālu*, "If a city is situated on a hill, the inhabitants of that city will be depressed; if a city is situated in a valley, that city will be elevated" is nonsense, because most cities in the ancient Near East were situated on a hill, as N. Veldhuis observes (1999: 170). He continues that "a city on a hill" and "a city in a valley" may well be understood as referring to moral maxims concerning pride and modesty (Veldhuis 1999: 170). When in the parallel passage Matthew 5:14 the teacher says to his disciples: "You are the light of the world. A city on a hill cannot be hidden," the saying follows the same pattern of exalting the humbled ones, which is also on the background of the Babylonian omen.

Proverbs and Counsels

Some omens listed in the compendia may have had a currency as proverbs and may have even their origin in proverbs. The proverbs or similes were traditional tools of ancestral and fatherly instruction in ancient Mesopotamian literature, from the Sumerian Instructions of Shuruppak to the Aramaic Teachings of Ahiqar. Some proverbs tend to relate specific actions to equally specific prognostics, which is a feature common to omen collections, with the difference that the proverbs are characteristically admonitory, rather than casuistic. Thus in the Instructions of Shuruppak, one finds a warning, "Do not curse a ewe, you will give birth to a daughter; do not throw a lump (of clay) into a money chest, you will give birth to a son" (lines 256–57). This example, which does not exhaust the available witness, is to be compared to many omens that bear on the question of the sex of future offspring (Cryer 1994: 192). The omen format is most transparently used by the famous Akkadian literary text known as Advice to a Prince, which lists a number of instances of princely behavior to be approved or censured, like "If the king does not heed justice, his people will become confused, and the country will be destroyed. If he does not heed his magnates, his own days will be shortened." These are statements of instruction, but they sound very much like conditionals used in omens.[9] The Advice to a Prince is a text in which didactic and ominous traditions flow together in the interests of political ideology which borders on forming a concept of natural law, above the demands of which not even the king is elevated (Cryer 1994: 193). More generally, many omens found in the compendia have their more natural origins in everyday common sense, in the instruction of proper behavior and the morals of the day.

Law Stipulations

Many scholars have noted the formal similarity between the casuistic form of omens and the law stipulations in so-called "law codes" of ancient Mesopotamia (Bottéro 1992: 187–94). According to A. Guinan, this similarity is deceptive because in individual laws "we can understand the connection between protasis and the apodosis. We can also deduce the underlying principles that govern the structure of the text" (Guinan 2002: 19), which is not always the case for the omen texts. However, J. Fincke has recently put forward a stronger argument for

---

[9] As Veldhuis observes: "The text differs from the omen collections proper by a few formal features — the sentences do not begin with *šumma* 'if,' even though these 'ifs' must be supplied to make the text intelligible. Advice to a Prince is a literary composition and does not belong to the inner core of the omen compendia. Yet given its contents the omen format is understandable" (Veldhuis 1999: 170).

defining the omens as laws, namely, as "the god-given laws of divination" (Fincke 2006–2007). As is pointed out above, there is some evidence that ancient Mesopotamians considered the future predicted by observed omens like sentences handed down by a divine court, and according to the texts pertaining to the release rituals *Namburbi*, the effects of sinister omens could be temporarily revoked by appealing to a higher divine court.

According to *Namburbis*, the person to whom the evil omen was announced had to placate the anger of the gods that had sent it to him and effect the gods' revision of their decision. By so doing, the person tried to achieve a correction of his fate which the gods had decreed. He or she had to appeal to the Judge of Heaven and Earth, the sun-god Šamaš, who was supposed to revoke the evil judgment against him (Maul 1999: 124–25). The divine triad Šamaš, Ea, and Asalluhi form the assembly for the person whom a sinister omen had threatened. He comes as plaintiff before the gods to implore them to change the evil fate which they had allotted him, a revision of the judgment. The next part of the ritual is a trial in which the affected person as well as his opponent, the omen carrier or its image, appear before the highest divine judge. The ritual before Šamaš had all the elements of a regular earthly trial, where the sun-god plays the part of the judge, whereas the person and the carrier are the two suitors of equal rights. There could be no appeal beyond the decision of this court, no other god could challenge or alter Šamaš's final judgment once it was rendered (Maul 1999: 126). Accordingly, the ancient Mesopotamians reacted to some evil omens as they were unfavorable judgments made by the court of gods, which may be similar to or even taken from the contemporary practice of law (Koch, this volume).

IS THERE A BABYLONIAN THEORY OF SIGNS?

As discussed above, the material gathered into Mesopotamian omen compendia is of heterogeneous origin, and consequently different groups of omens should be interpreted with different methods. Therefore, instead of attempting to discover one singular Babylonian omen theory which unifies all methods of divination, it seems more fruitful to give an account of many. In the following discussion, omens recording traditional wisdom or representing pieces of common sense in the ancient Mesopotamia are left out from consideration.

Mesopotamian scribes never expressed general principles of sign interpretation in abstract terms. Only when individual and groups of omens are contrasted and compared do systematic patterns of positive and negative meaning emerge (Guinan 1998: 40). Much of the learning of the Babylonian divination priest involved technical observational knowledge, such as sectors and zones in heaven, liver, or lung. The Babylonian scholars strove to cover the range of interpretation of the signs observed there by means of systematic permutations in pairs — such as left and right, above and below — or in long rows (Oppenheim 1964: 212). Despite some transparent principles of interpretation that scholars have identified in ancient omen texts, these texts are still often quite obscure. The most difficult problems to solve in the Mesopotamian divination are the theoretic and hermeneutic principles underlying the interpretation of omen texts, namely the kind of thinking or the system of ideas that connects protasis with apodosis. As Oppenheim wrote about a half of century ago:

> Only exceptionally are we able to detect any logical relationship between portent and prediction, although often we find paronomastic associations and secondary computations based on changes in directions of numbers. In many cases, subconscious

> association seems to have been at work, provoked by certain words whose specific connotations imparted to them a favorable or an unfavorable character, which in turn determined the general nature of the prediction (Oppenheim 1964: 211).

In various branches of Mesopotamian divination, some more or less universal principles apply that can easily be outlined. In general, the right side or part in Mesopotamian omen theory was considered to be related to good omens, and the left side to negative ones. Signs were divided into good, bad, and neutral. In some branches of divination, like Babylonian extispicy, signs were classified according to their intensity into stronger and weaker. Thus, a strong sign in the right side of the sacrificial animal was a favorable omen, but the same sign in the left side was unfavorable. The opposition of light and dark was also meaningful: a light color of the ominous organ conveyed favorable significance and dark color an unfavorable one. Dark color was essentially connected with the left side, and a light hue with the right side of the sacrificial animal's parts under examination. These principles were universally applied (Starr 1983: 18–19).

It is striking, however, how often — for example, in the physiognomic omen series *Alandimmû* — the right side is ill-omened and the left side favorable, and cases also exist where both sides are equally good or bad. Why is the usual pattern reversed? J. Scurlock suggests:

> ... there are in fact four types of signs, those that are good (and therefore good on either side, although usually somewhat less good on the left), those that are bad (and therefore bad on either side, although usually somewhat less bad on the right), those that are neutral (and become good only when placed on the right, and bad only when placed on the left), and those that are bad but not irreversibly so (that is, they are bad when placed on the right, but are transformed into good when placed on the left) (Scurlock 2003: 398).

The opposition of "right" and "left" is observed differently in omen texts and in scientific handbooks. In the scientific compendia, the signs are observed from the observer's point of view. In the physiognomic omen text *Alandimmû*, the "right" and "left" of the body of the observed human being is measured from the client's point of view, but in the diagnostic series *Sakikku* signs are influenced in a good or bad direction from the physician's, not the patient's, point of view:

> It follows that neutral signs are good on the observer's left (which would be observed's right) and bad on the observer's right, which would be the observed's left — apparently an inverted pattern but actually normal for *Alamdimmu*. Conversely, signs that are bad but not irreversibly so are good on the observer's right (which would be the observed's left) and bad on the observer's left (which would be the observed's right), apparently a normal pattern but actually inverted for *Alamdimmu*. It follows that the picture of the ideal woman should be modified to include only signs that are good on both sides, since ... all other signs are either bad (i.e., undesirable) or neutral (Scurlock 2003: 398).

Thus even the notions of "right" and "left" are not without difficulties and complexities in the knowledge texts. Ambivalences of reading the signs differently in different lights and contexts are deliberately used by the Babylonian diviners (Heeßel, this volume). This also applies to the medium of writing, because most of the cuneiform signs are polyphonous, and a different reading of the sign used in protasis could provide its interpretation in apodosis, thus creates a meaningful protasis-apodosis string (Frahm, this volume). The hermeneutical method of giving speculative Akkadian values to Sumerian logograms is well attested in Babylonian philology, most notably in the last two tablets of the Babylonian Creation Epic (Bottéro 1992: 87–102).

Puns and wordplays also played a role in omen interpretation. Thus the Assyrian Dream-Book says: "If a man dreams that he is eating a raven (*āribu*), he will have income (*irbu*). If a man dreams he is eating human flesh (*šêru*), he will have great riches (*šarû*)." Such wordplays are also used in explaining dreams in the Babylonian Talmud and in the *Oneirocritica* of Artemidorus Daldianus (Noegel 2002. 168–69). Rhyming or juxtaposition of similarly sounding words in oracular couplets was a well-known practice of divination in early China. The verbal methods of divination may easily become linked to poetry, in which an arousal of one poetic image, drawn usually from the animal or botanical world in China, associatively prepares the ground for another image that describes an event in the human world (Shaugnessy, this volume).

DIFFUSION OF BABYLONIAN OMENS IN EAST AND WEST

The diviners of Mesopotamian extispicy and lecanomancy were ideologically descendants of the antediluvian king Enmeduranki, who learned the art directly from the gods Šamaš and Adad at an audience in heaven (Lambert 1998). Biblical scholars generally agree that the religious-historical background of the figure of Enoch, the seventh antediluvian patriarch in Genesis 5:23f. and subsequently the apocalyptic authority in Enochic literature, lies in this seventh Mesopotamian antediluvian king (Collins 1998: 26, 45–46). Enmeduranki's connection with Enoch establishes a continuity of tradition from Mesopotamian divination to Jewish apocalyptic literature, where Enoch occurs as the seer and knower of divine secrets. Even in much later strata of Enochic mysticism, as in the third book of Enoch, traces can be found of the Mesopotamian divinatory traditions (Arbel 2008).

Apart from the figure of Enoch in Jewish literature, the omen branch of cuneiform sciences extensively influenced many other parts of ancient world. There is evidence in Aramaic, Greek, Hittite, Latin, Sanskrit, Sogdian, and in other languages that knowledge of Mesopotamian omen compendia was widespread both in space and time.

THE ARAMAIC WORLD

The Akkadian omen compendia must have been translated into Aramaic quite early, while the former was still a living language, and the Aramaic form gave to these texts much wider circulation. Evidence has been found for Mesopotamian physiognomic and astrological omens in Aramaic from Qumran (Greenfield and Sokoloff 1995), and for celestial omens in the texts of the Cairo Genizah (Greenfield and Sokoloff 1989). Jewish Aramaic parallels have been found to such omen series as *Šumma izbu*, *Šumma ālu*, dream omens, physiognomic omens, and astronomical omens. Rabbinic literature records many omens listed under the rubric *Darkei ha-Emori* "Amorite Practices," where the "Amorite" probably stands for speakers of a more ancient Aramaic. Many Talmudic omens have clearly Mesopotamian origins, such as one regarding a snake: if a snake fell on the bed, it says: "he is poor, but he will end up being rich. If (the woman) is pregnant, she will give birth to a boy. If she is a maiden, she will marry a great man" (Tosefta Shabbat 6, 16). The twenty-second tablet of the series *Šumma ālu* concerns itself with omens derived from snakes in the house, among which are omens in a broken passage which refer to a snake which falls upon a man's bed (Geller 2000: 3–4).

The later form of Aramaic, Syriac, preserved many forms of divinatory texts of Mesopotamian style, and the rich omen literature in Arabic mostly derives from Syrian antecedents. The most complete Syriac source is the Book of Prognostications of al-Hasan ben Bahlul, dating from the twelfth century A.D. (Fahd 1991).[10] There are Arabic manuscripts of *malhama* literature, some of the Ottoman period, which attest to the practice of reading astral and meteorological omens of an ancient Babylonian type. Other types of omens are also represented in Arab divination — from phenomena of animals, of human beings, of birds, the physiognomic and astrological omens. Certain magical practices were in use against unfortunate omens, like Mesopotamian *Namburbi*s (see Fahd 1966: 418–519). It is difficult to say anything for certain on the relationship between the Arab and earlier Mesopotamian omen collections, because the field remains understudied.

Inside the Aramaic world omens were transmitted from one culture to another both by means of written texts and orally. In the secret lore of the Mandaean priests, the tradition of omen interpretation persisted orally until modern times, and only some parts of it were written. Originally Mesopotamian elements may be traced in the Mandaean Book of the Zodiac (*Asfar / Sfar Malwašia*) of Sasanian origins, which is a compilation from various sources of astrological and divinatory content. The major Babylonian sources for the origins of the book are the celestial omen series *Enūma Anu Enlil* and its hemerological companion *Iqqur īpuš*. The last five chapters of the first part of the Mandaean book collect various omens which may be described as meteorological, astral, and at the end, a few "terrestrial" omens similar to those of the Babylonian series *Šumma ālu* (see Rochberg 1999). Not all omens were written in the Mandaean culture, as the priest in Ahwaz, speaking of secret knowledge transmitted from priest to priest, once vaunted to Lady Drower as follows:

> If a raven croaks in a certain *burj* (= astrological house) I understand what it says, also the meaning when the fire crackles or the door creaks. When the sky is cloudy and there are shapes in the sky resembling a mare or a sheep, I can read their significance and message. When the moon is darkened by an eclipse, I understand the portent: when a dust-cloud arises, black, red, or white, I read these signs, and all this according to the hours and the aspects (Drower 1937: 5).

India and Iran

According to D. Pingree, Mesopotamian omen literature was transmitted to India during the two centuries that followed the Achaemenid occupation of Gandhāra in northwestern India and the Indus Valley in the sixth century B.C. (see Pingree 1992: 376). As Pingree has pointed out, the author of the sermon *Brahmajālasutta*, allegedly delivered by Buddha and included in the collection *Dīghanikāya* (I 1.1–3.74) was very familiar with the contents of both Babylonian terrestrial and celestial omen compendia (Pingree 1997: 33). The sermon condemns some wandering diviners, Śramanas and Brāhmanas, who earn their living from the useless knowledge of omens. Almost every type of omen mentioned by the Buddha is found

[10] The best-known Syriac published manuscript containing omens and prognostications is the last part of the famous Syriac Book of Medicines (see Budge 1913).

both in cuneiform literature and in the later Sanskrit texts. The enumeration of the terrestrial omen carriers follows exactly the order of the tablets of the Akkadian compendium *Šumma ālu* — houses, ghosts, snakes, poisons, scorpions, mice, vultures, crows, and quadrupeds (see Pingree 1992). The transmission of Mesopotamian omen texts — both protases and apodoses — to India in the fifth and early fourth centuries B.C. is even clearer, for the contemporary Sanskrit and Prakrit literature is replete with references to and examples of such omens. In this period much of the Mesopotamian omen literature, perhaps from Aramaic versions, was translated into an Indian language, and these translations, though undoubtedly considerably altered to fit with Indian intellectual traditions and with the Indian society which the diviners had to serve, form the basis of the rich Indian literature on terrestrial and celestial omens. The Indian tradition also used pacification rituals comparable to Mesopotamian *Namburbi*, by which the anger of the god who sent the omen is appeased (Pingree 1997: 31–33).

The other examples of the diffusion of Babylonian omens in the East involve some lunar and snake omens that are found in Iranian texts (see Panaino 2005). A Christian Sogdian group of omens concerning calendrical prognostics based on the appearance of natural phenomena such as thunder, earthquakes, rainbows, and eclipses, has its origin in the Babylonian almanac *Iqqur īpuš* (see Sims-Williams 1995).

The Classical World

The traditional knowledge of Mesopotamian divination was transplanted to the classical world by wandering diviners; one such was likely the Chaldaean who visited Plato during his last night alive (Kingsley 1995: 199).[11] The Etruscan discipline of taking omens from liver inspection or hepatoscopy (*haruspicina* in Latin) shows remarkably close correspondence to the same form of divination developed in Mesopotamia. This can best be explained as the transmission of a "school" from Babylon to Etruria. The system of the slaughter of sheep, models of sheep livers of clay or metal, and the custom of providing them with inscriptions for the sake of explanation are peculiar things found precisely along the corridor from the Euphrates via Syria and Cyprus to Etruria. (Burkert 1992: 46–48).

The Etruscan written texts pertaining to hepatoscopy are lost and can be reconstructed only piecemeal from Latin and Greek texts. The internal tradition of the Etruscan discipline goes back to the seventh century, to precisely that period whose glory is reflected in many Near Eastern imports. It seems that hepatoscopy had no place in the older strata of Homeric epic, but it makes its appearance in the final version we have, dating to around 700 B.C. Calchas, Agamemnon's seer, is the best of the "bird-diviners," and by virtue of this art he has "led" the army (*Iliad* 1.69).[12] But a "sacrifice-diviner" (*thyoskoos*) is mentioned in the *Iliad* (24.221) and has a role in the *Odyssey* (21.145; 22.318–23). The observation of the liver remained by far the most predominant divination practice in Greece; from Plato (*Phaedrus* 244c) we learn that hepatoscopy enjoyed greater prestige than bird augury (Burkert 1992: 46–49).

The Mesopotamian divination by "lecanomancy" constituted a special art in Greece, whether in the pouring of oil onto water or the sprinkling of flour onto liquid. The liquids

[11] For the philosophical doctrines of signs in the Classical world, see Allen, this volume.

[12] A Greek inscription from Ephesus, from the sixth century B.C., published in Dittenberger 1924, vol. 3, no. 1167, lists some bird omens in Mesopotamian style, see Lonsdale 1979: 152–53.

were poured out into a dish, called *lekane* in Greek, a word which is cognate with Akkadian *lahannu* and Aramaic *laqnu*. "To pour vinegar and flour into same glass" and to watch their movements is mentioned by Aeschylus in *Agamemnon* 322. Such practices did not become as prominent as liver inspection in Greece (Burkert 1992: 53, 184).

The wandering diviners, sometimes called "Chaldaeans" in the Mediterranean sources, were often responsible for the dissemination of the Mesopotamian wisdom in the late antique world. An interesting question is possible Mesopotamian influence on the Stoic theory of signs given the circumstance observed already by F. Cumont that all first masters of the Stoic school were Orientals (Cumont 1912: 69–71, 81–82). The Stoic philosopher Chrysippus of Soli analyzed the conditional "If someone is born when Canicula (Sirius) is rising, he will not die in the ocean" (Cicero, *De fato* 12). This appears to be related to a record in a Babylonian principal manual of instruction "The place of Cancer: death in the ocean" (*Textes cunéiformes du Louvre* 6 14, obv. 23). This correlation shows that the Babylonian science of birth omens was known in the Greek world by the late third century B.C. Babylonian birth omens were probably known in Greece even long before the Stoic philosophers debated about their validity (Pingree 1997: 23). On birth omens in Cicero's *De divinatione*, see Jacobs, this volume.

Prophecy and Divination

Prophecy and divination are historically related to each other more closely than is generally assumed.[13]Apart from ancient kinds of prophetic literature, the Mesopotamian theology of signs, in which everything in the world can be viewed as a part of divine revelation, is persistent in different Middle Eastern theological schools using in their writings a Semitic idiom. The word for "sign" in Aramaic is *āthā*, in Hebrew *'ōth*, and in Arabic *āya*, all of which are etymologically related to the Akkadian word *ittu* "sign, omen." In Jewish writings of the Second Temple, there are plenty of references to signs and portents, which can be understood only by those skilled in interpreting them. For many theologians, the model interpreter of the divine signs is the apocalyptic authority Enoch, a figure modeled on Mesopotamian Enmeduranki. In Jewish apocalyptic literature, reading the signs of God mostly denotes the ability to predict the course of the world's eschatology. According to the Jewish historian Josephus, the divine or demonic beings reveal their warnings from time to time throughout the course of history. In his *Bellum Judaicum* (6.288–310) he enumerates the omens which preceded the destruction of the second Temple: a stationary comet, an abnormal light, a cow that gave birth to a lamb, a temple gate that opened automatically, chariots and armed men flying through the sky, a peasant who for some years prophesied disaster, etc. In Josephus' thought, the demonic communicated with men through omens, signs, portents, dreams, and prophecy, which are all closely related to one another (Smith 1987: 246).

The reputed theologians of Jewish, Christian, and Muslim traditions gave much higher regard to prophecies because of their alleged origin in monotheistic belief, and disregarded divination as pertaining to polytheistic past. However, Jewish, Eastern Christian, and Muslim traditions still enjoin believers to "ponder" or "reflect" on the natural world and its movements in order to discover the signs of God's omnipotence and appreciate his majesty. In 3 Enoch the terms such as "beholding," "seeing," and "looking" signify the act of discerning inner nature of things, accessing divine secrets about God's cosmic creation and plans (Arbel 2008:

[13] See Nissinen, this volume; and Scurlock, this volume.

310–11). In other texts, the ancient Mesopotamian divinatory traditions were modified by rejecting the practical side of omen divination, its apodoses, and every historical or natural portent became a sign of God's greatness. For the Babylonian priests everything could be read as a sign, and possibly everything becomes a sign of God for a monotheist, to the extent that all verses of the Quran are called by the term *āya*, just like all entries were called *ittu* in the Mesopotamian omen compendia. In the Islamic traditions, the multiplicity of the signs from God is successfully fitted in to tell the stories of Oneness:

> All the outward manifestations, the different forms of revelations, are signs ... the human being can only seize the hem of His favor and try to find the way to Him through His signs.... The plurality of signs is necessary to veil the eternal One who is transcendent and yet "closer than the neck vein" (Sura 50:16); the plurality of signs and the Unicity of the Divine belong together. The signs show the way into His presence, where the believer may finally leave the images behind (Schimmel 1994: xv).

The God in the Quran has some fiery manifestations of power, among his signs are thunderstorms and lightning (Sura 30:24), and thunder gives him praise (Sura 13:13). One finds the similar theology of thunder with Syriac authors, and it ultimately derives from Babylonian theology of Adad, the god of thunder and the giver of oracles and signs (see Annus 2006: 6–12). Often these signs were inscribed into the physical appearance of the world as cuneiform script, where Mesopotamian scholars could read them (see Frahm, this volume). A comparable concept is found in Jewish mysticism, where the creative power of the Hebrew alphabet establishes a connection of all worldly phenomena to certain letters. In the book of 3 Enoch, the letters are even conceived as something inseparable from natural phenomena. The book devotes considerable attention to presenting systematic lists of natural phenomena filled with meanings — terrestrial and celestial or meteorological phenomena, including stars and constellations, lightning and wind, thunder and thunderclaps, snow and hail, hurricanes and tempests (Arbel 2008: 309). When Enoch-Metatron is endowed with divine secrets in heaven, he receives the letters, by which these phenomena were created, which also means knowledge and power over them. The observing of letters implied beholding of the natural phenomena, on which God's secrets are inscribed and codified as signs (Arbel 2008: 309). These secret signs were also written on the heavenly *Pargod*, the curtain that separates God from the rest of heaven and which, like the Mesopotamian Tablet of Destinies, contains the hidden knowledge about divine decisions and plans regarding the course of human history (Arbel 2008: 312–13). Likewise, for Assyrian and Babylonian scholars, cuneiform signs were of divine origin and "capable of conveying, on various levels, completely incontestable eternal truths" (Frahm, this volume).

PROBLEMS OF DEFINITIONS

The Mesopotamian omen literature presents a problem to all who want to define the corpus from the point of view of the history of science and religion. The Mesopotamian omen compendia are highly complex phenomena that escape any precise and simple categorization. It can be said that from our contemporary perspective the Mesopotamian omen literature consists of a blend of observational sciences, common-sense attitudes, and religious beliefs. Even if not all Babylonian theories of signs make sense to a modern mind "etically," it may not be wrong to assume that they certainly did "emically" to the participants of that culture.

The first part of the original title of this seminar, "Science and Superstition," was deliberately chosen as provocative, in order to create some discussions about our inherited cultural biases. Whether a given statement represents a false belief or a scientific truth depends on a concrete epistemological situation, and can be ascertained only by some scientific proof or disproof, which may not be always available. As a modern online dictionary defines it, superstition is "a belief or practice resulting from ignorance" (Webster), and in this sense the term, as historically overloaded with negative connotations, is indeed useless in any serious discussion about ancient science (Rochberg, this volume). The philosophical or intellectual "superiority" of the monotheistic belief over any polytheistic system is often represented in the preconceived worldview of many textbooks as an axiom, thus it is often difficult to discard the popular prejudice that the science began with the Enlightenment.

It may be of interest, however, that the folklorist Alan Dundes has tried to define superstition technically as a folkloric genre. As much as I understand Dundes' effort, it is about defining superstition as a category of *knowledge* in folk religion. Without any regard to the validity of the practices and beliefs involved, Dundes argues, the category of superstition applies to the statements and practices making use of the logical fallacy *post hoc ergo propter hoc* (Dundes 1961: 27). Further, it interests Dundes to define superstitions formally at least to such extent that one would know a superstition when he came across it in folkloristic fieldwork. According to him, the formula — or rather the underlying thinking model — is a naively expressed and literally understood "If A, then B." This model, which is remarkably close to the form of a Babylonian omen, characterizes the sign superstitions for Dundes (Dundes 1961: 30). However, as I argue above, the "if ... then" format neither necessarily represents causality, nor prescribes any particular type of content. The use of conditionals is not the formal hallmark capable of sorting out superstitions from other types of knowledge, not even in folklore. Accordingly, the use of the term "superstitions" for folk beliefs in this restricted sense is not without problems either.

As I outline above, the omens present in the Mesopotamian compendia were collected from sources of heterogeneous origin. The Babylonian omens can therefore not be classified in an "either ... or" manner, for example, as mixes of "sciences" and "superstitions"; rather, they had manifold origins and functions. And most of all, they testify to the ample observational interests of ancient Mesopotamians, which in turn had a deep impact on the surrounding world. The results and inferences of such observations gained in the ancient world would not always count as scientific from our contemporary perspective, but these texts contain important raw data for the study of the history of the human mind and the functioning of the human brain. One can say metaphorically that as our own times will pass into antiquity, future scholars will look at our accomplishments in the field of intellectual culture with similar glasses — as a blend of true ("scientific") and false ("superstitious") beliefs, often mixed up without any clear distinction. In the end, the definitions are not as important as the content.

BIBLIOGRAPHY

Annus, Amar

2006 "The Survivals of the Ancient Syrian and Mesopotamian Intellectual Traditions in the Writings of Ephrem Syrus." *Ugarit-Forschungen* 38: 1–25.

Arbel, Daphna

2008 "Enoch-Metatron: The Highest of All *Tapsarim*? *3 Enoch* and Divinatory Traditions." *Jewish Studies Quarterly* 15: 289–320.

Bottéro, Jean

1992 *Mesopotamia: Writing, Reasoning, and the Gods*. Chicago: University of Chicago Press.

Brown, David

2000 *Mesopotamian Planetary Astronomy-Astrology*. Cuneiform Monographs 18. Groningen: Styx.

Budge, E. A. Wallis

1913 *Syrian Anatomy, Pathology and Therapeutics; or, "The Book of Medicines."* London: Oxford University Press.

Burkert, Walter

1992 *The Orientalizing Revolution: Near Eastern Influence on Greek Culture in the Early Archaic Age*. Cambridge: Harvard University Press.

Collins, John J.

1998 *The Apocalyptic Imagination: An Introduction to Jewish Apocalyptic Literature*. 2nd edition. Grand Rapids: Eerdmans.

Cooper, Jerrold S.

1980 "Apodotic Death and the Historicity of 'Historical' Omens." In *Death in Mesopotamia: Papers Read at the XXVIe Rencontre assyriologique internationale*, edited by B. Alster, pp. 99–105. Mesopotamia 8. Copenhagen: Akademisk Forlag.

Cryer, Frederick H.

1994 *Divination in Ancient Israel and Its Near Eastern Environment: A Socio-Historical Investigation*. Journal for the Study of the Old Testament, Supplement Series 142. Sheffield: Sheffield Academic Press.

Cumont, Franz

1912 *Astrology and Religion among the Greeks and Romans*. American Lectures on the History of Religions 8. New York; London: G. P. Putnam's Sons.

Dittenberger, Wilhelm

1924 *Sylloge inscriptionum Graecarum*. 3rd edition. Leipzig: Lipsiae Hirzel.

Drower, Ethel Stefana

1937 *The Mandaeans of Iraq and Iran: Their Cults, Customs, Magic, Legends, and Folklore*. London: Clarendon.

Dundes, Alan

1961 "Brown County Superstitions." *Midwest Folklore* 11: 25–50.

Fahd, Toufic

1966 *La divination arabe: Études religieuses, sociologiques et folkloriques sur le milieu natif de l'Islam*. Leiden: Brill.

1991 "Malhama." In *Encyclopaedia of Islam: New Edition*. Volume 6, p. 247. Leiden: Brill.

Falkenstein, Adam

1966 "'Wahrsagung' in der sumerischen Überlieferung." In *La divination en Mésopotamie ancienne et dans les régions voisines*, pp. 45–68. XIVe Rencontre Assyriologique Internationale. Paris: Presses Universitaires de France.

Fincke, Jeanette C.

2006–2007 "Omina, die göttlichen 'Gesetze' der Divination." *Ex Orient Lux* 40: 131–47.

Freedman, Sally

1998 *If a City is Set on a Height: The Akkadian Omen Series* Šumma Alu ina Mēlê Šakin. Volume 1: Tablets 1–21. Philadelphia: S. N. Kramer Fund.

Geller, Markham J.

2000 "The Survival of Babylonian Wissenschaft in Later Tradition." In *The Heirs of Assyria: Proceedings of the Opening Symposium of the Assyrian and Babylonian Intellectual Heritage Project Held in Tvärminne, Finland, October 8–11, 1998*, edited by S. Aro and R. M. Whiting, pp. 1–6. Melammu Symposia 1. Helsinki: The Neo-Assyrian Text Corpus Project.

Greenfield, J. C., and M. Sokoloff

1989 "Astrological and Related Omen Texts in Jewish Palestinian Aramaic." *Journal of Near Eastern Studies* 48: 201–14.

1995 "An Astrological Text from Qumran (4Q318) and Reflections on some Zodiacal Names." *Revue de Qumran* 69–70: 507–25.

Guinan, Ann K.

1998 "Auguries of Hegemony: The Sex Omens of Mesopotamia." In *Gender and the Body in the Ancient Mediterranean*, edited by M. Wyke, pp. 38–55. Oxford: Blackwell.

2002 "A Severed Head Laughed: Stories of Divinatory Interpretation." In *Magic and Divination in the Ancient World*, edited by L. Ciraolo and J. Seidel, pp. 7–40. Ancient Magic and Divination 2. Leiden, Boston, Cologne: Brill and Styx.

Kingsley, Peter

1995 "Meetings with Magi: Iranian Themes among the Greeks, from Xanthus of Lydia to Plato's Academy." *Journal of the Royal Asiatic Society* 5: 173–209

Koch-Westenholz, Ulla

1995 *Mesopotamian Astrology: An Introduction to Babylonian and Assyrian Celestial Divination*. Carsten Niebuhr Institute Publications 19. Copenhagen: Museum Tusculanum Press.

Kraus, Fritz R.

1936 "Ein *Sittenkanon* in *Omenform*." *Zeitschrift für Assyriologie* 43: 77–113.

Lambert, Wilfred G.

1998 "The Qualifications of Babylonian Diviners." In *Festschrift für Rykle Borger zu seinem 65. Geburtstag am 24. Mai 1994:* tikip santakki mala bašmu ..., edited by S. M. Maul, pp. 141–58. Cuneiform Monographs 10. Groningen: Styx.

Lonsdale, S. H.

1979 "Attitudes towards Animals in Ancient Greece." *Greece and Rome* 26: 146–59.

Maul, Stefan M.

1994 *Zukunftsbewältigung: Eine Untersuchung altorientalischen Denkens anhand der babylonisch-assyrischen Löserituale (Namburbi)*. Mainz am Rhein: Philipp von Zabern.

1999 "How the Babylonians Protected Themselves against Calamities Announced by Omens." In *Mesopotamian Magic: Textual, Historical, and Interpretive Perspectives*, edited by T. Absuch and K. van der Toorn, pp. 123–29. Studies in Ancient Magic and Divination 1. Groningen: Styx.

2003 "Omina und Orakel. A. Mesopotamien." In *Reallexikon der Assyriologie* 10: 45–88.

Oppenheim, A. Leo

1964 *Ancient Mesopotamia: Portrait of a Dead Civilization.* Chicago: University of Chicago Press.

1974 "A Babylonian Diviner's Manual." *Journal of Near Eastern Studies* 33: 197–220.

Panaino, Antonio

2005 "Lunar and Snake Omens among the Zoroastrians." In *Officina Magica: Essays on the Practice of Magic in Antiquity*, edited by S. Shaked, pp. 73–89. Institute of Jewish Studies in Judaica 4. Leiden: Brill.

Pingree, David

1992 "Mesopotamian Omens in Sanskrit." In *La circulation des biens, des personnes et des idées dans le Proche-Orient ancien*, edited by D. Charpin and F. Joannès, pp. 375–79. 38e Rencontre Assyriologique Internationale. Paris: Éditions Recherche sur les Civilisations.

1997 *From Astral Omens to Astrology. From Babylon to Bikaner.* Serie Orientale Roma 78. Rome: Istituto Italiano per l'Africa e l'Oriente.

Reiner, Erica

1998 "Apodoses and Logia." In *"Und Mose schrieb dieses Lied auf." Studien zum Alten Testament und zum Alten Orient: Festschrift für Oswald Loretz zur Vollendung seines 70. Lebensjahres mit Beiträgen von Freunden, Schülern und Kollegen*, edited by M. Dietrich and I. Kottsieper, pp. 651–54. Alter Orient und Altes Testament 250. Münster: Ugarit-Verlag.

Rochberg, Francesca

1999 "The Babylonian Origins of the Mandaean Book of the Zodiac." *ARAM* 11: 237–47.

2006 "Old Babylonian Celestial Divination." In *If a Man Builds a Joyful House: Assyriological Studies in Honor of Erle Verdun Leichty*, edited by A. K. Guinan, pp. 337–48. Cuneiform Monographs 31. Leiden: Brill.

Schimmel, Annemarie

1994 *Deciphering the Signs of God: A Phenomenological Approach to Islam.* Albany: State University of New York.

Scurlock, JoAnn

2003 Review of *Die babylonisch-assyrische Morphoskopie* (Vienna, 2000), by B. Böck. *Journal of the American Oriental Society* 123: 395–99.

Sims-Williams, Nicholas

1995 "Christian Sogdian Texts from the Nachlass of Olaf Hansen 2: Fragments of Polemic and Prognostics." *Bulletin of the School of Oriental and African Studies* 58: 288–302.

Smith, Morton

1987 "The Occult in Josephus." In *Josephus, Judaism, and Christianity*, edited by L. Feldman and G. Hata, pp. 236–56. Detroit: Wayne State University Press.

Starr, Ivan

1983 *The Rituals of the Diviner.* Bibliotheca Mesopotamica 12. Malibu: Undena.

Veldhuis, Niek

1999 "Reading the Signs." In *All Those Nations: Cultural Encounters within and with the Near East; Studies Presented to Han Drijvers at the Occasion of His Sixty-fifth Birthday by Colleagues and Students,* edited by H. L. J. Vanstiphout, pp. 161–74. Groningen: Styx.

2006 "Divination: Theory and Use." In *If a Man Builds a Joyful House: Assyriological Studies in Honor of Erle Verdun Leichty*, edited by A. K. Guinan, pp. 487–97. Cuneiform Monographs 31. Leiden: Brill.

Westbrook, Raymond

1985 "Biblical and Cuneiform Law Codes." *Revue Biblique* 92: 247–68.

2

"IF P, THEN Q": FORM AND REASONING IN BABYLONIAN DIVINATION

FRANCESCA ROCHBERG,
UNIVERSITY OF CALIFORNIA, BERKELEY

From the features and marks on the sheep's liver and other entrails to the characteristics of the human body and face to the behavior of animals and the appearances of stars and planets, the investigation of the meaning of ominous signs in ancient Mesopotamia took shape in serialized lists of omens arranged as correlations between the signs and what they signified. An omen is a pair of interdependent elements, on the one hand a sign in the natural world or social environment, and on the other an event in social life. The connection between the two elements is expressed by means of a conditional statement "If P, then Q." The signs collected in written lists of "If P, then Q" statements corresponded to visible, imaginable, or conceivable phenomena, but always grounded in consideration of or in relation to physical things. This paper is concerned with form and its effect as a systematizing device in omen texts. Form and system are two key aspects of what constitute the general principles of Mesopotamian omen divination as represented in omen text series (entitled *Šumma* P "If P"). These principles give us not only insight into the internal consistency and coherence of the texts, but also the styles of reasoning employed. The practice of divination is a separate issue and is not addressed here except in a minor way.

An omen statement, from a formal point of view, can be seen as a relationship between two propositions (P and Q) which function as premise and conclusion. Logically, the conclusion, or consequent, is inferable from the premise. In his study of theories of the sign in classical antiquity, G. Manetti drew the conclusion that,

> from the point of view of a historical reconstruction of the discipline of semiotics, the most significant aspect of Mesopotamian divination is that it is centered precisely on a distinctive and individual notion of the sign, which is a scheme of inferential reasoning that allows particular conclusions to be drawn from particular facts (Manetti 1993: 1–2).

One of the most basic of inference schemes, or rules of inference, is *modus ponens*. It is defined by its form, thus: If P, then Q. P, therefore, Q. This inference scheme was first defined as such in Stoic philosophy in the context of the investigation of the logic of propositions and inference from signs (Rochberg 2009: 14–15, n. 5). All Babylonian omens qualify. Thus, "If Jupiter becomes steady in the morning: enemy kings will be reconciled" (Reiner and Pingree 2005: 40–41 line 1, without indicating breaks). Jupiter is steady in the morning. Therefore, enemy kings reconcile. The "If P, then Q" statements of the omen lists relate sign and signified in the manner of the antecedent and consequent of inferences of this form. A temporal or sequential relationship between the sign and the signified may be read into the grammar of the Akkadian "if ... then," or *šumma*-clause, the antecedent expressed in the preterite, the consequent in the durative, though the temporal relation seems to be mitigated by the fact that the entire statement is hypothetical and can even contain an antecedent which cannot occur (is unobservable). The relation between P and Q remains, therefore, somewhat abstract from a temporal standpoint. Further consideration of the connections between P and Q (below) clarify this problem. Regardless of the temporal relation, antecedent and consequent in the omens maintain a certain logical relation, as any conditional statement does, and this logical relation will apply independently of phonetic, semantic, causal, or empirical connections between the statements P and Q (Rochberg 2009).

The question of what the conditional form might suggest about the meaning and purpose of omens has not been adequately addressed because of certain assumptions about the origins of omens in empirical connections enabling the prediction of Q on the basis of P and rationalizing future predictions of Q from P (Rochberg 2004: 268). A former consensus on this point no doubt underpins Manetti, who allows that the empirical connection constitutes one form of connective tissue between P and Q, or what he calls the "passage from protasis to apodosis" (Manetti 1993: 7). He said, "the first type of passage is linked to what is known as *divinatory empiricism*: the protasis and the apodosis record events which really occurred in conjunction in the past" (1993: 7, emphasis in the original). He takes as evidence of this divinatory empiricism the Mari liver models, whose interpretation has been subject to some difference in interpretation (Rochberg 2004: 269). Apart from this evidence, however, Manetti recognized a tropic associative connection, usually based in analogies of various kinds, between protasis and apodosis as well as the schematic expansion of elements of the antecedents (which he calls "codes") familiar from all omen series. The empirical, however, is viewed as original to the conception of the ominous sign and the other modes of relating P and Q are of secondary origin in a historical evolution of Mesopotamian divination (1993: 7).

In basic agreement with Manetti concerning non-empirical modes of relating P and Q in omen statements, I differ with his historical conclusions about an original empiricism underpinning divination by signs. The construction of omens in which paranomastic relations between a word in the protasis and one in the apodosis, or where various analogies made between elements of the sign and its portent, or, indeed, where "impossible" phenomena which cannot have been observed at any time are presented in omen protases, all demonstrate omen divination's independence from empiricism. Without any evidence in support of the actual observation of co-occurring phenomena the thesis of an original empirical relation remains purely conjectural. Though the non-empirical nature of the bulk of the cuneiform omens is clear, it is worth making explicit by a few examples. Let us again take the omen "If Jupiter becomes steady in the morning, enemy kings will be reconciled." To accept the empirical association of P and Q is to presume that at some time in the past it was observed that following the steadiness of Jupiter in the morning, enemy kings were reconciled, and further, to justify on the basis of that empirical connection future predictions about enemy kings being reconciled whenever Jupiter is "steady." But this omen is simply built upon an analogy drawn between the elements of the protasis, that is, Jupiter, Marduk's star, connoting rulership, and its "steadiness" (expressed with the verb *kânu*) connoting rectitude and stability, and the elements of the apodosis, that is, peace between enemy kings. The same is true for instances of paranomasia between words in the antecedent and consequent. For example, in the extispicy series (Clay 1923: no. 13:65): "If the coils of the intestine look like the face of Huwawa (written logographically ^{d}HUM.HUM): it is the omen of the usurper king (also written logographically, IM.GI = Akkadian *hammā'u*) who ruled all the lands."

Here the antecedent is related to the consequent by a wordplay based on the homophonous echo of HUM.HUM in *hammā'u*, not by any empirical connection between intestines coiled that way and a usurpation. The homophony pertains between the logogram ^{d}HUM.HUM in the

Figure 2.1. Clay mask of the demon Huwawa. Sippar, southern Iraq, ca. 1800–1600 B.C. 8.3 × 8.4 cm. ME 116624. Courtesy of the British Museum

protasis and the Akkadian reading of the logogram IM.GI in the apodosis. The antecedent-consequent connection, therefore, is based upon a homophonic play that requires and even presupposes a sensitivity to orthographic practice of the highly trained cuneiform scribe. Though the meaningful connection between antecedent (intestinal coils appearing as the face of Huwawa) and consequent (usurpation) is based on the phonetic play between words, the image (fig. 2.1) refers to the visual aspect of the imagery conjured by the protasis alone. Regarding the connection between protasis and apodosis, the omens illustrate scribal invention involving the sounds, meanings, writings, literary allusions (e.g., Clay 1923: no. 13:33, in which the coils looking like an eagle are read as "the omen of Etana," who ascended to heaven on the back of an eagle), as well as visual analogies between elements, such as might be constructed between the appearance of a cuneiform sign and what it signifies: "If the coils of the intestine look like a PAP-sign: your capital will prosper over the enemy's capital." Here the PAP-sign, two crossed wedges, is visually iconic for the notion of conflict. Or, coils that appear as a *kubšu*-cap (Clay 1923: no. 13:47), the headdress associated most particularly with royalty (or divinity), are read as significant for the "throne," again by an iconic means of sign representation.

To return to the question of the temporal relation of Q to P, then, if the omen consequent is meant to convey the meaning, or the reading (interpretation) of P, then we do not have a series of observation statements about what particular event in fact occurred following another particular event, but a series of hypothetical statements showing that P indicates Q. From such statements, however, one could come to expect Q in the event of P, and it is here that the potential for prediction is located.

The analogies drawn from sign to portent represent attention to particulars, but not necessarily to observable particulars, though visual analogies between elements of the protasis and apodosis are also attested. Associations of elements such as the sounds or meanings of words are not dependent upon empirical observation, yet, as the examples just mentioned illustrate, they construct meaningful and valid signification between antecedent and consequent that depend instead upon cultural or linguistic conventions. Analogic relationships construed between phenomena, especially analogies based on the sounds, spellings, or meanings of words for phenomena, are certainly subject to, but not wholly determined by sensory perception. Correspondingly, such relations are limited not by perception but by conception. As seen in some of the examples given, analogic connections made between particular elements of the protases and apodoses justify the inferential character of Babylonian omens. But the particularity of the analogous referents in the statements of protasis and apodosis (e.g., the homophonic relation between HUM.HUM and *hammā'u*) in no way compromises the general force of the omen. As T. Czeżowski observed,

> Mill claimed that reasoning by analogy — "from particulars to particulars," as he put it — is the fundamental form of reasoning, while reasoning by induction is in a sense a synthesis obtained by embracing a number of analogical cases together. To Mill a general statement is a conjunction of singular sentences which are subordinated to it. The train of reasoning is as follows: on the basis of a number of similar observations saying '*a* is *b*,' when there are no observations to the contrary 'we feel warranted — as Mill says — in concluding, that what we found true in those instances hold in all similar ones, past, present, and future, however numerous they may be" (Czeżowski 2000: 110, citing Mill 1886: 122).

The omen constructed by means of an analogical connection is assumed to apply "whenever P," and therefore has validity beyond any single occurrence.

The use of schematic relationships such as up-down, the four directions, the five colors, has been cited as a reason why ominous "phenomena" are not always observable in actuality. The celestial omens exhibit this characteristic. Phenomena such as the eclipse where the shadow moves in a direction opposite to that which occurs in reality, indeed, most of the extant Jupiter omens of *Enūma Anu Enlil* are "impossible." These have the planet "entering," "passing," "coming close to," or "being in the middle of" fixed stars whose latitudes with respect to Jupiter's path prevent this from ever occurring. In fact, as David Pingree pointed out (in Reiner and Pingree 2005: 28), "this choice of constellations far removed from the path of Jupiter seems to be deliberate," because when the planet is north of the equator (between the spring and fall equinoxes) the constellations it is associated with in these omens are to the south and vice versa. This can be explained in terms of the value placed by the scribes on conception as well as perception, and the omen corpus forces us to try to understand just what the relation is between the conceivable and the possible in ancient Mesopotamian thought, and how these categories map onto physical actuality. The character of the omen lists, which is the result of its formal as well as schematic nature, shows the importance not only of a different kind of knowledge, but also a different way of categorizing the physical.

That the relationships between the empirical, the actual, and the possible should be constructed differently in the Babylonian conception almost goes without saying. In later antiquity, for example, one can refer again to the Stoics, whose views on the actual and the possible also map differently from ours. The Stoic definition of the possible is rooted in the investigation of propositions (possible vs. necessary) and therefore has to do with the nature of predicates and their relation to principal (as opposed to initiating) causes. That the Stoic definition of possibility took shape in the context of the logic of propositions and how truth functions with respect to past or future events was furthermore of importance to the analysis of oracles and omens (Reesor 1965: 293). As in the Stoic discourse, the significance of the possible in cuneiform divination applies as well to the connection between antecedent and consequent in the context of making statements concerning future events. In light of the evident interest in possibility represented by the omens resulting from schematization without regard for actuality, the empirical dimension of omens hardly applies at the level of the connection between P and Q, even when the phenomenon of the protasis is observable. But in addition to the schemata which expand the possibilities for constructing signs, the many analogies and wordplays that connect P to Q by virtue of cuneiform cultural conventions, some of the nature of wordplay only evident to scribes (or Assyriologists), are also evidence of the relative unimportance of the empirical on the level of the connections made between P and Q. That each omen forms a valid conditional, however, is of the essence.

The analysis of the conditional form of Babylonian omens shows that though the omen statements certainly posit relations between phenomena that do not depend upon the physical and causal connections we ourselves would make, the relation between protasis and apodosis is a logically valid one that furthermore can be classified with inferences expressed in the form of conditionals. Inferential reasoning, sometimes embedding analogic reasoning, thereby lies at the basis of the connections between the propositions of antecedent and consequent. The claim that divination proceeds by means of a rational and systematic method is nothing new but perhaps shows from yet another standpoint that the particular difference in assumptions about the phenomenal world that we find in cuneiform divination texts are unrelated to cognition, being a function rather of culture. Second, and more interesting I think, is that the logical and systematic features of ancient Mesopotamian divination appear to be direct consequences of the use of the conditional as its form and mode of expression. Of course it is above all the logical and systematic nature of omen divination that has justified its classification as an ancient science.

Given the previous observation that despite its logical and systematic nature Mesopotamian divination does not conform to (modern) scientific standards of causality or knowledge, we might question whether the term "science" is too loaded, or simply anachronistic and inapplicable to an investigation of the human (cognitive) interaction with physical phenomena in ancient Mesopotamia. The same question has been addressed with respect to pre-nineteenth-century sciences in general (Cunningham 1988; Cunningham and Williams 1993; Cunningham and French 1996). But to limit the discussion of what the nature of ancient Babylonian divination is by erasing the term "science" from our discourse about it leads us back to the dichotomy of science and non-science, science and religion, or worse, science and superstition. If the term "science" is confined to the modern era, as Peter Dear has discussed in his critque of Cunningham's thesis (2001), medieval and renaissance science, including natural philosophy and the physical and mathematical sciences also end up on one side of a great divide between science and non-science. Dear's sensitive critique argues for further refinement of the categories science and natural philosophy and their relation to religion, and a finer-grained empirical as well as historicist treatment of sources in terms of which the sciences are defined.

Attempting such a finer-grained analysis of the sources for Babylonian divination as well as other ancient sciences (e.g., astronomy, magic, medicine) is a worthy goal. Focussing on formal considerations of the omen texts has uncovered the logical and systematic nature of these texts as a direct result of their conditional form. Their logical, systematic, and inferential character, I would argue, warrants classification with science. Other aspects of cuneiform divination, particularly those involving the practice (as opposed to the nature) of divination, indicate other possible classifications, for example, with magic or religion. The problem is that none of these categories are found in Akkadian terminology, though there are words for observe (*naṣāru*) and predict (*qabû*), apotropaic ritual (*namburbû*), incantation (*šiptu*), and gods (*ilū*).

The category "non-science," on the other hand, does not seem to be useful as its purpose is to set what we now hold to be justified correct scientific knowledge apart from unjustified or wrong belief. This has the mouthfeel of morality rather than history. For analyzing cuneiform omen texts, dichotomous models only generate and then perpetuate un-nuanced ideas about what the nature of Mesopotamian divination was, reminiscent of early anthropological characterizations of other divination systems as pre- or non-logical (such as Spencer, Frazer, Tylor and, most famously, Lévy-Bruhl) and therefore as invalid explanations of phenomena.

In light of the above analysis of the effect of the conditional on the logical structure of omens it would be difficult to sustain claims to pre-logical thinking, or the notion of a different rationality. It must be said that more recently it has been pointed out that Lévy-Bruhl did not promote a racist agenda, as did some in the early twentieth century, and ultimately, under pressure from some of his critics, came to think that his two types of "mentalités" (the pre-logical and the rational) coexisted within all societies. The result of this wholesale revision was that magical thinking, which was not genetic, cognitive, or evolutionary, was not replaced by non-magical thinking through the inexorable progress of cognitive evolution. Anthropology rid modern cognitive historians of the idea that "primitives" had a tremendous oral memory but a limited power of abstract reasoning (van der Veer 2003: 183; cf. Peek 1991).

Correspondingly, the history of the use of the term "superstition" further demonstrates its inapplicability to Mesopotamia. The pejorative meaning of the Latin *superstitio* stems from the first-century B.C. Roman condemnation of divination not sanctioned by the State, later having the force of "unreasonable religious belief," as opposed to *religio*, the reasonable, or proper, fear of the gods (Salzman 1987: 174 and nn. 10 and 14). Legislation in A.D. 297 against illicit divination and *superstitio* was an ideological and political tool, aimed against sorcerers and Manichaeans, not against the practice of divination in principle. Because of its origins, the use of the term "superstition" in historical analysis, unlike use of the term "science," can only have an invidious effect, connoting wrong belief. Despite the diversity of the cuneiform divination corpora, there is no evidence of ideological conflict such as that between orthodox and unorthodox divination in the Roman principate. More importantly, no distinction was ever invoked in cuneiform texts between say, astronomy and astrology. This is clear in the late Uruk tablet which gives effective rules not only for predicting month lengths and lunar eclipses from empirical data available in the astronomical diaries, but also contains sections for use in predicting worldly events of a political nature, such as we have in omen apodoses, and concludes with the subscript BE-*ma* EŠ.BAR 3,20 *ana* IGI-*ka šá* dUDU.IDIM.MEŠ *ina lu-maš* KIN.KIN-*ma* "In order for you to see a divine decision (*purussû*) about the king you seek (the positions) of the planets within the (zodiacal) constellations" (TU 11 rev. 37, Brack-Bernsen and Hunger 2002: 12). Whatever issues around which the terms "astronomy" and "astrology" later came to be distinguished, including implications about the nature of their knowledge, do not apply in cuneiform texts.

Furthermore, D. Martin has argued that the rejection of superstition was not "due to the rise of 'rationalism' or 'empiricism' in the ancient world" (2004: 230). He shows that the investigation of the natural causes of disease was due to a shift in belief about the nature of the gods, that they were incapable of perpetrating evil. Martin continues,

> ancient intellectuals never *demonstrated* that the gods were good; they assumed it. They did not discover new "evidence" about the nature of the divine.... No, the rejection of divine and daimonic causation of disease did not come about simply because certain Greek men were suddenly "rational" thinkers whereas all their countrymen were "irrational," nor because they suddenly became "empiricists" whereas their countrymen couldn't see nature in front of their faces. The modernist depiction of ancient "science" as caused by a development of "empiricism" or "rationality" is misleading and ultimately not supported by the evidence. Rather, we must look to ancient *social* and *cultural* sources for the invention of "superstition" (Martin 2004: 230).

Why this observation is relevant to the study of Mesopotamian divination is precisely that, even though our evidence does show an underlying rationality, its classification as "science" on that basis is only part of the story. We still need to look to the larger social and cultural context and put the rational dimension into a more complex whole of meanings, methods, and practices that constituted prognostication by means of ominous signs in ancient Mesopotamia.

The last generation of historians of science has rejected the science-superstition dichotomy and other such binaries as not terribly useful, especially when placed in an evolutionary scheme that has science's objective truths and transcendent achievements as triumphing over lower forms of thought. But science is no longer viewed as signaling a liberation from primitive or archaic thought. In fact, as Geoffrey Lloyd put it,

> the ideas that rationality is distributed unevenly across peoples or populations, that some are better endowed in this respect than others, that there are groups that exhibit an inferior rationality or are otherwise deficient in this faculty, those ideas look like the very worst kind of cognitive imperialism (Lloyd 2007: 151).

We do not want to project the defining features of modern science back into antiquity where knowledge takes other forms, is based on other methods, and has other aims. Nevertheless, in full awareness of the anachronism, ancient divination, astrology, and magic are now readily classified as sciences on the grounds that some characteristics of science are considered to be continuous over the course of history, even while its content or aim is discontinuous.

The purpose of the foregoing discussion was primarily intended to establish a formal unity across omen text genres by the use of the conditional statement and the implementation of reasoning styles (by analogy, and by inference). Anchored by its tight logical structure, the lists of conditionals "If P, then Q" proved to be an effective instrument for making connections, and also served as a systematizing device. If these applications of the conditional warrant categorization as science, perhaps it is more useful for the history of science, as illustration of its diversity, than it is for an analysis of Mesopotamian culture. But as science (to paraphrase Quine and Ullian 1978: 3–4) reveals what for a particular community constitutes knowledge, skill in reasoning, and, in some relative way, truth — specifically, truth derived from such reasoning — the thousands of conditional statements compiled in omen series are of the essence for understanding how Babylonian and Assyrian scribes perceived and conceived the world in which they functioned, how they thought about what connected or related the propositions comprising conditionals, and, consequently, what for them constituted knowledge, skill in reasoning, and even truth.

BIBLIOGRAPHY

Brack-Bernsen, L., and H. Hunger

2002 "TU 11: A Collection of Rules for the Prediction of Lunar Phases and of Month Lengths." *SCIAMVS* 3: 3–90.

Clay, Albert T.

1923 *Epics, Hymns, Omens and Other Texts*. Babylonian Records in the Library of J. Pierpont Morgan 4. New Haven: Yale University Press.

Czeżowski, Tadeusz

2000 *Knowledge, Science, and Values: A Program for Scientific Philosophy*. Edited by L. Gumański. Poznań Studies in the Philosophy of the Sciences and the Humanities 68. Amsterdam and Atlanta: Rodopi.

Cunningham, Andrew

1988 "Getting the Game Right: Some Plain Words on the Identity and Invention of Science," *Studies in History and Philosophy of Science* 19: 365–89.

Cunningham, Andrew, and Roger K. French

1996 *Before Science: The Invention of the Friars' Natural Philosophy*. Aldershot: Scolar Press.

Cunningham, Andrew, and P. Williams

1993 "De-centring the 'Big Picture': The Origins of Modern Science and the Modern Origins of Science." *British Journal for the History of Science* 26: 407–32.

Dear, Peter

2001 "Religion, Science, and Natural Philosophy: Thoughts on Cunningham's Thesis." *Studies in History and Philosophy of Science* 32: 377–86.

Lévy-Bruhl, Lucien

1922 *Les fonctions mentales dans les sociétés inférieures*. 6th edition. Travaux de l'Année sociologique. Paris: Alcan. First published 1910 by Félix Alcan.

1976 *La mentalité primitive*. Les classiques des sciences humaines. Paris: Retz. First published 1922 by Félix Alcan.

Lloyd, Geoffrey E. R.

2007 *Cognitive Variations: Reflections on the Unity and Diversity of the Human Mind*. Oxford: Clarendon Press.

Manetti, G.

1993 *Theories of the Sign in Classical Antiquity*. Translated by C. Richardson. Indianapolis: Indiana University Press.

Martin, D.

2004 *Inventing Superstition: From the Hippocratics to the Christians*. Cambridge: Harvard University Press.

Mill, J. S.

1886 *A System of Logic, Ratiocinative and Inductive*. London: Green.

Peek, Philip M., editor

1991 *African Divination Systems: Ways of Knowing*. Indianapolis: Indiana University Press.

Quine, W. V., and J. S. Ullian

1978 *The Web of Belief*. New York: Random House.

Reesor, M. E.

1965 "Fate and Possibility in Early Stoic Philosophy." *Phoenix* 19: 285–97.

Reiner, Erica, and David Pingree

2005 *Babylonian Planetary Omens: Part Four*. Cuneiform Monographs 30. Leiden: Brill; Boston: Styx.

Rochberg, Francesca

2004 *The Heavenly Writing: Divination, Horoscopy, and Astronomy in Mesopotamian Culture*. Cambridge: Cambridge University Press

2009 "Inference, Conditionals, and Possibility in Ancient Mesopotamian Science." *Science in Context* 22: 4–25.

Salzman, M. R.

1987 "'Superstitio' in the Codex Theodosianus and the Persecution of Pagans." *Vigilae Christianae* 41: 172–88.

van der Veer, R.

2003 "Primitive Mentality Reconsidered." *Culture and Psychology* 9: 179–84.

3
GREEK PHILOSOPHY AND SIGNS

JAMES ALLEN, UNIVERSITY OF PITTSBURGH

1

Our term "sign" comes, of course, straight from the Latin *signum*, which in turn renders the Greek σημεῖον, whose range of uses it tracks pretty closely. Not only the term, but the idea or complex of ideas for which it stands are an inheritance from Greco-Roman antiquity. If in this area as in so many others the Romans were indebted to the Greeks, here as elsewhere the Hellenic world was indebted to the ancient Near Eastern civilizations that preceded and coincided with it. The issues raised by these debts lie outside the scope of this essay, the aim of which is twofold. I want to sketch, in very rough outline, some of the main developments in ancient Greek thinking about signs. To that end, I shall be exploring some of the distinctions in which that thought is enshrined. But I also want to look at some corners of ancient Greek thought about this subject that are not captured, or at any rate are accommodated only with some strain, by the framework to which these distinctions belong. In the way of even the best and most illuminating efforts to distinguish and classify, these distinctions do not cover all cases equally well, and as often happens, it is the cases that impose the most strain on, a system or framework that are in some ways the most interesting.

2

As a first approximation, we might say that a sign is something that has or conveys meaning. This proposal is on the right lines, but baldly stated it has the potential to mislead. Talk of "meaning" inevitably brings to mind words, statements, and the like — in a word, language or language-like communication devices such as coded messages or signals.

It is not that we do not find the ancient term "sign" and the verb "signify" employed in this way. This use is well and amply attested. Plato's *Cratylus* was the most sustained and influential contribution to the long-running ancient debate about whether word-meaning is simply a matter of convention or there is, rather, a natural standard of correctness that governs the relation between words and their meanings so that some words are better suited by nature to mean certain things than others. The naturalist theory expounded and subjected to critical examination by Socrates in the dialogue envisages original legislators of names who are said to have fashioned "a sign and a name for each existing thing" (427c). In the passage in Plato's *Sophist* where for the first time the function of a name, viz. to pick out or refer to an object, is distinguished from that of a statement, wherein a predicate is joined to the name to assert something of the object designated by the name, the words composing the statement are described as "signs consisting in speech" (262d). Aristotle calls words "signs" in his discussion of the statements composed out of them in the *De interpretatione* (16a16, b7, 10). Stoic dialectic, which corresponds roughly to our discipline of logic but also covers much of the ground covered by grammar and theory of meaning, was concerned both with things that signify, that is, words, and what they signify or mean (Diogenes Laertius 7.62). And a good deal later, Saint Augustine (A.D. 354–430), who has much to say about signs, will treat scripture as a system of divinely given signs.

Yet another use of "sign" is at least as common. "Smoke is a sign of fire." "Tracks of this kind are a sign that a leopard has passed this way." "The fact that there is a ring around the moon is a sign that it will rain tomorrow." In cases like these there is, it seems, no question of anyone *meaning* something by the signs at issue. They serve, instead, as evidence or grounds for a conclusion — and this appears to be a very different thing indeed. Yet here too, even in the absence of someone who means something, we still speak of *meaning*. "The fact that there is a ring around the moon means that it will rain tomorrow," "Smoke means fire," and so on. These facts are the basis of the distinction between natural and non-natural meaning drawn in a celebrated article by H. P. Grice, who was himself looking back to a distinction of Saint Augustine's between natural and given signs (*signa naturalia*, *signa data*).[1] Very roughly speaking, natural meaning, which belongs to natural signs as such, is the evidential support that a sign furnishes for a conclusion, while given signs are used by humans, or beings relevantly like them, in order to convey their thoughts to other such beings, where it is somehow essential if this task is to be effected that the recipient grasp that this is the intention of the sign's user.[2]

The fact that the word "meaning," with its very different history, also extends across the divide separating the natural from the non-natural or given divide suggests that it is not an accident that the same term "sign" comes to be used of these very different cases. They have, and were felt to have, something important in common. Thus according to Augustine, "a sign is something that brings it about by itself that something apart from the impression it makes on the senses comes to mind" (*De doctrina christiana* 2.1.1). We shall come back to the distinction between natural and given signs, which is one of those that I mean to suggest comes under strain.

3

For the present, however, I shall concentrate on the natural side of the divide. A (natural) sign furnishes evidence: when all goes well, we come to know something distinct from it by inferring a conclusion from it. To discharge this function, it is not enough that the sign furnish grounds for the conclusion at issue, it must be better or more easily known than it, either in general or on the occasion of its use as a sign. This condition is enshrined in the requirement that a sign be *revelatory*, which is part of the Stoic definition of the sign as "a true antecedent in a sound conditional *revelatory* of the consequent."[3] So, for example, though the fact that

[1] Grice 1957; cf. Grice 1982.

[2] Note that on a naturalist theory of the kind examined in the *Cratylus*, words will not necessarily be classified as natural rather than given signs. According to the version of naturalism elaborated by Socrates, the naturalness of a word is its fitness to be used as an instrument by human beings to convey their thoughts to each other in the way that is characteristic of non-natural meaning (434e). By themselves independently of the use to which human beings put them, however, they do not mean something in the way that bearers of natural meaning do, except in the way that any vocal sound might. "Words (in a language unknown to me) are being produced on the other side of that screen. This means there is someone speaking there, or perhaps a parrot or a loudspeaker."

[3] Sextus Empiricus, *Outlines of Pyrrhonism* 2.104; *Adversus mathematicos* 8.245; [Galen] *Historia philosopha*, ch. 9.

it is light follows from the fact that is it day, the latter can hardly be a sign of the former. One cannot know that it is day without, at the same time, knowing that it is light. Compare the familiar examples cited earlier: smoke as a sign of fire, tracks as the sign of an animal's passage, and the like. Knowledge of the sign is, so to speak, given to us directly, while that of which it is a sign comes to be known through the sign.

The ancient Greek ἐνάργεια and Latin *evidentia* mean the quality of being evident or manifest, which I believe remains the dominant sense of "evidence" in modern European languages apart from English. To serve as *evidence for* or of a conclusion, a sign must exhibit evidence in this sense in addition to furnishing grounds for a conclusion, either absolutely or by comparison with the conclusion for which it is evidence, which fact seems to lie behind the sense of the term meaning evidence *for* a conclusion.

There is another pervasive, if not completely ubiquitous, feature of the ancient Greek philosophical thought about signs that calls for comment. Inference from signs often, though not always, makes up the inferior side of a contrast with forms of inference, sometimes called "demonstrations" (ἀπόδειξις), that are, in one way or another, superior to it. The version of this contrast that we find in Aristotle, where for the most part it is implicit, is representative. According to him, one has knowledge, at least in the strict and favored sense, not when one has a true belief and is justified in holding it — the condition that we tend to mean when we speak of knowledge and the focus of most contemporary epistemology — but rather when, in addition, one understands why matters are as one knows them to be, that is, grasps the cause or explanation for their being so. This is knowing *the because* as opposed to knowing (merely) the *that*, as Aristotle often puts it, and it is this condition that deserves above all to be called knowledge in his view.

The first principles of a science, in terms of which everything in the domain of that science is to be explained, are themselves self-explanatory, not by being self-evident, but in the sense that, while other things are explained and understood by reference to them, they are not understood or explained by reference to other more fundamental principles. When he is adhering strictly to his own technical terminology, Aristotle calls our grasp of them not "knowledge" (ἐπιστήμη) but νοῦς, "intuition" or however else we choose to translate this elusive term. Knowledge or ἐπιστήμη, most properly so called, is confined to derivative truths, which one must grasp as consequences of the first principles by which they are necessitated and explained if one is to know them in this favored sense. According to Aristotle, this condition consists in the grasp of an argument or syllogism of a special kind, viz., a demonstration, which in turn is defined as a syllogism by grasping which we know (*Nicomachean Ethics* 6.3, 1139b31–2; *Analytica posteriora* 1.2, 71b18).

Consider a favorite example of his: the demonstration that the planets do not twinkle (*Analytica posteriora* 1.13, 78a30–b4). Not-twinkling belongs to all that is near, nearness belongs to the planets; therefore the planets do not twinkle. Those familiar with Aristotelian logic will recognize this as a categorical syllogism in the first figure mood, *Barbara*. A crucial feature of a demonstration, according to Aristotle, is that the so-called middle term, in this case nearness, state the cause or explanation. It is *because* the planets are near that they do not twinkle, and it is, therefore, by grasping this syllogism that one understands why the planets do not twinkle at the same time as one grasps that they do not.

But suppose, says Aristotle, that the premise stating that not-twinkling belongs to all that is near converts, that is, not only does not-twinkling belong to everything that is near but nearness belongs to everything that does not twinkle. In these conditions, it is possible to construct an argument, also a syllogism in *Barbara*, that deduces the conclusion that the planets are near, one of the premises of the demonstration above, from the converted proposition, everything that does not twinkle is near, together with the fact, which can be established by observation, that the planets do not twinkle. Though the argument is no less valid and its premises and conclusion no less true, it is not a demonstration, strictly speaking, since the conclusion is not explained by the premises. The middle term, not-twinkling in this case, is not the cause; that is, it is not because the planets do not twinkle that they are near, though it is because they do not twinkle that, when guided by this argument, we are justified in concluding that they are near. In old-fashioned terms, not twinkling is the *ratio cognoscendi* not the *ratio essendi*.[4]

But though not the cause, not-twinkling is evidence for the nearness of the planets or, alternatively, a sign of their being near. Elsewhere Aristotle gives examples of pairs of syllogisms that share a conclusion, one of which is a demonstration, the other an inference from signs. For example, when the moon is eclipsed this can be demonstrated from the fact that it is undergoing interposition by the earth, which is the cause of the eclipse (*Analytica posteriora* 2.8, 93a36ff.). The same conclusion can also be deduced from the fact that the moon is unable to produce a shadow despite being full. But the latter, namely being unable to produce a shadow, is not the cause of the moon being eclipsed, but merely a sign of it.

Thus in Aristotle's hands talk of signs often signals a contrast between inferences that put us in a position to know the *that* and inferences that lay bare the causes thereby enabling us to understand the *why*. Signs are, if you will, mere evidence. Indeed the few remarks that Aristotle devotes explicitly to sign-inference are in passages concerned with forms of argument that are most prominent in rhetoric, where the object is not a deeper understanding of the kind sought in the sciences, but the simple establishing of the facts (*Analytica priora* 2.27; *Rhetorica* 1.2, 1357a33ff.; 2.25, 1402b12ff.).[5]

4

Two observations should be made before we proceed. First, some ancient philosophers, especially but not only the pre-Socratics, were happy to speak of signs in connection with inferences by means of which the sciences are constituted and an understanding of the ultimate causes at work in nature secured (if not quite in the Aristotelian way). This seems often to coincide with a tendency not to draw the kind of distinctions between types of inference and types of ground that we have been considering, or at least not to assign it a place of such central importance. Epicurus is an example, about whom I shall have more to say soon. Second, for those who do make the distinction, experience (ἐμπειρία, *experientia*) is an especially fruitful source of sign-inferences of the less exalted sort.

Since at least the time of Plato and Aristotle, experience was conceived in something like the following way. It arises out of repeated episodes of perception and is confined to the objects that fall under perception, which are, if you will, inferentially brute or discrete: by themselves and as such, they imply nothing substantively different from their own existence. Nevertheless, observation of recurring patterns of sequence and conjunction among such objects furnishes us with a stock of empirical generalizations, which are of great value not least in supporting sign-inferences like that from smoke to fire.

---

[4] Compare Patzig 1981.

[5] Compare Burnyeat 1982: 194–206.

According to the view in question, however, no amount of experience by itself is sufficient to uncover the underlying natures of things because of which they behave as they are observed to do; these natures are the causes in terms of which genuine explanations must be framed, and they can be revealed, if at all, only by the insights of a special faculty of reason. Plato, Aristotle and those who follow them on this point insist that a real art (τέχνη) and real knowledge (ἐπιστήμη) must go beyond experience to grasp the causes with the aid of reason conceived in this special way. The other distinction with which we shall be chiefly concerned is that between reason and experience.

5

These facts need to be kept in view as we turn to what is far and away the most extensive discussion of signs in surviving ancient Greek philosophical literature, that found in Sextus Empiricus, who was a Pyrrhonian Sceptic active, probably, in late second century A.D. His task as a sceptic was to call into question pretensions to knowledge in each department of philosophy. To this end, he adopts a framework dividing philosophy into parts, within which he expounds in enormous and enormously valuable detail the views of his dogmatic opponents before undertaking to refute them. He tackles epistemology first (which belongs to the logical division of philosophy as the ancient Greeks conceived it), and he treats as common ground a division of labor between the criterion, on the one hand, and signs and proofs on the other (*Adversus mathematicos* 7.24–26, cf. 396; 8.140, 319; *Outlines of Pyrrhonism* 2.96).

Knowledge of evident matters is the province of the criterion according to the framework that he adopts, and the truths won with its aid are in turn the basis of inferences by signs or demonstrations that promise to extend knowledge to the realm of the non-evident. It is plain that in setting up this framework Sextus does not distinguish between the function of signs and that of demonstrations and that he assigns to both an elevated part in the formation of natural philosophical theory.

The views that Sextus goes on to present and examine when he turns to signs do not really fulfill the corresponding expectation, however, and this is only the first in a series of peculiarities in his account. His discussion is framed in terms of a distinction between commemorative and indicative signs, only the former of which, he says, are acceptable to the Pyrrhonists (*Outlines of Pyrrhonism* 2.200–01; cf. *Adversus mathematicos* 8.154).

> A commemorative sign is: "that which, having been evidently co-observed with the signified, together with its occurrence when the signified matter is non-evident, leads us into a recollection of what was co-observed with it but is now not manifest."
>
> An indicative sign is: "that which has not been evidently co-observed with the signified, but from its own nature and constitution signifies that of which it is a sign."

Though this distinction is philosophical in the sense of being concerned with epistemological issues of completely general import, there are good reasons to believe that it was not the creation of professional philosophers, but rather had its origin in the context of the long-running debate between the self-styled Empirical school of medicine, which arose in the mid-third century B.C., and its opponents, the medical rationalists.[6]

---

[6] For arguments supporting this conclusion, see Allen 2001: 107ff., who follows Philippson 1881: 65ff.

The Empiricists accepted the challenge laid down by Plato and Aristotle and undertook to show that experience was entirely sufficient to give rise to an art by itself without the aid of reason in the special sense in which it refers to a faculty whose distinctive characteristic is the ability to grasp truths not accessible to observation. Rationalism, on the other hand, was not a single school, but a tendency common to medical thinkers of diverse views belonging to different schools who were united only by the conviction that a true art must go beyond experience and grasp the hidden natures and causes of things by means of reason.

The commemorative sign was, it seems, the favored tool of the Empiricists; the indicative sign that of the rationalists. Both seem to have their home in the *practice* of an art rather than the original process of constituting one. Commemorative signs point to evident events and conditions with which they have been conjoined in past experience. In the sphere of medicine, indicative signs reveal the hidden, pathological conditions underlying the patient's symptoms, which in turn *indicate* the appropriate therapy. To be sure, indicative signs could perhaps be viewed as playing a double role, as the means by which theory is applied to particular cases in practice and as the means by which elements in the theory are inferred from evident observation in the first place, which would make for closer fit with Sextus' framework. There is little evidence for this, however.

Let me mention two more important oddities. If there was a position that does meet the expectations created by Sextus' framework, it would seem to be that of Epicurus and his followers, who make explicit appeals to signs as the basis of their theories about non-evident matters in the realm of natural philosophy, atoms, and the motions of distant heavenly bodies, for instance. But though he mentions Epicurus a couple of times in passing, Sextus has nothing substantive to say about Epicurean views (*Adversus mathematicos* 8.177, 185).

On the other hand, he devotes much attention to the Stoics, whose definition of the sign I cited above. But this turns out to be perhaps the most puzzling thing of all in Sextus' treatment of signs. He has, as we have seen, no complaint against the commemorative sign and promises to direct his fire exclusively on indicative signification. The Stoic theory against which he argues should then be a theory of indicative signification, or at least have its primary application to indicative signs whether the Stoics used this terminology or not. And indeed the text of Sextus plainly states that the Stoic definition is merely an alternative characterization of the indicative sign (*Outlines of Pyrrhonism* 2.102). So awkward is the placement of this assertion, and so poorly does it fit its context, however, that scholars, including the editor of the standard edition, have rejected it as an interpolation. If this is right, as there is good reason to believe that it is, what we have is an ill-fated effort to paper over a gap between Sextus' avowed purpose to combat the indicative sign and the prominence he gives to the case against a Stoic theory whose relation to indicative signs is the opposite of clear.

6

Indeed, such evidence as we have points to a closer affinity with empirical reasoning of the kind that falls under the head of commemorative signification. Unlike the Empiricists, the Stoics did not question the possibility of grasping the hidden natures of things or reject causal explanations based on them. Indeed Sextus also preserves a Stoic theory of demonstration whose chief application appears to have been causal explanation in natural philosophy, which is accorded its own discussion by Sextus (*Outlines of Pyrrhonism* 2.134–92; *Adversus mathematicos* 8. 199–481).[7] But the Stoics seem to have supposed that we are in a position to grasp the causes far less often than many rationalists supposed. Thus Chrysippus (ca. 280–207 B.C.), the third scholarch of the Stoa and the philosopher most responsible for working out the orthodox Stoic position in detail, urges us to rely on *experience* and *history* — terms that figure prominently in the Empiricists' own self-description — in those all too frequent cases where causal speculation is likely to lead us into error (Plutarch, *De Stoicorum repugnantiis* 1047c). And Posidonius (ca. 135–50 B.C.), the most prominent Stoic of his time, could be faulted by other Stoics for aetiologizing in the Aristotelian manner rather than preserving a more authentically Stoic reserve before the hiddeness (ἐπίκρυψις) of the causes (Strabo 2.3.8)

As it happens, there is a Stoic discipline occupied with signs whose method was in good part empirical, namely divination, about which we know a good deal owing to Cicero's interest (106–43 B.C.). He tackled the subject in his work *De divinatione* where, proceeding as an Academic skeptic, he expounds the Stoic view before undertaking to refute it.[8] In a way that should sound very familiar by now, he distinguishes knowledge *that*, which is obtained through signs, from knowledge of causes, which, to be sure, when complete, would make it possible to know the future in every particular, but which, in this form, is available only to a god (*De divinatione* 1.127; cf. 12, 16, 29, 35, 86, 109). Much of the time, then, human beings are obliged to fall back on signs.

They are greatly helped by the fact that the signs in question were fashioned by divine providence for the benefit of humankind. According the Stoics, divination is the power to grasp and interpret the signs sent by Gods to human beings (*De divinatione* 2.130; Sextus Empiricus, *Adversus mathematicos* 9.132; Stobaeus, *Ekologai* 2.170). It has two parts, artificial and natural. The former is so-called because the signs with which it is occupied require specialized expertise to interpret, while the natural division relies on things like inspired utterances and dreams which do not (though there are, unsurprisingly, complications having to do with the skilled interpretation that dreams and prophetic utterances do sometimes require). Though artificial divination is also concerned with the interpretation of portents, much the largest share of its attention is absorbed by signs discovered by long observation, whose efficacy is explained along empirical lines and illustrated with examples drawn from medicine, viewed as an empirical art, and other arts viewed in the same way.

> Nor do I ask why this tree alone should flower three times nor why it makes the time for ploughing fit with the sign of its flowering. I am content with this, that, even though I do not know why this happens, I do know what happens. So for every kind of divination I shall give the same answer as I did for the things I have cited. I see the efficacy of the scammony root for purging and birthwort for countering snake bites ... and this is sufficient; I do not know why they work. In the same way I do not understand adequately the explanation for the signs of wind and rain.... I recognize, I know, and I vouch for the force and result of them (*De divinatione* 1.16; translation from Wardle 2006: 50).

Thus the Stoics came down squarely on the empirical side of a long-running debate about divination especially prominent in discussions of astrology. At issue was the question whether its efficacy is to be explained as the result of discovering the causal influences exerted on human beings and their affairs by heavenly bodies or rather merely a matter of grasping empirical correlations the causes responsible for which remain hidden.[9]

---

[7] Compare Brunschwig 1980; Barnes 1980.

[8] On this work, see Wardle 2006.

The fact that natural signs are the concern of artificial divination while natural divination is occupied with what look rather like bearers of non-natural meaning is perhaps only a superficial paradox. Yet the distinctions with which we began are bound to take on a different look in the context of a view like the Stoics', according to which the universe is governed down to the last detail by a providential deity whose benevolence extends to the provision of signs for us to read. The Stoics maintained that the world was so created at the beginning that certain signs run ahead of certain things (*De divinatione* 1.118, cf. 35). At the very least, the clean division between natural signs and bearers of natural meaning, which do not depend on intention for their significance, on the one hand, and given signs or bearers of non-natural meaning, on the other, which signify as a result of an intention to signify that must be grasped for this purpose to be effected, will not look quite the same.

One way to approach this point sets out from a familiar problem: How can experience of conjunctions among objects or events between which reason cannot discern any other relations furnish a ground or reason for inferring one from the other? One response, most famously associated with David Hume, is to deny that it can and insist that the observation of conjunctions does not put us in possession grounds for inferences properly so called, but rather gives rise to customs or habits by which practice is governed in the absence of reason. It is noteworthy that there was a prominent strand of radical anti-rationalism among the medical Empiricists, some of whom insisted that they were not engaged in the business of reasoning at all, but were instead guided by dispositions, implanted by experience, to be reminded of one thing by the perception of another with which it had been conjoined in past observation. Others were willing to speak of reasoning, but insisted that the kind of reasoning that they employed was of an ordinary, everyday sort restricted to the phenomena, which they called *epilogismos* in order to distinguish it from reason of the objectionable rationalist kind, which they called *analogismos*.[10] As we have seen, however, conspicuous correlations among events between which reason can discern no connection were, according to the Stoics, deliberately contrived for the benefit of humankind by god.

No doubt it is possible to be guided by these signs without being aware of or paying heed to the divine intention of which they are the expression. But one may also, and I take it the Stoic diviner will, go further and view divinatory signs as a system of divinely instituted signals, with the result that the faith he reposes in the signs that he studies will not be a matter of either rationally groundless custom, on the one hand, or conviction grounded in purely empirical reasoning — supposing there is such a thing —, on the other, but more like the trust one places in the testimony of an unimpeachable authority. Long observation and experience will for him be a source of clues about what the gods mean to tell us, rather than being viewed simply as the source of grounds to be exploited in empirical reasoning or the causal basis for mental habits of association.

Or rather, they will be this in addition to being that. The Stoics were far from repudiating the idea of the empirical. We have seen Chrysippus appealing to it. It is plain that even in the art of divination as the Stoics conceived it there will be an empirical aspect or dimension to what is known in the sphere of artificial divination and an empirical level to the diviner's understanding of it. This is implied by the comparison between divination and less exalted arts. The concern with divinely sent signs as such seems to be distinctive of the diviner's art

---

[9] Compare Long 1982; Adamson 2008.

[10] Galen, *De sectis ingredientibus* 3.10.23–24, 11.8–10 SM (in Marquardt, Mueller, and Helmreich 1967); Galen, *Subfiguratio empirica* 62, 24–3 (in Deichgräber 1965); Galen, *On Medical Experience* (in Frede and Walzer 1985: 133–35, 140); cf. Frede 1990.

— witness the Stoic definition of divination — though it is an intriguing question whether the regularities on which empirical arts of a less elevated kind rely are also deliberately contrived by divine agency for the benefit of humankind. Certainly Stoic views about providence are not incompatible with the suggestion. Yet there are some differences. The more ordinary empirical arts, or arts with a substantial empirical component, are only at one remove from a grasp of the nature of the matters with which they deal and the causes at work in them, whereas such an understanding may be in principle impossible for human beings in the sphere of divination. The divine intentions behind the regularities studied and exploited by, for example, the medical art are, one suspects, no business of the doctor as such. It is plausible to think that the perspective proper to medicine and other arts like it is a naturalistic one, even though to the Stoic way of thinking, this is a narrow or restricted way of viewing matters that can be subsumed in a broader perspective from which nature is seen as the expression of divine reason, indeed, in a sense, identical to it.

If this suggestion is on the right lines, the distinction between the natural and the non-natural does gain a purchase in Stoicism. Not only can there be analogues of indicative signification, which do not raise the question that we have been considering — the conclusion of the sign-inference will be accepted on the strength of the rationally compelling grounds afforded by the sign, but the presumably much larger mass of signs grasped through long observation can be understood along purely empirical lines. What is more, they will be so understood much of the time and by human beings reasoning in most capacities. What is striking and distinctive about the Stoics, however, is that one branch of divination as they conceive it is both an impeccably rigorous application of empirical method and a means of interpreting divinely given signals. Understood in one way and viewed from one perspective, the signs with which it is occupied are or are used as natural signs. Viewed in broader perspective, however, the empirically grounded sign-inferences that the diviner draws are not natural in a way that can be sharply contrasted with the non-natural. For they are not only the product of divine intentions, but of intentions whose divine author intends that they be recognized, at least by diviners, whose other tasks, it will be recalled, include interpreting other kinds of message from the gods, for example, portents.

7

Matters are otherwise when we turn to the Epicureans, whose views about the gods could hardly be more different from the Stoa's. The gods of Epicurus, such as they are, did not create the world, exert no influence on it, and could not care less about human beings. Nothing in the world observed by human beings is the product of divine intention, and there is, as a result, a clean break between natural signs and the signs human beings create and give to one another, even if the Epicureans do not themselves speak of "signs" in this connection. The break stands out that much more clearly as, in the Epicurean view, the development of the latter depends on the prior existence of the former. Epicurus' pioneering account of the origin of speech and language envisages a transition from an early phase in which human beings' spontaneous vocal utterances serve as what we would call natural signs of their mental states and emotions, to later phases where the possibility of conveying information that is revealed in this way is deliberately exploited by human beings, who now fashion and use words in order to communicate their thoughts to each other (*Letter to Herodotus* 75–76; cf. Lucretius, *De rerum natura* 5.1056–90).[11]

Our attempts to understand Epicurean views about sign inference have been greatly assisted by the survival, in the form of a papyrus buried at Herculaneum by the eruption of Mount Vesuvius in A.D. 79, of a work by the first-century B.C. poet and Epicurean philosopher Philodemus: *On Signs and Sign-inferences* (the *De signis* for short).[12] Among the problems presented by what we find in it is one that has to do with the distinction between the empirical and the rational, or rather its apparent absence. As we have already seen, the Epicurean position would seem at first to be a paradigmatic example of rationalist thought. According to empiricism, knowledge is confined to the phenomena, which are accessible to perception, and the patterns of conjunction and sequence that are observed to obtain among them and does not extend to so-called non-evident matters.

A very large part, perhaps the largest part, of Epicurus and his followers' energies were occupied with natural philosophy. Their motives were idiosyncratic to be sure, namely, by offering a purely naturalistic account of nature and natural phenomena to remove divine agency from the picture and so free human beings from superstition, which was in their — the Epicureans' — view the principal obstacle to happiness. To this end, Epicurus elaborated an atomic theory of matter and offered explanations for natural phenomena, paying special attention to heavenly phenomena.

To show how we could in fact know the contents of his theory, he also developed an epistemology. This theory seems to fit very comfortably in Sextus' epistemological framework. Direct observation of the phenomena secures ground-level truths, which in turn serve as points of departure for sign-inferences and demonstrations by means of which truths about the non-evident realm are won, whether about atoms, rendered inaccessible to perception by their smallness or heavenly bodies, put beyond the reach of observation by their distance from us (Epicurus, *Letter to Herodotus* 38, 39; *Letter to Pythocles* 87, 97, 104; Diogenes Laertius 10.32). It looks very much as if the Epicureans are to be classified as rationalists who subscribed to a theory of indicative signs, as Sextus conceived it, even if they did not describe themselves in this way or use the term "indicative sign" itself (and those who did held a view in some ways different from what Sextus leads us to expect).

To judge by Philodemus' testimony and hints from other Epicurean works, however, this expectation was not fulfilled. We search in vain for the contrast that defined the controversy between rationalism and empiricism. The position that we find instead appears to occupy a no-man's land that should not exist according to the framework of assumptions in terms of which rationalists and empiricists defined their opposition to each other. The medical Empiricists define experience as knowledge of what has been observed to occur in the same way many times. That a ring around the moon precedes rain or that venesection is followed by the remission of fever become part of experience by being observed repeatedly. No amount of observation, however, can make these anything other than empirical generalizations by grasping which we know *that* without being any closer to understanding the underlying causes and natures because of which things are as they are observed to be and in terms of which a genuine explanation of *why* they are would have to be formulated. One important consequence is that the so-called transition to the similar whereby we take things similar to those of which we have had experience to be similar to them cannot be a source of new knowledge by itself,

[11] Compare Verlinsky 2005.

[12] An edited text with translation and explanatory essays is contained in De Lacy 1978.

but only a source of hypotheses which must be confirmed by observation before they become known by becoming part of experience.[13]

According to the Epicurean views preserved by Philodemus, sign-inferences, whether about humdrum matters like smoke and fire or the fundamental truths of physics, are all grounded in what looks very much like the repeated observation of the same thing that is the Empiricists' point of departure. Indeed, the Epicureans sometimes speak, as the Empiricists did, of experience and history. Yet somehow the result of such observation is that it becomes inconceivable that things could be other than they have been seen to be. And the scope of the inferences that we are entitled to draw on the basis of observation is not confined to items of precisely the same type as those that have been observed. Not only may we infer that all human beings are mortal wherever they may be from the fact that those we have observed are, but our knowledge of atoms and the void is based on inferences from the observed behavior of medium-sized bodies in our vicinity. What is more, the knowledge we gain in this way far from being restricted to facts *that* — empirical truths as we have been calling them — embraces necessary truths about the ultimate causes of things in terms of which everything else is to be explained and understood.

That this runs counter not only to our expectations but to those of the Epicureans' philosophical contemporaries is plain from the form and content of the *De signis* itself. The work takes the form of series of objections to Epicurean views with replies by Epicurean authorities. The opponents are not specified by name. They are usually thought to be Stoics, though it has been plausibly suggested that they were Academic skeptics. Be that as it may, they appear to have been moved by concerns of just the kind that we would expect, as we can see from the questions with which they challenge the Epicureans. "Why should the fact that all the human beings whom we have observed are mortal exclude the possibility that human beings whom we have not observed might be immortal?" "Why should the fact that bodies of observable size move only through surroundings relatively empty by comparison with them entitle us to infer that atoms move through absolutely empty space, that is, a void?" And "If the observed behavior of visible bodies is the basis of inferences to conclusions about the atoms, should we not infer that the so-called atoms are in fact breakable like all bodies in our experience without exception?"

The Epicureans had much to say in their own defense as the *De signis* makes clear. One way of describing their position would be to say that it defies or overcomes the limitations on experience as they are understood in the debate between rationalism and empiricism in both its ancient and modern versions. This way of putting things is, however, misleading if it suggest that the Epicureans made larger claims for what went under the name of "experience." So far as one can tell, they understood terms like "experience" and "observation" as others did. Rather, they seem to have supposed that observation furnished the basis for a grasp of the phenomena that was, if you will, more than empirical because it amounted to a limited grasp of the natures and causes at work in what was observed, which in turn furnished the basis for inferences to conclusions about the unobserved and the unobservable. A part in their account was played by *epilogismos*, which, however, differs in ways that are hard to get a fix on from what went under that head among the medical Empiricists.[14] The account as a whole presents many difficulties, and not only because of the poor state of the mainly papyrlogical evidence on which we are obliged to rely.

---

[13] Galen, *Subfiguratio empirica* 70 (in Deichgräber 1965: 14ff.).

[14] Compare Schofield 1996; Allen 2004.

Grappling with those difficulties is a task for another day, however. The object of this essay is not to get to the bottom of these problems, but to draw attention ancient Greek philosophical views about signs that do not fit easily with our assumptions, even though those assumptions belong to a framework that we have largely inherited from the Greeks. The existence of such views does not show that the framework is anything other than sturdy and useful in the extreme, but rather that it was not obvious or inescapable.

BIBLIOGRAPHY

Adamson, P.

2008 "Plotinus on Astrology." *Oxford Studies in Ancient Philosophy* 35: 265–91.

Allen, James

2001 *Inference from Signs: Ancient Debates about the Nature of Evidence*. Oxford: Oxford University Press.

2004 "Experience as a Source and Ground of Theory in Epicureanism." In *Re-inventions: Essays on Hellenistic and Early Roman Science*, edited by P. Lang, pp. 89–106. Apeiron 37.4. Kelowna: Academic Printing and Publishing.

Asmis, Elizabeth

1984 *Epicurus' Scientific Method*. Cornell Studies in Classical Philology 42. Ithaca: Cornell University Press.

Barnes, Jonathan; Myles F. Burnyeat; and Malcolm Schofield, editors

1980 *Doubt and Dogmatism: Studies in Hellenistic Epistemology*. Oxford: Oxford University Press.

Barnes, Jonathan; Jacques Brunschwig; Myles F. Burnyeat; and Malcolm Schofield, editors

1982 *Science and Speculation: Studies in Hellenistic Theory and Practice*. Cambridge: Cambridge University Press.

Barnes, Jonathan

1980 "Proof Destroyed." In *Doubt and Dogmatism: Studies in Hellenistic Epistemology*, edited by J. Barnes, M. F. Burnyeat, and M. Schofield, pp. 161–81. Oxford: Oxford University Press.

1988 "Epicurean Signs." In *Oxford Studies in Ancient Philosophy*, supplementary volume, edited by J. Annas and R. H. Grimm, pp. 91–134. Oxford: Oxford University Press.

Brunschwig, J.

1980 "Proof Defined." In *Doubt and Dogmatism: Studies in Hellenistic Epistemology*, edited by J. Barnes, M. F. Burnyeat, and M. Schofield, pp. 125–60. Oxford: Oxford University Press.

Burnyeat, Myles F.

1982 "The Origins of Non-deductive Inference." In *Science and Speculation: Studies in Hellenistic Theory and Practice*, edited by J. Barnes, J. Brunschwig, M. F. Burnyeat, and M. Schofield, pp. 193–238. Cambridge: Cambridge University Press.

Deichgräber, Karl, editor

1965 *Die griechische Empirikerschule: Sammlung der Fragmente und Darstellung der Lehre*. Berlin: Weidmann.

De Lacy, Phillip H.; and Estelle A. De Lacy

1978 *Philodemus: On Methods of Inference*. Scuola di Epicuro 1. Naples: Bibliopolis.

Frede, Michael

1990 "An Empiricist View of Knowledge: Memorism." In *Epistemology*, edited by S. Everson, pp. 225–50. Companions to Ancient Thought 1. Cambridge: Cambridge University Press.

Frede, Michael, and Richard Walzer, translators

1985 *Galen: Three Treatises on the Nature of Science*. Indianapolis: Hackett.

Grice, H. P.

1957 "Meaning." *Philosophical Review* 67: 377–88; reprinted in Grice 1989: 213–23.

1982 "Meaning Revisited." In *Mutual Knowledge*, edited by N. V. Smith, pp. 223–50 (New York: Academic Press); reprinted in Grice 1989: 283–303.

1989 *Studies in the Way of Words*. Cambridge: Harvard University Press.

Long, A. A.

1982 "Astrology: Arguments Pro and Contra." In *Science and Speculation: Studies in Hellenistic Theory and Practice*, edited by J. Barnes, J. Brunschwig, M. F. Burnyeat, and M. Schofield, pp. 165–92. Cambridge: Cambridge University Press.

Marquardt, I.; I. Mueller; and G. Helmreich

1967 *Scripta minora*. Bibliotheca scriptorum Graecorum et Romanorum Teubneriana I–III. Amsterdam: A. M. Hakkert (reprint of 1884–1893 edition).

Patzig, G.

1981 "Erkenntnisgründe, Realgrunde und Erklärungen (zu *Anal. Post.* A 13)." In *Aristotle on Science: The Posterior Analytics*, edited by E. Berti, pp. 141–56. Studia aristotelica 9. Padua: Antenore.

Philippson, R.

1881 *De Philodemi libro, qui est* Περὶ σημειῶν καὶ σημειώσεων *et Epicureorum doctrina logica*. Berlin: Berliner Buchdruckerei Actien-Gesellschaft.

Rochberg, Francesca

2004 *The Heavenly Writing: Divination, Horoscopy, and Astronomy in Mesopotamian Culture*, Cambridge: Cambridge University Press

Schofield, Malcolm

1996 "Epilogismos: An Appraisal." In *Rationality in Greek Thought*, edited by M. Frede and G. Striker, pp. 221–37. Oxford: Oxford University Press.

Sedley, D. N.

1982 "On Signs." In *Science and Speculation: Studies in Hellenistic Theory and Practice*, edited by J. Barnes, J. Brunschwig, M. F. Burnyeat, and M. Schofield, pp. 239–72. Cambridge: Cambridge University Press.

Verlinsky, Alexander

2005 "Epicurus and His Predecessors On the Origin of Language." In *Language and Learning: Philosophy of Language in the Hellenistic Age*, edited by D. Frede and B. Inwood, pp. 56–100. Cambridge: Cambridge University Press.

Wardle, David

2006 *Cicero on Divination: De divinatione, Book 1*. Clarendon Ancient History Series. Oxford: Oxford University Press.

4

THREE STRIKES AND YOU'RE OUT! A VIEW ON COGNITIVE THEORY AND THE FIRST-MILLENNIUM EXTISPICY RITUAL

ULLA SUSANNE KOCH, INDEPENDENT SCHOLAR

In the past decades scholars from fields such as anthropology, science of religion, and psychology have sought to understand — or "explain" as it is often put — religious and magical phenomena in the framework of "cognitive science"; inspired by the advances in areas of research within neuroscience and cognitive psychology.[1] At the same time, as this symposium illustrates, the study of the well-nigh ubiquitous phenomenon of divination has also blossomed in recent years. However, most research of a more theoretical nature has been done within the study of contemporary, mostly African, divination systems.[2] Why could cognitive theory be relevant for divination? For one thing, cognitive theory is a way of getting past the sometimes more confusing than enlightening discussions of definitions. The very nature of divination is a topic that has often been discussed. It has been described as having, or uniting, traits which are characteristic of religion, magic, science,[3] or scholarship — or quite the reverse, it has been defined as something of a bastard phenomenon NOT quite belonging to the domain of religion, magic, science, or scholarship. Divination can also be described from a purely functionalist perspective, as a way of dealing with social or cognitive uncertainty, or a way of controlling the environment, for example, protecting the king, "making it so" by a performative magical act (Cryer 1994). These purposes it undoubtedly also served, but that does not explain its expressions or content, neither are these functions characteristic only of divination but are equally valid for a range of other cultural and/or religious phenomena. It could also be argued that divination is not only a way of reducing anxiety but could also equally well be a way of generating it. The reports of the astrologers to the Neo-Assyrian court amply demonstrate that assiduous observation of the earth and sky for ominous signs ensures no lack of new topics for worry. Furthermore, it has been posited that religion is "a manifestly practical enterprise" (Tremlin 2006: 112). It can be argued that the primary function of everyday religious practice is not to ease existential angst, to hold societies together, or to answer cosmological questions — it plays this and other roles — but "the central role that religion plays in peoples'

[1] For a good introduction to cognitive theory applied to religion, see Tremlin 2006.

[2] The application of anthropological approaches to the practice of divination in the ancient world is well under way, but has mainly been attempted in the field of classical antiquity (e.g., the studies by Lisdorf 2007 and Rosenberger 2001) but also to some extent in Assyriology (e.g., Cryer 1994; Guinan 2002; and elsewhere).

[3] For example, Jeyes 1991–92. Tedlock 2001: 194: "Impressed with the systematic divination procedures or "the orderliness which it may ascribe to the universe" a number of researchers have allowed divination at least a tentative space within the objective sphere of Western science." A. K. Guinan (2002: 18–19) stresses the importance of discussing divination per se, not "subsumed into these larger cultural categories" (i.e., magic, science, religion). Science and divination are similar in that they both are casuistic and paradigmatic in form "but [divination] cannot do what it claims." This is of course an objection raised against magic of all sorts.

lives is to get things done, to make things right, and to keep them that way." I believe that to a certain extent this function at least holds true for divination. Among other things, divination has been interpreted as primarily a heuristic pursuit, as a form of sense-making involving a categorization of the universe.[4] Divination analyzed from the point of view of hermeneutics, divination viewed as a semantic system, is certainly rewarding and relevant. The reading of signs according to a fixed semantic code is central to many divinatory systems, not least the Mesopotamian, and in Mesopotamian divination it cuts across such distinctions as *signa impetrativa* and *oblativa*, provoked/induced and unprovoked omens. Both induced signs as well as signs sent outside the frame of a ritual setting were read according to a fixed code.[5]

Categorization and manipulation of symbols have long been of central concern for cognitive psychologists,[6] and unraveling the semantic code utilized in a given divinatory system can yield insight into the social, ethical, and other normative bias of the culture from which it springs.[7] The diviner holds the "hermeneutic keys" to the divinatory code. The various hermeneutic practices used for instance within Mesopotamian divination as a means of revealing layers upon layers of meaning in the divinatory system are themselves worthy of study. Some, but not all, are explained and attested in the letters from ancient scholars as well as in commentaries and esoteric texts. However, this approach is in danger of neglecting the functions mentioned as well as the undeniable magical/religious aspects of many divinatory practices, as, for instance, extispicy. Divination is in fact so complex and multifaceted a phenomenon, that I believe it would be overly reductionist to explain it with reference to a single theory. Like "religion," divination is what Boyer called an "impure object"[8] exactly because it can not be explained or described by a single theoretical framework. However, I believe there is general consensus that whatever roots divination may have, and whatever purposes it may serve — be they epistemological, psychological, social, political, or religious — divination is certainly a practical means of obtaining otherwise inaccessible information: "divination is a way of exploring the unknown in order to elicit answers (that is, oracles) to questions beyond the range of ordinary human understanding."[9] Even this simple view on divination — as a means of gathering information — presents a very confused picture. The confusion is immediately apparent already from a cursory look at the evidence. The kind of knowledge concerned can pertain to the future, the present, or the past; the source can be intentional agents: gods, ancestors, spirits, or there may be no personified interlocutor as such; the privileged knowledge can be obtained by various means, ranging from such quiet pursuits as studying the sky or reading other environmental cues, performing an experiment using a special technique, to the more spectacular or even violent in the form of possession and ecstasy. Divination can involve elaborate rituals performed by specialists or it can be part of daily life accessible to Everyman.[10]

[4] For instance, already the French scholars Durkheim and Mauss (1903: 40ff.) argued that divination was a system of classification.

[5] The terminology used to describe various types of divination is described, for example, in Rochberg 2004: 47ff. For a full discussion of the many terms used to distinguish different types of divination based on the divinatory method, see, for example, Lisdorf 2007: chapter 3.

[6] For example, the works of C. S. Peirce, J. Skorupski, D. Sperber, and others.

[7] For example, Sørensen (1999: 187) arguing that divination gets its authority from its close connection with cosmology — the celestial and mythical exemplar of any human situation are found by divination. "This constitutes the very *raison d'être* of a divination system." See also Peek 1991.

[8] Sørensen, in press; and Boyer 1994.

[9] For example, Tedlock 2001: 189.

[10] Compare Tedlock 2001. For an introduction to the history of research into divination as a general phenomenon, see, for example, Cryer 1994; Lisdorf 2007: chapter 2.

Extispicy was one of the most pervasive and successful of the many Mesopotamian divinatory practices. With roots going back to the third millennium, it gained in importance over the millennia and became an important element in decision-making at the Neo-Assyrian court. This may have been because it was a practical means of obtaining privileged information concerning matters of immediate urgency to the individual or the state. In the following I try to apply elements from cognitive theory of religion to see if they can help shed light on a particular question posed by the Mesopotamian ritual of extispicy viewed in this light, namely why the only remedy for an unfavorable extispicy was to perform another? If necessary we know the diviner could repeat the procedure up to three times in a row, but in the worst case, when the answers were consistently against the client's hopes and desires, he just had to wait patiently and not try again until after the stipulated term had expired.[11] The gods did not like too-persistent questioning: "If the diviner constantly performs extispicy, he dies the death of transgression (*arnu*)"; three chances were all he had.[12]

First we must test if asking again, perhaps rephrasing the question, really was the only option open to the diviner and his client. If we accept that extispicy was not countered by apotropaic or appeasement rituals, the next question is, why? That this should be so is in my opinion by no means self-evident. Alone from a purely theological point of view one could argue that in extispicy you ask the gods for their decision, but in other forms of divination the will of the gods is no less directly expressed — in astrology the gods themselves signal their intentions with their celestial manifestations. Why is it possible to counter the expressed will of the gods in one case and not in the other? It is necessary to take a look at the kind of information obtained by extispicy, was it somehow different from that gained by other kinds of divination? Did the divinatory technique itself play a role? And finally, what was the relationship to the structure of the apotropaic rituals themselves?

Is there any evidence that extispicy was countered by apotropaic rituals? One of the characteristics of divination is that it serves as a guide to action, often ritual action. As put by Ann Guinan, "magic and divination operate from the same semantic foundation, but always bear an inverse relationship to each other" ... "what divination reveals, magic can resolve" (Guinan 2002: 18). From the ethnographic record we know that very often the results of a divinatory session are indeed closely linked with specific apotropaic or appeasement rituals. Divination itself and the ritual actions responding to the information gained by divination thus form part of the same event frame[13] but are not identical. Indeed, an Assyrian scholar stresses the role of the god Ea as sender of both omens and corresponding apotropaic rituals: "Ea has done, Ea has undone. He who caused the earthquake has also created the apotropaic ritual against it" (Parpola 1993: no. 56 rev. 9–12). It is often more or less automatically assumed that

---

[11] According to, for example, *Multābiltu* in the case of a given joker-sign (*pitruštu*): "It (the extispicy) has turned for you. For undertaking an enterprise: drop it until its term (i.e., date set by the omen), do it only after its term (has passed)," CT 31 46–48:12′–13′; see Koch 2005: 139. In an Old Babylonian letter to Zimri-Lim the god Addu is quoted for this admonition to the king with what seems to me to be a reference to extispicy: "When you go on a campaign, do not set out without an oracle (*tērtu*). If I am present in your oracle you shall go on the campaign, otherwise, do not go outside the gate"; see Durand 1993: 44.

[12] Zimmern 1901: no. 11 col. iii lines 18–19; cf. also CT 51 147:39′.

[13] Compare Sørensen, in press, p. 324: "Divinatory practices are often an integrated part of a large series of event frames involving ritual actions 'responding' to causes revealed through divinatory practices." The frame as metaphor for a set of socially constructed understandings that make up the context for any specific interaction was developed by E. Goffman (1974).

apotropaic rituals were associated also with extispicy. For instance, Erica Reiner[14] suggested that one might expect all the major omen compendia to have had parallel apotropaic rituals, and she assumes that they existed for both astrological omina and for the omina collected in the extispicy series *Bārûtu*. *Namburbi*s are of course well attested for "everyday divination" of the kind found in the series *Šumma izbu* or *Šumma ālu*. Whereas the letters and reports from Assyrian and Babylonian scholars demonstrate that aversive action in the form of various rituals, including *namburbi*s, was not uncommon in connection with astrological omina,[15] there is no similar evidence that apotropaic or appeasement rituals were ever performed in connection with extispicy. Aversive action in response to unfavorable extispicy is never explicitly mentioned in the scholarly correspondence of the Neo-Assyrian kings, nor to my knowledge are they attested to in texts from the second millennium.

*Namburbi*s that explicitly mention extispicy do exist but are in fact quite rare. As far as I can tell there were actually two different types of *namburbi*s directly connected with some aspect of extispicy:

1. Prophylactic rituals performed to safeguard the diviner and the extispicy
2. Apotropaic rituals performed to avert the evil portended by a failed extispicy

The prophylactic type of *namburbi* was quite rare, it included rituals for brisk trade and for bringing distant people near. The diviner could perform a *namburbi* before a divination session in order to prepare himself properly for performing extispicy, for instance, washing his leather bag[16] which contained the cultic implements of his trade such as cedar wood.[17] He could also perform rituals which safeguarded him from failure when serving an important client like the king. In the early morning before an extispicy, he could perform a *namburbi* to ensure that Shamash and Adad would stand by him in his "verdict," that he may experience renown in extispicy (*tanatti bārûti amāru*) and make himself famous (*šuma rabâ leqû*).[18] The apotropaic type of *namburbi* with reference to extispicy is structured like any other *namburbi* used to avert evil omens. The *namburbi*s seem to refer to phenomena that prevented the proper performance of the sacrifice and obstructed a reliable reading of the extispicy. This would include extreme anomalies of the entrails. The semantic code of extispicy involved the study of tiny variations on a theme; in general, serious malformations were of no relevance, or rather, they could change the whole session into something completely different and in itself ill-portending. I suggest that the purpose of these *namburbi*s therefore was not to counteract an unfavorable extispicy as such but to protect against the evil portended by

---

[14] Reiner 1995: 82–84. Caplice (1974: 7f.) commented upon the fact that the *namburbi*s themselves commonly refer to terrestrial omina, whereas the letters and reports most often mention *namburbi*s in connection with astrological omina.

[15] For examples of apotropaia mentioned in connection with astrological omina, compare, for example, Koch-Westenholz 1995.

[16] Reverse of Zimmern 1901: no. 11, and duplicates; see Zimmern 1901: 112ff.; and Farber 1987: 240f.

[17] Cedar wood apparently played an important role even though we do not know exactly how. "To raise the cedar" (*erēna našû*) appears to be a *pars pro toto* term for performing divination, whether it means to perform an incense offering or simply to raise a rod made of cedar. Compare the discussion by Starr (1983: 48). Cedar wood is already mentioned in connection with what appears to be a reference to extispicy in a Sumerian source, Poebel 1914: no. 76 col. vi 2–10: *me-bi šu mu-na-ab-d*[u_7] *máš-gíd-gíd a d.utu-šè mu-un-zi-*[*x*] *gudá šu-sikil-gim máš-gíd-gíd-e giš.eren d.utu-šè mu-un-zi-zi-i* u_4 *ti-la ku-li-ni-im en-na úš-a* gal_5*-la gal-ni*$^!$*-im* "He made its rituals perfect for him, the diviner rises before father Utu, like a guda-priest with clean hands the diviner raises cedar wood to Utu again and again."

[18] Zimmern 1901: nos. 75–78.

technical problems connected with the performance of the divinatory ritual. For instance, a *namburbi* could be performed if the slaughter itself was somehow defective — if no blood ran from the veins when the neck of the sacrificial animal was cut, if important organs were missing, or if they were seriously deformed.[19] This view is in agreement with Maul (1994: 432), who suggested that the *namburbi*s were performed due to the "Schweigen des Šamaš," that is, when the extispicy ritual failed to produce an answer. He does, however, assume that *namburbi*s could also be used to counteract the evil omens of an unfavorable extispicy, and he suggests that a *namburbi* amulet[20] and a universal *namburbi*[21] with reference to extispicy illustrates this. I believe that neither the amulet nor the universal *namburbi* are actually directed against an unfavorable extispicy result, but like the rest are directed against a failed or flawed performance of extispicy. The amulet mentions ill omens stemming from "the evil of flawed, terrifying signs, evil and unfavorable (signs) from performing the ritual (*lipit qāti*), or from the lamb having a disease (*hiniq immeri*) or from making the sacrifice (*nīqa naqû*) or from anything else in performance of extispicy (*nēpešti bārûti*)." All this could well refer to evil portended by signs observed in connection with the performance of extispicy, not the extispicy result itself. In the *namburbi*s the evil omens stem from flesh which is described as *šīru hatûti pardūtu*[22] "flawed or terrifying" flesh, or as *haliqti šīri*[23] missing flesh. Neither *haṭû* nor *pardu* are normal terms for unfavorable signs found in the protases of extispicy omina or in the extispicy reports. Circumstances surrounding the performance of divination were themselves observed and interpreted as ominous signs, as we know was the case with the behavior of the sacrificial animal itself.[24] This resembles the way we take omens from the act of catching the bride's bouquet — something which is totally unrelated to the efficacy of the Christian marital ritual. The ill omen averted is thus not the result of an extispicy, and is not interpreted as such, but rather as an individual unfavorable sign which could be countered by an apotropaic ritual. The two known *namburbi* catalogs, one from late Uruk, the other from Assurbanipal's library, include references to exactly these two types of *namburbi* in connection with extispicy and can therefore not be taken as evidence that *namburbi*s associated with the extispicy series itself existed.[25]

Interestingly, the ancient Greek version of divination by the entrails of a sacrificial animal used in warfare also had no link with apotropaia. M. Flower suggests that extispicy was the last of the major divinatory practices to reach Greece from the Near East. The Greeks themselves

---

[19] Compare the *namburbi*s edited by Maul 1994: 432–38: no bleeding, missing gall bladder, parts of the liver missing, missing kidney; and Maul 1994: 439–44; compare also 185:3.

[20] Edited by Maul 1994: 185–90.

[21] Edited by Maul 1994: 495ff.

[22] The universal *namburbi* (VAT 13988:2) mentions uzu.meš *hu-uṭ-ṭu-te*; see Maul 1994: 495. Such signs could as mentioned also be called "flawed and frightening" (KAR 26:41 uzu *ha-ṭu-te pár-du-te* nu dùg.ga.meš); cf. also the duplicate passage in Goetze 1939: 12:5; KAR 286:12 (universal *namburbi*); and Maul 1994: 185:3. *Pardu* is a term most commonly used of dreams; compare CAD P 183.

[23] See the discussion in Maul 1994: 439. This term is also found in two letters, in fragmentary context, in Parpola 1993: no. 200, and no. 212, both from an exorcist. It is impossible to tell from the context whether they refer to extispicy.

[24] Omina pertaining to the "behaviour of the sacrificial animal" were collected in a small compendium independent from the main series of extispicy omina *Bārûtu*. See Jeyes 1980: 13.

[25] Contra Reiner 1995: 83. The Uruk catalog mentions "If in the house of a man or the palace of the king missing flesh (*ha-liq-ti* uzu) seizes him" and "If a man brings an offering and when cutting the neck of the sheep no blood pours" (W 22279 8′–9′; see Maul 1994: 192). The Niniveh catalog mentions "When the diviner [washes] his bag" and "When the diviner [---] his divination" (K2389+: 19–20; see Maul 1994: 198. Both as suggested by Maul connected with the ritual preparation of the diviner before performance.

considered the art of divination to be either a homegrown idea or imported from Egypt, by the classical period extispicy was certainly a fully integrated part of Greek culture, whatever its origins.[26] From Xenophon's *Anabasis* we have a description of how the generals of the famous army of 10,000 Greek mercenaries practiced divination from "bloody sacrifice" on the route into and out of Babylonia in 401 B.C. Since the mercenaries were under Spartan leadership the practices described probably are closest to Lacedaemonian customs rather than Athenian but we know that the practice of divination by inspection of the entrails, primarily the liver, was widespread in classical antiquity. (Pseudo-) Xenophon elsewhere describes how the Spartan king would perform sacrifices before every decisive step of a military campaign:[27]

- At home before taking off.
- At the boundary of the city-state (*polis*) before crossing.
- At the river.
- In the camp.
- At the front lines before joining battle.
- After the victory (of course).

Most of these are decision points to which any Assyrian king would nod his head in recognition. The rituals and sacrifices differed from Mesopotamian practice in many respects; for one thing they seem to always have been addressed to the god most closely involved or relevant to the situation at hand. En route, Xenophon and the other generals performed sacrifices almost every day and sometimes many times a day. At one point they were so low on livestock suitable for sacrifice and eating that they bought a draught animal simply to perform divination in order to know whether it would be a good idea to go out foraging (pillaging the locals, that is). At no time, even when facing the enemy or hunger, could anything avert an unfavorable sign. The Greek soldiers wait and starve, and their generals perform one sacrifice after the other, sometimes rephrasing the question, until they get a favorable sign in an offering.[28] As in Mesopotamia, the limit seems to have been three performances of divination a day in the context of warfare as described by Xenophon. Apparently, however, it was possible in other contexts to avert unfavorable omens by acts of expiation and sacrifice before performing a renewed extispicy (Flower 2008: 80–84).

Extispicy was not the only kind of Mesopotamian divination with no known associated apotropaia. There exist no *namburbi*s that mention signs obtained by two other forms of induced omina: lecanomancy (oil divination) and libanomancy (smoke divination), and also none for the physiognomic omen series *Alamdimmu* and other omina concerned with the behavior or appearance of a person.[29] Well aware that the absence of evidence is not evidence of absence, Reiner suggested that the distinction between which omina required aversive action and which did not could be due to the character of the divination itself, whether it was "prognostic" or "diagnostic." The assumption is that since a diagnostic omen would be more concerned with a cause in the past, it was perceived as not possible to change the result anyway, hence no reason for apotropaic rituals. A common topic of lecanomancy is the gender of one's offspring, and no amount of ritual action could apparently change that. This may be so for the physiognomic omina: there is not much you can do about your features — there

[26] See Flower 2008: 25, 44; see also Burkert 1992: 46ff.

[27] See Egense 2002: 6ff., for Xenophon, *The Polity of the Athenians and Lacedaemonians.*

[28] See Egense 2002; also Jameson 1991.

[29] Compare Reiner 1995: 84.

certainly is not much point in cutting off your nose, even if it has an ill-favored shape.[30] In general, the explanation is not valid and I suspect another explanation must be found at least for lecanomancy and libanomancy. Finding the cause or nature of the evil is often the first step to curing it, and aversive rituals are commonly connected with diagnostic divination. The link between ritual aversive action and divination has nothing to do with the temporal orientation of the divination, whether it is retrospective of prospective,[31] but the idea that the nature of the divinatory practice plays a role merits further investigation.

When we look at the range of questions asked in the first-millennium Mesopotamian extispicy queries, *tamītus*, and reports, we see that even though a wide variety of topics are represented, the knowledge sought after is always of relevance to the health and happiness of the individual, be it as a private person or as *persona publica* — as in the case of, for instance, the Assyrian kings — or it relates to the larger social environment. The purpose of the Old Babylonian diviner's ritual is simply to decide the case of "the well-being of NN son of NN" (Starr 1983: 31). Even if we regard divination such as extispicy that can be classfied as relying on *signa impetrativa* from a functionalist point of view, as a magical confirmation of a proposed action (performative utterance),[32] it still supplies knowledge which falls within these categories. The standard topics for extispicy according to, for example, *Multābiltu* are the well-being of the king, the land, the camp, the patient, for warfare, for taking a city, healing the sick, rain, and "undertaking an enterprise or whatever else." The *tamītus*[33] give a more detailed picture. The questions were always very meticulously formulated to minimize ambiguity. Basically, there were two types of questions. The first type are questions concerning a special situation or undertaking; the second type regards a specified period of time, detailing any imaginable calamity and asking whether it would occur within that period. These examples stem from the *tamītus*:

FITNESS OF THE INDIVIDUAL

- Safe night-watch.
- Personal safety for one year "at the command of god, goddess, king, noble, and prince."
- Lunar eclipse (Sin).
- Ambition to be a temple administrator (temple personnel).
- Outcome of river-ordeal — to some degree dependent on the "mind of his accuser" and the river.
- Hunting.
- Horse appropriate for god.
- Risk of flooding.
- Marriage (acceptance by father-in-law).

[30] See also the discussion by Rochberg 2004: 50f.

[31] For example, in Nyole (Whyte 1991) and Ndembu (Turner 1975) divination.

[32] For example, Cryer 1994: 117 et passim. See critique of this approach by Joel Sweek (2000).

[33] Similar lists of reasons for divination have been compiled in the anthropological literature; see, e.g., Lisdorf 2007: 59. Lisdorf suggest that divination is used as recourse when the "life model" (i.e., ideal circumstances in life according to norms of a given culture) clashes with reality; cf. also Turner 1961: 16. For summaries of purposes of Babylonian extispicy, see Koch-Westenholz 2002: 140ff., with previous literature.

- Male offspring.
- Survival of pregnant woman.
- Taking a second wife.
- Recovery from illness.
- Faithfulness of servant.
- Truthfulness of wife.
- Sending a messenger.
- Reliability of physician.

FITNESS OF ORGANIZATION

- Military campaign (enemy, advisors, divine assistance).
- Safety of city from enemy action.
- Safety from enemies for people leaving the protecting wall of the city.
- Safety of watch from enemy attack.
- Safety of fort from the enemy.
- Damming a river.
- Mutiny.

As mentioned, on a very general level, what is of interest are matters to do with the physical and social well-being of the individual and his/her immediate social and physical environment.[34] Very often the first category is of course implicitly contained in the second. When keeping watch, personal safety is also involved; when the king goes on a campaign he may well fall in battle himself; defeat of the army can have terrible consequences for the community and its members individually. So far this kind of information is fully in accordance with what we would expect from any "successful divinatory practice" and is not essentially different from what other Mesopotamian divinatory practices supplied (Sørensen, in press). Knowledge of this kind is what Boyer has termed "strategic social information" (e.g., Boyer 2001: 173). The ability to process strategic social information can be argued to be a prerequisite for successful human interaction and ultimately survival, and therefore could be an example of an adaptive cognitive faculty as argued by Boyer. To succeed as a social animal it is necessary to read others, to read the "signs, signals, and minds" of others, and "to pair implicit knowledge with explicit information" (Tremlin 2006: 33ff.).

The intention and will of others are of vital importance but can be hard to define and identify. What is significant depends entirely on context and experience. Strategic information has two important features: it is often obtained through indirect sources (so indeed why not divination?), and generally it is of lasting value (Tremlin 2006: 115ff.). Cognitive science operates with two fundamental "mental mechanisms," the Agency Detection Device (ADD) and the Theory of Mind Mechanism (ToMM). ADD is eager to spot intentional agents in the world and ToMM normally works in unison with ADD supplying agents with minds, but at the same time, may supply minds even where no agent is identified. ToMM is seen, for instance, in perceptions of deceased persons as having wishes and emotions even though manifestly dead.[35] In view of this we would expect many of the *tamītu* questions to imply the action and/or

[34] As holds true for most kinds of divination; see Sørensen, in press, p. 323; Lisdorf 2007: 53.

intention of human-like agents. Indeed, in many cases agents are mentioned, either individual humans (wife, servant, temple personnel, father-in-law), groups (typically the enemy), or superhuman agents as gods (Sin or the River). The advantage of framing an intangible threat in terms of intentional agents is that it moves possible countermeasures from the physical to the social domain and thereby facilitates representations of possible control. This matches the well-known picture from Babylonian apotropaic and other rituals including *šurpû* and *maqlû*, where misfortune, ill health, etc., are described as the result of malevolent or angered human or superhuman agents. Sørensen suggests that a divinatory system that transforms threats to individual into previously undisclosed interactions between intentional agents is especially strong-lived (Sørensen, in press, p. 324). Even though intentional agents are represented in extispicy queries, this cannot be said to be very evident from the queries, it is a little more apparent in the *tamītus* (see list above). Intentional agents often figure in extispicy omen apodoses: witches, demons, oaths, kings, or angry gods. However, the transformation of threats to the social domain is perhaps clearest in the extispicy ritual itself and I suggest that exactly this transformation is what makes the kind of information extispicy supplied different.

The extispicy ritual itself was presented as a dialogue. The diviner asked (*ša'ālu*) and the god answered (*apālu*), preferably with a "firm yes." In the queries the question is formulated thus: "Does your great divinity know it? Is it decreed and confirmed in a favorable case (of extispicy) by the command of your great divinity, Shamash, great lord? Will he who can see, see it? Will he who can hear, hear it?" The Akkadian phrase is not necessarily to be understood as a question, but either way the implication is that the god has access to the answer and can make it known to the questioner.[36] The closing formula of queries sums up: "Be present in this ram; place an affirmative answer (*anna kēna*), favorable, propitious omens of the flesh of the query (*tāmītu*) by the command of your great divinity so that I may see them." But this was not a straightforward way of communicating. The diviner had to perform an elaborate ritual in order to obtain the desired knowledge. The first-millennium rituals collected in Zimmern 1901: nos. 1–20, show that divination could be performed in the frame of a complex ritual lasting from sunset to sunrise, in which one or more sheep were sacrificed to Shamash, Adad, and other gods and other offerings were brought as well. Apart from the ram that was used for divination, other lambs were also slaughtered and sacrifices were made. The distinction between divination and magic rituals, that gifts go from man to god in the latter not the former,[37] does not hold for extispicy: "The diviner shall not approach the place of judgment, he should not lift the cedar, without present and gifts, they (the gods) will not reveal to him the secret answer to his question" (*tāmīt pirišti*) (Zimmern 1901: 118 [no. 24]).

Interestingly, the extispicy ritual has one important thing in common with *namburbi*-rituals, namely, that the ritual is metaphorically described as a judgment (Maul 1999: 126ff.). The answer the diviner established was commonly referred to as a divine judgment or a "decision" (*purussû*). Shamash was the "lord of verdict" (*bēl dīni*), the "Judge of Heaven and Earth."[38] In Zimmern 1901: no. 11 rev. line 1, the diviner is instructed to "perform a sacrifice, establish

[35] As evidenced by, for example, ancestor cult also in Mesopotamia. See Tremlin 2006: 102ff.; compare also Sørensen 2007: 33ff.

[36] Lambert translates this phrase differently: "Your great divinity knows. The seer will see, the hearer will hear." Lambert (2007: 17), interprets it as an implied threat to the gods — if they do not answer or get the answer wrong, it will not be good for their reputation.

[37] Guinan 2002: 18.

[38] *Tamītus* and *ikribu*-prayers in the rituals of the diviner are addressed to Shamash and Adad, "queries" only to Shamash.

a verdict" (*dīna eppuš*), and in one of the rituals of the diviner he is told to "sit on the seat of the judge" in front of Shamash and Adad (Zimmern 1901: 104 [nos. 1–20 line 122]). The ritual scene is called either "the place of decision by extispicy (*bārûtu*)" (Zimmern 1901: 96 [nos. 1–20 line 6]), or "the place of judgement" (Zimmern 1901: 96 [nos. 1–20 line 16]). In the Old Babylonian ritual of the diviner,[39] the diviner prays to Shamash to "place a true verdict" in the sacrificial lamb, to judge the case in the divine assembly, and have the verdict recorded by the divine scribe Nisaba on the tablet of the gods. The terminology is the same as was used in connection with secular judgment: *arkata parāsu* "investigate the circumstances," *dīna dânu* "give a verdict," or *purussâ parāsu* "make a decision," and so on. Similar terminology is also found in other divinatory disciplines,[40] indeed, the metaphor is a central part of the conceptual underpinnings of Mesopotamian divination. The casuistic structure itself, characteristic both of omina and the law codes, has often been commented upon. But within the divinatory disciplines the metaphor of the court of law is most consequently and consistently used in extispicy, and the extispicy ritual actually *mise en scène*.

According to the theory of conceptual blending,[41] the cognitive process that attributes efficacy, authority, and credibility to a session of extispicy would be a cognitive integration of diverse conceptual spaces or domains. There are always at least four spaces at play which interact in a cognitive blend: two (or more) input spaces, a generic space which contains the elements common to the two input spaces, and the emerging blended space. In the case of the ritual of extispicy and the *namburbi*s, a blend between at least five domains would be present: a "mythic/sacred space," a "juridical space," and a "present social space" would merge with the "generic space" to form the "ritual space." During different phases of the ritual, different cognitive blendings would be viable and activated. In my opinion, the mapping of conceptual blendings can never be anything but a snapshot of one of many possible interpretations of the cognitive processes at play.

In order to enter the "ritual space" and through that be connected with the "sacred space" both the diviner and the client had to perform certain cleansing procedures. After the performance of the ritual the diviner probably also had to go through some steps to sever the connection to the sacred space, as is seen in other rituals, for example, the *namburbi*s. We have no description of this procedure, however the ritual described in Zimmern 1901: nos. 1–20 lines 126–227 details how the altars and incense burners for various gods had to be dismantled in reverse order from how they had been set up, so at least it seems that the diviner had to retrace his steps in order to leave the "ritual space." In the "ritual space" there are mappings between mythic and present space. The cultural hero Enmeduranki (the seventh antediluvian king) and the present-day diviner are linked by a metonymic link: blood, since ideally the diviner is a descendant of Enmeduranki.[42] This establishes a generic link between them; they

[39] Edited by Starr (1983).

[40] See, for instance, Rochberg 2004: 193ff.

[41] Fauconnier and Turner 2002: 45ff. Jesper Sørensen (2007) has drawn upon the theories of Lawson and McCauley 1990 concerning ritual action representation and Boyer's (1990; 1994; 1999; and 2001) theories of religious ideas combining them with concepts from cognitive psychology such as the theory of conceptual blending developed by Gilles Fauconnier and Mark Turner.

[42] Zimmern 1901: no. 24; compare Lambert 1998: 142f. and 149ff. In practice, this descent was not a prerequisite for practicing or discussing divination. That the Assyrian kings could show a keen interest and were permitted to discuss the secrets of extispicy with their scholars, is not necessarily due to their social status. We know from Old Babylonian sources (e.g., the Mari letters) that ordinary citizens also could discuss details of an extispicy and the interpretation of omina, but we do not know if they

partake of the same essence. The tools of the diviner — the stylus, the tablet, the bag, and the cedar wood — serve to reinforce this mapping, functioning as an iconic link between them. But though the person of the diviner is important for ritual efficacy (if anything is wrong with him, the ritual is a no-go) the primary source of ritual agency lies in the ritual action. The act of extispicy and the interpretation of the entrails were mapped by iconic identity connectors, since the art of extispicy itself, and certainly the code or technique applied in the interpretation of the entrails, were *identical* to the code given to mankind in mythic times by Enmeduranki. The implements again function as reinforcing iconic links. That the correct procedure was followed, the prayers pronounced clearly, and the diviner himself being in the right physical and mental state were of higher significance for giving the desired result — a reliable answer — than was the person of the diviner himself.

Just like a *namburbi,* the extispicy ritual activated a conceptual blending between the juridical domain and the sacred domain. A court case implies two intentional agents; and typically two parties will be represented at court: the accuser and the accused, or the victim and the culprit. Sometimes one party will not be present or may be represented by witnesses or symbolically by hem and hair or nail-imprint, just as in an extispicy ritual.[43] In a *namburbi* the ill-portending object would physically be present during the ritual. Even though the "attacker" is not physically present in an extispicy ritual, the blending with the juridical domain could suggest the existence of an opponent. The actions and intentions of the parties are laid open to judgment, and the divine judge is asked to rule in favor of the client. The transformation of the ominous sign from the physical to the social domain takes place in the ritual space through the cognitive blending with the judicial space.

I posit that the *namburbi*s were primarily used in connection with the kind of divination where the presentation of intentional agents is the weakest. There the blending with the domain of the courtroom has a similar effect as in the case of the extispicy ritual, it serves to remove troubles from the uncontrollable physical world to the more manageable social world. In *namburbi*s the signifier — the harbinger of the evil omen, whether this is a strange bird or seriously malformed entrails of the sacrificial lamb that renders it unsuitable for extispicy — is transformed into an intentional agent. The ritual is presented as a court of law with the signifier and the person to whom it occurred cast in the roles of the two contestants. As opposed to a performance of extispicy, in the context of a *namburbi* ritual, both suitors could be physically present. The metaphor of the court of law at the same time promotes the presentation of the omen as a communicative sign sent by an angry god whom the ritual serves to appease; in extispicy I suggest this is already inherent in the ritual with its many sacrifices and offerings.

Furthermore, according to McCauley and Lawson's action theory system, any action, including ritual action, has a simple syntax consisting of three or four basic elements. According to their theory, a small number of basic cognitive functions account for the similarities found in rituals all over the world and allow people to make intuitive judgments about the proper

kept on doing it in the first millennium. In ancient Greece divination was also a topic that could be discussed and practiced by laymen, even though there were traditions concerning the special qualities and genealogies of diviners. Experts would be called upon depending on the circumstances; see Flower 2008: chapter 2, esp. pp. 53ff.

[43] The client did not always have to be present in person, in the *tamītu*s and *ikribu*s the client was referred to as "the owner of this (black) wool and hem (of the garment)," or he could be represented by an imprint of his nail (Zimmern 1901: no. 11 line 3) on the tablet where his question was written.

forms, relationships, and efficacy of religious rituals.[44] This hinges on the understanding that religious rituals, though special actions, remain "actions" — people extend their skills for judging everyday actions to religious actions. What makes ritual action different from ordinary action they argue, is that it involves the "Principle of Superhuman Agency."[45] A "culturally postulated superhuman (CPS) agent."[46] of some kind plays a role as the source of efficacy. A CPS agent can and will always have a special connection with either of the elements involved.

In the case of extispicy these would be:

Agent	*Action / Instrument (Object)*	*Patient*
Diviner	Extispicy involving sacrifice and offerings / cedar wood	Client (can be represented by hem of clothing or nail impression)

According to one of the propositions of McCauley and Lawson's action theory system, there is a direct connection between how people judge the reversibility and repeatability of rituals and which of the three elements the CPS agent is perceived as most closely connected with.[47] The theory runs that if the CPS agent is involved most closely with the agent, the ritual is reversible but not repeatable: what god has done, god can undo, but god does not repeat himself. This would be true for initiation rites — a priest or diviner can only be initiated once, but it should be possible to throw him out of the community of people "in the know"[48] if he seriously violates the trust and secrets confided to him. An initiation should be reversible. "Special action / instrument" rituals and "special patient" rituals are, on the other hand, generally judged to be repeatable but not reversible. McCauley and Lawrence (2002: 26) suggest that sacrifices and rituals of penance fall within the group "special patient" rituals, since the CPS agent affects the patient most directly. Rituals of divination and blessing, on the other hand, generally fall in the category "special instrument" rituals. I would suggest that extispicy rituals actually span both the "special instrument" and the "special patient" categories. The closest connection with the "superhuman agent" in the extispicy ritual lies in the ritual act and the objects involved in the ritual; it thus falls under the "special instrument" or "special action" category. The diviner uses his special implements (cedar wood and leather bag), he applies the code of extispicy (a divine revelation and a "secret of heaven and earth"), and he performs multiple sacrifices and slaughters a very special lamb in which the gods are expected to be present and use for writing

[44] Compare Tremlin 2006: 166; McCauley and Lawson 2002. Lawson and McCauley's theory of religious ritual competence, a universal syntax of actions, is similar to Chomsky's structural description of language. Chomsky introduced the idea of an innate and thus universal grammar. The "universal grammar" is a stipulated system of simple cognitive rules that governs the structure of all the different actual grammars of the world, present and past (Chomsky 1975).

[45] For a further discussion of the nature of ritual, especially magical actions, see Sørensen 2007: chapter 6. Sørensen stresses that ritual action is characterized by a "transformation of the relation between the intention and the actual actions performed" (2007: 150).

[46] McCauley and Lawson 2002: 14, fig. 1.1. The term "CPS agent" goes back to Spiro's definition of religion as "an institution consisting of culturally patterned interaction with culturally postulated superhuman beings" (Spiro 1966: 96). "CPS agent" is yet another term for "superhuman agent," also referred to as a CIA, "counter-intuitive agent," by some cognitive scientists.

[47] See Whitehouse 2004: 33ff.

[48] The Geheimwissen formula found in the colophons of many Mesopotamian divinatory texts has also been taken as indication of some kind of initiation: "he who knows may see it, he who does not know, may not."

messages. At the same time it must fall in the same category as other kinds of sacrifice would, not only because of the very substantial sacrifices that could form part of a divinatory session, but also because the patient is put on trial before the divine judge. As mentioned, both "special patient" and "special action / instrument" rituals are, according to the theory, repeatable but not reversible.[49] Whether we interpret the extispicy ritual as a "special action/instrument" or a "special patient" ritual the same applies, you can not undo having performed extispicy, but you can repeat it. It is perhaps due to this dual function of extispicy that it could be used to inquire about unprovoked omens, for instance, the appearance of a lunar eclipse?[50]

The argument should not be pushed too far. I doubt that signs such as astrological omina should be seen as non-repeatable "special agent rituals." But then again, perhaps they might. A case could be made that any kind of *oblativa* is less dependent on a "special instrument" or "special action" than an induced omen. An epiphany is totally dependant on there being an agent to hear it or observe it, thus strengthening the link between CPS agent and human agent. No point in burning a bush or going into eclipse if there is nobody around to see it. However this may be, I do believe it is reasonable to accept that extispicy in itself provided a setting that transformed intangible threats to "strategic information" and acted upon it. The extispicy ritual spanned both parts of the event frame into which any divinatory practice normally falls: that of information-gathering on the one hand and that of sacrifices/aversive rituals on the other; performing further apotropaia just would not make sense.

ABBREVIATIONS

CT	Cuneiform Texts from Babylonian Tablets in the British Museum (London 1896–)
K	Tablets in the collections of the British Museum
KAR	Keilschrifttexte aus Assur religiösen Inhalts
W	field numbers of tablets excavated at Warka/Uruk

[49] This hypothesis has some empirical verification; see Whitehouse 2004: 40ff.

[50] For example, Lambert 2007: no. 2.

BIBLIOGRAPHY

Boyer, Pascal

1990 *Tradition as Truth and Communication: A Cognitive Description of Traditional Discourse.* Cambridge Studies in Social Anthropology 68. Cambridge: Cambridge University Press.

1994 *The Naturalness of Religious Ideas: A Cognitive Theory of Religion.* Berkeley; Los Angeles; London: University of California Press.

1999 "Cognitive Aspects of Religious Ontologies: How the Brain Processes Constrain Religious Concepts." In *Approaching Religion* 1, edited by Tore Ahlbäck, pp. 53–72. Turku: Åbo Akademi University Printing Press.

2001 *Religion Explained: The Human Instincts that Fashion Gods, Spirits and Ancestors.* London: Heinemann.

2003 "Religious Thought and Behaviour as By-Products of Brain Function." *Trends in Cognitive Sciences* 7: 119–24.

2005 "A Reductionistic Model of Distinct Modes of Religious Transmission." In *Mind and Religion: Psychological and Cognitive Foundations of Religiosity*, edited by H. Whitehouse and R. N. McCauley, pp. 3–30. Walnut Creek: Altamira.

Burkert, Walter

1992 *The Orientalizing Revolution: Near Eastern Influence on Greek Culture in the Early Archaic Age.* Cambridge: Harvard University Press.

Caplice, Richard I.

1974 *The Akkadian* namburbi *Texts: An Introduction.* Sources from the Ancient Near East 1/1. Los Angeles: Undena.

Chomsky, Noam

1975 *Reflections on Language.* New York: Plenum Press.

Cryer, Frederick H.

1994 *Divination in Ancient Israel and Its Near Eastern Environment: A Socio-Historical Investigation.* Journal for the Study of the Old Testament, Supplement Series 142. Sheffield: Sheffield Academic Press.

Durand, Jean-Marie

1993 "Le mythologème du combat entre le dieu de l'orage et la mer en Mésopotamie." *Mari: Annales de recherches interdisciplinaires* 7: 41–61.

Durkheim, Emile, and M. Mauss

1903 "De quelques formes primitives de classification: Contribution à l'étude des représentations collectives." *L'année sociologique* 6: 1–72. Paris: Presses Universitaires de France.

Egense, Ebbe

2002 "Divinatoriske Ofringer i Xenofon's Anabasis." In *AIGIS 2.1.* University of Copenhagen online journal: http://www.igl.ku.dk/~aigis/

Farber, Walter F.

1987 "Rituale und Beschwörungen in akkadischer Sprache." In *Texte aus der Umwelt des alten Testaments* II/2: *Rituale und Beschwörungen* I, edited by O. Kaiser, pp. 212–81. Gütersloh: Gütersloher Verlagshaus.

Fauconnier, Gilles, and Mark Turner

2002 *The Way We Think: Conceptual Blending and the Mind's Hidden Complexities.* New York: Basic Books.

Flower, Michael Attyah

2008 *The Seer in Ancient Greece*. Berkeley: University of California Press.

Gadd, C. J.

1948 *Ideas of Divine Rule in the Ancient East*. The Schweich Lectures of the British Academy. London: Oxford University Press.

Goetze, Albrecht

1939 "Cuneiform Inscriptions from Tarsus." *Journal of the American Oriental Society* 59: 1–16.

Goffman, Erving

1974 *Frame Analysis: An Essay on the Organization of Experience*. New York: Harper & Row.

Guinan, Ann K.

2002 "A Severed Head Laughed: Stories of Divinatory Interpretation." In *Magic and Divination in the Ancient World*, edited by L. Ciraolo and J. Seidel, pp. 7–40. Ancient Magic and Divination 2. Leiden: Brill; Boston: Styx.

Jameson, Michael H.

1991 "Sacrifice before Battle." In *Hoplites: The Classical Greek Battle Experience*, edited by V. D. Hanson, pp. 197–227. London: Routledge.

Jeyes, Ulla

1980 "The Act of Extispicy in Ancient Mesopotamia: An Outline." *Assyriological Miscellanies* 1: 13–32.

1991–92 "Divination as a Science in Ancient Mesopotamia." *Ex Oriente Lux* 32: 23–41.

Koch, Ulla

2005 *Secrets of Extispicy: The Chapter* Multābiltu *of the Babylonian Extispicy Series and* Niṣirti bārûti *Texts mainly from Aššurbanipal's Library*. Alter Orient und Altes Testament 326. Münster: Ugarit-Verlag.

Koch-Westenholz, Ulla

1995 *Mesopotamian Astrology: An Introduction to Babylonian and Assyrian Celestial Divination*. Copenhagen: Museum Tusculanum Press.

2000 *Babylonian Liver Omens: The Chapters* Manzāzu, Padānu *and* Pān tākalti *of the Babylonian Extispicy Series Mainly from the Aššurbanipal's Library*. Copenhagen: Museum Tusculanum Press.

2002 "Old Babylonian Extispicy Reports." In *Mining the Archives: Festschrift for Christopher Walker on the Occasion of his 60th Birthday, 4 October 2002*, edited by C. Wunsch, pp. 131–45. Babylonische Archive 1. Dresden: ISLET.

Lambert, Wilfred G.

1962 "A Catalogue of Texts and Authors." *Journal of Cuneiform Studies* 16: 59–77.

1967 "Enmeduranki and Related Matters." *Journal of Cuneiform Studies* 21: 126–38.

1998 "The Qualifications of Babylonian Diviners." In *Festschrift für Rykle Borger zu seinem 65. Geburtstag am 24. Mai 1994:* tikip santakki mala bašmu..., edited by S. M. Maul, pp. 141–58. Cuneiform Monographs 10. Groningen: Styx.

2007 *Babylonian Oracle Questions*. Mesopotamian Civilizations 13. Winona Lake: Eisenbrauns.

Lawson, Jack N.

1994 *The Concept of Fate in Ancient Mesopotamia of the First Millennium: Toward an Understanding of* "Šīmtu." Orientalia Biblica et Christiana 7. Wiesbaden: Harrassowitz.

Lisdorf, Anders
2007 The Dissemination of Divination in Roman Republican Times: A Cognitive Approach. Ph.D. dissertation, University of Copenhagen.

Maul, Stefan M.
1994 *Zukunftsbewältigung: Eine Untersuchung altorientalischen Denkens anhand der babylonisch-assyrischen Löserituale (*Namburbi*)*. Mainz am Rhein: Philipp von Zabern.
1999 "How the Babylonians Protected Themselves against Calamities Announced by Omens." In *Mesopotamian Magic: Textual, Historical, and Interpretative Perspectives*, edited by T. Abusch and K. van der Toorn, pp. 123–48. Ancient Magic and Divination 1. Groningen: Styx.

McCauley, Robert N., and E. Thomas Lawson
2002 *Bringing Ritual to Mind: Psychological Foundations of Cultural Forms*. Cambridge: Cambridge University Press.

Oppenheim, A. Leo
1974 "A Babylonian Diviner's Manual." *Journal of Near Eastern Studies* 33: 197–220.

Parpola, Simo
1993 *Letters from Assyrian and Babylonian Scholars*. State Archives of Assyria 10. Helsinki: Helsinki University Press.

Peek, Philip M., editor
1991 *African Divination Systems: Ways of Knowing*. Indianapolis: Indiana University Press.

Poebel, Arno
1914 *Historical and Grammatical Texts*. Publications of the Babylonian Section 5. Philadelphia: University Museum.

Reiner, Erica
1995 *Astral Magic in Babylonia*. Transactions of the American Philosophical Society 85/4. Philadelphia: American Philosophical Society.

Rochberg, Francesca
2004 *The Heavenly Writing: Divination, Horoscopy, and Astronomy in Mesopotamian Culture*. Cambridge: Cambridge University Press.

Rosenberger, Veit
2001 *Griechische Orakel: Eine Kulturgeschichte*. Darmstadt: Wissenschaftliches Buchgesellschaft.

Sørensen, Jesper
2007 *A Cognitive Theory of Magic*. Walnut Creek: Altamira.
in press "Cognitive Underpinnings of Divinatory Practices." In *Unveiling the Hidden: Contemporary Approaches to the Study of Divination*, edited by A. Lisdorf and K. Munk. Berlin: Walter de Gruyter. Pre-print from conference is cited.

Sørensen, Jørgen Podemann
1999 "On Divination: An Exercise in Comparative Method." In *Approaching Religion*, Part 1, edited by T. Ahlbäck, pp. 181–88. Turku: Åbo Akademi University Printing Press.

Spiro, M. E.
1966 "Religion: Problems of Definition and Explanation." In *Anthropological Approaches to the Study of Religion*, edited by M. Banton, pp. 85–126. Association of Social Anthropologists of the Commonwealth, Monograph 3. London: Tavistock

Starr, Ivan
1983 *The Rituals of the Diviner*. Bibliotheca Mesopotamica 12. Malibu: Undena.

1990 *Queries to the Sungod: Divination and Politics in Sargonid Assyria*. State Archives of Assyria 4. Helsinki: Helsinki University Press.

Sweek, Joel

2000 Review of *Divination in Ancient Israel and Its Near Eastern Environment: A Socio-Historical Investigation*, by Frederick H. Cryer. In *Review of Biblical Literature* 07/31/2000. http://www.bookreviews.org/pdf/2389_1622.pdf

Tedlock, Barbara

2001 "Divination as a Way of Knowing: Embodiment, Visualisation, Narrative, and Interpretation." *Folklore* 112: 189–97.

Tremlin, Todd

2006 *Minds and Gods: The Cognitive Foundations of Religion*. Oxford: Oxford University Press.

Turner, Victor

1961 *Ndembu Divination: Its Symbolism and Techniques*. Manchester: Manchester University Press.

1968 *The Drums of Affliction*. Oxford: Clarendon Press.

1975 *Revelation and Divination in Ndembu Ritual*. Ithaca: Cornell University Press.

Weidner, Ernst F.

1967 *Gestirn-Darstellungen auf babylonischen Tontafeln*. Sitzungsberichte Österreichischer Akademie der Wissenschaften. Philosophisch-Historische Klasse 254. Vienna: Böhlau in Kommission.

Whitehouse, Harvey

2004 *Modes of Religiosity: A Cognitive Theory of Religious Transmission*. Walnut Creek: Altamira.

Whyte, Susan Reynolds

1991 "Knowledge and Power in Nyole Divination." In *African Divination Systems: Ways of Knowing*, edited by P. M. Peek, pp. 153–72. Indianapolis: Indiana University Press.

Zimmern, Heinrich

1901 *Beiträge zur Kenntnis der Babylonischen Religion: Die Beschwörungstafeln* Šurpu, *Ritualtafeln für den Wahrsager, Beschwörer und Sänger*. Leipzig: J. C. Hinrichs.

5

AROUSING IMAGES: THE POETRY OF DIVINATION AND THE DIVINATION OF POETRY

EDWARD L. SHAUGHNESSY, UNIVERSITY OF CHICAGO

Ancient China shows evidence of numerous types of activities that involve aspects of divination (the attempt to use signs, whether natural or artificial, to understand and/or influence — in a word, to determine — events, present or future): pyromancy, sortilege, oneiromancy, chronomancy or hemerology, geomancy in all of its particulars (from the lay of the land and the nature of vapors emanating from it to the growth of vegetation and motion of animals on it), astromancy or astrology, physiognomy (of animals as well as of humans), and analysis of Chinese characters, would all have to be mentioned in any thorough survey of Chinese divination, and a real understanding of even any one of these practices would doubtless require at least one monographic study.[1] Rather than viewing the flowers while racing along on horseback, as the Chinese saying puts it, I propose herein to touch on just the first two of these types of divination — pyromancy and sortilege — and even at this I will not attempt to give any sort of systematic introduction to them.[2] Rather, I will try to show how they shared a common language of expression, a language that they shared in turn with the more general language of early Chinese poetry. I hope through this to be able to see how both diviners and poets viewed the world, and how they attempted to bring it under control.

Pyromancy, the scorching or burning of bone or shell in the attempt to cause cracks to appear in them that could then be read as signs, was practiced, sometimes extensively, sometimes intermittently, across broad stretches of northern Eurasia from no later than 3500 B.C. until well into the Qing dynasty (1644–1911).[3] The best-known manifestation of pyromancy in China is found on the plastrons of turtles and the scapula bones of oxen dating to the last stage of the Shang dynasty (ca. 1200–1050 B.C.). These shells and bones were often inscribed with the text of the divination (and thus are known in Chinese as *jiaguwen* or "writing of shell and bones"), which is still the earliest evidence of writing in China.[4] Known since the very end of the nineteenth century, it was once thought that the practice of inscribing pyromantic

[1] For earlier surveys, see Van Xuyet 1976; Loewe 1981: 38–62; DeWoskin 1983; Smith 1991; Kalinowski 1991; Loewe 1994; Chemla, Harper, and Kalinowski 1999; Strickmann 2005; Field 2008.

[2] For still the finest introduction in English to the most important manifestation of Chinese pyromantic practices — the oracle bones of the Shang dynasty — see Keightley 1978. For a more recent survey, very thorough in a different way, see Flad 2008: 403–37. For sortilege divination, especially that associated with the *Yi jing* or *Classic of Changes*, perhaps the best overview in English is Smith 2008.

[3] For Neolithic and early Bronze Age evidence, see Flad 2008: 405–11. Hu Xu, *Bu fa xiang kao* (Siku quanshu ed.), 4.2a, mentions a type of turtle-shell divination performed in the Qing period in the area around the delta of the Yangzi River.

[4] While Western-language research on these inscriptions has waned in recent years, there has blossomed a vigorous debate as to the place of these inscriptions in the rise of writing in China. For two opposing views, see Boltz 1994: esp. 31–52 (arguing for their place as the earliest writing), and Bagley 2004: 190–249 (arguing for the existence of earlier forms of writing).

shells and bones, if not the practice of pyromancy itself, died out with the end of the Shang dynasty. However, over the last thirty years numerous examples of Western Zhou dynasty (1045–771 B.C.) oracle bones have been uncovered from across north China (and especially in the Zhou homeland of Shaanxi), and there has also been plentiful other evidence of the continued practice of turtle-shell divination throughout the remainder of the Zhou dynasty (i.e., until 256 B.C.).[5]

While these archaeologically recovered records of divination properly command the greatest attention from contemporary historians, I propose to begin my examination of turtle-shell divination with a slightly later account, recorded in the history *Shi ji* or *Records of the Historian* (ca. 100 B.C.).[6] This concerns a divination performed on behalf of Liu Heng (died 157 B.C.), one of the sons of Liu Bang (247–195 B.C.), the founder of the Han dynasty (reigned 202–195 B.C.). After the death of Liu Bang, the Han ruling house fell into a fifteen-year-long period of civil war between the Liu family and the family of Liu Bang's empress, Empress Lü. With the death of Empress Lü in 180 B.C. and the subsequent elimination of her family, emissaries from the imperial court approached Liu Heng, then serving as the king (*wang*) of the state of Dai, and invited him to become the new emperor. Well aware of the precariousness of the position of emperor, Liu Heng at first resisted this offer. Eventually he was persuaded to accept it. According to the narrative of the *Shi ji,* one of the factors in his decision was a turtle-shell divination that he had performed about it. The account in the *Shi ji* reads as follows:

> The king of Dai consulted with the queen-mother about (whether to accept the emperorship), but he was still not decided about it. He divined it with a turtle, the divination omen obtained being the "Grand Transversal." (The diviner) prognosticated saying:
>
> > The Grand Transversal *geng-geng* (*geng*/*kəng[7]):
> > I will be the heavenly king (*wang*/*jwang),
> > Qi of Xia thereby shining (*guang*/*kwâng).
>
> The King of Dai said: "Given that I am already a king, what further kingship could there be? The diviner said, "What it means by 'heavenly king' is being the Son of Heaven."[8]

There is evidence from other accounts of divination, both archaeological and traditional, that this divination would have opened with a "command" or "charge" (*ming*) to the turtle that first announced an intended action, and then ended with a formulaic prayer seeking a successful outcome. Although the charge is not recorded here, it was doubtless something like "I will become emperor; would that it be successful." After the pronouncement of this charge, a red-hot brand would have been applied to the turtle-shell to cause a crack to appear in it. It was this crack — the omen (*zhao*) — that the divination official would have interpreted by way of a pronouncement that we might best translate as "oracle" (*yao*). This took a

---

[5] For still the only English-language discussion of these oracle bones, see Shaughnessy 1985–87: 146–194. There have been several piecemeal discoveries in the last few years, all reported only in the Chinese scholarly press; for one of the most important of these reports, see Cao 2003: 43–49.

[6] Over the years, I have explored these issues in several studies, perhaps most directly in Shaugnessy 1995: 223–40. Inevitably, I will need to repeat some earlier discussions, but I hope I will be able to introduce enough new evidence and new perspectives so that the present study is not entirely redundant.

[7] The reconstructions of archaic pronunciation presented here are taken from Schuessler 2007.

[8] *Shi ji* (Zhonghua shuju ed.), 10.414.

conventional form with an introductory four-character phrase often describing the crack in the turtle shell (or, in other forms of divination, of some omen in the natural world), followed by a couplet of rhyming four-character phrases relating the significance of that crack to the topic of the divination, in this case Liu Heng's intention to become emperor. The description of the crack, here "The Grand Transversal *geng-geng*," is apparently multi-dimensional: "Grand Transversal" (*da heng*) is a term that occurs in another chapter of the *Shi ji* — the "Biography of Turtle-(Shell) and Stalk (Diviners)" ("Gui ce liezhuan"), which includes a handbook of different crack shapes and their significances for various topics — and apparently refers to a crack that extends horizontally from the vertical shaft of the divination crack, perhaps in the shape of ├ but with a longer horizontal line.[9] "*Geng-geng*" presumably indicates the sound that the turtle shell made when the crack appeared in it.[10] Although the character used to write the sound here (*geng* 庚) is more or less meaningless, several commentators on the *Shi ji* point out that it is homophonous with another word (*geng* 更) that means "to succeed" (as in "to inherit"), as a son would "succeed" a father. It is perhaps easy to see how both of these omens might be interpreted to mean that Liu Heng should succeed his father Liu Bang and continue the Liu-family line of emperors. Certainly this is how the divination official who presided over the divination interpreted them. The couplet that he presumably extemporized, "I will be the heavenly king, Qi of Xia thereby shining" (*yu wei tian wang, Xia Qi yi guang*), refers explicitly to the reputed first case of father-son kingship succession in Chinese history, when Qi succeeded his father Yu to initiate the Xia dynasty. That his succession should be termed "shining" (*guang*), one of several terms in what one astute reader of early Chinese poetry has called "the key of '*wang*,'" *wang* being the word for "king,"[11] suggests that the diviner here intended this oracle to be encouraging. Nevertheless, Liu Heng continued to resist accepting the emperorship, pretending not to understand the significance of the oracle and pressing the diviner to explain it further. With the diviner's assurance that the oracle pertained to the "Heavenly King" (*tian wang*), obviously another term for *tianzi* "Son of Heaven" or "emperor" and not just any ordinary "king" (*wang*), and after still further consultations with close companions of his father, Liu Heng eventually did agree to become emperor, being known to history as Emperor Wen of the Han dynasty (reigned 180–157 B.C.).

Another account of a turtle-shell divination that is said to have taken place almost four hundred years earlier is similar in many respects. This is found in the *Zuo zhuan*, a lengthy historical narrative that serves in some respects as a commentary on the *Chunqiu* or *Spring and Autumn Annals,* under the tenth year of Duke Xiang of Lu (reigned 572–542 B.C.; i.e., 563 B.C.). It describes a divination performed on behalf of Sun Wenzi, ruler of the state of Wey, as he deliberated whether to counter an attack on his state by Huang'er of the state of Zheng. The account reads as follows:

> Sun Wenzi divined by turtle-shell about pursuing them. He presented the crack to Ding Jiang. Madame Jiang asked about the oracle. They said:

---

[9] See, for example, *Shi ji*, 128.3241.

[10] While it is well known that the character *bu* 卜 is a pictograph of the general shape that pyromantic cracks always took in China, it is worth noting as well that its archaic pronunciation, something like *puk, probably was onomatopoeia for the sound made by the shell when the crack appeared in it; see Keightley 1978: 21 n. 93.

[11] Saussy 1997: 540.

> The crack is like a mountain peak (*ling*/*ljəng):
> There is a fellow who goes out to campaign (*zheng*/*tsjäng),
> But loses his leader (*xiong*/*jung).

> Madame Jiang said: "That the campaigner loses his leader is the benefit of resisting robbers; the great ministers should make plans for it." The men of Wey pursued, and Sun Peng captured Huang'er of Zheng at Quanqiu.[12]

Again we can surmise that the command to the turtle shell must have been a statement akin to "We will counter-attack Zheng; would that we defeat them." This would have been followed by the cracking of the turtle shell, the shape of the crack being explicitly described in the oracle. We learn of this oracle only retrospectively when someone other than the divination official is called on to interpret the crack, presumably because the oracle was regarded as ambiguous. Again the oracle takes the form of a four-character phrase describing the crack as being in the shape of a mountain peak (*zhao ru shan ling*), perhaps something like |\ or |\. This omen is followed by a couplet of four-character phrases relating it to the topic of the divination. It is perhaps easy to see that "There is a fellow who goes out to campaign, But loses his leader" might be ambiguous; which fellow going out on campaign would lose his leader: the attackers from Zheng or the counter-attackers from Wey? For this reason, Sun Wenzi consulted a woman named Ding Jiang to provide the definitive interpretation: "That the campaigner loses his leader is the benefit of resisting robbers" (*zheng zhe sang xiong, yu kou zhi li ye*).

This prognostication is a simple transformation of a phrase that occurs formulaically in the *Zhou yi* or *Zhou Changes:* "beneficial to resist robbers" (*li yu kou*). The *Zhou Changes,* better known in the West as *Yi jing* (or *I Ching*) or *Classic of Changes,* is ancient China's premier divination text, originally produced and used in conjunction with sortilege divination (i.e., divination by counting, in the case of the *Zhou Changes* originally counting stalks of the yarrow plant). As is well known, the *Zhou Changes* consists of sixty-four "hexagrams" made up of six solid or broken lines in the shape of ䷗ or ䷱. Each hexagram has a general statement, usually quite formulaic, attached to it, while each line also has a statement attached to it, referred to as an "oracle" (*yao* 爻, a different character but almost certainly the same word as the *yao* 繇 or "oracle" referred to in the *Zuo zhuan* passage above) and usually describing some omen in the natural world. A good example of a *Zhou Changes* line statement is one of the line statements that contains the prognostication "beneficial to resist robbers." It occurs in the third line of *Jian* "Advancement" hexagram (#53 in the traditional sequence):

> Nine in the Third: The wild goose advances to the land (*lu*/*ljuk):
> The husband campaigns but does not return (*fu*/*bjuk),
> The wife is pregnant but does not give birth (*yu*/*jiuk).
> Baleful. Beneficial to resist robbers.

It is easy to see that the main portion of this line statement or "oracle" has the same form as the oracles seen above in the two accounts of turtle-shell divination: a four-character phrase describing an omen (in this case, one in the natural world rather than the shape of the crack in the turtle shell), followed by a rhyming couplet of four-character phrases relating it to

---

[12] *Chunqiu Zuo zuan zhengyi* (*Shisan jing zhushu* ed.), vol. 2, 1648 (31.246); see also Legge 1872: 443, 447.

some topic in the human realm. We can surmise that the divination that inspired this oracle was concerned with either a military campaign or birth-giving (or perhaps a general topic of marital fidelity), for which the movement of the wild goose (or geese) had a specific — and inauspicious — significance.[13] We can also deduce from the cases of turtle-shell divination examined above that the remaining words of the line statement, the prognosticatory formulas "baleful" (*xiong*) and "beneficial to resist robbers," reflect a secondary composition, presumably added by a subsequent prognosticator.

Many line statements in the *Zhou Changes* reflect this oracular format, the following being just a few of the more illustrative examples:

- *Tai* Top Six: The city wall returns to the moat: Do not use the army, From the citadel announce the command. Divining: A pity.
- *Xikan* Top Six: Tied using rope and twine: Place it in the thicket thorn, For three years you will not get it. Baleful.
- *Kun* First Six: The buttocks fastened to the stumpy tree: Entering into the dark valley, For three years you will not see him.
- *Ding* Nine in the Second: The caldron has substance: My enemy has an illness, It will not reach us. Auspicious.
- *Ding* Nine in the Third: The caldron's ears are stripped off: Its motion is blocked, The pheasant fat is inedible. The borderland rains diminish. Regret, in the end auspicious.
- *Ding* Nine in the Fourth: The caldron's broken leg: Overturns the duke's stew, Its form is glossy. Baleful.
- *Feng* Nine in the Third: Abundant its bubbles: In the day seeing the murk, Breaks his right arm. There is no trouble.
- *Feng* Nine in the Fourth: Abundant its canopy: In the day seeing the Dipper, Meeting his barbarian ruler. Auspicious.

Although these line statements all follow a standard format — one that I believe would have been normative for the divinations from which the text was created, one should hasten to note that most line statements in the *Zhou Changes* are not as complete as these. Many if not most line statements in the text are as simple as the following examples, drawn almost randomly from throughout the book:

- *Qian* Top Nine: Throated Dragon. There is regret.
- *Meng* Six in the Fourth: Fastened youth. A pity.
- *Gu* Nine in the Second: The pestilence of the stem mother. One cannot divine.
- *Shihe* Six in the Second: Biting the skin and cutting off the nose. No trouble.
- *Ben* Six in the Second: Decorating his beard.

[13] On several occasions, I have discussed the symbolic significance of the wild goose in ancient China; see, for instance, Shaughnessy 1992: 594.

- *Fu* Six in the Second: Successful return. Auspicious.
- *Fu* Six in the Third: Repeated return. Danger. No trouble.
- *Daguo* Nine in the Third: Bowed rafter. Baleful.

These are all omens of one sort or another, the significance of many of which is by no means immediately discernible. However, by comparing several line statements within the single hexagram *Tong ren* "Together with Men," it is possible, I believe, to reconstruct the process by which they were created. The text of the entire hexagram reads as follows:

- Together with men in the wilds. Receipt. Beneficial to ford the great river. Beneficial for the lord to divine.
- First Nine: Together with men at the gate. No trouble.
- Six in the Second: Together with men at the ancestral temple. A pity.
- Nine in the Third: Crouching enemies in the grass: Ascending its high hill, For three years it will not arise.
- Nine in the Fourth: Astride its wall, It cannot be attacked. Auspicious.
- Nine in the Fifth: Together with men, First crying and later laughing. The great armies can meet each other.
- Top Nine: Together with men in the suburbs. No regret.

Even though the Nine in the Third line employs a different image than the other lines, it is easy to see that it constitutes the sort of two-part oracle seen above, "Crouching enemies in the grass" (*fu rong yu mang*) being the description of the omen, and "Ascending its high hill, For three years it will not arise" (*sheng qi gao ling, san sui bu xing*) being the couplet that apparently comments on this omen's significance for the topic of the divination. The other lines are all less complete. Nevertheless, I think it is still possible to see that the various "Together with men" phrases must have served as the omen portion of the oracles. Depending on the topic of any given divination, an omen such as "Together with men in the wilds" (*tong ren yu ye*) or "Together with men at the gate" (*tong ren yu men*) would have prompted a divination official to compose a couplet of the sort "Astride its wall, It cannot be attacked" (*cheng qi yong, fu ke gong*) seen in the Nine in the Fourth line statement. Indeed, the rhyme in this latter couplet (*yong*/*jiwong and *gong*/*kung) suggests that it was probably originally attached to the image "Together with men at the ancestral temple" (*tong ren yu zong*; i.e., *zong*/*tsuong) of the Six in the Second line statement. Similarly, rhyme might suggest that the fifth and sixth lines were split from an original complete oracle:

> Together with men in the suburbs (*jiao*/*kau): First crying (*tao*/*dâu) and later laughing (*xiao*/*sjäu). The great armies can meet each other (*yu*/*ngju). No regret.

While the phrase "The great armies can meet each other" does not seem to be part of this oracle and should perhaps be understood as the same sort of injunction as the "beneficial to resist robbers" formula seen in the Nine in the Third line of *Jian* hexagram, it may well be that its near rhyme (*yu*/*ngju) influenced its insertion here.

Part of the appeal of the *Zhou Changes* is doubtless the incomplete state in which it has come down to us. This is not to say that any significant portion of it has been lost or that many line statements have been split or otherwise deformed, but rather that the text simply never underwent the sort of systematic editing that would have filled in all of the blanks. Long before post-modern literary critics began to discuss the authority of the reader, readers and especially people who have used the *Zhou Changes* to perform divinations have assumed the lion's share of responsibility for creating an intelligible text. This intelligibility has doubtless changed over the course of the centuries that the text has been read, and much of the original symbolic significance is lost to us. For instance, we cannot be sure at all how the various omens came to be associated with the different hexagrams. However, by learning as much as we can about how natural omens were viewed at the time that the *Zhou Changes* was created, we can at least come to some appreciation of how the couplet that relates the omen to the topic of the divination may have been understood. To learn more about these omens, there is probably no source better than the contemporary poetry, and especially the *Shi jing* or *Classic of Poetry*. When no less a figure than Confucius himself said that study of the *Poetry* would teach his disciples about the names of birds and animals, plants and trees,[14] his was almost certainly not the interest of a zoologist or a botanist; rather, he was urging his disciples to understand the symbolic meaning of the world around them, which is most immediately visible in the different natures of the goose and the grackle, the osprey and the oriole, or the pine and cypress. In the remainder of this study, I propose to turn my attention to these poetic images, and to suggest that just as divinations could partake of the language of poetry, so too could poems be divinatory.

Before examining the *Classic of Poetry* itself, I would like to begin with a "children's oracle" (*tong yao*) recorded in the *Zuo zhuan*. This is an example of a more or less extensive genre of folk-song that was regarded as prophetic. This particular song is said to have been occasioned by two events that took place in 517 B.C. in the state of Lu, the homeland of the *Spring and Autumn Annals*. In the autumn of that year, the lord of the state, Duke Zhao (reigned 541–510 B.C.) fled into exile after unsuccessfully challenging the great families that wielded real power in the state. Earlier in the year, a type of mynah bird or grackle (*quyu*) theretofore unknown in northern China was spotted nesting in the state. The music master regarded it as fabulous, but is said to have recalled the following folk song from about a century earlier than his own time. I present it in the inimitable translation of James Legge (1815–1897), the Scottish missionary who contributed so much to our understanding of ancient China through his translations of the Confucian classics.

> Here are grackles apace! The duke flies in disgrace.
> Look at the grackles' wings! To the wilds the duke flings, A horse one to him brings.
> Look how the grackles go! In Kan-how he is low, Wants coat and trousers now.
> Behold the grackles' nest! Far off the duke doth rest.
> Chow-fu has lost his state, Sung-foo comes proud and great.
> O the grackles so strange! The songs to weeping change.[15]

I have preserved even Legge's Victorian transliterations of Chinese words, but I have rearranged his line breaks so as better to show the rhyme scheme. I think it is easy to see how stanzas such as *quyu zhi yu* (*ju), *gong zai wai ye* (*jia), *wang kui zhi ma* (*ma) translated by Legge as "Look at the grackles' wings! To the wilds the duke flings, A horse one to him brings" or *quyu zhuzhu* (*tju), *gong zai Ganhou* (*yəu), *zheng qian yu ru* (*nzju) "Look how the grackles go! In Kan-how he is low, Wants coat and trousers now" (a more literal translation would be "The grackle goes hopping, The duke is in Ganhou, Seeking gown and jacket") are similar to line statements of the *Zhou Changes*, beginning with a description of

---

[14] *Analects* 17/9.

[15] Legge 1872: 709.

a natural omen and then correlating it — by way of a rhyming couplet — with a situation in the human realm. Whether this poem should be viewed as prophecy, as it has been portrayed in the Chinese literary tradition, or as historical comment (written after the event) as a more cynical reading might suggest, is perhaps irrelevant. Whether the human event comes after or before the omen, in ancient China at least it was felt that there was a necessary connection between them.

When we look at the images of still more traditional ancient Chinese poems, I think we will see the same connection between natural omen and human society. The most striking feature of poems in the *Classic of Poetry,* poems generally contemporary with the oracles of the *Zhou Changes,* is known in Chinese as their *xing*, a word that means "to raise up," "to cause to arise," and which I translate nominally as "arousal." The arousal routinely comes at the beginning of a stanza, which is often as short as four lines (of four characters each, or two lines of eight-character couplets). It takes the form of an opening couplet describing some nature image, drawn usually from the animal or botanical world (although astral and geomantic images also occur), and is then followed by another couplet, always rhyming, that describes an event in the human world. Although some readers have dismissed these arousals as essentially meaningless, designed simply to set the rhyme scheme,[16] I think a more sympathetic reading can readily see connections between the natural and human worlds, and — perhaps more important — can also see how the people of the time could have perceived connections between them. A few other poems, chosen almost at random from among the opening poems of the collection, will illustrate how these arousals work.

The first takes up again the nesting of a bird (or, in this case, two different types of birds): the magpie (*que*) and the dove (*jiu*). Arthur Waley (1889–1966), in his translation of the *Classic of Poetry,* points out that the dove, or the cuckoo, as he calls it, is known for settling in the nests of other birds, which Chinese tradition asserts those other birds regard as an honor.[17] Here the association between the dove's arrival in the magpie's nest and the marriage of the "girl" does not seem to have any of the pejorative connotations that are common in the European tradition; it simply portended a woman from another family, as all brides needed to be, coming to take up residence in her husband's home.

"The Magpie's Nest" (*Que chao*; Mao 12)

The magpie had a nest,
A dove settles in it (*ju*/*kjwo).
This girl goes to marry,
A hundred carts drive her (*yu*/*njwo).

The magpie had a nest,
A dove takes it over (*fang*/*pjwang).
This girl goes to marry,
A hundred carts lead her (*jiang*/*tsjang).

The magpie had a nest,
A dove fills it all up (*ying*/*jiäng).
This girl goes to marry,
A hundred carts place her (*cheng*/*zjäng).

---

[16] See, for instance, Gu 1925: 672–77. For an excellent discussion of the nature and history of the arousal trope, see Yu 1987: 44–83.

[17] Waley 1996: 13–14.

Another wedding song is introduced with a different sort of nature image, one that I suspect is less culturally specific: the various attributes of the peach.

"The Peach is Yummy" (*Tao yao*; Mao 6)

The peach is so yummy,
Blush red are its flowers (*hua*/*xwa).
This girl goes to marry;
Fitting her house and home (*jia*/*ka)

The peach is so yummy,
So bulbous is its fruit (*shi*/*dzjet).
This girl goes to marry;
Fitting her home and house (*shi*/*sjet)

The peach is so yummy,
Its leaves are so glist'ning (*zhen*/*sjɛn).
This girl goes to marry;
Fitting her home and man (*ren*/*nzjen)

While fruit ripe for the picking might turn a young man's thoughts to spring, other fruit falling from the vine could suggest to a young girl that she had missed her chance.

"Falling are the Plums" (*Biao you mei*; Mao 20)

Falling are the plums;
Oh, seven are its fruit (*shi*/* dzjet).
The many sirs seeking me;
Oh, would that one be fine (*ji*/*kjiet).

Falling are the plums;
Oh, but three are its fruit (*san*/*sâm).
The many sirs seeking me;
Oh, would that it be now (*jin*/*kjəm).

Falling are the plums;
The slant basket takes it (*xi*/*kjei).
The many sirs seeking me,
Would that one might say it (*wei*/*jwei).

Even without knowing that in later Chinese sex texts a "slant basket" (*qing kuang*) was a euphemism for the vagina,[18] it is probably not hard to see in this poem the despairing prayer — and I use the word "prayer" deliberately — of the last women to be chosen at the dance. I would like to suggest that we might compare this poem to the sort of divination that young children in the West have performed for generations: picking the petals off of a daisy and chanting "she loves me, she loves me not, she loves me." To be sure, this was a song or a poem, but the singer was also hoping that by employing this particular nature image — by catching a plum in her basket — that she could induce a suitable boy to come to her.

---

[18] For instance, the term appears written as *cheng kuang* "receiving basket" in the Mawangdui text *He yin yang* (Conjoining yin and yang); see Harper 1998: 413.

A similar magic, whether of word or of action, is to be seen in the poem "The Plantain" (*Fuyi*; Mao 8).

"The Plantain" (*Fuyi*; Mao 8)

Picking, picking plantain,
Going out picking it.
Picking, picking plantain,
Going out plucking it.

Picking, picking plantain,
Going out gath'ring it.
Picking, picking plantain,
Going out c'llecting it.

Picking, picking plantain,
Going out breasting it.
Picking, picking plantain,
Going out girdling it.

No one would claim that this is great poetry, but it does serve to illustrate how poetic images could stimulate — arouse — desired responses. There are two different identifications of the *fuyi* that is the focus of this poem: The Mao Commentary, the earliest commentary on the text identifies it as the "plantain" (*cheqianzi*), while other texts identify it as a type of pear.[19] However, both of these identifications agree that eating it induced pregnancy. As noted by Wen Yiduo (1899–1946), arguably modern China's most insightful reader of the *Classic of Poetry,* this was doubtless because the name of the fruit was closely homophonous in archaic Chinese with the word for fetus (*peitai*; indeed, the original characters were essentially the same for both words). In this simple poem, the woman wishing to become pregnant went out to gather the *fuyi,* which for convenience sake I have translated as "plantain." In the first two stanzas, she picks it off the tree or bush, in the next two stanzas she gathers several together, and then in the final two stanzas she tucks them into her clothing: first into her blouse near to her breasts, and then finally into her girdle at her waist. She must have understood that by singing this song as she gathered the plantain that she would have activated whatever medical properties it may have possessed, progressively making it more and more personal. Just as the diviner sought to use the image in the shell or in nature to influence the future course of events, so too did this poetess seek to use nature to bring about the result that she desired.

It is not possible in this brief paper to supply anything like an inventory of nature images in ancient China. However, to give one final example of how they work in the *Classic of Poetry*, let me finish with the best-known case, the poem *Guanju* "The *Join*ing Osprey," the first poem in the collection. It too is a wedding song, beginning with yet another avian image and then concluding in the last two stanzas with the male protagonist providing musical entertainment for the woman he seeks throughout the poem, first with strings and then percussion instruments, said to be appropriate first for courtship and then for a wedding feast.

[19] For the Mao Commentary, see *Mao Shi Zheng jian* (Sibu beiyao ed.), 1.7b. The "Wang hui" chapter of the *Yi Zhou shu* (Sibu beiyao ed., 7.10a) identifies its fruit as being similar to a pear.

"The *Join*ing Osprey" (*Guanju*; Mao 1)

"*Join, Join,*" calls the osprey,
On the river's island:
Luscious is the young girl,
The lordson's loving mate.

Up, down, the water cress;
Left and right, chasing it.
Luscious the young girl,
In and out of sleep seeking her.

Seeking, not getting her;
In out of sleep I think.
Longing, oh, longing, oh!
Toss turn, over myself.

Up, down, the water cress;
Left and right, picking it.
Luscious is the young girl;
Zither and lute befriend her.

Up, down, the water cress;
Left and right, gath'ring it.
Luscious is the young girl;
Bell and drum amuse her.

In the interests of brevity, I will ignore traditional interpretations and will assume simply that this poem concerns a man's yearning for a woman.[20] Also in the interests of brevity, I will also disregard all the other images in the poem, natural and otherwise, and focus only on the call of the osprey at the very beginning of the poem. However, to understand fully the meaning of this call, it will be necessary to consider first the nature of the osprey.

Most of the interpretation of this opening image has focused on this question: the nature of the bird. Although there have been some differences of detail, virtually all interpreters agree that the bird is a fish-eating raptor. Although the osprey is said to have various virtues and characteristics, I would prefer to focus just on this one point of agreement: that the bird eats fish. I have already mentioned above the modern scholar Wen Yiduo. In a classic essay of his entitled "On Fish,"[21] he demonstrated that in the *Classic of Poetry* fish consistently evoke sexual relations, and that the eating of fish evokes the consummation of those relations. He sees this illustrated, for instance, in the poem "Transverse Gate" ("*Heng men*"; Mao 138), the title of which refers to the "eastern gate" that led in ancient Chinese cities to what we would call the "red light district."

"Transverse Gate" (*Heng men*; Mao 138)

Beneath the Transverse Gate,
You can roost leisurely;

[20] For the most recent discussion of these interpretations, though one that takes the most traditional interpretation in the most untraditional of directions, see Chin 2006: 53–79.

[21] Wen 1948: 117–38.

By the spring's full flowing,
You can sate your hunger.

Could it be fish to eat
Must be the River's bream?
Could it be wives to take
Must be a Jiang of Qi?

Could it be fish to eat
Must be the River's carp?
Could it be wives to take
Must be a Zi of Song?

In several different discussions of this fish arousal, Wen notes that it seems also to inform some poems which do not mention fish explicitly, as for instance in the poem "The Men at Waiting" ("*Hou ren*"; Mao 151, the title of which might also be construed as "Waiting for Someone").

"The Men at Waiting" (*Hou ren*; Mao 151)

Oh, those men at waiting,
Carrying daggers and spears.
Those young men over there:
Three hundred red knee-covers.

There's a pelican on the bridge
Who doesn't wet his wings.
That young man over there
Doesn't fit his clothing.

There's a pelican on the bridge
Who doesn't wet his beak.
That young man over there
Doesn't pursue his date.

Oh, how dense; oh, how lush,
South Mountain's morning mist.
Oh, how cute; how charming,
Is the young girl's hunger.

The two central stanzas of this poem are both introduced by the image of a pelican, which, as Wen notes, is a fish-eating bird. However, in this poem the pelican does not deign to dip its head into the water to take its fish. So too, the young man preening in his guardsman's uniform, disregards the young girl who hungers for him; indeed, what I have translated as "Doesn't pursue his date" literally means "does not follow through with the sexual intercourse."

This evocative quality of the fish image would seem to be one of those cases of an interpretation so obvious that it needed but to be pointed out. Yet, it is curious that Wen himself seems to have overlooked the equally obvious parallel between the pelican in "The Man at Waiting" and the osprey in "The *Join*ing Osprey." Although fish are not mentioned in "The *Join*ing Osprey," their signification of sexual desire is not far beneath the surface of the poem.

Despite the concern among both traditional and modern interpreters of the *Classic of Poetry* over the identification and nature of the bird image in "The *Join*ing Osprey," there has been very little attention to its action: its calling *guan-guan*. The Mao Commentary remarks that this is "the concordant sound of the male and female responding to each other," and most subsequent interpreters have been content to accept this.[22] It seems to me, however, not well to evoke the mood of unrequited love that persists throughout much of the poem. Instead, I would suggest that the poet, in the person of the poem's male protagonist, heard the osprey, and presumably only the male osprey, seeking "to join" (*guan* 關) with its mate. The character with which this sound is written, which means generally "to close" a door, refers originally to the crossbar which locks a two-fold gate (*guan* 丱). If the phallic significance of this is not apparent enough, the word is also perfectly homophonous with the word *guan* 貫 (originally written 串), which means generally "to pierce the center of," but which in ancient China was also the standard euphemism for sexual penetration. Whatever sound the wild goose actually made, we can tell at least what the poet wanted to hear.

As in the "children's oracle" poem quoted above, this call of the osprey predicts what will happen in the human world, or at least what the young man contemplating — desiring — the young girl wanted to happen. And just as the grackle's "wings" suggested somehow the flight of the lord or its "hopping" the unusual appearance of the lord, so too, I would suggest, should we hear the call of the osprey here — written with the Chinese character that means "to close together" or "to join" — to predict the union of the "young girl" and the "lordson," consummated at the end of the poem by the banging of bells and drums. Of course, with a language such as Chinese, in which there is no alphabet with which to write value-neutral sounds, the sounds of nature can only be rendered with Chinese words. Whether for the poets or the diviners of ancient China, ospreys could only speak Chinese and anyone who spoke that language could understand them. But those attentive to nature did not need to wait for it to speak. Nature revealed itself also in the movement of the wild geese, the hopping of the grackle, the shape of the peach, the dropping of the plums. But more than this, it could be seen also in the belly of the caldron, the rise of a rafter, the biting of flesh, and the crack in the turtle-shell. To be sure, these images could be confusing. That is why then — as now — it was the job of the diviners and the poets to listen to them, to see them, to interpret them, and in turn to tell us what they mean.

[22] The only other interpretation that I have seen is that of Zheng Qiao (1108–1166) in the *Tong zhi*: "In all species of geese and ducks, since their beaks are flat their sound is *guan-guan*; in species of chickens and pheasants, since their beaks are pointed, their sound is *yao-yao*; these are natural sounds. The beak of the osprey resembles that of ducks and geese, therefore its sound is like this, also getting the sense of the water's edge"; quoted in Xiang 1986: 144.

BIBLIOGRAPHY

Bagley, Robert W.

2004 "Anyang Writing and the Origin of the of the Chinese Writing System." In *The First Writing: Script Invention as History and Process*, edited by S. D. Houston, pp. 190–249. Cambridge: Cambridge University Press.

Boltz, William G.

1994 *The Origin and Early Development of the Chinese Writing System.* American Oriental Series 78. New Haven: American Oriental Society.

Cao Wei

2003 "Zhouyuan xin chu Xi Zhou jiaguwen yanjiu." *Kaogu yu wenwu* 2003: 43–49.

Chemla, Karine; Donald Harper; and Marc Kalinowski, editors

1999 *Divination et rationalité en Chine ancienne.* Saint-Denis: Presses Universitaires de Vincennes.

Chin Tamara

2006 "Orienting Mimesis: Marriage and the *Book of Songs.*" *Representations* 94: 53–79.

DeWoskin, Kenneth J.

1983 *Doctors, Diviners, and Magicians of Ancient China: Biographies of Fang-shih.* New York: Columbia University Press.

Field, Stephen L.

2008 *Ancient Chinese Divination.* Honolulu: University of Hawaii Press.

Flad, Rowan K.

2008 "Divination and Power: A Multiregional View of the Development of Oracle Bone Divination in Early China." *Current Anthropology* 49: 403–37.

Gu Jiegang

1925 "Qi xing," *Ge yao zhoukan* 94. Reprint in *Gu shi bian*, vol. 3, Beijing: Pu she, 1931; Reprint, Shanghai: Shanghai Guji chubanshe, 1982.

Harper, Donald

1998 *Early Chinese Medical Literature: The Mawangdui Medical Manuscripts.* London: Kegan Paul.

Kalinowski, Marc

1991 *Cosmologie et divination dans la Chine Ancienne: Le compendium des cinq agents (*Wuxing dayi, *Vie siècle).* Paris: École Française d'Extrême-Orient.

Keightley, David N.

1978 *Sources of Shang History: The Oracle-Bone Inscriptions of Bronze Age China.* Berkeley: University of California Press.

Legge, James

1872 *The Ch'un Ts'ew with the Tso Chuen.* Reprint. Hong Kong: Hong Kong University Press, 1960.

Loewe, Michael

1981 "China." In *Divination and Oracles*, edited by M. Loewe and C. Blacker, pp. 38–62. London: George Allen and Unwin.

1994 *Divination, Mythology and Monarchy in Han China.* Cambridge: Cambridge University Press.

Saussy, Haun
1997 "Repetition, Rhyme, and Exchange in the *Book of Odes*." *Harvard Journal of Asiatic Studies* 57: 519–42.

Schuessler, Axel
2007 *ABC Etymological Dictionary of Old Chinese*. Honolulu: University of Hawaii Press.

Shaughnessy, Edward L.
1985–87 "Western Zhou Oracle-Bone Inscriptions: Entering the Research Stage?" *Early China* 11–12: 146–94.
1992 "Marriage, Divorce, and Revolution: Reading between the Lines of the *Book of Changes*." *Journal of Asian Studies* 51: 587–99.
1995 "The Origin of an *Yijing* Line Statement." *Early China* 20: 223–40.

Smith, Richard J.
1991 *Fortune-Tellers and Philosophers: Divination in Traditional Chinese Society*. Boulder: Westview Press.
2008 *Fathoming the Cosmos and Ordering the World: The* Yijing *(*I Ching, *or* Classic of Changes*) and Its Evolution in China*. Charlottesville: University of Virginia Press.

Strickmann, Michel
2005 *Chinese Poetry and Prophecy: The Written Oracle in East Asia*. Edited by B. Faure. Stanford: Stanford University Press.

Van Xuyet, Ngo
1976 *Divination, magie et politique dans la Chine ancienne*. Paris: Presses Universitaires de France.

Waley, Arthur
1996 *The Book of Songs*. New York: Grove Press.

Wen Yiduo
1948 *Wen Yiduo quanji*. Reprint. Beijing: Sanlian shudian, 1982.

Xiang Xi, editor
1986 *Shijing cidian*. Chengdu: Sichuan Renmin chubanshe.

Yu, Pauline
1987 *The Reading of Imagery in the Chinese Poetic Tradition*. Princeton: Princeton University Press.

6

THE THEORY OF KNOWLEDGE AND THE PRACTICE OF CELESTIAL DIVINATION

NIEK VELDHUIS, UNIVERSITY OF CALIFORNIA, BERKELEY

The letters and reports by Assyrian and Babylonian scholars to the Neo-Assyrian king provide a unique window to the relationship between a body of scholarly texts and the practice of actual scholarship. The theory of knowledge as adhered to by the experts of the king was founded upon a body of immutable texts ultimately derived from the god Ea himself. The scholars of the time dealt with the practical problem of using this ancient corpus for addressing current issues at the royal court by creating additional layers of textual interpretation. As it turns out, the practice of ancient scholarship did not coincide with its theory.[1]

THE THEORY OF KNOWLEDGE

The travails of Gilgameš, who in his search for life traveled to the edges of the earth and beyond, made him a better king, a man who had experienced everything and had achieved wisdom. The first-millennium version of the Gilgameš story emphasizes this wisdom aspect in its introduction (lines 1–8):[2]

> He who saw the deep, the foundation of the country
> who knew the proper ways, was wise in all matters;
> Gilgameš, who saw the deep, the foundation of the country,
> who knew the proper ways, was wise in all matters,
> he explored everywhere the seats of power.
> He knew the totality of wisdom about all things,
> He saw the secret and uncovered the hidden,
> He brought back a message from before the flood.

The reference to the flood connects this introduction to the Utanapištim passage in tablets 10–11, where Gilgameš learns from the survivor of the flood how the latter was saved and received eternal life and why his, Gilgameš', quest is in vain. More importantly, however, the antediluvian report (*ṭēmu*) that Gilgameš brings back refers to a well-known motif in first-millennium scholarly literature. All the important knowledge was revealed by the gods before the time of the flood and the scholars and kings of the present day owe their knowledge, directly, to primordial sages (Lenzi 2008b). This knowledge, in first-millennium scribal circles, is called *nēmequ* "wisdom" (Parpola 1993b; Beaulieu 2007).

[1] I wish to thank Alan Lenzi and Chessie Rochberg for their criticism and comments — and for being wonderful colleagues.

[2] After George 2003: vol. 1, 538–39; and George 2007; see van der Toorn 2007: 23, with further literature.

As van der Toorn (2007) has pointed out, this same first-millennium introduction specifically makes Gilgameš into a *literate* hero, one who wrote down his adventures and thus allowed later generations to profit from the lessons that he learned (lines 24–28):

> [Find] the tablet-box of cedar,
> [release] its bronze clasps!
> [Open] the lid of its secret,
> [pick] up the lapis lazuli tablet and read aloud
> all the travails of Gilgameš, all that he went through!

Through this introduction, Gilgameš' adventures are related to the self-consciousness of first-millennium scholars who referred to themselves as the guardians of the Wisdom of Adapa, the paradigmatic *apkallu*, or primordial sage.

The knowledge or wisdom (*nēmequ*) that is defined this way consists of the handbooks of the scholars at the Assyrian court: astrologers (*ṭupšarrūtu*), diviners (*barûtu*), exorcists (*ašipūtu*), lamentation priests (*kalûtu*), and physicians (*asûtu*).

The perception of the technical corpora of these five groups of experts may be further illustrated by various other pieces of evidence. Several of these corpora are attributed to the god Ea in the so-called Catalog of Texts and Authors (Lambert 1962; see Rochberg 1999), of Neo-Assyrian date:

> [The excorcists'] corpus; the lamentation priests' corpus; When Anu and Enlil;
> Figure; Not Completing the Months; Diseased Sinews;
> [Utte]rance; O king, the splendour of whose storm is majestic; Fashioned like An
>
> ---
>
> These are from the mouth of Ea

The list of compositions attributed to Ea includes the corpus of incantations and rituals to be used by the exorcist (plausibly restored by Lambert in the break), the corpus of laments meant to appease the anger of the gods, a variety of divination texts, and two myths around the god Ninurta. The divination compendia listed are *Enūma Anu Enlil* (When Anu and Enlil), the main compilation of astronomical omens; *Alamdimmû* (Figure), the body of physiognomic omens; *Saĝ iti nutila* (Not Completing the Months), the collection of omens from monstrous births otherwise known as *Šumma izbu*;[3] *Sagig* (Diseased Sinews), the compendium of diagnostic omens; and *Kataduga* (Utterance), a collection of omens derived from speech habits, usually perceived as a chapter of the physiognomic series *Alamdimmû*.

The two Ninurta narratives listed in this same section (conventionally known as Lugal-e and An-gin$_7$, respectively) depict Ninurta as a heroic warrior who goes to battle and defeats monstrous opponents. Sumerian versions of these narratives are known as Old Babylonian literary compositions. In the late second millennium the texts were provided with interlinear Akkadian translations and that is how the compositions circulated in the first millennium. These narratives are among a small group of Old Babylonian Sumerian composition that had survived the ages and they are the only two that were still regularly copied in both Babylonia and Assyria.[4]

---

[3] The identification of Not Completing the Months with *Šumma izbu* was already suggested by Lambert (1962: 70) and was confirmed by Biggs (1968). For the text published by Biggs, see now Böck 2000.

[4] For these compositions and their history, see Streck 2001 and Annus 2002.

The Catalog of Texts and Authors continues with two otherwise unknown compositions (both in Sumerian) authored by Adapa, the prototypical sage or *apkallu* (lines 5–7):[5]

> "[In triumph], Enlil"; "It is me, supreme divine power."
> [These are the ones which] Oannes-Adapa
> [...] spoke.

The rest of the Catalog of Texts and Authors, as far as preserved, mentions a variety of literary texts, some known, some otherwise unknown, and links these to human authors, some well attested as legendary figures of the ancient past (such as king Enmerkar), others apparently more recent in date.

Van der Toorn (2007) has argued that the classification of the compositions in this catalog "is by presumed antiquity, which is also an order of authority." The handbooks of the scholars, authored by the god Ea, come first. Literary compositions such as Gilgameš, Etana, proverb collections (the series of Sidu),[6] and others are supplied with human authors and are placed in the very last section of the text.

The Catalog of Texts and Authors thus throws some indirect light on the self-perception of the scholars of the time. The diviners, astrologers, excorcists, physicians, and lamentation priests saw themselves as the guardians and administers of the most ancient and most prestigious knowledge, based, ultimately, on the authority of Ea himself. This picture is confirmed by several other pieces of evidence (collected in Rochberg 1999), including the legend of Enmeduranki, which relates how the knowledge of libanomancy (observation of oil on water) and extispicy (reading of the entrails, in particular the liver, of a sacrificial animal) was revealed to Enmeduranki, the sixth antediluvian king who reigned at the city of Sippar for 54,600 years (Lambert 1998).[7]

Lenzi (2008a) has collected a broad spectrum of evidence to argue that all five scholarly disciplines at the Assyrian court claimed an authoritative body of secret texts, given by the god Ea to the *apkallu*s, or sages. This "mythmaking strategy" (in Lenzi's terminology) served to distinguish these scholars from mere scribes and provided them with the authority and competence to serve as an intermediary between the king and the gods. The secrecy of these texts was occasionally emphasized in the colophon: "Secret of the great gods. An expert may show it to another expert. A non-expert may not see it." Against most earlier interpretations, Lenzi argues that such secrecy colophons should be taken seriously, that indeed the entire scholarly corpora of astrologers, diviners, physicians, excorcists, and lamentation priests

---

[5] The beginning of line 5 is to be restored [u$_3$-ĝa$_2$-e ^{d}en-l]il$_2$-la$_2$ :: ĝa$_2$-e-me-en nam-^{d}en-lil$_2$-l[a$_2$]. These two titles are listed adjacently in the late Assyrian catalog published by Lambert 1976: 315 lines 8–9. Provisionally, I have taken u$_3$-ĝa$_2$ as a variant writing of u$_3$-ma = *irnittum*. The alternative reading u$_3$ ĝa$_2$-e ("and I myself") results in a rather unlikely opening of a composition. Lambert's original reading of line 5 of the Catalog of Texts and Authors ([ud-sar an ^{d}en-l]il$_2$-la$_2$) was based upon the parallel in Nabonidus Verse Account. Machinist and Tadmor (1993) have argued that the title mentioned in the Verse Account is not a real composition, but a polemic and intentional distortion of *Enūma Anu Enlil* (see also Lenzi 2008a: 101 n. 184).

[6] Finkel 1986.

[7] Enmeduranki is found in the list of antediluvian kings in the Babylonian Royal Chronicle, known from Neo-Assyrian and Neo-Babylonian sources (Glassner 2004: 126–34 with further literature). In the Old Babylonian Sumerian King List he is known as Enmeduranna (see Glassner 2004: 120), but at least one text has the variant Enmeduranki (Finkelstein 1963: 42).

were considered to be secret — even though the great majority of such tablets had no explicit secrecy colophon.[8]

Lenzi's argument defines the *ummânū* or scholars of the Assyrian court as the bearers and transmitters of textualized secret knowledge given by Ea, god of wisdom, to the primordial sages (*apkallū*) with whom the scholars identified. Exact transmission of this secret knowledge was, therefore, an important concern. As Lenzi demonstrates, some of the secrecy colophons and secrecy labels are attached to Kassite tablets[9] and thus the idea of secret knowledge is older than the Neo-Assyrian period. The Kassite evidence, however, is too isolated to understand how this secret knowledge functioned or was used. By contrast, the correspondence of the Neo-Assyrian kings and the tablet collections from this period provide a wealth of evidence that allows us a view of various aspects of the use and perception of this prestigious, secret body of knowledge.

SCHOLARLY PRACTICE: QUOTATION AND INTERPRETATION

The scholarly tradition that was thus imagined to derive from Ea and the primordial sages was actively used by specialists who were in service of the crown. Several hundreds of letters and reports sent by those specialists to the kings Esarhaddon and Assurbanipal reveal much that is of relevance for understanding the complexity of the written scholarly corpus and the way this corpus was used in the Neo-Assyrian period.[10] The letters and reports reflect on all five scholarly disciplines and they provide evidence how this secret knowledge was used in practice.

The letters and reports contain many quotations of omens, in particular (but not exclusively) celestial omens. They provide a glimpse at the relationship between a corpus of traditional texts and the process of actual decision-making at the court, between the theory of divine (secret) wisdom and the practice of royal counsel. In the present section I focus on the corpus of celestial omens and its uses, because that is where our evidence leads us.[11] It is possible that in other areas of scholarly specialization theory and practice developed other kinds of relationships — the important aspect to note is that any such relationship is complex and cannot be read or guessed from the theoretical (traditional) scholarly texts alone.

The scholars clearly quote omens as literarily as possible — "as it was written on the tablet," as Mar-Issar puts it (SAA 10, 362) — rather than giving a summary or paraphrase. The omen quotations are always in Standard Babylonian, the language used for all traditional texts, and commonly use the technical (heavily logographic) writing style of the divination compendia. Other parts of the letters and reports are in the local (Neo-Assyrian or Neo-Babylonian) dialect; the contrast is particularly clear in the letters and reports written in Assyrian. The

---

[8] On secrecy, see also Rochberg 2004: 210–19.

[9] The medical tablet BAM 385 (see Lenzi 2008a: 180) and the expository text PBS 10/4, 12 (see Lenzi 2008a: 188).

[10] The letters by Assyrian scholars were first edited by Parpola (1970 and 1983). These texts were re-edited in Parpola 1993a, with the addition of letters from Babylonian scholars. The reports were edited by Hunger (1992). These letters and reports have been studied in much detail and from various points of view. See, for instance, Brown 2000; Rochberg 2004 (in particular chapter 6); and Robson, forthcoming.

[11] Robson (2008) developed a similar argument on the relationship between the medical corpus and the practice of physicians, as attested in their letters. See also Jean 2006 on the exorcists' corpus and the practice of exorcism; and Robson, forthcoming.

quotations are thus set apart as being different from the voice of the scholar himself, coming from a more authoritative source.[12]

The celestial omens quoted in the letters and reports frequently do not come directly from the main series of *Enūma Anu Enlil,* but from one of the derived compositions, primarily from the commentary series *Šumma Sîn ina tāmartīšu*. The material that was at the disposal of the scholars of the king may be divided into the following main categories:[13]

1. the series *Enūma Anu Enlil*
2. the extraneous (*ahû*) tablets of *Enūma Anu Enlil* (containing additional omens, but not considered to be part of the main series)
3. the excerpt series *rikis girri Enūma Anu Enlil* (following the order in the main series)
4. excerpts which contain just a few omens from one or more tablets of the main series, concentrating on a single topic
5. factual commentaries (*mukallimtu*), usually quoting full omens, plus explanation
6. linguistic commentaries (*ṣâtu*), often in the form of word lists
7. the explanatory series *Šumma Sîn ina tāmartīšu*, which has the form of a *mukallimtu* commentary[14]

The boundaries between the various types of commentaries seem to be fluid and the relationships between the text categories are often unclear. One may note that even the main series contains rather heterogeneous material, such as the daylight tables in Tablet 14[15] and the tablet that associates certain stars with certain terrestrial events, not in the usual format of an omen, but rather as an abstract statement ("The Raven star is for a steady market").[16] Notwithstanding the high prestige enjoyed by *Enūma Anu Enlil*, and the scribal myth making that traced the composition all the way back to Ea, it was never truly standardized. Fincke (2001) has shown that there existed multiple versions of *Enūma Anu Enlil* in Assyria: one from Assur and two from Nineveh (one in Assyrian, the other in Babylonian ductus).[17] All versions follow the same general order of topics, but differ in the arrangement of tablets. As a result there is widespread confusion in the assignment of tablet numbers within the series, which further frustrates attempts to clearly understand how the various text types dealing with celestial omens are related to each other. There is a contradiction here between the internal literary history of the omen compendia, that asserts a direct connection with the god Ea, making the text "fundamentally unalterable" (Rochberg 1999), and the external literary history that shows divergent lines of development, even within the same library at Nineveh. The scribal myth depicts a very orderly world in which the omens that deliver messages from the gods are collected in compendia authorized by those same gods — copied and guarded through the ages by the scribes. In reality, the corpus of celestial omens is chaotic and difficult to navigate.

---

[12] For an excellent discussion of this phenomenon, see Worthington 2006.

[13] For these categories and for further information about their format and contents, see Weidner 1942: 182; Koch-Westenholz 1995: chapter 4.

[14] For this series, see Koch-Westenholz 1999; and Gehlken 2007.

[15] See Al-Rawi and George 1991–1992; and Hunger 1998.

[16] For this tablet and other unusual formats, see Reiner and Pingree 1981: 24–26. The example comes from Reiner and Pingree 1981: 40–41 line 3. Note that the format is already attested in an Old Babylonian text (Rochberg 2004: 68–69).

[17] Note, however, that Fincke's reconstruction was criticized as being too schematic by Gehlken (2005: 252 n. 81) in his detailed discussion of the tablet numbers of the Adad section in *Enūma Anu Enlil*.

In the letters and reports scholars rarely specify where their citations come from. If they do, however, they distinguish between *iškaru* "the series," *ahû* "extraneous omens," and (factual) commentaries, usually referred to as *ša pî ummâni* (from the mouth of a master),[18] but once as *mukallimtu* commentary (SAA 10, 23).[19] Mar-Issar, in a letter to the king, reports that Jupiter appeared five days late; it had been invisible for thirty-five days, while the normative period of disappearance (as he explains) was twenty to thirty days (SAA 10, 362). He quotes various applicable Jupiter omens, some of which have been identified in the omen literature.[20] He continues (in the translation by Parpola 1993a: 299):

> Furthermore, when it had moved onwards 5 days, (the same amount) by which it had exceeded its term, it completed 40 days. The relevant interpretation runs as follows:
>
> r. 3 "If Neberu drags: the gods will get angry, righteousness will be put to shame, bright things will become dull, clear things confused; rains and floods will cease, grass will be beaten down, (all) the countries will be thrown into confusion; the gods will not listen to pray[ers], nor will they ac[cept] supplications, nor will they an[swer] the queries of the haruspices."
>
> 11 [This interpretation I have ex]tracted and [sent] to the king, [my lo]rd, (exactly) as it was wr[itten] on the tablet (SAA 10, 362 obv. 19–rev. 12).

The assurance that he copied the omen "as it was written on the tablet" is unusual, because that was what scholars simply were supposed to do. He may have been inspired to add the remark by the gravity of the situation predicted, implying that the channels of communication with the divine world were to be closed.[21]

Ulla Koch-Westenholz has demonstrated that quite a few of the references to celestial omens do not come from the main series, but rather from *mukallimtu* commentaries (Koch-Westenholz 1995: 82–83), in particular from *Šumma Sîn ina tāmartīšu* (Koch-Westenholz 1999). Many quotations appear more than once in the correspondence, often by different scholars, and very frequently such quotations go back to commentaries. The following report contains two such omens (SAA 8, 10):[22]

> 1 If the moon becomes visible on the 1st day: reliable speech; the land will become happy.
> 3 If the day reaches its normal length: a reign of long days.
> 5 If the moon at its appearance wears a crown: the king will reach the highest rank.
> 7 From Issar-šumu-ereš.

The first omen is attested in *Šumma Sîn ina tāmartīšu* tablet 1 line 116 (Koch-Westenholz 1999: 161), and is quoted in three different reports by this same scholar, but also by others.[23] Other scholars tend to quote the variant omen "If the moon at its appearance is seen on

[18] That the expression refers to the commentaries rather than to a parallel oral tradition was argued with good evidence by Koch-Westenholz (1999: 151).

[19] For such references, see Koch-Westenholz 1995: 94–95.

[20] See Reiner and Pingree 2005: 10.

[21] See Reiner 2007; the omen in question has been identified by Koch-Westenholz (2004) on a fragment that includes another Jupiter omen quoted twice in the reports. Although the fragment is clearly part of the astrological corpus, we do not know what type of composition it belongs to.

[22] Translation by Hunger 1992: 10.

[23] Balasî (SAA 8, 86), Nabû-mušeṣi (SAA 8, 148–49), Bulluṭu (SAA 8, 116–19), Nergaleṭir (SAA 8, 256–57), Nabû-iqiša (SAA 8, 290–91), Zakir (SAA 8, 303), Munnabitu (SAA 8, 318), Ašaredu the older (SAA 8, 329–30), Ašaredu the younger (SAA 8, 342), Rašil (SAA 8, 389 and 409), Nabû-iqbi (SAA 8, 420–23), Ṭabiya (SAA 8, 439), Ṭab-ṣilli-Marduk (SAA 8, 445–46) and Bel-naṣir (SAA 8, 463).

the first day: good for Akkad, bad for Elam," which is the preceding line in *Šumma Sîn ina tāmartīšu*.[24] These reports originate both in Assyria and in Babylonia and clearly belong to the standard omen repertoire to be quoted when new moon happens at the right time (that is, when the preceding month had thirty days).

The second omen quoted by Issar-šumu-ereš is at least as frequent among the reports. This omen comes from *Šumma Sîn ina tāmartīšu* tablet 6 (see Gehlken 2007), a commentary to *Enūma Anu Enlil* tablet 36–37.[25] In the commentary the omen reads:

> If the day reaches its normal length: a reign of long days; the thirtieth day completes the measure of the month.[26]

The final phrase is the explanatory part, which renders the omen relevant for observations of the new moon on the first day. One may well doubt the appropriateness of this explanation. Tablet 36 of *Enūma Anu Enlil* talks about daylight, influenced by fog and other phenomena — it does not seem to imply anything about the length of the *month*. The explanation, however, is clearly adopted by Issar-šumu-ereš in his report, and in fact several Assyrian and Babylonian scholars quote this omen with the explanation included.[27]

Some of the interpretations in the commentaries and in the quotations in the reports are quite a bit more sophisticated or convoluted than what we have seen so far. The omen quotation "If the moon rides a chariot in month Sililiti: the dominion of the king of Akkad will prosper, and his hand will capture his enemies" is in need of several pieces of explanation. The Elamite month name Sililitu is explained by its common name Šebat (month 11) and the moon riding a chariot turns out to mean that it is surrounded by a halo while standing in Perseus (*Šību*):

^{ITI}*si-li-li-ti* ^{ITI}ZIZ$_2$	Sililiti = Šebat
ša$_2$ ^{ITI}ZIZ$_2$ *ina* ŠA$_3$-*bi* ^{MUL}ŠU.GI	That is: In Shebat, within Perseus
TUR$_3$ NIGIN-*mi-ma*	it (the moon) was surrounded by a halo.

This piece of explanation probably comes from *Šumma Sîn ina tāmartīšu* tablet 11[28] and is quoted in different reports by different scholars, located in different parts of the empire: Nabû-iqiša of Borsippa (SAA 8, 298), Akkulanu of Assur (SAA 8, 112), and Aplaya, again from Borsippa (SAA 8, 364).

An explanatory entry in SAA 8, 304 obv. 3–rev. 4, is derived from *Šumma Sîn ina tāmartīšu* tablet 1 lines 68–71:

> [If the moon's] horns at its appearance are very dark:
> [disbanding of the fortified] outposts, [retiring of the guards];
> there will be reconciliation [and pea]ce in the land.
>
> ---
>
> GI = to be dark
> GI = to be well

[24] Nabû-ahhe-eriba in SAA 8, 57; Akkullanu in SAA 8, 105; Nabû-šuma-iškun in SAA 8, 372–73. An unknown Assyrian scholar uses both variants (SAA 8, 188).

[25] In the tablet numbering by Gehlken 2005: 258.

[26] See Virolleaud 1907–1912, Adad section XXXIII (K.50), line 26.

[27] Balasî (SAA 8, 87), Akkulanu (SAA 8, 106), Nergal-eṭir (SAA 8, 251 and 257), Nabû-iqiša (SAA 8, 290–91), Nabû-šuma-iškun (SAA 8, 372), and an unknown scholar (SAA 8, 506). On this omen, see Koch-Westenholz 1995: 102.

[28] See Gehlken 2007; and Verderame 2002: 91 with n. 285.

GI = to be stable
Its horns are stable.

The various interpretations of GI in the report come straight from the commentary text,[29] although formulated slightly differently:

GI *ka-a-nu lu ta-ra-ku* GI *ša-la-mu*

GI = to be stable or to be dark. GI = to be well.

The commentary basically explains why darkness of the moon's horns can be interpreted as "Its horns are stable" and why this relates to peace or well-being in the apodosis, thus establishing a link between protasis and apodosis.[30] The connection between the words "to be dark," "to be well," and "to be stable" is that all can be equated with a logogram that has a value GI. The equation GI = *kânu* = "to be stable" is indeed common throughout the cuneiform tradition. "To be dark" may be written GI_6 and finally *šalāmu* "to be well," is related to *šullumu*, "to repay" or "to compensate," which equals Sumerian šu ... gi_4. The commentary thus uses complex associations between signs and words in which homographs (GI, GI_4, and GI_6) may substitute for each other in order to demonstrate the connection between Akkadian words. Although such associations are ultimately grounded in the kind of knowledge that lexical texts provide, they do not immediately depend on such texts. They use the kind of reasoning that is best known from "The Fifty Names of Marduk" in the final section of the Babylonian Epic of Creation (Bottéro 1977).[31]

It seems that *Enūma Anu Enlil*, the text authored by Ea and transmitted via the primordial *apkallu*s through a lengthy sequence of generations of scholars, was the ultimate authority in theory but that a second tier of compositions, more geared toward the actual practice of celestial divination, was primarily used for the day-to-day business of the scholars' craft.[32] This second tier, in particular the series *Šumma Sîn ina tāmartīšu* contained a selection of the more frequently quoted omens, explaining in more detail what the expressions in the protasis meant in terms of observation and adding some learned commentary. This second tier had authority enough to be quoted in letters to the king, yet it did not define the identity of the scholarly community in the same way that *Enūma Anu Enlil* did.[33]

Šumma Sîn ina tāmartīšu offered standardized solutions for some problems that were involved in the practical use of *Enūma Anu Enlil*. On the one hand, the complexity of *Enūma Anu Enlil* and the availability of a hermeneutical system that allowed for various interpretational strategies, implied that a single observation could be related to multiple omens in various chapters of the omen handbook (Koch-Westenholz 1995: 140–51; and Frahm 2004: 49).[34] On the

[29] The commentary in *Šumma Sîn ina tāmartīšu* is considerably longer because the omen, apparently, had variant applications and interpretations, corresponding to different pieces of explanation. The omen is indeed used for different kinds of observations in the reports (see Koch-Westenholz 1999: 158 with n. 67).

[30] See Al-Rawi and George 2006: 42.

[31] See now Seri 2006.

[32] A good number of quotes in the reports come from *Šumma Sîn ina tāmartīšu*, rather than from *Enūma Anu Enlil* or any of the other textual categories listed above. Since *Šumma Sîn ina tāmartīšu* has only partly been edited (Koch-Westenholz 1999; Borger 1973) and is only partly preserved (see Gehlken 2007), the origin of many quotations remains unclear at this moment. Quotations of thunder omens in the reports seem to come directly from the main series (see Gehlken 2008).

[33] See the discussion in Lenzi 2008a: 212–13.

[34] In his discussion Frahm emphasized the advantage of this "divinatory anarchy" to the king: it enabled him to choose the more convenient option from alternative interpretations.

other hand, *Enūma Anu Enlil* may not always have had available omens for what was normal and expected — such as the appearance of the new moon at the regular time. In other words, *Enūma Anu Enlil* offered both too much and too little. *Šumma Sîn ina tāmartīšu* provided a first selection of relevant omens (not all omens actually receive commentary) and supplied an initial interpretation. The fact that the same entries were used by scholars all over the place may imply that the commentary was part of the education of astronomers, as a tool for putting *Enūma Anu Enlil* to practice. *Šumma Sîn ina tāmartīšu* is a relatively rare text, which is consonant with its more practical function. Libraries primarily collect the most authoritative and ancient knowledge.

Šumma Sîn ina tāmartīšu was well suited for the purposes of the scholars corresponding with the Assyrian king, whose task was not only to find and quote the appropriate omens, but also to interpret them. Divination compendia that were less frequently used may not have had such an authoritative interpretational body of knowledge and thus the scholars were forced to provide such interpretations themselves. The following letter, SAA 10, 42, includes a quotation from the series of terrestrial omens *Šumma ālu*,[35] as well as a discussion by Balasî, the chief scribe of the king, of the applicability of the omen, the ritual countermeasures that might be taken (even though Balasî does not believe it is necessary) and an unrelated calendrical issue.

> 1 To the king, my lord: [your servant] Balasî. Good health to the king, my lord! [May Nabû and Marduk bless] the king, my lord!
>
> 5 As to what the king, m[y lord, wr]ote [to me]: "[In] the city of H[ar]ihumba lightning struck and ravaged the fields of the Assyrians" — why does the king look for (trouble), and why does he look (for it) [in the ho]me of a tiller? There is no evil inside the palace, and when has the king ever visited Harihumba?
>
> 16 Now, provided that there is (evil) inside the palace, they should go and perform the (ritual) "Evil of Lightning" there. In case the king, my lord, says: "How is it said (in the tablets)?" — (here is the relevant interpretation): "If the storm god devastates a field inside or outside a city, or if he puts down a ... of (his) chariot, or if fire burns anything, the said man will live in utter misery for 3 years." This applies (only) to the one who was cultivating the field.
>
> r. 10 Concerning the adding of the intercalary month about which the king wrote to me, this is (indeed) a leap year. After Jupiter has become visible, I shall write (again) to the king, my lord. I am waiting for it; it will take this whole month. Then we shall see how it is and when we have to add the intercalary month (translation by Parpola 1993a: 32–33).

In this letter Balasî's interpretation of the omen text is based on common-sense reasoning, not on the quotation of a commentary. In a similar letter Issar-šumu-ereš answers a query by the king about the applicability of an omen about a mongoose that appears between the legs of a man. The mongoose came out from under the chariot of the king, and according to Issar-šumu-ereš' opinion the omen is applicable in such a case (SAA 10, 33).

Comparing the celestial omens and their interpretation through *Šumma Sîn ina tāmartīšu* with the letters quoted above, we see that in both cases issues of applicability are addressed.

---

[35] The omen is attested in a slightly different form in CT 39 4 31–33.

What is different about *Šumma Sîn ina tāmartīšu* is that it was created (or compiled) as a second *textual* layer, largely standardized and thus delimiting the interpretational authority of the experts. The importance of texts and writing in this whole process is emphasized by the use in these commentaries of complicated sign equivalences, such as the analysis of GI discussed above. We may adduce one more example here from what may be the third tablet of the commentary series *Šumma Sîn ina tāmartīšu*.[36]

> DIŠ 30 TAB-*ma ba-ra-ri it-ta-ʾ-dar*
> AN.MI LUGAL URI.KI
> ba-ra : *la-a* : ri : *a-dan-nu*
> *ina la a-dan-ni-šu*$_2$ UD 12-KAM UD 13-KAM AN.MI GAR-*ma*
> *ina* EN.NUN AN.USAN$_2$ AN.MI GAR-*ma*
>
> If the moon is early and is eclipsed at the time of the evening watch:
> eclipse of the king of Akkad.
> ba-ra = "not"; RI = "period"
> an eclipse occurs not according to its period on the 12th or 13th day;
> (variant): an eclipse occurs in the evening watch.

The commentary refers to the first omen of *Enūma Anu Enlil* tablet 15; it analyses the rare (and probably technical astronomical) Akkadian word *barāri* ("at the time of the evening watch") first by analyzing it into its component syllables and then by giving a more conventionally written synonym (*ina* EN.NUN AN.USAN$_2$ "during the evening watch"). The analysis of *ba-ra-ri* takes the first two syllable of the word as the Sumerian verbal prefix ba-ra- , which is a negative modal and may thus be translated by Akkadian *lā*. Although RI does not seem to correspond to a Sumerian word meaning "period," its use as a logogram for Akkadian *adannu* (period) is well attested.[37]

Although such lexical gymnastics may seem rather farfetched to the modern observer, it should be noted that these comments do not play out in the context of fanciful academic speculation, but are found in the context of the actual *practice* of celestial divination in reports and commentary texts (see Frahm 2004).

In one case, *Šumma Sîn ina tāmartīšu* refers to the source of one of these lexical equations, explaining ITI.NE (normally a writing for the month name Abu) as "this month." "ITI.NE means 'this month,' NE means 'this,' it is said in the *ṣâtu*-commentary" (Koch-Westenholz 1999: 156 47–50). Significantly, the source is not a lexical text, but rather another type of commentary (a linguistic commentary or word list) within the realm of the celestial divination corpus.[38]

In a recent article Eleanor Robson (2008) has demonstrated that the relationship between the traditional corpus of *asûtu* and *ašipūtu* on the one hand, and the practical roles of experts who are identified as *asû* or *āšipu*, on the other, is weak at best. Such a discrepancy between theory and practice may not be surprising. The scholarly corpora may be understood as foundational texts that define the self-understanding of a profession, rather than their practice. The scholarly texts belong to the area of scribal myth-making, but are not necessarily the ones

[36] Virolleaud 1907–1912, Sin section XXXI; edited by Rochberg-Halton 1988: 80–81 lines 1–4. This passage is discussed by Koch-Westenholz 1995: 83. For the possibility that this is *Šumma Sîn ina tāmartīšu* tablet 3, see Gehlken 2007. Confusingly, the same omen is quoted in *Šumma Sîn ina tāmartīšu* tablet 1 with an abbreviated commentary (Koch-Westenholz 1999: 155 line 32).

[37] See CAD A/1, 99 2a–1′.

used in the day-to-day business of divinatory observation and reporting. We see a similar gap between *Enūma Anu Enlil* as a foundational text and the practice of celestial divination at the Assyrian court. What makes this case different, though, is that the gap is filled with written texts. The heavens are a tablet on which the gods write their messages, "heavenly writing" (*šiṭir šamê*),[39] legible for those who are initiated into its secrets. The practice of this reading refers from one text to another: from the heavenly writing itself to the core series (*iškaru*), from the core series to the *mukallimtu* commentaries, and from the *mukallimtu*s to the commentary word list (*ṣâtu*). It is hard to over-emphasize, indeed, how much this whole enterprise is textualized the final step in the process is a letter or report sent in writing to the king. The very practice of reading the skies is grounded in a text — in *Enūma eliš* — where Marduk determines the proper periods of the heavenly bodies, thus establishing the basic determinants of a system based on interpreting deviations from the standard period schemes that had been divinely imposed.[40]

During the first millennium, authoritative knowledge was located in traditional texts, which were carefully transmitted from one generation to another — at least in theory. Such an immutable concept of knowledge and authority is a valuable tool for collecting libraries, for foundational narratives, or for displaying universal knowledge through intertextual references. When it comes to practical application, however, knowledge from before the flood is a burden more than an asset. *Šumma Sîn ina tāmartīšu* represents the middle ground between the "heavenly writing" in the stars, the traditional knowledge "from the mouth of Ea" in *Enūma Anu Enlil,* and the actual responsibilities of scholars at the royal court.

ABBREVIATIONS

BAM	Köcher 1963–2005
CAD	A. Leo Oppenheim et al., editors, *The Assyrian Dictionary of the Oriental Institute of the University of Chicago*
CT	Cuneiform Texts from Babylonian Tablets in the British Museum
PBS 10/4	Langdon 1919
SAA 8	Hunger 1992
SAA 10	Parpola 1993a

[38] It is possible, however, that in this case *ṣâtu* does refer to a lexical text; see Frahm 2004: 46 n. 15.

[39] The metaphor has been discussed most recently by Rochberg 2004: 1–2.

[40] See Brown 2000: 113–22 (period schemes) and 253 (*Enūma Anu Enlil*).

BIBLIOGRAPHY

Al-Rawi, Farouk N. H., and Andrew R. George

1991–1992 "Enuma Anu Enlil XIV and Other Early Astronomical Tables." *Archiv für Orientforschung* 38–39: 52–73.

2006 "Tablets from the Sippar Library XIII: *Enuma Anu Enlil* XX." *Iraq* 68: 59–84.

Annus, Amar

2002 *The God Ninurta in the Mythology and Royal Ideology of Ancient Mesopotamia*. State Archives of Assyria Studies 14. Helsinki: The Neo-Assyrian Text Corpus Project.

Beaulieu, Paul-Alain

2007 "The Social and Intellectual Setting of Babylonian Wisdom Literature." In *Wisdom Literature in Mesopotamia and Israel*, edited by Richard J. Clifford, pp. 3–19. Society of Biblical Literature Symposium Series 36. Atlanta: Society of Biblical Literature.

Biggs, Robert D.

1968 "An Esoteric Babylonian Commentary." *Revue d'Assyriologie et d'Archéologie Orientale* 62: 51–58.

Böck, Barbara

2000 "'An Esoteric Babylonian Commentary' Revisited." *Journal of the American Oriental Society* 120: 615–20.

Borger, Rykle

1973 "Keilschrifttexte verschiedenen Inhalts." In *Symbolae Biblicae et Mesopotamicae Francisco Mario Theodoro De Liagre Böhl Dedicatae*, edited by M. A. Beek, A. A. Kampman, C. Nijland, and J. Ryckmans, pp. 38–55. Leiden: Brill.

Bottéro, Jean

1977 "Les noms de Marduk; L'écriture et la 'logique' en Mésopotamie ancienne." In *Essays on the Ancient Near East in Memory of J. J. Finkelstein*, edited by M. De Jong Ellis, pp. 5–28. Hamden: Archon Books.

Brown, David

2000 *Mesopotamian Planetary Astronomy-Astrology*. Cuneiform Monographs 18. Groningen: Styx.

Fincke, Jeanette C.

2001 "Der Assur-Katalog der Serie *enuma anu enlil (EAE)*." *Orientalia*. Nova Series, 70: 19–39.

Finkel, Irving L.

1986 "On the Series of Sidu." *Zeitschrift für Assyriologie* 76: 250–53.

Finkelstein, J. J.

1963 "The Antediluvian Kings: A University of California Tablet." *Journal of Cuneiform Studies* 17: 39–51.

Frahm, Eckart

2004 "Royal Hermeneutics: Observations on the Commentaries from Ashurbanipal's Libraries at Nineveh." *Iraq* 46: 45–50.

Gehlken, Erlend

2005 "Die Adad-Tafeln der Omenserie *Enuma Anu Enlil*. Teil 1: Einführung." *Baghdader Mitteilungen* 36: 235–73.

2007 "Die Serie DIŠ *Sîn ina tamartišu* im Überblick." *Nouvelles Assyriologiques Brèves et Utilitaires* 2007: no. 4, pp. 3–5.

2008 "Die Adad-Tafeln der Omenserie *Enuma Anu Enlil*, Teil 2: Die ersten beiden Donnertafeln (EAE 42 und EAE 43)." *Zeitschrift für Orientarchäologie* 1: 256–314.

George, Andrew R.

2003 *The Babylonian Gilgamesh Epic: Introduction, Critical Edition and Cuneiform Texts.* Oxford: Oxford University Press.

2007 "Gilgameš Epic at Ugarit." *Aula Orientalis* 25: 237–54.

Glassner, Jean-Jacques

2004 *Mesopotamian Chronicles.* Writings from the Ancient World 19. Atlanta: Society of Biblical Literature.

Hunger, Hermann

1992 *Astrological Reports to Assyrian Kings.* State Archives of Assyria 8. Helsinki: Helsinki University Press. http://cdl.museum.upenn.edu/saa

1998 "Zur Lesung sumerischer Zahlwörter." In *Dubsar anta-men: Studien zur Altorientalistik; Festschrift für Willem H. Ph. Römer zur Vollendung seines 70. Lebensjahres mit Beiträgen von Freunden, Schülern und Kollegen,* edited M. Dietrich and O. Loretz, pp. 179–83. Alter Orient und Altes Testament 253. Münster: Ugarit-Verlag.

Jean, Cynthia

2006 *La magie Néo-Assyrienne en contexte: Recherches sur le métier d'exorciste et le concept d'ašiputu.* State Archives of Assyria Studies 17. Helsinki: The Neo-Assyrian Text Corpus Project.

Koch-Westenholz, Ulla

1995 *Mesopotamian Astrology: An Introduction to Babylonian and Assyrian Celestial Divination.* Carsten Niebuhr Institute Publications 19. Copenhagen: Museum Tusculanum Press.

1999 "The Astrological Commentary *Šumma Sîn ina Tamartišu* Tablet 1." In *La science des cieux: Sages, mages, astrologues,* edited by R. Gyselen, pp. 149–65. Res Orientales 12. Bures-sur-Yvette: Groupe pour l'étude de la civilisation du Moyen-Orient.

2004 "A Fragment of *Enuma Anu Enlil* Concerning Jupiter." *Nouvelles Assyriologiques Brèves et Utilitaires* 2004, no. 45: 43.

Köcher, Franz

1963–2005 *Die babylonisch-assyrische Medizin in Texten und Untersuchungen.* 7 volumes. Berlin: Walter de Gruyter.

Lambert, Wilfred G.

1962 "A Catalogue of Texts and Authors." *Journal of Cuneiform Studies* 16: 59–77.

1976 "A Late Assyrian Catalogue of Literary and Scholarly Texts." In *Kramer Anniversary Volume: Cuneiform Studies in Honor of Samuel Noah Kramer,* edited by B. L. Eichler, J. W. Heimerdinger, and Å. W. Sjöberg, pp. 313–18. Alter Orient und Altes Testament 25. Neukirchen-Vluyn: Neukirchener Verlag.

1998 "The Qualifications of Babylonian Diviners." In *Festschrift für Rykle Borger zu seinem 65. Geburtstag am 24. Mai 1994.* tikip santakki mala bašmu..., edited by S. M. Maul, pp. 141–58. Cuneiform Monographs 10. Groningen: Styx.

Langdon, Stephen

1919 *Sumerian Liturgies and Psalms.* Publications of the Babylonian Section 10/4. Philadelphia: University Museum.

Lenzi, Alan

2008a *Secrecy and the Gods: Secret Knowledge in Ancient Mesopotamia and Biblical Israel.* State Archives of Assyria Studies 19. Helsinki: The Neo-Assyrian Text Corpus Project.

2008b "The Uruk List of Kings and Sages and Late Mesopotamian Scholarship." *Journal of Ancient Near Eastern Religions* 8: 137–69.

Machinist, Peter, and Hayim Tadmor

1993 "Heavenly Wisdom." In *The Tablet and the Scroll: Near Eastern Studies in Honor of William W. Hallo*, edited by M. E. Cohen, D. C. Snell, and D. B. Weisberg, pp. 146–51. Bethesda: CDL.

Parpola, Simo

1970 *Letters from Assyrian Scholars to the Kings Esarhaddon and Assurbanipal*, Part 1: *Texts*. Alter Orient und Altes Testament 5/1. Kevelaer: Butzon & Bercker.

1983 *Letters from Assyrian Scholars to the Kings Esarhaddon and Assurbanipal*, Part 2: *Commentary and Appendices*. Alter Orient und Altes Testament 5/2. Kevelaer: Butzon & Bercker.

1993a *Letters from Assyrian and Babylonian Scholars*. State Archives of Assyria 10. Helsinki: Helsinki University Press. http://cdl.museum.upenn.edu/saa

1993b "Mesopotamian Astrology and Astronomy as Domains of Mesopotamian 'Wisdom.'" In *Die Rolle der Astronomie in den Kulturen Mesopotamiens*, edited by Hannes D. Galter, pp. 47–59. Grazer morgenländische Studien 3. Graz: GrazKult.

Reiner, Erica

2007 "Another Harbinger of the Golden Age." In *Studies Presented to Robert D. Biggs*, edited by M. T. Roth, W. Farber, M. W. Stolper, and P. von Bechtolsheim, pp. 201–05. From the Workshop of the Chicago Assyrian Dictionary 2. Assyriological Studies 27. Chicago: The Oriental Institute.

Reiner, Erica, and David Pingree

1981 *Babylonian Planetary Omens*, Part 2. *Enuma Anu Enlil, Tablets 50–51*. Bibliotheca Mesopotamica 2/2. Malibu: Undena Publications.

2005 *Babylonian Planetary Omens*, Part Four. Cuneiform Monographs 30. Leiden: Brill, Styx.

Robson, Eleanor

2008 "Mesopotamian Medicine and Religion: Current Debates, New Perspectives." *Religion Compass* 2/4: 455–83. http://dx.doi.org/10.1111/j.1749-8171.2008.00082.x

forthcoming "Empirical Scholarship in the Neo-Assyrian Court."

Rochberg, Francesca

1999 "Continuity and Change in Omen Literature." In *Munuscula Mesopotamica: Festschrift für Johannes Renger*, edited by B. Böck, E. Cancik-Kirschbaum, and T. Richter, pp. 415–25. Alter Orient und Altes Testament 267. Münster: Ugarit-Verlag.

2004 *The Heavenly Writing: Divination, Horoscopy, and Astronomy in Mesopotamian Culture*. Cambridge: Cambridge University Press.

Rochberg-Halton, Francesca

1988 *Aspects of Babylonian Celestial Divination: The Lunar Eclipse Tablets of Enuma Anu Enlil*. Archiv für Orientforschung, Beiheft 22. Horn: F. Berger.

Seri, Andrea

2006 "The Fifty Names of Marduk in *Enuma eliš*." *Journal of the American Oriental Society* 126: 507–20.

Streck, Michael P.

2001 "Ninurta/Ningirsu. A I. In Mesopotamien." *Reallexikon der Assyriologie* 9: 512–22.

van der Toorn, Karel

2007 "Why Wisdom Became a Secret: On Wisdom as a Written Genre." In *Wisdom Literature in Mesopotamia and Israel*, edited by R. J. Clifford, pp. 21–29. Society of Biblical Literature, Symposium Series 36. Atlanta: Society of Biblical Literature.

Verderame, Lorenzo
2002 *Le Tavole I–VI della serie astrologica Enuma Anu Enlil*. Nisaba 2. Messina: Di.Sc.A.M.

Virolleaud, Charles
1907–1912 *L'astrologie chaldéenne: Le livre intitulé "Enuma (Anu) ilu Bêl*." Paris: P. Geuthner.

Weidner, Ernst F.
1942 "Die astrologische Serie Enûma Anu Enlil." *Archiv für Orientforschung* 14: 172–95; 308–18.

Worthington, Martin
2006 "Dialect Admixture of Babylonian and Assyrian in SAA VIII, X, XII, XVII and XVIII." *Iraq* 68: 59–84.

7

READING THE TABLET, THE EXTA, AND THE BODY: THE HERMENEUTICS OF CUNEIFORM SIGNS IN BABYLONIAN AND ASSYRIAN TEXT COMMENTARIES AND DIVINATORY TEXTS

ECKART FRAHM, YALE UNIVERSITY

INTRODUCTION

The Sumerian epic Enmerkar and the Lord of Aratta, composed sometime in the second half of the third millennium B.C., provides a famous etiology of the cuneiform writing system. It reports that the art of writing was invented by Enmerkar, a legendary early ruler of Uruk, because the couriers he used to send to the land of Aratta were not able to accurately memorize his messages:

> bar kin-gi$_4$-a ka-ni dugud šu nu-mu-un-da-an-gi$_4$-gi$_4$-da-ka
> en kul-ab$_4$ ^{ki}-a-ke$_4$ im-e šu bí-in-ra inim dub-gin$_7$ ⌜bí-in⌝-gub
>
> Because the messenger's mouth was too *heavy*, and he could not repeat it (the message),
> The lord of Kulab (Enmerkar) patted some clay and put the words on it as on a tablet (Vanstiphout 2004: 84–85, lines 502–03).

In the view of the author of these lines, Enmerkar, whose alleged impact on (scribal) culture, if not on writing itself, remained part of Mesopotamia's cultural memory until very late times,[1] had created the cuneiform writing system for one main reason: because it had the potential to serve as a far more reliable medium for communication over large distances of space and time than the human memory.

---

[1] In a Seleucid list of kings and scholars from Uruk (van Dijk 1962: 44–52), Enmerkar is the first and only postdiluvian king associated with an *apkallu*, one of the semi-divine sages from whom mankind took over the basic elements of civilization, including literature and scholarship. All the other *apkallu*-sages mentioned in the list are linked to antediluvian kings, and all the other postdiluvian kings to human *ummânu*-scholars. While Enmerkar's *apkallu* in the Uruk list is the rather insignificant Nungalpiriggal, a historical-literary text known from first-millennium copies from Uruk and Nineveh (Foster 2005: 531–32, with further literature), and a chronicle composed in the form of a fictitious royal letter some time after 1100 B.C. (Glassner 2004: 263–69), both badly broken, make Enmerkar a contemporary of the first and most important *apkallu*-sage, Adapa. The first-millennium "Catalogue of Texts and Authors" makes the even more remarkable claim that Enmerkar was the author of Sumerian poetic texts (Lambert 1962: 64–65 [III 3–5], 74). Given his association with writing and scholarship, it is somewhat ironic that the Cuthean Legend of Narām-Sîn blames Enmerkar for having failed to compose a monumental inscription (*narû*) addressed to posterity (Westenholz 1997: 264) — or does this story reflect, as suggested to me by Kathryn Slanski, that according to tradition Enmerkar invented writing on clay but not on stone? For a discussion of some other texts dealing with the origins of Uruk's association with scribal learning, see now George 2009: 110–11.

It is obvious that a script suitable for such a purpose should have been, ideally, both simple and precise. But the repertoire of cuneiform signs as we know it from the earliest written records is full of intricacies and ambiguities, and even though it underwent some systematization over time, eventually becoming capable of expressing linguistic data quite accurately, it remained tantalizingly complex until the end of its history.[2] One factor that makes the cuneiform writing system so complicated is that there are various types of signs: logograms (meaningful autonomous graphemes), determinatives (meaningful non-autonomous graphemes), phonograms (non-meaningful autonomous graphemes), and phonetic complements (non-meaningful non-autonomous graphemes).[3] What is even more bewildering is that one and the same sign can fulfill several of these functions and can have, within one and the same category, several different readings. The sign UD, for instance, can serve as a logogram for "sun," "day," and "white," and as a phonogram with the values u_4, utu, tam, tú, par, laḫ, and ḫiš, among others. Only the context determines which reading is correct.[4]

The Mesopotamian literati were clearly aware of the possibility of drastically simplifying their writing system, at least with regard to Akkadian texts. In fact, during the Old Babylonian period, Assyrian and Babylonian letter writers made do with a repertoire of no more than 68–82 syllabic signs, all of them representing a very restricted number of different values — and even though this meant that they used less than 10 percent of the 954 graphemes constituting the repertoire of cuneiform signs from all ages,[5] the clarity of their messages was not in the least compromised (Charpin 2008: 39, 53). Scribes who composed administrative texts during the same time employed a higher percentage of logograms, but the number of different signs used by them was small as well. Akkadian scholarly texts from the early Old Babylonian period are likewise written with a fairly limited selection of characters — 112 syllabic and 57 logographic signs in the case of the Old Babylonian omen corpus (Charpin 2008: 53). In the extispicy texts of this era, only one of the fifteen most important technical terms was written logographically (Goetze 1947: 5).

It would have been easy to reduce the complexity of the cuneiform writing system even further, but somewhat surprisingly, this did not happen. No systematic attempt was ever made by the scribes to dispose of the hundreds of signs and the thousands of possible readings associated with them that were for all intents superfluous. On the contrary: starting with the later Old Babylonian period, when logographic writings of technical terms in the aforementioned extispicy texts became the rule (see Richardson, this volume) and then for more than a thousand years, from the middle of the second millennium to the end of the first millennium B.C., the repertoire of signs used by the scribes, not so much for letters and documents but for scholarly texts, became progressively more complex. For instance, 84 percent of the signs of a typical first-millennium tablet of the terrestrial omen series *Šumma ālu* are logograms (Civil 1973: 26), and while in the Old Babylonian period most syllabic values belonged to the rather

[2] For a modern view of the origins of the cuneiform writing system, see Glassner 2000; for a list of archaic signs, see Green and Nissen 1987. There is no comprehensive treatment of the development of cuneiform writing through the ages, but the basic trends are conveniently outlined in Edzard 1980; see also Gong 1993. Borger 2003 contains a state-of-the-art sign list focusing on the Assyrian and Babylonian writing system, but useful for all periods of cuneiform writing; on pp. 624–25, the book provides information on additional sign lists dealing with specific periods.

[3] For this classification, see Kammerzell 1998.

[4] Borger 2003: no. 596. The lexical tradition offers many additional values, not attested in actual texts. Aa = *nâqu* 6, for instance, lists almost two hundred equations for the sign BAR (MSL 14, 229–35).

[5] This is the number of signs considered in Borger 2003.

simple CV (consonant — vowel) and VC types (*ba*, *ab*, etc.), scribes now employed a much larger number of CVC values (*bar*, *šad*, etc.). This development is all the more remarkable if one takes into account that the Aramaic alphabet, which became widely used in Mesopotamia in the first millennium B.C., operated with an extremely limited repertoire of characters.

It seems the main reason why the Babylonian and Assyrian scholars continued to cultivate this graphemic *embarras de richesse*, and even added to it in later periods, was that they regarded the overabundance of possible meanings associated with the polysemy of the cuneiform writing system as an inexhaustible source of knowledge and wisdom. The Mesopotamian literati of later times believed that language and writing were intimately connected, and that their basic elements, words and signs, were not arbitrarily chosen conventions, as claimed by Aristotle and Saussure, but representations that denoted their objects by nature.[6] Consequently, Sumerian and Akkadian words, however obscure and rare, had to be collected in lexical lists to be never forgotten, and so had the numerous signs used to write them. Giving up any of them, or reducing the complexity of their meanings, would have meant to lose access to some particular truth they conveyed.

COMMENTARIES

The so-called Esoteric Commentary from the Late Babylonian period (Biggs 1968; Böck 2000b) — which, in fact, is not a commentary proper but a treatise in its own right — provides a good example of this idea of "grammatology." It associates, in lines 14–18, the sign sequence *tu* : *ta* : *ti* — the *incipit* of an acrophonic sign list mostly known from the Old Babylonian period —, and the sequence *ù* : *a* : *ia* : *e* — Sumerian affixes listed in the beginnings of the first twelve entries of the Neo-Babylonian Grammatical Text no. I (MSL 4, 130)[7] — with cosmic abodes and what appears to be a Mesopotamian version of the four elements of Greek tradition: fire, water, air, and "earth" (*ḫuršānu*, lit., "mountain"). Both individual cuneiform signs and specific elements of Sumerian, a language that remained a central pillar of Mesopotamian scholarship up to the end of cuneiform civilization, are presented in this entry as being deeply meaningful and transcending their function as phonetic indicators and grammatical morphemes.

The "grammatology" underlying Babylonian and Assyrian text commentaries is informed by the same ideas that can be found in the Esoteric Commentary. Text commentaries, now attested on more than a thousand clay tablets and fragments, were introduced in Mesopotamia in the early centuries of the first millennium B.C.[8] The ancient scribes who composed them

[6] The same belief is, at least to some extent, behind the tenacity with which the Chinese, Japanese, and Koreans stick to their highly complex writing systems; see Taylor and Taylor 1995.

[7] The grammatical text has *i* instead of *ia*. A different interpretation has been advanced by Scurlock and Al-Rawi (2006: 371–72), who explain *ù* : *a* : *ia* : *e* as a rendering of the magical formula *eioiae* (or *eiaeioiae*) found in magical papyri from Egypt and associated with the name of Yahweh (for more evidence for the magical use of vowel sequences in the ancient world, see Dornseiff 1925: 35–60). I would not exclude that the author of the Esoteric Commentary wanted to make such a connection, but that his primary point of reference was the text on Sumerian grammar, still in use in Late Babylonian times, is all the more likely in the light of the preceding reference to the Mesopotamian *tu* : *ta* : *ti* lists.

[8] A comprehensive study of Babylonian and Assyrian text commentaries is currently prepared for publication by the present author.

often focused on the phonemic and graphemic "fabric" of their base texts, and not just on contents. To simplify a rather complicated matter, one could argue that the explanations in Babylonian and Assyrian commentaries are, for the most part, based on two complementary hermeneutical procedures: the finding of synonyms on one hand, and of homonyms on the other. Synonymity was used by the commentators in order to clarify the literal meaning of obscure words or expressions through the act of providing more common equivalents, often excerpted from lexical lists. Homonymity, in contrast, was employed whenever a commentator wished to establish a non-literal explanation of a given passage. In these cases, he would choose a word that sounded similar to the lemma in question, but meant something completely different. Closely related to this "etymological" (or pseudo-etymological) approach is an "etymographic" method of explanation.[9] Here, the commentator would analyze the signs used to write specific lemmata with an eye on the many other meanings these signs could have. Often etymological and etymographic modes of interpretation were combined and based not only on an Akkadian, but also a Sumerian reading of the lemmata that required explanation.

One of the main goals of commentaries employing etymology and etymography was to produce the illusion of an esoteric inner coherence of the texts they dealt with. A late Nippur commentary,[10] now accompanied by a partial duplicate from Ur,[11] on a collection of incantations and magico-medical prescriptions to help a woman in childbirth provides a good example. Among the ingredients recommended in the base text for the treatment of the woman is oil, Akkadian *šamnu*. The commentary entry on this word (lines 11–12) reads as follows:

> *šá-am-nu* : ni-ig GAR *sin-niš-tì* : *am* : *ze-ri* : nu : *ba-nu-u šá-niš* i NI / *šá-am-nu* : i : *a-ṣu-u šá* NUMUN
>
> "Oil" (*šamnu*, written *šá-am-nu*) — (this is what it means): (the sign) GAR (which is identical with *šá*), (when read) $nig_{(2)}$, (means) "woman," *am* (means) "offspring," (and) *nu* (means) "to create." (The sign) NI, (when read) $i_{(3)}$, (means) "oil," (while) $i_{(1)}$ (means) "to emerge," with regard to offspring.

The commentator deals with the word *šamnu* in two steps. He first dissects it along the boundaries of its syllabic spelling, and then refers to a homophone of the Sumerian reading of the logogram used to write the word, i_3. The putative background of the equations provided in the entry has been discussed by Civil (1974) and needs no reassessment here; most of them are taken from — bilingual and monolingual — lexical lists. The goal of the entry is obvious: the commentator wants to demonstrate that there is an immediate connection between the name of the ingredient used in the magico-medical ritual described in the base text, and the effect it was supposed to produce, namely the easy birth of the child. His interpretation is, for the most part, based on etymological speculation, but in the first explanation, where *šá* is

---

[9] The term "etymography" was introduced by Assmann (2003) in reference to ancient Egyptian hermeneutics. It should be noted that I am using it in this article in a restricted sense. Etymography, for me, is a method of producing or discovering additional levels of meaning by bringing into play the multitude of readings a specific grapheme can have within the writing system to which it belongs. Readings based on a code applied to a grapheme from outside this system, for example interpretations focused exclusively on the shape of a sign, are not regarded as "etymographical" here.

[10] 11N-T3, published in transliteration and with commentary in Civil 1974: 331–36.

[11] Ur Excavation Texts 6/3, no. 897, identified by Stol (see Römer 2007: 182).

read as níg and explained as *sinništu* "woman,"[12] etymography accompanies the etymological approach.

In some instances, text commentaries analyze the individual components of composite signs. A rather complex example of this procedure can be found in a commentary from Assurbanipal's library that deals with omens from the astrological series *Enūma Anu Enlil*. The entry in question explains the protasis DIŠ GI$_6$ *ni*$_5$(NE)-*pí-iḫ* IZI SÌG-*ma ḫa*(*ʾa*$_4$)-*ku*$_6$-*ku*$_6$-*tu*$_4$ *nap-ḫat* "If the night (sky) is tinged with fiery light and an abnormally red glow (*akukūtu*) blazes." It reads (Virolleaud 1907–1909: no. 33, K 50, rev. 10′–11′):

> mu-U+PA+KAB(copy: DI EN) *ḫa-ku*$_6$-*ku*$_6$-*tu*$_4$ mu *i-šá-tu*$_4$ eme-sal / *gi-ra-a* [*g*]*i*-⸢*kur-ru-ú*(?)⸣ *ge-eš-tar-kap-pa-ak-ku šá-mu-ú*
>
> The sign sequence mu-U+PA+KAB (represents) (*ḫ*)*akukūtu* (because), (in) Emesal, mu (means) "fire" (*išātu*), (and) *gigurû geštarkappaku* (i.e., the sign U+PA+KAB), (when read) *gi-ra-a*, (means) "sky" (*šamû*).

The aim of this explanation is to clarify the meaning of the word *akukūtu* by demonstrating that the two main components of its complicated logographic spelling provide the meaning "fire of the sky." The entry is based on passages from the lexical lists Antagal and Aa.[13]

Even more sophisticated is the analysis of a cuneiform sign found in a late Uruk commentary (and its partial duplicate) on the first tablet of the diagnostic series *Sa-gig* (Hunger 1976: no. 27, rev. 23–26; George 1991: 161). One of the entries of this tablet reads: DIŠ ^{giš}GIGIR IGI GIG BI ŠU ^{d}*Iš*$_8$-*tár* "If (the exorcist on his way to the patient) sees a chariot, that patient suffers from the hand of Ištar." The commentary, after establishing other links between the chariot mentioned in the protasis of the omen and the goddess Ištar featured in its apodosis, concludes with the statement:

> $^{\text{ú-bu}}$ubu$_x$(U) : *di-l*[*i-pat* / *aššu*(?) *ú*]-*bu* : (1)bán 3 *qa* : *ú-bu* : 15 : ^{d}15
>
> (The sign) U, (when read) ubu$_{(x)}$, (means) Dilipat (Venus), [*for*] ubu (corresponds to) one *seah* and three liters, (so) ubu is 15 (and thus represents) Ištar (^{d}15).

As shown by Hunger and George, this explanation is apparently based on an older form of the sign GIGIR, the logogram used to write *narkabtu* "chariot." This older form consists of a frame, not with an inserted BAD, as in the form common in the first millennium, but with a single Winkelhaken, which has the reading U, inside. It seems the commentator took this U as a depiction of the planet Venus residing in Auriga, the constellation representing a chariot. His identification of the U-sign with Ištar was based on the idea that U could also be read ubu, a Babylonian surface and capacity measure. By making use of the same metrological calculations that are preserved in the Uruk colophon of the Esagil tablet (George 1992: 118, line 3), the commentator claimed that one ubu corresponded to 15 *qû* or liters[14] — and 15 was the

---

[12] There is no lexical list that equates níg with *sinništu*. The commentator may have arrived at his explanation through a process of phonetic and semantic associations based on the Sumerian words nin "lady" or nig "bitch."

[13] The quotations from these series seem to be marred by major mistakes, though (collation necessary). Antagal C 101 (MSL 17, 197) reads: mu-gira(U-MAŠ-KAB) | *a-ku-ku-t*[*u*$_4$], and Aa II/4: 141 (MSL 14, 284): *gi-ra-a* | U+MAŠ+KAB | *ge-eš-pu maš-kab-ba-ku* | *šá-mu-u*. The commentator probably had quoted the lexical entries from memory.

[14] The equation is rather problematic; it mixes up an earlier Kassite and Early Neo-Babylonian metrological system and a later Neo-Babylonian one (see George 1992: 434).

holy number of the goddess Ištar. The explanation does obviously not reflect the thoughts of the author of the base text. Originally, the protasis-apodosis string of the omen may have been motivated by the fact that both the chariot and the deity were associated with warfare.

By using pseudo-etymological speculation as well as etymography in order to extract various meanings from such entries, the Mesopotamian commentators anticipated a hermeneutical strategy well known from classical and medieval Christian exegesis, where it is rooted in the Platonic semiotics of immediate signification, and also from rabbinical interpretation (Lieberman 1987; Cavigneaux 1987). In these traditions, however, with their far more one-dimensional writing systems, the application of *notarikon*, *gematriah*, and other forms of grapheme-related hermeneutical techniques seems rather artificial, while the multiple meanings of most of the cuneiform signs provide every Babylonian text in a far more organic way with an inherent set of possible alternative readings.

DIVINATION AND WRITING

The hermeneutic sensitivity that characterizes the Babylonian and Assyrian text commentaries of the first millennium derived from a long tradition of divinatory interpretation. From early on, Mesopotamian scholars believed that the gods left signs on the exta of the sacrificial animal, in the life of plants, the behavior of animals, the movement of heavenly bodies, and in dreams.[15] These signs reminded them in many respects of the signs of the cuneiform writing system. The scholars regarded nature as a book, or rather a tablet, that could be read by those who knew the underlying code.[16] Haruspices occasionally called the liver a "tablet of the gods" (*ṭuppu ša ilī*) and claimed that the signs they were able to detect on it were "written" on it by the sun-god Šamaš (Starr 1983: 30, lines 16–17; 53–57). Astrologers spoke of the "writing of the firmament" (*šiṭir šamê*, *šiṭir burūmê*) when referring to the starry sky from which they took their forecasts (see CAD Š/3, 146a).[17] Not surprisingly, then, there are cases in the Mesopotamian textual record in which the starting point for a divinatory quest was the observation, on objects of various types, of writing in its most literal sense, that is, of individual or multiple cuneiform signs.

References to written messages of a certain length that were deemed to have divinatory relevance occur in a few Mesopotamian dream reports. Two passages from inscriptions of the Assyrian king Assurbanipal can serve as examples. In the first, Assurbanipal writes that a man,

---

[15] For a convenient introduction to the various branches of Mesopotamian divination, and further bibliography, see Maul 2003.

[16] For further thoughts on this issue, see, inter alia, Bottéro 1974; Rochberg 2004: 1–13, 165–81; and Noegel 2007.

[17] It should, of course, not be overlooked that there were also differences between the interpretation of natural phenomena in divination and the exegesis of written texts, and that these differences are mirrored in the terminology used by the ancient scholars. The natural sign expounded in the protasis of an omen was called *ittu* in Akkadian and giskim in Sumerian, while the cuneiform sign was called *miḫiṣtu* (lit., "strike" [on the tablet]) in Akkadian (only once, in the Aa 16 commentary BM 41286, *ittu* seems to be used in this context; see MSL 14, 323–26) and gù-sum ("sound-giver") in Sumerian (see CAD I/J, 306–08, M/2, 54). It is also noteworthy that *pišru*, the *terminus technicus* for the interpretation provided for an ominous phenomenon in the apodosis of an omen entry (Parpola 1983: 40), is never used to label Mesopotamian text commentaries, which are called *ṣâtu*, *mukallimtu*, or *multābiltu* instead. This is all the more remarkable as in later Semitic cultures, terms for text commentaries such as Hebrew *pešer* and Arabic *tafsīr* are actually derived from the root *pšr*.

while dreaming, saw a cult pedestal of Sîn on which was written that the moon-god would persecute and destroy all the enemies of the king who refused to submit to him (Borger 1996: 40–41, 233).[18] In the second passage, Assurbanipal claims that the Lydian king Gyges sent messengers to him after he had seen the Assyrian king's "name" (*nibīt šumi*), apparently in some written form, in a dream (Borger 1996: 30–31, 218).[19] Both episodes are reminiscent of the famous "writing on the wall" in the Belshazzar story of the Bible, even though the latter does not feature dreams.[20]

The "texts" in the dream reports communicated by Assurbanipal are straightforward and non-enigmatic, quite in contrast to another type of script-related divination: the references in treatises on extispicy and physiognomy to features in the shape of cuneiform signs that were observed by experts on the exta of the sacrificial lamb or the body of a human being. My goal in the following sub-sections is to collect these references and to analyze the principles underlying the links between the protases referring to specific graphemes and the predictions based on their occurrence.[21] We have seen that Babylonian and Assyrian text commentaries often deduce new meanings from secondary values of cuneiform signs, and such an "etymographical" approach is what we would expect to find as the main rationale of omen entries mentioning cuneiform signs as well. But a closer look at the evidence, first from extispicy and then from physiognomic omens, will demonstrate that the situation is, in fact, somewhat less straightforward.

For the convenience of readers not acquainted with the cuneiform writing system, the Old Babylonian forms of the signs discussed in the following sub-sections are reproduced in figure 7.1.

EXTISPICY

Extispicy treatises are known from the Old Babylonian to the Late Babylonian period, and references to cuneiform signs are attested in texts from all phases of this tradition.[22] The earliest relevant entries occur in three Old Babylonian treatises on liver omens published in Goetze 1947.[23] They present the signs either in the form of the actual graphemes or invoke them by their ancient names.[24] Two of the texts describe the shape of what was called the *naplastum* in Old Babylonian times, a groove on the *lobus sinister* of the liver of the sacrificial lamb. The small tablet Goetze 1947: no. 14 (whose sign forms display archaizing tendencies) includes the following omens:

---

[18] In an alternative version of the passage, it was the god Nabû, patron of the scribes, who read the inscription to the dreamer.

[19] The episode has a somewhat miraculous character, which brings to mind that Gyges later became a legendary figure in other traditions as well, not only in the famous stories told about him by Herodotus and later classical sources, but also in the biblical book of Ezekiel, where he appears in the garb of the apocalyptic ruler Gog (*Gwg*), king of Magog. For details, see Lipiński 1998.

[20] For a discussion of the respective passage and some references to the massive scholarly literature dealing with it, see Noegel 2007: 160–62.

[21] While there are, undoubtedly, additional references overlooked by me, it is hoped that the entries discussed here provide a fairly representative sample of the evidence.

[22] For a very concise overview, see Nougayrol 1945–46: 79.

[23] For a learned treatment of the respective passages, see Lieberman 1977; see also Noegel 2007: 12–13.

[24] On the ancient names of the cuneiform signs, see Gong 2000. As shown above, first-millennium text commentaries would sometimes refer to sign names as well.

1) BAD IGI.BAR *ki-ma* BAD *a-ša-at* LÚ *i-ni-ak* (line 5)

If the *naplastum* is like (the grapheme) BAD, the man's wife will have (illicit) sexual intercourse.

No etymographic link between protasis and apodosis. Given that the BAD sign consists of a straight horizontal wedge ending in a hole-like Winkelhaken, it seems quite conceivable that the entry is informed by sexual symbolism of a Freudian type. The prediction is negative.

2) BAD IGI.BAR *ki-ma* BAD-*ma ù ši-lum i-na* ŠÀ-*ša na-di aš-ša-at* LÚ *i-ni-a-ak-ma / mu-sà i-ṣa-ba-as-sí-i-ma i-da-ak-ši* (lines 6–7)

If the *naplastum* is like (the grapheme) BAD and a hole is in its center, the man's wife will have (illicit) sexual intercourse, and her husband will seize her and kill her.

The reference to the killing of the wife could be related to the reading of BAD as ÚŠ = *mâtum* "to die" (and similar meanings of the sign), but whether the author of the text had really intended such a link is doubtful. If the interpretation provided in the preceding note is correct, it may be more likely that he regarded the BAD sign as a representation of the illicit sexual union, and the hole in its center as an expression of its violent termination by the husband. The prediction is negative.

3) BAD IGI.BAR *ki-ma* KASKAL *šar-ru-um ka-ab-tu-ti-šu i-da-ak-ma / bi-ša-šu-nu ma-ku-ur-šu-nu a-na bi-ta-at i-la-ni i-za-az* (lines 8–9)

If the *naplastum* is like (the grapheme) KASKAL, the king will kill his magnates and distribute their goods and possessions to the temples of the gods.

Lieberman (1977: 149–50) suggested that the prediction is based on paronomasia, with KASKAL (which was apparently read *kaškaš* in Old Babylonian, see below no. 7) being associated with the Akkadian verb *kašāšu* "to gain control of, to acquire." This explanation is ingenious, but since *kašāšu* does not occur in the apodosis, not completely convincing. The prediction is negative.

4) [B]AD ⌈IGI.BAR *ki*⌉-*ma* BAD *mar-ṣa-*⌈*am*⌉ ^giš^NÁ *i-ka-la-šu* (line 14)

If the *naplastum* is like the grapheme BAD, the bed will confine the sick man.

The apodosis could be motivated by a reading of BAD as *mâtum* "to die" (see no. 2), but the link is not obvious. The prediction is negative.

5) [BAD IGI.BA]R ⌈*ki-ma* x⌉ *sà-ap-ḫu-ut* LÚ *i-pa-ḫu-[ur]* (line 15)

[If] the *naplastum* is like (the grapheme) x, the man's scattered (relatives?) will come together again.[25]

Lieberman (1977: 149) argued that the protasis, like the preceding one, refers to a grapheme. The respective sign is damaged but could be PAB/KÚR, in which case there would be no obvious etymographic link between protasis and apodosis.[26] The prediction is positive.

[25] The translation of the apodosis follows CAD S, 164a.

[26] Collation of the tablet in the Yale Babylonian Collection established that Goetze's copy of the

Another Old Babylonian tablet dealing with the *naplastum* is Goetze 1947: no. 17, likewise written in an archaizing script:

6) BAD IGI.BAR *ki-ma pa-ap-pi-im* ⸢*ug*⸣*-ba-ab-tam* DINGIR *i-ri-iš* (line 47)

If the *naplastum* is like (the grapheme named) *pappum* (i.e., PAB), the god wants an *ugbabtum*-priestess.

As recognized by Lieberman (1977: 148 n. 19), the entry is based on paronomasia between the grapheme name and the second syllable of *ugbabtum*. The prediction is positive.

7) BAD IGI.BAR *ki-ma ka-aš-ka-aš* dIŠKUR *i-ra-ḫi-iṣ* (line 48)

If the *naplastum* is like (the grapheme named) *kaškaš* (i.e., KASKAL),[27] the god Adad will inundate.

As recognized by Lieberman (1977: 148), the prediction is based on the sign name's resemblance with *kaškaššu* "overpowering," a frequent epithet of Adad. The prediction is negative.

Two more graphemes are mentioned in the small Old Babylonian tablet Goetze 1947: no. 61, which deals with the liver's *lobus quadratus*, called *šulmum* "Well-being" in Akkadian:

8) *šum-ma i-na ma-aš-ka-an šu-*⸢*ul*⸣*-mi-im* ḪAL / LUGAL *ki-ša-ti i-na ma-ti i-li-am* (lines 9–10)

If in the place of the Well-being there is (the grapheme) ḪAL, a king of the world will arise in the land.

No etymographic link between protasis and apodosis. The prediction is positive.

9) *šum-ma i-na ma-aš-ka-an šu-ul-mi-im* / [*ḫ*]*a-lu-um pa-li a-ka-di-im ga-mir-ir* (lines 11–12)

If in the place of the Well-being there is (the grapheme named) *ḫallum* (i.e., ḪAL), the dynasty of Akkad is ended.

Noegel (2007: 13) suggests this protasis-apodosis string could be based on a reading of ḪAL as *zâzu* "to divide," a verb sometimes used to describe how countries lost their territorial integrity. This explanation, while not impossible, remains conjectural. The prediction is negative.

Lieberman (1977: 149) assumed that the first entry of the text, [*šum-m*]*a i-na ma-*[*aš*]*-ka-*[*an š*]*u-ul-mi-*⸢*im*⸣ PA, refers to a grapheme as well, but it seems more likely that PA is to be understood as a logogram for *larûm* "branch, bifurcation," and that the phrase means: "If in the place of the Well-being there is a 'branch.'"[28] Lieberman is right, however, when he

---

passage is very accurate; the space with the traces of the sign is indeed quite narrow. If one read ḪAL, one could construct a link with the apodosis (tablet 14 of Aa equates ḪAL with *paḫāru*, see MSL 14, 290 line 24), but the traces do not really favor this reading.

[27] According to the lexical tradition of the first millennium, the sign name of KASKAL was *kaskala* and not *kaškaš* (see Gong 2000: 144), but the grapheme KASKAL occurs in the preceding line and is therefore, most likely, referred to in this entry as well.

[28] Cf. line 6 of the tablet: [*š*]*u-ul-mu-um la-ri-am na-*⸢*di*⸣.

points out (1977: 149) that the *kakkum* ("Weapon"), an often mentioned small piece of liver tissue that sticks out in the form of a club or peg (Koch-Westenholz 2000: 48–51) and is usually regarded as inauspicious, probably owes its name to the cuneiform grapheme GAG, even though the word is later written with the logogram ^{giš}TUKUL. The occurrences of *kakkum* in extispicy texts are far too numerous to be listed here.

Neo-Assyrian and Neo- and Late Babylonian extispicy texts include more references to cuneiform graphemes than the Old Babylonian treatises so far available to us. We begin our overview with texts that describe the *manzāzu*, or Presence, a designation of the groove on the liver's *lobus sinister* that came to replace the Old Babylonian term *naplastum* (see above, nos. 1–7). Koch-Westenholz 2000: no. 11, one of the manuscripts of *Manzāzu*, the third chapter of the extispicy series of the first millennium, includes the following entry:

10) BAD NA GIM PAB/KÚR *šu-bat-ka* [*ana šubat nakrīka iššir*] (line 10′)

If the Presence is like (the grapheme) PAB/KÚR, your camp [will charge the camp of your enemy].

The restoration of the apodosis (which is missing in Koch-Westenholz's publication) is based on nos. 12 (a commentary on this entry) and 44. The reading of PAB/KÚR as *nakru* "enemy" provides an etymographic link between protasis and apodosis, but the shape of the sign, two wedges crossing each other, might have played a role as well — the wedges symbolize quite well the attack of one army on another. The prediction is positive. For an essentially identical protasis, with a different prediction, see above, no. 6 (see also no. 5).

Two first-millennium commentaries on *Manzāzu* include references to omen entries dealing with cuneiform graphemes. These commentaries are of particular interest because they provide us with explicit information on how the Babylonian and Assyrian scholars of the first millennium interpreted such omens. The first commentary is Koch-Westenholz 2000: no. 20:

11) [*šumma*] 5-*šú* NA GIM ḪAL UMUŠ KUR MAN-*ni* ḪAL *za-a-zu bé-e-ru pa-šá-ṭu* (line 20)

[If], fifth, the Presence is like (the grapheme) ḪAL, the political situation of the land will change. ḪAL (means) "to divide, to select, to efface."

The unraveling of the political situation predicted in the apodosis could be seen as being mirrored by the ḪAL sign with its notions of division. But the commentary is not interested in focusing on this link. Instead, it explains that the comparison in the protasis refers to a Presence that is split and (partially) effaced.[29] This is not surprising since the entry is part of a longer commentarial section listing older omens that were regarded as equivalent to the omen commented on in the first place, *šumma manzāzu ina qablīšu pašiṭ kakkī rabṣūti aḫītu* "If the Presence is effaced in its center, (there will be) idle weapons — inauspicious" (line 16). The shape of the ḪAL sign provides a good illustration of this particular condition of the Presence.[30] The prediction, the same as in no. 46 (which is likewise based on the occurrence of a ḪAL), is negative.

---

[29] For a similar explanation of ḪAL, see below, no. 27. While *zâzu* and *bêru* are well-attested renderings of ḪAL (see, e.g., MSL 14, 290, Aa 14, i 17, 21), the equation between ḪAL and *pašāṭu* is not known from the lexical tradition (see CAD P, 249) and probably an ad hoc explanation based on semantic association; it provides the link to the omen in line 16 of the commentary.

[30] It is not completely clear, though, if the entry refers to the late form of the sign (which is used in the

An entry in line 70 of the text has been claimed to refer to a grapheme as well, but this seems doubtful:

> BAD NA 3-*ma* BAR.MEŠ ŠUB.MEŠ DIŠ *e-liš* DIŠ *šap-liš* DIŠ *ina bi-ri-šú-nu re-diš* (var. om.) GÍR 3-*ma* GIM *an-nim-ma* (var.: AN-*a-n*[*im*]) GIŠ.ḪUR-*šú-nu*
>
> Koch-Westenholz translates this difficult passage as follows: "If there are three Presences and they lie separately, one above, one below, one *parallel* between them, three Paths and their design is like the sign AN(?)." It is true that AN was named *an(n)u* in ancient Mesopotamia.[31] Nonetheless, it seems unlikely that the entry, apparently a commentary on Koch-Westenholz 2000: no. 7 line 11, really refers to the AN sign — which, whether in its earlier or in its later form, simply does not look like the configuration observed here. Probably, we should rather normalize the last words of the entry as *kīma annîmma uṣurtašu* and translate: "Its drawing is like this." If understood correctly, the phrase would refer to a sketch, to be consulted by the reader of the commentary, of the ominous configuration described in the omen. In fact, ms. I of the text, K. 12845+, has an empty space, traversed by a horizontal ruling, before *kīma*, a feature that could reflect the occurrence of such a sketch on the tablet from which the manuscript was copied.[32] Note, furthermore, that in the preceding entry of the commentary (line 69), there is an unmistakable reference to a sketch, even though it is phrased somewhat differently: GIŠ.ḪUR-*šú-nu ana* IGI-*ka* "you have their design before you." The writing AN-*a-nim* in ms. I remains strange, however, and one cannot completely exclude the possibility that the scribe who wrote this tablet might mistakenly have taken what was originally a reference to a sketch as a statement about the grapheme AN.

12) BAD NA GIM PAB/KÚR KI.TUŠ-[*ka šubat nakrīka* SI].SÁ-*ir* : BE MAN-*ú* NA GIM BAR (line 104)

If the Presence is like (the grapheme) PAB/KÚR, [your] camp will charge [the camp of your enemy] — if, second, the Presence is like (the grapheme) BAR.[33]

This is a commentary on example no. 10. It establishes that the occurrence of a BAR on the Presence has the same — in this case apparently auspicious — significance as that of a PAB.

13) [*šumma manzāzu kīma* PAB(?) *ilu* NIN].DINGIR.RA APIN-*eš ú-lu* AN.MI (line 107)

[If the Presence is like (the grapheme) PAB(?), the god] wants an *ugbabtu*-priestess, or (there will be) an eclipse.

---

text) or an older one. The late ḪAL is a sequence of two horizontal wedges, which could represent the two elements of the split Presence, but it is also possible, as pointed out to me in a personal communication by A. R. George, that the horizontal wedge of the earlier form of the sign represents the *manzāzu*-crease, while the oblique wedges of this form make a cross that obliterates (*pašāṭu*) its middle part.

[31] For the sign name (often written ^{d}*a-nu*(*m*)), see Gong 2000: 102.

[32] See the photo in Koch-Westenholz 2000: pl. 49. Note, however, that K. 7149, Koch-Westenholz's ms. G, has no empty space in the relevant line; see the copy in Starr 1977: 164.

[33] One could also take the BAR in this line as a logogram for *pillurtu* "cross," but the next entry, which clearly refers to a *pillurtu*, uses the writing BAR-*ti*, indicating that the BAR without phonetic complement in line 104 rather represents the — cross-shaped — grapheme.

The restoration of the protasis is uncertain; it is based on the assumption that the omen is essentially identical with the Old Babylonian omen entry quoted above as no. 6, with *manzāzu* replacing *naplastum* in the protasis and the subject preceding the object in the apodosis. Note that there seem to be no other references to *ugbabtu*-priestesses in first-millennium extispicy texts, and that the entry occurs in a commentary section that refers several times to cuneiform graphemes (lines 104, 113, and perhaps other badly damaged lines). In the light of example no. 19, the grapheme mentioned in the protasis could, however, also have been a KUR. The first prediction is positive, the second negative.

14) BAD *šal-šú* NA GIM BAD ŠUB-*ti* ERIM-*ni* (line 113)

If, third, the Presence is like (the grapheme) BAD (there will be) a defeat of the army.

The entry may display the same rather vague etymographic link between protasis and apodosis that we have discussed above under no. 2. The protasis is essentially identical with that of nos. 1 and 4. The commentary quotes the entry because it regards it as equivalent to the badly broken omen presented in line 111.[34] The prediction is negative.

The *Manzāzu* commentary Koch-Westenholz 2000: no. 19 includes two additional references to cuneiform graphemes:

15) BAD MAN-*ú* MU.NI NA GIM AN NUN KUR [*ibbalkitūšu ileqqe*] (line 38)

If, second, the Presence is like (the grapheme) AN, the prince [will take] the land [that rebelled against him].

Restored after another *Manzāzu* commentary, Koch-Westenholz 2000: no. 25 line 29.[35] No obvious etymographic link between protasis and apodosis. The entry is presented in a section with omens deemed equivalent to the enry "If the Presence is long, the days of the prince will be long."[36] The prediction is positive.

16) BAD NA GIM BAD *ina* SUḪUŠ-*šú ka-ra-šu-ú* GAR (line 97)

If the Presence is like (the grapheme) BAD at its base,[37] there will be disaster.

The entry may display the same rather vague etymographic link between protasis and apodosis that we have discussed above under no. 2. The protasis is similar to that of nos. 1, 4, and 14. The prediction is negative.

The Well-being, already known to us from the Old Babylonian examples nos. 8 and 9, is associated with cuneiform graphemes in later texts as well. The *bārûtu* excerpt KAR 423 from Assur, its partial duplicate K. 10137 (Koch-Westenholz 2000: no. 105), and Koch-Westenholz 2000: no. 64 all include the following three short entries:[38]

---

[34] Theoretically, the protasis of that omen (which ends with *nadi*) could be identical with that of our example no. 2, but this remains very uncertain.

[35] In that entry, *ši-bu-šú* "its old version" replaces MAN-*ú* MU.NI.

[36] Considering that the AN sign does not really resemble a "long" Presence, this is rather surprising.

[37] "At its base" is missing in Koch-Westenholz's translation.

[38] Note, though, that the sequence of the signs discussed is not the same everywhere. In KAR 423 and K. 10137, it is AN, ḪAL, KUR; in Koch-Westenholz 2000: no. 64, KUR, AN, ḪAL.

17) BAD SILIM GIM AN DÙG(-*ub*) *lìb-bi* (KAR 423 ii 53; Koch-Westenholz 2000: no. 105 line 2´; no. 64 line 44)

If the Well-being is like (the grapheme) AN, (there will be) happiness.

For the same apodosis, see examples no. 80 (grapheme: IGI) and 86 (graphemes: ŠE and PI). No obvious etymographic link between protasis and apodosis. The prediction is positive.

18) BAD SILIM GIM ḪAL *tam-ṭa-a-ti/tu*$_4$ (KAR 423 ii 54; Koch-Westenholz 2000: no. 105 line 3´; no. 64 line 45)[39]

If the Well-being is like (the grapheme) ḪAL, (there will be) deprivation.

The wording of the apodosis may have been inspired by the fact that "division," a concept indicated by the sign ḪAL, implied the dispersal of an original total. The prediction is negative.

19) BAD SILIM GIM KUR AN.MI (KAR 423 ii 55; Koch-Westenholz 2000: no. 105 line 4´; no. 64 line 43)

If the Well-being is like (the grapheme) KUR, (there will be) an eclipse.

No etymographical link between protasis and apodosis. The prediction is negative.

Koch-Westenholz 2000: no. 64 includes five additional omens referring to cuneiform graphemes, one of which is also attested in KAR 423 and Koch-Westenholz 2000: no. 105:

20) BAD SILIM GIM BAD *ina* ^{giš}TUKUL ERIM-*ni* NUN *i-ger-ri-ma* $^{\textit{he-pí eš-šú}}$ (Koch-Westenholz 2000: no. 64 line 36)

If the Well-being is like (the grapheme) BAD, my army will turn against the prince in battle — *new break*.

For the possibility that there is a vague etymographical link between protasis and apodosis, see above, no. 2. The prediction is apparently negative.

21) BAD SILIM GIM PAB/KÚR DU IGI ERIM-*ni* LAL-*mu* (Koch-Westenholz 2000: no. 64 line 38)

If the Well-being is like (the grapheme) PAB/KÚR, the leader of the army will be captured.

There is no obvious etymographical link between protasis and apodosis, even though one could speculate that the latter, with its indirect reference to an important capture made by the enemy, could have been to some extent inspired by the well-known equation PAB/KÚR = *nakru* "enemy." The prediction is negative.

---

[39] As recognized by Koch-Westenholz, this omen is also quoted in a Query to the Sungod from Nineveh; see Starr 1990: no. 317, obv. 8.

22) BAD SILIM GIM GAM KUR NUN *ana* BAD_4 NIGIN-*ḫur* (Koch-Westenholz 2000: no. 64 line 39)

If the Well-being is like (the grapheme) GAM, the land of the prince will gather in a fortress.

There is no obvious etymographical link between protasis and apodosis, but note that GAM means, inter alia, *mâtu* "to die," a connotation that might have influenced the negative prediction.

23) BAD SILIM GIM U GU_4.UD-*iṭ* UR.MAḪ *kaš-du*(var. KUR-*du*) (Koch-Westenholz 2000: no. 64 line 41; KAR 323, ii 56; Koch-Westenholz 2000: no. 105 line 5′)

If the Well-being is like (the grapheme) U, (there will be) a successful attack by lions.

The translation follows Koch-Westenholz's. Instead of U, a sign that looks like a hole, one could also read BÙR[40] and assume that the protasis refers to a real hole (*šīlu*), but since the preceding and the following lines include references to graphemes, this seems less likely. There is no obvious etymographical link between protasis and apodosis. The prediction is negative.

24) BAD SILIM GIM U-*ma ke-pi* GU_4.UD-*iṭ* UR.MAḪ NU *kaš-du* (Koch-Westenholz 2000: no. 64 line 42)

If the Well-being is like (the grapheme) U but blunt, (there will be) a non-successful attack by lions.

Compare no. 23. There is no obvious etymographical link between protasis and apodosis. The prediction is positive.

Another *šulmu*-omen mentioning a grapheme is attested in KAR 423 ii 60–61 and in Koch-Westenholz 2000: no. 105 lines 9′–10′:

25) BAD SILIM GIM TAR ^{dug}ÚTUL *nap-tan* LUGAL GAZ-*pi šá-ri-ip nu-ri* / *i-⌈nar*?⌉-*ru-uṭ ú-lu* GÚ.ZI *ina* $ŠU^{II}$ ^{lú}ŠU!.SÌLA!.GAB *i-tar-ru-ur*

If the Well-being is like (the grapheme) TAR, a dish at the king's meal will break, the lamplighter will *tremble*, or the cup will shake in the cupbearer's hand.[41]

There are obvious etymographical links between the protasis and two of the predictions. TAR, with the reading ḫaš, means *šebēru* "to break," a synonym of the verb *ḫepû*, which is used in the first apodosis to describe the breaking of the royal dish.

[40] Cf. Koch-Westenholz 2000: no. 64 lines 53–61, a passage that clearly refers to "holes" on the Well-being.

[41] For the reading and translation of this entry, see CAD N/1, 323a, and CAD T, 208a. The interpretation of the first word in ii 61 poses a problem — instead of *i-⌈nar*?⌉-*ru-uṭ*, the reading presented above, CAD N/2, 350a, offers *i-par*?-*ru-ud* ("he will become afraid"?). While the final verdict on the correct understanding of the verb has to await collation of the tablet, it should be noted that a trembling lamplighter (who might spread fire all over the place) seems scarier — and therefore a better fit for a negative apodosis — than one who is merely afraid. Furthermore, the semantically related verbs *narāṭu* and *tarāru* are attested together elsewhere, in K. 9759 line 9 (see CAD T, 208a, 1d).

TAR is, furthermore, the Sumerian equivalent (and logographic writing) of *tarāru*, the verb employed in the third apodosis, which, in addition, begins with *tar*. All the predictions are negative.

The *Pān tākalti* commentary Koch-Westenholz 2000: no. 79 from Nineveh explains some of the examples presented above as nos. 17–25. The explanations are preceded by a badly damaged phrase that seems to refer to graphemes and may have functioned as a heading of the section following it:

[*šumma* ... *mi*?-*ḫi*?]-*il-ti ṣa-a-ti* / [*ú*]-*lu* EME [... *ša* (...)] *iq-bu-ú ana* IGI-*ka* (line 8)

[If] you have before you [...] *cuneiform sign*(*s*) (with explanations from) (bilingual) *ṣâtu*-lists or (monolingual) *lišānu*-lists [..., *which* ...] *said*.[42]

After a horizontal ruling, the text includes various entries on cuneiform graphemes observed on the Well-being:

26) BAD SILIM GIM AN AN *šá-mu-ú* [(... AN)] *e-lu-ú a-šá-re-du* / EN SIG ZÉ *i-šaq-qu-ma* [(...)] *a-šá-re-du-tú* DU-*ak* (line 9)

If the Well-being is like (the grapheme) AN: AN (means) "sky," [(... AN (means))] "upper" (and) "first in rank"; it (the Well-being) rises towards the thin part of the Gall Bladder [(...) — the ...] will reach the highest rank.[43]

Compare no. 17. If understood correctly, this passage provides one of the few examples of an explicit link based on etymography between a protasis referring to a grapheme, in this case AN, and its apodosis. The commentary begins with listing a number of Akkadian renderings of AN, of which *šamû* "sky" and *elû* "upper" are well attested in lexical and bilingual texts, while the reference to *ašarēdu* seems to be based on semantic association. Apparently drawing on the equation of AN with *elû*, the commentary then claims that the omen refers to a Well-being "rising" towards the Gall Bladder. The positive prediction referring to *ašarēdūtu* at the end of the entry (cf. the apodosis in example no. 17) is justified by the preceding equation of AN with *ašarēdu*. For similar explanations, see below, nos. 36 and 40.

27) BAD SILIM GIM ḪAL ḪAL *za-a-zu* ḪAL *bé-*[*e*?-*ru*? (ḪAL)] *bé-e-šú pa-šá-ṭu* / *tam-ṭa-a-tu*$_4$ BAR-*ma* MURUB.MEŠ-[*šú*] *pa-áš-ṭu* (line 11)

If the Well-being is like (the grapheme) ḪAL: ḪAL (means) "to divide," ḪAL (means) "*to select*," [(ḪAL (means))] "to fork" (and) "to efface" — (there will be) deprivation; it (the Well-being) is divided and [its] center effaced.

Compare no. 18. The equations given for ḪAL are very similar to the ones provided in example no. 11 and must go back to the same learned tradition. No attempt is made to create an explicit link between protasis and apodosis. Compare also the following entry.

42 Restorations and translation by the present author. For a fuller discussion of the difficult terms *ṣâtu*, *lišānu*, and *ša iqbû*, see my forthcoming study of Babylonian and Assyrian text commentaries.

43 Koch-Westenholz translates: "it rises till the Narrow of the Gall Bladder and reaches the highest position," but it seems more likely that *ašarēdūtu illak* is part of an apodosis, referring to a man, the king, or the land; see CAD A/2, 418–19.

28) BAD MAN-*ú* MU.NI SILIM GIM TAR [(...)] (line 12)

If, second, the Well-being is like (the grapheme) TAR [(...)].

Compare no. 25. It is possible that neither an apodosis nor an explanation is to be restored at the end of the line, and that the commentator quoted this protasis only because he thought it was equivalent to the preceding one (no. 27).

29) BAD SILIM GIM PAB/KÚR *e-ge-ru e-de-ru e*-x-[...] / *a-ḫa-meš šap-ṣu šá-pa-ṣu e-ge-ru* [...] (line 13)

If the Well-being is like (the grapheme) PAB/KÚR: "to cross" (and) "to wind around," ... [...] they grip each other; "to grip" (is synonymous with) "to cross" [...].

Compare no. 21. The commentary tries to clarify the nature of the configuration described in the omen by associating the sign PAB with *egēru* "to cross" (cf. nos. 30, 42) and other, similar verbs. The equations seem to be based solely on the shape of the sign and not on any lexical references.

30) BAD MAN-*ú* MU.NI SILIM 2-*ma* GIM PAB/KÚR *it-gu-ru tam-ṭ*[*a*?-*a*?-*tu*? ...] / [...] ⌈x⌉-gi SILIM RA-*iṣ-ma* PIŠ_{10} NU TUKU? [...] / [...] ⌈x⌉ *pe-tu-ú u ra-ḫa-*[*ṣu* ...] (line 14)

If, second, there are two Well-beings and they are crossed like (the grapheme) PAB/KÚR, (*there will be*) *deprivation* [...] ... the Well-being is submerged and *has* no bank [...] ... "to open" and "to submerge" [...].

Compare the preceding entry — the present one was apparently regarded as equivalent. There is no obvious etymographical link between protasis and apodosis (if the latter is correctly restored).

The *Multābiltu* commentary Koch 2005: no. 25 includes a broken reference to yet another grapheme observed in connection with the Well-being (line 89):

31) [... *mi*]-*ḫi-il-tu* SILIM GIM GI

[...] cuneiform sign, the Well-being is like (the grapheme) GI.

Too little is preserved to make much sense of this entry.

Another feature of the liver occasionally associated with cuneiform signs is the *piṭir šumēli* or "Left Split," a fissure half a finger long.[44] The first entries of the second tablet of *Multābiltu*, the tenth chapter of the extispicy series (Koch 2005: no. 3), read as follows:

32) BAD DU_8 2, 30 GIM AN DAM [*amīli* DAM-*s*]*à uš-dak* (line 1)[45]

If the Left Split is like (the grapheme) AN, [the man's] wife will have her [husband] killed.

No etymographical link between protasis and apodosis. The prediction is negative.

[44] See Koch-Westenholz 2000: 61. In first-millennium extispicy texts, the Left Split is more often mentioned than the Right Split.

[45] See also line 16 of the catalog Koch 2005: no. 1. Note (here and in example no. 35) the archaizing writing *-sà*.

33) BAD DU_8 2, 30 GIM ḪAL DAM LÚ [*ana ḫa*]-*ri-mu-ti* È (line 2)

If the Left Split is like (the grapheme) ḪAL, the man's wife will become a prostitute.

No obvious etymographical link between the protasis and the apodosis (unless one argued that the apodosis implies a "divided" loyalty on the part of the wife). The prediction is negative.

34) BAD DU_8 2, 30 GIM BAD URU KÚR DAB-*bat* (line 3)

If the Left Split is like (the grapheme) BAD, you will seize the enemy city.

No obvious etymographical link between protasis and apodosis (but cf. the remarks on no. 2). The prediction is positive.

35) BAD DU_8 2, 30 GIM ḪA DAM LÚ DAM-*sà ú-kaš-šap* (line 4)

If the Left Split is like (the grapheme) ḪA, the man's wife will cast a spell on her husband.

No obvious etymographical link between protasis and apodosis. The prediction is negative.

Koch 2005: no. 25 provides an unfortunately severely damaged commentary on these entries:

36) BAD DU_8 2, 30 GIM AN AN *šá-m*[*u*?-*ú*? (AN) *e*?-*lu*?]-*ú* / *ul-lu-ma* IGI-*et* É [*zitti* ...] DU_8 (line 2)

If the Left Split is like (the grapheme) AN: AN (means) "*sky*," [(AN means)] "*upper*" ([*el*]*û*); it (the Split) is elevated (*ullû*), and next to the "House [of Division" ...] *it is split.*

Compare no. 32. The explanation is reminiscent of the one provided in example no. 26, on which my restoration *šá-m*[*u-ú*] is based.[46] Unlike there, the present entry seems not to deal with the apodosis, though; it simply states that the occurrence of the sign AN, because it means, among other things, "upper," points towards a Split that is elevated. For a very similar commentary on the same entry, see no. 40.

37) BAD DU_8 2, 30 GIM ḪAL BAR-*ma* [...] DU_8 (line 3)

If the Left Split is like (the grapheme) ḪAL: it is divided[47] [...] *it is split.*

Compare no. 33. The explanation seems to focus on the shape of the sign ḪAL, but there may also be an etymographical component, since both ḪAL and BAR are logograms representing *zâzu* "to divide."

---

[46] Koch reads: "an *šá-a*[*m* x x x x] / *ul-lu-ma*," and her copy on plate 11 seems to indicate that the last sign before the gap is indeed rather an *a*[*m* than a *m*[*u*. Collation is required to establish whether there are two horizontal wedges or only one, but in the light of the parallel from example no. 26, the latter seems more likely to me.

[47] Koch translates: "If the Left Split like the sign ḪAL is split in the middle," but since the protasis of the entry commented on ends with ḪAL, one must assume that BAR-*ma* belongs to the explanation.

38) BAD DU_8 2, 30 GIM BAD *ana* ⌈x⌉[48] [...] sag (line 4)

If the Left Split is like (the grapheme) BAD: *towards* ... [...] ....

Compare no. 34. Too broken for an analysis.

39) BAD DU_8 2, 30 GIM ḪA D[AM ...] ri (line 5)

If the Left Split is like (the grapheme) ḪA, [the man's] wife [...] ....

Cf. no. 35. If this entry, unlike the preceding ones, really quoted the complete apodosis, it would have provided little space for explanations.

Another commentary on example no. 32 can be found in Koch 2005: no. 30 i 5´; it is very similar to no. 36:

40) [*šumma* (...) D]U_8 2, 30 GIM AN AN [*šá-mu*]-*u e-lu-ú ul-lu-ma* IGI-*et* KUR ŠU.S[I ...]

[If (...)] the Left Split is like (the grapheme) AN: AN (means) "*sky*" (and) "upper" (*elû*); it (the Split) is elevated (*ullû*), and next to the area of the Finger [...].

Note the reference to the "area of the Finger" instead of the "House [of Division]," mentioned in no. 36.

One text, ms. I of the *Padānu* commentary Koch-Westenholz 2000: no. 42, includes a sketch of a Left Split looking like a grapheme.[49] The entry shows a horizontal line with a bifurcation on the left side, followed by the words:

41) BAD DU_8 2, 30 GIM BAD (rev. 3)

If the Left Split is like (the grapheme) BAD.

Note that the drawing looks like a BAD rotated 180 degrees. This is so because the diviner studied the liver with the sacrificial animal lying on its back (Koch-Westenholz 2000: 39).

One omen, Koch-Westenholz 2000: no. 27, refers to a grapheme to describe a configuration on the *padānu*, or Path (like the *manzāzu* a groove on the liver's *lobus sinister*):

42) BAD GÍR 2-*ma* GIM PAB/KÚR *it-gu-ru* KÚR *ina ri-ʾi-i-ti ana* KUR MÁŠ.ANŠE *i-ḫab-bat* (line 18)

If there are two Paths and they are crossed like (the grapheme) PAB/KÚR, the enemy will steal cattle from the land on the pasture.

[48] Koch reads *ana* K[I.TA and translates "down[wards]," but the traces could also be interpreted in other ways.

[49] Sketches of configurations observed on the exta are attested in quite a few extispicy texts, especially in treatises that deal with the Weapon (*kakku*) (for discussion and an overview, see Nougayrol 1974), but also, for instance, in the *Padānu* commentary Koch-Westenholz 2000: no. 42 lines 151–65. The sketches bring to mind the Mesopotamian clay models of livers and other organs, which were often inscribed, usually with omens; see Meyer 1987; Wiseman and Black 1996: no. 60. To my knowledge, cuneiform signs observed on the exta are never referred to in the texts on these objects, but the very existence of inscribed liver models and models of other parts of the exta may have contributed to the diviners' interest in grapheme-related omens.

The mentioning of an enemy — KÚR = *nakru* — in the apodosis is probably based on the reference to the respective sign in the protasis. For the association of PAB with lines crossing each other, see also nos. 29, 30, 43, 54, and 55. The omen following in line 19 is similar; it reads: BAD GÍR 2-*ma* GIM BAR-*tu*$_4$ *it-gu-ru* GAL-^{giš}GAG EN-*šú* *i-bar* "If there are two Paths and they are crossed like a Cross (*pillurtu*), the *rab-sikkati*-official will revolt against his lord." The choice, in the apodosis of this entry, of the predicate *i-bar* is clearly inspired by the cross-shaped logogram BAR, used to write *pillurtu*; but the entry does not directly refer to a grapheme.

Koch-Westenholz 2000: no. 88 includes a grapheme-related omen referring to the Path to the left of the Gall Bladder (*padān šumēl marti*), a groove on the *lobus dexter* of the liver (iv 8–9):

43) BAD MAN-*ú* MU.NI GÍR 2, 30 ZÉ 2-*ma* GIM PAB/KÚR GIB.MEŠ / NUN *re-ṣu-šú* TAG$_4$.MEŠ-*šú*

If, second, there are two Paths to the left of the Gall Bladder and they lie crosswise like (the grapheme) PAB/KÚR, the auxiliaries of the prince will abandon him.

No obvious etymographical link between protasis and apodosis (but see the remarks on no. 21). The prediction is negative.

Several references to graphemes are included in Clay 1923: no. 13, a treatise on the coils of the convolutions of the sacrificial animal's colon (*tīrānu*):

44) BAD ŠÀ.NIGIN GIM PAB/KÚR KI.TUŠ-*ka a-na* KI.TUŠ KÚR-*ka* SI.SÁ (line 28)

If the coils of the colon are like (the grapheme) PAB/KÚR, your camp will charge the camp of your enemy.

Compare nos. 10 and 12, with the same etymographical link between protasis and apodosis. The prediction is positive.

45) BAD ŠÀ.NIGIN GIM AN ERIM-*ni* NUN GABA.RI NU TUKU-*ši* (line 29)

If the coils of the colon are like (the grapheme) AN, the army of the prince will have no rival.

No etymographical link between protasis and apodosis. The prediction is positive.

46) BAD ŠÀ.NIGIN GIM ḪAL UMUŠ KUR MAN-*ni* (line 30)

If the coils of the colon are like (the grapheme) ḪAL, the political situation of the land will change.

Compare no. 11, which, after a reference to ḪAL, offers the same apodosis. The prediction is negative.

K. 85 (Koch 2005: no. 75), a small tablet from Nineveh, deals with the occurrence of eight graphemes, all of them inauspicious, in the center of the right side of the Gall Bladder. The first entry reads:

47) BAD *ina* MURUB$_4$ 15 ZÉ AN$^!$ GAR NU SILIM-*at* / *ina* NU SILIM-*ti* SILIM-*at* (obv. 1–2)

If there is (the grapheme) AN in the center of the right side of the Gall Bladder,[50] it is unfavorable, in an unfavorable (extispicy), it is favorable.

Koch interprets the grapheme referred to in the entry as a QA, but the sign on the tablet most probably represents the ancient form of AN, as already recognized by Lieberman (1977: 148). Otherwise, with the exception of the sign ḪAL in line 3 (see below), the tablet is written in the Neo-Assyrian ductus.

The following six entries in K. 85, written in an abbreviated way, are identical with the first one, but mention different graphemes. Their contents can be summarized as follows:

48–53) BAD *ina* MIN ḪAL! (obv. 3) / PAB (obv. 4) / KASKAL (obv. 5) / NI (obv. 6) / U (obv. 7) / EN IN (obv. 8) GAR MIN (obv. 3–8)

If *ditto*, (and) there is (the grapheme) ḪAL / PAB / KASKAL / NI / U / EN (or) IN, *ditto* (applies).

Koch interprets the grapheme referred to in obv. 3 as KUD, but the sign on the tablet represents almost certainly the ancient form of ḪAL. Note that the two signs mentioned in obv. 8, EN and IN, are listed together not because they look similar or have the same meaning, but apparently because of their almost identical phonetic values. The lines following the quoted passage refer to occurrences of a piece of flesh (*šīru*) (obv. 9), a "cuneiform sign" (*miḫiltu*)[51] (rev. 1), and a white Gall Bladder (rev. 3); two entries (rev. 2, 4) remain unclear. All these configurations are regarded as inauspicious.

Two further references to the sign PAB, one of which is related to the Throne Base (*nīdi kussê*, perhaps the liver's *impressio renalis*), while the other occurs in connection with Feet (*šēpu*, apparently a groove in the form of a throw-stick), can be found on a tablet from Susa and another from Assur. Both tablets are written in Middle Babylonian script:

54) DIŠ ŠUB.BA GU.ZA 2-*ma* GIM PAB/KÚR *šu-te-gu-ru* ARAD.MEŠ 3, 20 *aš-ma-mi-iš* GAZ-*ku* (Labat 1974: no. 4, obv. 9)

If there are two Throne Bases, and they are crossed like (the grapheme) PAB/KÚR, the servants of the king will kill one another.

No etymographical link between protasis and apodosis (what matters, instead, is the symbolically charged configuration of the two Throne Bases). The prediction is negative.

55) BAD *i-na* GÙB ZÉ 2 GÌR.MEŠ GIM PAB/KÚR *it-gu-ra ana* IGI KÚR È-*ma ḫe-pí* ka ⸢x⸣ [...] (KAR 454, obv. 30)

If there are two Feet to the left of the Gall Bladder and they lie crosswise like (the grapheme) PAB/KÚR, you will go forth towards the enemy, *broken* ... [...].

The grapheme KÚR in the protasis mirrors the reference to the enemy (KÚR = *nakru*) in the apodosis. The prediction is probably positive, but this is not completely certain.

[50] "The center of" is inadvertently omitted in Koch's translation.

[51] Koch translates "a Scratch," but since K. 85 refers to so many graphemes, the translation "cuneiform sign" seems more appropriate. A *miḫiltu* is also referred to, in broken context, in line 72 of tablet 1 of *Multābiltu* (Koch 2005: no. 2).

Several conclusions can be drawn from this sample of grapheme-related extispicy omens. One is that the number of different signs mentioned in the texts is fairly small, with a few dominating the corpus. In the sequence of their frequency, the graphemes are:[52] PAB (twelve times),[53] BAD (eight times),[54] ḪAL (seven times),[55] AN (six times),[56] KASKAL (three times),[57] U (three times),[58] and BAR, EN, GAM, GI, ḪA, IN, KUR, NI, and TAR (each one time).[59] Example nos. 47 and 48, from a tablet otherwise inscribed in the Neo-Assyrian ductus, render the signs AN and ḪAL in their "Old Babylonian" forms, and it cannot be excluded that other signs mentioned in the post-Old Babylonian texts, even though they are written in their later forms, referred the diviners to configurations on the exta that they thought resembled the older sign forms as well.[60] PAB, BAD, ḪAL (in its old form), AN, KASKAL, and BAR are all very simple signs consisting of a few wedges crossing each other,[61] and it is most probably the resemblance of these signs to certain lesions or cysts on the exta that explains why they are so frequently invoked. Like the *pillurtu*, or Cross, a symbol associated with concepts such as mutiny, murder, and chaos,[62] the signs in question were usually regarded as inauspicious, the only clear exceptions being examples nos. 5(??), 6, 8, 10, 15, 17, 24, 26, 34, 44, and 45, which have positive predictions.

Of particular interest for our investigation is the question to what extent the apodoses of the omens seem to be "etymographically" derived from the signs mentioned in the protases. Overall, obvious links of this type can be found in only a few omen entries. Examples nos. 3(?), 6 (= 13?), 7, 25 (two apodoses motivated etymographically), and 26 are based on rather sophisticated philological associations, whereas examples nos. 10 (= 12, 44), 42, and 55 are less creative. In these latter cases, the link between the observations and the predictions depends on a reading of the PAB sign as *nakru* "enemy," a word that occurs in the apodoses. This reading may also have informed several entries whose apodoses do not include the term *nakru* but refer to situations in which enemies play a role, and some apodoses in omens referring to the observation of a BAD and a ḪAL sign might have been based on such rather loose associations as well; but this is far from certain.[63]

In the case of the references to the grapheme PAB, there seems to be a tendency for positive predictions (nos. 6, 10, 44, and perhaps 55) to be more often informed by etymography than negative ones. Since the sign was, apparently, inauspicious in general, it seems that positive interpretations of it had to be based on some additional hermeneutical effort. Given its cross-like shape, one would have expected the sign AN to be normally inauspicious as

[52] Commentary entries are only counted in the following if they include new omens.

[53] Nos. 5(??), 6, 10, 13(?), 21, 30, 42, 43, 44, 49, 54, and 55; see also the commentary entries nos. 12 and 29.

[54] Nos. 1, 2, 4, 14, 16, 20, 34, 41; see also the commentary entry no. 38.

[55] Nos. 8, 9, 11, 18, 33, 46, 48; see also the commentary entries nos. 27 and 37.

[56] Nos. 15, 17, 26, 32, 45, 47; see also the commentary entries 36 and 40.

[57] Nos. 3, 7, and 50.

[58] Nos. 23, 24, and 52. The numerous references to the U-shaped "hole" (*šīlu*) are not counted here, but it should be noted that it is not always easy to distinguish between references to a "hole" and to the grapheme U.

[59] Nos. 12, 53, 22, 31, 35 (see also the commentary entry no. 39), 53, 19, 51, and 25 (see also the commentary entry no. 28). With regard to the sign GAG, see my remarks under example no. 9.

[60] See Lieberman 1977: 148.

[61] GAM, KUR, NI, and TAR are similar to them in shape. The sign U, as stated before, represents a hole (*šīlu*), an inauspicious configuration when observed on the exta.

[62] See Jeyes 1989: 86–87.

[63] See example nos. 2, 4, 9, 11 (= 46), 14, 16, 18, 20, 21, 22, 33, 34, and 43.

well (which it is in examples nos. 32 and 47), but strikingly, most omens mentioning it have a positive prediction (see nos. 15, 17, 26, and 45). This may be due to the sign's Akkadian readings *ilu* "god," *elû* "upper," and *šamû* "heaven," all imbued with positive connotations, even though these words do not occur in the apodoses in question. In a few cases, we find references to cuneiform signs observed in different contexts followed by the same apodosis (see nos. 10, 12, and 44; and 11 and 46). Here, an interpretative tradition seems to have developed around the signs at some point.

A few extispicy commentaries from the first millennium B.C.[64] show us how Babylonian and Assyrian diviners interpreted omen entries referring to cuneiform signs. Interestingly, only one commentary entry, example no. 26, establishes a link between a grapheme-related protasis and an apodosis. All the others (nos. 27, 29, 30, 36, 37, 40) have a different purpose. Often drawing on Akkadian readings of the sign in question, they try to elucidate the exact nature of the ominous configuration associated with it.[65] While at first glance surprising, this hermeneutical approach is, in fact, quite in line with the main goal of extispicy commentaries in general: to illuminate the exact meaning of the various protases, and to adduce differently phrased but equivalent omens. Since the wording of the apodosis did not really matter in extispicy — of interest was only whether it was positive or negative — the commentators of the *bārûtu* corpus usually abstained from a careful analysis of the predictions.

Cuneiform characters are featured in yet another extispicy treatise. The Late Babylonian "orientation tablet" BM 32268+, published in Koch 2005: no. 107 (ms. A), associates various graphemes, in iii 24′–28′ (a partly broken passage), "first with a feature of the Liver in the order of inspection, secondly with another part of the intestines in what could be reverse order, and finally with yet another feature of the Liver" (Koch 2005: 71). KU is linked to the Presence, the Coils of the Colon, and the Path to the right of the Gall Bladder, TE to the Path, the Door Beam, and the right Seat, BAR to the Pleasing Word and the left Seat, GU to the Strength, the Rib Cage, and the Back [of one side of the lungs?], and A to the Palace Gate, the Breast Bone, and the Weapon. The rationale behind these associations remains obscure.

PHYSIOGNOMY

Cuneiform signs are also mentioned in treatises on physiognomy, the intellectual discipline that explains how to infer the qualities and future prospects of human beings from physical features of their body, especially the face. The most important Assyro-Babylonian treatise on physiognomy is the series *Alamdimmû* ("physique"), now available in a new edition by Böck (2000a). The third chapter of this text includes a long section on facial marks reminiscent of cuneiform signs observed on the forehead. The passage is preserved in two manuscripts, K. 8071 and K. 3815+, both from Assurbanipal's library and written throughout in Assyrian script. It has recently been discussed by Bilbija (2008), but since his article focuses exclusively on cases in which the protasis and the apodosis of the omens seem to be linked with each other through etymography, a new and more complete evaluation of the evidence (which will give Bilbija credit for his insights, of course) seems to be called for.

---

[64] For a preliminary assessment of the genre, see Koch-Westenholz 2000: 31–36.

[65] Example no. 26 deals with this issue as well, and not only with the apodosis.

A conspicuous aspect of the passage, briefly discussed by Bilbija but not fully investigated, is that quite a few of the entries mention not just one but two or even three signs, all of them apparently holding the same ominous significance. In the following overview of the passage, which is based on Böck's edition (2000a: 92–97), I discuss both the potential links between protases and apodoses and the connections between these variant signs. To facilitate referencing, the numbering of the examples continues that of the extispicy omens in the preceding section. The first entry of the text provides the protasis in full, while the later ones present it in an abbreviated version.

56) [DIŠ *a*]*lam-dím-me-e* SAG.KI NA *ina* SAG.KI NA AN ŠUB NA BI ḪUL (line 76)

[Concerning] the appearance of the forehead of a man: (If the grapheme) AN appears on the forehead of a man, this man will experience misfortune.[66]

No etymographical link; the prediction is negative.

57) [DIŠ] ŠID NA BI ŠU LUGAL KUR-*ád* (line 77)

[If] (there is the grapheme) ŠID, the hand of the king will reach this man.

Bilbija (2008: 22–23) suggests the apodosis is based on the fact that *šarru* "king" is semantically related to the word *iššakku* "city ruler," one of the readings of ŠID. While not impossible, this explanation remains doubtful since the two words are otherwise clearly distinguished; ŠID does not occur among the numerous logograms listed in lexical texts as representing *šarru* (see CAD Š/2, 76–78). The prediction is negative.

58) [DIŠ] BA NA BI ḪUL IGI : GE_6 IGI IGI-*mar* (line 78)

[If] (there is the grapheme) BA, this man will face misfortune; var.: he will face rage (*ṣulum pāni*).

No etymographical link; the prediction is negative.

59) [DIŠ] ZI DUMU.MEŠ É AD-*šú-nu i-za-aq-qà-pu* (line 79)

[If] (there is the grapheme) ZI, the sons will raise the house of their father.

As seen by Bilbija (2008: 23), the apodosis could be based on the fact that ZI corresponds to Akkadian *tebû* "to arise," which is semantically related to *zaqāpu* "to raise." The prediction is positive.

60) [DIŠ] MU : BI DUMU.MEŠ É AD-*šú-nu* ZÁḪ.MEŠ (line 80)

[If] (there is the grapheme) MU (or) BI, the sons will ruin the house of their father.

The signs MU and BI, semantically unrelated, look rather similar, especially in Old Babylonian cursive script. No etymographical link; the prediction is negative.

[66] Böck translates "ist dieser Mann böse," and Bilbija (2008: 19) follows her, translating: "that man is evil." My own translation is based on AHw, 542b.

61) [DIŠ B]U? MU-*šú* NU GÁL-*ši* (line 81)

[If] (there is the grapheme) *BU*, he will not maintain his name.

Reading of the sign uncertain, no obvious etymographical link; the prediction is negative.

62) [DIŠ] ⌈x⌉ DUMU.MUNUS.MEŠ É AD-*ši-na i-za-aq-qá-pa* (line 82)

[If] (there is the grapheme) x, the daughters will raise the house of their father.

Compare no. 59; the prediction is positive.

63) DIŠ [x] DUMU.MUNUS.MEŠ É AD-*ši-na i-kab-ba-sa* : ZÁḪ.ME (line 83)

[If] (there is the grapheme) [x], the daughters will tread down, var.: they will ruin the house of their father.

Compare no. 60; the prediction is negative.

64) DIŠ ⌈GIŠ : UŠ⌉ EGIR É LÚ GÁL-*ši* (line 84)

If (there is the grapheme) GIŠ (or) UŠ, the legacy of the house of the man will remain.

In the Old Babylonian cursive (but not in later Babylonian or Assyrian script), the — semantically unrelated — signs GIŠ and UŠ look quite similar. No obvious etymographical link;[67] the prediction is positive.

65) DIŠ TAB : PA EGIR É LÚ ZÁḪ (line 85)

If (there is the grapheme) TAB (or) PA, the legacy of the house of the man will perish.

TAB and PA, semantically unrelated, have similar shapes throughout the history of cuneiform writing. Bilbija (2008: 24) argues that "the apodosis ... can be linked to the sign TAB if it is read as *ḫamāṭum* 'to burn (up),' and the head carrying the sign is interpreted as the man's house," but this explanation seems rather far-fetched to me. The prediction is negative.

66) DIŠ EN RI ḪU LÚ BI *be-en-nu* ⌈x⌉ [...] (line 86)

If (there is the grapheme) EN, RI, (or) ḪU, this man [(...)] epilepsy [(...)].[68]

The three graphemes, semantically unrelated, have similar shapes throughout the history of cuneiform writing. No obvious etymographical link;[69] the prediction is probably negative.

---

[67] *arki redû* means "to follow after," a concept not unrelated to a "legacy," but it seems doubtful that a reading of UŠ as *redû* is behind the entry.

[68] CAD B, 206a, restores at the end ⌈*i*⌉-[*ṣab-bat-su*] "will seize him."

[69] One could speculate that the protasis-apodosis string is based on paronomasia between the grapheme EN and the middle part of the word *bennu* (cf. example no. 6, above), but such an explanation would be highly conjectural.

67) DIŠ UR : IB ŠU.BI.AŠ.À[M] (line 87)

If (there is the grapheme) UR (or) IB, the same.

UR and IB, semantically unrelated, have similar shapes throughout the history of cuneiform writing. Their shapes also resemble to some extent those of the graphemes from the preceding entry, which has the same apodosis. No etymographical link; the prediction is probably negative.

68) DIŠ GÁN : UD LÚ BI *ša* ^{d}30 *i-ma-*⌈*at*?⌉ (line 88)

If (there is the grapheme) GÁN (or) UD, this man *will die* (...) of Sîn.[70]

In the Old Babylonian cursive (but not in later Babylonian or Assyrian script), the — semantically unrelated — signs GÁN and UD look quite similar. No obvious etymographical link;[71] the prediction is negative.

69) DIŠ MA : LU : KU NA BI ÚŠ *ḫi-bil-ti* : [... *imât*] (line 89)

If (there is the grapheme) MA, LU, (or) KU, this man [will die] violently, var. [...].

In the Old Babylonian cursive, MA and KU can look very much alike, and LU has a similar shape; in other periods of cuneiform writing, the similarities are less pronounced. No etymographical link; the prediction is negative.

70) DIŠ KI ÚŠ ŠÀ ḪUL UG_7 : ÚŠ *ḫi-ṭi* [(...) *imât*] (line 90)

If (there is the grapheme) KI, he will die of grief, var.: [he will die] in a sinful way [(...)].

No etymographical link; the prediction is negative.

71) DIŠ KA NU *mit-gur-ti ina* É NA GÁ[L-*ši*] (line 91)

If (there is the grapheme) KA, there will be discord in the house of the man.

According to Bilbija (2008: 23–24), this protasis-apodosis string may be based on the widely attested readings of KA as gù = *šasû* "to shout" and *rigmu* "voice, noise," possibly indicative of loud altercations. This interpretation is ingenious, but not completely compelling. One could also argue that a reading du_{11}(KA)-du_{11}(KA) = *dabābu* "to litigate" is behind the entry. Perhaps, there is, in fact, no etymographical link at all. The prediction is negative.

---

[70] The restoration and translation are uncertain. For illnesses associated with the moon-god, see Stol 1993: 121–30. Perhaps, the line refers to another form of epilepsy, the subject of the two preceding apodoses — as pointed out by Stol, the *seleniasmos* — or "lunacy" — described in the gospel of Matthew (17:14–18) can be identified as an epileptic disease.

[71] The sign for "month," a word semantically related to "moon," is ITI, written UD×EŠ(= 30), but it seems unlikely that this explains why the UD sign is mentioned in the protasis.

72) DIŠ AB : UM *muš-ke-nu i-šár-*[*ru*] (line 92)

If (there is the grapheme) AB (or) UM, the poor man will become rich.

In the Old Babylonian cursive, but usually not in other periods, AB and UM can have the same shape. No etymographical link; the prediction is negative.

73) DIŠ AD : ÍL *bi-ir-ta ú-šá-kal ša bu-tuq-qé-*⸢*e*⸣ [...] (line 93)

If (there is the grapheme) AD (or) ÍL, he *will provision the fortress*, of the losses [...].

The signs AD and ÍL look quite different in all periods of Mesopotamian writing, but in Old Babylonian, there is a certain similarity between them (see Kraus 1935: 22). No etymographical link. The prediction seems to be positive, but its meaning is not completely certain.

74) DIŠ BI : GA ŠUB IBILA NA DAM NA ⸢x⸣ [...] (line 94)

If (there is the grapheme) BI (or) GA, the man's heir will fall, the man's wife [...].

In Babylonian script, but not in Assyrian, BI and GA look rather similar. No etymographical link; the prediction is negative.

75) DIŠ UL DINGIR KI LÚ BI SILIM [...] (line 95)

If (there is the grapheme) UL, the god will make peace with this man [...].

No etymographical link;[72] the prediction is negative.

76) DIŠ NA DUMU.MEŠ-*šu* UG_7.UG_7 [...] (line 96)

If (there is the grapheme) NA, his sons will die [...].

No obvious etymographical link;[73] the prediction is negative.

77) DIŠ TAB : UB NU Ù.TU Ù.TU NU SI.SÁ SI.[SÁ] (line 97)

If (there is the grapheme) TAB (or) UB, an infertile woman will have a child, a woman having difficulties in childbirth will easily give birth.

In Babylonian script, but not in Assyrian, TAB and UB have similar shapes. No etymographical link; the prediction is negative.

78) DIŠ URU : GUR ÚŠ ^{giš}DAL [*imât*] (line 98)

If (there is the grapheme) URU (or) GUR, [he will die] through a *crossbeam*.

The shapes of URU and GUR are similar throughout the history of Babylonian and Assyrian cuneiform writing. As for a possible link between the protasis and the apodosis, one could point to the readings RÍ of URU and RI of DAL, but this remains speculation. The prediction is negative.

---

[72] It seems unlikely that UL was associated phonetically with *ilu*, which sounds somewhat similar.

[73] It would be far-fetched to assume that association of the grapheme NA with the Sumerian prohibitive prefix na- might explain the negative apodosis.

79) DIŠ NI : IR BA.UG$_7$ KIMIN MUNUS *ina ḫi-ṭi* LÚ ⌜x⌝ [...] (line 99)

If (there is the grapheme) NI (or) IR, he will die, *ditto*, a woman, through a crime [(...)] the man [(...)].

The shapes of NI and IR are similar throughout the history of Babylonian and Assyrian cuneiform writing. No obvious etymographical link;[74] the prediction is negative.

80) DIŠ IGI DU$_{10}$-*ub lìb-[bi]* (line 100)

If (there is the grapheme) IGI, there will be happiness.

For the same apodosis, see examples no. 17 (grapheme: AN) and 86 (graphemes: ŠE and PI, both similar to IGI); compare also no. 122. No obvious etymographical link. The prediction is positive.

81) DIŠ KI É LÚ IZI *[ikkal]* (line 101)

If (there is the grapheme) KI, a fire [will devour] the house of the man.

No etymographical link; the prediction is negative.

82) DIŠ LA : ŠU *dan-na-tu*[75] LÚ BI *i-ra-am-[mi]* (line 102)

If (there is the grapheme) LA (or) ŠU, this man will dwell in a fortress.

The shapes of LA and ŠU are similar throughout most of the history of Babylonian and Assyrian cuneiform writing. No obvious etymographical link. The prediction is apparently negative.

83) DIŠ AL ÚŠ KI.ḪUL *[imât]* (line 103)

If (there is the grapheme) AL, [he will die] through mourning.

No etymographical link; the prediction is negative.

84) DIŠ SAG ÚŠ *šu-ub-ti* U[G$_7$] (line 104)

If (there is the grapheme) SAG, he will die *in (his) dwelling*.[76]

No etymographical link; the exact meaning of the prediction is unclear.

85) DIŠ Ú ÚŠ *a-ši-i [imât]* (line 105)

If (there is the grapheme) Ú, [he will die] through the *ašû*-illness.

Bilbija argues the entry is based on the fact that Ú is read *šammu* "plant" in Akkadian, and that the plant used to cure the *ašû*-illness was called *šammi aši*; this explanation, however, seems rather far-fetched. The prediction is negative.

---

[74] IR means, among other things, *tabālu* "to take away," but it would be rather far-fetched to assume that this is the reason why the apodosis refers to a death.

[75] The reading *-tu* follows Böck's edition (2000a), which is based on collation. The copy has *-at*.

[76] One wonders if *šu-ub-ti* could be a mistaken rendering by the ancient scribe of an original ŠUB-*ti* = *miqitti* "defeat," but the expression *mūt miqitti* does not seem to be attested elsewhere.

86) DIŠ ŠE : PI DU_{10}-*ub lìb*-[*bi*] (line 106)

If (there is the grapheme) ŠE (or) PI, there will be happiness.

There is a certain similarity between the two graphemes from the Old Babylonian period onward. For the same apodosis, see examples no. 17 (grapheme AN) and 80 (grapheme IGI, similar to ŠE and PI), cf. also no. 122. No obvious etymographical link. The prediction is positive.

87) DIŠ ŠÀ *ba-la-aṭ* ŠÀ [*amīli*(?)[77]] (line 107)

If (there is the grapheme) ŠÀ, a healthy life (lit., life of the heart) [(*is in store*) *for the man*].

There is an obvious link between protasis and apodosis, as pointed out by Bilbija (2008: 22, n. 12): both include the sign ŠÀ. The prediction is positive.

88) DIŠ DA ŠE *ina la ša-at-ti* Š[U? ...] (line 108)

If (there is the grapheme) DA (or) ŠE, [he will] ... [...] in the wrong year.

The two graphemes do not resemble each other. Unlike other variant signs, they are not divided by separating cola, and one wonders if the ancient scribe (or one of his predecessors) may have copied the beginning of the line incorrectly. Alternatively, one could suppose that ŠE introduces the apodosis, and translate: "If (there is the grapheme) DA, the barley [will ...] ... outside the season [...]" (see CAD Š/2, 206a). No etymographical link; the prediction is probably negative.

89) [DIŠ] DAR LÚ *ina ḫi-ṭi* [...] (line 109)

[If] (there is the grapheme) DAR, the man [will ...] through a crime.

Too broken for an analysis. The prediction is probably negative.

90) [DIŠ A]L? *ra-bu* É LÚ *i-b*[*a*? ...] (line 110)

[If] (there is the grapheme) *AL*, *a magnate* will [...] the house of the man [...].

Too broken for an analysis.

91) [DIŠ] ⌜x⌝ LÚ BI ^{giš}GI *ina*? ⌜x⌝ [...] (line 111)

[If] (there is the grapheme) x, this man [...] *a reed* [...].

Too broken for an analysis.

92) DIŠ [x] KIMIN ne ne[78] *ina* ŠÀ ⌜x⌝ [...] (line 112)

If (there is the grapheme) [x], *ditto*, ... *in the heart* ... [...].

Too broken for an analysis.

---

[77] Restoration based on the apodosis of example no. 107. Böck restores [TUKU?-*ši*?].

[78] Theoretically, one could read KÚM.KÚM, which would yield a Gtn form of *emēmu* "to be constantly feverish," but this remains very uncertain.

93) DIŠ MI ÚŠ *ḫi-it-nu-*[*qí imât*] (line 113)

If (there is the grapheme) MI, [he will die] through strangulation.

Bilbija (2008: 23) argues that MI, read GE_6 = *ṣalāmu* "to become dark," could "describe the effects of strangulation," but this is again a rather speculative idea. The prediction is negative.

94) DIŠ GAN/KÁM TÉŠ LÚ [...] (line 114)

If (there is the grapheme) GAN/KÁM, the *potency* of the man [will ...].

Too broken for an analysis.

95) DIŠ U *ṣal-tú* ZI.GA [...] (line 115)

If (there is the grapheme) U, there will be quarrel, loss [...].

No obvious etymographical link. The prediction is negative.

96) DIŠ ḪAR : AḪ ÚŠ *ši-il-la-ti* [U]G_7 (line 116)

If (there is the grapheme) ḪAR (or) AḪ, he will die a death (caused by) blasphemy.

The graphemes resemble each other in Babylonian, but not in Middle and Neo-Assyrian script. No etymographical link; the prediction is negative.

97) DIŠ AZ : LUGAL ÚŠ *šar-ri* ÚŠ *bu-ri* UG_7 (line 117)

If (there is the grapheme) AZ (or) LUGAL, he will die a death (*caused by*) the king (or) a death (caused by) *a well/a calf/hunger.*

The two graphemes resemble each other most closely in the Old Babylonian cursive. The reference to the king in the apodosis is clearly motivated by the occurrence of LUGAL in the protasis. The prediction is negative.

98) DIŠ LI : TU ÚŠ ÍD ÚŠ *ḫa-am-ṭa* UG_7 (line 118)

If (there is the grapheme) LI (or) TU, he will die a death (caused by) the river (or) a speedy death.

The two graphemes resemble each other throughout much of the history of Babylonian and Assyrian writing, but most closely in the Old Babylonian cursive. No etymographical link; the prediction is negative.

99) DIŠ ZA ÚŠ *ṣú*(A, B: *ṣu*)*-um-me*(A, B: *mé*)*-e* UG_7 (line 119)

If (there is the grapheme) ZA, he will die from thirst.

No etymographical link; the prediction is negative.

100) DIŠ BAD GIG.MEŠ LÚ DAB.MEŠ (line 120)

If (there is the grapheme) BAD, diseases/wounds will seize the man.

Compare example no. 4. BAD, read úš, means *mâtu* "to die" in Akkadian, but one wonders if this really explains the (negative) prediction.

101) DIŠ Ù : LÚ LÚ BI *ina* É TUŠ-*ab* (line 121)

If (there is the grapheme) Ù (or) LÚ, this man will live in a house.

The two graphemes do not resemble each other. The reference to the man in the (positive) apodosis could be motivated by the occurrence of LÚ in the protasis (see Bilbija 2008: 21), but, obviously, most of the predictions deal with a "man."

102) DIŠ TAR : GAM i kúr id ZI.GA LÚ NA UG_7 (line 122)

If (there is the grapheme) TAR (or) GAM, ... loss for the man, the man will die.

The two graphemes resemble each other in Babylonian writing, but not so much in Assyrian. Bilbija (2008: 21) argues that the last two apodoses are based on readings of GAM as *pilšu* "breach" and *mâtu* "to die." TAR/KUD, with its reading *parāsu* "to cut off," is semantically not too far off, but this may be simply by chance. The prediction is negative.

103) DIŠ NU i kúr id ZI.GA LÚ È (line 123)

If (there is the grapheme) NU, ... the man will experience loss.

Especially in Old Babylonian, NU looks quite similar to TAR and GAM, the signs featured in the preceding entry, which has a similar apodosis. NU means *lā* "not," and this negative connotation *could* have inspired the prediction, but if it really did remains doubtful.

104) DIŠ UD *ú-la-lu-tam*(B, A: ⌈*ú*? :?⌉ *i-la-lu-tam*) LÚ GIN (line 124)

If (there is the grapheme) UD, the man will become helpless.

No etymographical link; the prediction is negative.

105) DIŠ NINDA LÚ NINDA *i-be-ru* (line 125)

If (there is the grapheme) NINDA, the man will hunger for bread.

The reference to the bread (NINDA, *akalu*) in the apodosis is clearly motivated by the occurrence of NINDA in the protasis. The prediction is negative.

106) DIŠ GÌR : UG (A, B: AZ) : BAN (A, B: GIM) ÚŠ *re-i-ib-ti* LÚ UG_7 (line 126)

If (there is the grapheme) GÌR, UG (A) / AZ (B), or BAN (A) / GIM (B), the man will die from the *reʾibtu*-disease.

GÌR, UG, and AZ look similar in Old Babylonian, but not so much in later phases of cuneiform writing. BAN and GIM are similar to each other throughout most of the history of Babylonian and Assyrian cuneiform, and in Old Babylonian, the signs also look to some extent similar to the other three characters. No etymographical link; the prediction is negative.

107) DIŠ TI : IM *ba-la-aṭ* ŠÀ(B, A adds *-bi*) NA(A, B: LÚ) (line 127)

If (there is the grapheme) TI (or) IM, a healthy life (lit., life of the heart) (is in store) for the man.

Compare no. 87. There is a certain, even though somewhat superficial, similarity between the shapes of TI and IM. TI is often rendered as *balāṭu* "life" in Akkadian, which explains the reference to *balāṭu* in the apodosis (see Bilbija 2008: 22). The prediction is positive.

108) DIŠ EŠ ZI.GA ŠU NA (line 128)

If (there is the grapheme) EŠ, there will be losses *for the hand* of the man.

EŠ consists of three "Winkelhakens" (U), and it is interesting that in example no. 95, the grapheme U indicates losses (ZI.GA) as well. No etymographical link; the prediction is negative.

109) DIŠ MEŠ ŠU DINGIR LÚ DAB-*bat* : KUR-*ad* (line 129)

If (there is the grapheme) MEŠ, the hand of the god will seize, var.: reach the man.

No etymographical link; the prediction is negative.

110) DIŠ A *na-mar* É LÚ *ana ṣa-a-tim* (line 130)

If (there is the grapheme) A, the man's house will be bright forever.

No etymographical link; the prediction is positive.

111) DIŠ MAN *bu-tuq-ti*(A, B: *tum*) É LÚ GAR-*an* (line 131)

If (there is the grapheme) MAN, a *breach*[79] will be made in the man's house.

No etymographical link; the prediction is negative.

112) DIŠ NA(A, B: BA) : MA *li-iʾ-bu* É(B, A om.) LÚ *i-la-ib* (line 132)

If (there is the grapheme) NA (A) / BA (B) (or) MA, the (household of) the man will suffer from the *liʾbu*-disease.

While BA and MA look similar in Babylonian script, NA does not. However, NA does look similar to BA in Assyrian script, suggesting that the reading NA in ms. A goes back to a mistake made by an Assyrian scribe copying an Assyrian manuscript. No etymographical link; the prediction is negative.

113) DIŠ *ḫe-pí* DAM.MEŠ LÚ(A, B om.?) UG_7.MEŠ (line 133)

If (there is the grapheme) — broken —, the wives (of the man) will die.

The prediction is negative.

Another passage referring to cuneiform characters observed on the body of a man occurs in the Assur text KAR 395, edited by Böck (2000a: 290–95).[80] This is the second tablet of a series, but not the canonical *Alamdimmû* series as we know it from Nineveh. As in the case of *Alamdimmû* III, the section on the signs occurs toward the end of the tablet. Its beginning is lost, and it is not completely clear which body part it describes. Most probably, though,

[79] Böck's translation "Einbuße" (which is probably based on CAD B, 358a, s.v. *butuqtu* B) would require *butuqqû* instead of *butuqtu*.

[80] The fragment VAT 11291 (Heeßel 2007: no. 49) may be part of the same tablet. KAR 395 is not considered in Bilbija 2008.

the section deals with cuneiform characters on the cheek. Kraus (1935: 52–53), pointing out that the catchline of KAR 395 refers to the *usukku*, or upper cheek, suggested, quite convincingly, that this word may also occur in rev. iv 2´, which is followed by the section on the graphemes.[81] The passage includes the following omens, all referring to one grapheme only (the line numbering follows Böck 2000a):

114–16) DIŠ NU [...] / DIŠ KUR ⸢x⸣ [...] / DIŠ NE LÚ B[I ...] (lines 69–71)

If (there is the grapheme) NU, [...]. / If (there is the grapheme) KUR, ... [...]. / If there is the grapheme NE, this man [...].

Too broken for analysis.

117) DIŠ IGI IGI^{II}.BI [...] (line 72)

If (there is the grapheme) IGI, *his* eyes [...].

The occurrence of IGI (= *īnu* "eye") in the protasis is mirrored by the reference to eyes in the apodosis.

118) DIŠ GAG *ina-kud* KUR UŠ$_{11}$ ŠU ⸢x⸣ [...] (line 73)

If (there is the grapheme) GAG, he will become anxious, (*there will be*) *an attack* through sorcery, *the hand* [...].

No etymographical link; the prediction is negative.

119) DIŠ NÍGIN *me-si-ru* DAB-*su* (line 74)

If (there is the grapheme) NÍGIN, confinement/hardship will befall him.[82]

The reference in the apodosis to *mēsiru* "confinement" seems to be based on the well-established reading of NÍGIN as *esēru* "to confine" (but cf. the discussion below). The prediction is negative.

120) DIŠ SAG AD$_6$! KUR-*su* (line 75)

If (there is the grapheme) SAG, a corpse will reach him.

No etymological link; the prediction is negative.

121) DIŠ LAL *al-ma-nu-tam* GIN-*ak* (line 76)

If (there is the grapheme) LAL, he will become a widower.

The sign LAL is associated with notions of poverty and dearth; it can be read *maṭû* "to become little" and *qalālu* "to become weak." These connotations might have inspired the apodosis, but this is not certain.

---

[81] Kraus wanted to read [DIŠ TE.MU]RUB$_4$(= [ÚN]U)-*šu* "If (on) his upper cheek" at the beginning of rev. iv 2´. This seems reasonable, and one could go even further and assume that the A after -*šu* is the first grapheme discussed in this section — note that it is followed by an empty space before the line breaks off. Böck, however, does not follow Kraus, reading instead [... MU]RUB$_4$-*šu a*-[...] in rev. iv 2´ and translating "... seiner Mitte ...."

[82] A very similar omen occurs in VAT 11291 (which may form an indirect join with KAR 395, see n. 80) line 1: DIŠ GIM NÍGIN *me-sír* [...]. Heeßel (2007: 122) reads *kīma šibirti* (LAGAB) and translates "wie ein Klumpen," but it seems more likely that the entry refers to the cuneiform sign NÍGIN, as does example no. 119. Quite possibly, then, the text represented by KAR 395 and VAT 11291 originally included yet another section on cuneiform signs, probably observed on some other part of the face.

122) DIŠ UD ŠÀ.BI DU_{10}.GA (line 77)

If (there is the grapheme) UD, he will be happy.

Compare example nos. 80 and 86, where the analogous apodosis *ṭūb libbi* "happiness" is preceded by references to the signs IGI, ŠE, and PI, all similar to UD. No etymographical link; the prediction is positive.

123) DIŠ BAR *ina la-li-šu* BA.UG_7 (line 78)

If (there is the grapheme) BAR, he will die in his prime.

No etymographical link (but the cross-like shape of the sign may have played a role); the prediction is negative.

124) DIŠ PA ŠU DINGIR KUR-*su* (line 79)

If (there is the grapheme) PA, the hand of a god will reach him.

No obvious etymographical link; the prediction is negative.

125) DIŠ RA ÚŠ *ša-ga-aš-ti* BA.UG_7 (line 80)

If (there is the grapheme) RA, he will die through murder.

One could speculate that a reading of RA as *maḫāṣu* "to beat, smite" influenced the negative apodosis, but this remains uncertain.

126) DIŠ BA[83] U_4.MEŠ-*šu* TIL.MEŠ (line 81)

If (there is the grapheme) BA, his days will come to an end.

No obvious etymographical link; the prediction is negative.

127) DIŠ ZU *ra-ga-am* DINGIR *ana* NA (line 82)

If (there is the grapheme) ZU, there will be divine prosecution against the man.

No etymographical link; the prediction is negative.

128) DIŠ GAN? ŠU LUGAL KUR-*su* (line 83)

If (there is the grapheme) *GAN*, the hand of the king will reach him.

No etymographical link; the prediction is negative.

The two texts presented here mention the following graphemes (in alphabetical order): AB (72), AD (73), AḪ (96), AL (83, 90[?]), AN (56), AZ (97, 106), BA (58, 112, 126), BAD (100), BAR (123) BI (60, 74), BU (61?), DA (88), DAR (89), EN (66), EŠ (108), GA (74), GAG (118), GAN (128), GÁN (68), GIM (106), GÌR (106), GIŠ (64), GUR (78), ḪAR (96), ḪU (66), IB (67), IGI (80, 117), ÍL (73), IM (107), IR (79), KA (71), KI (70, 81), KU (69), KUR (115), LA (82), LAL (121), LI (98), LU (69), LÚ (101), LUGAL (97), MA (69, 112), MAN (111), MEŠ (109), MI (93), MU (60), NA (76, 112 [scribal mistake]), NE (116), NI (79), NÍGIN (119), NU (103, 114), PA (65, 124), PI (86), RA (125), RI (66), SAG (84, 120), ŠÀ (87), ŠE (86, 88[?]), ŠID (57), ŠU (82), TAB (65, 77), TAR (102), TI (107), TU (98), U (95), Ú (85),

[83] Böck reads NA, but the copy has a clear BA.

Ù (101), UB (77), UD (68, 104, 122), UG (106), UL (75), UM (72), UR (67), URU (78), UŠ (64), ZA (99), ZI (59), ZU (127). Forty-nine of the apodoses are inauspicious, fourteen are auspicious, and nine remain unclear.

The preceding overview clarifies a number of issues. First, it is obvious that the signs analyzed in the physiognomic texts differ substantially from those of the extispicy treatises. In the latter, the number of different graphemes observed on the exta is fairly small, with the same characters reoccurring again and again, apparently because of their similarity with certain lesions and grooves typically found on the liver and other organs. In the case of *Alamdimmû* III, the author/compiler of the text was interested in the analysis of a much larger sample of signs. His goal was to point out with regard to each of them what its specific meaning was when it occurred, most probably in the form of wrinkles, on a man's forehead. Only a few signs are mentioned two or three times.

What governs the sequence of the signs investigated in *Alamdimmû* III remains unclear — no lexical list seems to have provided the model. In a few instances, the entries seem to be organized according to acrophonic principles reminiscent of the Old Babylonian *tu* : *ta* : *ti* lists,[84] but these principles are not applied with any consequence. The same holds true for the rare cases in which sign sequences mirror those of Proto-Ea.[85] There is no question, however, that the bulk of the text's section on graphemes goes back to Old Babylonian times. As outlined in my notes (and already recognized in Kraus 1935: 22, but not taken into account by Bilbija 2008), the many variant signs mentioned in the omens resemble one another, almost without exception, in the Old Babylonian cursive script of the time of Ḫammurapi and his successors, but not necessarily in other periods of Babylonian writing, and even less so in the Neo-Assyrian script used in the two Nineveh manuscripts that preserve the passage.[86] This insight, unfortunately, does not settle the question of when the variant signs were actually added. Theoretically, they could already have been part of the original Old Babylonian version of the passage, with a scribe assuming that similarly shaped graphemes observed on the forehead all had the same import. It is also possible, however, that a later redactor of the text, perhaps even the famous scholar Esagil-kīn-apli, who according to Mesopotamian tradition edited the canonical series *Alamdimmû* in the eleventh century B.C. (see Finkel 1988), provided the variants. Working with older manuscripts, the redactor in question may no longer have been able to establish the exact nature of the decontextualized graphemes, and this uncertainty may have prompted him to give every possible reading of them in his new compilation. The truth could also lie somewhere in between, with some variants being old and some of a later date.[87]

[84] See KU, KI, KA (nos. 71–73), BA, BI, BU (nos. 58, 60, 61), and ŠI(= IGI), ŠU, ŠE, ŠÀ (nos. 80, 82, 86, 87).

[85] For instance, LI, TU in no. 98 (cf. MSL 14, 58 lines 681–87) and GAM, NU in nos. 102–03 (cf. MSL 14, 49 lines 448–50). For sign sequences apparently governed by the shape of individual graphemes, see the discussion below.

[86] The Old Babylonian origin of the passage can also be inferred from certain orthographic peculiarities (see nos. 59, 62, 99) — even though most of the writing conventions reflect later standards — and from the contents of a few apodoses (see, for example, no. 72).

[87] That the matter may be fairly complicated is indicated by example nos. 106 and 112, where the two Neo-Assyrian manuscripts provide different variants.

Whatever the exact editorial history of *Alamdimmû* III, the fact is that the variant signs mentioned in many of its entries are grouped together because of their shape, and not because their logographic or phonetic readings share some *tertium comparationis*. This strongly mitigates against the idea that "etymography" is to be regarded as the main rationale behind the protasis-apodosis strings of the various entries. To be sure, there are a few cases where etymography does seem to play a role. In example nos. 87, 97, 101, 105, 107, and 117, the grapheme of the protasis is either repeated or rendered syllabically in the apodosis, and in example nos. 59, 102(?), 119, 121(?), and 125(?), somewhat more subtle links seem to exist.[88] But these are only eleven out of seventy-three entries (some, admittedly, badly broken), representing exceptions rather than the rule.

Unfortunately, what *is* the rule, in the other cases, remains difficult to establish. Apparently the sign's shape, in the Old Babylonian cursive, played a major role; yet why, for instance, the shape of the KI sign, in no. 81, points to a future conflagration remains obscure to the present writer.

Here and there, however, some vague patterns seem to emerge. Nos. 59 and 60, for example, provide very similar apodoses, one positive and the other negative, and it is noteworthy that the graphemes adduced in these entries, ZI and MU, resemble each other. In the Old Babylonian cursive, ZI looks like a MU supplied with two additional vertical wedges. Could ZI therefore symbolize the "raising" (*zaqāpu*) of the house mentioned in the particular apodosis,[89] while MU signifies the exact reverse? Example nos. 64–65 provide a comparable pair of omens with opposite predictions, and again, the signs, GIŠ and UŠ in no. 64 and TAB and PA in no. 65, have similar shapes; yet TAB and PA, unlike GIŠ and UŠ, are "open" on the right side, a feature that might have indicated to the ancient experts that the legacy of the house dealt with in the omen entry was about to "flow out" and perish.[90] Another reference to TAB, in no. 77, is followed by a positive prediction: a woman having difficulties in childbirth will easily give birth (*šutēšuru*). Could it be that in this case, the two parallel wedges of the TAB sign signaled a smooth delivery? Example no. 119 is also of interest. The link between the sign NÍGIN in the protasis and the word *mēsiru* "confinement" in the apodosis could be based on etymography, as argued above, but also on the shape of the sign, a square formed by four wedges "confining" an empty space in the center. And finally, it is noteworthy that the rather similar signs IGI, ŠE, PI, and UD in nos. 80, 86, and 122, for whatever exact reason, all refer to happiness (*ṭūb libbi*).[91]

There is one more physiognomic text that needs to be taken into account here: the highly unusual Nineveh manuscript K. 2087(+?)K. 2088, copied by Kraus (1939: pls. 35–36; see also figs. 7.2–3 below), and edited by Böck (2000a: 258–61). Its section on cuneiform graphemes

[88] Bilbija (2008) claims that this is also the case in nos. 65, 71, and 93, but I remain somewhat skeptical. Other highly questionable cases include nos. 64, 66, 68, 75, 78, 79, 100, and 103, all discussed above. It is true, as pointed out by Bilbija, that the modern scholar trying to pinpoint implicit connections between protases and apodoses of Babylonian omens runs the risk of being rather subjective, but the fact that *Alamdimmû* III includes so few unequivocal links calls for caution when it comes to searching for highly speculative ones.

[89] But note that the respective omen entry can, in fact, also be explained through etymography.

[90] Other sequences of similarly shaped signs can be found in nos. 66–67 (EN/RI/ḪU — UR/IB, identical apodoses); nos. 69–70 (MA/LU/KU — KI, similar apodoses); nos. 72–73 (AB/UM — AD); nos. 74–75 (BI/GA — UL); nos. 83–85 (AL — SAG — Ú, similar apodoses); and nos. 102–103 (TAR/GAM — NU, similar apodoses).

[91] It must be stressed that all these suggestions are highly conjectural. Future analysis of the evidence, hopefully facilitated by the present contribution, may well arrive at more convincing conclusions.

differs from the corresponding passages in *Alamdimmû* III and KAR 395 in several respects. First and most conspicuously, while otherwise written in Neo-Assyrian script, the tablet presents the graphemes it discusses in forms that seem to be based on an attempt to reconstruct the earliest, essentially pictographic stages of cuneiform writing, even though closer inspection reveals them to be artificial concoctions of a younger age that do not match the real sign forms of the late fourth millennium. Second, while some entries seem to have the usual omen format, others do not. And third, quite a few of the entries display very clear examples of "etymographical" thinking.

The section on graphemes is introduced, in K. 2087, rev. i´(?), "III´",[92] by the heading *alam-dím-me-e* SAG.KI N[A ...] "(Concerning) the appearance of the forehead of a man [...]," a line highly reminiscent of the introduction to the analogous passage in *Alamdimmû* III (see above, no. 56). Then, in IV´, follows the entry (**129**)[93] DIŠ *ina* SAG.KI NA BAD ŠUB U$_{4}$.MEŠ-[*šu*...] / ÚŠ ⌈di?⌉-⌈x⌉ [...] / EN(*adi*?) *kim-ti*-[*šu*? ...] "If (the grapheme) BAD appears on the forehead of a man, [his] days [*will be short* (...)], death through ... [...] *together with* [*his*] family[94] [...]." A drawing of a BAD that resembles an arrow accompanies the entry.[95] The reference to death (BAD = ÚŠ = *mūtu*) seems to be based on etymography. Entry no. V´ (**130**) reads: DIŠ KIMIN SIG$_{7}$ ŠUB [...] "If *ditto* (the grapheme) SIG$_{7}$ appears [...]." Entry no. VI´ (**131**) refers to the sign GIŠIMMAR, and entry nos. VII´ and VIII´ (**132–33**) to signs mostly broken away. The apodoses of these last entries are lost, and of the drawings only modest traces remain.

K. 2087 rev. i´ breaks off at this point. The text seems to continue, after a gap, with K. 2088, a fragment with remains of one column, probably the last of the reverse. Entry I´ of this piece (**134**) is mostly lost. Entry II´ (**135**) deals with the sign TUK, presented both in an archaizing and in its Assyrian form. The short text passage accompanying these sign forms is badly damaged and largely unintelligible, but it includes the logographic writing NÍG.TU[KU] = *išarru* "he will become rich," indicating that there is an etymographical link between the sign and the text passage. It is also clear that the passage, like the ones in the following entries, does not have the omen format found in the entries in rev. i´. We cannot be absolutely sure, therefore, even though it seems likely, that we are still dealing with signs observed on a man's forehead. Entry no. III´ (**136**) provides an archaizing drawing of a sign interpreted by Böck as KUM, with an inscribed smaller sign resembling a monumental Babylonian NÍG and another, badly broken sign on the right. The accompanying short text — *ku-um-ma*! / *ib-ta-ni* "He built a shrine (*kummu*)" — is clearly linked to the sign through paronomasia.[96] Entry no. III´ is followed by a subscript (IV´) explaining that the preceding section presented "four cuneiform signs from a second *liginnu*-tablet" (4 GÙ.SUM *šá* KA 2-*ti* IM.GÍ[D.DA]).[97] The

[92] My reconstruction of the sequence of the columns differs from Böck's edition; it is in line, though, with Kraus 1935: 48–50. The roman numerals beginning with III´ follow the numbering of individual passages that was introduced by Kraus and is also used by Böck.

[93] I continue here the numbering used for the omen entries discussed before.

[94] Kraus (1935: 49) reads *bēl kim-ti* "Herr der Familie," but this expression seems not to be attested elsewhere. Böck, reading EN DÍM TI, does not offer a translation.

[95] The tip of the arrow is, correctly, on the right side, not on the left as in example no. 41.

[96] Note that the CAD and Böck interpret the text differently. CAD K, 534b, translates: "(if the mark on a person's forehead?) forms (the cuneiform sign) *k*.," while Böck offers "Das Zeichen *kummu* ist geformt." Given the context of the passage, both renderings seem unlikely to me.

[97] A reference to the source used by the scribe. My translation follows Kraus 1935: 50, 108. Böck translates: "vier Keilschriftzeichen als Erklärung der zweiten Exzerpt-Tafel."

following entry, V´ (**137**), presents another, unidentifiable archaizing sign form, and a short text too badly damaged to make much sense of it.

K. 2088 breaks off at this point. After what may have been an extremely small gap, the left column of the tablet continues with K. 2087 rev. ii´.[98] Entry no. I´ of this section (**138**) reads: *tu-kul-ta-šú* / *^{d}asari-ma* / *i-da-aṣ* ḪUL.GÁL.BI / ḪUL.ḪUL.BI "He treated (or: he will treat) the god Asari (i.e., Marduk), who supports him, with disregard — *misfortune for him, evil for him.*" The archaizing sign accompanying this sentence is tentatively identified by Böck as UB, but Kraus's suggestion (1935: 50) to read it as ḪUL would provide a better etymographical link. Entry no. II´ (**139**) shows a stylized palm tree that is supposed to represent the sign GIŠIMMAR, whose Neo-Assyrian form is given as well. A short text on the left reads: *dum-qa* / *ú-šat-lim-šú* / *ú-kin-šu* / *tak-li-me* "He provided him with good things, established for him the *taklīmu*-offering." Since *damāqu* can be written with the GIŠIMMAR sign, read sa_6, there is again an obvious link between text and grapheme.[99] Entry no. III´ (**140**) offers an archaizing and a Neo-Assyrian version of the sign DU, accompanied by the phrase *al-la-ku* / *ša ur-ḫi* / *i-du-uš-šu* / *i-ba-a*ʾ "A traveler went (or: will go) at his side"; it is linked to the sign through the well-established reading of DU as *alāku* "to go." This part of the text comes to an end with yet another subscript (IV´), which states that the "four graphemes" treated in the preceding lines were taken "from the third *liginnu*-tablet."

The last preserved section of the fragment seems to contain nothing but drawings of pseudo-archaic signs and their Neo-Assyrian equivalents. Entry no. V´ (**141**) presents the Neo-Assyrian form of the sign MAḪ and a drawing that looks like a hill, perhaps because MAḪ = *ṣīru* means "exalted, high(-ranking)." No. VI´ (**142**) offers the sign RAD/ŠÌTA and two horizontal lines possibly symbolizing an irrigation channel (note that the sign represents the word *rāṭu* "water-channel"). No. VII´ (**143**) has yet again GIŠIMMAR, this time accompanied by a drawing of a half-circle, and VIII´ (**144**) has SA, in its Neo-Assyrian form, a fairly realistic archaic version, and the pseudo-archaic shape, probably based on the latter, of a triangular structure. The remaining entries are mostly damaged and obscure. IX´ (**145**) presents GA and a drawing made up of horizontal wedges, X´ (**146**) TUK(?) and IL with two small stars in between, XI´[100] (**147**) a DU inscribed in a rectangular configuration, together with NÍGIN(?) KIB(?) written on the right, XII´ (**148**) GIM with a drawing of a pseudo-archaic form of the sign, and XIII´ (**149**) LIL Ú KÚR(?), together with a drawing that is mostly lost. After another — badly damaged — subscript (XIV´) probably stating that the preceding section included "nine cuneiform signs from the forth *liginnu*-tablet," K. 2087 rev. ii´ breaks off.

The graphemes mentioned in K. 2087(+) are (in alphabetical order): BAD (129), DU (140, 147), GA (145), GIM (148), GIŠIMMAR (131, 139, 143), ḪUL(?) (138), IL (146), KIB(?) (147), KUM(?) (136), KÚR(?) (149), LIL (149), MAḪ (141), NÍGIN(?) (147), RAD (142), SA (144), SIG_7 (130), TUK (135, 146(?)), and Ú (149). Omen no. 129 has a negative prediction, while of the intelligible short texts of the left column nos. 135, 136, 139, and 140 seem to be positive and no. 138 negative.[101]

---

[98] It cannot be completely excluded that K. 2087, rev. ii´ actually precedes K. 2088, but this seems unlikely.

[99] Note that the Late Babylonian extispicy text Clay 1923: no. 13 line 32 refers to a date palm as well, in an attempt to describe a specific configuration of the coils of the colon: BAD ŠÀ.NIGIN GIM ^{giš}GIŠIMMAR. Interestingly, three of the four omens preceding this entry deal with cuneiform signs (see above, example nos. 43–45).

[100] Entries XI´–XIV´ are missing in Böck's edition of the tablet.

[101] Most of the short texts, maybe all, use past tense forms, an indication that they are probably not predictions but rather general statements about the character

The highly archaizing sign forms listed in K. 2087(+) seem to indicate, at first glance, that K. 2087(+) represents a tradition that precedes *Alamdimmû* III with its Old Babylonian background. But in reality, the text probably originates from a later period. Quite a few of the signs analyzed in it were usually employed as logograms or CVC signs, grapheme types more widely used in post-Old Babylonian Akkadian writing. The text's focus on "etymography" points to a later stage of cuneiform culture as well. And finally, attempts by Mesopotamian scholars to systematically reconstruct the original forms of cuneiform graphemes are otherwise known only from first-millennium sources, most prominently from a number of Neo-Assyrian and Late Babylonian syllabaries with added columns featuring what the scribes apparently believed were those forms,[102] but also from a small fragment from Kalḫu inscribed with what appears to be a first-millennium historical text written in extremely archaic characters.[103] The text represented by K. 2087(+) was probably composed by scribes who, aware of the tradition of analyzing "Old Babylonian" sign forms on the face of human beings, felt motivated to replace them with even older forms, which they believed were closer to the beginnings of all wisdom.

INSCRIBED BODIES IN EVERYDAY LIFE

Originally, Mesopotamian physiognomists may have found the inspiration for their interest in graphemes "inscribed" on the human body in their everyday experience of encountering (runaway) slaves, prisoners, and temple oblates who were tattooed or branded[104] with the names of their owners (or the institution they belonged to), or with some other inscription. Skin is "the most obvious canvas upon which human differences can be written and read,"[105] and it is therefore not surprising that the ancient Babylonians and Assyrians, like the people of later ages, used it in this capacity, and, in addition to finding on it imaginary signs, also inscribed it with real ones.

A Mesopotamian branding iron from the third millennium(?) that was used to apply the name of a certain Duggani on cattle or slaves to document his ownership claims is the most tangible testimony of the gruesome but widespread practice of branding; it is also the oldest object of its kind.[106] A passage in *Ana ittīšu*, a collection of legal phrases reflecting judicial

---

and disposition of the individual on whose body the signs accompanying them were observed.

[102] See, inter alia, the fragments published in CT 5, nos. 7–16; Wiseman and Black 1996: no. 229; and von Weiher 1993: nos. 212, 216. A comprehensive study of the corpus remains a desideratum. The often almost pictographic sign forms of the Syllabary A fragment edited by Wiseman and Black (and its join, K. 8250) and those found in 81-7-27, 49+ (CT 5, pl. 7) look very similar to the characters presented in K. 2087(+) and may well represent the tradition on which the latter text drew; but the *liginnu*-tablets referred to in the subscripts of K. 2087(+) cannot be identified as excerpt tablets of specific syllabaries.

[103] Wiseman and Black 1996: no. 229; with remarks by Finkel 1997. There are, of course, many more first-millennium texts that use archaizing characters, but they are usually more "realistic."

[104] Which method exactly was applied is often unclear; scarification is another possibility.

[105] Schildkrout 2004: 319. Schildkrout's article provides an excellent overview of the current state of anthropological and historical studies of the inscribed body, a topic to which assyriologists have much to contribute.

[106] The object is kept in the Schøyen Collection; for a photo and a short discussion, see http://www.schoyencollection.com/smallercollect2.htm#3032 (07/19/2009). The Web site ascribes the object to the period between 2600 and 2300 B.C., a dating that may be subject to future revision.

customs of the Old Babylonian period, includes the words: *ḫalaq ṣabat ina pānīšu iqqur* "'He is a runaway, seize him,' he engraved (i.e., tattooed?) on his (the slave's) face,"[107] an entry that provides clear proof that in the first half of the second millennium, fugitive slaves could carry cuneiform signs on precisely the same body part that is analyzed in *Alamdimmû* III and K. 2087(+). In the first millennium, such signs were apparently more often tattooed on the hands and wrists of slaves, but their faces could still be inscribed as well.[108] A letter from Nineveh (Parpola 1993: no. 160) mentions an eminent scholar and exorcist who, for unknown reasons, had become a fugitive from Assyria and, now apparently a slave, "was inscribed on his face and hand" (*pa-ni-šú u r*[*i*]*t-ti-šú šaṭ-ru*, rev. 11). One can only hope that this pitiful man found a way to use his learnedness to discover some auspicious meaning behind the characters that were so crudely written on his body. A bill of sale from Borsippa dated to the reign of Xerxes mentions a slave "who is inscribed with the name of his owner ... on the right and left (hand?) and on the cheek (*lētu*) of his left and right side,"[109] indicating that the body part analyzed in the physiognomic treatise KAR 395, namely the cheek, could be inscribed in a very literal sense as well. The slaves and temple oblates of the Neo-Babylonian and Late Babylonian period could carry inscriptions in cuneiform, Aramaic, and even Egyptian characters, but they were also often marked with symbols, for example, a star representing the goddess Ištar that signaled an ownership claim of the Eanna temple in Uruk.[110] Sometimes, slaves became, quite literally, human palimpsests, inscribed with the symbols or names of their successive owners one above the other.[111] Given how widespread the practice was to tattoo Babylonian slaves, it is certainly not by chance that the famous Greek playwright Aristophanes, in his (mostly lost) comedy "The Babylonians" from 426 B.C., seems to apply to Babylonians emerging from a mill the term *polygrámmatos* "(multi)-lettered," apparently referring to slave marks on their foreheads.[112]

Tattooing and branding were also known in ancient Israel and the classical world. Leviticus 19:28, using the word *ktbt*, which refers to writing, contains a prohibition against tattooing of the human body, while Isaiah 44:5, quite in contrast to this injunction, anticipates the glorious times when an Israelite "shall write on his hand: 'the Lord's.'" Since Isaiah 40–55 reflects experiences of the Babylonian exile, it is quite feasible that the quoted passage was inspired by encounters between Judeans and Babylonian temple oblates whose hands bore inscriptions or symbols referring to the religious institution they belonged to. Finally, in Ezekiel 9:4, god tells a faithful angelic scribe: "Go through the midst of the city, the midst of Jerusalem, and set a mark (lit., mark [the grapheme?] Tau) upon the foreheads of those who grieve and lament over all the detestable things that are done in it." Again, a Babylonian background

---

[107] *Ana ittīšu* II iv 13´–14´, see MSL 1, 29 and Reiner 2004. The accompanying Sumerian text reads: lú-zu-záḫ giš e-dab / igi-ni ‹‹na-ni›› in-bal.

[108] For a thorough investigation of the evidence, see Stolper 1998.

[109] See Stolper 1998: 135, n. 7.

[110] The texts normally use the expression *šimtu ... šamātu* to refer to the marking of slaves and cattle with symbols, and (*ina*) *šumi ... šaṭāru* to indicate the marking with writing; see Stolper 1998: 135–36. Reiner (2004: 477–79) points out that the identification marks on cattle were often just painted. For Aramaic signs mentioned in Neo- and Late Babylonian texts in the context of the marking of animals, see Jursa 2000 (note that the Šin on the neck of the horse that is described in the text published in this article is most probably an abbreviation for the name of the sun-god Šamaš, whose temple owned the animal) and Jursa 2002.

[111] Stolper 1998: 136–37.

[112] See Jones 1987: 149–50. "*Polygrámmatos*" also means "learned," but it is unclear if this *double entendre* is deliberately applied to the Babylonians or to the Samians to whom they are compared in the passage in question.

seems possible, and it cannot, in fact, be excluded that some popular form of Mesopotamian physiognomics informed this enigmatic passage.[113] A Jewish treatise describing twelve or thirteen Hebrew letters observed on the forehead of a man, and what they meant with regard to his character and destiny, is known from a manuscript from the Cairo Genizah. The exact origins of the treatise remain obscure (it is ascribed to Rabbi Ishmael, who lived in the late first and early second century A.D.), but the parallels with the Babylonian texts presented above are of course rather intriguing.[114]

As for the classical world, it seems that the Greeks borrowed tattooing for identification and punishment from the Babylonians and Persians and used it in ways very similar to theirs, as did the Romans who borrowed it from the Greeks. In Greece and Rome, penal tattoos, called *stígmata*, a term later applied to the wounds of the crucified Jesus, marked primarily the forehead, the neck, and the wrists of slaves, much like in Mesopotamia.[115] Reiner (2004) has pointed out that according to a scholion to Aeschines, the forehead of a runaway slave was marked with the Greek words *kátekhé me, pheúgô* "Seize me — I am a runaway," a phrase almost exactly identical with the phrase *ḫalaq ṣabat* used on the forehead of fugitive slaves in Mesopotamia according to the *Ana ittīšu* passage quoted above. Roman slaves could wear a ring around their neck inscribed with the same words in Latin, *fugi tene me*.

CONCLUSION

Undoubtedly, Babylonian and Assyrian scholars regarded their writing system, first and foremost, as a tool that provided them with the opportunity to accurately reproduce language. But this was not the only function cuneiform writing fulfilled for them. Drawing on the polysemy and polyphony inherent in the repertoire of cuneiform signs, and inspired by the belief that the many alternative readings of each of these signs conveyed to them a secret message on how things were actually connected, they found ways to imbue the texts they wrote, by using particular characters, with additional layers of meaning,[116] and to discover such layers, through the application of creative hermeneutics, in the foundational texts they read and commented on.[117] Cryptographic writing was employed to make certain texts inaccessible to everybody except a small group of initiates.[118] And finally, as demonstrated in our preceding overview of omens dealing with graphemes, there were also traditions that applied completely alien "codes" to cuneiform writing. In the case presented here, scholars employed

[113] The main function of the mark in Ezekiel 9:4 is, however, quite clearly apotropaic; see Bodi 1991: 49. Because of the originally cruciform shape of the letter Tau, Bodi discusses a possible connection with Mesopotamian amulets inscribed with a cross, and amulet-shaped tablets inscribed with the Erra epic.

[114] For a translation and discussion of the treatise, which also deals with chiromancy (a field unknown from cuneiform sources), see Scholem 1969.

[115] For a detailed study of branding and tattooing in the classical world, see Jones 1987.

[116] See Maul 1999. The word *u'iltu* ("debt-note"), for example, usually rendered *ú-il-tu* or *ú-il-tu*, could also be written *ú-íl-tu*, with the sign ÍL (otherwise only rarely employed syllabically) replacing IL. Since Sumerian íl means "to carry," this writing indicated to an ancient reader the heaviness of the financial burden the debtor had to shoulder. For additional examples, including some from omen texts, see Noegel, this volume.

[117] See the commentary entries discussed earlier in this paper.

[118] For discussions of cuneiform cryptography, see Weidner 1964 and Westenholz 1998 (with further literature).

a code in which, as far as we can determine, the shape of the signs was the primary factor that determined their meaning.[119] This peculiar "grammar" of the visual appearances of cuneiform signs was part of the much larger system of analogies governing the Mesopotamian omen corpus.[120] Another code unrelated to the established conventions of cuneiform writing seems to be used in a few cuneiform syllabaries from the first millennium B.C. that associate individual graphemes with numbers. The principles behind the equations presented in these texts are still obscure to us.[121]

Given the ever increasing complexity of Mesopotamian "grammatology," it is not surprising that the etiological tale the Enmerkar epic gave with regard to the cuneiform writing system — that it was invented to ease long-distance communication — was eventually replaced by another story. The most prominent version of it can be found in Berossos's famous "Babyloniaka," written at the beginning of the Seleucid era and in Greek language, but in the spirit of Babylonian scholarship. Berossos reports that in the early days of mankind, the semi-divine sage Oannes-Adapa, emerging from the sea, had taught the people how to found cities, establish temples, introduce laws, and measure land, had inaugurated sciences and crafts of all kinds — and had given men the knowledge of letters.[122] For Berossos, and many other Babylonian and Assyrian scholars, the cuneiform writing system was not a human creation, compromised by all the imperfections of mortal striving, but a gift of the gods, originating in a period that preceded historical times, and capable of conveying, on various levels, completely incontestable eternal truths.

ABBREVIATIONS

AHw	W. von Soden, *Akkadisches Handwörterbuch*
BM	Tablets in the collections of the British Museum
CAD	A. Leo Oppenheim et al., editors, *The Assyrian Dictionary of the Oriental Institute of the University of Chicago*
CT	Cuneiform Texts from Babylonian Tablets in the British Museum
K.	Tablets in the Kouyunjik collection of the British Museum
KAR	Keilschrifttexte aus Assur religiösen Inhalts
MSL	Materials for the Sumerian Lexicon

[119] Looking at the evidence from a diachronic perspective, it is certainly not by chance that this code seems to have been established in the Old Babylonian period, when Akkadian texts were written in a rather unsophisticated and simple orthography. "Etymographical" approaches became more popular with the subsequent emergence of increasingly complex orthographical conventions.

[120] For some thoughts on this matter, see Glassner 1984.

[121] For presentations of the relevant texts, see Oelsner 1995 and Pearce 1996; for an attempt to explain at least one of the grapheme-number equations, see Cavigneaux 1996.

[122] See Burstein 1978: 13–14.

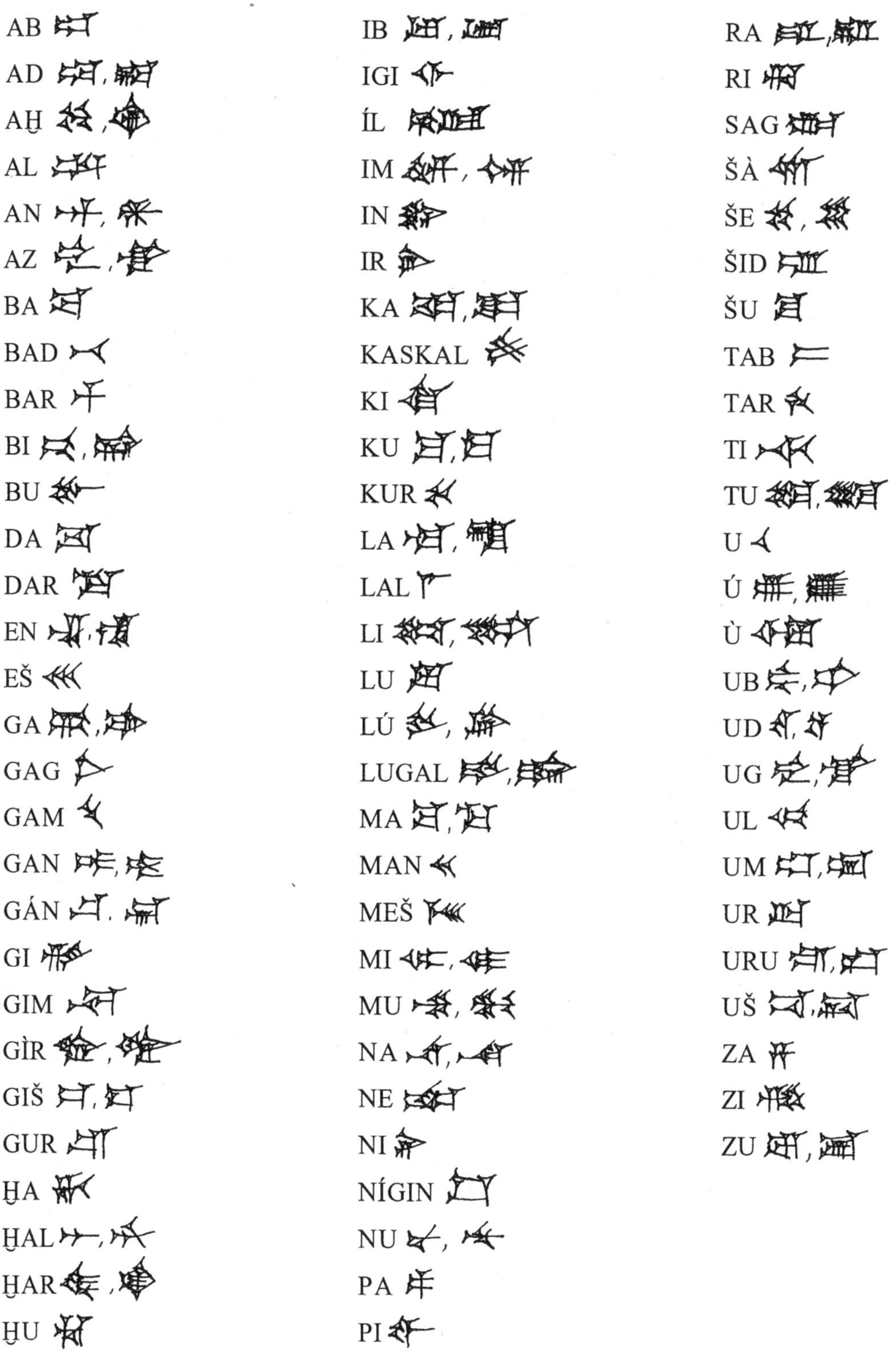

Figure 7.1. Cuneiform graphemes mentioned in the extispicy texts, *Alamdimmû* III, and KAR 395, in alphabetical order. The sign forms, for the most part taken from Goetze 1947, pls. 127–32, are those of the Old Babylonian younger cursive and the so-called "archaic cursive."

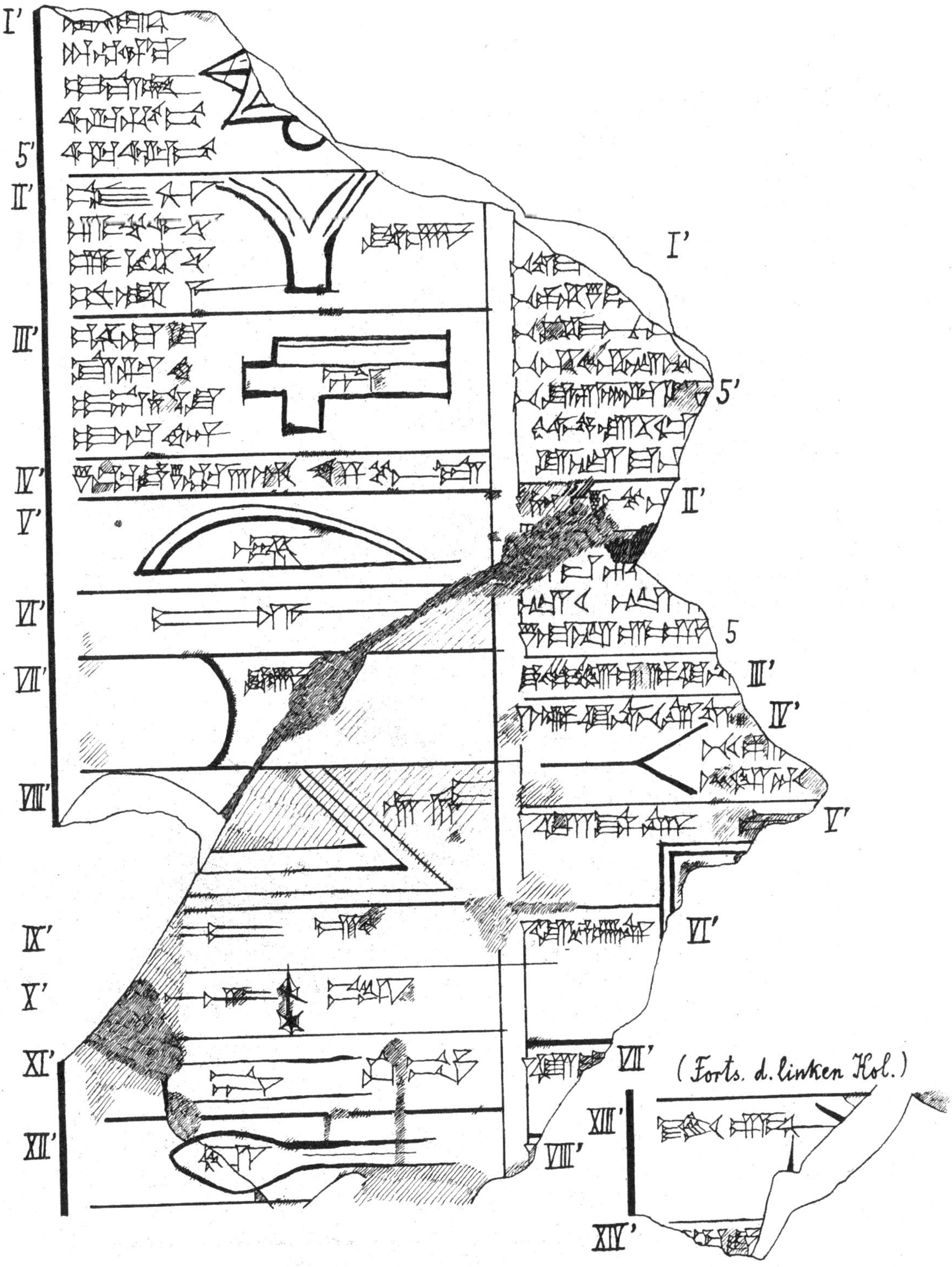

Figure 7.2. Cuneiform autograph of K. 2087 (after Kraus 1939, pl. 35, no. 27a)

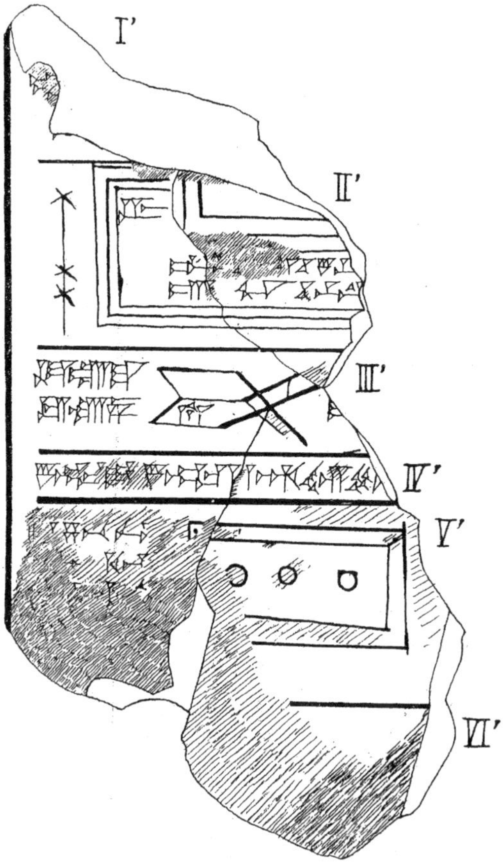

Figure 7.3. Cuneiform autograph of K. 2088 (after Kraus 1939, pl. 36, no. 27b)

BIBLIOGRAPHY

Assmann, Jan

2003 "Etymographie: Zeichen im Jenseits der Sprache." In *Hieroglyphen: Stationen einer anderen abendländischen Grammatologie*, edited by A. Assmann and J. Assmann, pp. 37–63. Munich: Fink.

Biggs, Robert D.

1968 "An Esoteric Babylonian Commentary," *Revue d'Assyriologie* 62: 51–58.

Bilbija, Jovan

2008 "Interpreting the Interpretation: Protasis-Apodosis-Strings in the Physiognomic Omen Series šumma alamdimmû 3.76–132." In *Studies in Ancient Near Eastern World View and Society Presented to Marten Stol on the Occasion of his 65th Birthday*, edited by E. J. van der Spek, pp. 19–27. Bethesda: CDL Press.

Böck, Barbara

2000a *Die babylonisch-assyrische Morphoskopie*. Archiv für Orientforschung, Beiheft 27. Vienna: Institut für Orientalistik der Universität Wien.

2000b "'An Esoteric Babylonian Commentary' Revisited." *Journal of the American Oriental Society* 120: 615–20.

Bodi, Daniel

1991 *The Book of Ezekiel and the Poem of Erra*. Orbis Biblicus et Orientalis 104. Freiburg: Universitätsverlag; Göttingen: Vandenhoeck & Ruprecht.

Borger, Rykle

1996 *Beiträge zum Inschriftenwerk Assurbanipals*. Wiesbaden: Harrassowitz.

2003 *Mesopotamisches Zeichenlexikon*. Alter Orient und Altes Testament 305. Münster: Ugarit-Verlag.

Bottéro, Jean

1974 "Symptômes, signes, écritures en Mésopotamie ancienne." In *Divination et rationalité*, edited by J. P. Vernant, pp. 70–197. Sources orientales 2. Paris: Seuil.

Burstein, Stanley M.

1978 *The* Babyloniaka *of Berossus*. Sources from the Ancient Near East 1/5. Malibu: Undena.

Cavigneaux, Antoine

1987 "Aux sources du Midrash: L'herméneutique babylonienne." *Aula Orientalis* 5: 243–55.

1996 Review of *Uruk*: *Spätbabylonische Texte aus dem Planquadrat U 18*, Teil IV, by E. von Weiher. *Zeitschrift für Assyriologie* 86: 148–50.

Charpin, Dominique

2008 *Lire et écrire à Babylone*. Paris: Presses Universitaires de France.

Civil, Miguel

1973 "The Sumerian Writing System: Some Problems." *Orientalia* 42: 21–34.

1974 "Medical Commentaries from Nippur." *Journal of Near Eastern Studies* 33: 329–38.

Clay, Albert T.

1923 *Epics, Hymns, Omens and Other Texts*. Babylonian Records in the Library of J. Pierpont Morgan 4. New Haven: Yale University Press

Dornseiff, Franz

1925 *Das Alphabet in Mystik und Magie*. Leipzig and Berlin: Teubner.

Edzard, Dietz Otto

1980 "Keilschrift." *Reallexikon der Assyriologie* 5: 544–68.

Finkel, Irving L.

1988 "Adad-apla-iddina, Esagil-kīn-apli, and the Series SA.GIG." In *A Scientific Humanist: Studies in Memory of Abraham Sachs*, edited by E. Leichty, M. de Jong Ellis, and P. Gerardi, pp. 143–59. Philadelphia: The University Museum.

1997 "Practical Political Paleography." *Nouvelles Assyriologiques Brèves et Utilitaires* 1997: no. 1.

Foster, Benjamin R.

2005 *Before the Muses: An Anthology of Akkadian Literature*. 3rd edition. Bethesda: CDL Press.

George, Andrew R.

1991 "Babylonian Texts from the Folios of Sidney Smith, Part Two: Prognostic and Diagnostic Omens, Tablet I." *Revue d'Assyriologie* 85: 137–63.

1992 *Babylonian Topographical Texts*. Orientalia Lovanensia Analecta 40. Leuven: Peeters.

2009 *Babylonian Literary Texts in the Schøyen Collection*, Cornell University Studies in Assyriology and Sumerology 10. Bethesda: CDL Press.

Glassner, Jean-Jacques

1984 "Pour un lexique des termes et figures analogiques en usage dans la divination mésopotamienne." *Journal asiatique* 272: 15–46.

2000 *Écrire à Sumer: L'invention du cunéiforme*. Paris: Seuil.

2004 *Mesopotamian Chronicles*, edited by B. R. Foster. Writings from the Ancient World 19. Atlanta: Society of Biblical Literature.

Goetze, Albrecht

1947 *Old Babylonian Omen Texts*. Yale Oriental Series 10. New Haven: Yale University Press.

Gong, Yushu

1993 *Studien zur Bildung und Entwicklung der Keilschriftzeichen*. Hamburg: Kova.

2000 *Die Namen der Keilschriftzeichen*. Alter Orient und Altes Testament 268. Münster: Ugarit-Verlag.

Green, Margaret W., and Hans J. Nissen

1987 *Zeichenliste der archaischen Texte aus Uruk*. Ausgrabungen der Deutschen Forschungsgemeinschaft in Uruk-Warka 11. Berlin: Mann.

Heeßel, Nils P.

2007 *Divinatorische Texte* I: *Terrestrische, teratologische, physiognomische und oneiromantische Omina*. Keilschrifttexte aus Assur literarischen Inhalts 1. Wiesbaden: Harrassowitz.

Hunger, Hermann

1976 *Spätbabylonische Texte aus Uruk*, Part 1. Ausgrabungen der Deutschen Forschungsgemeinschaft in Uruk-Warka 9. Berlin: Gebruder Mann.

Jeyes, Ulla

1989 *Old Babylonian Extispicy: Omen Texts in the British Museum*. Istanbul: Nederlands Historisch-Archaeologisch Instituut te Istanbul.

Jones, Christopher P.

1987 "Stigma: Tattooing and Branding in Graeco-Roman Antiquity." *Journal of Roman Studies* 77: 139–55.

Jursa, Michael

2000 “Der ‘Zahn’ des Schreibers: Ein aramäischer Buchstabenname in akkadischer Transkription.” *Zeitschrift für Assyriologie* 90: 78–84.

2002 “Weitere aramäische Buchstabennamen in akkadischer Überlieferung.” *Nouvelles Assyriologiques Brèves et Utilitaires* 2002: no. 13.

Kammerzell, Frank

1998 “The Sounds of a Dead Language: Reconstructing Egyptian Phonology.” *Göttinger Beiträge zur Sprachwissenschaft* 1: 21–41.

Koch-Westenholz, Ulla

2000 *Babylonian Liver Omens: The Chapters Manzāzu, Padānu and Pān tākalti of the Babylonian Extispicy Series Mainly from Aššurbanipal's Library*. Copenhagen: Museum Tusculanum Press.

Koch, Ulla

2005 *Secrets of Extispicy: The Chapter Multābiltu of the Babylonian Extispicy Series and Niṣirti bārûti Texts Mainly from Aššurbanipal's Library*. Alter Orient und Altes Testament 326. Münster: Ugarit-Verlag.

Kraus, Fritz R.

1935 *Die physiognomischen Omina der Babylonier*. Mitteilungen der Vorderasiatisch-Ägyptischen Gesellschaft 40/2. Leipzig: C. Schulze.

1939 *Texte zur babylonischen Physiognomatik*. Archiv für Orientforschung, Beiheft 3. Berlin.

Labat, René

1974 *Textes littéraires de Suse*. Mémoires de la Délégation en Perse 57. Paris: Geuthner.

Lambert, Wilfred G.

1962 “A Catalogue of Texts and Authors.” *Journal of Cuneiform Studies* 16: 59–77.

Lieberman, Stephen J.

1977 “The Names of the Cuneiform Graphemes in Old Babylonian Akkadian.” In *Essays on the Ancient Near East in Memory of Jacob Joel Finkelstein*, edited by M. de Jong Ellis, pp. 147–54. Memoirs of the Connecticut Academy of Arts and Sciences 19. Hamden: Archon Books.

1987 “A Mesopotamian Background for the So-Called *Aggadic* ‘Measures’ of Biblical Hermeneutics?” *Hebrew Union College Annual* 58: 157–225.

Lipiński, Edward

1998 “Gyges et Lygdamis d'après les sources néo-assyriennes et hébraïques.” In *34ème Rencontre Assyriologique Internationale - 34. Uluslararasi Assiriyoloji Kongresi - Türk Tarih Kurumu Yayinlari 26*, edited by H. Erkanal, V. Donbaz, and A. Uguroglu, pp. 159–65. Ankara: Türk Tarih Kurumu Basimevi.

Maul, Stefan M.

1999 “Das Wort im Worte: Orthographie und Etymologie als hermeneutische Verfahren babylonischer Gelehrter.” In *Commentaries — Kommentare*, edited by G. W. Most. Aporemata 4: 1–18. Göttingen: Vandenhoeck & Ruprecht.

2003 “Omina und Orakel.” *Reallexikon der Assyriologie* 10: 45–88.

Meyer, Jan-Waalke

1987 *Untersuchungen zu den Tonlebermodellen aus dem Alten Orient*. Alter Orient und Altes Testament 39. Kevelaer: Butzon & Bercker; Neukirchen-Vluyn: Neukirchener Verlag.

Noegel, Scott B.

2007 *Nocturnal Ciphers: The Allusive Language of Dreams in the Ancient Near East*. American Oriental Series 89. New Haven: American Oriental Society.

Nougayrol, Jean

1945–46 "Textes hépatoscopiques d'époque ancienne conservés au musée du Louvre II." *Revue d'Assyriologie* 40: 55–97.

1974 "Deux figures oubliées (K 2092)." *Revue d'Assyriologie* 68: 61–68.

Oelsner, Joachim

1995 "'Number Syllabaries': Das Keilschrift-Syllabar A mit Zahlwerten." In *Meilenstein: Festgabe für Herbert Donner zum 16. Februar 1995*, edited by M. Weippert and S. Timm, pp. 154–63. Ägypten und Altes Testament 30. Wiesbaden: Harrassowitz.

Parpola, Simo

1983 *Letters from Assyrian Scholars to the Kings Esarhaddon and Assurbanipal*, Part 2: *Commentary and Appendices*. Alter Orient und Altes Testament 5/2. Kevelaer: Butzon & Bercker; Neukirchen-Vluyn: Neukirchener Verlag.

1993 *Letters from Assyrian and Babylonian Scholars*. State Archives of Assyria 10. Helsinki: Helsinki University Press.

Pearce, Laurie E.

1996 "The Number Syllabary Texts." *Journal of the American Oriental Society* 116: 453–73.

Reiner, Erica

2004 "Runaway — Seize Him." In *Assyria and Beyond: Studies Presented to Mogens Trolle Larsen*, edited by J. G. Dercksen, 475–82. Leiden: Nederlands Instituut voor het Nabije Oosten.

Rochberg, Francesca

2004 *The Heavenly Writing: Divination, Horoscopy, and Astronomy in Mesopotamian Culture*, Cambridge/New York: Cambridge University Press.

Römer, Willem H. Ph.

2007 Review of *Ur Excavation Texts* VI/3, by A. Shaffer. *Bibliotheca Orientalis* 64: 180–82.

Schildkrout, Enid

2004 "Inscribing the Body." *Annual Review of Anthropology* 33: 319–44.

Scholem, Gershom

1969 "Ein Fragment zur Physiognomatik und Chiromantik aus der Tradition der spätantiken jüdischen Esoterik." In *Liber Amicorum: Studies in Honour of Professor Dr. C. J. Bleeker*, pp. 175–93. Studies in the History of Religions 17. Leiden: Brill.

Scurlock, JoAnn, and Farouk N. H. Al-Rawi

2006 "A Weakness for Hellenism." In *If a Man Builds a Joyful House: Assyriological Studies in Honor of Erle Verdun Leichty*, edited by A. K. Guinan et al., pp. 357–81. Cuneiform Monographs 31. Leiden: Brill.

Starr, Ivan

1977 "Notes on Some Published and Unpublished Historical Omens." *Journal of Cuneiform Studies* 29: 157–66.

1983 *The Rituals of the Diviner*. Bibliotheca Mesopotamica 12. Malibu: Undena.

1990 *Queries to the Sungod: Divination and Politics in Sargonid Assyria*. State Archives of Assyria 4. Helsinki: Helsinki University Press.

Stol, Martin

1993 *Epilepsy in Babylonia*. Cuneiform Monographs 2. Groningen: Styx.

Stolper, Matthew W.

1998 "Inscribed in Egyptian." In *Studies in Persian History: Essays in Memory of David M. Lewis*, edited by M. Brosius and A. Kuhrt, pp. 133–43. Achaemenid History 11. Leiden: Nederlands Instituut voor het Nabije Oosten.

Taylor, Insup, and M. Martin Taylor
1995 *Writing and Literacy in Chinese, Korean and Japanese*. Studies in Written Language and Literacy 3. Philadephia: John Benjamins.

van Dijk, Johannes J. A.
1962 "Die Inschriftenfunde." In *18. vorläufiger Bericht über die Ausgrabungen in Uruk-Warka*, edited by H. Lenzen, pp. 39–62. Berlin.

Vanstiphout, Herman L. J.
2004 *Epics of Sumerian Kings: The Matter of Aratta*. Edited by J. S. Cooper. Writings from the Ancient World 20. Atlanta: Society of Biblical Literature.

Virolleaud, Charles
1907–09 *L'astrologie chaldéenne, le livre intitulé "enuma (Anu) ^{ilu}Bêl": Adad*. Paris: Geuthner.

von Weiher, Egbert
1993 *Uruk: Spätbabylonische Texte aus dem Planquadrat U 18*, Teil IV. Ausgrabungen in Uruk-Warka, Endberichte 12. Mainz: Philipp von Zabern.

Weidner, Ernst F.
1964 "Geheimschrift." *Reallexikon der Assyriologie* 3: 185–88.

Westenholz, Joan Goodnick
1997 *Legends of the Kings of Akkade*. Mesopotamian Civilizations 7. Winona Lake: Eisenbrauns.
1998 "Thoughts on Esoteric Knowledge and Secret Lore." In *Intellectual Life of the Ancient Near East: Papers Presented at the 43rd Rencontre Assyriologique Internationale*, edited by J. Prosecký, pp. 451–62. Prague: Oriental Institute.

Wiseman, Donald J., and Jeremy A. Black
1996 *Literary Texts from the Temple of Nabû*. Cuneiform Texts from Nimrud 4. Oxford: British School of Archaeology in Iraq.

8

"SIGN, SIGN, EVERYWHERE A SIGN": SCRIPT, POWER, AND INTERPRETATION IN THE ANCIENT NEAR EAST[1]

SCOTT B. NOEGEL, UNIVERSITY OF WASHINGTON

As the title of this study indicates, my primary aim is to shed light on ancient Near Eastern conceptions of the divine sign by bringing into relief the intricate relationship between script, power, and interpretation. At the seminar organizer's request I have adopted a comparative approach and herein consider evidence from Mesopotamia, Egypt, and Israel.[2]

I divide my study into three parts. In the first, I argue that we obtain insight into the interpretive process of ancient diviners by recognizing the cosmological underpinnings that inform the production of divinatory and other mantic texts. Among these underpinnings is an ontological understanding of words and script as potentially powerful.

In the second part of the essay, I should like to show that the ontological understanding of words and script provides a contextual framework that permits us to see the exegetical process as a ritual act of performative power that legitimates and promotes the cosmological and ideological systems of the interpreter.

In my third and final section, I argue that recognizing the process of exegesis as an act of power provides insights into the generative role that scripts (or writing systems) play in shaping ancient Near Eastern conceptions of the divine sign.

---

[1] I take this opportunity to thank Amar Annus for the invitation to participate in the annual Oriental Institute Seminar and the Oriental Institute for its hospitality. I also thank my graduate students Karolien Vermeulen and Jacob Rennaker, and my colleague Dr. Gary Martin for lending their editorial eyes to various versions of this paper.

[2] There is more evidence for divination in Mesopotamia than in Egypt, and far more publications on the subject. Nevertheless, our understanding of Egyptian divination is changing drastically with the publication of previously unknown texts. Currently, the earliest evidence for divination in Egypt appears in the form of kledonomancy and hemerology texts of the Middle Kingdom (von Lieven 1999). Thereafter, we have a dream omen text that dates to the New Kingdom (Gardiner 1935; Szpakowska 2003; Noegel 2007: 92–106), and an increasing number of divinatory texts of the Late Period and beyond, mostly unpublished (Volten 1942; Andrews 1993: 13–14; Andrews 1994: 29–32; Demichelis 2002; Quack 2006). With regard to the Israelites, it is largely recognized that they also practiced divination, even though scholars debate its extent and role in Israelite religion (see Cryer 1994; Jeffers 1996; Noegel 2007: 113–82). Regardless of what constitutes divination in ancient Israel, my focus in this study is on the exegesis of divine signs (often in visions), for which there is ample evidence in the Hebrew Bible. For a discussion on the taxonomic relationship between visions and prophecy in ancient Israel, see Noegel 2007: 263–69.

COSMOLOGY AND THE POWER OF WORDS

It is well known that the literati of the ancient Near East regarded words, whether written or spoken, to be inherently, and at least potentially powerful (see already Heinisch 1922; Dürr 1938; Masing 1936). With reference to Mesopotamia, Georges Contenau explains:

> Since to know and pronounce the name of an object instantly endowed it with reality, and created power over it, and since the degree of knowledge and consequently of power was strengthened by the tone of voice in which the name was uttered, writing, which was a permanent record of the name, naturally contributed to this power, as did both drawing and sculpture,[3] since both were a means of asserting knowledge of the object and consequently of exercising over it the power which knowledge gave (Contenau 1955: 164).

Statements by scribal elites concerning the cosmological dimension of speech and writing are plentiful in Mesopotamia. A textbook example is the Babylonian creation account, which characterizes the primordial world of pre-existence as one not yet put into words.

> *enūma eliš lā nabû šamāmu*
> *šapliš ammatum šuma lā zakrat*
>
> When the heavens above had not yet been termed
> Nor the earth below called by name
>
> — *Enuma Elish* I 1–2

Piotr Michalowski has remarked about this text that it "... contains puns and exegeses that play specifically on the learned written tradition and on the very nature of the cuneiform script" (Michalowski 1990b: 39). Elsewhere we hear that writing is *markas kullat* or "the (cosmic) bond of everything" (Sjöberg 1972) and the secret of scribes and gods (Borger 1957; Lenzi 2008a).[4] Moreover, diviners in Mesopotamia viewed themselves as integral links in a chain of transmission going back to the gods (Lambert 1957: 1–14), and in some circles, traced their genealogy back to Enmeduranki, the antediluvian king of Sippar (Lambert 1967: 126–38; Lenzi 2008b). Elsewhere, we are told that diviners transmitted knowledge "from the mouth of the God Ea" (Michalowski 1996: 186). The Mesopotamian conception of divine ledgers or "Tablets of Life" on which gods inscribed the destinies of individuals similarly registers the cosmological underpinnings of writing (Paul 1973: 345–53). One could add to this list many Mesopotamian incantations that presume the illocutionary power of an utterance.[5]

---

[3] On the power of images in Mesopotamia, see Bahrani 2003.

[4] The *markasu* also appears in *Enuma Elish* V 59–60, VII 95–96, as the means for holding the earth, heavens, and the *apsû* in place (CAD M/1, 283 s.v. *markasu*; Horowitz 1998: 119–20). It also appears in reference to temples (CAD M/1, 283–84 s.v. *markasu*; George 2001–2002: 40). Like the cosmological cable (i.e., *markasu*) and temple, writing was a linking device that permitted the diviner to connect and communicate with the gods. The comment by Rochberg concerning the worldview of Mesopotamian celestial diviners is apropos: "A central feature of this relation to the world is the attention to the divine and the assumption of the possibility of a connection and communication between divine and human. In the specific case of celestial divination, that form of communication connected humans not only to gods but to the heavens wherein the gods were thought to make themselves manifest and produce signs for humankind" (Rochberg 2003: 185).

[5] The study of the "illocutionary" power of language was inaugurated by Austin (1962) and Searle (1969); but it received its most influential stamp from Tambiah (1968, 1973, 1985). See also Turner 1974. For an excellent synopsis on the various ancient and

A similar cosmology undergirds the Egyptian conception of text, as David Frankfurter points out:

> ... Egyptian letters were the chief technology of a hierocratic scribal elite who preserved and enacted rituals — and by extension the cosmic order itself — through the written word (Frankfurter 1994: 192).

The Egyptians referred to the hieroglyphic script as *mdw nṯr*, literally, "the words of the gods" and the scribal art was to them an occupation without equal. The ibis-headed god Thoth, who is credited with the invention of writing, is said to be "excellent of magic" (*mnḫ ḥkꜣ*) and "Lord of hieroglyphs" (*nb mdw nṯr*) (Ritner 1993: 35). He is depicted (see fig. 8.1) writing the hieroglyphic feather sign  [6] representing *maat* (*mꜣʿt*), a word that stands for the cosmic force of equilibrium by which kings keep their thrones and justice prevails (Assmann 1990; Teeter 1997).[7]

Figure 8.1. Thoth writing the hieroglyphic sign for *mꜣʿt*

The link between writing and *maat* underscores how integral the scribal art was perceived for maintaining the cosmic order in Egypt (Hodge 1975). The spoken word too was capable of packing power in Egypt, as countless ritual and "magic" texts make clear. In the words of Geraldine Pinch, "In the hieroglyphic script, the power of the image and the power of the word are almost inseparable" (Pinch 1994: 69).

According to Isaac Rabinowitz, the Israelites shared this ontological understanding of words:

> ... words were not merely presumed to have the properties of material objects, but might be thought of as foci or concentrations of dynamic power. They were plainly regarded as not only movable but mobile, not only susceptible to being acted upon, but capable of acting upon other entities in ways not confined to communication, of producing and enacting effects, conditions, circumstances and states (Rabinowitz 1993: 16).

modern approaches to this topic, see Leick 1994: 23–55; and Greaves 1996. On the relationship between Mesopotamian conceptions of words as power and the later Greek doctrine of the logos, see already Langdon 1918; Hehn 1906; Böhl 1916; and more recently Lawson 2001. Images, like text, could also serve as loci of divine power in Mesopotamia. See Bahrani 2008: 59–65.

6 All references to Egyptian signs follow the sigla of Gardiner 1988.

7 *Maat* was also personified as Thoth's wife.

The conceptual link between a word and an object is reflected most clearly in the Hebrew word דבר (*dābār*), which means "word" and also "thing, object." Of course, this notion of words contextualizes Yahweh's creation of the universe by fiat in Genesis 1 (Moriarty 1974).[8]

Like the Mesopotamians and Egyptians, the Israelites also attribute a cosmologically powerful role to writing (Rabinowitz 1993: 33–36). One could cite many proof texts, such as the role that divine writing plays in issuing the Ten Commandments (Exodus 31:18), or Yahweh's heavenly text in which he keeps the names of the sinless (Exodus 32:32–33), or the priestly curses that must be written on a scroll, dissolved in water, and imbibed by a wife tested for unfaithfulness (Numbers 5:23–24), or the many prophecies that Yahweh orders his prophets to utter before an audience and put into writing (e.g., Jeremiah 36:18, 36:27–28).

Perhaps one of the best demonstrations of the cosmological dimension of the written word in Israel appears in Numbers 11, in which we hear how Yahweh gave a portion of Moses' spirit to seventy leading Israelites so they could help bear the people's burdens (Numbers 11:17). In this story, the names of the seventy men are written on a list at the Tent of Meeting, *outside* the camp. As the text tells us:

> Now two men stayed behind in the camp, one named Eldad, the second Medad; but as they were among those written (on the list), the spirit rested upon them even though they had not gone out to the Tent; so they were prophetically possessed within the camp. Thereupon a lad ran and told Moses, and said, "Eldad and Medad are prophesying *within* the camp" (Numbers 11:26–27).

This text illustrates that the written names of the seventy men alone sufficed to bring on the spirit of prophesy (Rabinowitz 1995: 34). The expectation was that prophesying would occur close to the Tent of Meeting and not in the camp.[9]

Such references could be multiplied, but these should suffice to show that speaking and writing in the ancient Near East, especially in ritual contexts, could be perceived as acts of cosmological power. This ontological conception of words would appear to be a necessary starting point for understanding the perceived nature of language, writing, and text in the ancient Near East. Nevertheless, it is seldom integrated into studies of scribal culture or textual production, and even more rarely into studies of ancient divination, despite the importance that language, writing, and text play in the ritual process (see Noegel 2004).

INTERPRETATION OF DIVINE SIGNS AS AN ACT OF POWER

The exegesis of divine signs is often treated as if it were a purely hermeneutical act. However, recognizing the cosmological dimension of the spoken and written word naturally forces us to reconsider the ontological and ritual dimensions of the interpretative process. Indeed, I believe it is more accurate to think of the exegesis of divine signs as a ritual act,[10] in

---

[8] This view also is found in Ugaritic texts. See Sanders 2004.

[9] For additional demonstrations of the power of the written word in Israel, see the insightful work of Rabinowitz 1995: 34–36. On the longevity of the power of names in Israelite religion in later Judaism note the comment of Bohak 2008: 305: "Of all the characteristic features of Jewish magic of all periods, the magical powers attributed to the Name of God are perhaps the longest continuous practice."

[10] Definitions of ritual have multiplied and expanded in recent years. I refer the reader to the taxonomy of

some cases, as one chain in a link of ritual acts. In Mesopotamia, for example, exegesis could be preceded by extispicy or other ritual means for provoking omens and followed by *namburbû* rituals when something went wrong or the omen portended ill (Maul 1994). Therefore, the exegesis of divine signs is cosmologically significant and constitutes a performative act of power.

Until one deciphers them, omens represent unbridled forms of divine power. While their meanings and consequences are unknown they remain liminal and potentially dangerous. The act of interpreting a sign seeks to limit that power by restricting the parameters of a sign's interpretation.[11] A divine sign cannot now mean *anything*, but only *one* thing. Seen in this way, the act of interpretation — like the act of naming — constitutes a performative act of power; hence the importance of well-trained professionals and of secrecy in the transmission of texts of ritual power.

Moreover, the performative power vested in the interpreter is both cosmological and ideological. It is cosmological in the sense that the interpreter takes as axiomatic the notion that the gods *can* and *want to* communicate their intentions through signs, and that the universe works according to certain principles that require only knowledge and expertise to decode. Insofar as the process of interpretation reflects a desire to demonstrate that such principles continue to function, it also registers and dispels ritual or mantic insecurities.[12] The Mesopotamian and Egyptian lists of omens that justify titling this essay "Sign, Sign, Everywhere a Sign,"[13] not only demonstrate that virtually anything could be ominous when witnessed in the appropriate context, they also index a preoccupation with performative forms of control.[14] To wit, all signs, no matter how bewildering or farfetched they might appear, not only *can* be explained, they *must* be explained.

Moreover, to understand the cosmological context of words of power within ancient interpretive contexts, it is important to recognize that acts of interpretation are also acts of divine judgment. In Mesopotamia, diviners use the word *purussû* "legal decision" or "verdict" to refer to an omen's prediction. As Francesca Rochberg has shown, divinatory texts also share in common with legal codes the formula *if x, then y*.[15]

Snoek (2008), who lists twenty-four characteristics that one might find in most (but not all) rituals. I assert that the interpretation of divine signs in the ancient Near East exhibits most of these characteristics. I treat this topic more directly in Noegel, in press.

[11] This perspective also sheds light on why diviners recorded protases that appear "impossible." For a convenient summary of scholarship on these protases, see Rochberg 2004: 247–55.

[12] This may explain why some anthropologists have conceived of divination as a blaming strategy. See Leick 1998: 195–98. On the mantic anxieties that underlie divination generally in Mesopotamia, see Bahrani 2008: 183–89.

[13] This portion of the article's title detourns a lyric from the song "Signs" by the Five Man Electrical Band (1970).

[14] A preoccupation with performative forms of control also might explain the format and organization of the divinatory collections, especially in Mesopotamia. Mogens T. Larsen has described the compiling of lexical lists as presenting "... a systematic and ordered picture of the world" (Larsen 1987: 209–12). Joan G. Westenholz's remarks concerning the practice of listing is equally apposite: "... the earliest lexical compilations may have been more than a utilitarian convenience for the scribes who wrote them; that they may have contained a systematization of the world order; and that at least one was considered as containing 'secret lore'"; and "On the intellectual level, knowing the organization of the world made it possible to affect the universe by magical means" (Westenholz 1998: 451, 453). See also Rochberg 2004: 214.

[15] On the relationship between law codes and omens, see Rochberg 1999: 566: "The formulation itself gives the omens a lawlike appearance, especially when it is further evident that predictions derivable from the relation of x to y are the goal of the inquiry into the set of x that bear predictive possibilities." See also Rochberg 2003, 2004. Reiner (1960: 29–30), shows

In fact, Babylonian oracle questions (i.e., *tamītu*) specifically request judgments (i.e., *dīnū*) from the god Shamash (Lambert 2007: 5–10). Therefore, within this performative juridical context, all means of connecting protases to apodoses constitute vehicles for demonstrating and justifying divine judgment.[16]

The cosmological underpinnings that connect interpretation, power, and judgment in Mesopotamia were no more present than during an extispicy, as Alan Lenzi tells us:

> ... only the diviner had the authority to set the king's plans before the gods via an extispicy and to read the judgment of the gods from the liver and other exta of the animal. In this very act ... the diviner experienced the presence of the divine assembly itself, which had gathered about the victim to write their judgments in the organs of the animal (Lenzi 2008a: 55).

In Egypt there is a great deal of evidence for viewing the interpretation of divine signs as an act of judgment. The very concept of judgment is embedded in a cosmological system that distinguishes sharply between justice or cosmic order (i.e., *mꜣꜥt*) and injustice or chaos (i.e., *jsft*). According to Egyptian belief, *maat* was bestowed upon Egypt by the creator god Atum. Therefore, rendering justice was a cosmological act. For this reason, judicial officials from the Fifth Dynasty onward also held the title "divine priest of *maat*" (*ḥm-nṯr mꜣꜥt*) (Morenz 1973: 12–13). Moreover, since the interpretation of divine signs fell under the purview of the priests, it was they who often rendered judgment in legal matters. Serge Sauneron observes:

> ... divine oracles were often supposed to resolve legal questions. In the New Kingdom, cases were frequently heard within the temples or in their immediate vicinity. Moreover, in every town, priests sat side by side with officials of the Residence on judicial tribunals (Sauneron 2000: 104).

Potsherds discovered at Deir el-Medina also show that priests served as oracular media for obtaining divine judgments (MacDowell 1990: 107–41). Petitioners would inscribe their queries on the potsherds in the form of yes or no questions and the priests would consult the gods before pronouncing their verdicts.

In Israel, interpreting divine signs and judgment also were intimately connected. This is in part because the Israelites regarded Yahweh as both a king and a judge. So close is this connection that the pre-exilic prophetic oracles have been classified as *Gerichtsrede* "lawsuit speeches" (Nielsen 1978). The conceptual tie between the interpreters of divine signs, cosmological power, and judgment continued long after the post-exilic period, as we know from Talmudic texts that discuss the rabbinic interpreters of divinely sent dreams. About the rabbinic interpreter, Philip Alexander remarks:

> He wields enormous power — the power of performative speech. The dream creates a situation in which — like the act of blessing and cursing, or the act of pronouncing judgment in a court of law — speech can lead directly to physical results. And the dream-interpreter exercises this power in virtue of the knowledge and the tradition

---

that *purussûs* could come from stars, birds, cattle, and wild animals as well.

[16] Compare the remark of Shaked 1998: 174, with respect to the language of magic: "... spells are like legal documents ... in that they have the tendency to use formulaic language, and that the language they use creates, by its mere utterance, a new legal situation." See also the comment of Mauss 1972: 122: "... all kinds of magical representations take the form of judgments, and all kinds of magical operations proceed from judgments, or at least from rational decisions."

which he has received from hoary antiquity as to how dreams are to be understood (Alexander 1995: 237–38).[17]

Of course, as this statement also reveals, the power of the interpreter is as much ideological as cosmological. Throughout the ancient Near East the knowledge and expertise required for decoding divine missives typically comes from a privileged few literati, masters of the scribal arts, and/or disciples who keep their knowledge "in house."[18] We may characterize this as an ideology of privilege and erudition.[19] In order to ascertain the meaning of a divine sign, one *must* go to *them*.

Contributing to the ideological power of the interpreter is the role that deciphering divine signs plays in shaping behaviors and beliefs (Sweek 1996). By harnessing the performative power of words, interpreters determine an individual's fate. Thus, the interpretation of signs also can function as a form of social control.[20]

Therefore, we may understand the process of interpreting divine signs as a performative ritual act that empowers the interpreter while demonstrating and promoting his/her cosmological and ideological systems.

THE GENERATIVE ROLE OF SCRIPT

Up to this point I have focused primarily on the cosmological and ideological contexts that inform the interpretation of signs in the ancient Near East. I have underscored the illocutionary power of words and the cosmic dimension of writing, and I have suggested that we see the interpretation of divine signs as a performative ritual. These considerations lead me to the third and final section of this study, an explorative look at the role that writing systems play in shaping ancient Near Eastern conceptions of the divine sign.

Since interpreting divine signs is a semiotic process, it is worthwhile considering how writing systems inform this process. In Mesopotamia, the divination of omens and the process of writing were conceptually linked, even though the Akkadian words for "omenological sign" (i.e., *ittu*) and "cuneiform sign" (i.e., *miḫiṣtu*) were not the same. The conceptual overlap likely derives from the pictographic origins and associations of cuneiform signs (Bottéro 1974). Bendt Alster's comment on the associative nature of the script is apposite: "Cuneiform writing from its very origin provided the scribes with orthographical conventions that lent notions to the texts which had no basis in spoken language" (Alster 1992: 25).

---

[17] Note also that a number of scholars have observed a correlation between the hermeneutics of omens in Mesopotamia and the *pesher* genre found among the Dead Sea Scrolls. See Finkel 1963; Rabinowitz 1973; Fishbane 1977; Geller 1998; Noegel 2007: 24–26, 131, n. 73; Jassen 2007: 343–62; Nissinen forthcoming.

[18] In Mesopotamia the link between secrecy and the reading of omens also is reflected in the Akkadian word for "omen" (i.e., *ittu*), which also can mean "password" or "inside information." See CAD I/J s.v. *ittu* A.

[19] On the relationship between ideology and divinatory ritual in Mesopotamia, see Bahrani 2008: 65–74.

[20] On the use of other omens as vehicles of social control, see Guinan 1996: 61–68. On the increasing complexity of the cuneiform script and the roles of elitism and literacy as mechanisms of social control, see Michalowski 1990a; Pongratz-Leisten 1999.

The dialectic between ominous signs and linguistic signs was so close in Mesopotamia that some extispicy omens were interpreted based on a similarity in shape between features of the exta and various cuneiform signs (Noegel 2007).[21]

a. When the lobe is like the grapheme (named) PAB (*ki-ma pa-ap-pi-im*), (then) the god wants an *ugbabtum*-priestess (YOS 10 17:47).[22]

b. When (the) lobe is like the grapheme (named) *kaškaš*, (then) Adad will inundate (with rain) (YOS 10 17:48).[23]

c. When (the) lobe is like a particular grapheme [here we have the grapheme itself (i.e., *kaškaš*), not its name], then the king will kill his favorites in order to allocate their goods to the temples of the gods (YOS 10 8–9).[24]

Also demonstrating a close relationship between divine signs and cuneiform signs are a number of omens that suggest that diviners either wrote down the omen in order to interpret it or at least conceived of it in written form. These omens derive their interpretations from the polyvalent readings of cuneiform signs in their protases (Noegel 2007: 20–03; Bilbija 2008). Witness the following dream omen.

> If a man dreams that he is traveling to Idran (*id-ra-an*); he will free himself from a crime (Á-*ra-an*).[25]
>
> — K. 2582 rev. ii, x + 21

This omen exploits the cuneiform sign *id* for its multiple values (in this case as Á), which enables the interpreter to read it as an altogether different word. The apodosis illustrates erudition and the importance of understanding the polyvalent values of individual signs. It is reminiscent of the interpretive strategy that appears in Mesopotamian mythological commentaries by which scholars obtain divine mysteries (Lieberman 1978; Tigay 1983; Livingstone 1986). In fact, many omen texts reveal knowledge of a vast array of lexical and literary traditions.[26]

---

[21] Mesopotamian divinatory professionals considered their literate gods capable of using a variety of writing surfaces to communicate their intentions, from clay and stone to animal livers and constellations. The Akkadian term for "liver" (i.e., *amūtum*) may be related etymologically to *awātu* "word," as suggested first by Nougayrol (1944–45: 14, n. 54). Cited also in Jeyes 1989: 17, see also 46. Moreover, the Sumerian sign MUL can refer to a "cuneiform sign" and also a "star" (see Roaf and Zgoll 2001) and astronomical portents and constellations were called the "writing of heaven" (*šiṭir šamê*). See Reiner 1995: 9; Rochberg 2004.

[22] Lieberman (1977: 148, n. 19) notes a pun between the grapheme name and the second syllable of *ugbabtum*. Discussed also in Noegel 2007: 12.

[23] Lieberman (1977: 148, n. 24) observes that the grapheme *kaškaš* puns on *kaškaššu*, which is an epithet used of the storm-god Adad. Discussed also in Noegel 2007: 12.

[24] The omen appears in Lieberman 1977: 148. A pun between the grapheme *kaškaš* and the verb *kašāšu*, "exact services for a debt or fine, hold sway, to master," is discussed in Noegel 2007: 13.

[25] Translations and transliterations of this omen appear in Oppenheim 1956: 268, 313. The siglum K. = tablets in the Kouyunjik collection of the British Museum.

[26] See the remark of Nissinen (2000b: 108): "What united the scholars of different kinds (astrologers, haruspices, and exorcists) was their scholarship, the profound knowledge of traditional literature, and a high level of literacy ..."

An even more sophisticated example of polyvalent reading appears in the following dream omen.

> If he seizes a fox (KA$_5$.A = *šēlibu*); he will seize a Lamassu (AN.KAL), but if he seizes a fox in his hand (ŠU), and it escapes; he will have seized a Lamassu, but it also will escape from his hand (ŠU)[27]
>
> — Sm. 801 rev. iii, x + 10

Though the protasis records the image of a fox, written with the Sumerogram KA$_5$.A (= Akkadian *šēlibu*), its interpretation derives from understanding the Akkadian counterpart *šēlibu* as if it were written syllabically. When written as *še$_7$-líb-bu* the same signs can be read as (A).AN.KAL-*u*, that is, "Lamassu."[28] Moreover, though the Sumerogram ŠU here stands for the Akkadian word *qātu* "hand," one lexical list gives us the equation ^{d}LAMMA = ^{d}ŠU.[29] Like the previous example, this omen's interpretation derives from the divine sign conceived of in written form.

Though unrelated to cuneiform, hieroglyphic Egyptian also began and continued as a pictographic system. The connection between the name of an object and its pictographic form similarly led to a conception of texts as images, but also images as texts. The Egyptian word *tjt* means both "written word" or "letter," and also an artistic "image, form, or sign." Sculpted images too could be read as hieroglyphic signs and drawings functioned as tools of performative power (Ritner 1993: 111–43). As Robert Ritner notes: "The very notions of divinity and imagery are cojoined in Egyptian thought; the conventional term for 'god' (*nṯr*) has as its root meaning 'image'" (Ritner 1995: 51).

As in Mesopotamia, some Egyptian omens derive their interpretations solely from their written forms as in the following dream omen.

> ... *ḥr mꜣꜣ jꜥḥ wbn=f; nfr ḥtp n=f jn nṯr=f*
>
> ... seeing the moon when it is risen; good, (it means) being clement to him by his god.[30]
>
> — Papyrus Chester Beatty III recto 5.22

Of note is the determinative of the falcon-god Horus 𓅆, which occurs after the word *wbn* "risen" in the protasis. This is not the usual determinative for this word (which is 𓇶). Nevertheless, it provides the interpreter with a reason for interpreting the omen as the sign of a "god" (*nṯr*). Like the Akkadian examples, this interpretation derives from the omen's written form.

---

[27] Translations and transliterations of this dream omen appear in Oppenheim 1956: 281, 326. On the clever reading of signs in this omen, see Noegel 1995; 2007: 21. The siglum Sm. = tablets in the collections of the British Museum.

[28] For a similar divinatory pun on this word, see the omen series *Šumma ālu* I 178, "If, before the daises of my city, a dog yelps and a [fox(?) = KA$_5$.A = *šēlebu*] answers it; the king of Lullubu (*lul-lu-bu*) will die." The pun hinges on the reading KA$_5$.(LUL).A. Noted in Freedman 1998: 41. On the integrated use of Sumerian and Akkadian in the scribal schools of the ancient Near East, see Rubio 2006: 49.

[29] Matouš and von Soden 1933: 2, 285 and 4 iv 16. Cited in CAD L s.v. *lamassu*.

[30] Noegel and Szpakowsa 2006: 205.

Another example appears on the same scroll.

> ... *ḫr fꜣj-ṯꜣ.w m ḫd; ḏw, ʿnḫ pw nj sḫḫ*
>
> ... sailing downstream; bad, (it means) a life of running backward.[31]
>
> — Papyrus Chester Beatty III recto 8.3

This omen employs the words for "sailing" (*fꜣy-ṯꜣ.w*, lit., "carrying the wind), which is the usual way of writing "upstream" since the wind flows north to south in Egypt. Yet the omen also employs the term *ḫd* with the boat and oars determinative , which only can mean flowing downstream from south to north. In this way the omen offers contradictory directions in its hieroglyphic signs and suggests the use of sails to go downstream. For this reason the omen is interpreted as going backward, a reading that is given further visual support by the determinative of backward-facing legs following the word for "running" (*sḫḫ*).

These Mesopotamian and Egyptian examples demonstrate the centrality of writing and the generative role of script in the interpretive process. Despite their differences, the cuneiform and hieroglyphic writing systems both have a large repertoire of signs with polyvalent, logographic, and determinative values. Since divination aimed to control the power inherent in the divine word, and since words and images shared the same ontological framework, the pictographic associations of individual *linguistic* signs were naturally exploited when interpreting *divine* signs.

Viewed from this perspective, the Israelites appear as something of an anomaly, for the Bible's Ten Commandments specifically prohibit the creation of images,[32] but demand the transmission of divine knowledge by way of the written and spoken word. While the legal code rejects all forms of "magical" praxis and divination (e.g., Deuteronomy 18:10–14), the very presence of laws prohibiting such practices, and references to speech and words found elsewhere in the Bible, as I have shown above, imply a belief in the power of words on par with Mesopotamian and Egyptian dogmata. Moreover, while the Hebrew word for a "written mark" אות (*ʾôt*) also means "sign, portent,"[33] the Bible connects the two semantic ranges only in reference to oneiromancy. Thus, Deuteronomy 13:2–6 states that the Israelites perceived dream interpreters as providing אות או מופת (*ʾôt ôw mōfēt*) "a sign or portent." Unlike the Mesopotamians and Egyptians, therefore, the Israelites appear to have reserved

---

[31] Noegel and Szpakowsa 2006: 205–06.

[32] On the conceptual overlap between iconic images and the veneration of the Torah, see van der Toorn 1997.

[33] Though the biblical Hebrew word for "alphabetic letter" is unknown, it is highly likely that it was אות (*ʾôt*). Not only does this word mean "alphabetic letter" in Middle Hebrew (e.g., Babylonian Talmud *Bava Batra* 15a, *Shabbat* 103a, and *Qiddushin* 30a), it derives from a root, i.e., אוה (*ʾāwāh*), which means "inscribe a mark." Thus, some biblical passages employ the word אות (*ʾôt*) in a way that suggests inscribing or writing (e.g., Exodus 13:9, 13:16). The word's appearance for the mark of Cain (Genesis 4:15) has resulted in a variety of interpretations (see Mellinkoff 1981), of which some included writing (e.g., Rashi, Ibn Ezra). Compare the related root תאה (*tāʾāh*) "leave a mark" used in conjunction with the letter ת (*tāw*) in Ezekiel 9:4–6 (spelled out as תו, i.e., *tāw*). See also Job 31:35 where the word תו means "written document" or "signature." The connection of the Hebrew word אות (*ʾôt*) to writing finds support also in the cognate data. In Babylonian Aramaic, אתא (*ʾātāʾ*)is used for a consonantal letter. See Sokoloff 2002: 175, s.v. אתא. The related form יותא *yūtāʾ* means "constellation" (see Sokoloff 2002: 532, s.v. יותא, and compare the Akkadian *šiṭir šamê* "writing of heaven"). The Syriac cognate *ʾātuw* also occurs for "sign," "alphabetic letter," and "constellation." See Smith 1903: 32, s.v. *ʾātuw*. The Arabic cognate too (i.e., *ʾāyat*) means "sign," "mark," and also a Quranic verse(!). See Wehr 1976: 36, s.v. *ʾāyat;* Lane 1968: 135, s.v. *ʾāyat*.

the performative power of the written word for divination by dreams and for texts perceived as authored by Yahweh (see Noegel 2007: 113–82).[34]

I believe that this distinction can be explained, at least in part, by acknowledging the generative role of scripts in shaping Near Eastern conceptions of the divine sign. The Israelites used a consonantal script. Though the Hebrew script evolved from pictographic signs, by the time of the Israelites it had lost its pictographic associations. Consequently, its associative dimension was limited largely to sound devices like paronomasia and polysemous homonyms.

See, for example, a vision of the prophet Amos in which Yahweh shows Amos a basket of "summer fruits" (קיץ, *qayiṣ*), objects that are interpreted as signaling the "end" (קץ, *qēṣ*) of Israel (Amos 8:1–2).[35]

Similarly, in the book of Jeremiah Yahweh shows the prophet an "almond branch" (שקד, *šāqēd*), which is decoded as meaning that Yahweh will "watch" (שקד, *šōqēd*) to ensure that his word is fulfilled (Jeremiah 1:11–12). Like the vision of Amos, the interpretation exploits the phonetic similarity of these homonyms (Noegel 2007: 265).[36]

The examples from Amos and Jeremiah do not entirely rule out the notion that divine signs were written down or conceived of in writing before interpreting them, because homonyms also operate on a visual level. Nevertheless, they do appear to place a greater emphasis on orality in the interpretive process.[37]

Moreover, unlike the Egyptian conception of creation, which permits a role for writing (Frankfurter 1994), the book of Genesis reports creation as solely an oral work, though later Jewish tradition recalls the role of the alphabet in the creative process (Babylonian Talmud *Menahot* 20b; *Midrash Rabbah* 1:10). It therefore seems likely that in the same way that pictographic scripts played formative roles in Mesopotamian and Egyptian conceptions of the divine sign, the non-pictographic script played a role in shaping the Israelite conception.

The Hebrew Bible's preference for referencing oral as opposed to written modes of performative power also might represent a conceptual shift with regard to the perceived locus of this power. In Mesopotamia and Egypt, performative power was centered in the divine sign and script, and was activated by the professional during the processes of speaking, writing, and decoding. Israel inclined toward oral modes of performative power, which naturally centered the locus of power more firmly on the speaker. Consequently, an Israelite could embody the same performative power that a cuneiform or hieroglyphic sign could in Mesopotamia and

---

[34] A related use of ritualistic writing in the ancient Near East, including Israel, is the composing of devotional prayers, see van der Toorn 2008.

[35] Though the two words contain different Proto-Semitic phonemes (i.e., קיץ [*qyẓ*] and קץ [*qṣ*]), by Amos's time the phonemes had merged.

[36] As in the previous example, the two words contain different Proto-Semitic phonemes (i.e., "almond" [*ṯqd*] and "watch" [*šqd*]), but these phonemes already had merged.

[37] The two passages might also reflect an effort to distance Amos and Jeremiah from other divinatory experts, for in both cases, Yahweh both provides the sign and interprets it.

Egypt. This explains why Isaiah could refer to himself and his children as לאות ולמופתים, *lĕʾôt ul-mōftîm* "signs and portents" (Isaiah 8:18),[38] and Ezekiel could be called a אות *ʾôt* "sign" while personifying the siege of Israel (Ezekiel 4:3).[39]

CONCLUSION

In this essay I argue for the importance of viewing the divinatory enterprise through a cosmological lens that brings into focus an ontological understanding of words and script as potentially powerful. I argue for the centrality of writing in the exegetical process and I suggest that we see the interpretation of divine signs as an act of ritual and ideological power that serves to promote the cosmological system upon which divination is based. Building upon these observations, I offer some explorative thoughts on the generative role that scripts play in shaping ancient Near Eastern conceptions of the divine sign. As research continues on this subject it is my hope that scholars pay greater attention to such topics and test the framework I provide here.

[38] It is important to distinguish here what I have called the locus or embodiment of divine power from the perceived source of this power. As abundant biblical texts make clear, the Israelite prophets and their audiences perceived the power to be divine in origin even if embodied in a prophet. Yet, the fact that prophets could be called an אות *ʾôt* "sign" means that their bodies served to encode divine meaning in a way that the cuneiform and hieroglyphic scripts did in Mesopotamia and Egypt. This does not mean that writing did not retain its cosmological significance for the prophets. As we see in Isaiah 8:1, Yahweh commanded Isaiah to write the divine signs on a large scroll. The signs (i.e., מהר שלל חש בז *mahēr šālāl ḥāš baz* "swift is the booty, speedy is the prey") would later become the name of his son. Note also that in Isaiah 8:19 the function of Isaiah and his children as "signs and portents" is placed in contradistinction to those who seek oracles from necromancers and other diviners.

[39] Note also that even an idolatrous man could become an אות *ʾôt* "sign" (Ezekiel 14:8). It also is of considerable interest that at Mari a prophet also could be called an *ittu* "sign." See Durand 1982: 44 and the Epic of Zimri-Lim, line 139, cited in Nissinen 2000a: 263. Curious is the mention in Atrahasis I 215–16 of a human ghost proclaiming the living human as *ittaša* "its sign." In Israel, the shift in the locus of performative power from the written sign to spoken word to the individual perhaps prefigures the role of the rabbi in late antiquity who embodied for his disciples the Oral Torah (Jaffee 2001).

ABBREVIATIONS

CAD	A. Leo Oppenheim et al., editors, *The Assyrian Dictionary of the Oriental Institute of the University of Chicago*
YOS 10	Goetze 1947

BIBLIOGRAPHY

Alexander, Philip

1995 "*Bavli Berakhot* 55a–57b: The Talmudic Dreambook in Context." *Journal of Jewish Studies* 46: 231–48.

Alster, Bendt

1992 "Interaction of Oral and Written Poetry in Early Mesopotamian Literature." In *Mesopotamian Epic Literature: Oral or Aural?*, edited by M. E. Vogelzang and H. L. J. Vanstiphout, pp. 23–69. Lewiston: Edwin Mellen.

Andrews, C. A. R.

1993 "Unpublished Demotic Texts in the British Museum." In *Life in a Multi-Cultural Society: Egypt from Cambyses to Constantine and Beyond*, edited J. H. Johnson, pp. 9–14. Studies in Ancient Oriental Civilization 51. Chicago: The Oriental Institute.

1994 "Unpublished Demotic Papyri in the British Museum." In *Acta Demotica: Acts of the Fifth International Conference for Demotists. Pisa, 4th–8th September 1993*, edited by E. Bresciani, pp. 29–37. Egitto e Vicino Oriente 17. Pisa: Giardini.

Assmann, Jan

1990 *Ma'at: Gerechtigkeit und Unsterblichkeit im alten Ägypten*. Munich: C. H. Beck.

Austin, J. L.

1962 *How To Do Things with Words*. The William James Lectures 1955. Cambridge: Harvard University Press.

Bahrani, Zainab

2003 *The Graven Image: Representation in Babylonia and Assyria*. Philadelphia: University of Pennsylvania Press.

2008 *Rituals of War: The Body and Violence in Mesopotamia*. New York: Zone Books.

Bilbija, Jovan

2008 "Interpreting the Interpretation: Protasis-Apodosis-Strings in the Physiognomic Omen Series *Šumma Alamdimmû* 3.76–132." In *Studies in Ancient Near Eastern World View and Society Presented to Marten Stol on the Occasion of His 65th Birthday, 10 November 2005, and His Retirement from Vrije Universiteit Amsterdam*, edited by R. J. van der Spek, pp. 19–27. Bethesda: CDL Press.

Bohak, Gideon

2008 *Ancient Jewish Magic: A History*. Cambridge: Cambridge University Press.

Böhl, Franz M. Th.

1916 "Mummu = Logos?" *Orientalistische Literaturzeitung* 19: 265–68.

Borger, Rykle

1957 "*Niṣirti bārûti*, Geheimlehre der Haruspizin." *Bibliotheca Orientalis* 5/6: 190–95.

Bottéro, Jean

1974 "Symptômes, signes, écritures en Mésopotamie ancienne." In *Divination et rationalité*, edited by J. P. Vernant, pp. 70–197. Sources orientales 2. Paris: Seuil.

Budge, E. A. Wallis

1913 *The Papyrus of Ani*, Vol. 3. New York: G. P. Putnam's Sons; London: Philip Lee Warner.

Contenau, Georges

1955 *Everyday Life in Babylon and Assyria*. London: Edward Arnold.

Cryer, Frederick H.

1994 *Divination in Ancient Israel and Its Near Eastern Environment: A Socio-Historical Investigation*. Journal for the Study of the Old Testament, Supplement Series 142. Sheffield: Sheffield Academic Press.

Demichelis, S.

2002 "La divination par l'huile à l'époque ramesside." In *La magie en Égypte: À la recherché d'une définition; Actes du colloque organisé par le musée du Louvre les 29 et 30 septembre 2000*, edited by Y. Koenig, pp. 149–65. Paris: Musée du Louvre.

Durand, Jean-Marie

1982 "In Vino Veritas." *Revue d'Assyriologie* 76: 43–50.

Dürr, Lorenz

1938 *Die Wertung des göttlichen Wortes im Alten Testament und in antiken Orient*. Mitteilungen der Vorderasiatisch-ägyptischen Gesellschaft 42/1. Leipzig: Hinrichs.

Finkel, Asher

1963 "The *Pesher* of Dreams and Scriptures." *Revue de Qumran* 15: 357–70.

Fishbane, Michael

1977 "The Qumran *Pesher* and Traits of Ancient Hermeneutics." In *Proceedings of the Sixth World Congress of Jewish Studies, Hebrew University of Jerusalem, 13–19. August, 1973*, edited by M. Jagendorf and A. Shinan, pp. 97–113. Jerusalem: World Union of Jewish Studies.

Frankfurter, David

1994 "The Magic of Writing and the Writing of Magic: The Power of the Word in Egyptian and Greek Traditions." *Helios* 21: 189–221.

Freedman, Sally M.

1998 *If a City Is Set on a Height: The Akkadian Omen Series* Šumma Ālu ina Mēlê Šakin, Vol. 1, *Tables 1–21*. Occasional Publications of the Samuel Noah Kramer Fund 17. Philadelphia: University of Pennsylvania Museum.

Gardiner, Alan H.

1935 *Hieratic Papyri in the British Museum, Third Series: Chester Beatty Gift*. 2 volumes. London: British Museum.

1988 *Egyptian Grammar*. Oxford: Griffith Institute.

Geller, Markham J.

1998 "New Documents from the Dead Sea: Babylonian Science in Aramaic." In *Boundaries of the Ancient Near Eastern World: A Tribute to Cyrus H. Gordon*, edited by M. Lubetski, C. Gottlieb, and S. Keller, pp. 224–29. Journal for the Study of the Old Testament, Supplement 273. Sheffield: Sheffield Academic Press.

George, Andrew

2001–2002 "Palace Names and Epithets, and the Vaulted Building." *Sumer* 51: 38–42.

Goetze, Albrecht
1947 *Old Babylonian Omen Texts*. Yale Oriental Series, Babylonian Texts 10. New Haven: Yale University Press. Second printing, 1966.

Greaves, Sheldon W.
1996 The Power of the Word in the Ancient Near East. Ph.D. dissertation, University of California, Berkeley.

Guinan, Ann K.
1996 "Social Constructions and Private Designs: The House Omens of *Šumma Ālu*." In *Houses and Households in Ancient Mesopotamia: Papers Read at the 40e Rencontre Assyriologique Internationale, Leiden, July 5–8, 1993*, edited by K. R. Veenhof, pp. 61–68. Istanbul: Nederlands Historisch-Archaeologisch Instituut te Istanbul.

Hehn, J.
1906 "Hymnen und Gebete an Marduk." *Beiträge zur Assyriologie* 5: 279–400.

Heinisch, P.
1922 "Das 'Wort' im Alten Testament und im alten Orient." *Biblische Zeitfragen* 10/7–8: 3–52.

Hodge, Carleton T.
1975 "Ritual and Writing: An Inquiry into the Origin of Egyptian Script." In *Linguistics and Anthropology: In Honor of C. F. Voegelin*, edited by M. D. Kinkade, pp. 331–50. Lisse: Peter de Ridder.

Horowitz, Wayne
1998 *Mesopotamian Cosmic Geography*. Winona Lake: Eisenbrauns.

Jaffee, Martin S.
2001 *Torah in the Mouth: Writing and Oral Tradition in Palestinian Judaism, 200 BCE–400 CE*. Oxford: Oxford University Press.

Jassen, Alex P.
2007 *Mediating the Divine: Prophecy and Revelation in the Dead Sea Scrolls and Second Temple Judaism*. Leiden and Boston: Brill.

Jeffers, Ann
1996 *Magic and Divination in Ancient Palestine and Syria*. Leiden: Brill.

Jeyes, Ulla
1989 *Old Babylonian Extispicy: Omen Texts in the British Museum*. Istanbul: Nederlands Historisch-Archaeologisch Instituut te Istanbul.

Lambert, Wilfred G.
1957 "Ancestors, Authors, and Canonicity." *Journal of Cuneiform Studies* 11: 1–14.
1967 "Enmeduranki and Related Matters." *Journal of Cuneiform Studies* 21: 126–38.
2007 *Babylonian Oracle Questions*. Winona Lake: Eisenbrauns.

Lane, Edward William
1968 *Arabic-English Lexicon*, Part 1. Beirut: Librairie du Liban.

Langdon, S.
1918 "The Babylonian Conception of the Logos." *Journal of the Royal Asiatic Society* July 1918: 433–49.

Larsen, Mogens Trolle
1987 "The Mesopotamian Lukewarm Mind: Reflections on Science, Divination, and Literacy." In *Language, Literature, and History: Philological and Historical Studies Presented to Erica Reiner*, edited by F. Rochberg-Halton, pp. 203–25. New Haven: American Oriental Society.

Lawson, Jack N.

2001 "Mesopotamian Precursors to the Stoic Concept of Logos." In *Mythology and Mythologies: Methodological Approaches to Intercultural Influences; Proceedings of the Second Annual Symposium of the Assyrian and Babylonian Intellectual Heritage Project Held in Paris, France, October 4–7, 1999*, edited by R. M. Whiting, pp. 69–91. Melammu Symposia 2. Helsinki: The Neo-Assyrian Text Corpus Project.

Leick, Gwendolyn

1994 *Sex and Eroticism in Mesopotamian Literature*. London: Routledge.

1998 "The Challenge of Chance: An Anthropological View of Mesopotamian Mental Strategies for Dealing with the Unpredictable." In *Intellectual Life in the Ancient Near East: Papers Presented at the 43rd Rencontre Assyriologique Internationale, Prague, July 1–5, 1996*, edited by J. Prosecky, pp. 195–208. Prague: Academy of Sciences of the Czech Republic, Oriental Institute.

Lenzi, Alan

2008a *Secrecy and the Gods: Secret Knowledge in Ancient Mesopotamia and Biblical Israel*. State Archives of Assyria Studies 19. Helsinki: Neo-Assyrian Text Corpus Project.

2008b "The Uruk List of Kings and Sages and Late Mesopotamian Scholarship." *Journal of Ancient Near Eastern Religions* 8: 137–69.

Lieberman, Stephen J.

1977 "The Names of the Cuneiform Graphemes in Old Babylonian Akkadian." In *Essays on the Ancient Near East in Memory of Jacob Joel Finkelstein*, edited by M. de Jong Ellis, pp. 147–54. *Memoirs of the Connecticut Academy of Arts and Sciences* 19. Hamden: Archon Books.

1978 "A Mesopotamian Background for the So-Called *Aggadic* "Measures" of Biblical Hermeneutics?" *Hebrew Union College Annual* 58: 157–225.

Livingstone, Alasdair

1986 *Mystical and Mythological Explanatory Works of Assyrian and Babylonian Scholars*. Oxford: Clarendon Press.

MacDowell, A. G.

1990 *Jurisdiction in the Workmen's Community of Deir el-Medînah*. Egyptologische Uitgaven 5. Leiden: Nederlands Instituut voor het Nabje Oosten.

Masing, Hugo

1936 *The Word of Yahweh*. Tartu: Mattiesen.

Matouš, Lubor, and Wolfram von Soden

1933 *Die lexikalischen Tafelserien der Babylonier und Assyrer in den Berliner Museen*. Vol. 2, *Die akkadischen Synonymenlisten*. Berlin: Staatliche Museen.

Maul, Stefan M.

1994 *Zukunftsbewältigung: Eine Untersuchung altorientalischen Denkens anhand der babylonisch-assyrischen Löserituale (Namburbi)*. Mainz am Rhein: Philipp von Zabern.

Mauss, Marcel

1972 *A General Theory of Magic*. London: Routledge and Kegan Paul.

Mellinkoff, Ruth

1981 *The Mark of Cain*. Berkeley: University of California Press.

Michalowski, Piotr

1990a "Early Mesopotamian Communicative Systems: Art, Literature, and Writing." In *Investigating Artistic Environments in the Ancient Near East*, edited by A. C. Gunter, pp. 53–69. Washington, D.C.: Smithsonian Institution.

1990b "Presence at the Creation." In *Lingering Over Words: Studies in Ancient Near Eastern Literature in Honor of William L. Moran*, edited by T. Abusch, J. Huehnergard, and P. Steinkeller, pp. 381–96. Harvard Semitic Studies 37. Atlanta: Scholars Press.

1996 "Sailing to Babylon: Reading the Dark Side of the Moon." In *The Study of the Ancient Near East in the Twenty-First Century: The William Foxwell Albright Centennial Conference*, edited by J. S. Cooper and G. M. Schwartz, pp. 177–93. Winona Lake: Eisenbrauns.

Morenz, Siegfried

1973 *Egyptian Religion*. Translated by Ann E. Keep. Ithaca: Cornell University Press.

Moriarty, F. L.

1974 "Word as Power in the Ancient Near East." In *A Light Unto My Path: Old Testament Studies in Honor of J. M. Myers*, edited by H. N. Bream, pp. 345–62. Philadelphia: Temple University.

Nielsen, Kirsten

1978 *Yahweh as Prosecutor and Judge: An Investigation of the Prophetic Lawsuit (Rîb Pattern)*. Translated by Frederick Cryer. Journal for the Study of the Old Testament, Supplement 9. Sheffield: Journal for the Study of the Old Testament Press.

Nissinen, Martti

2000a "Spoken, Written, Quoted, and Invented: Orality and Writtenness in Ancient Near Eastern Prophecy." In *Writings and Speech in Israelite and Ancient Near Eastern Prophecy*, edited by E. Ben Zvi and M. H. Floyd, pp. 235–71. Society of Biblical Literature, Symposium Series 10. Atlanta: Society of Biblical Literature.

2000b "The Socioreligious Role of the Neo-Assyrian Prophets." In *Prophecy in Its Ancient Near Eastern Context: Mesopotamian, Biblical, and Arabian Perspectives*, edited by M. Nissinen, pp. 89–114. Society of Biblical Literature, Symposium Series 13. Atlanta: Society of Biblical Literature.

Forthcoming "*Pesharim* as Divination: Qumran Exegesis, Omen Interpretation and Literary Prophecy." In *On Prophecy in the Dead Sea Scrolls and in the Hebrew Bible*, edited by K. de Troyer and A. Lange. Leuven: Peeters.

Noegel, Scott B.

1995 "Fox on the Run: Catch a Lamassu by the Pun." *Nouvelles Assyriologiques Brèves et Utilitaires* 1995/4: 101–02.

2004 "New Observations on Scribal Activity in the Ancient Near East." In *Voice, Text and Hypertext at the Millennium: Emerging Practices in Textual Studies*, edited by R. Modiano, L. F. Searle, and P. Shillinsburg, pp. 133–43. Seattle: University of Washington Press.

2007 *Nocturnal Ciphers: The Allusive Language of Dreams in the Ancient Near East*. American Oriental Series 89. New Haven: American Oriental Society.

In press "The Ritual Use of Linguistic and Textual Violence in the Hebrew Bible and Ancient Near East." In *Ritual and Violence*, edited by Margo Kitts. Ritual Dynamics and the Science of Ritual 3. Wiesbaden: Harrassowitz.

Noegel, Scott B., and Kasia Szpakowsa

2006 "'Word Play' in the Ramesside Dream Manual." *Studien zur altägyptischen Kultur* 35: 193–212.

Nougayrol, Jean

1944–45 "Note sur la place des 'présages historiques' dans l'extispicine babylonienne." *École pratique de hautes études, 5e section, Annuaire* 1944–45: 1–41.

Oppenheim, A. Leo

1956 *The Interpretation of Dreams in the Ancient Near East: With a Translation of the Assyrian Dream Book*. Transactions of the American Philosophical Society 46/3. Philadelphia: American Philosophical Society.

Paul, M.

1973 "Heavenly Tablets and the Book of Life." *Journal of the Ancient Near Eastern Society of Columbia University* 5: 345–53.

Pinch, Geraldine

1994 *Magic in Ancient Egypt*. Austin: University of Texas Press.

Pongratz-Leisten, Beate

1999 *Herrschaftswissen in Mesopotamien: Formen der Kommunikation zwischen Gott und König im 2. und 1. Jahrtausend v. Chr.* State Archives of Assyria Studies 10. Helsinki: The Neo-Assyrian Text Corpus Project.

Quack, Joachim Freidrich

2006 "A Black Cat from the Right, and a Scarab on Your Head: New Sources for Ancient Egyptian Divination." In *Through a Glass Darkly: Magic, Dreams, and Prophecy in Ancient Egypt*, edited by K. Szpakowska, pp. 175–87. Wales: Classical Press of Wales.

Rabinowitz, Isaac

1973 "*Pēsher/Pittārōn*": Its Biblical Meaning and Its Significance in the Qumran Literature." *Revue de Qumran* 8: 219–32.

1993 *A Witness Forever: Ancient Israel's Perception of Literature and the Resultant Hebrew Bible*. Bethesda: CDL Press.

Reiner, Erica

1960 "Fortune Telling in Mesopotamia." *Journal of Near Eastern Studies* 19: 23–35.

1995 *Astral Magic in Babylonia*. Transactions of the American Philosophical Society 85/4. Philadelphia: American Philosophical Society.

Ritner, Robert K.

1993 *The Mechanics of Ancient Egyptian Magical Practice*. Studies in Ancient Oriental Civilization 54. Chicago: The Oriental Institute.

1995 "The Religious, Social, and Legal Parameters of Traditional Egyptian Magic." In *Ancient Magic and Ritual Power*, edited by M. Meyer and P. Mirecki, pp. 43–60. Religions in the Graeco-Roman World 129. Leiden: Brill.

Roaf, Michael, and Annette Zgoll

2001 "Assyrian Hieroglyphs: Lord Aberdeen's Black Stone and the Prisms of Esarhaddon." *Zeitschrift für die alttestamentliche Wissenschaft* 91: 264–95.

Rochberg, Francesca

1999 "Empiricism in Babylonian Omen Texts and the Classification of Mesopotamian Divination as Science." *Journal of the American Oriental Society* 119: 559–69.

2003 "Heaven and Earth: Divine-Human Relations in Mesopotamian Celestial Divination." In *Prayer, Magic, and the Stars in the Ancient and Late Antique World*, edited by S. B. Noegel, J. Walker, and B. Wheeler, pp. 169–85. University Park: Pennsylvania State University Press.

2004 *The Heavenly Writing: Divination, Horoscopy, and Astronomy in Mesopotamian Culture*. Cambridge: Cambridge University Press.

Rubio, Gonzalo

2006 "Writing in Another Tongue: Alloglottography in the Ancient Near East." In *Margins of Writing, Origins of Cultures*, edited by S. Sanders, pp. 33–66. Oriental Institute Seminars 2. Chicago: The Oriental Institute.

Sanders, Seth
2004 "Performative Utterances and Divine Language in Ugaritic." *Journal of the Ancient Near Eastern Society of Columbia University* 63: 161–81.

Sauneron, Serge
2000 *The Priests of Ancient Egypt*. Translated by David Lorton. Ithaca: Cornell University Press.

Searle, John R.
1969 *Speech Acts: An Essay in the Philosophy of Language*. London: Cambridge University Press.

Shaked, Shaul
1998 "The Poetics of Spells: Language and Structure in Aramaic Incantations of Late Antiquity, 1: The Divorce Formula and its Ramifications." In *Mesopotamian Magic: Textual, Historical, and Interpretive Perspectives*, edited by T. Abusch and K. van der Toorn, pp. 173–95. Studies in Ancient Magic and Divination 1. Groningen: Styx.

Sjöberg, A. W.
1972 "In Praise of the Scribal Art." *Journal of Cuneiform Studies* 24: 126–31.

Smith, J. Payne
1903 *A Compendious Syriac Dictionary*. Oxford: Clarendon Press.

Snoek, J. A. M.
2008 Defining "Rituals." In *Theorizing Rituals: Issues, Topics, Approaches, Concepts*, edited by J. Kreinath, J. Snoek, and M. Stausberg, pp. 3–14. Leiden: Brill.

Sokoloff, Michael
2002 *A Dictionary of Jewish Babylonian Aramaic*. Ramat Gan: Bar Ilan University Press; Baltimore: Johns Hopkins University Press.

Sweek, Joel
1996 Dreams of Power from Sumer to Judah: An Essay on the Divinatory Economy of the Ancient Near East. Ph.D. dissertation, University of Chicago.

Szpakowska, Kasia
2003 *Behind Closed Eyes: Dreams and Nightmares in Ancient Egypt*. Swansea: Classical Press of Wales.

Tambiah, Stanley J.
1968 "The Magical Power of Words." *Man* 3: 175–208.
1973 "The Form and Meaning of Magical Acts: A Point of View." In *Modes of Thought: Essays on Thinking in Western and Non-Western Societies*, edited by R. Horton and R. Finnegan, pp. 194–229. London: Faber.
1985 *Culture, Thought and Social Action: An Anthropological Perspective*. Cambridge: Harvard University Press.

Teeter, Emily
1997 *The Presentation of Maat: Ritual and Legitimacy in Ancient Egypt*. Studies in Oriental Civilization 57. Chicago: The Oriental Institute.

Tigay, Jeffrey H.
1983 "An Early Technique of Aggadic Exegesis." In *History, Historiography, and Interpretation: Studies in Biblical and Cuneiform Literatures*, edited by H. Tadmor and M. Weinfeld, pp. 169–89. Jerusalem: Magnes Press.

Turner, Victor
1974 *Dramas, Fields, and Metaphors: Symbolic Action in Human Society*. Ithaca: Cornell University Press.

van der Toorn, Karel

1997 "The Iconic Book: Analogies between the Babylonian Cult of Images and the Veneration of the Torah." In *The Image and the Book: Iconic Cults, Aniconism, and the Rise of Book Religion in Israel and the Ancient Near East*, edited by Karel van der Toorn, pp. 229–48. Leuven: Peeters.

2008 "Votive Texts and Letter-Prayers: Writing as a Devotional Practice." In *Studies in Ancient Near Eastern World View and Society Presented to Marten Stol on the Occasion of His 65th Birthday, 10 November 2005, and His Retirement from Vrije Universiteit Amsterdam*, edited by R. J. van der Spek, pp. 39–46. Bethesda: CDL Press.

Volten, Aksel

1942 *Demotische Traumdeutung (Pap. Carslberg XIII und XIV Verso)*. Analecta Aegyptiaca 3. Copenhagen: Einar Munsgaard.

von Lieven, A.

1999 "Divination in Ägypten." *Altorientalische Forschungen* 26: 77–126.

Wehr, Hans

1976 *Arabic-English Dictionary*. Ithaca: Spoken Language Services.

Westenholz, Joan Goodnick

1998 "Thoughts on Esoteric Knowledge and Secret Lore." In *Intellectual Life in the Ancient Near East: Papers Presented at the 43rd Rencontre Assyriologique Internationale, Prague, July 1–5, 1996*, edited by J. Prosecky, pp. 451–62. Prague: Academy of Sciences of the Czech Republic, Oriental Institute.

9

THE CALCULATION OF THE STIPULATED TERM IN EXTISPICY

NILS P. HEEßEL, UNIVERSITY OF HEIDELBERG

Among the many different divinatory methods used in Mesopotamia, the practice of extispicy stands apart. It has always been of special importance to society as it represents the only means of direct communication between mankind and the realm of the gods. While other divinatory genres are concerned with signs as messages from the gods and sacrifice represents a human way to beseech the gods, they remain techniques for a one-way contact. Quite on the contrary, extispicy functions in both directions and therefore it is real communication: A human being formulates a question that can be answered with "yes" or "no," the gods decide upon the answer and write their decision within the entrails of a sacrificial animal. Extispicy makes it possible to communicate with the divine sphere in order to find out the will of the gods concerning specific events and to align one's deeds with it. Therefore, extispicy has been called a "checking technique,"[1] which coordinates a planned action with the will of the gods. This possibility to communicate with the divine sphere can be seen as a highly stabilizing factor for a community, as the society could be sure to live in accordance with the decrees of the gods.

However, the will of the gods, even when formulated as a simple yes-or-no answer to a predetermined question, was not easy to read. For the gods gave their answers not for free, but only after a sacrifice had been made; a sacrifice that represented something valuable for the person seeking a divine answer to a question, be it cedar from a diviner, flour from a widow, oil from a poor woman, or a lamb from a rich man.[2] No matter how poor or rich a person might be, in order to get an answer from the gods one had to sacrifice something valuable for oneself. And the answer of the gods was not communicated by a dream or a revelation, in a form that anyone could easily understand, but it was written within the physical material of the sacrifice, in the shape of either sprinkled flour, the smoke generated by burned cedar wood, or oil poured in water. However, the most sophisticated technique was always to read the entrails of a sacrificial lamb, into which the gods wrote the answer to a question. Numerous passages illustrate that especially the liver of the sacrificial lamb was regarded as the "tablet of the gods."[3] And, therefore, the different elements of the liver surface, its marks, colors, sizes, and so on, could be viewed as a script that like cuneiform signs could be pieced together into a meaningful whole. In order to be able to read the answer, one had to be initiated in the art of extispicy and have a thorough understanding of the correct interpretation of extispicy results. These hermeneutics of extispicy are quite straightforward at first glance, as the rules

[1] Pongratz-Leisten (1999: 12, 14) uses the German term "Vergewisserungssystem," which describes extispicy well, contra Brown 2004: 113f.

[2] *na-šak-ka* DUMU ^{lú}ḪAL ^{giš}EREN ^{munus}*al-mat-tú* ZÌ.MAD.GÁ *la-pu-un-tú* Ì+GIŠ *šá-ru-u ina šá-ru-ti-šú na-ši* ^{udu}SILA$_4$ "(Oh Šamaš,) the diviner brings you cedar, the widow roasted flour, the poor woman oil, the rich from his wealth brings you a lamb" K. 3333 iii 9′–10′ // KAR 252 iii 21–23 // K. 3286 (Gray 1900/1: pl. 3) 3–6; see Oppenheim 1956: 301 and 340.

[3] Lambert 1998, 148, line 8, 149 lines 14 and 16; Maul 2003–05: 76f.

of interpretation follow the basic principles of society which are at the same time the basis for the interpretation of other divinatory genres. Simple examples are: right is positive, left is negative, white is good, black is bad, etc.[4] But it does not end with this simple interpretation. Certain marks had their own value of interpretation that might affect the basic rules,[5] signs had to be evaluated according to their exact location, different signs had to be balanced against each other, and certain signs called *nipḫu* or *pitruštu* could affect and, indeed, change the result of the whole extispicy to the opposite[6] — and it is here at the latest where it becomes increasingly difficult for modern scholars to understand the rationale of Babylonian extispicy. And so Babylonian scholars put layer on layer of interpretation and the implications of each layer need to be assessed for their impact on the preceding layers of interpretation. One of the particularly enigmatic layers of interpretation is set forth in a group of texts called "Calculation of the Stipulated Term" that problematize the time period in which a given extispicy result can justly expect validity.

The earliest references to the use of a certain time period in extispcy can be found in Old Babylonian Mari, where extispicies are said to be taken for a specified time, for example for the well-being of a city or an area "for one month."[7] However, in Mari the technical term *adannu* for the "stipulated term" is not (yet) used, but the time period for the validity of the extsipicy result is usually rendered as: *têrētim ana šulum alim*/*ṣabim*/GN *ana* U_4 X-KÁM *ēpuš* "I made extispicies for the well-being of the town/troops/GN for x days/months." In the extispicy queries taken at the court of the Sargonid kings the "stipulated term" (*adannu*), is mentioned frequently as a predetermined period of time, which is often well defined.[8] This chronological range shows that the idea of a certain time period, for which a given extispicy was considered valid, had already been developed when the first extispicy texts were written down and that it was carried on until the end of cuneiform culture.

In the Old-Babylonian texts from Mari as well as in the extispicy queries from Ninive the time period for the validity of extispicies could be artificially defined by the person carrying out the extispicy. However, in addition to this simple system of fixing a certain time period for the extispicy, a handful of texts present us with more elaborate rules for the calculation of the stipulated term. These texts have been recently edited by Ulla Susanne Koch;[9] while Koch was not the first in editing a text of this particular enigmatic group of extispicy treatises — this was Ernst Weidner already in 1917 — she was first in putting them in a coherent context and to explain the basic rules governing the texts. This group of texts makes it clear that the stipulated term can be extrapolated by the appearance of the finger (*ubānu*), one of the basic elements of the sheep's liver. The finger, today called the *processus caudatus* by veterinary surgeons,[10] is a piece of flesh sticking out of the liver, having three rather flat sides or surfaces. All these texts use the most common marks — *piṭrū* "notches," *šīlū* "holes," and *kakkū* "weapons" — placed on the three zones (top, middle, basis) of the two outer surfaces of the finger to calculate the stipulated term. As Ulla Koch has shown, the significance of

[4] For these basic rules of interpretation, see Starr 1983: 15–24.

[5] The different marks have been studied, inter alia, by Meyer 1987; Leiderer 1990; Koch-Westenholz 2000: 43–70.

[6] For *nipḫu* and *pitruštu*, see Koch 2005: 10–22, with older literature.

[7] See the examples listed in Starr 1990: p. XVII, and add the information compiled in Durand 1988: 57–59.

[8] See Starr 1990: pp. XVIf.

[9] Koch 2005: 459–79.

[10] For the identification of *ubānu*, see Jeyes 1989: 65; Leiderer 1990: 119–34; and Koch-Westenholz 2000: 69f. For a good picture of the "finger" (*ubānu*), see Leiderer 1990: 182f.

the zones of the finger is quite straightforward, as the stipulated term depends on how many marks appear in which zone of the finger:[11]

	Right/Left Surface 1 mark	*Right/Left Surface 2 marks*	*Right/Left Surface 3 marks*
Top	1	4	7
Middle	2	5	8
Basis	3	6	9

But in order to calculate the stipulated term another factor has to be known. This is the *rēš adanni* "the basis for (the calculation of) the stipulated term." The *rēš adanni* again depended on two factors:

1. The time period for which the extispicy should be performed, usually a day, a month, or a year. This is phrased in the texts as "If you perform the extispicy for a day/a month/a year."
2. The *uddazallû*, the "correction," which represents the constant coefficient.

The time period for which the extispicy is performed is multiplied with the *uddazallû*, the constant correction, as well as with a certain number, and the result of this multiplication is in turn multiplied with the number gained from the observation of the marks on the outer surfaces of the finger. This result then represents the *adannu*, the time period for which the extispicy is actually valid.

But what exactly is the *uddazallû*, the constant correction in extispicy, and with what exact value is it to be multiplied? Ulla Koch has shown that the *uddazallû* in extispicy differs from the *uddazallû* for astronomical purposes as laid down in the astronomical compendium Mul.apin.[12] In extispicy the *uddazallû* according to the text K. 4061, published in CT 31/16, and 18[13] that lays down these rules, seems to be 6 2/3 (or: 6,666) for one day. However, the relevant passage in K. 4061, which might explain why this is the value of the *uddazallû*, is broken, as K. 4061 is only the lower left edge of the original tablet. However, while looking for parallels to the extispicy texts from Assur among the Ninive texts in the British Museum (siglum K.) I was able to find the missing right side of that tablet. By this new join (K. 4061 + K. 10344) it becomes clear that the *uddazallû* was multiplied with three times the *šikin ubāni* "shape of the finger" (see the Appendix and figs. 9.1–2). The relevant passage reads:

7′ *šum-ma a-na* MU 1-KÁM DÙ-*uš* 0;6,40 *ud-da-zal-le-e* u_4*-mi a-na* 6 UŠ u_4*-mi* 0;6,40 ÍL-*ma*

8′ 0;6,40 A.RÁ 360 40 *tam-mar* 40 *ud-da-zal-le-e* MU 1-KÁM <u>*a-na* 3 *ši-kin* ŠU.SI *i-ši-ma*</u>

9′ 40 A.RÁ 3 120 *tam-mar* 120 4 ITI *ina* NÍG.KA_9 *i-ta-bal*

10′ *ana* MU 1-KÁM *a-dan-na* GAR-*an* SAG *a-dan-ni-ka* 120

[11] Koch 2005: 65.

[12] Koch 2005: 64.

[13] Transliterated and translated by Koch (2005: 471–74).

7′ If you perform (the extispicy) for one year, then 1/9 is the correction of a day, multiply (it) with 360 days and

8′ you will see that 1/9 times 360 is 40. 40 is the correction (*uddazallû*) for one year; multiply (it) with the three shapes of the finger (*šikin ubāni*) and

9′ you will see that 40 times 3 is 120. 120 corresponds to four months in the result.

10′ (If) you determine the period for a year, (then) the basis for (the calculation of) your period is 120.

The still enigmatic term *šikin ubāni* appears several times in the so-called DUB ḪA.LA texts, but we are far from really understanding what it means.[14] According to K. 4061 + K. 10344 obv. 8′, it seems reasonable to view *šikin ubāni* as a synonym to the surface of the finger (*ṣēr ubāni*). This would further support the convincing idea put forward by Ulla Koch, that the reciprocal of the *uddazallû* in extispicy being 9 corresponds to the three surfaces of the finger and their subdivision into the zones top/middle/basis.[15]

But this new join also puts into question the previously assumed number for the *uddazallû* in extispicy. In his first edition of this text Ernst Weidner (1917: 260) read the number of the *uddazallû* as 6 2/3 and all scholars followed him. However, a given number in the cuneiform sexagesimal writing system has many possible readings, as, for example, one vertical wedge can stand for the numbers 1, 60, 3600 and so on or even 1/60, 1/3600, etc.[16] The actual value, be it 60 times higher or lower, can only be determined through the context. The new text K. 4061 + K. 10344 shows that the *uddazallû* is to be multiplied with the three *šikin ubāni* and not, as was formerly surmised, with the number 3/60 (or 1/20). Since it is much more likely that there are three *šikin ubāni* and that they refer to the surfaces of the finger, we have to lower the *uddazallû* by the factor 60, which is perfectly possible in all texts. So instead of the formerly assumed *uddazallû* of 6 2/3 for a day, 200 for a month and 2400 for a year we now have an *uddazallû* of 1/9 for a day, 3 1/3 for a month, and 40 for a year.

Now, having established the actual value of the *uddazallû* and its multiplication with the three shapes of the finger (*šikin ubāni*), we can derive a formula for the "calculation of the stipulated term":

(planned time period × *uddazallû* × 3 *šikin ubāni*) × marks on the finger = *adannu*

The first multiplications in the parentheses constitute the *rēš adanni*, the basis for the stipulated term, which is then multiplied with the value of the marks on the finger. To illustrate this, we can now analyze lines 7′–16′ of the obverse of K. 4061 + K. 10344, which in its first section explains the rules for the calculation of the *rēš adanni*, which we have used to derive the formula, and in the second section actually calculates the stipulated term (*adannu*) by multiplying the *rēš adanni* with the results from the observed marks on the finger.

7′ If you perform (the extispicy) for one year, then 1/9 is the correction (*uddazallû*) of a day; multiply (it) with 360 days, and

8′ you will see that 1/9 times 360 is 40. 40 is the correction (*uddazallû*) for one year; multiply (it) with the three shapes of the finger (*šikin ubāni*) and

[14] For *šikin ubāni*, see the discussion in Borger 1957: 191f. For the DUB ḪA.LA texts, see the edition in Koch 2005: nos. 90–95.

[15] Koch 2005: 64f.

[16] See Friberg 1987–90: 533f.

9′ you will see that 40 times 3 is 120. 120 corresponds to four months in the result.

10′ (If) you determine the period for a year, (then) the basis for (the calculation of) your period (*rēš adanni*) is 120.

11′ If a hole lies in the top of the right surface of the finger: 120 times 1 is 120, 4 months. The enemy will besiege and seize the town,

12′ in battle: defeat of the army, it will rain, a patient will recover.

13′ If a hole lies in the middle of the right surface of the finger: 120 times 2 is [240], 8 months. The enemy will besiege and seize the town,

14′ in battle: defeat of the army, it will rain, a patient will recover.

15′ If a hole lies in the basis of the right surface of the finger: 120 times 3 is [360, one ye]ar. The enemy will besiege and seize the town,

16′ in battle: defeat of the army, it will rain, a patient will recover.

The planned time period is a year or 360 days, the *uddazallû*-correction is 1/9 and this together with the 3 *šikin ubāni* gives a number of 120 for the basis of the calculation (*rēš adanni*). This is now multiplied with the value gained from one hole in the different zones[17] of the finger in order to get the result for the stipulated term (*adannu*).

From these texts for the calculation of the stipulated term, two important aspects for the Babylonian understanding of extispicy can be deduced: First, the *adannu*, the time period in which the extispicy is actually valid, is not necessarily identical with the time period for which the extispicy is performed. Even if a diviner "performs the extispicy for a year," its *adannu* can be shorter or longer, or it can be identical, but this depends on the calculation of the stipulated term and, therefore, on the observation how many marks are located on the different surfaces of the finger. When a Babylonian diviner "performs an extispicy for a year," this extispicy is not necessarily valid for a year. Basically, he is proposing a time period he is interested in. However, it is the part of the gods to decide how long the extispicy is actually valid. And they place their verdict into the appearance of the finger of the liver. The diviner, then, calculates this time period for the validity of the extispicy result according to the planned period and the *uddazallû*-correction. In this case, the *adannu* is not determined by the diviner or the client, but by the gods.[18]

The second aspect concerns the fact that the *adannu* not only indicates the time period of validity of the extispicy result, but it also determines the maximum time period that will elapse until a certain dreaded or hoped for event will happen. This is made clear by many entries in the texts for calculation of the stipulated term, speaking of "in x hours/days/months you will besiege and seize the enemy town."[19]

---

17 See the table above.

18 This is also illustrated by passages in the chapter *Šumma multābiltu* of the series *Bārûtu*, which tell the diviner to wait for the time period set by the god(s): *a-dan ili*(DINGIR) *ú-qa-a-a*; see Koch 2005: 7/1 and 8/1.

19 See K. 4061 + below, obv. 24′–rev. end, and VAT 9492 (KAR 452), for which see Heeßel, forthcoming, no. 64.

This layer of interpretation called the "calculation of the stipulated term" again calls to mind the fact that Babylonian extispicy was never used to gain secure, unchangeable statements about the future. Extispicy results had a limited validity that seldom exceeded one year.[20] Therefore, extispicy was not used to make general statements about the far away future, but on the contrary was indicating the result of a development, which was viewed as threatening or desirable in the present. This might be regarded as one of the main reasons for its success with the common people as well as the ruling class, as it answered to the current needs and hopes of people.

APPENDIX

Edition of K. 4061 (CT 31/16, 18 [Koch 2005: 471–74]) + K. 10344

K. 4061+K. 10344, represents the lower half of a one-column tablet. The joined fragment measures 92 × 95 × 20 mm (see figs. 9.1–2).

Obv. 1′ ⸢BE *ina* MURUB$_4$ EDIN 15 ŠU.SI BÙR ŠUB⸣-[*di*] ⸢URU NIGIN-*mi*⸣ D[AB-*bat*]

2′ *ina* ^giš^TUKUL ŠUB-*ti* ÉRIN-*ni* [AN-*ú* SUR]-*nun* GIG T[I.LA]

3′ BE SUḪUŠ EDIN 15 ŠU.SI BÙR ŠUB-*di* 10 A.RÁ ⸢3 30⸣ [ITI 1-KÁM/30 u_4-*mi* KÚ]R URU NIGIN-*ma* DAB-[*bat*]

4′ *ina* ^giš^TUKUL ŠUB-*ti* ÉRIN-*ni* AN-⸢*ú*⸣ [SUR]-*nun* GIG TI.[LA]

5′ *šum-ma a-na* ITI 2-KÁM DÙ-*uš* SAG *a-dan-ni-ka* 20 20 u_4-*m*[*i*] EN MU 1-KÁM *tu-mal-lu-*⸢*ú*⸣

6′ 40 *ud-da-zal-le-e* MU 1-KÁM GUB-*ma* 3,20 *ud-da-zal-le-e* ITI 1-KÁM *tuš-te-qa*

7′ *šum-ma ana* MU 1-KÁM DÙ-*uš* 0;6,40 *ud-da-zal-le-e* u_4-*mi a-na* 6 UŠ u_4-*mi* 0;6,40 ÍL-*ma*

8′ 0;6,40 A.RÁ 360 40 *tam-mar* 40 *ud-da-zal-le-e* MU 1-[KÁ]M *a-na* 3 *ši-kin* ŠU.SI *i-ši-ma*

9′ 40 A.RÁ 3 120 *tam-mar* 120 4 ITI *ina* NÍG.KA$_9$ *i-ta-bal*

10′ *ana* MU 1-KÁM *a-dan-na* GAR-*an* SAG *a-dan-ni-ka* 120

11′ BE SAG EDIN 15 ŠU.SI BÙR ŠUB-*di* 120 A.RÁ ⸢1 120 4 ITI⸣ KÚR URU NIGIN-*ma* DAB-*bat*

12′ *ina* ^giš^TUKUL ŠUB-*ti* ÉRIN-*ni* ⸢AN-*ú*⸣ SUR-⸢*nun*⸣ GIG TI.LA

13′ BE MURUB$_4$ EDIN 15 ŠU.SI BÙR ŠUB-*di* 120 A.RÁ ⸢2⸣ [240] 8 ITI [K]ÚR URU NIGIN-*ma* DAB-*bat*

14′ *ina* ^giš^TUKUL ŠUB-*ti* ÉRIN-*ni* AN-⸢*ú* SUR⸣-*nun* GIG TI.LA

15′ BE SUḪUŠ EDIN 15 ŠU.SI BÙR ŠUB-*di* 120 A.RÁ ⸢3 360⸣ [MU 1]-KÁM KÚR URU NIGIN-*ma* DAB-*bat*

---

[20] See Starr 1990: p. 16.

16′ *ina* ^{giš}TUKUL ŠUB-*ti* ÉRIN-*ni* AN-[*ú* S]UR-*nun* GIG TI.LA

17′ *šum-ma a-na* MU 2-KÁM DÙ-*uš* SAG *a-dan-ni-ka* 240 8 ITI *a-dan-ni ana* MU 1-KÁM

18′ EN UD.LÁ-*a* GAR-*an*

19′ BE *lu ina* SAG EDIN 15 U *lu ina* MURUB$_4$ EDIN 15 U *lu ina* SUḪUŠ E[DIN] 15 U BÙR.MEŠ

20′ *ú-lu* 1 *ú-lu* 2 *ú-lu* 3 ŠUB.MEŠ KÚR URU NI[GIN-*m*]*a* DAB-*bat*

21′ *ina* ^{giš}TUKUL ŠUB-*ti* ÉRIN-*ni* AN-⸢*ú*⸣ SUR-[*nu*]*n* GIG TI.LA

22′ *šum-ma ana* U$_4$ 1-KÁM DÙ-*uš a-dan-ni* u_4-*mi* 0;20$^{!}$(Text: 0;10) ⸢150⸣ ŠUB-*ku*

23′ BE *ina* SAG EDIN 150 U BÙR ŠUB-*di* 0;20 A.RÁ 1 0;20 *ina* 4 DANNA u_4-*mi* URU KÚR NIGIN-*ma* DAB-*bat*

24′ *a-na* ^{giš}TUKUL ŠUB-*ti* ÉRIN KÚR AN-*ú* NU [SU]R-*nun* GIG BA.ÚŠ

End of obv.

Rev. 1 BE *ina* MURUB$_4$ EDIN 150 U BÙR ŠUB-*di* 0;20 A.RÁ 2 0;40 *ina* 8 DANNA u_4-*mi* URU (erasure) KÚR NIGIN-*ma* DAB-*bat*

2 *a-na* ^{giš}TUKUL ŠUB-*ti* ÉRIN KÚR AN NU SUR-*nun* GIG BA.ÚŠ

3 [BE *ina* S]UḪUŠ EDIN 150 U BÙR ŠUB-*di* 0;20 A.RÁ 3 1 *ina* 12 DANNA u_4-*mi* [*ga*]*m*$^{?}$-*mar-ti a-dan-ni* URU KÚR NIGIN-*ma* DAB-*bat*

4 [*šum-m*]*a ana* ITI 1-KÁM DÙ-*uš a-dan-ni* <<10>> ITI 10 150 ŠUB-*ku*

5 ⸢BE⸣ *ina* ⸢SAG⸣ EDIN 150 [U B]ÙR ŠUB-*di* 10 A.RÁ 1 10 *ina* 10 u_4-*mi* URU KÚR NIGIN-*ma* DAB-*bat*

6 *ina* ⸢^{giš}⸣T[UKUL ŠUB-*ti* É]RIN KÚR AN-*ú* NU SUR-*nun* GIG BA.ÚŠ

7 BE [*ina*] ⸢MURUB$_4$⸣ [EDIN 15]0 U BÙR ŠUB-*di* 10 A.RÁ 2 20 *ina* 20 u_4-*mi* URU KÚR NIGIN-*ma* DAB-*bat*

8 *ina* ⸢^{giš}TUKUL ŠUB-*ti*⸣ ÉRIN KÚR AN-*ú* NU SUR-[*nun*] GIG BA.ÚŠ

9 BE *ina* SUḪUŠ EDIN 150 U BÙR ŠUB-*di* 10 A.RÁ 3 30 *in*[*a* 30 u_4-*mi* URU KÚR NIGIN-*ma* DAB-*bat*

10 *ina* ^{giš}TUKUL ŠUB-*ti* ÉRIN KÚR AN-*ú* [NU SUR-*nun* GIG B]A.ÚŠ

---

11 *šum-ma ina a-dan-ni* MU 1-KÁM [ ]

12 BE *ina* SAG EDIN 150 U BÙR ŠUB-*di*-⸢*ma*⸣ [ ]

13 *a-na* ^{giš}TUKUL ŠUB-*ti* ÉRIN [KÚR]

14 BE *ina* MURUB$_4$ EDIN 150 [U BÙR ŠUB-*di-ma*]

15 *a-na* ^{giš}TUKUL [ ]

16 BE *ina* SUḪUŠ EDI[N 150 U BÙR ŠUB-*di-ma*]

17 *a-na* [^{giš}TUKUL]

---

18 BE *ina* SAG [ ]

19 BE *ina* [ ]

20 B[E]

TRANSLATION

Obv. 1′ If a hole lies in the middle of the right surface of the finger: [… … : The enemy] will besiege the town, he will t[ake (it)],

2′ in battle: defeat of the army, [it will ra]in, a patient will rec[over].

3′ If a hole lies in the basis of the right surface of the finger: 10 times 3 is 30 [days … … : The ene]my will besiege and seize the town,

4′ in battle: defeat of the army, it will rain, a patient will rec[over].

5′ If you perform (the extispicy) for two months, then the basis for (the calculation of) your period is 20, 20 days until one year you make full,

6′ 40 is established as the correction for one year, 3 1/3 is the correction for one month, you let it pass.

7′ If you perform (the extispicy) for one year, then 1/9 is the correction of a day, multiply (it) with 360 days and

8′ you will see that 1/9 times 360 is 40. 40 is the correction for one year; multiply (it) with the three shapes of the finger (*šikin ubāni*) and

9′ you will see that 40 times 3 is 120. 120 corresponds to four months in the result.

10′ (If) you determine the period for a year, (then) the basis for (the calculation of) your period is 120.

11′ If a hole lies in the top of the right surface of the finger: 120 times 1 is 120, 4 months. The enemy will besiege and seize the town,

12′ in battle: defeat of the army, it will rain, a patient will recover.

13′ If a hole lies in the middle of the right surface of the finger: 120 times 2 is [240], 8 months. The enemy will besiege and seize the town,

14′ in battle: defeat of the army, it will rain, a patient will recover.

15′ If a hole lies in the basis of the right surface of the finger: 120 times 3 is [360, one ye]ar. The enemy will besiege and seize the town,

16′ in battle: defeat of the army, it will rain, a patient will recover.

17′ If you perform (the extispicy) for two years, then the basis for (the calculation of) your period is 240, 8. The period for one year

18′ together with the correction you determine.

19′ If holes lie either in the top of the right surface of the finger or in the middle of the right surface of the finger or in the basis of the right surface of the finger

20′ either one, two, or three: The enemy will besiege and seize the town,

21′ in battle: defeat of the army, it will rain, a patient will recover.

22′ If you perform (the extispicy) for one day, then the period for one day is 1/3, the left side occurs for you

23′ If a hole lies in the top of the left surface of the finger: 1/3 times 1 is 1/3. In 4 double-hours of a day you will besiege and seize the enemy town,

24′ in battle: defeat of the enemy army, it will not rain, a patient will die.

End of obv.

Rev. 1 If a hole lies in the middle of the left surface of the finger: 1/3 times 2 is 2/3. In 8 double-hours of a day you will besiege and seize the enemy town,

2 in battle: defeat of the enemy army, it will not rain, a patient will die.

3 [If] a hole lies [in the b]asis of the left surface of the finger: 1/3 times 3 is 1. In the 12 double-hours of a day, in the completion of the period, you will besiege and seize the enemy town.

4 [I]f you perform (the extispicy) for one month, then the period for one month is 10, the left side occurs for you.

5 If a [hole l]ies in the top of the left surface of the finger: 10 times 1 is 10. In 10 days you will besiege and seize the enemy town,

6 in ba[ttle: defe]at of the enemy army, it will not rain, a patient will die.

7 If a hole lies [in the] middle [of the lef]t [surface] of the finger: 10 times 2 is 20. In 20 days you will besiege and seize the enemy town,

8 in battle: defeat of the enemy army, it will not rain, a patient will die.

9 If a hole lies in the basis of the left surface of the finger: 10 times 3 is 30. In 30 days you will besiege and seize the enemy town,

10 in battle: defeat of the enemy army, it will [not rain, a patient will d]ie.

---

11 If in the period of one year [… …].

12 If a hole lies in the top of the left surface of the finger and [… …],

13 in battle: defeat of the [enemy] army, [… …].

14 If [a hole lies] in the middle of the left surface [of the finger and … …],

15 in battle: [… …].

16 If [a hole lies] in the basis of the [left] surf[ace of the finger and … …],

17 in b[attle: … …].

---

18 If in the top [… …].

19 If in [… …].

20 I[f … …].

COMMENTARY

obv. 1′ Despite the fact that this line is broken it is clear that the scribe wrote URU NIGIN-*mi* and not, as in obv. 3′ etc., URU NIGIN-*ma*.

22′ Here and in rev. 4 the phrase 150 ŠUB-*ku* shows that concerning the calculation of the stipulated term the right side refers to the enemy and the left side to the client of the extispicy, contrary to the usual custom in extispicy.

rev. 1 The scribe erased the sign NIGIN after URU as he had forgotten to write KÚR before NIGIN.

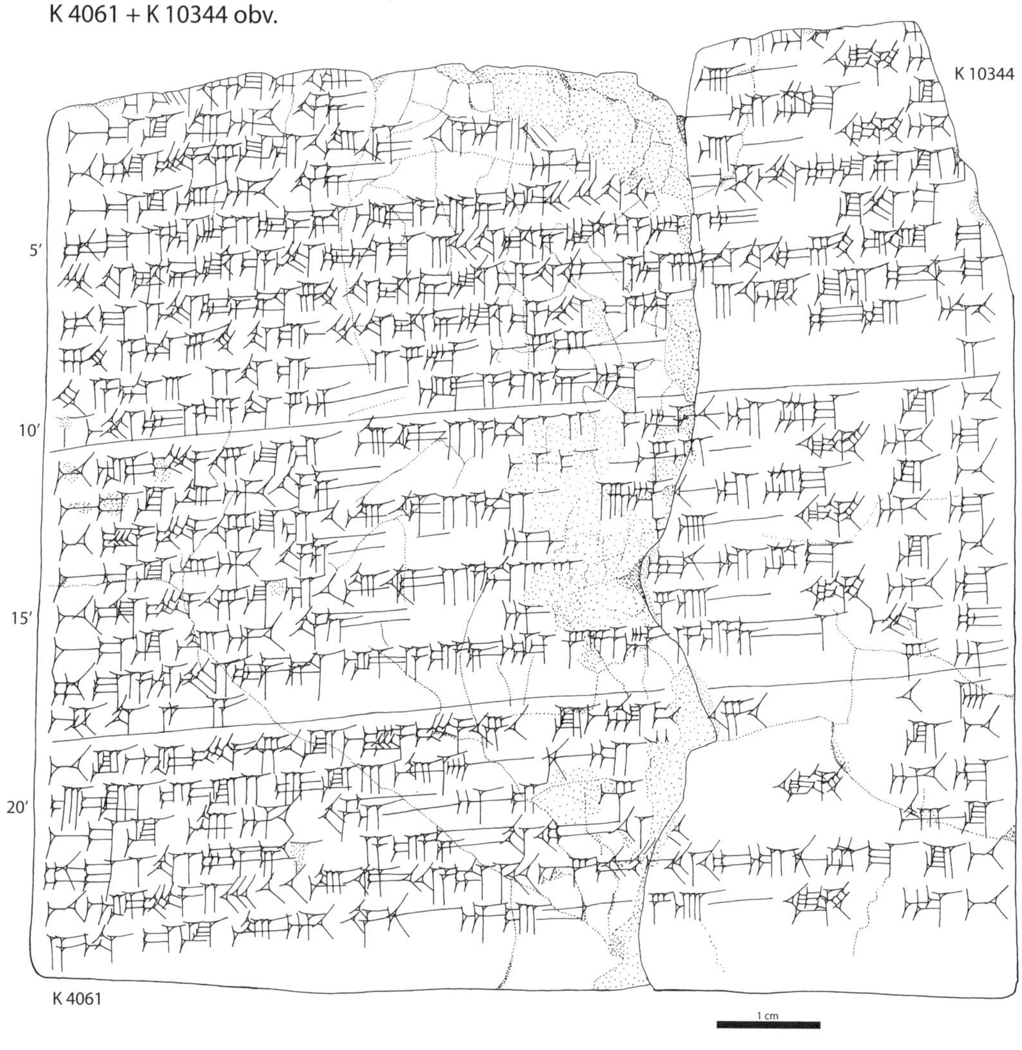

Figure 9.1. K. 4061+K. 10344 obverse

K 4061 + K 10344 rev.

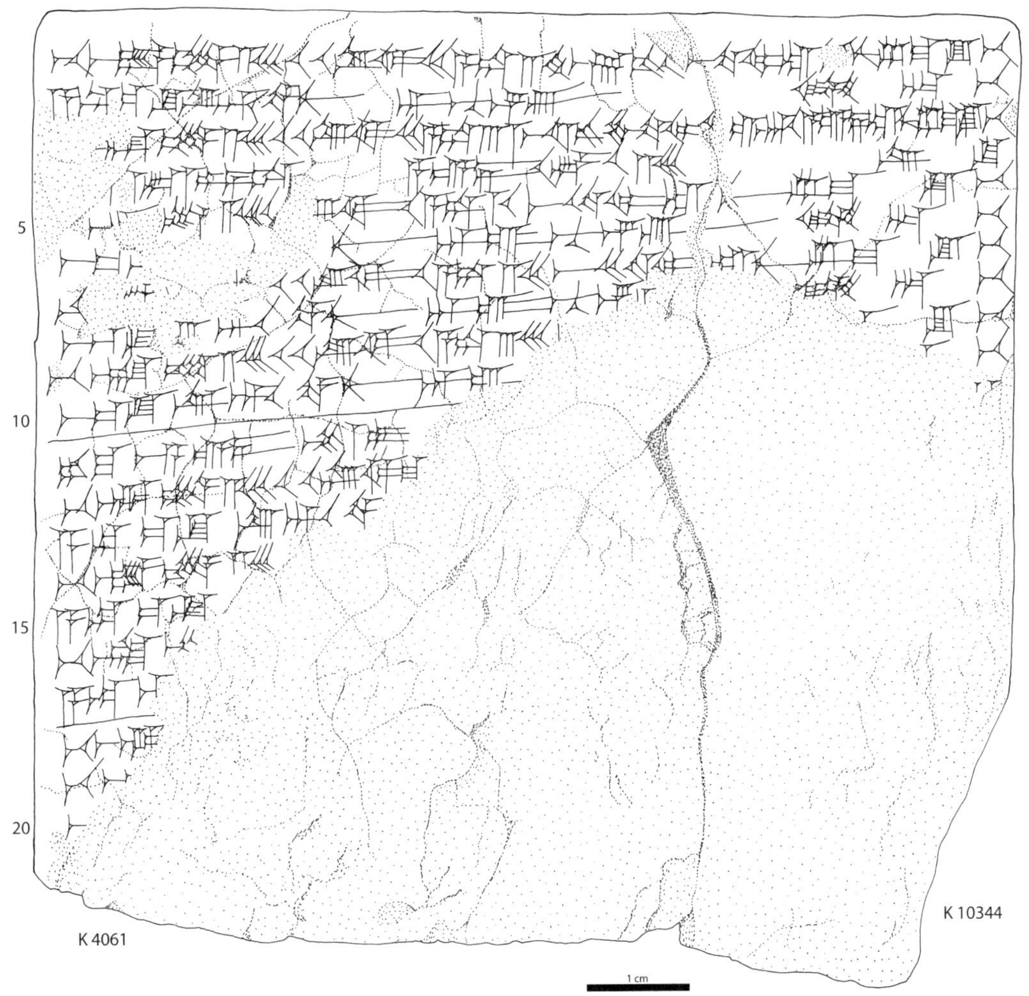

Figure 9.2. K. 4061+K. 10344 reverse

BIBLIOGRAPHY

Borger, Rykle

1957 "*niṣirti bārûti*, Geheimlehre der Haruspizin (Zu Neugebauer-Sachs, MCT, V und W, und einigen verwandten Texten)." *Bibliotheca Orientalis* 14: 190–95.

Brown, David

2004 Review of *Herrschaftswissen in Mesopotamien*, by B. Pongratz-Leisten. *Zeitschrift für Assyriologie* 94: 112–21.

Durand, Jean-Marie

1988 *Archives épistolaires de Mari* I/1. Archives Royales de Mari 26/1. Paris: Éditions recherche sur les civilisations.

Friberg, Joran

1987–90 "Mathematik." *Reallexikon der Assyriologie* 7: 531–85.

Gray, Clifton D.

1900/01 "The Šamaš Religious Texts." *American Journal of Semitic Languages and Literatures* 17: 129–45 and 222–43.

Heeßel, Nils P.

forthcoming *Divinatorische Texte* II: *Opferschau-Omina*. Keilschrifttexte aus Assur literarischen Inhalts, Wissenschaftliche Veröffentlichungen der Deutschen Orient-Gesellschaft.

Jeyes, Ulla

1989 *Old Babylonian Extispicy*. Publication de l'Institut historique-archéologique néerlandais de Stamboul 64. Leiden: Nederlands historisch-archeologisch Instituut te Istanbul.

Koch(-Westenholz), Ulla Susanne

2000 *Babylonian Liver Omens: The Chapters* Manzāzu, Padānu *and* Pān tākalti *of the Babylonian Extispicy Series Mainly from Aššurbanipal's Library*. Carsten Niebuhr Institute Publications 25. Copenhagen: Museum Tusculanum Press.

2005 *Secrets of Extispicy: The Chapter* Multābiltu *of the Babylonian Extispicy Series and* Niṣirti bārûti *Texts mainly from Aššurbanipal's Library*. Alter Orient und Altes Testament 326. Münster: Ugarit-Verlag.

Lambert, Wilfred G.

1998 "The Qualifications of Babylonian Diviners." In *Festschrift für Rykle Borger zu seinem 65. Geburtstag am 24. Mai 1994.* tikip santakki mala bašmu ..., edited by S. M. Maul, pp. 141–58. Cuneiform Monographs 10. Groningen: Styx Publications.

Leiderer, Rosemarie

1990 *Anatomie der Schafsleber im babylonischen Leberorakel*. Munich: Zuckerschwerdt.

Maul, Stefan M.

2003–05 "Omina und Orakel. A. Mesopotamien." *Reallexikon der Assyriologie* 10: 45–88.

Meyer, Jan-Waalke

1987 *Untersuchungen zu den Tonlebermodellen aus dem Alten Orient*. Alter Orient und Altes Testament 39, Neukirchen-Vluyn: Neukirchner Verlag.

Oppenheim, A. Leo

1956 *The Interpretation of Dreams in the Ancient Near East, with a Translation of an Assyrian Dream-book*. Transactions of the American Philosophical Society, n.s., 46/3: 177–373. Philadelphia: American Philosophical Society.

Pongratz-Leisten, Beate

1999 *Herrschaftswissen in Mesopotamien*. State Archives of Assyria Studies 10. Helsinki: Helsinki University Press.

Starr, Ivan

1983 *The Rituals of the Diviner*. Bibliotheca Mesopotamica 12. Malibu: Undena Publications.

1990 *Queries to the Sungod. Divination and Politics in Sargonid Assyria*. State Archives of Assyria 4. Helsinki: Helsinki University Press.

Weidner, Ernst F.

1917 "Zahlenspielereien in akkadischen Leberschautexten." *Orientalistische Literaturzeitung* 20: 258–66.

10

THE DIVINE PRESENCE AND ITS INTERPRETATION IN EARLY MESOPOTAMIAN DIVINATION*

ABRAHAM WINITZER, UNIVERSITY OF NOTRE DAME

1

Divination, if one seeks to define it, is less difficult a task than is the counterpart for its alleged parent, religion — though perhaps only marginally so. After all, one can approach the topic from virtually every entryway through which the drive to understand religion is tackled. Whether via its mythology or ritual, its accompanying liturgy, or the treatises its record may leave behind, the complexity of the phenomenon is such that it should give anyone deluded in believing that the meaning of divination is somehow self–evident room for pause. Still, no matter the approach to which one resorts, a central tenet that must be confronted at some point concerns not merely the existence of a divine realm, but of its willingness to reveal something of itself in the natural order, something perceivable to man; this, perhaps, does stand in contrast with religion.

And so questions concerning the proclamation or signs of the divine's manifestation or "presence" in divination systems, including those from ancient Mesopotamia, must be understood as basic to the broader enterprise. In a very real sense what enabled Mesopotamian diviners to proceed with their queries was the fundamental assumption of and hope for the divine's manifestation via one of the various divinatory channels, of and for the divine's virtual "presence" in the examined media, in the form of a sign.

When, however, one turns to the omen collections from ancient Mesopotamia — by far the most elaborate testimony of divinatory interest stemming from this civilization — it is the relative silence concerning the mention of deities that is striking. On occasion one does encounter statements exhibiting an interest in this basic theological premise, though frequently upon their assessment it becomes clear that these are marginal to the broader enterprise of the collections. And perhaps most telling of the divine realm's place in these texts are those omens whose forecasts herald the presence of this or that deity but immediately see fit to gloss these statements, as if to reconfigure them, subsuming in the process proclamations of "divine presence" in the literature's deep technical sea.

In the following I attempt to explore this discrepancy, something that may be seen as one between Mesopotamian divination theory and practice, as Niek Veldhuis put it recently.[1] In particular, I try to posit an explanation for it and to provide a model for its development. In so doing I hope that some light may be shed on the following two questions: What does the evolution in the place of the divine mean for an understanding of divination in ancient

* This paper draws on two previous ones given at the Harvard Workshop on the Religion of Ancient Mesopotamia and Adjacent Areas, in October 2002, and February 2004, and is the beneficiary of feedback received in that venue.

[1] Veldhuis 2006.

Mesopotamia? Is there a way in which this development reflects a change in attitude in Mesopotamia concerning the way by which divinatory knowledge was accessed, perhaps even about the very meaning of divination?

2

We might begin with a consideration of the testimony from the theoretical side of things. A recent study by Piotr Steinkeller (2005) presents a comprehensive picture of the conceptual setup of early Mesopotamian divination, at least for its most significant channel, extispicy. This reconstruction, it should be noted at the outset, is not without its drawbacks. One may quibble with particular aspects in Steinkeller's overall model or even object to his synchronic approach; what follows, in fact, raises some challenges to his overall scheme. Still, Steinkeller's contribution to the understanding of the overall picture cannot be overestimated; more to the point, for the present purposes his reservations about it, even if ultimately justified, prove to be tangential. Accordingly, it is recapped in what follows.

Table 10.1. The gods of Mesopotamian divination (following Steinkeller 2005)

Major Gods:	**Šamaš**	**Adad**(?)[2]
Description:	*bēl dīnim*	*bēl bīrim/bēl ikribī u bīrim*
	"Lord of Judgment"	"Lord of (extispicy) Inspection/Petitions and Inspection"
Other Deities:	**Ištar**...(Venus), **Šulpae** (Jupiter), **^{mul}gal.si.sá** (Sirius [Ninurta]), **Sîn** (Moon), etc.	
Description:	*ilū mušītim*	*bēl têrtim*
	"Gods of the Night" (Collective)	"Lord of the Omen" (Individual)

In his work, Steinkeller sought to understand the place of Šamaš, the sun-god, Adad, the weather-god — respectively the *bēl dīnim* "lord of judgment" and the *bēl bīrim/bēl ikribī u bīrim* "lord of (extispicy) inspection/petitions and inspection" — as well as the so-called Gods of the Night in the Mesopotamian conception of the divinatory universe. In particular, it is the pairing of the former two that appears in many of extant prayers and prayer rituals of Old Babylonian divination (including *ikribu*- and *tamītu*-prayers, and other related material), something even more appreciable now with the recent publication of the *tamītu* (oracle) texts by Lambert.[3] As Steinkeller explains it, this Šamaš-Adad duo operates in tandem — with Adad providing for Šamaš, the real actor, a turbo-like boost — to enable the cosmic process. That divination takes place at night owes itself to the belief that at this time Šamaš traverses the

[2] See below.

[3] See Lambert 2007: esp. 5–9, 12–14, for a description of the genre and related materials. See also the subscript in text VI of the MDAI 57 Susa omens, *šurri Šamaš u Adad*, perhaps "if statement(s) (= casuistic omen sentences) of Šamaš and Adad," discussed recently in Michalowski 2006.

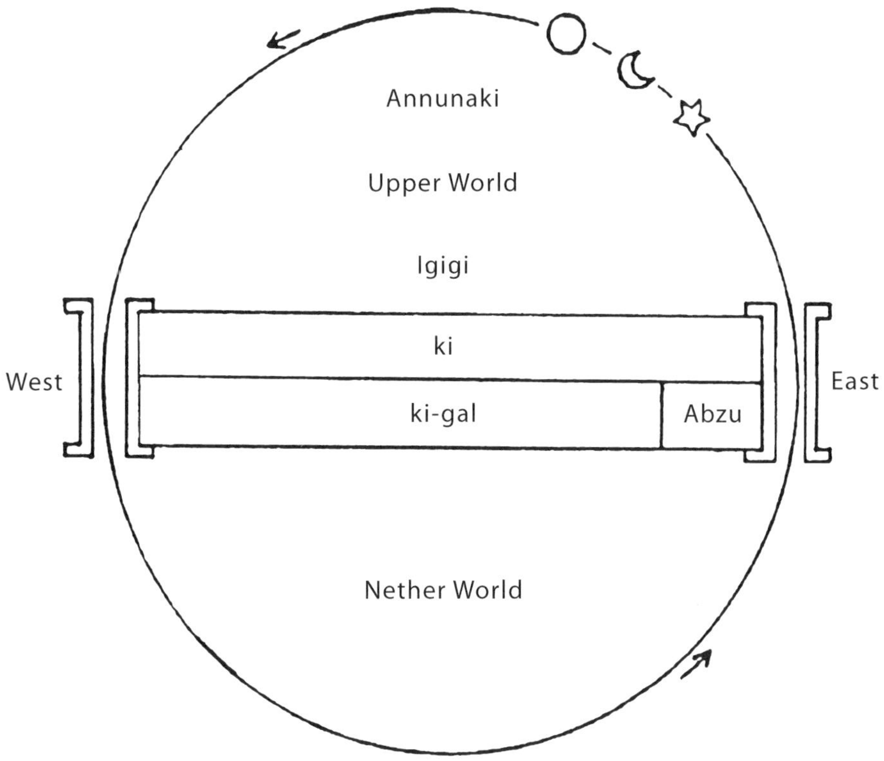

Figure 10.1. The Babylonian universe (after Steinkeller 2005)

Netherworld's horizon, a mirror image of the one visible in daytime (fig. 10.1). At this time, when earthly judgment ceases, the interest of the cosmic judge turns to divinatory matters, the heavenly counterpart of legal verdicts.[4] The Gods of the Night, according to Steinkeller, are the selfsame deities named in many extispicy reports — including Ištar (in her various guises), Šulpae, Ninurta, Sîn, and so on — that are also to be equated with the night's stars (thus Ištar = Venus, Šulpae = Jupiter, Ninurta = Sirius, Sîn = Moon, etc.). For a given extispicy one of these functions as the *bēl têrtim*, or the deity responsible for that extispicy, perhaps in accordance with personal proclivity or with astronomical and/or meteorological realities.[5] In all the system is, Steinkeller claims early on, "highly coherent and ... internally logical,"[6] and, more significant for the present purposes, unequivocal about the place of the divine realm in it.

Further evidence of the centrality of the idea of divine manifestation or presence in Mesopotamian divination may be witnessed when one turns to the phenomenology of the divinatory act, at least as it is met — *faute de mieux* — in the accompanying prayers and related literature. In this respect, the transformation inherent in the extispicy act must be understood as a quasi-transfiguration for its practitioner and the conceptual universe he inhabits. Accordingly, the rooftop that provided the setting for the event serves as the *axis mundi* where the gods encounter the human realm. Indeed, the texts all but spell out the fulcrum on which the cosmic beam rests: having concluded the preparatory ritual, the diviner moves on to beseech the gods to have "truth" (*kittum*) established — or, perhaps better, materialized

[4] For a recent word of this epistemological metaphor in its broader context, see Wilcke 2007: 224ff.

[5] Steinkeller 2005: 41–42.

[6] Steinkeller 2005: 17.

— before him. The coda of the well-known Prayer (to the Gods) of the Night[7] (example 1) makes the point clearly:

1. In the extispicy I am performing / In the lamb I am offering[8] / Establish truth (*kittum*) *for me*![9]

So, too, for the Old Babylonian prayer of the divination priest YOS 11 22 (example 2), where this last imperative functions as the refrain of the entire text. The diviner beseeches the gods to establish truth (*kittam šakānum*) within his reach:

2. In the *ikrib*-blessing I am pronouncing / In the extispicy I am performing / Establish truth (*kittam šuknam*) for me![10]

And what is here understood as "truth" is qualified elsewhere even further. Thus, upon the appeal for the establishment of truth via the extispicy performed, the petitioner turns to the gods in the initial prayer of the great Old Babylonian extispicy liturgical manual YOS 11 23 (and //)[11] with the following plea (example 3):

3. Cause the god, the lord of the omen I am performing, to be present for me!
In the extispicy I am performing establish truth for me!
In the *manifestation*(*s*)[12] of the great gods (*šiknāt ilî rabûtim*), in the tablet of the gods (*ṭuppi ša ilī*),
May a *takaltum* be present![13]

The precise identification of the term *takaltum* in this passage has been a matter of some debate. If one follows the view espoused most recently by Steinkeller, then in the present context the word should be understood as a euphemism for the (whole) liver, this on analogy with its primary meaning, a carrying bag for storage of small tools.[14] Accordingly, the un-inscribed liver was envisaged as the depository of equipment of a different sort, namely,

[7] Following the recent edition and sigla ([a] AO 6769 // [b] Erm 15642) in Wilcke 2007: 225–28.

[8] In one version (a): "In the *ikrib*-blessing I am pronouncing."

[9] Ibid., lines 22–24. On the unusual *-ān* dative dual ending on the imperative (directed at Šamaš and Adad) in version (b), see Wilcke 2007: 227 n. 82; and, better, Lambert 2007: 8. The same formula with this ending appears repeatedly in YOS 11 23, for which see Starr 1983 (full edition); Wilcke 2007: 233–38 (updated, partial edition).

[10] Wilcke 2007: 230–33, (text) lines 12–13, 17–18, 31–33, 40–41, 49, 52–53, 56–57, 64–66.

[11] Wilcke 2007: 233–38.

[12] Or perhaps "creation(s)"; *pace* CAD Š/2, 431b: "decree(?)."

[13] Ibid., ms. A (= YOS 11 23), lines 15–16.

[14] Steinkeller (2005: 30 and n. 43) cleverly understands the enveloping *ṭuppi ša ilī* in this image as referring to the lamb itself; cf. earlier Lambert 1967: 133; Starr 1983: 53–56; Vanstiphout and Veldhuis 1995: 31–32. Note in particular the equation giš. tùn = *takaltum* in various (native) lexical lists, especially those in Hh, cited in CAD T, 61, s.v. *takaltu* A, already noted in Starr, ibid., 53–54 n. 98; also Vanstiphout and Veldhuis, ibid., p. 31 n. 9.

At issue is the relation between the *takaltum* (*ta-ka-al-tum*) and the *ṭuppi ša ilī*. If the latter is taken as a metaphor for the liver itself, then one must either: (a) interpret the *takaltum* as a subset of the liver or as something in its interior (so, e.g., Glassner 2002: 10 "les viscères"; Wilcke 2007: 236 "Tasche"), or (b), more radically, read the word in the genitive (*ta-ka-al-tím*) so as to have it in apposition with the *ṭuppi ša ilī* (so Lambert 1998: 147).

The first of these options is possible, though it is not without its problems. It seems unlikely that the prayer would have in mind here either the liver's "organs" generally (whose sound presence, though certainly meaningful and desirable [see further below], did not articulate on its own the precise signification for which the diviner frequently awaited), or, alternatively, the (non-"canonical") zone by the same name (for which see, e.g., Jeyes 1989: 76), to the exclusion of all the others. Less likely is Lambert's solution to

the divine message, with the liver amounting to a veritable *tabula rasa*, an empty slate upon which this message was recorded. Elsewhere too, in a tale intended to provide an etiology for divination, it is likened to nothing less than the Tablet of the Gods. This tale (example 4), the opening of a text concerned with proper diviner qualifications and procedures, which was re-edited not long ago by Lambert,[15] tells how Enmeduranki, the legendary king of Sippar, was given "the Tablet of the Gods, the liver, secret (or, just below in the same text: mystery) of Heavens and Earth," along with instructions about how to conduct the craft of various sorts of divination and determine who might be their respective practitioners.

4. Šamaš in the Ebabbara [*appointed*] Enmeduranki, [King of Sippar], the beloved of Anu, Enlil, [and Ea]. Šamaš and Adad [brought him in] to their assembly, Šamaš and Adad [*honored* him], Šamaš and Adad [seated him] before [them] on a golden throne. They showed him how to observe oil in water, a mystery of Anu [Enlil and Ea]. [Th]ey gave him the Tablet of the Gods, the *liver*, a secret of Heaven and the Netherworld (*ṭuppi ilāni takalta pirišti šamê u erṣeti* [*i*]*ddinūšu*), they put the cedar in his hands, beloved by the great gods.
   And he, [in accordance with] their [*command*], brought into his presence the citizens of Nippur, Sippar, and Babylon, and *honored* them, he seated them before him on thrones, he showed them how to observe oil in water, a mystery of Anu, Enlil, and Ea, he gave them the Tablet of the Gods, the *liver*, a secret of Heaven and the Netherworld (*ṭuppi ilāni takalta pirišti šamê u erṣeti iddinšunūti*), he put the cedar in their hand, beloved by the great gods, the Tablet of the Gods, the *liver*, a mystery of Heaven and the Netherworld (*ṭuppi ilāni takalta niṣirti šamê u erṣeti*)....[16]

Now Lambert was astute to note similarities between some of the qualifications of would-be divination-priests and those incumbent upon Levitical priests in the Bible.[17] Actually, a broader comparison — note: functional, not genetic — may be suggested, one that sheds further light on divination's theoretical conceptual stance. After all, as presented in the legends and prayers surveyed,[18] the entire extispicy event parallels much of what is the defining event in the biblical text, indeed of all revealed religions: revelation and transmission of the divine word from the god(s) to his/their select group of people.[19] And if one accepts the premise that the Mesopotamians reckoned the sign or signs detected via extispicy, or through any divinatory channel, as divinely inspired in some transcendent fashion, then logically it follows that extispicy, or divination in general, is nothing less than a source of revelation, its product tantamount to the divinely revealed word. In fact this point was made long ago,[20]

read TUM as *tím*, which loses strength when one notes the regular use of TIM for *tim* elsewhere in this text, indeed even in the very same line (*ra-bu-tim*). The tentative suggestion in CAD (ibid.) that the bag in question was intended for the (diviner's?) reed stylus seems still less likely.

[15] Lambert 1998; originally Lambert 1967.

[16] Lambert 1998: 148–49, lines 1–16.

[17] Lambert 1998: 147–48.

[18] There are still others, for which see Lambert 2007: 13–14.

[19] In fact this too had occurred to Lambert, and even earlier at that (1967: 127), though he drew the parallel to a more explicit instance of this idea, namely, the famous "chain of tradition" in Mishnah *Avot* describing the transmission of the Torah.

[20] For example, Moran 1969: 23. Compare Durand 1988: 25 (also idem 2008: 492), who, unfortunately, still subordinates the stature of divinatory-based revelation to that from realm of prophecy ("Dans certains cas privilégiés, la réponse à l'interrogation oraculaire se mue en un véritable discours prophétique.

but appears underappreciated for its basic phenomenological significance.[21] All the same, of its basic truth there can be no doubt. And if, arbitrarily or from a comparatist's standpoint, divination is not included among the premier league of moments of the divine's manifestation in the human realm — those including revelation, incarnation, transubstantiation, or an ongoing mystical divine presence (the *šᵉḵīnā* in Jewish Kabbalistic terminology, a cognate of the aforementioned *šiknātu* "manifestation(s)" of the *ilī rabûtim*[22]) — then at least within a more modest Mesopotamian scope one is wise to include this version of Michelangelo's "touch of God."[23]

Dans ce dernier cas, le devin est doublé, cependant, par un autre personnage, le 'Répondant du Dieu,' l'âpilum").

[21] By contrast, much has been made of the sociological context and ideological manipulation of this knowledge by select parties. With respect to the Old Babylonian period, understandably these matters were first tackled at length by Durand (1988: 3–68, esp. 11–24), whose publication of the divinatory epistolary and related materials afforded a previously unimaginable window into Old Babylonian diviners as well as their machinations and relations to the state and state affairs. The latter angle, drawing further support from the more recent edition of prophecy texts from Assyria (Parpola 1997), has been developed further, especially in Pongratz-Leisten 1999; also Lenzi 2008; and now Richardson in this volume.

Needless to say, the question of how to approach the study of Mesopotamian divination must not proceed along "either"-"or" lines. Generally speaking in the study of religion, the idea that specialized secret knowledge attributed to divine sources could be and was manipulated for political purposes, with a developing "guild" around it cultivating a certain clout for itself in the bargain, is clear and legitimate — if not new. Yet this must not deny or even overshadow the religious dimension to a particular phenomenon, in this case the possibility of a legitimate belief in divinatory-based revelation by the ancients. To assume otherwise risks a misunderstanding of the very nature of divination and its place in ancient thought.

This same issue, but with respect to the oracle at Delphi in terms of its modern investigation, was articulated effectively by Hugh Bowden not long ago. As Bowden observes (2004: 122–23), not merely have historians underestimated what, in terms of subject, represents the largest category of consultations, namely, religious; they have also misrepresented the very nature of the oracular activity, assuming a distinction between consultations more secular in nature and those concerned, *prima facie*, with the divine realm. He writes:

> The analysis of Athenian consultations of Delphi has divided them into categories that involved political, military and diplomatic issues as well as 'religious' ones. However, in every case where we know the terms of the enquiry, and quite probably in all the cases where we don't know, the actual question asked of Delphi is directly about relations with the gods (Bowden 2004: 132).

The point is illustrated even further if, upon returning to the Mesopotamian sphere, we consider an analogous situation from a comparable phenomenon: the record of prophecy and prophetic activity, along with the transmission of this information, at Mari. In one well-known instance known from this corpus, an episode involving the deliberations of (king) Zimri-Lim in a foreign-policy matter, reports of a certain prophetic utterance reach the king from multiple sources. The events surrounding these missives, if one follows their explication in Sasson 1995; also van der Toorn 2000: 230–33; idem 2007: 112–13, are intricate, and offer a supreme example of self-interest and crafty diplomacy by politically savvy parties. But this does not gainsay the existence of an enigmatic prophetic utterance at the core of the matter (*šapal tibnim mû illakū* "waters run beneath straw"), even if, as Sasson (ibid., 607–08) and van der Toorn (2000: 232–33; 2007: 113) wonder, it may be impossible even in this instance to settle on the *ipsissima verba* (assuming there was more to it than the above-mentioned aphorism!).

[22] Already noted in Starr 1983: 53. To be sure, earlier reflexes of this idea abound in biblical writings, from Deuteronomy's so-called Name Theology (*šikkēn šēm*) to the initial promise by the Israelite deity of presence in the portable sanctuary (Exod. 25:8) and, indeed, to the basic term for this "tabernacle" (*miškān*).

[23] Compare Durand 2008: 431–33.

3

Of course all this rests on a model of the theoretical conception of Mesopotamian divination. As such, its value may be challenged on two fronts. First, there is the question of the model's accuracy: to what extent have we represented its basic ingredients correctly and proportionally? And there is a second question, one involving the degree to which theory reflects and matches practice. A word on each of these matters is in order.

Concerning the model's accuracy one might consider, by way of example, the question of the place of Adad within the conceptual framework. As described above, Steinkeller had contended that numerous references to this god as the *bēl bīrim*, or "lord of divination," are not incidental to the overall setup. And yet in numerous texts and even entire text genres that bear on the issue of the theoretical framework, Adad does not figure as Šamaš' counterpart.[24] Even in the Enmeduranki etiology, connected as it is to Šamaš and his Sippar home, the Ebabbar temple, the place of Adad should probably be seen as an external intrusion to a native theology, as Lambert observed recently.[25] It is thus not unlikely that his place in the Babylonian divinatory universe, and even his title *bēl bīrim*, represents a specific historical development, and not something that can be deemed autochthonous.[26]

---

[24] For example, the Middle and Neo-Babylonian "Gods of the Night" prayers (for which see Lambert 2007: 13) where Adad does not appear, and especially the so-called "Queries to the Sungod" (Starr 1990), the first-millennium large collection of oracle questions by diviners in the Sargonid court that, as their modern designation suggests, address Šamaš — alone.

[25] Lambert 2007: 8.

[26] Compare Schwemer 2007: 149. Note also objection raised by Durand (1997: 278; 2008: 220–21) concerning the understanding of *bīrum* in the title *bēlet bīri/bīrī* ("lady of ... ") as "divination." According to Durand, this is to be understood as "well(s), pit(s)," with the deity in question — elsewhere a reference to Išḫara — one in command of water sources ("la divinité des points d'eau"). That this deity and title became associated with divination (Steinkeller 2005: 15 n. 6) may be entirely secondary, whether owing to her association with Adad (connected in his own right with underground water; see Schwemer 2001: 170 and n. 1202) or otherwise, in the reinterpretation of *bīrum* in light of parallel developments in Adad's character.

Not included in this assessment, though perhaps deserving of brief mention, are the many passages from non-divinatory literary genres that refer to divination, and in particular extispicy. One thinks, for instance, of the well-known passages in Gudea Cylinder A (Edzard 1997: 69–88) describing his divinatory inquiries, extispicy included (xii 16–17; xiii 16–17; xx 5), concerning the rebuilding of the Eninnu temple. These are silent as regards the conceptual framework of the divinatory act. Granted, from the standpoint of the narrative, this may well have been deemed beside the point. Then again, the text, which spares little in conveying Gudea's piety throughout his sacred task, certainly does not refrain elsewhere from the mention of other deities. One finds the major gods of the Lagaš pantheon to be sure, but also others, parenthetically mentioned, including Nisaba, Ištarān and Šamaš, Ninzaga and Ninsikila, etc., each in connection to his/her defining attribute (respectively, writing, justice, relation to Dilmun). Why, then, no mention should have been made of the gods of divination in the telling of events is worth considering.

And elsewhere where the performance of extispicy is described this matter is even more curious. A case in point is the intriguing portion of a school letter "by" Ibbi-Sîn, recently published in Michalowski 2006a. There Ibbi-Sîn reports of having received a favorable omen via extispicy. The deity responsible for this, we are told, is Enlil, who, Ibbi-Sîn swanks, "has looked upon me with grace and has taken my supplication in (his) holy heart; he established for me in my omens the favorable parts..." (ibid., 251). The verisimilitude of this omen, to put it mildly, is problematic; at the very least the issue must be considered in the context of the Old Babylonian scribal curriculum and in light of the literary and historiographic conventions of the royal letter genre (Michalowski 1976: 3–16, 27; 2006a: 256–57). Nevertheless, the question may still be raised as regards its image of extispicy therein, since, as Michalowski rightly observes, its language does contain elements that capture accurately both the technical side of extispicy and the reporting of extispicy omens in the (non-literary) Old Babylonian epistolary. Why then, in this light, is it Enlil who is depicted fashioning the liver's regions (uzu zid/gub...ak) and setting signs in it (kin-gi$_4$-a/

One is thus left to wonder what other aspects of the theoretical setup are secondary to native ideas of Mesopotamian divination, or, for that matter, whether such a "trait-list" investigative approach is prudent in any case. Now happily, this skepticism too has its limits. Certainly for divination literature in broad terms Steinkeller's model is defensible for the early second millennium B.C., such that at least conceptually it may be said, in the spirit of Paul Veyne, that the Mesopotamians did indeed believe in their divination myth.

But then there remains the second, larger matter, the one concerning the relevance of any of this for the understanding of the place of the divine in "practical" Mesopotamian divination. Theories of all kinds run their course,[27] and in any case in practice things typically operate differently. With respect to the topic at hand one must ask to what extent the theoretical framework can serve as the guide to ideas about the place of the divine realm in Mesopotamian divination. In other words, at some point our quest must shift its focus onto other facets of the phenomenon of divination, lest we be fooled by the "fantastic screen" of the conceptual setup, to borrow Leo Oppenheim's metaphor,[28] and equate Mesopotamian divinatory mythology with Mesopotamian divination.

So what place exactly did the divine realm hold in the eyes of its practitioners? What of the petitioners for whom the divination was performed? After all, if, as suggested by the theoretical framework, divine "presence" was a basic, even determinative, fact to the broader enterprise, then should one not anticipate a continuous and explicit witness to divine manifestation, whether in accounts of divinatory activity or, better yet, in the omens themselves? Might we not expect omen literature to be, in a word, more "theological" — and considerably less "technical"?[29]

4

Naturally, a comprehensive answer to this question must build on different areas of data, of which two in particular stand out. These are: (1) the testimony of or about diviners and divinatory concerns, especially that appearing in the considerable divinatory epistolary corpus from the Mari archives,[30] and (2) the Mesopotamian omen collections themselves. Unfortunately, the present setting cannot take up both these angles, but rather must limit itself to only the latter of these.[31]

As is well known, Mesopotamian divination left an immense corpus of omen collections, from various divinatory channels, beginning apparently in the Old Babylonian period.

uzu...gar)? That this is to be read in the light of his role in the historiographic depiction of the unraveling of the Ur III state (cf., for the earlier case of the collapse of Akkad, Enlil's depiction in the Curse of Agade, lines 98–99 [Cooper 1983: 54–55, and earlier 22]) may not explain this question away. The issue may ultimately find resolution in our accepting the possibility that Steinkeller's model, ingenious though it is, did not extend far beyond the parameters of the divination literature itself.

[27] Enjoyably, as even Terry Eagleton now tells it (Eagleton 2003).

[28] Oppenheim 1977: 177, there applied more generally to significance of Mesopotamian myths to the understanding of Mesopotamian religion.

[29] Compare Jacobsen 1976: 84

[30] Collected for the most part in Durand 1988; additionally Glassner 2005: 281 n. 22, to which additional letters may be added, including some published earlier and treated in Durand 2000: 98 (no. 949), 100–04 (nos. 952–56); 259–60 (no. 1174), and still others, appearing in the more recent editions of Mari letters; e.g., FM 7 and 8; see esp. FM 7 50 (Durand 2002:167–68).

[31] I hope to return to the issue regarding the Mari evidence in the near future. See, meanwhile, Durand 2008, in the aptly named chapter, "Le contact avec la divinité," especially pages 492–94.

To be sure, these cannot be conceived as the direct testimony of Mesopotamian divination or diviners. They represent, rather, part of the scientific literature of ancient Mesopotamia. More broadly this means the Mesopotamian penchant to organize data in massive lists, what at times is labeled *Listenwissenschaft*; more specifically, the collections form a subset of the casuistic literature — of which the law "codes" are better-known examples — and are the product of scribes, who organized and, on the basis of hermeneutic principles and deductive reasoning, generated the overwhelming majority of this material from an empirically based kernel.[32] Nevertheless, a relation between Mesopotamian divination and the omen collections is beyond dispute,[33] such that, if properly executed, the gleaning of details from the collections can serve as a legitimate source of information on Mesopotamian divination, especially in terms of its broader assumptions.

Let us turn, then, to the omen collections, and specifically to a branch of the literature that has not received the attention of extispicy but which exists from the early periods of Mesopotamian divination and which, if the tradition reflected in the Enmeduranki etiology can serve as any guide, enjoyed a privileged status in the eyes of the ancients.[34] This is lecanomancy, or the divinatory method studying the configuration of oil poured in water. Though its place in the first-millennium divinatory sciences or in the cuneiform "stream of tradition" appears negligible,[35] there exists a respectable corpus of oil omens from the Old Babylonian period. These were the subject of a comprehensive edition and study by Giovanni Pettinato (1966), now over forty years ago, though apparently they have not inspired much interest since. For the present purposes their significance stems from the fact that they contain a considerable number of individual entries, each in the classic casuistic logic-sentence form, whose interpretations bear statements about the "presence," or *manzāzum* (or: *mazzāzum*), of particular deities, literally their "stand." Now similar statements, it is noted below, are not absent in extispicy, but when comparing the sizes of the respective corpora it is clear that such statements figure more prominently in lecanomancy.[36]

Concerning such *manzāzu*-formulas, the question to be posed is a simple one: what is their meaning? How to interpret apodoses professing a particular god's "presence?" Can one justly speak of these as conveying an early sort of what later theological reflection might label an epiphany? To answer these questions one must contend with another matter that frequently presents itself in those omens mentioning the *manzāzum* of particular gods. This involves the mention of "requests" (singular: *erištum*) for specific items that accompany statements of divine "presence." As the following demonstrates, the understanding of the relation between these terms sheds considerable light on the meaning of the *manzāzu*-formulas themselves,

---

[32] With respect to the omen literature, see provisionally Winitzer 2006. For a recent and excellent overview of the scribal curriculum's role in this process, see van der Toorn 2007: 54–70, 109–41.

[33] See most recently Winitzer 2006: 234ff.

[34] On the presumed antiquity of the Enmeduranki tradition, see Lambert 2007: 4. For another indication of the place of lecanomancy early on, see Šulgi C line 102 (ETCSL's numbering): ì-gíd níg-na de$_5$-ga IGI PI/x-re á-bi-šè in-ga-zu "Moreover, I properly know the *inspecting* of lecanomancy and libanomancy," following roughly the interpretation first suggested in Klein 1980: xv–xvii; more recently Sallaberger 2005: 237 (with additional bibliography); also Volk 1996: 210 n. 187.

[35] Even though in practice this technique remained common; for which, and on post-Old Babylonian lecanomancy generally, see Maul 2003: 83. The most significant witness of interest in the scholastics of lecanomancy comes from the diviner's "manual" KAR 151, discussed and edited most recently (with parallels) in Koch 2005: 39–45, 273–96; to be re-edited by Nils Heeßel in the forthcoming volume of the KAL.

[36] An explanation for this discrepancy is suggested below in section 6.

and also on the broader issue of the place of the very expression of "divine presence" in the omen collections.

5

From almost the very beginnings of the study of Mesopotamian divination, a relation was observed between statements about a deity's request and those of its presence. Jastrow, in his pioneering work on Mesopotamian divination,[37] had already qualified the relation between *manzāzum* and *erištum* as the deity's "Bestand" and "aktive Tätigkeit," respectively.[38] Pettinato advanced this idea in his study of the lecanomancy corpus, observing that in these omens the *manzāzu*-formula was at times clarified and/or made more specific, most frequently via a statement describing a request, *erištum*.[39] The evidence from the oil-omens corpus is instructive for the present purposes. Its reassessment, conducted below, provides an opportunity to test Pettinato's observation systematically. More importantly, it sheds additional light on the ancients' attempts to contend with the root of the problem: the meaning of divine presence in Mesopotamian divination.

Within the lecanomancy corpus, apodoses with *manzāzu*-formulas and/or *erištu*-statements are attested in distinct types, summarized in the following (table 2), where an element Y somehow qualifies or is qualified by a statement about a deity X:

Table 2. Synopsis of *manzāzum* and *erištum* attestations in Old Babylonian lecanomancy omen collections

	Syntagm	Examples (= Apodoses)
(a)	*manzāz* X	*manzāz Sîn*[40]/*Šamaš*[41]
(b_1)	*manzāz* X *erišti* Y	*manzāz Šamaš erišti šamšim*[42]/ *manzāz Ea erišti nārim*[43]
(b_2)	*manzāz* X *erišti* Y′	*manzāz Sîn*[44]/*Ištar*[45] *erišti kaspim*
(c)	*manzāz* X (*ana*) Y	*manzāz il awīlim ana damiqtim*/*lemuttim*[46]/ *manzāz Adad ana damiqtim*[47]
(d)	*manzāz* Y *erišti* X	*manzāz ṣēni*[48]/*erṣetim*[49] *erišti Sumuqan*
(e)	Y *erišti* X	*mukīl rēš damiqtim erišti Sîn*[50]/ *mukīl rēš lemuttim erišti Šamaš*[51]

[37] Jastrow 1905–12, vol. 2.

[38] Ibid., 775, and see the even earlier effort to understand these terms in Hunger 1903: 25–27.

[39] Pettinato 1966, vol. 1: 192–93; more recently Durand 1997: 281.

[40] E.g., Ölwahrsagung I 58.

[41] E.g., Ölwahrsagung I 60.

[42] Ölwahrsagung I 59; cf. ibid., I 6 and II 65.

[43] Ölwahrsagung I 61; on the variant in ms. C, see ibid., 41.

[44] Ölwahrsagung I 57.

[45] Ölwahrsagung II 53.

[46] Ölwahrsagung IV rev. 12–13.

[47] Ölwahrsagung IV rev. 5.

[48] Ölwahrsagung I 56.

[49] Ölwahrsagung II 52; cf. ibid., II 50. The "Land" certainly refers to the Netherworld (so Pettinato 1966, vol. 2: 72), with which Sumuqan (Sum. Šakkan) is associated in the Sumerian tale of the Death of Gilgameš; see further George 2003, vol. 2: 850–51.

[50] Ölwahrsagung II 48.

[51] Ölwahrsagung II 49.

Most frequently attested are apodoses where a simple statement about the "presence" of a particular deity (DN), expressed by way of a *manzāz* X formula, appears unqualified (a), for example, *manzāz Sîn/Šamaš*, "(it represents) the presence of Sîn/Šamaš." Of the qualified variety (b–e), most common are cases where an *erištu*-statement appears to comment on a preceding *manzāz* X formula (b_{1-2}). At times this is achieved via a paranomastic hermeneutic (b_1) like the phrase *erišti šamšim*, "(it is) a request of/for the sun disk (written: *ša-am-ši-im*)," that follows *manzāz Šamaš*, "presence of Šamaš (written: ^{d}utu)," or *erišti nārim*, "(it is) a request of/for the canal," apparently as commentary the preceding *manzāz Ea*, "the presence of Ea." In other instances of this type (b_2) the qualification of the *manzāz* X formula by the *erištu*-statement does not seem to be based on paranomastic grounds: the presence of Sîn/Ištar, *manzāz Sîn/Ištar*, is followed by a request (*erištum*) of/for silver, *erišti kaspim*. Still elsewhere the *manzāz* DN formula may be qualified without resort to an *erištu*-statement: for example, in (c) the phrases "for good/bad" qualify the previous *manzāz* X formulas. In a couple of cases (d) the *manzāzum* and *erištum* appear crisscrossed: in the apodoses *manzāz ṣēni/erṣetim erišti Sumuqan* "the presence of the flock/Land; (it is) the request of Sumuqan," the DN appears as part of the *erištu*-statement, seemingly as an explanation of the previous *manzāzu*-formulas. Finally, in the apodoses *mukīl rēš damiqtim erišti Sîn / mukīl rēš lemuttim erišti Šamaš* (e), an *erišti* X statement also appears to explain a preceding element, though in this case this element is not bound with *manzāzum*.

A number of general observations may be made from this survey. First, it is apparent that an *erištu*-statement, where it appears (b_{1-2}, d, e), *follows* some component of the apodosis, whether a *manzāzu*-formula (b_{1-2}, d) or merely the element Y (e).[52] Second, it is also evident that a *manzāzu*-formula, where it appears and is qualified by (or, less likely, qualifies) another element in the apodosis (b_{1-2}, c, d), *precedes* any other component of the apodosis, whether an *erištu*-statement (b_{1-2}, d) or merely Y (c). Third, it is plain that the *manzāz* DN formula can be qualified, for example by *ana damiqtim/lemuttim*, that is, as positive or negative, and thus cannot be understood, in and of itself, as having an absolute value.[53] From these observations it follows that the *erištu*-statements fill a fundamentally different role from those of *manzāzu*-formulas (notwithstanding the cases [d–e] where a divine name appears as part of the *erištu*-statement). It is also apparent that the same *erištu*-statement can follow two alternative *manzāzu*-formulas (b_2, d); the converse, however, is not attested. Finally, on the basis of all these factors it seems likely that, if at least for the oil omens, Pettinato's judgment stands: where they appear, the *erištu*-statements clarify or specify a preceding element — the latter often a *manzāz* DN formula.

Yet, as noted above, this examination of the oil omens is instructive in another manner, one dovetailing with the preceding observation and illuminating the broader underlying issue of the meaning of divine-presence formulas. In at least two pairs of omens from this corpus an inverse relation seems to operate between interpretive *erištu*-statements in apodoses and the appearance of similes or metaphors in the counterpart protases. One reads (example 5):

5 [1.] If from the middle of the mass a(n oil) bubble came up[54] and has burst ⇒ (it represents) the presence of Sîn: a request of/for silver (*erišti kaspim*).

---

[52] To my knowledge no example occurs in the lecanomancy corpus of an unqualified *erištu*-statement. Certainly elsewhere in early divination literature, e.g., in the extispicy corpus, this is not the case.

[53] So, too, Pettinato 1966, 2: 193.

[54] In another version: "detached."

2. If the oil, in your pouring water (on it), has taken (the shape of) two horns (*qarnīn*[55]) ⇒ (it represents) the presence of Sîn ø.[56]

3. If in your pouring water into the middle of the oil one fourth of the oil separated ⇒ (it represents) the presence of Šamaš: a request of/for the sun disk (*erišti šamšim*).

4. If in your pouring water into the middle of the oil (the oil bubble) came up like a star (*kīma kakkabim išḫiṭ*) ⇒ (it represents) the presence of Šamaš ø.[57]

Notably, *erištu*-statements appear in the apodoses of the first omens of each pair (lines 1, 3), while in the latter of each couple (lines 2, 4) they do not (indicated by ø above). What is remarkable about this is the relation of these apodoses with what precedes them. In the protases of the second omen of either pair one observes a transparent signification for the presence of Sîn and Šamaš: the metaphor of "horns" (*qarnū*) and the simile of a rising star (*kīma kakkabim išḫiṭ*), respectively; no such signification is found in the counterpart protases of omens (1) and (3). This finding can hardly be coincidental. Rather, one must assume that the appearance of the *erištu*-statements in the first of each pair, and their absence in the second, is directly related with the information given in the protases. To wit: where a sufficiently clear signification is offered in the protasis no explanatory gloss appears in the respective apodosis; where no such clarity is initially afforded on the other hand, one finds a compensatory explanation in the oracle itself.

In other words, statements of requests occur in these examples where formulas of divine presence appear but are not prompted by some unusual finding in the corresponding protasis. By "unusual" here what is meant is precisely what Nougayrol (1976) had in mind when describing his "*silhouettes dé référence*," those similes occurring in many omen protases that stood outside the standardized *metonymic* signification system of a given divinatory technique. With these for one reason or another a choice was made to keep things at the *metaphoric* level, that is, outside the bounds of the divinatory technique's established signification.[58] The divine-presence formulas in these examples represent the product of such cases. Their expression, when matched by the accompanying "silhouettes," appears foreign within the context of the established divinatory semiotics. Elsewhere, however, where found detached from their "silhouette" moorings, they are mediated by explanatory glosses. Such instances, as already observed, represent the majority among the overall number of occurrences of divine-presence formulas. From this picture it thus seems that not only do *erištu*-statements clarify often-preceding formulas of divine presence; they appear to do so when the accompanying *manzāz* DN formulas are not heralded by — one is tempted to say: have lost — metaphorical signs promoting various divine-presence significations.

This evidence, then, though limited in scope, nonetheless points to a metaphorically based connection between statements concerning divine "presence" in certain omen apodoses and particular signs in the matching protases. This connection seems to represent an exception to the collection's metonymy-based interpretive apparatus, what elsewhere in divination literature is plainly one of its defining features (see below). One wonders whether the unevenness in these findings suggests that a reconfiguration of ideas concerning the divine presence was

55 Also written *qannīn* in one version; on which see Pettinato 1966, vol. 1: 66, 2:41; GAG §35d.

56 Ölwahrsagung I 57–58.

57 Ölwahrsagung I 59–60.

58 A similar point concerning the use of metaphor in celestial divination is made in Rochberg 1996: 476.

already underway in Old Babylonian lecanomancy, though with the data available, at least for the oil-omen corpus, this question must remain in the realm of speculation.

6

Indeed, it remains to be seen whether the observations witnessed above for the case of lecanomancy hold for other branches of divination, most significantly extispicy. Elsewhere I argue that in fact a similar picture may be gleaned from the extispicy omens.[59] One striking example involves the following passage, where one finds just the sort of reference to the divine presence that was encountered with the oil omens (example 6):

6. [1–2.] [If] in the back of the Crucible of the right side a foo[t(-mark)] (*šēpum*) has a [f]ork ([*la*]*riam*) ⇒ (it represents) the foot of Nergal.

   [3–4.] If in the back of the Crucible of the right side (there are) two feet(-marks) (*šēpān*) ⇒ Adad will devastate the *iškaru*-fields of the pa[lace].

   [5.] If in the back of the Crucible of the right side a foot(-mark looks) like a shawl with (of) a *parsikku-band* ((<*u*>)*pur parsikkim*)[60] ⇒ (it represents) the presence of Ištar.[61]

Of particular interest is the third entry (line 5). In this instance again one encounters an unusual simile in the protasis, describing an image well outside of the standard metonymy-based nomenclature and semiology of extispicy (something even more striking when compared with the standard marks in lines 1–2, 3–4: the "foot" [*šēpum*] and "fork" [*larûm*][62]). That it should thus be the subject of theological speculation about the "presence" of a deity, in this case Ištar — this over against more standard formulations as those in the preceding entries[63] — is therefore less surprising than before.[64]

And yet a comparison between lecanomancy and extispicy is actually neither fair nor valid, since in the case of the latter, which was not only the most significant in the early periods but also the most technically advanced, statements concerning divine presence and requests had assumed, via metonymy, a place within the technical apparatus itself. In the case of divine presence this was probably the secondary name — *manzāzum*, the "Presence" — of the first zone of the liver, *naplastum* (or: *naplaštum*, the "View"), as Nougayrol first suggested.[65]

---

[59] Winitzer, forthcoming b.

[60] On the reading and significance of this "silhouette," see Winitzer, forthcoming b.

[61] MAH 15994:1–5 (Nougayrol 1969: 153–56; for collations and analysis, see Winitzer, forthcoming b).

[62] On these marks, see, for example, Jeyes 1989: 83–84, 92–93.

[63] For apodoses based on the *šēp* X formula, see Richter 1994: 241 n. 87. The apodictic mention of Nergal and other gods of plague and pestilence — and pestilence itself — for which Nergal is probably the hypostasis (see the discussion of CT 29:1b [= AbB 2 118] apud Jeyes 1989: 121; Wiggermann 1999: 216–17), is well attested; see CAD A/2, 96 s.v. *amūtu* A, mng. 2a; M/2, 296b, s.v. *mūtānu* mng. b; AO 7539 rev. 67′ (Nougayrol 1971: 72–77); OBE 1 obv. 19′; 3 iv 11′; 16 obv. 4′. For attestations of the common Adad (X) *iraḫḫiṣ* formula and its variations in apodoses, see Schwemer 2001: 416–19.

[64] See further Winitzer, forthcoming b.

[65] Nougayrol 1950: 3–5, 23; idem 1967: 219 n. 6; so Labat 1974: 123; Starr 1983: 77; but compare Jeyes 1989: 53; and Koch-Westenholz 2000: 52, who seem to favor the factor of geographical-regional distribution for the variant appellations. Again, needless to say, the matter need not be mutually exclusive.

Additional support in favor of Nougayrol's proposal may be found if one considers the name of this

Concerning requests there existed a mark named *erištum*, or "Request," whose appearance in the protasis frequently coincided with a statement of request in the accompanying apodosis (see, e.g., example 7 below).[66] In short, "presence" begat "Presence"; divine (and other) "requests" engendered "(the) Request."

7. If at the View's head (is) a Request-mark (*erištum*) ⇒ (it is) a request by the great god (*erišti ilim rabîm*).[67]

Consequently, in terms of both protases and apodoses, omen statements from extispicy collections are highly systematized and rather predictable, certainly relative to contemporary divination from other avenues. One suspects, for instance, that were the technical apparatus of extispicy less advanced and abstract in this period, then the apodosis of an omen like that in example 7 might initially have made mention of the deity's "presence," and then follow with the request statement, perhaps: **manzāz* DN *erišti ginîm*, "presence of DN; request for an offering."

Remarkably, however, even among this highly standardized material one still finds traces of the old interest in the divine presence. Evidence of this appears in a number of the collections themselves, which entertain in various ways a deity's "standing," or presence, in the performed extispicy (examples 8–11).

8. 1. "If it has Palace Gate ⇒ in whichever stanc[e (lit., stand) you] take the deity will protect you."
2. "If it does not have a Palace Gate ⇒ the gods will abandon the land."[68]

9. 1. "[If it ha]s [a View] ⇒ the man's sacrifice for (lit., with) the god will be (lit., is) accepted."
2. "[If it does not have a View] ⇒ it (i.e., the man's sacrifice for the god) will not be accepted (lit., did not stand)."[69]

10. "If the Path is situated (normally) ⇒ the god will set straight the man's path."[70]

---

same zone at Mari: *sissiktum*, the "Hem" (on which see most recently Glassner 2005: 282–83). As is well known, the mention of a *sissiktum*, at times paired with a lock of hair (*šārtum*), is frequent at Mari and elsewhere, with these functioning as markers of personal identification (for references see CAD S s.v. *sissiktu*, mng. c). Undoubtedly this was the sense behind the name of the extispicy zone at Mari, which, consequently, must be understood as a secondary development, again via metonymy, to signify the same concept that is at issue with *manzāzum*: divine presence.

[66] Jeyes 1989: 86. The mark's logographic rendering as kam/kám(-tu) is perhaps to be explained as deriving from ak.am, that is, the genitive postposition followed by the copula, and thus meaning something like "concerning, regarding." Its writing as uru_4 (APIN) represents undoubtedly a confusion with the homonymous *erēšum* "to plow"; compare also the lexical equation níg.al.di = *erištum* (e.g., Hh 1 41 [MSL V 12]).

[67] Text: YOS 10 17:66; and cf. its parallel in AO 9066:26–28 (Nougayrol 1950: 26 and pl. 1):

> If at the View's head (is) a Request-mark (*erištum*) ⇒ (it is) a request by the great god (*erišti ilim rabîm*); the god requests a regular offering (*ša ginîm ilum irriš*).

Interestingly, the additional gloss (for which see Winitzer 2006: 153–54) in this version concerns the object of the divine request — no small matter, theologically speaking. And yet still one finds no proclamation of the very deity's presence.

[68] YOS 10 23:1–2.

[69] YOS 10 17:1–2; also compare the parallel to YOS 10 17:1, AO 9066:1–2 (Nougayrol 1950: 23 and pl. 1).

[70] YOS 10 11 i 1–2.

And compare:

[6 omen entries concerning the Path]

11. "If it has a Strength ⇒ divine umbrage [will b]e upon the man."[71]

What is particularly striking about these examples is their place in the respective collections in which they appear: these represent the very opening of each. Even an apparent exception proves to confirm to the rule upon closer examination. This is example 11, an entry from a collection studying two different zones, which, when concerned with only the presence of the "Strength," figures to be the very first in its respective section — immediately following a double line demarcating between the former and the current topics.[72] Following each of these entries their respective compendia turn to deal with more usual concerns, those describing abnormalities of one sort or another in the very zone for which the issue of normal presence had first been explored, though now in more specific terms and in greater detail. It would thus seem that in a very real sense the idea of a given zone's normal state with which certain collections commence was intended to define the compendia, and to spell out the structural opposition between soundness and abnormality that elsewhere in the extispicy collections was the underlying assumption, what has been dubbed the "first paradigm" of divination.[73]

This evidence represents, in a sense, a vestige of an older interest that has been fossilized in the collections. But it is all the more significant for it. On its basis it is possible to say that at a fundamental level the basic theoretical notion of the deity's presence remained the central — indeed foundational — tenet for the broader enterprise. That the collections are frequently anchored by this premise cannot be ignored; that soon thereafter they shift to more complex algebraic permutations is, in a real sense, secondary. One cannot, despite the immense technical sea that followed, overlook that which served as the foundation to it all: the belief in the theological notion of divine presence as *sine qua non* for Mesopotamian divination.

Evidently, in all these examples the reality of the zone's presence or absence was equated with the theological metaphor of divine presence or abandonment, respectively. One wonders to what extent this signification reflected an article of faith for the diviner-scholar, one that operated coherently and consistently within his system of hermeneutics, and, subsequently, from which additional theological ominous postulates were (or could be) generated. This question, too, cannot be entertained in the present context, and must await a full treatment elsewhere. Nevertheless, it already seems clear that its analysis will yield important findings, and not only for our understanding of the semiotics of divination literature. After all, in the final analysis, statements concerning the divine presence in Old Babylonian Mesopotamian divination bear more broadly on contemporary conceptions of religion and the divine realm within it.

---

[71] AO 7028:7 (9) (Nougayrol 1941: 80; idem 1946: 56–57 and pl. 1).

[72] Notably, another such instance, ARM 26 3:18, another apparent exception to this pattern, also follows a ruling and begins a new section in its collection ARM 26 3 (Durand 1988: 66–68). What is more, it comprises the first entry of a numerical gradation (on which see Winitzer 2006: 553–605). In all likelihood, therefore, its place in the collection is to be attributed to these factors, something that explains its apparent exception to the rule as just that.

[73] See Winitzer 2006: 234–47, building on Starr 1983: 18. Why no explicit statement to this effect is appears in the majority of the collections seems in keeping with the general attitude toward second-order thinking at this time, on which see Machinist 1986.

7

Our journey, which must end, has not been a fruitless one, for we have gathered from it an answer to our initial query. The notion of divine presence in Mesopotamian divination, it is now clear, was not limited to theory alone. This remained a central tenet of Mesopotamian divination, even after the latter was reconfigured in part, with its empirical record incorporated into the scribal curriculum and the Mesopotamian written sciences.[74] In that new context a branch of Mesopotamian divination developed which no longer resembled what had previously been: Mesopotamian divination literature. This omen literature describes a different sort of divination altogether, one whose theater of operation was the written text and whose reasoning was derivative of the words themselves. In this rich new literary world — a world, in the manner of language itself, limitless in its deductive bounds — the manifestation of the divine figured much less prominently. Indeed, the beginnings of this process were already encountered above. The appearance of interpretative glosses describing "requests" following statements of divine "presence" in some examples suggests that even within the conceptual framework of any given divination technique, this *Ursprache* was, simply put, not enough; commentary would be needed to explain revelation. And what, one might ask by way of conclusion, was the fate of the latter? This, in turn, was relegated, in the way of a *deus otiosus*, to a conceptual attic from which, on unprecedented occasions, it could scarcely mutter a thin, small voice.

Which reminds us of an old, if somewhat less ancient, Mesopotamian story, at first glance about an intellectual debate on an altogether different matter, unrelated to our subject:

> On that day Rabbi Eliezer brought forward every imaginable argument, but they [the other Rabbis] did not accept them. He said to them: "If the law is as I say, let this carob tree prove it!" Thereupon the carob tree was torn a hundred cubits out of place (others affirm: four hundred cubits). "No proof can be brought from a carob tree," they answered. Again he said to them: "If the law is as I say, let the stream of water prove it!" Whereupon the stream of water flowed backwards. "No proof can be brought from a stream of water," they answered. Again he argued: "If the law is as I say, let the walls of the schoolhouse prove it." Whereupon the walls inclined to fall. (But Rabbi Joshua rebuked them, saying: "When scholars are engaged in ... dispute, what have you to interfere? Hence they did not fall in honor of Rabbi Joshua, nor did they remain upright, in honor of Rabbi Eliezer, and they are still standing thus inclined.)
>
> Again he said to them: "If the law is as I say, let it be proved from heaven!" Whereupon a heavenly voice cried out: "Why do you dispute with Rabbi Eliezer, seeing that in all matters the law is as he says!" But Rabbi Joshua arose and exclaimed: "It is not in heaven (Deut. 30:12)." What did he mean by this? Said Rabbi Jeremiah: "That the Torah had already been given at Mount Sinai; we pay no attention to a heavenly voice, because You have long since written the Torah at Mount Sinai....
>
> Rabbi Nathan met Elijah and asked him: "What did the Holy One, blessed be He, do at that moment?" He replied: "He laughed, saying: 'My sons have defeated me, my sons have defeated me'" (Babylonian Talmud, *Bava Metzi'a* 59b).

[74] For ramifications of this reconfiguration, see, for example, Glassner 2005: 276–77; Winitzer, forthcoming a.

ABBREVIATIONS

AbB	Altbabylonische Briefe in Umschrift und Übersetzung
AHw	W. von Soden, *Akkadisches Handwörterbuch*
AO	Musée du Louvre tablet number
ARM 26	Durand 1988
CAD	A. Leo Oppenheim et al., editors, *The Assyrian Dictionary of the Oriental Institute of the University of Chicago*
CT	Cuneiform Texts from Babylonian Tablets in the British Museum
Erm	Hermitage Museum tablet number
ETCSL	The Electronic Text Corpus of Sumerian Literature
FM 7	Durand 2002
FM 8	Durand 2005
GAG	W. von Soden, *Grundriß der Akkadischen Grammatik*
Hh	ḪAR.ra = *ḫubullu* (lexical series)
KAL	Keilschrifttexte aus Assur literarischen Inhalts
KAR	Keilschrifttexte aus Assur religiösen Inhalts
MAH	Musée d'Art et d'Histoire (Geneva) tablet number
MDAI	Mémoires de la Délégation archéologique en Iran
MSL	Materials for the Sumerian Lexicon
OB	Old Babylonian
OBE	Jeyes 1989
Ölwahrsagung	Pettinato 1966
YOS 10	Goetze 1947
YOS 11	van Dijk, Goetze, and Hussey 1985

BIBLIOGRAPHY

Bowden, Hugh
2004 *Classical Divination and the Delphic Oracle: Divination and Democracy*. Cambridge: Cambridge University Press.

Cooper, Jerrold S.
1983 *The Curse of Agade*. The Johns Hopkins Near Eastern Studies. Baltimore: Johns Hopkins University Press.

van Dijk, Johannes J. A.; Albrecht Goetze; and Mary I. Hussey
1985 *Early Mesopotamian Incantations and Rituals*. Yale Oriental Series 11. New Haven: Yale University Press.

Durand, Jean-Marie
1988 *Archives épistolaires de Mari* I/1. Archives Royales de Mari 26/1. Paris: Éditions recherche sur les civilisations.
1997 "La divination par les oiseaux." *Mari: Annales de Recherches Interdisciplinaires* 8: 273–82.
2000 *Documents épistolaires du palais de Mari*, Volume 3. Littératures anciennes du Proche-Orient 18. Paris: Éditions du Cerf.
2002 *Florilegium marianum* VII: *Le culte d'Addu d'Alep et l'affaire d'Alahtum*. Mémoires de N.A.B.U. 8. Paris: Société pour l'étude du Proche-Orient ancien.
2005 *Florilegium marianum* VIII: *Le culte des pierres et les monuments commémoratifs en Syrie amorrite*. Mémoires de N.A.B.U. 9. Paris: Société pour l'étude du Proche-Orient ancien.
2008 "La religion amorrite en Syrie à l'époque des archives de Mari." In *Mythologie et religion des sémites occidentaux*, Volume 1: *Ébla, Mari*, edited by G. del Olmo Lete, pp. 161–716. Orientalia Lovaniensia Analecta 162. Leuven: Peeters.

Eagleton, Terry
2003 *After Theory*. New York: Basic.

Edzard, Dietz Otto
1997 *Gudea and His Dynasty*. The Royal Inscriptions of Mesopotamia, Early Periods 3/1. Toronto: University of Toronto Press.

George, Andrew R.
2003 *The Babylonian Gilgamesh Epic: Introduction, Critical Edition and Cuneiform Texts*. 2 volumes. Oxford: Oxford University Press.

Glassner, Jean-Jacques
2002 "*takāltu*." *N.A.B.U.: Nouvelles Assyriologiques Brèves et Utilitaires* 8: 9–10.
2005 "L'aruspicine paléo-babylonienne et le témoignage des sources de Mari." *Zeitschrift für Assyriologie* 95: 276–300.

Goetze, Albrecht
1947 *Old Babylonian Omen Texts*. Yale Oriental Series 10. New Haven: Yale University Press. Second printing, 1966.

Hunger, Johannes
1903 *Becherwahrsagung bei den Babyloniern nach zwei Keilschrifttexten aus der Hammurabi-Zeit*. Leipziger semitistische Studien I/1. Leipzig: J. C. Hinrichs.

Jacobsen, Thorkild
1976 *The Treasures of Darkness: A History of Mesopotamian Religion*. New Haven: Yale University Press.

Jastrow, Morris
1905–12 *Die Religion Babyloniens und Assyriens*. 2 volumes. Giessen: Alfred Töpelmann.

Jeyes, Ulla
1989 *Old Babylonian Extispicy: Omen Texts in the British Museum*. Publication de l'Institut historique-archéologique néerlandais de Stamboul 64. Istanbul: Nederlands Historisch-Archaeologisch Instituut te Istanbul.

Klein, Jacob
1980 "Some Rare Sumerian Words Gleaned from the Royal Hymns of Šulgi." In *Studies in Hebrew and Semitic Languages Dedicated to the Memory of Prof. Eduard Yechezkel Kutscher*, edited by P. Artzi et al., pp. 9–28. Bar-Ilan Departmental Researches Department of Hebrew and Semitic Languages. Ramat Gan: Bar-Ilan University

Koch(-Westenholz), Ulla
2000 *Babylonian Liver Omens: The Chapters* Manzāzu, Padānu *and* Pān tākalti *of the Babylonian Extispicy Series Mainly from Aššurbanipal's Library*. Carsten Niebuhr Institute Publications 25. Copenhagen: Museum Tusculanum.
2005 *Secrets of Extispicy: The Chapter* Multābiltu *of the Babylonian Extispicy Series and* Nisirti bārûti *Texts mainly from Assurbanipal's Library*. Alter Orient und Altes Testament 326. Münster: Ugarit-Verlag.

Labat, Rene, with the assistance of Dietz Otto Edzard
1974 *Textes littéraires de Suse*. Mémoires de la Délégation archéologique en Iran 57. Paris: Paul Geuthner.

Lambert, Wilfred G.
1967 "Enmeduranki and Related Matters." *Journal of Cuneiform Studies* 21: 126–38.
1998 "The Qualifications of Babylonian Diviners." In *Festschrift für Rykle Borger zu seinem 65. Geburtstag am 24. Mai 1994:* tikip santakki mala bašmu..., edited by S. M. Maul, pp. 141–58. Cuneiform Monographs 10. Groningen: Styx.
2007 *Babylonian Oracle Questions*. Winona Lake: Eisenbrauns.

Lenzi, Alan
2008 *Secrecy and the Gods: Secret Knowledge in Ancient Mesopotamia and Biblical Israel*. State Archives of Assyria Studies 19. Helsinki: Helsinki University Press.

Machinist, Peter
1986 "On Self-Consciousness in Mesopotamia." In *The Origins and Diversity of Axial Age Civilizations*, ed. by S. N. Eisenstadt, pp. 183–202, 511–18. Albany: State University of New York Press.

Maul, Stefan M.
2003 "Omina und Orakel. A." *Reallexikon der Assyriologie* 10, 1/2: 45–88.

Michalowski, Piotr
1976 The Royal Correspondence of Ur. Ph.D. dissertation, Yale University.
2006 "The Scribe(s) of MDAI 57 Susa Omens?" *N.A.B.U.: Nouvelles Assyriologiques Brèves et Utilitaires* 41: 39–40.
2006a "How to Read the Liver — in Sumerian." In *If a Man Builds a Joyful House: Assyriological Studies in Honor of Erle Verdun Leichty*, edited by A. K. Guinan et al., pp. 487–97. Cuneiform Monographs 31. Leiden/Boston: Brill.

Moran, William L.
1969 "New Evidence from Mari on the History of Prophecy." *Biblica* 50: 15–56.

Nougayrol, Jean
1941 "Textes hépatoscopiques d'époque ancienne conservés au Musée du Louvre." *Revue d'assyriologie et d'archéologie orientale* 38: 67–83.

1946 "Textes hépatoscopiques d'époque ancienne conservés au Musée du Louvre (II)." *Revue d'assyriologie et d'archéologie orientale* 40: 56–97.

1950 "Textes hépatoscopiques d'époque ancienne conservés au Musée du Louvre (III)." *Revue d'assyriologie et d'archéologie orientale* 44: 1–40.

1967 "Rapports paléo-babyloniens d'haruspices," *Journal of Cuneiform Studies* 21: 219–35.

1969 "Nouveaux textes sur le *ziḫḫu* (I)." *Revue d'assyriologie et d'archéologie orientale* 63: 149–57.

1971 "Nouveaux textes sur le *ziḫḫu* (II)." *Revue d'assyriologie et d'archéologie orientale* 65: 67–84.

1976 "Les 'silhouettes de référence' de l'haruspicine." In *Kramer Anniversary Volume: Cuneiform Studies in Honor of Samuel Noah Kramer*, edited by B. L. Eichler, pp. 343–50. Alter Orient und Altes Testament 25. Kevelaer: Butzon & Bercker; Neukirchen-Vluyn: Neukirchener.

Oppenheim, A. Leo

1977 *Ancient Mesopotamia: Portrait of a Dead Civilization*. 2nd edition. Chicago: University of Chicago Press.

Parpola, Simo

1997 *Assyrian Prophecies*. State Archives of Assyria 9. Helsinki: Helsinki University Press.

Pettinato, Giovanni

1966 *Die Ölwahrsagung bei den Babyloniern*. 2 volumes. Studi Semitici 21–22. Rome: Istituto di studi del Vicino Oriente.

Pongratz-Leisten, Beate

1999 *Herrschaftswissen in Mesopotamien: Formen der Kommunikation zwischen Gott und König im 2. und 1. Jahrtausend v. Chr.* State Archives of Assyria Studies 10. Helsinki: Helsinki University Press.

Richter, Thomas

1994 "Zu einigen speziellen Keulenmarkierungen." *Altorientalische Forschungen* 21: 212–46.

Rochberg, Francesca

1996 "Personifications and Metaphors in Babylonian Celestial *Omina*." *Journal of the American Oriental Society* 116: 475–85.

Sallaberger, Walther

2005 "The Sumerian Verb na de_5(-g) 'To Clear.'" In *"An Experienced Scribe Who Neglects Nothing": Ancient Near Eastern Studies in Honor of Jacob Klein*, edited by Y. Sefati et al., pp. 229–53. Bethesda: CDL Press.

Sasson, Jack M.

1995 "Water beneath Straw: Adventures of a Prophetic Phrase in the Mari Archives." In *Riddles and Untying Knots: Biblical, Epigraphic, and Semitic Studies in Honor of Jonas C. Greenfield*, edited by Z. Zevit et al., pp. 599–608. Winona Lake: Eisenbrauns.

Schwemer, Daniel

2001 *Die Wettergottgestalten Mesopotamiens und Nordsyriens im Zeitalter der Keilschriftkulturen: Materialien und Studien nach den schriftlichen Quellen*. Wiesbaden: Harrassowitz.

2007 "The Storm-Gods of the Ancient Near East: Summary, Synthesis, Recent Studies, Part I." *Journal of Ancient Near Eastern Religions* 7: 121–68.

Starr, Ivan

1983 *The Rituals of the Diviner*. Bibliotheca Mesopotamica 12. Malibu: Undena.

1990 *Queries to the Sungod: Politics and Divination in Sargonid Assyria*. State Archives of Assyria 4. Helsinki: Helsinki University Press.

Steinkeller, Piotr

2005 "Of Stars and Men: The Conceptual and Mythological Setup of Babylonian Extispicy." In *Biblical and Oriental Essays in Memory of William L. Moran*, edited by A. Gianto, pp. 11–47. Biblica et Orientalia 48. Rome: Pontifical Biblical Institute.

van der Toorn, Karel

2000 "From the Oral to the Written: The Case of Old Babylonian Prophecy." In *Writings and Speech in Israelite and Ancient Near Eastern Prophecy*, edited by E. Ben Zvi and M. H. Floyd, pp. 219–34. Society of Biblical Literature, Symposium Series 10. Atlanta: Society of Biblical Literature.

2007 *Scribal Culture and the Making of the Hebrew Bible*. Cambridge: Harvard University Press.

Vanstiphout, Herman L. J., and Niek Veldhuis

1995 "ṭuppi ilāni takāltu pirišti šamê u erṣetim." *Annali* 55: 30–32.

Veldhuis, Niek

2006 "Divination: Theory and Use." In *If a Man Builds a Joyful House: Assyriological Studies in Honor of Erle Verdun Leichty*, edited by A. K. Guinan et al., pp. 487–97. Cuneiform Monographs 31. Leiden/Boston: Brill.

Volk, Konrad

1996 "Methoden altmesopotamischer Erziehung nach Quellen der altbabylonischen Zeit." *Saeculum* 47: 178–216.

Wiggermann, F. A. M.

1999 "Nergal. A." *Reallexikon der Assyriologie* 9, 3/4: 215–23.

Wilcke, Claus

2007 "Das Recht: Grundlage des sozialen und politischen Diskurses im Alten Orient." In *Der geistige Erfassen der Welt im Alten Orient*, edited by C. Wilcke, pp. 209–44. Wiesbaden: Harrassowitz.

Winitzer, Abraham

2006 The Generative Paradigm in Old Babylonian Divination. Ph.D. dissertation, Harvard University.

Forthcoming a "Writing and Mesopotamian Divination: The Case of Alternative Interpretation." *Journal of Cuneiform Studies*.

Forthcoming b "More on Inanna's Symbol as Sign, and Her 'Presence' in OB Divination."

11
PHYSIOGNOMY IN ANCIENT MESOPOTAMIA AND BEYOND: FROM PRACTICE TO HANDBOOK*

BARBARA BÖCK, CSIC, MADRID

Big head, little wit,
Small head, not a bit.[1]

INTRODUCTION

Physiognomy — the art of reading the face and general appearance as well as the idea that specific body characteristics are indicative of personality traits and man's future and fate — is deeply rooted in ancient cultures and still persistent in our day within the discipline of psychology, albeit in a marginal position. Not only the idea to judge other people's destiny and personality by visual inspection is a recurrent element in societies, but also the contexts in which physiognomic information has an effect are remarkably consistent. Ancient Mesopotamia has produced an ample amount of physiognomic omens. Although they are not as large in extent as extispicy, astronomical omens, or predictions drawn from occurrences in the human environment — such as the observations of the *Šumma ālu* corpus — the portents of human face and appearance are comparable in size to the teratological omens compiled in the *Šumma izbu* treatise. Despite the amount of physiognomic omens, there is hardly any evidence on how physiognomy was put into practice in ancient Mesopotamia. Neither the nature of the cuneiform sources nor the quality of information permits us to safely draw conclusions about reasons, circumstances, and individuals involved in performing the art of physiognomy. The present article suggests plausible situations for carrying out physiognomic evaluation in ancient Mesopotamia in the light of ancient and early Chinese and Sanskrit literature on body divination. Another aspect I treat is related to the authoritative character of divination. I also include some reflections on cuneiform handbooks as representational objects.

THE CUNEIFORM CORPUS

The first systematic treatment of physiognomic omens is owed to F. R. Kraus. In his work *Die physiognomischen Omina der Babylonier* (1935), Kraus provides an introduction to the handbook, which includes descriptions of its internal organization, function, and textual

* This article is part of the research project FFI 2008-00996. CSIC = Consejo Superior de Investigaciones Científicas.

[1] The quote is taken from the review article "Genius as to Feet and Inches: Is It the Tall Man or the Short One Who Is Great — Famous Men and Their Measurements," published in *The New York Times* on July 31, 1897.

history. Some years later, in 1939, appeared his *Texte zur babylonischen Physiognomatik* (= TBP), which contains a catalog of all physiognomic texts and fragments known to him at that time. The material Kraus has published in the form of cuneiform autographs is about 66 percent of the corpus we know today.[2] The present author has identified some 18 percent, which are included in *Die babylonisch-assyrische Morphoskopie*.[3] Single contributions and text editions carried out by a number of scholars amount to 16 percent of the material.[4] Now, as regards the critical text edition of this corpus, 5 percent have been treated by various scholars, 15 percent are owed to Kraus, and the remaining 80 percent have been published by the present author.

Physiognomic omens are first attested in the Old Babylonian period. The bulk of text material, however, dates from the first millennium B.C., like most of cuneiform scholarly literature. The great majority of copies comes from Esarhaddon's and Assurbanipal's libraries at Nineveh, others have been unearthed at the ancient cities of Assur, Nimrud, Sultantepe, Sippar, Babylon, Kiš, Ur, and Uruk. The handbook *Alandimmû* contains various sub-series, one entitled like the whole series of twelve tablets on the physical appearance of male anatomy, another sub-series of two tablets called in Akkadian *Šumma nigdimdimmû* ("If the outward look"), the sub-series *Kataduggû* "Statement," the sub-series on women's physiognomy, the sub-series of birthmarks, and, finally, the sub-series on muscle twitching. There are twenty-seven chapters in total, twenty-two of which are still preserved. Moreover, a considerable amount of commentaries and extra-serial tablets are to be added to this corpus.

The physiognomic handbook was arranged and edited, as it seems, by a single scholar, a certain Esagil-kīn-apli, exorcist at the court of the eleventh-century Babylonian king Adad-apla-iddina. Esagil-kīn-apli was also responsible for the redaction of the corpus of diagnostic and prognostic texts *Sakikkû*.[5] As far as the number of tablets comprised in both handbooks is concerned, J. Scurlock has put forward that the forty tablets constituting *Sakikkû* refer to the god Ea, whom some traditions consider as the author of the handbook. Accordingly, the number of tablets of the handbook *Alandimmû* should also implicitly be linked to a god. She proposed thirty tablets evoking the moon-god Sîn.[6] There is, however, no space for thirty incipits in the catalog of Esagil-kīn-apli. At most, twenty-seven incipits can be restored in the broken passage quoting the titles of the different sub-chapters on omens from flecks and macula. This number, furthermore, is reconstructed on the basis of the preserved colophons. I should add that there are traditions that also attribute the *Alandimmû* handbook to the god of wisdom and magic.

---

[2] Further texts have been published in Kraus 1936a; Kraus 1936b; Kraus 1947.

[3] See Böck 2000 and Böck 2004.

[4] The following contributions include text editions with translations: Köcher and Oppenheim 1958; Labat and Edzard 1974: 177–94; Hunger 1976: 85–98 (nos. 82 and 83); Arnaud 1985: 343; Arnaud 1987: 309; von Weiher 1993: 65–80 (nos. 149, 150, and 151). Translations have been offered by von Soden (1981) and Reiner (1982).

[5] See Finkel 1988.

[6] See Scurlock 2003: 396.

ALANDIMMÛ: FROM PRACTICE TO HANDBOOK

Alandimmû:

> Tablet III line 63 "If the curl in his front points downwards: losses, he will become worried."[7]
> Tablet VIII line 69 "If his right eye is long: he will become rich."[8]

Spot omens:

> *Šumma tirku* line 8 "If (a black birthmark) is (above his) left (eyebrow): he will be contented."[9]
> *Šumma kittabru* (said of women) line 9 "If she has a small birthmark on her right ear: she will make mischief."[10]

Twitching muscle:

> *Šumma šer'ān pūtīšu* line 1 "If the muscle of the right side of his forehead twitches: god [will give him happiness]."[11]

Behavioral omen:

> *Kataduggû* line 63 "If he often acts humbly: god will have mercy with him."[12]
> *Kataduggû* line 117 "If he is lavish: he [will suffer] losses."[13]

ON THE NATURE OF PHYSIOGNOMIC OMENS

If we had to characterize the omens included in the different sub-series and chapters of the physiognomic handbook, we would certainly have the impression that they smack of popular wisdom and appear to be widespread maxims, aphorisms, and common-sense truths. Instead of folklore, we prefer another term, which has been coined by the classicist scholar Gilbert Murray and applied by E. R. Dodds in his classic study *The Greeks and the Irrational*, namely, "inherited conglomerate." The expression refers to the folklore or the mass of experiences and forces, which have worked on a community in the past and left their mark on the minds and habits of thought of individuals. We would then describe the statements included in the physiognomic text corpus as inherited conglomerate of the ancient Mesopotamian insights into human condition and character.

Thanks to its visual, even non-literate nature, physiognomy is easily spread and accessible. Indeed, parts of the physiognomic text corpus are characterized by a certain transparency of what we could term the otherwise hidden webs of divination, which is due to a somewhat straightforward surface connection between portents of the human face and body and their respective interpretations. We are referring to predictions that result from commonplace associations of contents that account for an immediate access to the meaning of a portent. As can be observed, omens describing freckles and flecks of different nature located around the

[7] See Böck 2000: 92.
[8] See Böck 2000: 112.
[9] See Böck 2000: 204.
[10] See Böck 2000: 230.
[11] See Böck 2000: 234.
[12] See Böck 2000: 134.
[13] See Böck 2000: 138.

mouth are often linked with statements involving speech or food references. Some predictions derived from macula omens, which are observed on the feet, play with formulations that contain *verba movendi*, metaphorical expressions for legs and feet, or refer to motion and immobility. On the other hand, the size of the male member sheds light on virility and accounts for the number of children, while the form of breast and navel of women stands for fertility and the capacity of birthing.

Mouth

"If it (= *umṣatu* fleck) is on the surface of his tongue on the right side: he will be overwhelmed by blasphemy."[14]

"If it (= *umṣatu* fleck) is below his tongue: he will swear and god will not seize him."[15]

"If there is a *kittabru* fleck on his upper lip, be it inside, be it outside: god will provide him with plenty of food."[16]

"If there is a *kittabru* fleck above and below his lips: aphasia will seize him."[17]

"If there is a *kittabru* fleck on his upper gums, be it on the right, be on the left side, he will have plenty of food."[18]

Feet

"If they (= *umṣatu* flecks) cover his ankles: he will be confined in bed."[19]

"If there is a *kittabru* fleck on the right or left heel: he will follow the road of success."[20]

"If there is a *kittabru* fleck on the side of his feet, be it up, be it down: wherever he goes it will be propitious for him."[21]

"If there is (a dark spot) on his left foot: he will not follow the road of success."[22]

"If there is a *kittabru* fleck on the right side of the sole of her feet: solid fundaments will be assigned to her."[23]

Primary genitalia and breast

"If his penis looks like a fish: he will become powerful and have sons."[24]

"If his penis is long and thick: he will beget males."[25]

"If it (= *liptu* fleck) is on the right side of his penis: he will have few sons."[26]

"If it (= dark spot) is on the left side of his penis: he [will have] sons."[27]

---

[14] See Böck 2000: 188 (line 70).

[15] See Böck 2000: 188 (line 73).

[16] See Böck 2000: 216 (line 30).

[17] See Böck 2000: 216 (line 31).

[18] See Böck 2000: 216 (line 32).

[19] See Böck 2000: 192 (line 146).

[20] See Böck 2000: 227 (line 120). Note that the Akkadian phrase plays with the term *tallaktu* "way" and the Gtn stem of *alāku*.

[21] See Böck 2000: 227 (line 121).

[22] See Böck 2000: 210 (line 96).

[23] See Böck 2000: 232 (line 38).

[24] See Böck 2000: 122 (line 77).

[25] See Böck 2000: 122 (line 84).

[26] See Böck 2000: 175 (line 30).

[27] See Böck 2000: 209 (line 86).

> "If there is a *kittabru* on the upper side of his penis, be it up or down / be it right or left: he will have sons and daughters, he will make profit."[28]
>
> "If a woman's navel is hard: she is a woman who has difficulties to give birth."[29]
>
> "If a woman's navel is soft: she is a woman who brings her pregnancy to term."[30]
>
> "If *umṣatu* flecks cover (the nipples) of a woman: she is barren."[31]

But it is not only the issue of visibility that demarcates physiognomic omens from other divinatory treatises in which the perceptible world appears only as a small part of reality and whose hidden realms clearly require understanding and unraveling by experts. It is the nature and appearance of the object of physiognomy — namely, a normal physique, a healthy complexion, and an able-bodied person — that stand out against truly disturbing and ominous observations such as "a ewe that gives birth to a lion, and it has the face of an ass,"[32] or "an anomaly has three extra ears behind both of its ears and they face its back,"[33] or the prospect of "a goat-like catcher demon which is seen in a man's house,"[34] or "a ghost crying out a good deal in a man's house."[35]

Yet one more characteristic of the physiognomic text corpus should be mentioned: all predictions refer exclusively to the person who is object of or subject to visual inspection. In other words, as compared to predictions referring to king and country compiled in omen handbooks such as *Šumma izbu, Šumma ālu, Enūma Anu Enlil*, or extispicy, the impact of physiognomic omens was very limited and reduced: whether a man had a black fleck behind or on top of his left ear scarcely concerned anybody else but him, since he would have to cope with the consequences. The question of who might be affected by an omen was a serious matter and it was apparently one of the first issues addressed by the expert. Quite illustrative in this regard is one of the letters of the astrologer Balasî who wrote in early 670 B.C. to king Esarhaddon:

> As to what the king, m[y lord, wr]ote [to me]: "[In] the city of H[ar]ihumba lightning struck and ravaged the fields of the Assyrians" — why does the king look for (trouble), and why does he look (for it) [in the ho]me of a tiller? There is no evil inside the palace, and when has the king ever visited Harihumba?[36]

---

[28] See Böck 2000: 222 (lines 87–88).

[29] See Böck 2000: 163 (line 188). In her recent translation of some of the omens included in the chapter on women's physiognomy, R. Pientka-Hinz (2008: 46–47 with fnn. 87 and 92) translates the apodosis *mulamminat* with "ist sie eine, die Böses tut" referring to AHw 542. W. von Soden, however, states in AHw 542b s.v. *lemēnu*(*m*) D 2, that the meaning of the participle in the D-stem stative is unclear. CAD L 118a s.v. *lemēnu* 5a) 5′, in turn, suggests the meaning "she will have a difficult time giving birth." The translation chosen here and in Böck 2000: 163 follows CAD and takes into account the opposition between *mulamminat* and *mušallimat* in the follwing line. As for *mušallimat*, we prefer to follow CAD Š/1 s.v. *šalāmu* 226b 11f., which gives for *šalāmu* in D-stem the meaning "to bring to term" and preserves more accurately the basic meaning; AHw 1145a s.v *šalāmu*(*m*) D 5 c translates "gesund gebären" which is also the translation of R. Pientka-Hinz.

[30] See Böck 2000: 163 (line 189).

[31] See Böck 2000: 162 (line 169).

[32] The quote is from Leichty 1970: 78 (V line 53).

[33] The quote is from Leichty 1970: 142 (XI line 138′).

[34] The quote is from Freedman 1998: 276 (XIX line 1).

[35] The quote is from Freedman, 1998: 280 (XIX line 65′).

[36] See Parpola 1993a: 32–33 no. 42 lines 5–15.

WAS THERE AN ORAL PHYSIOGNOMICAL TRADITION?

I have stated that physiognomy formed part of the Mesopotamian inherited conglomerate and assumed that it had its roots in and arose partly from popular wisdom and general notions of physiognomical characteristics, though distinct for ancient Mesopotamians. Our arguments referred to a certain transparency and immediacy of the divinatory speech — as it may be observed in some omens — as well as to the modes of interpreting physical signs based on associations or wordplays that must have been common to all people.[37] In order to prove the assumption that physiognomy grew in part out of folklore, I should wonder now how significant oral tradition was and what was its relationship with the physiognomy described in the handbook of physiognomic omens.

There are two text corpora representative of oral traditions, which seem to have absorbed some ideas incorporated later in *Alandimmû*. Remnants of oral tradition in both physiognomy and human behavior have been handed down in the form of proverbs, and other physiognomical expressions have penetrated one of the lexical texts, namely the Old Babylonian List of Human Classes — the so-called lú ázlag : *ašlākum*. It is worth noting that all in all there are only very few parallels that can be drawn and, as shown below, correspondences between proverbial *sagesse* and the physiognomic omen handbook are confined to the section on behavioral omens only. As for the Old Babylonian lexical texts, they echo either the physical descriptions or the state and fate of the person, but they do not provide a link between the signifier and the thing signified. It should also be emphasized that there is a temporal gap between the proverbs and the lexical text on the one hand, and the *Alandimmû* handbook on the other. Finally, there is also a difference in language.

As discussed further below, there are no exact parallels, but rather what we might call "variations on a theme." Examples are taken from the Sumerian proverb collection quoting the B. Alster's 1997 *Proverbs of Ancient Sumer* and those proverbs W. G. Lambert included in his 1960 *Babylonian Wisdom Literature*.

Example 1:

Proverbs: (a) Alster 1997: 20; (b) K. 4347+16161, Lambert 1960: 240

(a) line 78 "He hurled his insult, and (soon) there was a curse (on him)."

(b) ii lines 15–17 "Slander no one, and then grief [will not] reach your heart."

F. R. Kraus' *"Sittenkanon"* (Kraus 1936a): *Šumma kataduggû* lines 27, 32, 141, 142, 191, 192[38]

"If he slanders and causes troubles: his god will oblige him to corvee work."

"[If he] slanders someone: he will die due to denouncement."

"If he constantly hurls insults: it will turn against him, [...]."

"If he calumniates someone: *ditto*."

"If he is a calumniator: he will be denounced."

[37] For association as one of the principles of order in Hammurabi's law code, see Petschow 1968; for association based on the shape of cuneiform signs, see Edzard 1982; for the role of phonological association and semantic attraction in lexical lists, see Finkel 1982: 23–36; for analogy as one of the decoding/encoding devices in divination, see Glassner 1984.

[38] See Böck 2000: 132, 140, 142.

"If he hurls insults: he will be denounced."

Example 2:

Proverbs: Alster 1997: 87

3.33 "(He who says) 'Let me live today' is bound like a bull to a leash."

F. R. Kraus' *"Sittenkanon"* (Kraus 1936a): *Šumma kataduggû* line 4[39]

"If he says 'I shall live!': he will not live."

Example 3:

Proverbs: (a) Alster 1997: 216; (b) Lambert 1960: 263

(a) 14.1 "Let kindness be repaid to him who repays a kindness."

(b) Obv. lines 12–13 "May kindness be repaid to him who does a kindness."

F. R. Kraus' *"Sittenkanon"* (Kraus 1936a): *Šumma kataduggû* line 58[40]

"If he repays kindness: he will be completely pleased."

Example 4:

Proverbs: K. 4347+16161, Lambert 1960: 240

ii lines 11–14 "Commit no crime, and fear [of your god] will not consume you."

F. R. Kraus' *"Sittenkanon"* (Kraus 1936a): *Šumma kataduggû* lines 87, 145[41]

"If he hates wrongdoing: his god will go together with him."

"If he is a criminal: he will be discontent."

The other text corpus, which presents some physiognomical references, is the Old Babylonian List of Human Classes.[42] Since I have already treated resemblances between this lexical text and expressions in the omen handbook,[43] I refer to a few examples in order to illustrate the degree of comparability. A person whom god has rejected is called lú dingir.zag.tag.ga : *ša ilum iskipu*[*šu*] (OB Lú rec. A 380). The same phrase occurs as omen apodosis in the Old Babylonian treatise on flecks called in Akkadian *umṣatum*: "If there is an *umṣatum* fleck on the right side of his breast: he is rejected by his god."[44] A bashful person is referred to in the lexical entry lú téš.tuku.tuku : *bajjišum* (OB Lú B ii 25). Compare the two omens "If a man has long eyelashes: he is bashful; if they are thick: he is bashful and fears god."[45] The last example is a person with a particular hair growth called in Akkadian (*ḫ*)*apparû*(*m*). The lexical entry reads lú sík.guz.za : *ḫapparrû* (OB Lú C_5 22) and the omen "if a man's head is shaggy: happiness."[46]

[39] See Böck 2000: 130.

[40] See Böck 2000: 134.

[41] See Böck 2000: 137, 140.

[42] See Landsberger, Reiner, and Civil 1969.

[43] See Böck 1999: 60–67.

[44] See Böck 2000: 303 (line 10).

[45] See Böck 2000: 290 (line 21) and 292 (line 23).

[46] See Böck 2000: 76 (*Alandimmû* II line 52).

To finish this part, we include a proverb about a wife who is quite extravagant, which is in turn one of the arguments that speaks in favor or against her being chosen as bride.

Proverbs: Alster 1997: 31; BM 38539 4–7; Lambert 1960: 266 lines 4–7 (first-millennium version)

line 151 "In marrying a thriftless wife, in begetting a thriftless son, an unhappy heart was assigned to me."

line 154 "A thriftless wife living in a house is worse than all diseases."

Physiognomic omens on women: *Šumma sinništu qaqqada rabât* lines 4, 6, 70, 74[47]

"If there is a red *umṣatu* fleck on her right ear: she is marriageable but thriftless."

"If there is a yellow *umṣatu* fleck on her right ear: she is marriageable but thriftless."

"... are beclouded: she will ruin the house where she will be living."[48]

"...: she will ruin the house she enters."[49]

There are strikingly few comparable statements between the physiognomic handbook and the text corpora of proverbs and the Old Babylonian List of Human Classes. Since any resemblance or link between the oral folk tradition preserved in proverbs and the knowledge assembled in *Alandimmû* is more arbitrary than natural, we can merely deduce that oral tradition on physiognomy has not been captured in text genres of folklore, such as the collections of proverbs, and has thus been lost. There is, however, one commentary to physiognomic omens preserved which according to its colophon goes back to oral interpretive tradition.[50] Whether also other parts of physiognomic lore were handed down orally, we will never know.

THE LANGUAGE OF PHYSIOGNOMIC OMENS AND THE ISSUE OF STANDARDIZATION

The sayings and statements of the physiognomic handbook were, in all likelihood, rather familiar to the members of ancient Mesopotamian society. One should add that this is a feature that can be found in other divinatory treatises, too. This proximity to or familiarity with

[47] See Böck 2000: 152, 154, 156.

[48] The apodosis allows two translations; the one given here and the passive version "the house in which she will live, will be ruined" as given in Böck 2000: 155.

[49] Again, the apodosis allows two translations; the one given here and the passive version "the house in which she will enter, will be ruined" as given in Böck 2000: 157.

[50] The text is published in Hunger 1976: 87 (no. 83); the reference is in rev. 28: NIG$_2$.ZI.GAL$_2$.EDIN.NA *šu-ut pi-i u maš-a-a-al-tum šá um-man-nu šá* DIŠ SAG.DU *ḫu-la-mi-šú* GAR "Word list, oral explanation and examination of a scholar for 'If he has a head like a chameleon.'" The text comments, words, and expressions to the tablet published by Kraus as TBP 17 (Kraus 1939: pl. 24), which is an explanatory text (perhaps a *mukallimtu* commentary) to the second tablet of the *Alandimmû* handbook. See for both texts also Böck 2000: 246–49, 254–56.

physiognomy is corroborated by the terminology used for the different terms of face and body, which do not require any specific anatomical knowledge.[51] Rather, as I have already put forward by comparing physiognomic terminology with the list on human anatomy, *Ugu.mu* — a lexical text that was part of the basic learning in schools — physiognomy-related words form part of "everyday language."[52]

As for the complete omen sentences, they are certainly not the everyday language of the period to which most written testimonies of physiognomy and the physiognomic handbook itself date, that is, around the time of Assurbanipal. This is best attested by the various commentaries to physiognomic omens dating roughly from the time of Assurbanipal to the fourth century B.C. In these commentaries, the Assyrian and Babylonian scholars explained the lost meaning of some obscure, difficult, or obsolete expressions and phenomena.[53] Note, for example, a commentary of the Urukaen exorcist Anu-ikṣur, where the typically Old Babylonian writing *wa-ṣu-ú*, which was not any more understood, is explained by spelling it out *a-ṣu-u*.[54] It is, however, not beyond doubt that spellings such as this actually point to an Old Babylonian precursor of the text. It is also likely that scribes used old-fashioned writings intentionally in order to demonstrate their learnedness or to make the text appear older and antiquated.

Apodoses found in the physiognomic handbook are characterized by standard formulations which are also found in other omen treatises such as *Šumma ālu* and *Šumma izbu*. The same phraseology entered into the genre of *Šuila*-prayers, which also formed part of apotropaic *namburbi* rituals that were performed to avert the evil predicted by an ominous sign.[55] As compared to the Old Babylonian apodoses of the physiognomic corpus, which are more varied as regards themes and formulations, the first-millennium versions seem, from a subjective point of view, unoriginal, repetitive, and rather simplified.[56]

Yet the standardized written form of expressions did not only facilitate the association between the divinatory literature and formal prayers such as the *Šuila* type, but it also helped foster traditional texts. The importance of preserving these "ancient beliefs," entailing thus the need for scholarship, becomes more evident if we consider the language or dialect in which the texts are written. Divinatory texts were like Akkadian first-millennium literature composed in the Standard Babylonian dialect, which differed formally, grammatically, and lexically from the Assyrian and Babylonian vernacular dialects. To keep alive a rich written culture in Akkadian (Standard Babylonian) and Sumerian had an impact on the position and authority of specialists and experts in the respective fields of knowledge, as amply testified by the number of scholars attached to the court of the Assyrian kings.

---

[51] This observation as well as a comparison between medical and physiognomical texts will be further developed in a forthcoming article.

[52] See, for a comparison between some terms attested in *Ugu.mu* and in the physiognomic omen corpus, Böck 2000: 45–46.

[53] For a study of Babylonian and Assyrian hermeneutics, see Frahm, in press.

[54] The text is Hunger 1976: 86–89 (no. 83); the text is a *ṣâtu*-commentary, for which see Frahm 2004: 46–47 n. 15.

[55] See Böck 2002 for a comparison of the terminology; for a thorough study of apotropaic rituals, see Maul 1994.

[56] It is worth noting that a somewhat similar process took place in the transmission of Akkadian literary texts. J. S. Cooper (1977: 509), in his study of the Old Babylonian and Standard Babylonian version of the Myth of Anzu, observes "the OB version chose to phrase similar ideas differently in different contexts, whereas the SB text conflates and homogenizes, albeit artfully, producing a text in which subtly different expressions become monotonously identical. The narrative not only becomes less interesting, but may be impoverished as well."

There are few reflections about the effect and circumstances of the process of fixing texts. A. L. Oppenheim pointed to the "freezing" impact of writing, relevant for certain text genres, keeping "a specific wording and an established arrangement of content," which he situates into the third quarter of the second millennium B.C. As for the consequences, he further explains, "standardization effectively maintained the original contents against the pressure of changing concepts and attitudes, preserving obsolete text material that otherwise certainly would have disappeared."[57] In his study *The Logic of Writing and the Organization of Society*, J. Goody takes up the issue of the fixedness of text, referring especially to prayers. Once a prayer such as the Lord's Prayer is fixed, it requires exact repetition regardless of whether the words are understood or if they are suitable for specific times and occasions. This "repetitious diction" tends, as Goody describes, "to simplify complex procedures (...) for which end the Book is highly instrumental."[58]

I would like to add two more aspects to the discussion, which involve the advantages of standardization and the intention of divination language. Standardizing texts or languages has undoubtedly the advantage that it eases learning. This is an issue that is often overlooked since we do not have any data about how much an expert scribe learned, memorized, or internalized throughout his career. We can certainly reconstruct the school *pensum* of scribes and we also know from texts, such as the catalog of works belonging to the art of exorcism (*āšipūtu*), what an incantation priest was supposed to have studied.[59] Despite this information, the picture of how many texts were actually known by expert scholars by heart remains somewhat blurred.

Quite instructive in this regard is the number of text verses W. Bascom gives in his study on casting cowrie divination among the Yoruba in Nigeria. His main source is the Nigerian diviner Salakho who could recite for him more than 12,000 lines of divinatory text.[60] Just to compare, if the physiognomic handbook were completely preserved, it would include about 2,000 lines of text. Additional information for memorizing comes from the corpus of propitious rituals, the so-called *namburbi*. At least two tablets could have been used as memory prop, as S. M. Maul suggests. Both texts are *Sammeltafeln* and seem to be concise versions of several rituals containing keywords and incipits of prayers, which in their full form would have occupied the space of ten to twelve tablets.[61] In all likelihood, *Alandimmû* had to be learned and memorized for quotation. The catalog of incipits of both the diagnostic and prognostic, and the physiognomic handbook provide support for this assumption. The catalog states, "one who does not achieve a certain degree of knowledge shall not pronounce the *Sakikkû* handbook and shall not recite *Alandimmû*."[62]

As we may observe, quite a number of physiognomic predictions display "philological" knowledge, which — as it is generally assumed — was only accessible to the scholarly elite

---

[57] Oppenheim 1975: 18; see also Oppenheim 1978: 642 on the standardization of omen apodoses. For the process of "canonization," see Leichty 1993: 24.

[58] Goody 1986: 39.

[59] See Gesche 2001 for first-millennium schools. For the curriculum of an *āšipu*, compare the works listed in KAR 44 and duplicates, for which see the edition Geller 2000: 242–54.

[60] The transliteration and translation of the divination verses occupy most of the study; see Bascom 1980: 54–773.

[61] Maul (1994: 203–04) suggests that the tablets K. 9718(+) and K. 9789+ "waren für einen Beschwörer von Nutzen, der die Ritualtexte beherrschte und den Text der Tafel lediglich als Gedankenstütze benötigte."

[62] Quoted are lines A 64–65 / B 27′–28′ according to the edition of Finkel 1988: 148. The first verb is *dabābu*(*m*) written logographically DU_{11}.GA, the second *nabû*(*m*).

and enabled them thus to provide interpretations. By philological knowledge, I mean the different hermeneutical techniques such as association, analogy, and bringing into play language and writing. Unlike the use of writing skills, association, analogy, and wordplay were common devices of dialog, interpretation, and understanding that had to be shared by any Mesopotamian. It is precisely this graphic level that allows us to re-assess the nature of *Alandimmû*. It seems that, in the process of compiling and composing the handbook of physiognomic omens, the Assyrian and Babylonian scribes would have attributed a scholarly rationalization later, with the benefit of hindsight. There are several omens in which the scribe stressed or playfully hid, through the choice of cuneiform signs, an association or interpretation.[63] Perhaps one could say that the impetus for intellectual endeavors and aspirations of the Assyrian and Babylonian scholars lay not so much in the formation and creation of omens but rather in demonstrating their — writing — skills of reasoning, corroborating thus the prediction.[64] The following examples demonstrate this assumption.

Example 1: *Alandimmû* II line 107, text duplicate D[65]

DIŠ SIK$_2$ *bi-tam na-da-at ek-liš* GAL$_2$ *ina tam-ṭa-a-ti* GEN.MEŠ

"If the hair turns inside: he will be gloomy, he will suffer losses."

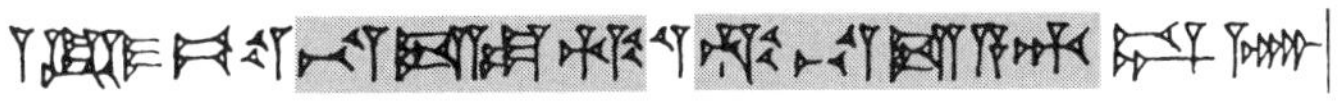

Figure 11.1. Kraus 1939: pl. 4, text 3b rev. iii line 10

A closer look at the cuneiform writing reveals how the expert scribes played with the signs or rather chose them deliberately, as if to show the evident connection between protasis and apodosis on the written level. In order to demonstrate the visual effect, the words and signs are transliterated regardless of their correct reading.

The verbal form written *na-da-at* in the protasis is graphically resumed in the apodosis. If we compare the appearance of the signs, what is read *ina tam-* looks very much like the NA-sign. We would then have, on a graphic level, the sequence NA-DA-A-TI which has to be correctly read *ina tam-ṭa-a-ti*. Another graphic play is the writing of *ek-* in *ek-liš* in the protasis and GAL$_2$ in the apodosis, both being the same cuneiform sign.

Example 2: *Šumma umṣatu* line 3[66]

DIŠ SAG.DU-*su ma-la-a* ḪUL.GIG *uḫ-tam-maṭ-su ma-la-a* IL$_2$.MEŠ

"If his head is covered (with *umṣatu* flecks): rancor will make him restless, he will wear the hair gear of mourning."

The verb *malû* is attested seventy times in the physiognomic handbook; in fifty-eight occasions it is written logographically with DIRI and in twelve times it is spelled syllabically. In the *Šumma umṣatu* section DIRI is attested twelve times and *malû* in syllabic writing, three

[63] See Eckart Frahm, "Reading the Tablet, the Exta, and the Body," in this volume.

[64] See also the discussion of Larsen 1987: 222–25 on the role of writing and literacy in Mesopotamian divination.

[65] See Böck 2000: 82.

[66] See Böck 2000: 184.

times. The chapter on the *kittabru* fleck does not use *malû* syllabically spelled but nine times uses the logogram. Though in roughly 17 percent of all preserved passages *malû* is written syllabically, I believe that it is noteworthy that it is spelled out in the line under discussion. It seems that the scribe intended to stress the validity of the interpretation by choosing the same spelling for the homonymous forms of *malû* "hair dress of mourners" in accusative singular and of *malû* "to cover" stative G in plural feminine.

Example 3: *Šumma umṣatu* lines 6–8 (and lines 1–14)[67]

DIŠ *ina* GU_2.TAL_2 ZAG GAR *mu-kil ku-tál-šú* UG_7 $ŠA_3$ ḪUL IGI

DIŠ *ina* GU_2.ḪAŠ KIMIN SAG.ḪUL.ḪA.ZA SIG_3-*su-ma* UG_7-*su*

DIŠ *ina* GU_2.ḪAŠ : GU_2.TAL_2 GUB_3 GAR KIMIN SI.SA_2 : ŠUB EN INIM-*šú*

"If it (= the *umṣatu* fleck) is on the right side of the back of his head: the one who supports him will die, he will experience worry."

"If it (= the *umṣatu* fleck) *ditto* (= is on the right side of the back of his head): the demon called 'the one who provides evil' will affect him and he will die."

"If it (= the *umṣatu* fleck) is on the left side of the back of his head: *ditto* (= the demon called 'the one who provides evil') will advance against him, defeat of his enemy in court."[68]

What marks the composition of these lines is the use of the term *kutallu*. A writing play is included in line 6 with the logogram GU_2.TAL_2 instead of the rather common GU_2.ḪAŠ in the protasis, which is taken up again in the apodosis with *ku-tál-šú*. This writing is clearly a wordplay since one would rather expect the correct spelling *ku-tál-li-šú*. The connection from line 6 to line 7 is on an associative level linking the expression *mukil kutalli* with the name of the demon *mukil rēš lemutti* which is repeated in line 8. On the writing level it should be noted that the logogram ḪUL of the demon SAG.ḪUL.ḪA.ZA appears in the preceding line in the expression $ŠA_3$ ḪUL.

A closer look at the whole section of TBP 36 i 1–14 (Kraus 1939: pl. 40) seems to suggest that the scribes were guided by keywords, in particular by logograms. Once a term is introduced, it comes up again in the following line(s). The apodosis in line 1 contains the expression ḪUL $ŠA_3$ GIG, some of these logograms appear in the following omens, namely, in line 2 GIG, in line 3 ḪUL.GIG, and in line 6 $ŠA_3$ ḪUL. In line 4 appears the term ŠUB KA which is used in line 5, too. In line 8 we find ŠUB EN INIM-*šú*, the following line 9 and also line 13 refer to EN INIM. In order to better visualize the occurrences of logograms in *Šumma umṣatu* lines 1–19, Kraus' copy is included below. Only parallel logograms and syllabic writings have been transliterated.

---

[67] See Böck 2000: 184.

[68] The apodosis allows two translations since the KIMIN sign can refer to both the name of the demon only or the name of the demon and the following verb *maḫāṣu*. In the translation here I have given preference to the first option; the logogram SI.SA_2 has been equated with the verb *kašādu*. In Böck 2000: 184 (line 8), however, I understood that KIMIN would include the whole expression and the following logogram SI.SA_2 would stand in opposition to *matū* "to die" in the preceding line. Accordingly, I read the logogram as *iššer* derived from the verb *ešēru* "to get well."

Šumma umṣatu, text duplicate K. 12548+ (= TBP 36)

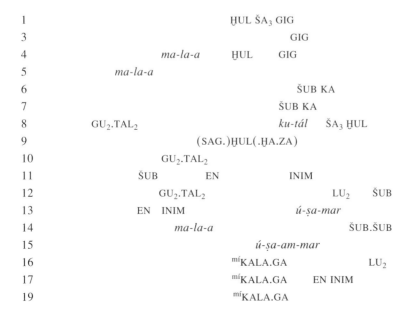

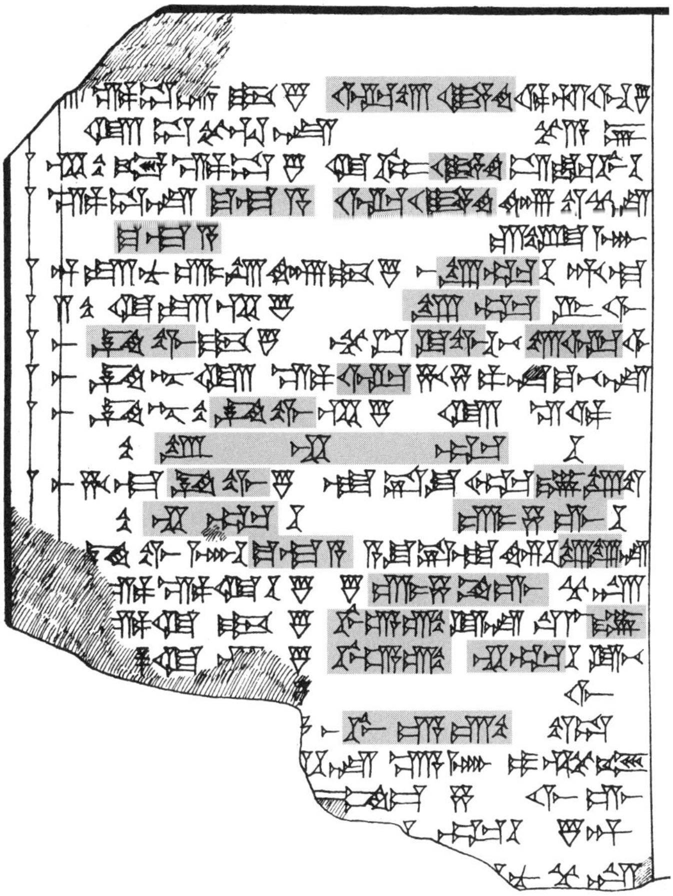

Figure 11.2. Kraus 1939: plate 39, text 36 obv. i 1–23

1 ḪUL ŠA$_3$ GIG
3 GIG
4 *ma-la-a* ḪUL GIG
5 *ma-la-a*
6 ŠUB KA
7 ŠUB KA
8 GU$_2$.TAL$_2$ *ku-tál* ŠA$_3$ ḪUL
9 (SAG.)ḪUL(.ḪA.ZA)
10 GU$_2$.TAL$_2$
11 ŠUB EN INIM
12 GU$_2$.TAL$_2$ LU$_2$ ŠUB
13 EN INIM *ú-ṣa-mar*
14 *ma-la-a* ŠUB.ŠUB
15 *ú-ṣa-am-mar*
16 ^{mí}KALA.GA LU$_2$
17 ^{mí}KALA.GA EN INIM
19 ^{mí}KALA.GA

Example 4: Second excerpt tablet of the series of extra-serial *Alandimmû* omens

TBP 23 (Kraus 1939: pl. 29)[69]

line 8 [DIŠ U.]MEŠ GIR$_3$.II.MEŠ-*šú* TUR.MEŠ NIM.MEŠ UGU ŠEŠ.MEŠ-*šú i-šaq-qu*

line 9 [DIŠ U.MEŠ] GIR$_3$.II.MEŠ-*šú* TUR.MEŠ *šag-ga-ma* (…)

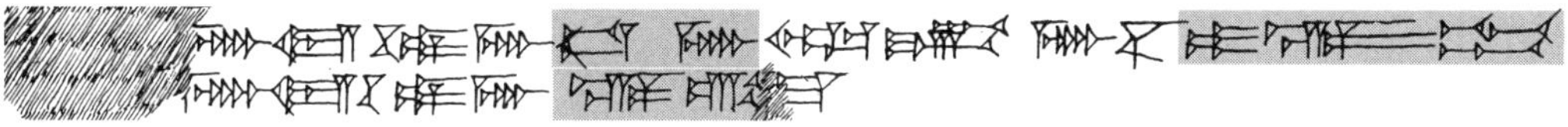

Figure 11.3. After Kraus 1939: plate 29, text 23 obv. lines 8–9

In line 8 the scribal play is about the different writing forms of the verb *šaqû*: as logogram NIM in the protasis and syllabically spelled in the apodosis. In accordance with the following lines, the form in the protasis should be transliterated as stative plural feminine *šaqâ*. It is worth noting that the verbal form *šaggā-ma* in the succeeding line 9 is a sound play on *šaqâ* and at the same time a graphic play on *išaqqû*, both being spelled with the SAG sign.

Another aspect of the study of physiognomic texts relates to the language of divination and the identity of the "author" of the prediction. Although divination is associated with the divine realm, as discussed below, the gods are not considered the authors of omens but rather supervisors of a divinatory procedure. As for the physiognomic handbook, the god Ea or the great gods are not specific to physiognomy or divination in general. The formulation and style of predictions rather point to anonymity for which no one accounts. There are no personal intentions behind the words; no one appears to be responsible either for the selection of words or for their consequences and no one questions the validity of a prediction. On the contrary, a sign and its prediction could only be canceled out or counterbalanced by another sign and experts could manipulate a meaning by searching for alternative interpretations.[70] As stated by Ulla Koch-Westenholz concerning the interference of Assyrian and Babylonian experts in astrology, "the individual astrologer's judgment of what seems relevant plays a decisive role in what omina are selected."[71] It seems that what authorizes divination is the absence of human responsibility which is best demonstrated by the reliance on texts full of old-fashioned, learned, and obscure meanings.

THE PHYSIOGNOMIC HANDBOOK AS REPRESENTATIONAL OBJECT

The corpus of physiognomic texts appears as an amalgam of ideas, beliefs, and customs that, having received the sanction of tradition, was systematically established, documented and copied using eventually a sophisticated writing system. Physiognomy became thus the book *Alandimmû*. The fact that scribes took care in writing and highly regarded the contents of their tablets turned the tablet handbook into a representational object. Although because of their material cuneiform manuals lack artistic decorations and colorful illustrations, as compared with the masterpieces of Eastern and Western literature written on papyrus, parchment, and paper,

[69] See Böck 2000: 280 (with text duplicate TBP 69).

[70] See Koch-Westenholz 1995: 146 for the issue of cancellation and a discussion of the so-called Diviner's Manual.

[71] Koch-Westenholz 1995: 150.

which are in the truest sense representational objects, they do actually share some features with the latter. Needless to say, no cuneiform handbook could ever equal a manuscript such as the famous Kennicott Bible, one of the most costly medieval Spanish manuscripts, copied by Moses Ibn Zabara in La Coruña in the province of Galicia in northwest Spain. Cuneiform texts are not as beautifully written as the aforementioned Hebrew Bible manuscript, but at least, as far as the tablet collection of Assurbanipal and his father is concerned, the tablets are distinguished by a stylistic calligraphy that allows even tiny fragments to be easily identified as belonging to one of the Nineveh libraries.[72] Admitting the somewhat inappropriate comparison, I believe that the binding of the Kennicott Bible into a splendid morocco goatskin box is certainly rivaled by the skillfully and delicately carved ivory boards sheeted with wax, which Sir Max Mallowan discovered at Nineveh.[73]

Another characteristic feature of books as representational objects concerns how much their owners valued them. As for cuneiform handbooks, this is evident from colophons stating the name of the owner and copyist of a tablet, stressing that the text was neatly written, collated, and copied from an older *Vorlage*, describing the purpose and circumstances of writing, and adding expressions of desire and exhortation for the one handling the tablet. Finally, the warning to keep the contents secret and the admonition to pronounce them correctly is undoubtedly a sign of the reverence and high prize that cuneiform manuals meant to their owners.[74]

I include below some examples of colophons from the *Alandimmû* handbook. The so-called Assurbanipal colophon d) is attested or preserved three times in the handbook, namely, in *Alandimmû* tablets 2 and 3, and at the end of the *liptu* fleck chapter. The restored version reads as follows:

> Palace of Assurbanipal, king of the universe, king of the land of Assur, whom Nabû and Tašmetu bestowed with understanding and whom they granted bright eyes — the highest level of scribal art which no-one of the kings preceding me had achieved in this discipline. I have laid down on tablets the wisdom of Nabû, the writing of cuneiform sign as many as there are, I have checked and collated them. In order to read aloud, (this tablet) is deposited in my palace.[75]

We seldom find because of lack of preservation colophons mentioning the scholar who has copied the tablet. *Alandimmû* tablet 5 has the following colophon:

> Not completed. Copy from a wax tablet ..., tablet of Anu-ikṣur ..., Hand of Anu-...[76]

The reading of cuneiform handbooks as representational objects is supported by a number of texts that delegate their auspices to the divine realm. The claim of divine patrons or supervisors of the divinatory procedure certainly served to express that the tradition of divination was authoritative and sanctioned. And it is probably safe to say that this form of authorizing turned the possession of such a handbook into the intellectual delectation and spiritual

---

[72] This holds also true for those Nineveh texts written in Babylonian ductus. In comparison with contemporary and younger tablets from Sippar, the Babylonian tablets in the Nineveh library show slightly different proportions of widths and lengths of the cuneiform signs.

[73] Mallowan 1966: 148–63, 278.

[74] For the themes treated in colophons, see Hunger 1968: 3–15. See also the contributions of Leichty 1964; and Pearce 1993; for texts labeled as secret or esoteric knowledge, see Westenholz 1998.

[75] For the colophon in *Alandimmû*, see Böck 2000: 88, 96, and 178. See also Hunger 1968: 97–98.

[76] See Böck 2000: 98.

edification of the owner. Of interest for the present discussion, are those passages that refer to the handbook *Alandimmû* as well as to other divinatory treatises. The well-known catalog of texts and authors, as termed by W. G. Lambert (1962), is one of the examples. The text opens with all those works that have been revealed by Ea, who, as Lambert formulates "has the place of honor at the head of the list," and includes the handbook of astrological omens, the series *Alandimmû, Šumma izbu, Sakikkû, Kataduggû*, and the mythological narrations *Lugale* and *Angindima*. Similarly, Enmeduranki and Related Matters, another text which has been brought to light by Lambert (1967), attributes liver and oil divination, but also astrological omens to the gods Adad and Šamaš. The divine patronage of physiognomic omens is corroborated by the introduction to the *Kataduggû* part of the handbook, which opens with a phrase relating to the great gods: "When the great gods prepared the soul of man or *human character* to exercise the divine power of ruling, they established as guideline for him *Kataduggû*."[77]

Physiognomic Omens in Ancient Mesopotamia: Who, Why, and How

There are only a few text passages that allude to the setting of the physiognomic omen handbook and besides the two references preserved have more than one possible reading. One is the aforementioned paragraph from the *Kataduggû* section pointing to the use of speech and behavioral omens, which, if we take the line literally, seems to have been meant as a sort of instructions for ruling and decision-making. The line could be equally interpreted as a reference to the mythological and divine realm in order to provide authority to both the omens and the experts who handled this knowledge. Also, the other textual reference relating to the usage of physiognomic omens has these two readings, which do not exclude each other and intersect in some way.

The reference is included in the already-mentioned catalog of the wise scholar Esagil-kīn-apli, which states:

> "Let the exorcist, who makes decisions and who watches over people's lives,
>
> Who comprehensively knows the *Sakikkû* and *Alandimmû* handbooks, inspect (the patient) and check (the appropriate series),
>
> Let him ponder, and let him put his diagnosis at the disposal of the king."[78]

Again, we may take the lines plainly: the king would be the beneficiary of the examination of people and an exorcist trained in the lore of *Alandimmû* and *Sakikkû* would have to carry out the inspection. The assumption that such experts were needed at the Assyrian royal court is supported by a letter from a certain Marduk-šapik-zēri addressed to king Esarhaddon or Assurbanipal. He describes all the fields in which he is learned including the physiognomic treatises *Alandimmû*, *Kataduggû*, and *Nigdimdimmû*.[79] We could then create the scenario that the king drew upon *Kataduggû* for guidance in ruling, and upon *Alandimmû* for examining people. The expert who provided him with all the necessary information was the exorcist. How

[77] For the Akkadian, see Böck 2000: 130 (lines 1–2). The Akkadian allows, certainly, different interpretations since the terms used are difficult or obscure: *zaqīqu ša amēlūti* "soul of mankind," *ana illilūti šakānu* "to turn into supreme power," and the Gtn of the infinitive of *redû* "to lead."

[78] For the lines quoted, see Finkel 1988: 148 (A 69 // B31′ - A 71 // B33′).

[79] Parpola 1993a: 122 no. 160 obv. line 41.

the result and consequences of this inspection was put into practice, however, is not certain. Now, we also could interpret Esagil-kīn-apli's statement as an autobiographical reference, which was meant to stress his far-reaching importance for the king, demonstrating that his position at the royal court was essential. At least for the Neo-Assyrian royal court we know that, as for their livelihood, scholars depended heavily on the favor granted by the king. In this regard, it is not surprising that scholars insisted on their expertise and indispensability.[80]

The setting of physiognomic omens was certainly not restricted to the royal court, but it was neither too common; there was surely a physiognomist required to perform the physiognomical inspection. If this were certain, the circle of persons who could have had access to and afforded hiring an *āšipu* trained in physiognomic treatises would be reduced to what we might call the elite. Omens concerning women — as it has been long stated by Kraus and further developed by the present author — refer to the *marriageability* of the potential bride.[81] Predictions concerning fertility, easy birth, fidelity, conjugal care and affection, or ruling a household are all human universals.[82] Information about character or fate of the other could have been furthermore required in occasions such as accepting someone to join certain circles of people, admitting someone for employment, or choosing a bridegroom. Although, to the best of my knowledge, there are no cuneiform texts preserved that would describe any of the above-mentioned circumstances, the use of physiognomy to bring about a decision concerning a person is a feature of "culture, society, (...) behavior, and psyche found in all ethnographically or historically recorded human societies."[83] Because of the lack of sufficient information in cuneiform sources, we included in *Die babylonisch-assyrische Morphoskopie* a short description on the use of physiognomical literature and inspections in Greek, Hebrew, Aramaic, Syriac, and Arabic tradition. In the following section we add information about Sanskrit and Chinese sources. It is worth stressing that physiognomical knowledge in the West and East seemed to have been relevant mainly in secular contexts.

Physiognomy in the Far East

A glance at other cultures throughout the history shows that the different systems of physiognomy served to uncover the moral inclination and intelligence of individuals and to gain insight into the way people could act or what would happen to them. Physiognomic inquiries were not restricted to the classical or biblical and Middle Eastern world only: Iamblichos and Porphyrios reported about Pythagoras, who screened potential candidates before admitting them in his circle; Plato tells us that Socrates predicted the promotion of Alcibiades from his appearance; and Josephus Flavius describes in one of his accounts how Caesar detected the pretence of spurious Alexander from his rough hands and surface.[84] Both ancient India and China have produced an equally rich, if not vaster, amount of literature about the art of reading the face and general appearance of men and women and, in addition, provided information for reconstructing a physiognomic setting. I should say in advance that I am ignorant of ancient Chinese and Sanskrit so I cannot speak with authority of the literature of ancient China and

[80] See Parpola 1971: xviii.

[81] See Kraus 1935: 11; and Böck 2000: 58–59.

[82] For the aspects of affection, childcare, family and household, moral sentiments, and sexual attraction as common features of culture, society, and behavior, see Brown 1991.

[83] The quote is taken from Brown 2000: 157.

[84] See the discussion in Böck 2000: 61–69.

India. The following glimpse at some of the Far Eastern traditions of physiognomy is what I have gathered from reading secondary literature.

The evidence for commercial relations and political contacts between Mesopotamia and India in the second half of the third millennium B.C. and later, in Hellenistic times, has fostered and laid the basis for the interest of researching further cultural interferences. One of the most fervent defenders of Mesopotamian intellectual influence and the transmission of Mesopotamian omen texts in India was D. Pingree. He proposed that several Sanskrit treatises represent translations of recensions of terrestrial omens included in *Šumma ālu* and astrological omens from *Enūma Anu Enlil,* that were made under Achaemenid rule in Mesopotamia and whose cuneiform originals are not any longer preserved.[85] Recently, H. Falk (2000) challenged this transfer of ideas, as far as methods to measure time are concerned, and argued for the occurrence of independent internal cultural developments. However, it is not our purpose to compare the contents of Sanskrit and cuneiform material on physiognomy in order to establish possible interconnections or to rule out any direct borrowing.

As it has been stressed, studying a person's looks in order to determine his character, intelligence, or future is a fundamental desire of human beings. By reading physiognomic literature of different cultures, one gets the impression that the vocabulary to describe the face, body, and outward appearance is rather limited. The limited expressions of language result in terminological resemblances and parallels, though not exact, of other physiognomic treatises to the contents of the protases in cuneiform omens. The different corpora, however, differ from each other in the interpretation of single body features since the translation of an object into a portent underlies distinct theories and worldviews, which are as intrinsic to a culture as its language, and are bound up to different systems of thought.

Evidence for Indian physiognomy can be found in a variety of compositions.[86] One of the oldest sources are the *Purāṇa*s, a collection of various stories including myths, legends, and genealogies. The *Purāṇa*s are divided into eighteen major sections, containing each various sub-sections. The dating is somewhat problematic; they were written down roughly between A.D. 300 and 1100. Discussions on the physiognomy of prepubescent girls were included in the forty-eighth chapter of the *Gargasamhitā*, a compilation of a variety of different omens probably written in the first century B.C. or A.D.[87] Another work is the so-called *Jyotiḥśāstra*, a compilation of Hindu knowledge on astronomy and astrology which also includes a chapter on physiognomy.[88] The work is commonly dated into the sixth century A.D. An independent textbook on physiognomy is the *Sāmudrikatilaka*, attributed to the legendary Samudra who is regarded as the first author of physiognomy; the work dates from the twelfth century A.D.[89] Physiognomy also found its way into compilations on Hindu law and custom such as the late medieval work of Brahminic law *Smrtinibandha* or the *Ratiśāstra* on conjugal love. Following Zysk, there are mainly two techniques of physiognomy: one which involves numerology

---

[85] See Pingree 1992: 379. In many of his publications, Pingree put forward the idea that there existed intellectual ties between India and Mesopotamia which led to the adoption of Mesopotamian ideas in Vedic India; see, e.g., Pingree 1987: 293–315; or Pingree 1998: 125–37. An overview of cultural parallels is offered in Parpola 1993b.

[86] Especially helpful for this overview have been the works of Zysk 2005 and Zysk 2002. As Zysk (2005: 441) states, text-critical editions and translations of manuscripts on Indian physiognomy are a desideratum.

[87] See Pingree 1981: 69–71; Caquot and Leibovici 1968: 118, 127; Zysk 2002: 14.

[88] See Pingree 1981: 69; Zysk 2005: 430–32.

[89] As D. Pingree points out (1981: 76), the actual composer of the work, which began in about A.D. 1160, was Durlabharāja; the composition was finished by his son Jagaddeva.

counting the male's body parts up to thirty-two, and the other, including the examination of the body of men and women in order to predict their future. The check-up started by the sole of the feet and moved up to the hair of the head, that is to say, following the opposite direction of cuneiform physiognomy. It seems that only the privileged castes of ancient and medieval India made use of physiognomy, which served two purposes:

> one focused on the man in the establishment of his right succession and his suitability as a spouse; and the other concentrated on the woman as a partner in arranged marriages. It was used to determine a man's future prosperity and fitness to be a leader and head of the household, and a woman's fertility and suitability as a wife and mother (Zysk 2005: 428).

Ancient China has produced a large number and great variety of schools and manuals on physiognomy.[90] As L. Kohn remarks (1986), "hardly any of them have been brought to scholarly attention."[91] Readily available is the work of the anthropologist W. Lessa on *Chinese Body Divination* or, as he also terms it, "somatomancy."[92] One of the most complete and widespread Chinese works is the *Shenxiang quanbian*, dating to the early Ming dynasty (1367–1458) and still in use today. The earliest datable texts come from the tenth century A.D.;[93] information about the application of physiognomy is, however, older. In one of her contributions, L. Kohn points to a passage in the *Zuo zhuan, Chronicle of Zhuo* about the master of physiognomy Shu Fu, which represents one of the earliest-known references to the performance of physiognomic examination. The *Zuo zhuan* is not dated later than the fourth century B.C. Chinese historical and biographical accounts are full of references to practitioners of physiognomy and to physiognomic inspections predicting longevity, intelligence, and prosperity, ascertaining the nomination of heirs and supporting the appointment or demotion of officials and nobles. Suffice it to mention just two narrations in order to get an impression of the style of these sources. The *Records of the Grand Historian of China* have passed down an anecdote about Madam Wei and her daughter Bo who was to live in the palace of Wei Bao. Madam Wei took her daughter to be physiognomized in order to get to know her future.[94] In another story, included in the biography of Chu Chien-p'ing, a skillful physiognomist, it is reported that Cao Cao (A.D. 155–220), a regional warlord under the last Han emperor, named later Duke of Wei, summoned him to become a court gentleman and physiognomize the guests at his court. "'General,' Chien-p'ing began, 'your lifespan should be eighty years but at forty you will have a small crisis. Please take care to protect yourself.' He told Hsia-hou Wei, 'You will become a provincial governor. At the age of forty-nine, you will face a crisis, but if you manage to survive it, you will live to seventy and rise to the post of ducal attendant.' He then told Ying Ch'ü, 'Sir, at the age of sixty-two you will become a high attendant official and will face a crisis. A year before that happens, you will see an apparition of a white dog, but it

[90] For a short overview, see Needham 1956: 363–64.

[91] See Kohn 1986: 227.

[92] See also the critical review of Lessa 1968 by Feuchtwang (1970). Lessa includes in his book a brief survey into cuneiform omens that he considers to be the oldest sources for physiognomy. He even suggests that Chinese could have borrowed the idea of body divination from Mesopotamia by stimulus diffusion developing their own theories and interpretations of physiognomy; see Lessa 1968. The term "somatomancy" is introduced in Lessa 1952.

[93] So far twelve manuscripts on physiognomy have been discovered at Duhuang, a city in Jiuquan, Gansu province of China; for a recent overview, see Despeux 2005; see also Kohn 1988: 216–18.

[94] See Watson 1961: 381–82. See also the translation of this section included in Hardy 1999: 77.

will be invisible to the people standing around you.'" The biography goes on describing that Chien-p'ing's predictions were all fulfilled.[95]

ANCIENT MESOPOTAMIAN PHYSIOGNOMY IN RELIGIOUS CONTEXT?

Finally, we again raise the question whether physiognomy could have also been used in selecting candidates for religious positions as priests.[96] It is likely that tacit physiognomic knowledge played a certain role in choosing an appropriate aspirant. However, in light of those cuneiform tablets dealing with the physical appearance required from priests, it seems rather improbable that the result of an inquiry based on the physiognomic omen handbook had an impact on the consecration. The cuneiform texts in question resemble the specific instructions for priests as stated in Leviticus 21, namely, that the candidates must also be free from physical defects.[97] The documents refer to the condition for ordaining diviners (*bārû*) and *nêšakku-* and/or *pāšišu*-priests who serve at the temple of Enlil. The latter are excluded from service if they possess a face disfigured by mutilated eyes, and if they have brandings or irregular features.[98] There are probably more defects stated but the text is too fragmentarily preserved. The diviner, on the other hand, as far as his physical appearance is concerned, must be perfect as to his body and limbs — as also the *nêšakku*-priest; if he has an eye defect, chipped teeth, bruised fingers, or a damaged scrotum, he is to be excluded.[99]

It is tempting to interrelate these catalogs of physical conditions with the physiognomic omen corpus, but one should presumably distinguish the reasons for examining a priestly candidate from the art of physiognomy. The purpose of the former is to detect a blemish. It is not stated that the check-up of priests is meant to uncover the future or moral qualities of the candidate. The physiognomic omens, on the other hand, do not include descriptions of imperfect body parts, but refer to the natural looks and shapes of the human body. In the case of the diviner, it seems reasonable to assume that he should not suffer from defects of eyes and hands, which could deter him from correctly performing extispicy and other divinatory practices. As for his teeth, I would like to draw attention to the preparatory ritual of the *bārû* before he undertakes his inquiry: after having cleansed himself with holy water, anointed himself with purifying oil containing the plant "resisted 1,000 (diseases)," then dressed with a pure garment, purified with tamarisk and soap plant, he has to chew on an empty stomach chips of cedar or cypress in his mouth.[100] The latter act points to the fact that he was in need of good teeth. Concerning the ruptured testicles, one should consider the mythological text referring to the legendary king Enmeduranki, progenitor of all diviners. As stated, a rightful diviner assuming his ancestors' office should descend from a family rooted in the prestigious cities of Nippur, Sippar, or Babylon — a condition that implies procreative capacity. However,

---

[95] For the text quote, see DeWoskin 1982, 134–37.

[96] See, e.g., Veldhuis 1999: 169 n. 44; Böck 2000: 57–58; and most recently Popović 2007: 85.

[97] The relevant text material has been published in Borger 1957; Borger 1973; Lambert 1967; and Lambert 1998. See also my discussion in Böck 2000: 57–58.

[98] See Borger 1970: 164–65 col. i 9, 29–42.

[99] For the text, see Lambert 1998: 149 (lines 30–32). The Akkadian terms used are *ina gatti u minâtīšu lā šuklulu* "(who) is imperfect as regards his body and his limbs"; *zaq-tu īnī* "squinting eyes"; *ḫe-sír šinnī* "chipped teeth"; *nak-pi ubāni* "bruised finger"; *iška* DIR.KUR.RA "a ruptured testicle."

[100] See Zimmern 1901: 112 (no. 11 rev. lines 3–6).

as Lambert pointed out, in real life a *bārû* without children could have adopted a son to assist and succeed him in his profession.[101]

In view of the scanty cuneiform evidence and the use of physiognomy in secular settings, such as the choice of a bride and bridegroom in elite circles and royal courts and the appointment of personnel in Western and Eastern cultures of antiquity (and one should add up to the twenty-first century of our days),[102] we would presently consider the usage in religious context less probable.

[101] See Lambert 1998: 143.

[102] See, for example, for the role of physiognomy in employment matters in South Korea, Kim 2005: 291–92.

BIBLIOGRAPHY

Alster, Bendt

1997 *Proverbs of Ancient Sumer: The World's Earliest Proverb Collections*. Bethesda: CDL Press.

Arnaud, Daniel

1985 *Recherches au pays d'Aštata, Mission archéologique de Meskéné-Emar* VI/1–2: *Les textes sumériens et accadiens, planches*. Éditions Recherche sur les Civilisations, Synthèse 18. Paris: Éditions Recherche sur les Civilisations.

1986 *Recherches au pays d'Aštata, Mission archéologique de Meskéné-Emar* VI/3: *Les textes sumériens et accadiens, texte*. Éditions Recherche sur les Civilisations, Synthèse 18. Paris: Éditions Recherche sur les Civilisations.

1987 *Recherches au pays d'Aštata, Mission archéologique de Meskéné-Emar* VI/4: *Les textes sumériens et accadiens: Textes de la bibliothèque, transcriptions et traductions*. Éditions Recherche sur les Civilisations, Synthèse 18. Paris: Éditions Recherche sur les Civilisations.

Bascom, William

1980 *Sixteen Cowries: Yoruba Divination from Africa to the New World*. Bloomington: Indiana University Press.

Böck, Barbara

1999 "Homo mesopotamicus." In *Munuscula Mesopotamica: Festschrift für Johannes Renger*, edited by B. Böck, E. Cancik-Kirschbaum, and T. Richter, pp. 53–68. Alter Orient und Altes Testament 267. Münster: Ugarit-Verlag.

2000 *Die babylonisch-assyrische Morphoskopie*. Archiv für Orientforschung, Beiheft 27. Vienna: Institut für Orientalistik der Universität Wien.

2002 "Physiognomie und Schicksal? Oder wie der altmesopotamische Mensch mit einem durch ein physiognomisches Omen angekündigten Unheil umgegangen sein mag." *Sefarad* 62: 125–41

2004 "Weitere Texte physiognomischen Inhalts." *Sefarad* 64: 289–314.

Borger, Rykle

1957 "*niṣirti bārûti*, Geheimlehre der Haruspizin." *Bibiotheca Orientalis* 14: 190–95.

1973 "Die Weihe eines Enlil-Priesters." *Bibliotheca Orientalis* 30: 163–76.

Brown, Donald E.

1991 *Human Universals*. Philadelphia: Temple University Press.

2000 "Human Universals and Their Implications." In *Being Humans: Anthropological Universality and Particularity in Transdisciplinary Perspectives*, edited by N. Roughley, pp. 156–74. Berlin: Walter de Gruyter.

Caquot, Andre, and Marcel Leibovici

1968 *La divination*. Paris: Presses Universitaires de France.

Cooper, Jerrold S.

1977 "Symmetry and Repetition in Akkadian Narrative." *Journal of the American Oriental Society* 97: 508–12.

Despeux, Catherine

2005 "From Prognosis to Diagnosis of Illness in Tang China." In *Medieval Chinese Medicine: The Dunhuang Medical Manuscripts*, edited by V. Lo and Ch. Cullen, pp. 176–205. London and New York: Routledge Curzon.

DeWoskin, Kenneth J.

1982 *Doctors, Diviners, and Magicians of Ancient China: Biographies of* Fang-shih. New York: Columbia University Press.

Edzard, Dietz Otto

1982 "Der Aufbau des Syllabars 'Proto-Ea.'" In *Societies and Languages of the Ancient Near East: Studies in Honour of I. M. Diakonoff*, pp. 42–61. Warminster: Aris & Phillips.

Falk, Harry

2000 "Measuring Time in Mesopotamia and Ancient India." *Zeitschrift der Deutschen Morgenländischen Gesellschaft* 150: 107–32.

Feuchtwang, Stephan

1970 Review of *Chinese Body Divination*, by W. A. Lessa. *American Anthropologist*, n.s., 72: 427–29.

Finkel, Irving L.

1982 *The Series SIG_7.ALAN* = Nabnītu. Materials for the Sumerian Lexicon 16. Rome: Editrice Pontificio Istituto Biblico.

1988 "Adad-apla-iddina, Esagil-kīn-apli, and the Series SA.GIG." In *A Scientific Humanist: Studies in Memory of Abraham Sachs*, edited by E. Leichty, M. de J. Ellis, and P. Gerardi, pp. 143–59. Philadelphia: The University Museum.

Frahm, Eckhart

2004 "Royal Hermeneutics: Observations on the Commentaries from Ashurbanipal's Libraries at Nineveh." *Iraq* 66: 45–54.

In press *Origins of Interpretation: An Introduction to Assyrian and Babylonian Text Commentaries*. Münster.

Freedman, Sally M.

1998 *If a City Is Set on a Height: The Akkadian Omen Series* Šumma Alu ina Mēlê Šakin, Volume 1: *Tablets 1–21*. Philadelphia: S. N. Kramer Fund.

Geller, Markham J.

2000 "'Incipits and Rubrics.'" In *Wisdom, Gods, and Literature: Studies in Honour of W. G. Lambert*, edited by A. R. George and I. L. Finkel, pp. 225–58. Winona Lake: Eisenbrauns.

Gesche, Petra

2001 *Schulunterricht in Babylonien im ersten Jahrtausend v. Chr.* Alter Orient und Altes Testament 275. Münster: Ugarit-Verlag.

Glassner, Jean-Jacque

1984 "Pour un lexique des termes et figures analogiques en usage dans la divination mésopotamienne." *Journal Asiatique* 272: 15–46.

Goody, Jack

1986 *The Logic of Writing and the Organization of Society*. Cambridge: Cambridge University Press.

Hardy, Grant

1999 *Worlds of Bronze and Bamboo: Sima Qian's Conquest of History*. New York: Columbia University Press.

Hunger, Hermann

1968 *Babylonische und assyrische Kolophone*. Alter Orient und Altes Testament 2. Neukirchen-Vluyn: Neukirchener.

1976 *Spätbabylonische Texte aus Uruk* I. Ausgrabungen der Deutschen Forschungsgemeinschaft in Uruk-Warka 9. Berlin: Mann.

Kim, A. Eungi

2005 "Nonofficial Religion in South Korea: Prevalence of Fortunetelling and Other Forms of Divination." *Review of Religious Research* 46: 284–302.

Koch-Westenholz, Ulla

1995 *Mesopotamian Astrology: An Introduction to Babylonian and Assyrian Celestial Divination.* Copenhagen: Museum Tusculanum Press.

Köcher, Franz, and A. Leo Oppenheim

1958 "The Old Babylonian Omen Text VAT 7525." *Archiv für Orientforschung* 18: 62–77.

Kohn, Lisa

1986 "A Textbook of Physiognomy: The Tradition of the *Shenxiang quanbian*." *Asian Folklore Studies* 45: 227–58.

1988 "A Mirror of Auras: Chen Tuan on Physiognomy." *Asian Folklore Studies* 47: 215–56.

Kraus, Fritz R.

1935 *Die physiognomischen Omina der Babylonier.* Mitteilungen der Vorderasiatisch-ägyptischen Gesellschaft 40/2. Leipzig: C. Schulze.

1936a "Ein Sittenkanon in Omenform." *Zeitschrift für Assyriologie* 43: 77–113.

1936b "Babylonische Omina zur Ausdeutung der Begleiterscheinungen beim Sprechen." *Archiv für Orientforschung* 11: 211–30.

1939 *Texte zur babylonischen Physiognomatik.* Archiv für Orientforschung, Beiheft 3. Berlin.

1947 "Weitere Texte zur babylonischen Physiognomatik." *Orientalia,* n.s., 16: 172–206.

Labat, Rene, and Dietz O. Edzard

1974 *Textes littéraires de Suse.* Mémoires de la Délégation archéologique en Iran, Mission de Susiane. Ville Royale de Suse 11. Mémoires de la Délégation archéologique en Iran 57. Paris: P. Geuthner.

Lambert, Wilfred G.

1960 *Babylonian Wisdom Literature.* Oxford: Clarendon Press.

1962 "A Catalogue of Texts and Authors." *Journal of Cuneiform Studies* 16: 59–77.

1967 "Enmeduranki and Related Matters." *Journal of Cuneiform Studies* 21: 126–38.

1998 "The Qualifications of Babylonian Diviners." In *Festschrift für Rykle Borger zu seinem 65. Geburtstag am 24. Mai 1994*, tikip santakki mala bašmu ..., edited by S. M. Maul, pp. 141–58. Cuneiform Monographs 10. Groningen: Styx.

Landsberger, Benno; Erica Reiner; and Miguel Civil

1969 *The Series* lú = ša *and Related Texts.* Materials for the Sumerian Lexicon 12. Rome: Editrice Pontificio Istituto Biblico.

Larsen, Mogens Trolle

1987 "Reflections on Science, Divination and Literarcy." In *Language, Literature, and History: Philological Studies Presented to Erica Reiner*, edited by F. Rochberg-Halton, pp. 203–25. American Oriental Series 67. New Haven: American Oriental Society.

Leichty, Erle

1964 "The Colophon." In *Studies Presented to A. Leo Oppenheim, June 7, 1964.* From the Workshop of the Assyrian Dictionary 1, pp. 147–54. Chicago: University of Chicago Press.

1970 *The Omen Series* Šumma izbu. Texts from Cuneiform Sources 4. New York: J. J. Augustin.

1993 "The Origins of Scholarship." In *Die Rolle der Astronomie in den Kulturen Mesopotamiens: Beiträge zum 3. Grazer Morgenländischen Symposium (23.–27. September 1991)*, edited by H. D. Galter, pp. 21–29. Graz: GrazKult.

Lessa, William A.

1952 "Somatomancy: Precursor of the Science of Human Constitution." *The Scientific Monthly* 75/6: 355–65.

1968 *Chinese Body Divination: Its Forms, Affinities, and Function*. Los Angeles: United World.

Mallowan, Max E. L.

1966 *Nimrud and Its Remains*. London: Collins.

Maul, Stefan M.

1994 *Zukunftsbewältigung: Eine Untersuchung altorientalischen Denkens anhand der babylonisch-assyrischen Löserituale (*Namburbi*)*. Baghdader Forschungen 18. Mainz am Rhein: Philipp von Zabern.

Needham, John

1956 *Science and Civilization in Ancient China*, Volume 5, Part 2: *History of Scientific Thought*. Cambridge.

Oppenheim, A. Leo

1977 *Ancient Mesopotamia. The Portrait of a Dead Civilization*. Chicago: University of Chicago Press.

1978 "Man and Nature in Mesopotamian Civilization." *Dictionary of Scientific Biography* 15: 634–65.

Parpola, Simo

1971 *Letters from Assyrian Scholars to the Kings Esarhaddon and Assurbanipal*. Alter Orient und Altes Testament 5. Neukirchen-Vluyn: Neukirchener.

1993a *Letters from Assyrian and Babylonian Scholars*. State Archives of Assyria 10. Helsinki: Helsinki University Press.

1993b "Cultural Parallels between India and Mesopotamia: Preliminary Considerations." *Studia Orientalia* 70: 57–64.

Pearce, Laurie

1993 "Statements of Purpose: Why the Scribes Wrote." In *The Tablet and the Scroll. Near Eastern Studies in Honor of William W. Hallo*, edited by M. Cohen, D. Snell, and D. Weisberg, pp. 185–93. Bethesda: CDL Press.

Petschow, Herbert

1968 "Zur Systematik und Gesetzestechnik im Codex Hammurabi." *Zeitschrift für Assyriologie* 57: 146–72.

Pientka-Hinz, Rosel

2008 "Omina, Orakel, Rituale und Beschwörungen. 1.1.8. Physiognomische Omina und Verhaltensomina." In *Texte aus der Umwelt des Alten Testaments,* Neue Folge, 4, edited by B. Janowski and G. Wilhelm, pp. 40–47. Gütersloh: Gütersloher Verlagshaus.

Pingree, David

1981 *Jyotiḥśāstra, Astral and Mathematical Literature*. History of Indian Literature, Volume 6, Part. 4. Wiesbaden: Harrassowiṭz.

1987 "Venus Omens in India and Babylon." In *Language, Literature, and History: Philological Studies Presented to Erica Reiner*, edited by F. Rochberg-Halton, pp. 293–315. American Oriental Series 67. New Haven: American Oriental Society.

1992 "Mesopotamian Omens in Sanskrit." In *La circulations de biens, des personnes et des idées dans le Proche-Orient ancien*, edited by D. Charpin and F. Joannès, pp. 375–79. Paris: Éditions Recherche sur les Civilisations.

1998 "Legacies in Astronomy and Celestial Omens." In *The Legacy of Mesopotamia*, edited by S. Dalley, pp. 125–37. Oxford: Oxford University Press.

Popović, Mladen

2007 *Reading the Human Body: Physiognomics and Astrology in the Dead Sea Scrolls and Hellenistic-Early Roman Period Judaism*. Studies on the Texts of the Desert of Judah 67. Leiden: Brill.

Reiner, Erica

1982 "A Manner of Speaking." In *Zikir Šumim*. Assyriological Studies Presented to F. R. Kraus on the Occasion of His Seventieth Birthday, edited by G. van Driel et al., pp. 282–89. Leiden: Brill.

Scurlock, JoAnn

2003 Review of *Die babylonisch-assyrische Morphoskopie*, by B. Böck. *Journal of the American Oriental Society* 123: 395–99.

Veldhuis, Niek

1999 "Reading the Signs." In *All Those Nations...: Cultural Encounters within and with the Near East*, edited by H. L. J. Vanstiphout, pp. 161–74. Groningen: Styx.

von Soden, Wolfram

1981 "Die 2. Tafel der Unterserie *Šumma Ea liballiṭ-ka* von *alandimmû*." *Zeitschrift für Assyriologie* 71: 109–21.

von Weiher, Egbert

1993 *Spätbabylonische Texte aus Uruk* IV. Ausgrabungen in Uruk-Warka 12. Mainz am Rhein: Philipp von Zabern.

Watson, Burton

1961 *Records of the Grand Historian of China. Translated from the* Shih chi *of SSu-ma Ch'ien*, Volume 1: *Early Years of the Han Dynasty 209 to 141 B.C.* New York: Columbia University Press.

Westenholz, Joan Goodnick

1998 "Thoughts on Esoteric Knowledge and Secret Lore." In *Intellectual Life of the Ancient Near East: Papers Presented at the 43rd Rencontre Assyriologique Internationale, Prague, July 1–5*, edited by J. Prosecky, pp. 451–62. Prague: Oriental Institute.

Zimmern, Heinrich

1901 *Beiträge zur Kenntnis der babylonischen Religion*. Assyriologische Bibliothek 12. Leipzig: J. C. Hinrichs.

Zysk, Kenneth G.

2002 *Conjugal Love in India*. Sir Henry Wellcome Asian Studies 1. Leiden: Brill.

2005 "Indian Traditions of Physiognomy: Preliminary Remarks." In *Theory and Practice of Yoga: Essays in Honour of Gerald James Larson*, edited by K. A. Jacobsen, pp. 425–42. Studies in the History of Religions 110. Leiden: Brill.

12

ON SEEING AND BELIEVING: LIVER DIVINATION AND THE ERA OF WARRING STATES (II)*

SETH F. C. RICHARDSON, UNIVERSITY OF CHICAGO

"The Beginning of the War Will Be Secret"
— Jenny Holzer, "Survival," 1983[1]

1.0 HISTORICISM AND A "CREATED" OLD BABYLONIAN DIVINATORY LITERATURE

A number of postulates about Mesopotamian divination and divinatory literature rest uncomfortably together, even though they are by now standard equippage in Assyriological discussions. There is a general, but not exclusive, sense that divinatory literature first arose in the Old Babylonian period. This idea does not preclude the possibility or even probability, for some scholars, that the Old Babylonian texts drew on earlier traditions or an oral background. There is the further idea that the divinatory arts in ancient Mesopotamia constituted a "scientific" form of inquiry or discourse, or stood in an analogous cultural position. Of all the formal devices divinatory literature deployed and which puzzle scholars, the largest — really the meta-device — was that omens were ever written down in the first place. Yet it is this topic which has received the least attention, and probably for the very good reason that this event or process is not visible in any textual precipitate.

Still, this entextualization is a change in both composition and praxis, and it is to these changes that this essay turns its attention. I argue (section 2.0) that our understanding of extispicy should assume the deliberate composition of the compendious texts (manuals) without prior written source material, and not any continuous, scholarly transmission of observational forerunners. The hodgepodge of evidence that is often used to discuss early extispicy can be shown to be either a) not extispicy, or b) extispicy, but not emphatically non-textual. The importance of this argument is that the moment of this literature's composition must be understood (section 3.0) in a wholly other context, in the political crises that afflicted the age of its creation. The Old Babylonian period, Mesopotamia's own "Warring States" epoch, was a time in which many third-millennium cultural forms were being transformed by programmatic revision and political appropriation in the contest to restore geopolitical equilibrium. Extispicy was just such a revolution.

* The first part of this study was published as Richardson 2006.

[1] I extend thanks to all those who helped me clarify this study through conversations and comments, especially Joan Westenholz and Piotr Michalowski, but also Christopher Woods, Marc Van De Mieroop, Steven Garfinkle, Martha Roth, Nat Levtow, Beate Pongratz-Leisten, Gertrud Farber, Seth Sanders, Eva Von Dassow, Ann Guinan, Eckart Frahm, Nils Heeßel, Ulla Koch, Martti Nissinen, Francesca Rochberg, Abraham Winitzer, and Amar Annus for his work in organizing the seminar. None of them is responsible for the opinions or errors herein, which are mine alone.

2.0 A TRANSMITTED LITERATURE? EVIDENCE FOR EXTISPICAL TEXTS PRIOR TO THE OLD BABYLONIAN PERIOD

The understanding of extispicy as a transmitted literature fundamentally depends on the existence of forerunners[2] to the three forms of technical literature we see arising in the Old Babylonian period: liver-omen models, compendia, and reports. Models are those clay objects which, whether schematically or realistically representing the organs of a sheep, are labelled to indicate signs and marks typical of protases.[3] Compendia are defined as those long and serialized lists of casuistic theoretical statements which link (in theory, observed) phenomena in the organs to the detemporalized existence or eventuation of other (observable) happenings and (non-observable) qualities. Reports are those texts which record specific, historically unique readings of protastic signs in organs; though these encompass a variety of occasions, forms, and purposes, sometimes omitting even the most summary apodictic statements, they purport to record signs of relevance.[4]

It has been a problem of many analyses of these three text-types that they freely compare terms and features of texts from different times, places, and text-types on a presumption of fixed meanings and direct transmission. Dispensing with a historically critical approach, this presumption does not reduce, but rather increases, the possibility of creating anachronisms and contextual noncomparabilities. Lexical and semantic understandings in extispical texts are often reconstructed by referring between Mariote, northern and southern Babylonian corpora, between the three text types mentioned above, and/or between Old Babylonian and Neo-Assyrian attestations. So eager are we to know what the "Comb" of the lung is — to resolve definitional problems through intertextual references — that we have ignored large problems of synchronic and diachronic comparability: the terms of compendia rarely appear in the reports (and vice-versa); the omens of Larsa do not show up in Sippar; the proportion of hapaxes is through the roof; and so forth. The comparability of these texts is in general very low (see below, section 3.2). Nor should we expect a total correspondence — but if the conceit of extispicy was that specific observations were to be preserved for future use, one ought to expect a much higher proportion of overlap between materials than exists.

If a unitary and accumulated literature existed, it should be demonstrable in some measure — but what evidence for a pre-Old Babylonian literature do we have? Eight categories of evidence will be discussed relative to arguments supporting the existence of extispical literature prior to the nineteenth century:[5]

---

[2] By "forerunners," I mean here any text that employs an observational principle, to record an observed signifier with some connection to its signified meaning; for an example of a text which discusses extispicy but nevertheless falls outside this definition, see the discussion of the Ebla "omen" below (section 2.4).

[3] Some early liver models, cast as "historical" observations (i.e., regarding specific kings), speak in the voice of reports, as defined below; as I argue, since I view these omens as fictional texts, I see their compositional intention to have been identical to other liver models: to teach and to demonstrate features to diviners. Such models are not in general to be understood as "reports," though some ambiguity persists in the Daduša liver-model, discussed in section 2.2.

[4] Of the three text types, reports have been the most resistant to disclosing their purpose: for instance, although Koch-Westenholz's (2002) survey of Old Babylonian reports is helpful, it is not really possible to summarize the wide range of purposes cataloged there, much less answer the deceptively simple question: why were these results written down at all?

[5] Throughout this study, some slightly differing shorthand terms are used to refer to the period preceding the essential change that I understand to have taken place ca. 1850 B.C.: "prior to the nineteenth century," "pre-Old Babylonian," and "third millennium" should all be understood as having equivalent meanings for our present purposes. For the sake of convenience, all dates here employ the Middle Chronology.

2.1 The appearance of diviners in third-millennium professional lists
2.2 Third-millennium references to animal omens
2.3 Third-millennium references to liver divination
2.4 Purported examples of third-millennium extispical texts
2.5 The appearance of third-millennium kings in Old Babylonian "historical" omens
2.6 The size, extent, and comprehensiveness of the Old Babylonian extispical compendia
2.7 Later references to extispicy's antiquity
2.8 Procedural dissimilarities to scientific method with respect to observationalism

2.1 The Appearance of Diviners in Third-Millennium Professional Lists

The earliest evidence for extispicy is the appearance of diviners in Early Dynastic professonal lists, in the entries lú.máš.šu.gíd ("one who reaches the hand (in)to the goat") in Lu E from Ebla[6] and Lu C from Fara and Abu Ṣalabikh.[7] Yet while these entries attest to an identifiable class of ritualist at this early stage, they tell us nothing of the apparatus of ritual itself. If anything, Lu C, which displays some apparent groupings of professional types, lists the lú.máš.šu.gíd together with persons working with animals, not with professions more likely to have been working within a scribal or cult tradition.[8]

It also bears observation that, despite the early appearance of the professional name, it does not appear again until the middle of the Ur III period, when once again the documentation is strictly concerned with the administration of animal management, not with cult or ritual practice as such.[9] It is also not possible to locate diviners within rosters of cultic personnel at major temples.[10] Whatever the ritual functions of the professional *bārû* in the third millennium, we cannot point to any instance in which he functioned in a cultic or literate context with or within the institutional households where textual traditions were most prominently supported.

[6] Archi 1984: TM.75.G.1488.

[7] Fara = Civil 1969: 1.3, viii.63; Abu Ṣalabikh = Civil 1969: 1.5, 130; the title is not in the Gasur text ("Source C").

[8] Taylor 2003: lú.máš.šu.gíd among lines 10–15, including sipa.udu, muḫaldim, and lú.gú.šu.du; see also "animal-related" names in lines 32–38 and 52–54; cf. cult personnel in lines 1–2 and 47–49, and "music-related" personnel in lines 56–60. While it is not possible to discern in Lu E that lú.máš.šu.gíd (line 130) is grouped together with any particular professional names, the most identifiable group of cultic personnel appears at quite a remove, lines 64–80.

[9] Some forty-six attestations of the (lú.)máš.šu.gíd(.gíd) appear in Ur III documents according to the Database of Neo-Sumerian Texts (http://bdts.filol.csic.es) in March 2009. In the majority of cases, the activities of diviners are limited to the delivery of animals, animal products, or other goods; often other persons/professionals make identical deliveries alongside them in the same texts. A few of these animal deliveries (e.g., Legrain 1912: no. 313; TCL 2 5559) are indeed designated for the gods, but they in no way indicate any ritual role for or procedure of the diviner. In the remainder of cases, the appearance of the professional name simply appears in their sealings.

[10] Westenholz (1992), surveying the cultic personnel at the five major temples of Nippur from the mid-third millennium to the end of the Old Babylonian period, enumerates no diviners among them. One late exception is known, a ration list for the personnel of Ninurta's Ešumeša temple, from the reign of Damiq-ilišu, ca. 1800 B.C. (the latest of fourteen such tablets treated by Sigrist 1984b: 160–65), on which there is a single entry for a *bārû*.

2.2 Third-Millennium References to Animal Omens

A host of third-millennium references to omens procured through small livestock are often cited as evidence for early extispicy. Yet while some are undoubtedly liver divinations (see section 2.3), many others are not so clearly marked. This has produced some definitional drift when both extispicies and other ominous events or procedures are both simply translated as "omens" — and in any event none of these cases suggests or constitutes observational record-keeping or specific technical means.

Gudea's Cylinder A is commonly cited as providing evidence for third-millennium extispicy (as indeed it does: see section 2.3). What is commonly overlooked, however, is that in this one composition alone several *other* kinds of animal omens are also mentioned. In one instance, a goat is led to the brick shed to identify the pure brick for building.[11] Elsewhere, Gudea leads two sheep and a kid to lie down on animal skins to induce an omen in an incense ritual.[12] Within his initial dream, Gudea recalls seeing a donkey pawing the ground, a sign of his own eagerness to build Eninnu.[13] All these animal omen techniques also appear alongside several forms of non-animal divination used by Gudea: dream, grain, and *kledon* omens.[14] The existence of multiple formal procedures for procuring omens from animals should warn us away from a "presumption of extispicy" when extispicy is not specified (as Gudea elsewhere does): there clearly were a number of ways to get an omen out of a goat.

This in turn must cast some doubt on just what procedures were meant in the large number of southern Mesopotamian year-names from the Akkad, Lagaš, Ur, Isin, and Larsa dynasties referring to omens.[15] At least twenty-eight year-names — from Narām-Sîn's years "o" and "ll" (ca. 2250 B.C.),[16] as late as Damiq-ilišu of Isin's year 4 (1812 B.C.) — refer to sheep omens identifying cult officials to be appointed in temples, using the following formulae (see *Appendix 1* for a complete listing):

Narām-Sîn "o":	... **máš.e íb.dab$_5$.ba**
Narām-Sîn "ll":	... **maš.e íb.dab$_5$.ba**
Lagaš: Ur-Ningirsu I "a":	... **maš.e pà.da**[17]

[11] Edzard (1997: 77) supposed this was an extispicy by interpolating "(by means of) the kid('s liver)"; cf. Ur-Ningirsu I, in Edzard 1997: 8–9, where the same translator instead gives only "sacrifical animal." The verb, however, is ambiguously /pàd/: sig$_4$ máš.e bí.pàd (Gudea, Cyl. A xiii 17). In the technical literature of extispicy, however, ominous "behavior" of the animal only refers to how it acts while being slaughtered, not at any other time (see, for instance, the omens of YOS 10 47–49, incipiently: *šumma immerum ištu ṭabḫu…*).

[12] Gudea, Cyl. A viii 9. Jacobsen (1987: 398) surmises that the animals were to be sacrificed; cf. Edzard 1997: 74, which goes no further than the text. Gudea elsewhere sacrifices goats and bulls to induce a dream omen (Gudea Cyl. A i 14), but the goat is not the vehicle of the omen itself.

[13] Gudea Cyl. A v 10; vi 12.

[14] Gudea Cyl. A xx 7–8; xx 6; xx 2–3, respectively; see also "The Hymn to Enlil," Jacobsen 1987: 104, lines 47f., for *kledon*-oracles procured in temples.

[15] The temple-cities for which priestly appointment omens were procured were Nippur (northernmost), Isin, Uruk, Larsa, Lagaš, and Ur (southernmost); several year-names do not specifically name the temples or cities of appointed personnel.

[16] The designation of these year-names follows Frayne 1993: 85–87.

[17] Contrast this instance to the later dedication of a "sanctuary, the House chosen by her heart" (èš.gú.tùr é šà.ge pà.da.ni) by Ur-Bau; see Edzard 1997: 19.

Ur III: Ur-Namma "b": ... **maš.e ba.pà.da**

Isin/Larsa: Išbi-Erra 13: ... **máš.e ba.pà.da**

These year-names differ only in the type of priest and deity named,[18] the expression for goat (maš/máš), and the verb (Akkadian dynasty only: dab_5; thereafter: pàd), all meaning "Year in which NN-priest(ess) was named (dab_5: installed) by (means of) a goat."[19]

First, a literal-minded translation of these formulae must take note of the fact that extispicy per se (i.e., some variation on šu ... gíd) is not mentioned, though we know that the verbal formulation was in use at this time (see sections 2.1 and 2.3). A further question is raised by the ambiguities of the verb pàd "to call," which is most heavily employed in contexts which imply speaking (or, perhaps, bleating), though of course the semantic range of "calling" (both in Sumerian and English) affords the idea of "naming."[20] The meaning is thus unclear, and dab_5 is even more obscure as regards the ominous method. We must remain sensible that the "calling" in question is no more likely to have involved reading the entrails of a dead goat than of the other procedures illustrated in the Gudea cylinder.

Further problems arise that make this more than a matter of raising a reasonable doubt about the nature of the ominous procedure. Three disconnects — geographic, temporal, and functional — must be established between this class of year-names and the later technical literature; these disconnects substantially separate the nominative year-names from the later technical extispicy. First, the practice of choosing priests "by means of a goat" was restricted to southern Mesoptamian cities (Nippur, Isin, Uruk, Larsa, Lagaš, and Ur), which were not, with the exception of Larsa,[21] the cities from which the later technical literature is attested (Larsa, Mari, Sippar, Babylon, Ešnunna). Second, the technical literature post-dates the year-names with very little overlap.[22] Our latest-known sheep omen year-name is for Damiq-ilišu's year 4, 1812 B.C.; the earliest exemplars of technical literature probably date to nineteenth century Mari (see section 2.5); the earliest securely datable technical document for liver divination is now the omen for the accession of Daduša of Ešnunna, ca. 1800 B.C.[23]

Third, the apodoses of the technical literature are virtually silent about the concerns (so far as we know) of the third-millennium sheep omens, the appointment of priestly personnel or the identification of temple sites. Indeed, the classes of officials in the two sets of literature show almost no overlap: third-millennium references to extispicy address the choosing of cult figures such as the en, nin.dingir, lú.maḫ, $gudu_4$,[24] and išib; the later compendious texts (e.g.,

[18] At Ešnunna, several year-names of the king Šu-ilija referred to the selection of his "son" and "daughter."

[19] Occasionally year-names celebrated the installation/elevation of priestly officials without reference to omens; see, e.g., Ibbi-Sîn 4 (ba-ḫun), Išbi-Erra 31 (ba-íl), and Iddin-Dagan 9 (mu-un-íl).

[20] Edzard (1997), in virtually all other contexts, renders pà(d) as "called," rather than "chosen."

[21] Goetze (1947a) estimated the script of the most "archaic" extispical texts from Larsa to resemble the cursive in use at the time of Rīm-Sîn, thus post-dating the last omen year-name there by about seventy-five years and two changes of dynasty.

[22] Note that the Larsa year-names in question are quite early, corresponding to 1926 and 1895 B.C., respectively, prior to the development of the technical literature there around the time of Rīm-Sîn (i.e., the last third of the nineteenth century B.C.; Goetze 1947: 1). One other geographic overlap with a similar temporal gap should be noted: of OBE 10, probably from Ur, Jeyes (1989: 6) wrote that it was written in younger cursive, probably from the time of Hammurabi, thus significantly post-dating the latest sheep-omen year name for Ur (reign of Lipit-Ištar, ca. 1930 B.C.).

[23] Al-Rawi 1994: no. 5.

[24] See the curse formula of the Šu-Sîn inscription (Frayne 1997: 3.2.1.4.7, lines 27–32) which refers to a $gudu_4$-priest "chosen by oracular means."

YOS 10 and OBE) are concerned with non-temple officers such as the sukkal, *šakkanakku*, *šipru*, zabardab, nun, and lugal. This dichotomy is not without exceptions. Šulgi, for instance, boasts of using extispicy to determine not only cultic matters, but also military action (Šulgi Hymn B, lines 131–49).[25] On the Old Babylonian side, a very few omens from the technical literature do take priestly personnel as their subject matter in various contexts — but only three, out of perhaps three thousand omens,[26] for their selection or appointment. In all three cases, these omens are about *ugbabtu*-priestesses,[27] who are not among the personnel appearing within the nominative year-names.

Divination of the máš ... dab_5/pàd type should be understood as older, southern, and cultic, while literature of the máš šu ... gíd omens should be seen as newer, northern, and emphatically statist and non-cultic. The year-names and the Old Babylonian omens are mutually exclusive in terms of time, space, and subject, two fundamentally different sets of practices, neither precursor nor finished form.

2.3 Third-Millennium References to Liver Divination

Notwithstanding, there is no doubt that extispicy was practiced in the third millennium. Yet written references to the practice of the extispical craft cannot be regarded as evidence for a technical literature of liver divination. In fact, the undoubted antiquity of references to practice then makes the millennium-long absence of procedural and reference materials all the more remarkable, underscoring the nature of that practice as a craft.

The very diversity of contexts for these references (administrative documents, literary works, year-names — but see section 2.2, above) has been distracting. Two Early Dynastic pieces of evidence are, together with the appearance of diviners in Lu C and E, the oldest specific mentions of extispicy. The first is an enigmatic Sumerian proverb "The songs of a city are its omens (uru^{ki} èn-du-bi maš-šu-gíd-gíd-bi-im),"[28] which suggests only perhaps a likeness at the level of orality. The second is the cultic text OIP 99 114;[29] this composition probably names rituals for the reader to perform, but contains no information about method or

---

[25] This is not a máš ... pàd omen; on this passage, see Richardson 2006.

[26] Jeyes (1980: 107–08) estimates the total known Old Babylonian omens to number around 3,000.

[27] I am aware of no Old Babylonian omens regarding the suitability of sites, bricks, or times for the building of temples. A few Old Babylonian omens do mention en's and entu's: these can be typed as "appointment" omens (i.e., appointing priests) and "incidental" omens (i.e., omens which have nothing to do with cultic installation; e.g., the Old Babylonian liver model apodosis "... one who frequents the temple will repeatedly have sexual intercourse with the en-priestess" [CAD E s.v. *ēnu* 2 b) 1′-b′)). Not to be mistaken for appointment omens are those incidental omens simply predicting the death of priestly personnel, e.g., Nougayrol 1950: 43 (dupl. YOS 10 17 53–54; cf. Jeyes 1989: 104) and YOS 10 39 37. I know of three omens which are conceivably of the appointment type, all for *ugbabtu*-priestesses: the paired omen reading YOS 10 38 r. 11 and r. 16: "the high priestess will die, and an *ugbabtu*-priestess will [r. 16: will not] be installed"; and YOS 10 17 47, "If the *naplastum* is like a PAB-sign, the god wants an *ugbabtu*-priestess."

[28] Alster 1997: SP 1.70, II 348: "The songs serve as an indicator of the spirit and, thereby, of the future of the city"; cf. ETCSL, which gives "diviners" instead of "omens." This is the only máš ... gíd construction in the proverbs collection, where other omens are indicated by giškim. Like most other proverbs, this is only attested in later Old Babylonian copies of the collections, but was presumably part of the Early Dynastic corpus.

[29] Biggs 1974: 114 (4 references): iii.2 (maš šu nun gíd); iii.15 (maš nun me gíd); iv.11 (TUK NA_5 maš šu me gíd); v.13 (maš šu mu.gíd); see Alster 1976: 115. Cf. the duplicate Fara text with five references: Deimel 1969: no. 37 iii.10, 13 and vii.5, 13, 18; all máš šu mu.gíd.

procedure; though its contents are "obscure," as Alster notes, it is not itself a technical text.[30] What can be said about the proverb and the cultic text is that they point away from written technical instruments, and towards oral performance.

Throughout the third millennium, a host of literary compositions make reference to divination with varying emphasis. The most well-known extispicies among these are the two by Narām-Sîn in "The Cursing of Akkade,"[31] at least two performed by Gudea (Cyl. A xii 16–17; xx 5),[32] and those boasted of by Šulgi (Richardson 2006). In all these instances, the verbal formulae maš/máš šu gíd is used to designate the method used to gain an omen. In none of these instances is there any reference to textuality, nor could the passages themselves conceivably constitute any kind of observational document drawn on by future readers. The one exception to this state of affairs has long seemed to be a crucial passage in Šulgi's Hymn B ("I am the very Nintud of the omen collections (gìr-gin-na)"), which supported the idea that a fully serialized library of omens existed at least by Šulgi's time. My recent argument (Richardson 2006) that gìr-gin-na should be translated as "procedures" rather than "omen collections" considerably alters this picture. A mistaken conflation of Šulgi's learned skills with his innate ones in the secondary literature masked the emphasis on extipicy as a natural and intutive art, not a "book-learned" technical skill, nor an observational and documentary one.

Categorical errors about what skills and practices lay behind extispicy have been magnified by a definitional drift in which ominous procedures of all kinds have often loosely been translated simply as "omens." The tertiary effect has been for students, scholars, and editors to sometimes interpolate extispicies where other kinds of omens were actually meant (see *Appendix 2* for the effects of this problem in a particularly influential set of translations in Jacobsen 1987). The image produced has thus been one in which extispicy was practiced more often than it was and stood in some clearly preeminent position vis-à-vis other divinatory systems. It did not.

However: even were these instances all to be understood as liver divinations, what they have in common is that — though they would certify that extispicy was in use — none of them mentions or suggests the use of texts. In "The Cursing of Akkade," the evidence is equivocal on this point, since Narām-Sîn is simply said to "perform" extispicies. But for Gudea, the contexts point more toward an intuitive or memorized craft than a scholarly one. The omen of Cylinder A xii 16–17 is said to reveal Ningirsu's intention (šà-^{d}nin-gír-su-ka) which "stands out as clear as daylight" (u_4-dam mu-na-è), and that the revelation was due to Gudea's (repeatedly, emphatically) proclaimed qualities of "great knowing" (gal mu-zu) and "great carrying-out" (gal ì-ga-túm-mu), epithets which suggest an unmediated and untutored access to divine knowledge based on innate gnostic ability — not on learned knowledge.[33]

---

[30] Alster (1976: 114–15) suggests that the repetition of the terms from line to line may indicate a performative function for the two texts.

[31] Cooper 1983: 54–55 (lines 94–7), 244; these lines are not preserved in the Ur III copies (see Cooper 1983: 41–44, 70, 130–32), but for the sake of argument, I will assume they existed in the earlier version as well.

[32] Note also Jacobsen (1987: 442) translates Gudea's Cyl. B xx 12, a message from Ningirsu to Gudea that "The orders concerning [the temple] were not ones spoken by a diviner, I was not keeping [my heart] remote from [you]!" Edzard 1997 provided neither transliteration nor translation for these lines.

[33] The only tablets to be discussed within the lines of Gudea's Cylinders A and B are those held by Nidaba (A v 24–28) and Ninuruda (B vi 4–5). Throughout the poems, the dramatic device that makes Gudea an ideal man is his innate ability to receive messages from the gods, understand, and act correctly; in no instance does he make recourse to or boast of learned techniques. One might compare this to the slightly different emphasis on textuality expressed in Šulgi's hymns, throughout which the king dictates for others

2.4 Purported Examples of Third-millennium Extispical Texts

Two very different letters — one from Ebla, one a school text from the "royal correspondence" of Ur — have either been proposed as or pretend to be extispical texts dating to the third millennium. The first, however, is not an omen (though it is from the third millennium), and the second is not from the third millennium (though it is an omen). A third direct claim in Šulgi's hymns to have produced serial literature for extispicy is evidence I have disputed elsewhere on the grounds that the crucial Sumerian term gìr-gin-na, often translated as "collections" or "library" (of omens, in this case), should rather be understood as "procedures," relevant to extispicy's unwritten and performative protocols (Richardson 2006).

In the first case, the Ebla text TM.76.G.86 has been published as an "extispicy report."[34] Strictly speaking, it is a letter which refers to an extispicy. Coser asserts that a "structural analysis" reveals that the letter contains both protases and apodoses.[35] This is not the case. The letter refers to two inspections of sacrifices (no specific animal is mentioned) in II.2–3 (*wa* ḫul, "and (the omen result) was bad"), and III.7–IV.1 (*wa* igi.gar *gú-šum* ug_7 *áš-dag* igi.gar, "and, when he observed the victim, he saw death by your side"). An extispical procedure is discussed, but the relevant passages fall short of the operative criterion of extispical literature: to record a specific observation (a protasis, indispensible in reports, as Coser herself notes) in order to read a specific result (an apodosis, often, though not always, present in reports), reproducible conditions which can be consulted in the future. No sign or mark is recorded in the Ebla letter: there are no protases, and there are no technical terms of any kind.[36] No observation, as such, is recorded in TM.76.G.86: nothing from the document could be reproduced as an omen. The letter talks about an omen, but doesn't contain one.

A different case presents itself with the Old Babylonian school letter, in which an "omen" appears embedded within long and short versions of a putative royal letter of Ibbi-Sin of Ur:

> Enlil has looked upon me with grace and has taken my prayer to his holy heart; he established for me in my omens the favorable parts. *Furthermore*, he fashioned the right side for him, and the left side for me. He beautifully set there the Weapon on my favorable side with a straight flank; the Weapon on his unfavorable side was present and (looked over) to the other side, bound steadfast to the filament. (This means:) "My enemy will be delivered over to me and killed."[37]

---

to write, composes for others to sing, and whose knowledge is in general superior to the scribes and experts who surround him. Note, for instance, when he boasts of his excellent skill as a diviner, while "my diviner watches in amazement like an idiot" (Šulgi B 144).

[34] The text appears to date to approximately the twenty-fourth century B.C. (Bonechi and Catagnoti 1998: 37–38). Coser 2000: 169, "The other two typologies, i.e. liver models and omen collections or compendia, have not (yet) been attested at III millennium Ebla." See also Biga 1999, in which references to good omens (máš ... sa_6) are briefly mentioned in early Ebla texts.

[35] Coser 2000, lines i 5–ii 1: nídba nídba *áš-ti* / *wa* ḫul, "(the sacrifice was sacrificed on *my own initiative* / and (the omen result) was bad." Lines iii.3–iv.1: *wa* *Ìr-am$_6$-Ma-lik* nídba-*ma* nídba / *wa* igi.gar *gú-šum* ug_7 *áš-dag* igi.gar "And then Yir'am-Malik made a sacrifice / and, when he observed the victim, he saw death by your side."

[36] Coser (2000) discusses TM.76.G.86 by using the terms uzu.*tērtum* and *piqittum*, but the text does not use these (or any other) identifiably extispical terms.

[37] Michalowski 2006. The adumbrated version is less specific in its reference to extispical signs, reading: "He has established for me in my omens the favorable parts. *Furthermore*, when he fashioned in them the right side and the left side (the meaning of the omen became) 'My enemy will be captured and killed.'"

The passage (in contrast to the Ebla letter) refers to specific signs, employing a technical terminology, connected to specific results. Yet although it is genuinely extispical, it is not genuinely third millennium: eight copies of the long and short versions of the letter are known, and they all date closely to the latter half of the reign of Samsuiluna in the late eighteenth century B.C., and not to the twenty-first century B.C. reign of Ibbi-Sin. As Michalowski argues, the "omen" is one of a variety of Old Babylonian scribal exercises inserted within a school text, written in the "highly baroque style" of the Larsa court, an insertion fully consistent with the wider program of archaizing elements of the "royal correspondence."[38]

2.5 The Appearance of Third-Millennium Kings in Old Babylonian "Historical" Omens

Some of the very first written omens have been understood to require written third-millennium sources: these are the so-called "historical" omens, which mention the long-dead kings of Akkad and Ur, among others.[39] These omens themselves give not a hint of any contemporary conviction, however, that the observations had their origins in *histoire événementielle*. The "information" they provide better reflects scribal-scholarly interests in paronomasia (e.g., the Narām-Sîn omen about Apišal) and the historiographic tradition of *Heils/Unheilsherrschaft*, a dualistic scheme which fit well into the interpretive matrix of extispicy. It is also no accident that the kings of the historical omens were often the same famous kings who were the subjects of other literary compositions then popular in the Old Babylonian school curriculum — Gilgameš, the Akkadian kings, Ibbi-Sîn, etc.[40] — and visible in the statuary at Nippur. Though these ominous significations clearly referred to the past — as did literary tales of those kings — there was no claim that the texts (or even the omens) themselves had come from the past — as with the colophons that scrupulously marked the copying of original documents of other kinds, such as royal inscriptions.

From the start, the problematic datation of these historical omens has confused the historical/historiographic issue. The liver models found at Mari (the earliest-known documents to be inscribed with historical, indeed any, omens) were written in the *šakkanakku* script which does not clearly distinguish the century of their composition. It has thus been possible to suppose that the omens so inscribed had been composed contemporaneous with their subject matter. The pivotal historical figure here is Išbi-Erra:[41] his appearance among these omens has been used to argue that he marks a *teminus ante quem* for the liver omens, that is, that they had

---

[38] Michalowski (2006: 250) refers to the extispical terminology here as "invented": "the only way to solve the puzzles [of this passage] is to try to work out how the writer invented a Sumerian extispicy terminology in back translation from Akkadian"; cf. Jacobsen 1994: 147, where the historicity of the account is taken at face value. The date derives from one exemplar which bears a Samsuiluna date.

[39] Most firm in this opinion is Goetze (1947b: 264–65); cf. Cooper 1980.

[40] The omen purporting to mention the earliest "historical" king names ^{d}*Gi-il-ga* (= Gilgameš); see Goetze 1947b. While the omen with the latest king refers to Išbi-Erra, a separate mention of Sîn-iddinam of Larsa (Starr 1983: 13) is elsewhere known. To these we may now add Daduša of Ešnunna (Al-Rawi 1994: 38–40), though the inscription on this particular liver model bears many of the features of an extispical report (multiple observations rather than single protasis-apodosis construction) — and so its generic classification remains uniquely problematic.

[41] The Išma-Dagan who is the subject of Rutten 1938: no. 11, is probably the *šakkanakku* of Mari (fl. ca. 2050 B.C.) rather than the Isin king of a century later (who would then otherwise be the latest-dated king mentioned among these models). Gelb asserted this point on orthographic grounds (1956: 3 n. 1), but we can also observe that it is the only royal name among

all been composed between the time of Sargon and the death of the first king of Isin.[42] Gelb, to the contrary, argued that the liver models could not have been inscribed *before* the reign of Išbi-Erra — that the rebel king was simply the least venerable in the company of "historical" kings.[43] I feel this is the more sensible explanation: a group of texts, found together, all mentioning past events in similar form and script, are more likely to have been composed or compiled together soon after the latest recorded event among them, not from the earliest one and over a period of four centuries.[44]

Historians of these texts have asked why they were first composed. But given the above, we should perhaps invert the question: if "historical" omens were observational, why did they ever *stop*? If the scribes believed in the authenticity of observational omens, why were there never again recorded liver omens about any Old Babylonian kings who reigned during the time when the technical texts were actually being produced?[45] The "historical" liver-model omens of the twentieth/nineteenth century B.C.[46] have the highest comparability among the Old Babylonian technical texts[47] and are thus the strongest evidence that extispical literatures drew on common-culture sources. Liver models are also the first apparatus appearing among the technical types, with compendia surfacing only in the later nineteenth and early eighteenth centuries, and reports in the eighteenth and seventeenth centuries. Yet the kings who were treated as "historical," and whose significance was broadly similar from text to text, was limited: they reflected the Old Babylonian idea of what constituted history, that is, the events of the Akkad and Ur III dynasties. By contrast, when compendious texts were still in production in the seventeenth century, at a time when onomastica still reflected pious veneration of Hammurabi and Samsuiluna and the kings still traced their lineage through them, we never find any new ominous signs named for these or any other more recent kings. Thus, not only are the "historical omens" poor historical sources for those kings (as Cooper 1980 stated so succinctly), their temporal restriction to the pre-compositive phase of the literature also speaks

---

the Mari models to be afforded a divine determinative, and therefore more likely to refer to a native Mari ruler.

[42] E.g., Starr 1983: 4, stating that the Mari liver models "... cannot be dated later than the reign of Išbi-Erra, that is, they belong at the end of the third millennium at the latest"; more generally Starr 1991: 176: "the process of serialization was well advanced already in the Old Babylonian period." Goetze's opinion (1947a: 1–2) is more difficult to discern: he saw Išbi-Erra as the figure providing a *terminus post quem* for the texts in YOS 10 1–2, but held the opposite view for the composition of the Mari liver models, for which Išbi-Erra served as the *terminus ante quem*. See Goetze 1947b: 264–65, where he refers to them (linguistically) as "Old Akkadian" and concludes: "There is every reason to assume that it goes back to good tradition that was first drawn up contemporaneously with the respective event."

[43] Gelb 1956: 2–3, 7: "The composition of the liver models could not have taken place before the time of Išbi-Erra." He stated, on the one hand, that neither does this mean that certain "graphic and linguistic" features of the models might not indicate copying from earlier texts, but on the other hand noted the presence of deliberately archaizing features.

[44] Meyer, although treating the Mari liver models as Old Babylonian documents, ultimately admits that the question of their preservation from an older archive cannot now be answered (Meyer 1987: 8–11, 45–16); Cooper (1980: 99) does not hesitate to label them Old Babylonian.

[45] Hallo's (1967: 96–97) re-translation of the "Sîn-iddinam F" liver-model omen precludes an understanding of the text as a historical tradition about that king('s death) — rather, whether contemporary to the time of Sîn-iddinam or not (this is not clear), the omen purports to give a date for the omen, to historicize it, and in this sense is more akin to the omen of Daduša of Ešnunna.

[46] Regarding the assessment of comparability, see below, section 3.2.

[47] That is, ominous signs named for ancient kings are among the few types that show a high rate of duplicates and parallels between compendia, liver models, and reports.

against any ongoing interest in observable phenomena. The "historical" kings were chosen in a later period precisely for their historical veneer.

2.6 The Size, Extent, and Comprehensiveness of the Old Babylonian Extispical Compendia

The impression that forerunners for extispical literature existed is also suggested by the dramatic appearance of the extensive compendious literature; without antecedent materials, how could such a corpus be formed *ex novo*? The massive series from southern (nineteenth-century Larsa) and northern (eighteenth–seventeenth-century Babylon and Sippar) Babylonia are the earliest compendia known, yet these already display a series numbering nearly 10,000 omens. The texts appear to us so fully formed that it is hard to believe they were not the outcome of a long process of scholarly redaction or compilation. This seeming impossibility induces assumptions that earlier texts, though not yet found, nevertheless must have existed prior to the nineteenth century B.C. This is, of course, precisely the interpretation which the scattershot of earlier secondary references would seem to favor (but see sections 2.2–5, above).

And, indeed, some aspects of the internal, formal organization of the compendious series could be taken to mean that a few of the Old Babylonian texts known to us cannot be "first-generation" documents. Goetze (1947a) long ago pointed out the existence of both duplicates and variants, possibly indicating the existence of earlier recensions (cf. section 3.2),[48] and the arrangement of the compendia by the zones of the liver has encouraged an association of complex organization with antiquity. These have occasionally led to speculations about written[49] and oral[50] sources for the compilation of such texts.

Yet the hard fact remains that, while Assyriologists have been studying liver-omen literature for over a century, in this time no technical texts dating earlier than the Old Babylonian period have emerged.[51] Despite the propensity of third-millennium scribes to compile lists

---

[48] The admixture of archaic and younger orthographies within individual Old Babylonian texts is more likely to reflect deliberate archaizing than the preservation of original archaic forms. In the case of formal preservation, one expects a more uniform attempt to be true to an original, not permitting the neologisms and younger orthographies which characterize the texts Goetze discusses.

[49] Starr (1983: 6) views the omen series as having developed by the gradual accumulation of individual extispical observations in small tabulated collections, then collated into the Old Babylonian "chapters" organized by protastic features, and finally into Neo-Assyrian *Bārûtu*. Though acknowledging the absence of pre-Old Babylonian material, he writes only: "Such classification, systemization and serialization of omens could only have come at the end of a long process of evolution. When the process begins, we know not."

[50] Koch-Westenholz (2000: 11–15) has recently argued that Old Babylonian extispical texts were composed in close temporal proximity to a formative stage of oral tradition, but does not elucidate how or why the transition between these stages was accomplished. Both Koch-Westenholz and Starr (1983: 6) postulate that written and oral traditions of extispicy enjoyed some significant period of coexistence. The Kuhnian view would hold that the transition between the oral and written stages would have been punctative and culturally constructed, not gradual and evolutionary.

[51] This is the same period of scholarship during which the earliest-known dates of many compositions have been pushed back: the Sumerian King List (an Ur III copy now published by Steinkeller 2003), a Sumerian Gilgameš and Agga story published as early as 1949 (see Cooper 1981 for bibliography), Narām-Sîn and the Great Revolt appearing as an Old Akkadian school text (Gelb 1952: 172), and so forth.

and collections of many kinds, and the avidity of Old Babylonian scribes for copying them, no earlier lists of omens have emerged. Despite the antiquarianism abroad in the Old Babylonian period (especially at Nippur), we find little reflection in extispical texts (absent at Nippur) of the topoi which concerned the Sumerian literati (e.g., fertility, mortality, purity, cosmic order; see also sections 2.1–2); it is hard to see that the Sumerian *Weltanschauung* is reflected in the extispical corpus. In contrast to the wide variety of Old Babylonian texts coming out of a true scholastic tradition of copying (epics, hymns, prayers, commentaries, mathematical documents, lexical and other lists), no known Old Babylonian extispical text bears a colophon indicating it to have been copied from another source, nor is there any reasonable expectation that such sources will emerge.[52] This is especially strange when we consider the degree to which Old Babylonian omens were accurately transmitted to Neo-Assyrian *Bārûtu*: are we to understand that a great textual tradition, maintained and transmitted with a high degree of reliability in all periods when it is visible, is to be constructed where it is not visible?

One of the other great bodies of serialized Mesopotamian literature was similarly not preceded by materials identifiable as "forerunners": the Early Dynastic proverb collections were sizeable, extensive, and comprehensively organized, yet seem unlikely to have been compiled from any antecedent literature. The only "smaller" materials for the Early Dynastic corpus are a handful of school texts that are not earlier than the collections themselves, and perhaps later in date. Only the Old Babylonian proverb collections are accompanied by great numbers of excerpts and school tablets, that is, long after the collections themselves were well established.[53] While it has been debated whether or not Early Dynastic proverbs were collected from genuine phrases and sayings or were compiled for purely academic purposes, it is clear that they do not reflect other parts of the scribal curriculum — despite having been composed by scribes.[54] In the cases of both the omens and proverbs, there is no "primitive" literate background to these massive, well-organized corpora. This absence suggests that, while the compilations may have been genuine in the sense of collecting existing knowledge based on oral tradition, they did not emerge from a scholastic tradition over time, gathered from multiple sources.[55]

---

[52] Hunger (1968: 24–29) lists no colophons appearing on Old Babylonian ominous texts; such colophons appear beginning only with Middle Babylonian texts, not coincidentally the same period of the first known extispical school text (Veldhuis 2000). Old Babylonian extispical compendia of course bore rubrics indicating their serialization — cf. Goetze 1947a, with eight tablets marked ki.[number in series] and one marked šu.nigin 48 mu.bi.im 1 kam.ma; and Jeyes 1989: nos. 11 (r. 2′: DUB-*pí* 60+30) and 14 (85 mu.bi šà *ša* 1 dub) — but no colophons indicating copying from other tablets per se (i.e., those tablets which included incipits and/or formulae such as im.gíd.da/*qāt*/igi.kár PN). Lambert (1998: 147) notes ruefully: "Unfortunately, there are no Old Babylonian texts dealing specifically with qualifications of these diviners...." Nils Heeßel, in press and communicated privately, now adds that his collection of the OBE 11 colophon results in the reading DUB-*pí* ᴵ ᵈSîn(XXX)-⸢*ka*⸣-[ ], "Tafel des Sîn-ka[...]," with no supporting evidence for "tablet 90," as Jeyes translated; my thanks to him for sharing this information.

[53] This was, of course, also the era in which the syllabary was under reform.

[54] Alster (1997: xvi–xvii) argues for an oral and secular origin for these texts.

[55] A still more radical example might be the professional and lexical lists of the Late Uruk period. No precursors or forerunners were needed to develop these complex technical documents, which were among the earliest texts. It is, of course, an open question as to the process by which the brand-new technology of writing itself developed, but I prefer the position adopted by Glassner (2003: 216), which argues for a similarly "created" rather than an "evolving" technology.

2.7 Later References to Extispicy's Antiquity

Potency and legitimacy were accorded to Mesopotamian cultural forms for their venerability, and extispicy was indeed viewed as an ancient art — but only in the first millennium, when it was already more than a thousand years old. The claim of antiquity was advanced for the first and only time in a text from Aššurbanipal's seventh-century B.C. library, that the antediluvian king Enmeduranki was taught the art by the god Šamaš, the king then passing his knowledge on to wise scholars.[56] "Enmeduranki" is a slight corruption of the Enmeduranna known from the Sumerian King List. Yet though the Sumerian King List dates to at least the twenty-first century B.C., it mentions no wisdom traditions of any kind — only that Enmeduranna was a king ruling at Sippar for 21,000 years.[57] A third and final reference to Enmeduranna is in the King List compiled by Berossus in the third century B.C., but here again we find no reference to liver divination.[58]

As Pongratz-Leisten argues,[59] the Aššurbanipal-era claim has little value as historical evidence. The ancient pedigree of knowledge texts was part of a wider royal claim to hold independent access to divine will by privileging the past as a site of original knowledge production, such as with Aššurbanipal's famous boast to have "read tablets from before the Flood."[60] Earlier ages had in fact emphasized the antiquity of knowledge to a lesser degree. Neither within the Old Babylonian technical literature or in secondary references to liver divination are there any references to its antiquity, nor even to its general origins (see section 2.5 regarding the absence of colophons).[61] Old Babylonian scribes, like Neo-Assyrian ones, embraced antiquarian learning, but there is nothing to suggest that they looked on extispicy as an especially ancient tradition. This is reflected in the Old Babylonian use of the terms *bārû* and *bārûtu*: though we know of plenty of *bārû*s in the Old Babylonian period, the term *bārûtu* was little used.[62] We know the names of hundreds of Old Babylonian "diviners," but almost no abstract concept of "divination"; the Old Babylonian craft was still too heterodox (or newly orthodox) to admit abstraction.

---

[56] Zimmern 1901: no. 24 (= K. 2486); cf. Lambert 1969 and 1998. Starr (1983: 3) dubs Enmeduranki the "Prometheus" of extispicy.

[57] Jacobsen 1939; see Steinkeller 2003 for the Ur III fragment of the Sumerian King List. Sippar was not one of the cities associated with liver divination in the third-millennium year-names (rather, Nippur, Ur, Isin, and Larsa), but was later correctly associated with the first-known (Old Babylonian) extispical literature.

[58] Verbrugghe and Wickersham 1996: 19, 70: Enme(n)duranki/na is here "Euedorankhos of Pautibiblon." Though he is given one of the shortest antediluvian reigns in the Sumerian King List (21,000 years), he is tied (with the hero "Xisouthros of Larankhos") for the longest one in Berossus' list (64,800 years).

[59] Pongratz-Leisten 1999: ch. 6 passim, but esp. p. 309: "In seiner Zeit wird die Interdependenz von Selbstpräsentation im Umgang mit "Geheimwissen" und die terminologische Bezeichnung von Wissen, das als Teil des Herrschaftswissens betrachtet wird, offensichtlich."

[60] Lambert 1957: 7–8: One Koyunjik text (K. 4023) does claim that it was originally set down by an Enlil-muballiṭ, a "sage of Nippur knowledgeable in the craft of *bārûti*," and identified in the colophon as active in the time of Enlil-bani of Isin (ca. 1850 B.C.) — but note that the text itself is a medical text.

[61] E.g., in the *ikribu*-prayer of the diviner (Goetze 1968). The Sumerian used in Foxvog's (1989) "Manual of Sacrificial Procedure" is written with "at best only ad hoc approximations of the Akkadian"; see also section 2.4 on the "Sumerian Liver Omen."

[62] AHw 110 gives the first use of *bārûtu* as m/spB; CAD B 131–33 gives "from Old Babylonian on," but offers no pre-Kassite usages except Silbenvokabular A 39f.: nam.úzu = *ba*-[*ru-tu*].

2.8 Procedural Dissimilarities to Scientific Method with Respect to Observationalism

Finally, a theoretical problem: divination's similarity to scientific procedure, and the implication that observationalism was its underlying mechanism, has lent weight to the idea that its process was documentary in nature. The analogy to "science" is partly welcome. It sets liver divination at a distance from the semantic fields of "temple religion" and "magic." It is justifiably pinned on both a) science's similar status in modernity as an irreducible form of knowledge, and b) divination's likeness to the scientific method in its systematic organization of phenomena, causal association to other repeatable phenomena, the creation of extensible theoretical categories, and (apparently) in the employment of observation.[63] But the analogy is limited: absent are the critical methodologies which also characterize modern science: experimentalism, problematization, falsification, disproof.[64]

Observations of livers have been presumed to be the means by which the first omens were transferred to their place in the texts (e.g., "If X is observed, then Y"), but that process is not visible in the textual precipitate.[65] The presumption that a gradual process of accumulation and compilation retrojects observationalism into extispicy's genetic development.[66] A historicist point of view, however, looking at the concentration of early evidence into the century ca. 1850–1750 B.C., sees this idea as dubious: the absence of a documentary trail (as discussed above) itself militates against the existence of either an observational procedure or a principle of causation whose mechanism did not require the heavy framing of both scribe and specialist.[67]

It has been almost fifty years since Thomas Kuhn (1962) first critiqued the presumption of cumulative observationalism as the mode of progress in the sciences (*The Structure of Scientific Revolutions*). Kuhn argued that change in scientific knowledge is characterized by sudden crises in thought that demarcate otherwise long periods of quiescent paradigm.

---

[63] The most programmatic statement to this effect in recent times has been J. Bottéro's (1992) essay "Divination and the Scientific Spirit" (first published in 1975), but it is a sentiment echoed in many quarters, aimed at establishing divination's intellectual position (if not its technical history) as "science." Similar expressions may be found in Oppenheim 1964: 210–11; Starr 1983: 7–8; Bahrani 2003; though also as "philosophy" in this last case. Arrayed somewhat against these positions (though without intending to explain the entextualization of divination), are Koch-Westenholz 2000; Rochberg 1999; Pongratz-Leisten 1999: esp. chs. 1 and 6; and Farber 1995.

[64] Although verifications of individual omen *readings* are known from a relatively early point in the practice of extispicy, there never were attempts to verify the omens themselves — only to continually add to the corpus, to revise by increasing (rather than reducing) the likelihood of alternative explanations. In practice, the (always secondary) observation or observer could be wrong, but never the original observation.

[65] See Rochberg 1991 on the observational fallacy in astronomical omens.

[66] Commonly compounding this presumption is a conflation of the undoubted third-millennium practice of divination and a presumed early technical literature argued against above (sections 2.1–7). P. Michalowski (2006: 247): "Divination is commonly thought to be one of the salient characteristics of Mesopotamian culture and the great libraries of the late period were filled with long omen series. And yet all these omens were composed in the Akkadian language and not a single early omen in Sumerian has been found; the only such examples are very late bilingual texts that are clearly scholastic in nature. The distribution of omen texts as well as the exclusively Akkadian technical terminology of the craft contrast with the information gleaned from other sources that provide ample evidence of divinatory practices in early times."

[67] See Roth (2001: 248–52, 281), who argues that Mesopotamian legal and scientific collections did not grow as accretions of abstract, universal, and operational principles, but were gathered as particular "examples of successful practice."

Although this stance has not been adopted uncritically by intellectual communities,[68] one of Kuhn's most long-lasting and widely subscribed ideas is that observation has never been — can never be — free of theoretical framing. In these points — the punctative nature of scientific development on the one hand, and the rejection of some root of "pure" observationalism on the other[69] — extispical literature deserves the analysis of its entextualization, of its texts as a literature with a history, not as a unitary form that presumably existed from time immemorial. Someone created it, and for a reason.

2.9 SYNTHESIS

This part of the discussion has argued against the existence of any scholarly tradition for liver divination prior to the nineteenth century B.C. In so doing, it refutes no particular opinions to the contrary, but counters a scholarly discourse too accepting of certain very modern premises about the observational origin of the practices, amplified by some tendentious claims of later antiquity. Thus, though little that I have argued above has not been considered in some fashion elsewhere, it is my hope that there is a particular value in bringing all these strands of evidence together in a systematic fashion. It is not my purpose to destroy a "straw man": the next section turns its attention to the entextualization of liver divination, to thinking about the reasons why it came into being when and as it did. Central to the discussion is the coincidence of the rise of the extispical literature with the 150-year period during which Mesopotamia descended into intra-regional war.

3.0 A CREATED LITERATURE: EXTISPICY IN THE ERA OF WARRING STATES

The Old Babylonian era in which extispical texts first appeared was one which suffered from chronic warfare, and divination and diviners figured prominently in the courts and councils of the warring states of nineteenth- and early eighteenth-century Babylon, Mari, and Larsa. In my view, the divinatory craft was appropriated by competing Amorite courts, hungry for legitimizing devices. What we have missed in presuming a further antiquity to the corpus is that the redaction of divinatory arts into a technical literature was more a product of state competition and warfare, not the reification of a genuine set of Sumerian practices, precepts, or (least especially) observations. The project to deliberately encode and control this common-culture form enabled Old Babylonian kings to define alternative access to divine knowledge. These practices remained garbed in the clothing of a traditional craft, yet operated on new protocols of secrecy and deliberately blurred generic distinctions between magico-ritual, religious, legal, and scholarly traditions,[70] the influence of all of which have been noticed in extispicy and vice-versa. In this sense, the law codes of the same period (indeed, of the same *sub*-period of the Old Babylonian) should be seen as parallel projects, undertaking to establish ultimately unverifiable claims of authority through a legal voice.

---

[68] E.g., Horwich 1993.

[69] One might usefully compare this gradualist point of view with J.-J. Glassner's (2003) understanding of the origins of the Mesopotamian writing technologies.

[70] See Koch, this volume, p. 43.

It is *not* my opinion that divinatory texts formed a "secret code" of some kind. It *is* my opinion that the flexibility, secrecy, and privileged nature of the practice and the practitioners provided a screen behind which political objectives could be achieved without criticism. I turn my attention now to some characteristics of Old Babylonian liver divination that argue not only against third-millennium origins, but for a deliberate composition in the courts of the warring states. I focus first on three issues related to the technical literature itself, and then turn to two aspects of the social and political world of Old Babylonian divination:

3.1 Deliberate archaisms in liver models and omen compendia

3.2 Low comparability between and among extispical corpora

3.3 Military and political character of the OBE omens

3.4 The "secular" position of Old Babylonian diviners and divination

3.5 The information war and the "secrecy paradigm"

3.1 Deliberate Archaisms in Liver Models and Omen Compendia

Third-millennium orthographies and sign-forms make some appearances in Old Babylonian liver-omen texts. A few such features appear in the earlier Mari liver models[71] and more in the Larsa technical literature,[72] but in general are not so much a feature of the later Sippar compendia represented by OBE.[73] Since these features appear together with younger Old Babylonian forms within the same texts or between "duplicates," their inconsistent use has prompted puzzlement: were these features genuine relic forms preserved by scribal tradition?[74] Old Babylonian scribes were of course not only well practiced in copying tablets from the Sargonic and Ur III periods, but in reproducing antique forms and deploying them in specific contexts (perhaps most famously in the Codex Hammurabi). At a minimum we can say that archaisms were used, in Roth's words, to "magnify the authority of the composition."[75] It seems plausible that duplicates might appear in both archaic and younger cursive scripts,[76] but the preservation of such a miscellany of archaic forms in mixed-style points toward the deliberacy of an archaizing purpose.[77] Archaic forms were more likely ornamental to new compositions, not surviving relics of earlier ones.

---

[71] See esp. Gelb 1956: 7: "As against the few archaizing features of the Mari texts linking them with Sargonic, the majority of the features show post-Ur III innovations."

[72] Goetze 1947a: 1; note mixed-script (both archaic and cursive) appearing mostly on compendia (YOS 10, nos. 17, 22–23, 25–26, 29, 37, 39, 42, 44–45, 47–50, 55, and 61), but also on a liver model (no. 1), and an undated report (no. 19).

[73] Jeyes 1989: 9–14, where the similarity to Neo-Assyrian texts is stressed; see also Koch-Westenholz 2000: 17–18.

[74] Gelb 1956: 7.

[75] Roth 1995: 73, referring to the Codex Hammurabi, which uses an archaic ductus and orientation of the writing, as well as an "archaizing literary language" in the prologue and epilogue. The "hymnic-epic dialect" might be another example of a deliberate archaizing style, which depended on sign-form, morphology, and word choice (used in, e.g., the Elegy on the Death of Narām-Sîn; see Westenholz 1997: 25–26, 204–05).

[76] E.g., YOS 10 34, a later cursive partial duplicate of YOS 10 33, written in archaic script.

[77] E.g., YOS 10 22, in mixed script, partial duplicate of YOS 10 24 (archaic).

Another area in which archaization shows up is in the extispical *termini technici* themselves, which employ an artificial Sumerian jargon.[78] The zones and marks of the liver first appear almost entirely in Akkadian, but shift to an almost exclusively Sumerian terminology by the end of the Old Babylonian period: in the earliest phase of terminologies (Old Babylonian I), only one of fifteen terms (ká é.gal) was expressed ideographically; by the third phase (Late Old Babylonian), only one of ten terms (*tīrānū*) remained in Akkadian.[79] Far from reflecting an original technical vocabulary, anatomical similes like ki.gub, kal, or ká é.gal had no terminological use in the third millennium. The artificial nature of the terms is complemented by the failure of Old Babylonian extispicy to perpetuate pre-existing anatomical terms — notably the word for "liver" itself (bar).[80] A newly invented cryptolect had been preferred over an accepted terminology.

It is not an end in itself to observe the existence of archaisms as formal features; one must ask why the scribes chose to use them. Along with the use of historical kings in the omens and the conscious insertion of an artificial "omen" in the Ibbi-Sin letter, [81] it seems probable that the "antiqued" nature of extispical texts was window dressing meant to add to their authority. A deliberate attempt was made to present the technical literature as a genuine, transmitted antique — an intention scholarship sometimes reproduces in accepting its antiquity — and it is precisely this intentionality that points toward the original composition of the technical literature in the Old Babylonian period.

3.2 Low Comparability between and among Extispical Corpora

The lack of intertextual connections between extispical technical texts and their ephemeral literatures has been briefly noted above (section 2.0), but we should look more systematically at the low comparability between the Old Babylonian technical texts themselves:

1. between the Sippar corpus and other extispical traditions,
2. between the major types of contemporary technical literature, and even
3. between the variants and duplicates themselves.

I do not pretend to offer a full comparative analysis of this massive body of primary literature (about 3,193 published Old Babylonian omens[82]), but some general observations

[78] Koch-Westenholz 2000: 14, noting the "absence of [other] Sumerian terminology"; see also section 3.2 below regarding solecisms and hapaxes. The many unique similes compiled by Nougayrol (1976: 343–50) attest to the heterodox creativity of the literature; see also the many additions in Jeyes 1989, e.g., OBE 2 obv. 2′, in which the "View" (igi.tab) is uniquely "like a reed stylus" (*kīma qarṭuppim*). The problems noted in tracing the etymology of *ṣiḫḫum*, CAD Ṣ 178b–179a, may also reflect its origin as a neologism.

[79] Goetze, YOS 10 5.

[80] Compare the well-attested use of bar ("liver") in third-millennium literature to mean "spirits" or "mood" to the few second-millennium attestations of its use to mean "omen" or "portent," restricted to lexical lists (PSD B 107–109). Marcel Sigrist (pers. comm.) has also brought to my attention a comparison between BM 29663, an unpublished Ur III list of anatomical terms; cf. YOS 13 47–49, where only a minority of terms are shared.

[81] Michalowski (2006), positing that the "false" nature of the omen may have been a "hidden commentary on current events from the time of Samsuiluna." As he points out, the insertion cannot have been intended as a genuine omen, since the scribes who inserted it would have known it was not original.

[82] Jeyes (1980: 107) estimated 2,160 published Old Babylonian compendious liver omens, to which should be added the 402 omens she published in 1989, totalling about 26 percent (Jeyes 1989: 11) if 10,000 compendious omens ever existed. In addition

are in order. It becomes clear on reading through the specialized literature that, while some part-parallels and partial duplicates can be located within the many thousands of lines of omen texts, the number of *direct* duplicates across all three[83] of these comparable categories is simply too low to support the idea that any major effort was invested in actually copying omens. While it is true that some duplicates and varied parallels exist, two points may be made.

First, duplicates and omens are in the vast minority within an enormous technical literature whose signatures, if anything, are unique expressions. Most omens are *not* parallels or duplicates, even though much of what has been written about omens has focused on duplication.[84] When one peruses Starr 1983 or Jeyes 1989, for instance, one could gain the impression that a great deal of overlap exists between the primary sources they study because a great deal of ink in the notes is reserved for investigating links between extispical texts (notwithstanding the contrapuntal commentary on solecisms and hapaxes). This is a perfectly understandable feature of a scholarship which hopes to understand these most obscure practices by using allied information wherever it may be found. Yet in service of this goal, methodological concerns about anachronism are often suspended in the presumption of a greater background of copying; the likenesses are part of a greater unity of likeness, as it were, and the unalikenesses are seen as heterogeneously unalike.

Second, a definitional problem has persisted in referring to "duplicates" which has promoted an artificial appearance of overlap: the majority of claimed "duplicates" are omens reproducing or approximating only the apodosis or protasis of other omens. In my view, while this may indicate a literary or oral borrowing, it is not a duplicated omen per se: the comparability exists only on the level of signifier (protasis) or signified (apodosis), not on the level of the sign (omen). What we see is the emulation of literary motifs, not the copying of actual observations.

How much comparability should we really expect between these texts? Too stringent a definition, too literal a comparativism, runs the risk of overdefining a threshhold between "real" copying and a "phony" scribal erudition. Still, we ought to be able to see a much greater degree of overlap than we do if we are to preserve the idea that what was being recorded in these texts were, even partially or secondarily, observed and repeatable phenomena. In wanting some evidence that some texts were employed as the source material for other texts, we

to these 2,562 compendious omens, we know of some 37 published Old Babylonian extispical reports (see Koch-Westenholz 2002: 130 for a catalog; the reports contained in the relevant Mari letters might also be added to our totals), which range from as few as 10 to as many as 23 observations each, averaging around 16; from this I derive a working total of 592 more ominous passages. Finally, the published Old Babylonian liver models, which number around 39 (38 referred to by Meyer 1987: 11, and at least 1 more subsequent to his work; Jeyes 1989: no. 19), in many cases specify as few as 1 ominous sign; for the sake of convenience, I use the estimate of 39 to arrive at a total of 3,193 published omina. A full one-to-one analysis of these units would involve more than ten million comparisons!

[83] It would be irrelevant and anachronistic to consider, for our historical study of the Old Babylonian texts, the comparability to a fourth category, to Neo-Assyrian extispical texts (though these are the basis for many analytical comparisons in the secondary literature of these technical texts). Not surprisingly, however, it may be remarked that all aspects of a transmitted literature are in evidence in the later *bārûtu*, for which copying and transmission bespeaks a much more overtly antiquarian project.

[84] The variability within Old Babylonian technical literature is again reminiscent of the situation in early writing; Christopher Woods (pers. comm.) writes of UD.GAL.NUN values: "Typologically, writing systems reveal a high degree of variability and experimentation in their infancies, only later becoming confined by the conventions and standardizations that typify their mature phases."

are much more disappointed than satisfied. What is more in evidence are contemporaneous text series whose material was drawn out of the heterodox oral traditions of individuals and/or guilds who shared a common-culture craft.[85]

The differences between the Old Babylonian "northern" (i.e., Babylon and Sippar) and "southern" (i.e., Larsa) extispical traditions have long been noted, and there is little use in comparing two text traditions that were perhaps not fundamentally comparable.[86] Yet, taking the north-Babylonian compendia from Jeyes 1989 as a more manageable but still sizeable sample — 402 omens are substantially preserved on eighteen tablets[87] — it is striking how few observations are true duplicates or parallels. We can also point to the high incidence of hapaxes and unique phrases within the OBE texts. Extispical texts are filled with arcana and strange turns of phrase, of course, but I am not speaking of interpretive problems: at least nine terms or phrases are not otherwise known in Old Babylonian extispical literature,[88] and fourteen more are not known from extispical literature of any time or place.[89] Given that the same sample produces only one genuinely duplicate omen (see below), this already suggests more differences than similarities to other corpora.

Forty-seven OBE omens are partial duplicates or parallels: that is, protases and apodoses that are duplicated or paralleled outside the corpus, but without their partner clauses. In fifteen of those forty-seven cases, duplicates or parallels of OBE protases can be found elsewhere — but married to mismatched apodoses;[90] twenty-six apodoses are known in other texts, but now without the protases attached.[91] Only five full omens among 402 are duplicated within the same OBE texts,[92] and only one has a contemporary Old Babylonian parallel, where the

75 In this, we might draw a parallel to the Balkanization of the lexical tradition in the Old Babylonian, where local curricular traditions were privileged over any notion the more unified lexicographic practices observable in the third millennium (most recently, Veldhuis 1999: 102).

86 See especially Koch-Westenholz 2000: 17f. Among the relatively sparse technical literature originating at Mari, I am unaware of any parallels or duplicates with either the Sippar or Larsa corpora.

87 Jeyes 1989. Discussions of OBE texts here do not include Jeyes 1989: no. 10, from Ur. The remaining eighteen OBE texts only serve as a sample to suggest the direction that a full analysis of all Old Babylonian texts would take. The OBE texts may all derive from Sippar, but their use as a corpus has substantial methodological challenges: they are divided between two periods of composition (a group dated to the time of Samsuiluna, another to Ammiṣaduqa), by completeness (Jeyes expects these eighteen tablets should be part of a total of ca. 100 tablets), by series (the omens mostly address different zones of the liver), and by comprehensibility (31% of the omens are either broken [21.4%] or obscure [9.5%]). The thirty-seven compendia of YOS 10, most of them individually much longer, would probably present a superior sample for major research.

88 OBE 1 obv. 3′, 19′ and rev. 7′; 2 obv. 13′; 3 iv 5′, 15′; 14 rev. 19′; 15 rev. 20′; 18 rev. 20.

89 OBE 1 obv. 4′, 9′, 24′; 2 obv. 2′; 3 iv 14′; 6 obv. 2′; 7 obv. 8′; 12 obv. 6; 13 rev. 19′–20′; 14 obv. 11, 18, 36, 38.

90 The relevant OBE protases appear in: 2 obv. 3′, 8′–10′, 13′; 8 obv. 1′; 14 rev. 10′; 15 rev. 4′; 16 rev. 9′ and 27′. Five other possible parallels rely on restoration *from* the proposed parallel: 2 obv. 4′; 1 rev. 20′–21′; 2 obv. 7′; 4 obv. 14′.

91 The relevant OBE apodoses appear in: 1 obv. 7′, 10′, 13′; 2 obv. 14′; 5 obv. 4′, 7 obv. 10′; 9 obv. 16′; 13 rev. 7′, 9′; 14 obv. 19 and rev. 5′, 12′; 16 rev. 12′; 18 obv. 6–7; 19 obv. 1–2. Ten other possible parallels rely on restoration *from* the proposed parallel: 1 obv. 5′; 4 obv. 13′; 2 obv. 11′; 3 iii 15′; 4 obv. 10′, 12′; 9 obv. 24′; 11 obv. 8; 13 obv. 4′; and 16 rev. 25′.

92 One of these duplicates appears within the same text: OBE 1 rev. 15′ (among rev. 12′–15′, where an observation is duplicated). The other four omens are duplicated within short passages of OBE 13 and 14: 13 rev. 11′ (paralleled by 14 obv. 33), 13 rev. 17′–18′ (by 14 obv. 17), 13 rev. 19′–20′ (by 14 obv. 34–35), and 13 obv. 13′ (by 14 rev. 7′). Both OBE 13 and 14 are Late Old Babylonian observations from the same BM collection concerning the series SAG ŠÀ: given that OBE 13 preserves thirty-six omens, and OBE 14 preserves seventy-eight omens, the question should be: why are only *four* omens paralleled between the texts?

sense of the omen is identically intentioned (though not worded) — and significantly, it is a "historical omen" of Akkad, for which an oral rather than scribal tradition is not difficult to imagine.[93] Neither in part nor in whole do the other 349 OBE omens have evident parallels or duplicates anywhere outside the corpus.

Jeyes took passing note of both "partial duplicates" or "partial parallels,"[94] but the significance of these oddities has never been satisfactorily explained. Indeed, the problem becomes even stranger when we consider "partial duplicates" *within* the OBE corpus. Not enumerated above are six partial duplications of protases or apodoses in other OBE texts: in three cases we find the protasis duplicated without the apodosis; in two cases, the apodosis without the protasis; and in one case we find both halves of an omen duplicated — but split between two different omens![95] What seems impossible is to imagine a scribe who would borrow at will an extispical observation or its result, and freely marry it elsewhere if copying was the intellectual project. To refer to "duplicates" or "parallels" without a more stringent definition implies copying and observationalism, whereas what we see is re-editing and (by a standard of observationalism) outright original composition. To recap: of 402 OBE omens, there is one verifiable (if very general) parallel, but the other fifty-two known "duplicates" are *partial* duplicates which would of course violate the principles of causation that would be encoded in observational record-keeping. Whatever else this editing process can be called, it cannot be said that faithful transmission of data was a concern of the editors; creativity and reconfiguration of omens far outpaces genuine copying.

There also seems a very low incidence of comparability between Old Babylonian extispical reports (of which thirty-eight are known[96]) and compendia, though, once again, a full study is beyond the scope of this paper.[97] A modest experiment, however, suggests the result: using four Late Old Babylonian extispical reports as a sample,[98] we find forty-three individual observations that are preserved or dependably restored, thirty-four of which are the aberrant types that appear in compendious texts.[99] Among these, only one of those reported observations can be found within the protases of the OBE compendia (and it is the very common "there was a path to the left of the gall bladder").[100] Since these four reports are all Late Old Babylonian, all

[93] The omen is OBE 19 3–7, the very last in the volume. OBE 1 7′ has, Jeyes argued, four "parallels"; yet, while OBE 19 3–7 records a "Hole in the [x] of the Presence," its three "parallels" actually find the Hole in "the middle of the View to the right," "in the rim of the Path," and "in the middle of the View in its centre" — altogether different observations. Indeed, four other omens in OBE 16 (3′–5′ and rev. 20′) have genuine duplicates — but they are all later Neo-Assyrian ones.

[94] E.g., Jeyes' notes to OBE 14 rev. 5′ and 10′.

[95] Protasis only: OBE 1 obv. 18′; 13 obv. 3′ and 9′ (second protasis only). Apodosis only: OBE 1 obv. 23′; 7 obv. 7′. OBE 13 obv. 9′ also includes a protasis and apodosis which appear separately within the corpus. The situation of "partial duplicates" is reminiscent of several compendious texts found in YOS 10 (e.g., nos. 22, 24, and 26), which duplicate some sequences of omens, but not others.

[96] The thirty-seven cataloged by Koch-Westenholz 2002, plus one more in Richardson 2007.

[97] Using the following sample as the basis for an estimate, the thirty-eight known Old Babylonian reports contain approximately 323 aberrant observations; checking these against the estimated body of 3,193 published omens would require over a million individual comparisons.

[98] The reports in Richardson 2002. Although the sample size is not convincingly large in itself, it should be noted that two of those reports derive from the same museum collection as nine of the OBE compendia (nos. 1, 8–9, 11–16), thus probably belonging to the same archive. On this basis alone, some degree of comparability should present itself; it does not.

[99] That is, omitting from statistical consideration statements that certain features were simply "present," which are generally not represented in the compendia.

[100] This protasis should indicate the very general positive apodictic reading of "defeat for the enemy" (i.e., the enemy of the client — not to be confused with the more specific "defeat for the enemy army," found

from northern Babylonia, and half from the same divination archive as the OBE compendia, is it not reasonable to hope, if the reports were written to be "keyed" to the massive compendia, that more than *one* might be found among the 402 OBE omens?[101] Alongside the extremely low incidence of duplication and the high incidence of "partial duplication," the fact that the reports match up so poorly to the compendia does not lend much credence to the idea that a process of observation and verification was in use.

What small overlap exists between extispical series from different places, between technical types, between even duplicate texts of the same type from the same place, suggests much more of a common-culture tradition and scribal familiarity from use than it suggests these texts were a core source material for a scholarly project of continued observation. Of course, cuneiform literatures are entirely characterized by variability between recensions, allied text types, local traditions — but minor variations versus comparabilities as low as the ones outlined above have to suggest vastly different editorial processes. One crucial clue lies in the dates alone: no extispical report to our knowledge is dated before Ammiṣaduqa 2 (1645 B.C.), while compendia were in production from at least 1822 B.C. and mostly finished by 1712 B.C.[102] The compendia and the reports really belonged to different historical epochs, composed for different purposes (see section 4.0).

3.3 Military and Political Character of the OBE Omens

The formal aspects of extispical texts outlined above point away from the idea that even the earliest-visible stages of the project involved disinterested, scholarly observationalism. Yet if this was not its purpose, what was? One approach would be to return to look at the subject matter of the ominous apodoses; a topical analysis of the omens from OBE reveals a primary concern with political and military intelligence.

The concerns of the OBE texts are most economically represented in tabular form (see table 1). Type A subsumes those apodoses which are concerned with interstate competition: military action (A_1),[103] geopolitical affairs (A_2, including diplomacy, court intrigues, territorial dispositions), and the political affairs of "the prince" (i.e., the king, NUN/*rubûm* in northern Old Babylonian texts), especially news of and for him.[104] Although the subjects of domestic traitors, usurpers, border garrisons, etc. are not explicitly "interstate" concerns, they do reflect the competition between the royal courts of Mari, Ešnunna, Larsa, Elam, etc. Type B are those apodoses whose contents are either obscure and unintelligible (B_1) or simply too broken (B_2) to place in either Type A or Type C. Type C apodoses, finally, are those

elsewhere). For a survey of Old Babylonian extispical reports, see Koch-Westenholz 2002.

101 Though note a few instances in which the recorded protasis seems to anticipate or indicate prior knowledge of the associated apodosis (e.g., BM 97433; see Richardson 2002). Such protases do seem to indicate that the author of the report was the diviner himself, perhaps to some degree obviating the need for reference materials.

102 The range of dates for the compendia are established by their apparent earliest appearance in the time of Rīm-Sîn I of Larsa (reigned 1822–1763 B.C.), and their relatively isolated Old Babylonian production after the time of Samsuiluna (died 1712 B.C.); see Koch-Westenholz 2002: 132–33; Jeyes 1989: 5; Goetze 1947a: 1.

103 In this typology, a differentiation between apodoses mentioning the "enemy" (i.e., the enemy of the client, thus Type C) and the "enemy army" (Type A) has been strictly observed.

104 By "political affairs," I mean to exclude those apodoses about "the prince" which are not *prima facie* concerned with interstate competition.

Table 1. A brief typology of apodictic concerns in the extispical compendia published in OBE (Jeyes 1989)

Type A: Apodosis concerns interstate competition: Military action (A_1), geopolitical developments (A_2), "the prince" (A_3)
Type B: Apodosis may belong to either Type A or Type C due to uncertain meaning (B_1) or broken text (B_2)
Type C: Apodosis concerns matters other than statecraft: signs from the gods (C_1) and non-state affairs / *résults divers*

Aṣ = Ammiṣaduqa
Ha = Hammurabi
Si = Samsuiluna

OBE No.	*BM Collection*	*Date*	*Series*	A_1 *military*	A_2 *geopolitical*	A_3 *the prince*	B_1 *uncertain*	B_2 *broken*	C_1 *the gods*	C_2 résults divers
1	1902-10-11	Aṣ	KI.GUB	21	4	5	4	3	5	4
2	91-5-9	Si 20	IGI.TAB	4	6	—	3	2	—	—
3	94-1-15	Si 20	IGI.TAB	13	2	—	10	4	3	—
4	91-5-9	Si 20	IGI.TAB+ *puzrum*	5	—	—	2	5	—	3
5	94-1-15	Si 20	*puzrum*	4	1	—	—	2	—	—
6	94-1-15	Si 20	*puzrum*	2	—	—	2	—	—	1
7	83-1-21	Aṣ	KÁ.GAL	1	2	—	4	—	2	1
8	1902-10-11	Aṣ	mixed	1	2	—	1	30	—	—
9	1902-10-11	Aṣ	ŠU.SI	6	5	4	1	3	4	1
*10**	*Ur*	*Ha / earlier*	*ṣibtu*	—	*4*	—	*3*	*5*	—	*15*
11	1902-10-11	Aṣ	gišTUKUL	4	8	—	3	5	—	1
12	1902-10-11	Aṣ	ŠU.SI MUR *kīdītum*	5	—	—	1	—	—	—
13	1902-10-11	Aṣ	*tal*/SAG ŠÀ	12	4	3	3	10	2	2
14	1902-10-11	Aṣ	*tal/rēš* ŠÀ	17	7	33**	3	2	9	7
15	1902-10-11	Aṣ	BI.RI	5	7	4	—	—	1	1
16	1902-10-11	Aṣ	*kalītum / elibuḫḫum*	7	5	6	1	18	1	2
17	1900-10-16	OB	*šuḫḫum*	3	1	—	—	1	—	—
18	1900-10-16	OB	mixed	3	—	—	—	1	2	2
19	94-1-15	OB	*tākaltum* model	1	1	—	—	—	—	—
Totals			402 omens →	114 (28.4%)	55 (13.7%)	55 (13.7%)	38 (9.5%)	86 (21.4%)	29 (7.2%)	25 (6.2%)

* OBE 10, from the "southern tradition" (and note its emphasis on non-military matters) — is not included in the totals.

** Most of the OBE 14 apodoses about "the prince" are explicitly concerned with military and geopolitical matters.

Type A: 56% of apodoses concern state business

Type B: 31% of apodoses are unclear

Type C: 13% of apodoses do not concern state business

concerned with subjects that seem more epistemic in their intent to explain signs throughout the world at large — as an open system of knowledge, not a fixed or closed one.[105] Type C includes signs of the gods which do not clearly indicate whether the concern is either state or private business (C_1),[106] and the *résults divers* which more apparently have no connection to the state business of Type A omens (C_2). Some examples:

A_1	OBE 1 rev. 12′:	"my raid will search for much booty in the enemy's country"
A_2	OBE 9 obv. 21′:	"they will revolt against [the king] in the council"
A_3	OBE 14 obv. 37:	"the prince will get his advisers from his palace servants"
B_1	OBE 3 iv 6′:	"(or:) couriers"
B_2	OBE 7 12′:	"[…] the fall of […]"
C_1	OBE 3 iv 7′:	"the presence of Ištar"
C_2	OBE 1 obv. 3′:	"the son of a herald will die"

The results are quite lopsided: with almost a third (31%) of the apodoses of an undetermined nature (Type B),[107] the remaining subject matter is overwhelmingly concerned with state business (Type A with 56%, Type C with 13%, a 4:1 ratio). Of the omens whose subject matter can be clearly discerned, the focus is emphatically on the expedition of the army, palace coups, harem intrigues, on the fall of cities rather than on predictions of curses, abundance of the harvest, medical conditions, etc.

The most insistent concern of Type A omens is for two areas of action out of the direct sight of the king: the success of the army in the field, and stability within the loyalist class. The interest in military action is not hard to spot: omen after omen fears the "fall of the army while attacking" (OBE 1 obv. 15′), that the "army will not reach its destination (OBE 2 obv. 15′), that "the enemy will strike at the core of your army" (OBE 4 rev. 13′), that "you will lead away in captivity the population of the city you are besieging, but another will enter it" (OBE 13 obv. 8′) — information so specific that it borders on the tactical.

Loyalty is the other pre-eminent concern of the texts. Betrayals endangered the Amorite monarchies on many fronts: among the king's populace, officials, military, vassal kings, even the dynastic family itself. An emphasis persists throughout the compendia on tracking the movements of both people (logistically) and allegiances, in which the deceptions of friends are a prominent feature: "a servant of the king will slander him" (OBE 13 rev. 8′); "the sons of the prince will rise against their father with malevolence" (OBE 14 obv. 20); "the proletariat

[105] The crudeness of this typology is to an immediate purpose. The durability of divination was due in part to its use of deliberately enigmatic apodoses. These constructions, which permitted a great deal of flexibility in interpretation, were in practice precisely because of their metaphoric applicability as vehicles for perhaps limitless tenors; see Sasson 1995 for a discussion of enigmatic constructions in prophecy. These interpretive needs were manifested through cognitive biases such as illusory correlation, availability heuristics, and "hot" (e.g., emotional) cognition.

[106] Those omens mentioning divine signs explicitly related to Type A concerns have been counted there.

[107] I have been extremely conservative in apportioning cryptic or metaphorical apodoses away from Type B or C_1 to Type A, even though one gains the overall impression that "obscure" omens are couched in metaphorical language that were meant to be interpreted as referring to affairs of state, e.g. "a well-known woman will die."

[108] See also Koch-Westenholz 2000: 14, who sees in this a functional consistency with third-millennium

(*hupšum*) will rebel" (OBE 14 obv. 24); "his courtiers will kill him" (OBE 11 obv. 3); "an envoy telling dangerous lies will arrive" (OBE 13 rev. 12′–13′); "defection of a diviner" (OBE 14 rev. 48).

These concerns are very much of-the-moment: the omens are not really concerned with the far-flung future and "fortune-telling," but with a shifting status quo. They are consistent with what we know of Sumerian extispicy, that it was used to reveal what already existed, though hidden or unrecognized — not what would come to pass in the far future.[108] Our readings of many ancient Near Eastern omens and prophecies already expect that their authors intended them as messages about the present (often with reference to the past), couched in a future tense, *ex eventu* in their voice. In this connection, one should note the indistinction or ambivalence between the Akkadian verbal present and future tenses, and that the apodictic verb is also known to appear in the stative, the perfect, or even the preterite.[109] The presentist nature of extispical knowledge is now also forcefully underscored by Heeßel's study (this volume), which establishes that the "stipulated term" for which extispical readings were valid were limited to a maximum term of three years, and most often for much shorter periods of time.

The formal aspects of causation and future tense should not take our eyes from the content: Old Babylonian extispicy tried to determine courses of action for the conduct of statecraft in the here-and-now, having to do with the immediate outcomes of present conditions, in war, in diplomacy, in staffing. In reading an omen that said to the king "they will revolt against you in the council," we should understand that the real message was not to predict some future revolt, but to give notice that the council was at that moment or incipiently disloyal and plotting. That the omens took political and military intelligence as their subject matter should nevertheless not, I believe, direct us toward a strictly functional view of extispicy — that it had an exclusive, primary, or dispositive role in determining policy — but that it served a function parallel to civil and military channels of intelligence and political pressure. The paradigm of information-gathering for leaders of states at war is not to construct a single and infallible source, but to construct multiple, overlapping, and even competing branches to advise leadership.[110] Part of this structuring is functional (in the sense that it increases intelligence and offers verification),[111] part political (in that it polices and builds an image of total state knowledge), part hegemonic (in that divination specifically braids in and blurs distinctions between religious, military, political, and cultural forms of authority).

---

divination: "There is nothing to suggest a Sumerian practice of predicting future events."

[109] E.g., apodictic verbs in the stative: "the fall of my army," OBE 1 obv. 8′; "the prisoners of war are cowed," ibid., rev. 4′ (*qaddu*, adj.); in the perfect: "a snake has charged," OBE 1 obv. 9′, MUŠ *i-te-še-er*; in the preterite: "the discipline of the prince's army was not firm," OBE 12 obv. 1 (cf. Jeyes' translation, "will not be firm," but also OBE 18 21, *iq-bu-ú*, recognized by Jeyes). Both the stative and perfect are attested in the Mari omens: e.g., stative: ARM 26/1 2, 5 (*ṣabit*), 3, 10 (*radi*); perfect: ARM 26/1 3, 4 (*ittabal*). Where Sumerian verbs are employed, the prefix /ba-/ likely also reflects the perfect (OBE 1, passim: ba-ug_x).

[110] Most interesting among OBE omens are those which advise the king to trust or distrust the advice of his own retainers: e.g., OBE 16 rev. 25′, "the king will accept the word of his servants"; Jeyes 1989: 27. The presence of multiple diviners also attests to this chambered approach to political administration.

[111] What in modern intelligence analysis is referred to as "Analyses of Competing Hypotheses."

3.4 THE "SECULAR" POSITION OF OLD BABYLONIAN DIVINERS AND DIVINATION

The subject matter of the texts then match up very closely to the sociopolitical position of divination in an administrative economy fueled by secrecy, intrigue, and a concern for the secure transmission of information. In spirit, the technical literature better resembles the intelligence technologies of states at war[112] than, say, scholarly projects like medieval hagiographies or Enlightenment encyclopedias.[113] In this respect, the palace orientation of divination is probably reflected in what we know of third-millennium extispicy; while it is anachronistic to describe divination as "secular," I use it here to mark as erroneous any idea that its origins were essentially part of Babylonian religion.[114] While earlier liver divination indeed concerned temples, there is little evidence for it as *part* of temple cult: that is, extispicy was used to choose chief priests and sites or dates for temple-building by kings, but there is little indication that it was used by cult personnel. From earliest times, diviners had primarily been agents *exterior* to the temple household used by the palace for verification. The communicative mode of temple cult was sacrifice, but sacrifice was a distinctly secondary gloss on Old Babylonian extispicy. The communicative mode of extispicy was professional interpretation, and its incorporation of Babylonian gods and use of sheep and goats as media / *materia magica* resulted from orthopraxy, not orthodox theology.

In general, diviners appear in third-millennium contexts which are not cultic, and divination is also absent from divine hymns. No reference is made to divination in either royal letters or hymns to Utu (the god most commonly associated with divination), nor in temple hymns mentioning Utu of Sippar or Larsa,[115] nor indeed for any other gods.[116] I am aware of no incantation or ritual text from the Old Babylonian period (or earlier) which sets the work of the diviner inside a temple, nor any instance in which the title máš.šu.gíd.gíd is further clarified by an extended title "of Temple Name."[117] The gods, meantime, are in sparse attendance

[112] In the 1950s and 1960s Cold War, agencies such as the CIA did not limit their interests to "scientific" technologies like cryptography and handwriting identification, but conducted active research in the paranormal, magic, witchcraft, psychic ability, and psychoactive drugs. The fact that these were and are all discredited pseudo-sciences did not prevent the Agency from devoting significant resources toward researching them as potentially useful tools for intelligence-gathering. What is most directly analogous to the present argument is not so much that the appropriation of those arcane "knowledges" actually secured or verified information gathered otherwise, but that it helped to secure the Agency's pre-eminent position as a locus of secrecy, helping it to bypass political constraints on the pretext of secrecy-in-wartime.

[113] On the close alliance between classification and surveillance, however, see especially Lyon 2007.

[114] See section 3.0 and n. 65, and *pace* Winitzer, this volume. I do believe that a theological integration of divination was underway no later than the Late Old Babylonian period (that is, post-Samsuiluna), but that those were post-entextualization rationalizations. Notwithstanding, as is true of many *ex post facto* rationalizations, their constructedness is difficult to observe because of later belief in them.

[115] Note the following compositions among those translated on the ETCSL Web site: the "letter from Sîn-iddinam to the god Utu about the distress of Larsam" (3.2.05); Hymns Utu B, E, and F (4.32.2, .e, f); the "temple hymns" (4.80.1) lines 169–78 and 479–93 (and also lines 16–23).

[116] References to extispicy are similarly lacking in hymnic literature to the other gods associated with extispicy (Enlil, Inanna, and Iškur); the only possible exception of which I am aware is Enlil A (4.05.1) line 113 — yet it uses the máš.e ... dab_5 formula of Sargonic year-names about which I have expressed doubts above. Note also the heterogeneous distribution of addressees of Old Babylonian reports: Šamaš is found there, but also Sîn, Marduk, Annunītum, Nanaya, and Ištar (Goetze 1957).

[117] One may further compare the rare instances of máš.šu.gíd.gíd "of Divine Name" to the well-attested military-style title ugula máš.šu.gíd.gíd: I am aware of one "diviner of the god Marduk" mentioned in ARM 26/2 371 — though he appears, explicitly, in the palace gate.

within the lines of the omen literature: to be sure, they are routinely called upon at the outset of extispical reports, and the compendia do enumerate the occasional "sign of Ištar," but these features do not indicate institutionalism any more than a "weapon of Sargon" indicates specific historical knowledge about the dynasty of Akkad.[118] Secondary extispical literature (that is to say, not the technical literature, e.g., the "prayer of the diviner") may mention Šamaš, but never other priests, shrines, or temples. Rarely do the omens take cultic personnel as their apodictic subjects (see section 2.1); instead, in addition to military personnel (see section 3.3), they are concerned with councils, courtiers, cupbearers — the civil, military, and domestic servants of the Crown.[119]

Readers will already be familiar with the extensive network of diviners employed by the Mari kings, despatched to the courts (petty and great) of greater Mesopotamia. More than forty-five diviners are known by name from the court of Zimri-Lim alone, posted in more than two dozen foreign palaces, fortresses, and towns.[120] From the kingdom of Babylon, diviners are also primarily seen to be engaged in state business having to do with diplomacy and military matters, a picture derived not only from the technical literature,[121] but also from letters and administrative texts.[122] One may summarize the functional role of diviners in the vast majority of texts as being in service to the king in a variety of ways related to intelligence — as diplomats and spies in foreign courts, on the march with armies, in private council to kings, in charge of fortresses.[123] Diviners' chief concern with interstate affairs is also evident in terms of the environments in which they moved: the compendious texts discuss the cityscapes of palaces, gates, walls, harems, and storehouses — but not temples — and landscapes far beyond the city walls: garrisons and strongholds, borderlands, army bivouacs, battlefields, roads, and the open country. These latter places were, by the urban orientation of Mesopotamian theology, de facto relatively unprotected by the gods, spaces across which movement of goods and personnel was a dangerous business.[124] By a geography of knowledge, one would better

---

[118] Note, as Jeyes (1989: 30–31) does, the compendious preference to refer generically to "the gods," rather than any one specific god by name.

[119] See Jeyes 1989: 33–34 for the incidental figures who appear among the OBE omens, none of whom are cultic or temple personnel.

[120] Other than Ašqudum, whose missions are too numerous to mention here (to Aleppo, Emar, Qaṭṭunān, Saggarâtum, Karkemiš, Suḫû, Ḫana, etc.), some diviners acting as foreign agents for Mari include (but are not limited to): **Erīb-Sîn**, mission(?) to Babylon (ARM 27 161); **Hammī-esim**, mission to Mišlān (ARM 26/1 168); **Ilšu-nāṣir**, resident in Andarig (ARM 26/2 442), and mission to Ša Bāṣim (ARM 2 22); **Inib-Šamaš**, mission(?) to Babylon (ARM 26/1 102–04), in the field near Ḫirītum (ARM 27 151); **Išḫī-Addu**, mission to Dūr-Yaḫdun-Lîm (ARM 26/1 121), in the field at siege of Aḫunā (ARM 26/1 117), mission(?) to Emar (ARM 26/1 112); **Išmaḫ-Šamaš**, resident at Dir on the Baliḫ (ARM 26/1 247); **Kakka-Ruqqum**, in the field near Ḫanat (ARM 26/1 131); **Māšum**, resident at Mišlān (ARM 26/1 168–72); **Narām-Sîn**, mission to Terqa (ARM 26/1 137), and resident at Šitullum (ARM 26/1 138 bis); **Nūr-Addu**, mission to Qaṭṭunān (ARM 26/1 139–40); **Sîn-rēmēni**, resident at Kahat (ARM 26/1 108 bis); **Šamaš-īn-mātim**, resident in Terqa (ARM 26/1 142–44); **Šamaš-inaya**, resident at Dir on the Baliḫ (ARM 26/1 145); **Yamṣi-ḫadnu**, resident at Mišlān (ARM 26/1 168–72); **Zikri-Ḫanat**, resident in Suḫû (ARM 26/1 154), expedition to Yabliya (ARM 26/1 156); **Zimrī-Dagan**, resident at Tuttul (ARM 26/1 157). Many other Mari letters mention the dispatch to or residence of known diviners in unspecified locations, unspecified diviners in known locations, and unknown diviners to unknown locations.

[121] See Jeyes 1989: ch. 2 passim; at the apex of these duties, diviners could be appointed outright rulers of conquered cities, as with Aqba-Ḫammu's post at Qaṭṭarā after control fell to Hammurabi (Van De Mieroop 2005: 61).

[122] See Richardson 2002: ch. 4 "The Diviners' Archive."

[123] "Private" activity by diviners is not well represented until the Late Old Babylonian; see section 4.0.

[124] See the letters of the diviner Išḫi-Addu (including ARM 26/1 112–18, 123, 125), which are chiefly concerned with safe dispatch and travel — of troops,

contrast than compare temple religion (where truth was to be found with the god, in his cella, at the very heart of the city) to extispicy (where truth was to be found by a professional, inside a sheep, from the transhumant zones of the countryside).

Most critical to this study is that Old Babylonian diviners served these roles in an era of prolonged and aggravated crisis than that they were "secular" figures per se. The existence of divination as an already accepted form of para-knowledge made it an ideal vehicle for the ideological re-inventions and circumventions of the day. To make a categorical distinction between the "secular" and "sacred" would fall afoul of a modernist dichotomy that would have mystified an ancient Mesopotamian; yet to write a primarily "sacred" valence back into a history of Old Babylonian divination would be a correspondingly severe mistake. If we do not credit these actors with the intellectual, social, and political ability to consciously manipulate traditional signals for their immediate needs, we miss an opportunity to see how the forms that remain, dried in clay, began as impressionable substances in the hands of master scribes.

3.5 The Information War and the "Secrecy Paradigm"

Why should divination, first attested as a craft in the Early Dynastic period, only now in the Old Babylonian take on this new entextualized aspect? Why should the paradoxical dimensions of secrecy and a written tradition develop simultaneously after a thousand years of practice? An episode from the Mari letters first drew me to reflect on this apparent paradox. ARM 26/1 101–04 are letters from agents of Zimri-Lim on a diplomatic mission to Babylon; the last of these complains of Hammurabi's violation of secrecy protocols in favor of attachés from Ekallatum:

> The servants of Išme-Dagan (king of Ekallatum) ... have ousted the lords of the land and they themselves have become the masters of Hammurabi's council. He listens to their advice. Once or twice, when (Mari diviners) ... read the oracles and reported on them, [these men] were not asked to leave. As they were present, they heard the message of the oracles. What other secret is there beside the secret report of the diviners? *While his own servants do not hear the secrets of the diviners, these men do!*[125]

Both the process and results (sometimes even the practitioner) of liver divination were insistently secret. Divination was highly charged as a secret enterprise: a "secret" (*pirištum*, later *niṣirtu*) in extispical contexts could refer not only to the results of an inspection, but to the spoken word of the diviner, the written reports, the person of the diviner (*mukīl pirištīšu*),[126] even to the liver itself — secrets to be guarded against being "stolen," "betrayed," "leaked," or "seized."[127] Coupled with what we have observed above about the diviners' place in courts

---

female *aštalû*-singers, cattle, individual agents, and the king himself (cf. ARM 26/1 138 bis).

[125] ARM 26/1 104, translated by Van De Mieroop 2005: 58, after Charpin 1999; emphasis mine. In another letter, the two Mari diviners in question were forced by Hammurabi to reveal their extispicies in front of Babylonian diviners, who refused to divulge their own (ARM 26/1 102; cf. 96).

[126] The identity of many Babylonian diviner-agents was kept deliberately anonymous: several letters from the king to his *bārû* (including VS 16 27, 59, 60, 61, 97) were addressed only to, e.g., "the diviner living in Sippar-jaḫrurum," even though the other addressees in the letters were named by name.

[127] Jeyes 1989: 16–17, 23: the signs or answers designated *awātum* were implicitly synonymous with *pirištum*; note that, from what little reference there is to extispicy in the third millennium, there is nothing which suggests secrecy.

distant from their king's;[128] about Zimri-Lim's network of dozens of diviners throughout Syro-Mesopotamia; about their entrustment with troops, fortresses, and other materiel[129] — the context of intelligence for divination's "secrecy paradigm" is difficult to ignore.

Yet though it seems only natural that kings should hold secrets of state together with their advisors, and that those secrets were of a sensitive nature, Hammurabi's exclusion of the Babylonian councillors in favor of foreign agents in ARM 26/1 104 strikes a more discordant tone. It has been typical to think of divination as a form of knowledge that was sensitive due to its content, that what liver divination did was to passively reveal (rather than actively create and communicate) secrets.[130] Yet there has been remarkably little association of divination's emphasis on secrecy to its military-political subject matter. This reluctance may arise because a functional explanation of extispicy might seem to compromise or reduce the status of a classic Mesopotamian intellectual project, but knowledge forms are too much artifactualized if we do not approach them as historically contingent.

The century in which extispical literature first came to light is the same one in which the courts and scribaria of Mari, Babylon, Larsa, and Ešnunna were in such an unparalleled state of political and military flux that the atmosphere may fairly be said to have been revolutionary. In the sphere of ideological production, this revolution saw re-inventions of at least four major patterns of political power and legitimation. Political authority was established on hybrid grounds of both dynastic authority and genealogical descent.[131] The political envelope of city-state dynasticism was being pushed by the novelty of single cities with multiple dynasties (e.g., Mari, with two competing dynasties, and Larsa, with at least three successive ones) and single dynasties with multiple centers (e.g., Šamši-Adad and sons, Larsa and Jamutbal, Elam's *sukkal* and *sukkalmaḫ*).[132] An unstable system of vassalages, peerships, and royals-in-exile had grown up which encouraged a virtual marketplace competition for power. Fourth — and perhaps most relevant to our analysis here — this competition extended well below the level of kings and viziers, to courtly, military, and urban officials, who jockeyed not only for position relative to one another, but even marketed their loyalties between royal courts.[133] This is the political culture which forms the backdrop of extispical text-production in the palace sector.

I posit two different functions of the extispical literature in its creative period; these functions intersect in the issue of secrecy. On the level of ideology, extispical texts defined a body of knowledge independent of religious authority, control over which not only permitted kings a direct access to the divine will, but which was inaccessible to other authorities.[134] If the state arises by means of its monopoly of legitimate violence — that is, through a generalized,

[128] Jeyes 1989: 21–22.

[129] Richardson 2002: ch. 4.

[130] Jeyes 1989: 35, 70: "it was the access to state secrets which the court diviners had which made them [a risk]."

[131] Best represented by the Genealogy of the Hammurabi Dynasty and the sections of the Assyrian King List leading up to the reign of Šamši-Adad I; see Michalowski 1983.

[132] This fragmentation may be said to prefigure the rise of the territorial states of post-1500 Mesopotamia, which were never again founded on the primacy of single city-states as they were in the third millennium.

[133] The Mari letters of ARM 26/1 reveal this all-pervading atmosphere of distrust and competition in superabundance, but a few illustrative examples can be cited: for recruitment of spies, informers, and defectors, see ARM 26/1 35, 93, 140?, 381; for denunciations of officials and diviners, see ARM 26/1 4–6, 32, 45, 88, 101, ARM 26/2 302, 303, 312, 326, 380; for denunciations of kings, see ARM 26/1 40 and ARM 26/2 371.

[134] This may be contrasted with many of the references to "secrets" in Sumerian literature (ad-ḫal or líl), which are reserved for the gods.

coercive principle of inequality (Trigger 1985) — it can only do so by first controlling the terms of legitimacy (Kelly 2006). Securing structural inequality thus presupposes control over the *terms* of privilege, over access to knowledge: what the state finally requires is privileged knowledge, is secrecy.[135] Extispicy, through its explicit claims to secrecy but also through its voluminous and exclusive technical apparatus, helped to establish that equality gap for Old Babylonian kingship.

The principle of secrecy operated on a second level of praxis, too: claims of exclusivity allowed kings a very real free agency in the realm of intelligence. Control over extispical knowledge permitted the creation of a loyalist cadre of diviners, parallel to other cadres, who by definition operated on principles of secrecy for intelligence-gathering. This "secrecy paradigm" created opportunities for kings to establish

- internal policing to monitor staff loyalty and information security
- firewalls to encourage but control intra-organizational elite competition[136]
- opportunities for backchannel diplomacy
- free movement of political agents across non-urban and foreign zones
- permanent networks of agents whose activities could circumvent the strictures of courtly politics

The pre-eminence of these secrecy functions is made clear by the Mari "diviners' oath" (ARM 26/1 1), in which ritual and scholarly concerns go entirely unmentioned: the oathtaker swears not to hide information; to reveal information only to Zimri-Lim; to reveal the identity of diviners who have violated their disclosure oath; to report "evil rebels" who have "hostile mouths," especially those who have tried to use the divinatory apparatus for their own ends. That is, not only the secrets and the secret-holders were under royal authority, but the process itself.

Divination thus did not merely reflect the subject matter of the Mari letters when it read signs of warring states and secret news, it was the medium through which those struggles were processed. The vertical structures of command in dynastic city-states were simply not sufficient to meet the challenges of a continuous state of internecine war in nineteenth–eighteenth-century B.C. Babylonia. Divination afforded alternate avenues for kings to transmit information securely and quickly in insecure environments peppered with disloyal courtiers, traitors, and spies, and fast-marching armies. At the same time, divination ambiguated lines of control and clamped down on self-interest among internal elites by creating multiple channels of information, cross-checking, and verification.[137] The hallmark of this new tool was the simultaneous discursive power of truth *and* secrecy.

---

[135] Hence the Holzer quote at the outset of this article. Trigger (1985: 52) sees the state's appropriation of community practices in privileged forms as a hallmark of state authority claims; these knowledge forms then "cease to be [allies] of equality and become an adjunct of class privilege and state power."

[136] Myerson (2008) considers the "dynamic moral hazards" of leadership over elites through normative optimal incentives (such as delayed rewards) and sanctions such as randomized (but fair) trials; systems of unknown but ubiquitous monitoring may complement such techniques by encouraging participation controlled by fear or shame.

[137] One need only reflect briefly on the seemingly endless permutation and proliferation of contemporary intelligence agencies to see the need of political executives for alternative sources of information. At the beginning of the last century, the United States government staffed only a handful of very small offices, staffed by only a few dozen intelligence officers. By 2002, these had mushroomed into some twenty-two agencies employing almost 200,000

Secrecy is not disharmonious with ritualism, but it does not harmonize so well with the development of a massive literature consisting of hundreds of tablets, ±10,000 written omens, the communication of results in written and dated reports, the development of reference tools like liver models, or the discussion of omen results in letters. The "secrecy paradigm" is best revealed by its absence in two contexts. The first of these is its absence from the school curriculum: although, by our estimate above, some 3,200 Old Babylonian omens survive to this day, not a single extispical school text is known until the Kassite period.[138] Extispical knowledge was indeed produced by scribes, but the texts were not taught as a part of Old Babylonian scribal knowledge.

The second is extispicy's absence from Old Babylonian royal inscriptions. Though the craft had been acclaimed by Šulgi and Gudea[139] in ages past, extispicy was absent from this more public literature. Hammurabi (once) and Samsuiluna (twice) speak of "signs" (giškim/ *ittū*) signifying their legitimate power, but these almost certainly refer to celestial or terrestrial signs, not extispical ones.[140] Among all Old Babylonian kings, only Warad-Sîn mentions *têrtū* — probably liver omens, but rather vaguely.[141] The school curriculum and royal inscriptions addressed different audiences for different purposes, but divination's absence from both literatures emphasizes its isolation from persuasive efforts to speak through the literati or to the literate public. Old Babylonian kings never boasted or bragged about extispicy because it was *not* a public discourse of power like temple religion or patronage of ancient literature.[142] It was not meant to be publicly legitimizing (as remained the patronage of gods and temples); it was not yet a classical cultural form for junior scribes to master (as were royal hymns).

For whom, then, was extispical literature developed? Again, we should turn to divination's functional, political environment for answers. Though the need for quick transmission of news from city to city between political agents was paramount, the security of that information was mediocre at best. We know of paired messengers sent to corroborate the contents of letters, a kind of "double-key system";[143] we know of the capture and interrogation of envoys;[144] of decoy messages sent to courts in opposite directions at the same time;[145] of limitations placed on the movements of even allied ambassadors within the Babylonian cities;[146] of hidden

people, not including several agencies (e.g., the OWI, FIS, COI, OSS) that have come and gone in the intervening years. In recent years, bureaucratic competition and protectionism have come to be blamed more for intelligence failures than the politicization of intelligence — the structure and process more than the content. The 2003 and 2004 amendments to Executive Order 12333 restructured seventeen agencies under the authority of a Director of National Intelligence, but other agencies maintain some degree of structural autonomy.

[138] See above, section 3.2; Veldhuis 2000: 74, 82; further significance is discussed in section 4.0.

[139] Knowledge of extispicy had also been attributed to Narām-Sîn and Sîn-iddinam by Old Babylonian scribes.

[140] Frayne 1990: Hammurabi (E4.3.6.16) mentions giškim, Samsuiluna mentions once each (E4.3.7.7) *ittū* and (E4.3.7.8) giškim. *ittū* seems not to have been used to mean "signs" or "marks" in extispicy until first-millennium *Bārûtu*.

[141] á.ág in Frayne 1990: 4.2.13.17 and .27; as against .16 and .24, where he refers to giškim.

[142] Of course "temple religion" and "literature" were highly exclusive practices, but both were publicly valorized.

[143] E.g., ARM 26/2 384 (translated by Van De Mieroop, after Charpin 1999): "When Išme-Dagan's messengers told him [their message], Hammurabi replied: 'As you don't want to complete your message, my servant who has come with you will do so.' So Hammurabi fetched his servant who had come with them...."

[144] E.g., ARM 6 27 and 26/2 372, 383.

[145] Most famously, the double-cross of Elam against Larsa and Babylon reported in ARM 26/2 362 (when learned by Mari), and the triple-cross organized in turn against Elam by Rīm-Sîn and Hammurabi.

[146] ARM 26/2 370 (trans. by Van De Mieroop, after Charpin 1999; cf. ARM 26/2 361 and 363): "The man was sent as envoy from Eshnunna to Hammurabi. After he arrived in Babylon, Hammurabi released the

messages and messengers;[147] and, as mentioned above, the not-so-discrete method of barring some people from the council chamber while others got to stay in. The variety of means by which to improve and protect intelligence were many, but intrinsically limited to the reliability of people.

In claiming a perquisite of secrecy for their texts and procedures, diviners created "spaces" — legitimized secrecy-complexes of environment, personnel, opportunity, and action — in which the king could gain advice and information from people outside the normal channels of court and council, and sometimes without their knowledge altogether. (What I do *not* suggest is that divination texts were themselves a "secret code" or the like.) Extispical texts carved out an exceptional, secret space at the highest, most rarefied levels of power; divination's authority paralleled the military power of generals and political power of viziers, a flexible intelligence protocol developed to keep politburos in the dark and kings in the know. The "antiqued" cultural legitimacy of this new science of communication with the gods protected it as a *mysterium*, one tool among many enabling the king to move and communicate freely in an environment swimming with other political actors and agents.

CONCLUSION: ON SEEING AND BELIEVING

It was only a later development, under Ammiṣaduqa and Samsuditana, that reports were written for private clients; only in the Kassite period that we first find extispicy in school curricula. Not until these features arise can we speak of a scholarly and scientific category of knowledge called *bārûtu*. The historically attested distribution of texts referring to and constituting extispical practice conform to the following course of change:

- first, a third-millennium southern tradition of extispicy used within the old Sumerian temple-cities for the selection of cultic personnel, a procedure which was not committed to text but existed as a local, heterodox, and orally transmitted craft down into the nineteenth century;[148]
- second, the nineteenth/eighteenth-century appropriation of that craft tradition by newer, north-Babylonian courts at Ešnunna, Babylon, Mari, and Larsa,[149] entextualized in liver models and compendia, a new *techné* redeveloped in the context of Mesopotamian state struggle;[150]

Eshnunnan messengers and soldiers he held prisoner, but he still has limited their movements inside the city." See also ARM 26/2 420 (in which messengers of Ekallatum and Mari are kept separate from each other in Kurda) and 26/1 77, a prison detainment to solicit information.

[147] E.g., ARM 26/2 384 (in which messengers protest "We are not hiding a secret message!") and 414.

[148] Since orally transmitted cultural forms cannot be assessed for their similarity to standardized written forms, to refer to this as "oral tradition" would be oxymoronic.

[149] Since Larsa is the only city in which both the third- and second-millennium traditions are attested, it likely plays a crucial role in this transformation. Note that Larsa also boasts the last king from a "historical" omen, Warad-Sîn's *têrtū*, and the "outsider" status of the Kudur-mabuk dynasty as important features marking Larsa's central role.

[150] J.-J. Glassner (pers. comm., 2007) has taken the position that another change attending this historical phase of the literature was that "diviners began to understand the omens as written signs and no more as images."

- third, a gradual, Late Old Babylonian (seventeenth century) and Kassite-period re-transmission of this codified extispicy as an epistemic form of knowledge, represented newly within the scribal curriculum through school texts[151] and in civil society through extispical reports for private clients.[152]

Assuming for the moment that these stages represent fundamentally different uses of the same technology, we see not a unitary science of extispicy under a single process of gradual development, but three extispicies, each developed and put to its own end. In Kuhnian terms, the first and third stages were paradigms, the second revolutionary. Since all three stages may also be located within the Old Babylonian period itself — four centuries long, no small timeframe! — we are looking at a perfect illustration of how periodization can sometimes mislead our thinking. Historical periods are not necessarily coincident with paradigm; changes can come in the middle, and paradigms reign at beginnings and ends.

Do we do an injustice to divination to locate its compositional moments and purposes so precisely? After all, the system of omina ranks among the greatest signatures of Mesopotamian intellectual life. To see its composition determined by political exigencies will strike some as mechanical and reductive, eroding the "conceptual autonomy" of Mesopotamian culture, or failing to appreciate the emic sensibility of ancient beliefs and practices in needing a "practical" explanation. Yet what I argue for is to see a venerable and respected tradition from one time and place, borrowed and reconfigured in highly sophisticated ways in later times and other places. Mesopotamian kings drafted liver divination into service not simply because it was legitimate (all such knowledges propagated by political actors are legitimizing, so this is truistic) — not because it was infallible or irreducible (the question of belief cannot anyway be proved) — nor because it was mere political legerdemain — but because it offered them another choice, a "third way" between traditional kingship and rule by naked force, bases of legitimacy which were, now, equally shaky in this time of prolonged warfare. A strictly historicist and minimalist survey of the temporal and geographic evidence permits this reading without having to see any one period through the eyes of another. "Historicizing" has to require the interrogation of all documentary classes, all texts analyzed, questioned, doubted; "context" must be established without recourse to projection of fragmentary evidence generically and periodically, as if the distribution of what is recovered were purely circumstantial.

No form of human inquiry is autogenetic; since no form of knowledge is unconstructed, composition need not be at odds with belief when historical change occurs over time. As it came to be, seeing wasn't believing — but *believing* in seeing was believing. Within a very short period of time (indeed, before the end of the very dynasty which helped initiate the project), divination was released into the "stream of tradition," where it grew and flourished in a life of two thousand years.

---

[151] Veldhuis 2000.

[152] When written reports finally make their appearance almost two centuries after the first compendia are known, it seems significant that they are exclusively written for private clients. Conspicuously absent from the known reports is the person who was far and away the client most commonly identified in the compendia: the king. Reports thus constitute a different form of use for extispicy, marking its emergence into civil-social use only well after the era of warring states had come to an end.

APPENDIX 1

Mesopotamian year-names referring to priestly nominations via sheep omens.[a]

AKKAD:

Narām-Sîn: "o" variants: en/nin.dingir en.líl; "ll": en ^{d}nanna.

LAGAŠ II:

Ur-Ningirsu I: "a": šíta-ab.ba; "b": lú.maḫ ^{d}ba.ú; "c": išib ^{d}nin.gír.su / nin. dingir ^{d}iškur.*

Gudea: 19: lú.maḫ ^{d}inanna.[b]

Pirigme: "a": en nina^{ki}; "f": išib ^{d}nin.gír.su.

UR III:

Ur-Namma: "d": en ^{d}inanna unug^{ki}; "h": en ^{d}nanna; "j": nin.dingir ^{d}iškur.

Šulgi: 15 and 43: both en ^{d}nanna.

Amar-Sîn: 4: en ^{d}nanna.

Ibbi-Sîn: 2: en ^{d}inanna; 10: en ^{d}nanna / ^{d}inanna*; 11: en ^{d}enki eridu^{ki}.[c]

ISIN:

Išbi-Erra: 13: en.gaba ^{d}inanna; 22: en.bára an.na.

Iddin-Dagan: 3: nin-dingir ^{d}iškur; 5: en ^{d}inanna; 8: nin.dingir ^{d}nin.kilim.

Išme-Dagan: "a": en ^{d}nanna; "e": en ^{d}en.líl.

Lipit-Ištar: "g": en ^{d}nin.gublalaga úri^{ki}.

Damiq-ilišu: 4: lú.maḫ ^{d}nin.ì.si.in^{ki}.

LARSA:

Gungunum: 6: en ^{d}utu.

Abisare: 10: en ^{d}utu.

---

[a] This index compiles exempla of Frayne 1993; 1997; and 1990; Edzard 1997; and the year-names Web site of the CDLI project (http://cdli.ucla.edu/tools/yearnames/yn_index.html). Pains have been taken to ensure that multiple listings are not presented here, but the designations of individual year-names (especially where their order remains unknown) has inclined toward the CDLI site in the interests of clarity. Asterisks (*) designate directly contrary readings by those sources.

[b] A fragmentary year-name of Gudea may also be a nomination: mu nin.dingir [...] (Edzard 1997: 27).

[c] Unusually, this year-name identifies the nominee's previous position as šita-priest of Ibbi-Sîn.

APPENDIX 2

"Omens" from Jacobsen 1987 misunderstood as "extispicies."

Th. Jacobsen's oft-cited *The Harps That Once...* (1987) remains the most popular translations of Sumerian poetry. Yet what Jacobsen often translates as "omen," "diviner," or "divination," however, and then annotates as an extispical procedure, are either explicitly or probably non-extispical. This list of six passages from that work serves as an example of this definitional drift, not an exhaustive study:

1. In "Dumuzi's Dream," lines 17–25, Geštinanna is said to "know the writings" (Alster 1972: 55, "tablet-knowing"), but this is for the interpretation of a dream omen, not a liver omen.

2. The so-called "Eridu Genesis" was specifically understood by Jacobsen (1987: 145) to make reference to a liver divination, but this is apparently a confusion of ki-azag (= *amūtu*, the pure or precious metal) for *amūtu* "liver"; cf. Poebel (1914: 13, 17 line 9′: ki-azag-ga), who made no translation suggesting extispicy.

3. Jacobsen (1987: 290 and n. 30) more emphatically connects an epithet of Enki in "Enmerkar and the Lord of Aratta," to the (supposedly extispical) omen readings for the appointment of en-priests, translating "sagacious omen-revealed lord of Eridu." Vanstiphout's (2003: 65) translation, however, makes better sense of geštúg-ge pàd-da (line 153) as "chosen for wisdom" — and avoids the logical fallacy of a god said to be chosen by men through omens!

4. In the "Hymn to Enlil," Jacobsen's translation of line 56 (é-a en-bi é-da mú-a) is "the en-priest was a diviner," but the term for diviner there is mú, a kind of disputant seer, not a liver-omen diviner. Falkenstein (1960: 21) gave the altogether different "Der Herr des Hauses ist mit dem Haus zusammen großgeworden."

5. In the "Nanše Hymn," what Jacobsen translates in line 131 as "divination" is instead given by Heimpel (1981) as "decision" (eš-bar-kin), which is especially unlikely to be an extispical decision, since the message "comes out of the mouth of the Apsu." Like Šulgi's Hymn B, this hymn in general presents a strong contrast between the uses of writing (e.g., for administration) and memorized/intuitive knowledge in lines 110–35, where this reference to eš-bar-kin falls.

6. Jacobsen's (1987: 271; as van Dijk 1983: 145) translation of line 712 in "Lugal-e" mentions "the preeminent tablets, with series (with the rites of) enship and kingship" — but the closest indication of any divinatory pratice of Nidaba indicates only that she read stars (line 726), not livers.

ABBREVIATIONS

AHw	W. von Soden, *Akkadisches Handwörterbuch*
ARM	Archives Royales de Mari
CAD	A. Leo Oppenheim et al., editors, *The Assyrian Dictionary of the Oriental Institute of the University of Chicago*
CDLI	Cuneiform Digital Library Initiative (Web site: cdli.ucla.edu)
ETCSL	Electronic Text Corpus of Sumerian Literature (Web site: www-etcsl.orient.ox.ac.uk/)
OBE	Jeyes 1989
PSD	Åke W. Sjöberg, editor, *The Sumerian Dictionary of the University Museum of the University of Pennsylvania*
TCL	Textes cunéiformes du Louvre
VS	Vorderasiatische Schriftdenkmäler der Königlichen Museen zu Berlin
YOS 10	Goetze 1947a

BIBLIOGRAPHY

Al-Rawi, Farouk N. H.

1994 "Texts from Tell Haddad and Elsewhere." *Iraq* 56: 35–43.

Alster, Bendt

1972 *Dumuzi's Dream: Aspects of Oral Poetry in a Sumerian Myth.* Mesopotamia 1. Copenhagen: Akademisk Forlag.

1976 "On the Earliest Sumerian Literary Tradition." *Journal of Cuneiform Studies* 28: 109–26 (review of Biggs 1974).

1997 *Proverbs of Ancient Sumer: The World's Earliest Proverb Collections.* Bethesda: CDL Press.

Archi, Alfonso

1984 "The 'Names and Professions List': More Fragments from Ebla." *Revue d'Assyriologie* 78: 171–74.

Bahrani, Zainab

2003 *The Graven Image.* Philadelphia: University of Pennsylvania Press.

Biga, Maria G.

1999 "Omens and Divination at Ebla." *Nouvelles Assyriologiques Brèves et Utilitaires* 1999, no. 109.

Biggs, Robert D.

1974 *Inscriptions from Tell Abū Ṣalābīkh.* Oriental Institute Publications 99. Chicago: University of Chicago Press.

Bonechi, M., and A. Catagnoti

1998 "Magic and Divination at IIIrd Millennium Ebla, 1: Textual Typologies and Preliminary Lexical Approach." In *Magic in the Ancient Near East*, edited by S. Ribichini, pp. 17–39. Studi epigrafici e linguistici sul Vicino Oriente antico 15. Verona: Essedue Edizioni.

Bottéro, Jean

1992 "Divination and the Scientific Spirit." In *Mesopotamia: Writing, Reasoning, and the Gods,* by Jean Bottéro, pp. 125–37. Chicago: University of Chicago Press.

Castellino, G. R.

1972 *Two Šulgi Hymns (BC).* Studi Semitici 42. Rome: Istituto di studi del Vicino Oriente.

Charpin, Dominique

1999 "Hammu-rabi de Babylone et Mari: Nouvelles sources, nouvelles perspectives." In *Babylon: Focus mesopotamischer Geschichte, Wiege früher Gelehrsamkeit, Mythos in der Moderne; 2. Internationales Colloquium der Deutschen Orient-Gesellschaft 24.–26. März 1998 in Berlin*, edited by J. Renger, pp. 111–30. Saarbrücken: Saarbrücker Druckerei und Verlag.

Civil, Miguel

1969 *The Series* lú = *ša and Related Texts.* Materials for the Sumerian Lexicon 12. Rome: Pontificium Institutum Biblicum.

1976 "Lexicography." In *Sumerological Studies in Honor of Thorkild Jacobsen on His Seventieth Birthday, June 7, 1974*, pp. 123–57. Assyriological Studies 20. Chicago: University of Chicago Press.

Cooper, Jerrold S.

1980 "Apodictic Death and the Historicity of 'Historical' Omens." In *Death in Mesopotamia*, edited by B. Alster, pp. 99–106. Mesopotamia 8. Copenhagen: Akademisk Forlag.

1981 "Gilgamesh and Agga: A Review Article." *Journal of Cuneiform Studies* 33: 224–41.

1983 *The Curse of Agade*. Baltimore: Johns Hopkins University Press.

Coser, M.

2000 "An Extispicy Report in III Millennium Ebla." *Ugarit Forschungen* (Gordon Memorial Volume) 32: 169–76.

Deimel, Anton

1969 *Die Inschriften von Fara 2: Schultexte aus Fara*. Wissenschaftliche Veröffentlichungen der Deutschen Orient-Gesellschaft 43. Leipzig: Deutschen Orient-Gesellschaft. First printing 1923.

DeMeyer, L.

1982 "Deux Prières *ikribu* du temps d'Ammī-ṣaduqa." In *Zikir Šumim: Assyriological Studies Presented to F. R. Kraus on the Occasion of His Seventieth Birthday*, edited G. van Driel et al., pp. 271–78. Leiden: Brill.

Dossin, G.

1935 "Prières aux 'Dieux de la Nuit' (AO 6769)." *Revue d'Assyriologie* 32: 179–87.

Durand, Jean-Marie

1988 *Archives épistolaires de Mari* I/1. Archives Royales de Mari 26/1. Paris: Éditions recherche sur les civilisations.

Edzard, Dietz Otto

1997 *Gudea and His Dynasty*. Royal Inscriptions of Mesopotamia, Early Periods 3/1. Toronto: University of Toronto Press.

Falkenstein, Adam

1960 *Sumerische Götterlieder*. Part 1. Heidelberg: C. Winter.

Farber, Walter F.

1993 "'Forerunners' and 'Standard Versions': A Few Thoughts About Terminology." In *The Tablet and the Scroll: Near Eastern Studies in Honor of W. W. Hallo*, edited by M. E. Cohen, D. C. Snell, and D. B. Weisberg, pp. 95–97. Bethesda: CDL Press.

1995 "Witchcraft, Magic, and Divination in Ancient Mesopotamia." In *Civilizations of the Ancient Near East*, edited by J. Sasson, pp. 1895–1909. New York: Charles Scribner's Sons.

Foxvog, D. A.

1989 "A Manual of Sacrificial Procedure." In *Dumu-e$_2$-dub-ba-a: Studies in Honor of Åke W. Sjöberg*, edited by H. Behrens, D. Loding, and M. T. Roth, pp. 167–73. Occasional Publications of the Samuel Noah Kramer Fund 11. Philadelphia: University Museum.

Frayne, Douglas R.

1990 *Old Babylonian Period (2003–1595 B.C.)*. Royal Inscriptions of Mesopotamia, Early Periods 4. Toronto: University of Toronto Press.

1993 *Sargonic and Gutian Periods (2334–2113 B.C.)*. Royal Inscriptions of Mesopotamia, Early Periods 2. Toronto: University of Toronto Press.

1997 *Ur III Period (2112–2004 B.C.)*. Royal Inscriptions of Mesopotamia, Early Periods 3/2. Toronto: University of Toronto Press.

Gelb, Ignace J.

1952 *Sargonic Texts from the Diyala Region*. Materials for the Assyrian Dictionary 1. Chicago:University of Chicago Press.

1956 "On the Recently Published Economic Texts from Mari." *Revue d'Assyriologie* 50: 1–10.

Glassner, Jean-Jacques

2003 *The Invention of Cuneiform: Writing in Sumer*. Translated and edited by Z. Bahrani and M. Van De Mieroop. Baltimore: John Hopkins University Press.

Goetze, Albrecht

1947a *Old Babylonian Omen Texts*. Yale Oriental Studies 10. New Haven: Yale University Press. Second printing, 1966.

1947b "Historical Allusions in Old Babylonian Omen Texts." *Journal of Cuneiform Studies* 1: 253–65.

1957 "Reports on Acts of Extispicy from Old Babylonian and Kassite Times." *Journal of Cuneiform Studies* 11: 89–105.

1968 "An Old Babylonian Prayer of the Divination Priest." *Journal of Cuneiform Studies* 22: 25–29.

Hallo, William W.

1963 "On the Antiquity of Sumerian Literature." *Journal of the American Oriental Society* 83: 167–76.

1967 "New Texts from the Reign of Sin-iddinam." *Journal of Cuneiform Studies* (Goetze festschrift) 21: 95–99.

Heeßel, Nils P.

1981 "The Nanshe Hymn." *Journal of Cuneiform Studies* 33: 65–139.

Heimpel, Wolfgang

1981 "The Nanshe Hymn." *Journal of Cuneiform Studies* 33: 65–139.

2003 *Letters to the King of Mari: A New Translation, with Historical Introduction, Notes, and Commentary*. Mesopotamian Civilizations 12. Winona Lake: Eisenbrauns.

Horwich, Paul, editor

1993 *World Changes: Thomas Kuhn and the Nature of Science*. Cambridge: MIT Press.

Hunger, Hermann

1968 *Babylonische und assyrische Kolophone*. Alter Orient und Altes Testament 2. Kevelaer: Neukirchener Verlag.

Jacobsen, Thorkild

1939 *The Sumerian King List*. Assyriological Studies 11. Chicago: University of Chicago Press.

1987 *The Harps That Once...: Sumerian Poetry in Translation*. New Haven: Yale University Press.

1994 "The Historian and the Sumerian Gods." *Journal of the American Oriental Society* 114: 145–53.

Jeyes, Ulla

1980 "Death and Divination in the Old Babylonian Period." In *Death in Mesopotamia: Papers Read at the XXVIe Rencontre Assyriologique Internationale*, edited B. Alster, pp. 107–21. Mesopotamia 8. Copenhagen: Akademisk Forlag.

1989 *Old Babylonian Extispicy: Omen Texts in the British Museum*. Istanbul: Nederlands Historisch-Archaeologisch Instituut te Istanbul.

Kelly, John

2006 "Writing and the State: China, India, and General Definitions." In *Margins of Writing, Origins of Culture*, edited by S. Sanders, pp. 15–32. Oriental Institute Seminars 2. Chicago: The Oriental Institute.

Klein, Jacob

1981 *The Royal Hymns of Shulgi, King of Ur: Man's Quest for Immortal Fame*. Transactions of the American Philosophical Society 71/7. Philadelphia: American Philosophical Society.

Koch-Westenholz, Ulla
2000 *Babylonian Liver Omens: The Chapters* Manzāzu, Padānu *and* Pān tākalti *of the Babylonian Extispicy Series Mainly from Aššurbanipal's Library*. Copenhagen: Museum Tusculanum Press.
2002 "Old Babylonian Extispicy Reports." In *Mining the Archives: Festschrift for Christopher Walker on the Occasion of His 60th Birthday*, edited by C. Wunsch, pp. 131–45. Babylonische Archive 1. Dresden: ISLET.

Kramer, Samuel Noah
1942 "The Oldest Literary Catalogue." *Bulletin of the American Schools of Oriental Research* 88: 10–19.
1961 "Kataloge." In *Sumerische Literarische Texte aus Nippur*, Volume 1, edited by S. N. Kramer and I. Bernhardt, pp. 19–20. Berlin: Akademie-Verlag.

Krecher, J.
1980 "Kataloge, literarische." *Reallexikon der Assyriologie* 5: 478–85.

Kuhn, Thomas
1962 *The Structure of Scientific Revolutions*. Chicago: University of Chicago Press.

Lambert, Wilfred G.
1957 "Ancestors, Authors, and Canonicity." *Journal of Cuneiform Studies* 11: 1–14.
1969 "Enmeduranki and Related Matters." *Journal of Cuneiform Studies* 21: 126–38.
1998 "The Qualifications of Babylonian Diviners." In *Festschrift für Rykle Borger zu seinem 65. Geburtstag am 24. Mai 1994:* tikip santakki mala bašmu..., edited by S. M. Maul, pp. 141–58. Cuneiform Monographs 10. Groningen: Styx.

Legrain, Leon
1912 *Le temps des rois d'Ur: Recherches sur la société antique d'après des textes nouveaux*. Paris: H. Champion.

Lieberman, Stephen J.
1977 *The Sumerian Loanwords in Old-Babylonian Akkadian*. Harvard Semitic Studies 22. Missoula: Scholars Press.

Lyon, David
2007 *Surveillance Studies: An Overview*. Oxford: Polity.

Luckenbill, Daniel D.
1930 *Inscriptions from Adab*. Oriental Institute Publications 14. Chicago: University of Chicago Press.

Meyer, Jan-Waalke
1987 *Untersuchungen zu den Tonlebermodellen aus dem Alten Orient*. Alter Orient und Altes Testament 39. Kevelaer: Neukirchener Verlag.

Michalowski, Piotr
1983 "History as Charter: Some Observations on the Sumerian King List." *Journal of the American Oriental Society* 103: 237–48.
2003 "An Early Dynastic Tablet of ED Lu A from Tell Brak (Nagar)." *Cuneiform Digital Library Journal* 2003/3. http://cdli.ucla.edu/pubs/cdlj/2003/cdlj2003_003.pdf
2006 "How to Read the Liver — in Sumerian." In *If a Man Builds a Joyful House: Assyriological Studies in Honor of Erle Verdun Leichty*, edited by A. K. Guinan et al., pp. 247–58. Cuneiform Monographs 31. Leiden and Boston: Brill.

Nougayrol, Jean
1950 "Textes hépatoscopiques d'époque ancienne conservés au Musée du Louvre." *Revue d'Assyriologie* 44: 1–44.

1976 “Les ‘silhouettes de référence’ de l’haruspicine.” In *Kramer Anniversary Volume: Cuneiform Studies in Honor of Samuel Noah Kramer*, edited by B. L. Eichler, pp. 343–50. Alter Orient und Altes Testament 25. Kevelaer: Butzon & Bercker.

Oppenheim, A. Leo

1959 “A New Prayer to the ‘Gods of the Night.’” *Analecta Biblica* 12: 282–301.

1964 *Ancient Mesopotamia: Portrait of a Dead Civilization.* Chicago: University of Chicago Press.

Poebel, Arno

1914 *Historical Texts.* University of Pennsylvania Publications of the Babylonian Section 4/1. Philadelphia: The University Museum.

Pohl, A.

1937 *Rechts- und Verwaltungsurkunden der III. Dynastie von Ur.* Texte und Materialien der Frau Professor Hilprecht Collection of Babylonian Antiquities im Eigentum der Universität Jena, neue Folge, 1–2. Leipzig: J. C. Hinrichs.

Pongratz-Leisten, Beate

1999 *Herrschaftswissen in Mesopotamien: Formen der Kommunikation zwischen Gott und Konig in 2. und 1. Jahrtausend v. Chr.* State Archives of Assyria Studies 10. Helsinki: The Neo-Assyrian Text Corpus Project.

Richardson, Seth F. C.

2002a “The Diviners’ Archive.” In The Collapse of a Complex State, by Seth Richardson, Chapter 4. Ph.D. dissertation, Columbia University. University Microfilms no. 3053344.

2002b “Ewe Should Be So Lucky: Extispicy Reports and Everyday Life.” In *Mining the Archives: Festschrift for Christopher Walker on the Occasion of His 60th Birthday*, edited by C. Wunsch, pp. 229–44. Dresden: ISLET.

2006 “gir$_3$-gin-na and Šulgi’s ‘Library’: Liver Omen Texts in the Third Millennium (I).” *Cuneiform Digital Library Journal* 2006/3: 1–9. http://cdli.ucla.edu/pubs/cdlj/2006/cdlj2006_003.pdf

2007 “Omen Report No. 38.” *Nouvelles Assyriologiques Brèves et Utilitaires* 2007: no. 47.

Rochberg, Francesca

1991 “Between Observation and Theory in Babylonian Astronomical Texts.” *Journal of Near Eastern Studies* 50: 107–20.

1999 “Empiricism in Babylonian Omen Texts and the Classification of Mesopotamian Divination as Science.” *Journal of the American Oriental Society* 119: 559–69.

Roth, Martha T.

1995 *Law Collections from Mesopotamia and Asia Minor.* 2nd edition. Atlanta: Scholars Press.

2001 “Reading Mesopotamian Law Cases: PBS 5 100: A Question of Filiation.” *Journal of the Economic and Social History of the Orient* 44/3: 243–92.

Rutten, Maggie

1938 “Trente-Deux modèles de foies en argile inscrits provenant de Tell-Hariri (Mari).” *Revue d’Assyriologie* 35: 36–70.

Sasson, Jack

1995 “Water beneath Straw: Adventures of a Prophetic Phrase in the Mari Archives.” In *Solving Riddles and Untying Knots: Biblical, Epigraphic, and Semitic Studies in Honor of Jonas C. Greenfield*, edited by Z. Zevit, S. Gitin, and M. Sokoloff, pp. 599–608. Winona Lake: Eisenbrauns.

Sigrist, Marcel
1984a *Neo-Sumerian Account Texts in the Horn Archaeological Museum.* Andrews University Cuneiform Texts 1. Berrien Springs: Andrews University Press.
1984b *Les sattukku dans l'Ešumeša durant la période d'Isin et Larsa.* Bibliotheca Mesopotamica 11. Malibu: Undena Publications.

Starr, Ivan
1983 *The Rituals of the Diviner.* Bibliotheca Mesopotamica 12. Malibu: Undena Publications.
1986 "The Place of the Historical Omens in the System of Apodoses." *Bibliotheca Orientalis* 43: 628–42.
1990 *Queries to the Sungod: Divination and Politics in Sargonid Assyria.* State Archives of Assyria 4. Helsinki: Helsinki University Press.
1991 Review of *Old Babylonian Extispicy: Omen Texts in the British Museum*, by Ulla Jeyes. *Bibliotheca Orientalis* 48: 175–80.

Steinkeller, Piotr
1980 "The Old Akkadian Term for 'Easterner.'" *Revue d'Assyriologie* 74: 1–9.
2003 "An Ur III Manuscript of the Sumerian King List." In *Literatur, Politik und Recht in Mesopotamien: Festschrift für Claus Wilcke*, edited by W. Sallaberger, K. Volk, and A. Zgoll, pp. 267–92. Orientalia Biblica et Christiana 14. Wiesbaden: Harrassowitz.

Sweek, Joel
2002 "Inquiring for the State in the Ancient Near East: Delineating Political Location." In *Magic and Divination in the Ancient World*, edited by L. Ciraolo and J. Seidel, pp. 41–56. Ancient Magic and Divination 2. Leiden and Boston: Brill.

Taylor, J.
2003 "Collations to Lu C and D." *Cuneiform Digital Library Bulletin* 2003/3. http://cdli.ucla.edu/pubs/cdlb/2003/cdlb2003_003.pdf

Trigger, Bruce
1985 "Generalized Coercion and Inequality." In *Development and Decline: The Evolution of Sociopolitical Organization*, edited by H. J. M. Claessen, P. van de Elde, and M. E. Smith, pp. 46–61. South Hadley: Bergin and Garvey.

Van De Mieroop, Marc
2005 *King Hammurabi of Babylon: A Biography.* Oxford: Blackwell.

van der Meer, L. Bouke
1987 *The Bronze Liver of Piacenza: Analysis of a Polytheistic Structure.* Amsterdam: J. C. Gieben.

van Dijk, J. J. A.
1983 *Lugal ud me-lám-bi Nir-gál: Le récit épique et didactique des Travaux de Ninurta, de Déluge et de la Nouvelle Création.* Leiden: Brill.

van Dijk, J. J. A., and Markham J. Geller
2003 *Ur III Incantations from the Frau Professor Hilprecht-Collection, Jena.* Texte und Materialien der Frau Professor Hilprecht Collection of Babylonian Antiquities im Eigentum der Universität Jena, Neue Folge 6. Wiesbaden: Harrassowitz.

Vanstiphout, Herman L. J.
2003 *Epics of Sumerian Kings: The Matter of Aratta.* Writings from the Ancient World 20. Atlanta: Society of Biblical Literature.

Veldhuis, Niek

1999 "Continuity and Change in the Mesopotamian Lexical Tradition." In *Aspects of Genre and Type in Pre-Modern Literary Cultures*," edited B. Roest and H. L. J. Vanstiphout, pp. 101–18. Groningen: Styx.

2000 "Kassite Exercises: Literary and Lexical Extracts." *Journal of Cuneiform Studies* 52: 67–94.

Verbrugghe, Gerald P., and John M. Wickersham

1996 *Berossos and Manetho, Introduced and Translated: Native Traditions in Ancient Mesopotamia and Egypt*. Ann Arbor: University of Michigan Press.

Westenholz, Joan Goodnick

1992 "The Clergy of Nippur." In *Nippur at the Centennial: Papers Read at the 35[e] Rencontre Assyriologique Internationale, Philadelphia 1988*, edited by M. de Jong Ellis, pp. 297–310. Philadelphia: The University Museum.

1997 *Legends of the Kings of Akkade: The Texts*. Mesopotamian Civilizations 7. Winona Lake: Eisenbrauns.

Wilcke, C.

1976 "Kollationen zu den sumerischen literarischen Texten aus Nippur in der Hilprecht-Sammlung Jena." *Abhandlungen der Sächsischen Akademie der Wissenschaften* 65/4: 42.

Zimmern, Heinrich

1901 *Beiträge zur Kenntnis der babylonischen Religion*. Leipzig: J. C. Hinrichs.

13

DIVINATION AND ORACLES AT THE NEO-ASSYRIAN PALACE: THE IMPORTANCE OF SIGNS IN ROYAL IDEOLOGY

CYNTHIA JEAN, UNIVERSITÉ LIBRE DE BRUXELLES, FNRS

In everyday life and for (inter)national issues as well, Neo-Assyrian kings were eager to hear or read their scholars' reports and interpretations of omens. The royal letters and archives found at Nineveh give an idea about the Sargonid rulers' need to look for signs and understand their interpretations about matters of uttermost importance, such as the management of their state and their personal well-being.

What status was conferred to divination and oracles at the Neo-Assyrian court, and to what extent did the signs sent by gods have a decision-making value? From the end of the nineteenth century A.D. until the thirties of the twentieth century, when ancient sources about Greek, Egyptian, and Mesopotamian magic began to emerge and to be (often reluctantly[1]) edited, the finest debate among historians of religions and philologists was the opposition, or the relationship, of religion, science, and magic. Today we find these questions rather outdated, but we have to acknowledge that our will to classify and sort out ancient concepts may be misleading if we use our modern definitions and standards. Classification is indeed helpful in order to understand our ancient records, but it should be considered no more than an organizing tool.

As A. Annus put it,[2] the disciplines labeled as sciences during one period in history for one civilization will be considered as a blend of science and superstition by their followers or even by outsiders of their time, just as we are always someone else's best pagan or heretic. Our modern Western definition of science being irrelevant to ancient history, the appropriate issue is: what status is given to a discipline (our concern being divination, oracles, and any signs forecasting future) within a society (Mesopotamian civilization) during a certain period in history (Neo-Assyrian period)?

At the Neo-Assyrian court, the five disciplines of Assyrian wisdom, based on religious and metaphysical concepts, are represented by a chief scholar, the *ummānu*, and his assistants: the *āšipūtu* or "exorcistic lore," the *asûtu* or "medicine, therapy," the *bārûtu* or "divination, extispicy," the *kalûtu* or "science of lamentations," and *ṭupšarrūtu* or "science of the scribes," that is, astrology. In a sense, in our modern view, these disciplines were made up of religion, science, and superstition, since they all relied on the same faith (the henotheistic theology

[1] See, for example, Betz 1997: xliii. The French auction catalog of a Greco-Coptic magical papyrus described it as a "mystical cheese": "En tête sont trois pages de copte, qui débutent par l'histoire d'un fromage mystique (...). Ce fromage n'est autre que la gnose" (quoted from Lenormant, Catalogue 87, about PGM IV). The famous scholar U. von Wilamowitz-Möllendorf wrote that he once heard a well-known colleague complain about the edition of these papyri "because they deprived antiquity of the noble splendor of classicism" (Betz 1997: xliii and n. 31).

[2] See Annus, this volume.

of Aššur, blended with the deep-rooted Mesopotamian religious system in general), since they recorded observable evidence and analyzed facts, and since they acquired some of their interpretations of facts on common beliefs.

Should an apotropaic ritual, a therapy, an omen, or a lament turn out to be false or unsuccessful, it seldom brought a questioning about the validity of these disciplines. Failures were attributed to a lack of the scholars' skill, to a flaw in the ritual or to a god's will.[3] In every human system of knowledge, individuals need to stick to the social construction of reality, where the authority of a "brute fact," in J. Searle's words,[4] is equivalent to a self-referential or "institutional" fact.

When it comes down to studying the concept of knowledge and the systems of ideas in antiquity, we must analyze ancient sources to find out whether a discipline, whatever systems it relies on, begets a triple validation by a given society, that is, **political**, **social**, and **psychological** supports. If an ancient discipline obtains this validation, we can consider it *mutatis mutandis* a "science" in its broadest sense, that is, a knowledge or a practice relying on a system. From an Assyrian point of view then, the five disciplines mentioned above were sciences, because kings, scholars, and people back them up, giving them a triple validation. In the correspondence and scholarly reports of the Neo-Assyrian kings, we find many evidences that these disciplines had the highest status and influenced political decisions, warfare, royal ideology, and theology. The status of divination and oracles, the discipline of interpreting and asking for signs, had thus the status of a science due to the triple support of the Assyrian society.

THE PSYCHOLOGICAL SUPPORT OF DIVINATION

The reliability of divination is based on a technical lore,[5] which achieves recognition from a tradition written down by scholars throughout the centuries and passed down from the ancient times. Observations and omens were organized in series (labeled as ÉŠ.QAR). These series could be considered as canonical or non-canonical (*aḫi'u*).[6] The compiling habits of scholars made compendiums and anthologies available for themselves, their colleagues, and their successors. For example, the corpus of the *tamītu* has mostly a Babylonian origin, but these texts could be consulted in Neo-Assyrian libraries, where collections of *tamītu* were at hand.[7]

The conclusions of famous scholars of the past were also considered as significant (*ša pî ummāni*).[8] For example, the scribe Akkullanu writes to Assurbanipal that scanty rains are a good omen.[9] At first, this may sound weird and Akkullanu feels that the king will ask where

[3] See Ambos 2007; and my forthcoming paper "Healing Assyrian Kings: At the Crossroads of Technique and Psychology," to be published in the proceedings of the International Conference Ritual Dynamics and the Science of Ritual (Heidelberg, 29 September–2 October 2008).

[4] Searle 1995, especially chapters 4–5 (The General Theory of Institutional Facts).

[5] Implicitly it also requires the neutrality of the performer.

[6] Non-canonical texts were as authoritative as canonical ones, but came from "other" traditions. There is no "apocryphal text" from a Mesopotamian scholar's point of view; cf. Jean 2006: 56–57.

[7] Lambert 2007: 10–12.

[8] Cf. Elman 1975.

[9] SAA 10, 100; see commentary below.

he read it. This is why the scholar quotes his source in the following lines: this omen comes from a report of Ea-mušallim, the *ummānu* of the Babylonian king Marduk-nadin-aḫḫe, written more than 400 years ago.

Some tricky issues required the use of every kind of text. In an astrological report about retrograding planets, the scribe Issar-šumu-ēreš quotes three planetary omens due to the retrogradation of Mars and Jupiter with many explanations, the king being doubtful about the accuracy of the scribe's interpretation. This letter does not refer to genuine observations[10] but to similar situations:

SAA 10, 8 — Date: late Tebet (X) 672

> To the king, my lord: your servant Issar-šumu-ēreš. Good health to the king, my lord! May Nabû and Marduk bless the king, my lord!
>
> Concerning what the king, my lord, wrote to me: "Why have you never told me the truth? When will you (actually) tell me all that there is to it?" — Aššur, Sin, Šamaš, Bel, Nabû, Jupiter, Venus, Saturn, Mercury, Mars, Sirius, and ... be my witnesses that I have never untruly ... (...)
>
> ---
>
> If Mars, retrograding, enters Scorpius, do not neglect your guard; the king should not go outdoors on an evil day.
>
> ---
>
> This omen is not from the Series (ÉŠ.QAR); it is from the oral tradition of the masters (*ša pî ummāni*).
>
> When Mars, furthermore, retrogrades from the Head of Leo and touches Cancer and Gemini, its interpretation (*pišru*) is this:
>
> ---
>
> End of the reign of the king of the Westland.
>
> ---
>
> This is not from the series; it is non-canonical (*aḫi'u*). This aforesaid is the only area which is taken as bad if Mars retrogrades there. Wherever else it might retrograde, it may freely do so, there is not a word about it.
>
> And the matter of the planet Jupiter is as follows: If it turns back out of the Breast of Leo, this is ominous. It is written in the series as follows:
>
> ---
>
> If Jupiter passes Regulus and gets ahead of it, and afterwards Regulus, which it passed and got ahead of, stays with it in its setting, someone will rise, kill the king, and seize the throne.
>
> ---
>
> This aforesaid area is the only area which is taken as bad if Jupiter retrogrades there. Wherever else it might turn, it may freely do so, there is not a word about it. (...)

The scholar uses three kinds of source for his interpretation: the omens linked with the retrogradation of Mars are not omens from the series (ÉŠ.QAR, i.e., the series *Enūma Anu Enlil*) but from oral tradition of scholars (*ša pî ummāni*) and non canonical (*aḫi'u*) sources, but the omen concerning the retrogradation of Jupiter passing Regulus is quoted from "the series."

---

[10] Cf. the commentary of this letter in Parpola 1983: 16 (LAS 13).

Concerning oracles and dreams, these signs won recognition from their divine origin. The signs sent in oracles were often predicted by officials involved in the cult of Ištar[11] or by individuals possessed by a god, while prophetic dreams were sent by gods, on request or not.[12]

This psychological validation is particularly made obvious in the anxious reaction of Neo-Assyrian kings — especially Esarhaddon's — to the interpretations of omens. In a letter about the significance of a recent earthquake,[13] the scribe Balasî agrees that it is indeed a bad omen but fortunately, the gods also created the required rituals to dissipate the evil of an earthquake.[14] The scholar then emphasizes on the moral message of this event, which is sent by the gods: the king should watch out, even if all apotropaic rituals are performed.

THE SOCIAL SUPPORT OF DIVINATION

Various Mesopotamian sources demonstrate that every method foretelling future events — divination, oracles, and dreams — was fully validated socially, both on popular and scholarly levels. Questions asked by private persons are frequent in some corpuses, for example, in *tamītu* questions,[15] and prophets could be consulted in private at the temple of Ištar in Nimrud as a letter of an exorcist shows.[16] When confidence in *asûtu* or *āšipūtu* was fading away, divination about health was an easy way out and was quite common among private persons[17] and among members of the royal family.[18]

The faith of the society in the legitimacy of signs was so strong that their utterance had the authority of official statements. Esarhaddon's Succession Treaty states that any improper word heard from the mouth of a prophet (LÚ.*ra-gi-me*), of an ecstatic (LÚ.*maḫ-ḫe-e*), or of an inquirer of oracles (LÚ.*šá-'i-li a-mat* DINGIR) should not be concealed from the king.[19] A prophecy against the king could thus be interpreted as a plot by the people, as these prophets were seldom uttering alone, but preferably in public places where people would hear the prophecy. According to S. Parpola, an oracle delivered by La-dagil-ili was meant to "impress

[11] Parpola 1997: 47–48; Nissinen 1998: 10.

[12] Butler 1998: 2–7.

[13] SAA 10, 56. Another case is Assurbanipal's fear of an eclipse, about which two astrologers, Balasî (SAA 10, 57) and Nabû-aḫḫē-erība (SAA 10, 75), wrote similar reports.

[14] Cf. the well-known magical concept *Ea epuš Ea ipšur* ("Ea did it, Ea undid it") quoted here by Balasî.

[15] Cf. Lambert 2007: 7: "The topics vary from matters of state (Should the king undertake such-and-such a campaign?) to purely personal matters (Is my wife telling me the truth?)." On the contrary, queries to the sun-god (published in Starr 1990) seem to be a form of divination designed for the mighty only, since the texts we know deal with political matters or with the health of royal individuals, that is, the king, the princes, and the queen mother Naqia.

[16] Cf. the letter of the forlorn exorcist Urad-Gula, SAA 10, 294, lines 31–32: "[I turned to] a prophet (*raggimu*) (but) did not find [any hop]e, he was adverse and did not see much"; see commentaries in Parpola 1997: XLVII and n. 243; and Nissinen 1998: 86–88.

[17] Lambert 2007: *tamītu* 1, 20, 21, 22 (about personal safety and well-being); *tamītu* 12b–c, 13, 25 (about the survival or health of pregnant women); *tamītu* 14, 15, 16, 21 (about sickness); *tamītu* 25 (about the relevance of seeking out a physician).

[18] See, e.g., SAA 4, 183, "Is Esarhaddon ill because of the gods?"; SAA 4, 185, "Should Esarhaddon take this potion or not?"; SAA 4, 187, "Should Assurbanipal take this potion?"; SAA 4, 186(?), 276–278, medical queries for Assurbanipal; SAA 4, 190–191 (+ possibly 192–195), medical queries for the queen mother Naqia.

[19] SAA 2, 6, §10, lines 116–117. Cf. Nissinen 1998: 156–62.

on the audience the divine support for Esarhaddon's kingship,"[20] since his accession was controversial.

Some officials were supposed to report prophecies[21] and signs to the palace. Letters from priests inform the king about anomalies in offering animals, for example, priests mentioning a missing kidney in a sheep[22] or sending to the palace an abnormal kidney for inspection by the royal scholars.[23] Mar-Issar, the Assyrian emissary in Babylon, reports[24] that at the end of the performance of the substitute king ritual, a prophetess (*raggintu*) said that the son of Damqî (the substitute king) would take over kingship and that she had revealed the "thieving polecat(?)," probably referring to the king's opponents.[25] This prophecy, and the fact that Damqî is of noble origin, frighten the people in Babylonia, but Mar-Issar tells the king he is confident since the apotropaic rituals (*namburbî*) were appropriately performed. However, as Mar-Issar writes, it would be preferable for the king not to go out until the threat of the eclipse still ensues for 100 days, and to have a substitute for the king's cultic duties.

THE POLITICAL SUPPORT OF DIVINATION

As a matter of principle, a discipline validated psychologically and socially guarantees powerful effects when used in politics. However, in Neo-Assyrian society, kings and magnates validate in the discipline's efficiency and did not use it only for the public opinion's manipulation. A large array of the most important politic matters was decided as a result of scholarly advice and the interpretation of signs seemed to have had a huge influence on domestic and international affairs, religious issues, and triggered the performance of complex rituals.

Succession at the Neo-Assyrian court was sometimes a risky business and political choices were more easily accepted by the magnates and the people if backed by the gods' will. Some queries to the sun-god are questions about the rightful choice of a political heir. Before choosing Assurbanipal, Esarhaddon asked Šamaš if he should take his son Sin-nadin-apli as the crown prince or not.[26] Such an important decision was certainly left in the hands of top-ranking and reliable diviners,[27] whose confidence was also required in issues such as the loyalty of officials. During the year 671/670, insurrections occurred at the Neo-Assyrian court and suspicion arose about the loyalty of officials and priests in duty, or of prospective officials and priests. Queries to gods were considered the only reliable way to know the truth about these persons.[28]

At the international level, questions related to military campaigns are the most recurring themes. Various questions about warfare are settled with divination: what is the right moment to go to war, what are the required forces, which techniques and which itinerary would help,

[20] Parpola 1997: 64.

[21] SAA 13, 37; 139; 144; 148(?); cf. Cole and Machinist 1998: XVII.

[22] SAA 13, 133.

[23] E.g., SAA 13, 131.

[24] SAA 10, 352.

[25] About the meaning of *kakkišu šarriqtu* ("thieving polecat(?)"), see Nissinen 1998: 74–75.

[26] SAA 4, 149.

[27] Contra Lambert 2007: 10. Even if the ductus and style of the queries look rougher, I would not assume, as Lambert did in the introduction of the *tamītu*'s edition, that there were two sorts of Assyrian diviners, the skilled ones who performed the well-written *tamītu* and the lesser ones who clumsily wrote the queries to the sun-god.

[28] E.g., SAA 4, 150–182; 274–275; 299–311; *tamītu* 24 (in Lambert 2007: 126–29).

what is the level of safety, what are the enemies' intentions, what are the chances of success, and so on. These questions are by far the biggest group in the queries to the sun-god and the *tamītu*.[29] Some letters of astrologers and exorcists also deal with this matter, probably when the king is looking for additional reassurance. Akkullanu's letter about the portent of an Assyrian victory on Cimmerians (SAA 10, 100, dated to 15 Simānu 657) displays the scribe's ability to explain signs to the king and influence him to go to war. Assurbanipal's annals describe the Cimmerians as rebellious tribes, but we learn from this letter that they had conquered Syria at this period and that the king was waiting for good omens to grasp control over this region again (Parpola 1983: 308). In a long astrological report, Akkullanu explains to his king that according to several omens, the Westland will perish and the king of Assyria will succeed. Quite remarkable is the alternation of the interpretations of omens, negative for the Cimmerians and positive for Assyria, found in the *Enūma Anu Enlil*, in reports from famous scholars and other sources:

- The heliacal rising of Mars means a rebellion in the Westland, which is positive since the region is in Cimmerians' hands;
- The "strange star" (i.e., Mars) approaching Enmešarra[30] brings happiness in the country and an increase of population, which means good fortune for Assyria;
- When Mars is visible in the month Iyyar, it portends the destruction of Umman-Manda (glossed by Akkullanu as meaning the Cimmerians);
- The last solar eclipse was not in Subartu's quadrant and Jupiter was visible, which is propitious: the king will go to war;
- The scanty rains are, according to a report by the ancient scholar Ea-mušallim, a good omen, that the king will conquer everything he wants;
- When the new moon is visible, the Aḫlamû (i.e., Arameans = Assyrians) will consume the wealth of Westland, which is auspicious again.

This is why Akkullanu draws the conclusion that "The enemy will fall into the hands of the king, my lord."

The relationship between Assurbanipal and his brother Šamaš-šum-ukin may be considered as an international affair. When Šamaš-šum-ukin rebelled against his brother in 652 B.C., Assurbanipal put a query before Šamaš about his idea to capture his brother in Babylon, just as he would have asked about an enemy.[31] The query goes on with a question about the Sealand and Elam.

In religious affairs, the interpretation of expected and unexpected signs was of uttermost importance. For example, signs and oracles did play a role in the reintroduction of Marduk's cult in Babylon. An incident happened during Esarhaddon's reign, unexpected[32] and strange enough to stop the journey of Marduk's statue.[33] On the way to Babylon, a servant suddenly mounted the sacred horse of Marduk and said prophetic words: "Babylon — straight — the

[29] Lambert 2007; and Starr 1990, passim.

[30] The constellation of Enmešarra is the lower part of Perseus; cf. Parpola 1983: 309 (LAS 300+110).

[31] SAA 4, 279.

[32] Some official inscriptions take the return of Marduk's statue for granted; cf. Parpola 1983: 32–33 (LAS 29).

[33] SAA 10, 24.

loot of Kurigalzu." An official gives an explanation: on their way to Babylon, robbers are waiting for them in Dūr-Kurigalzu (a town on the way). The scribe Issar-šumu-ēreš, the king's exorcist Adad-šumu-uṣur, and the chief exorcist Marduk-šakin-šumi explain the incident to the king about the prophecy and wait for orders. The anxious Esarhaddon most probably made the expedition stop, as the cult was reintroduced after his death by his son Assurbanipal. In 668 B.C., Assurbanipal sought practical advice about the transfer of Marduk to Babylon[34] through a series of queries to the sun-god: should Šamaš-šum-ukin accompany him, should he go by boat, and which priest should we choose?

The substitute king ritual is probably the best evidence of the full political support achieved by the interpretation of signs. This complex ritual aimed to remove the evil omen due to an eclipse if the quadrant of the moon or the sun in the shadow matched the geographical area controlled by the king. It had implications in different fields — royal ideology, well-being of the king as an individual and as the human representative of divine power, and, in a sense, theology — and throughout the ritual, its performance involved a deep confidence in the systems of the *āšipūtu*, the *bārûtu*, the *kalûtu,* and the *ṭupšarrūtu* to relieve fear, evil, and prospective chaos. No wonder that many letters of the scribes and the exorcists deal with this ritual,[35] whose implications were sometimes not fully understood by the participants[36] or by the king himself.[37]

Actually, even if divination and oracles had a triple validation, it seems that the Neo-Assyrian society, with its typical skepticism, somehow reached the boundary of the system. On the one hand, Assyrian scholars sometimes seemed taken aback by some issues and were unable to make sure their interpretation of signs was right or comprehensive. On the other hand, individuals of royal origin or not cast doubt on the interpretation of a prediction.

During a ritual of the substitute king, the fake king complained about the relevance of a second enthronement in Akkad.[38] Since the lunar eclipse had been total, the evil omen pertained to Assyria and Babylonia. Esarhaddon was the king of both regions and this omen concerned him twice; the substitute king would in this case rule half of his "reign" in Assyria (50 days) and half in Babylonia (50 days) to fulfill the length of the apotropaic ritual. This was infrequent enough — only once in Esarhaddon's reign — to sound weird to the substitute king. This fake king was supposed to rule unnoticed and take the portents of the signs on him, but this time he rebelled against the performers and asked because of what sign (GIŠKIM) they wanted to re-enthrone him in Akkad, and then he revealed a conspiracy he had heard about. What is worth mentioning here is that the substitute king did not revolt against his forthcoming death, but against the procedure: lack of obvious signs for the second enthronement and relevance of the choice as a substitute of him, the faithful servant, when traitors are all around.

The technical limitations of Mesopotamian astrologers for predicting some eclipses,[39] seeing some heliacal risings,[40] and understanding certain disturbances such as sandstorms[41]

[34] SAA 4, 262–266.

[35] Cf. Parpola's (1983: XXII) excursus on the substitute king ritual.

[36] SAA 10, 2.

[37] SAA 10, 90 (reaction to SAA 10, 89).

[38] SAA 10, 2.

[39] E.g., SAA 10, 347, rev. 9′.

[40] E.g., SAA 10, 50, about an unpredictable heliacal rising of Mercury; cf. Parpola 1983: 60 (LAS 53): "they also were perfectly aware of the relatively great anomaly and inclination of the orbit of Mercury, which made even moderately accurate predictions of the planet's appearances impossible before the time of Ptolemy."

[41] E.g., SAA 10, 79; cf. Parpola 1983: 68 (LAS 64).

or meteors[42] could lead to inaccuracy. In this case, it was best to tell the king, try to explain the origin of the mistake,[43] and apologize (otherwise dear colleagues would be kind enough to emphasize your ignorance). A famous quarrel between three scribes about the visibility of Venus and Mercury came from the king's misunderstanding of an astrological explanation[44] given by one of them. In his fear to be fooled, Esarhaddon had the habit to check and re-check the predictions and prescriptions,[45] but since the scholars worked together, this could worsen the situation.

Eclipses could be predicted rather accurately, but sometimes scholars could not be sure about the visibility of the phenomenon. In a letter from Babylonia, the writer refers to the king being upset because the scholars are unable to tell him if the solar eclipse will occur or not.[46] The second *tamītu* in Lambert's edition asks Šamaš and Adad to confirm the coming of an eclipse with ominous consequences for the petitioner.[47]

Some situations were new to scholars and no reference was to be found in the tablets and series. The best solution was to find an omen resembling the signs observed. When the scribe Issar-šumu-ēreš was asked to determine if a mongoose passed under the king's chariot was the same omen as the well-known "If a mongoose passes between the legs of a man,"[48] he took it as the same portent, giving a poor explanation. The interpretation — the hand of the god will seize the king — is inauspicious for the forthcoming campaign of the king against the Nabateans: they will not submit to the king's chariot! Anyway, in each discipline, the king's will was to a certain extent superior to any sign or ritual. The priest Adad-aḫu-iddina was cautious about a prophecy of the *raggintu* Mullissu-abu-uṣri.[49] The middle of her utterance is broken, but the end says "Let the throne go! I shall overcome my king's enemies with it!" The priest wonders if he really has to let the god's throne go to Babylonia and writes to the king for his command.

ABBREVIATIONS

LAS	Parpola 1983
PGM	Papyri Graecae Magicae
SAA 2	Parpola and Watanabe 1988
SAA 4	Starr 1990
SAA 8	Hunger 1992
SAA 10	Parpola 1993
SAA 13	Cole and Machinist 1998

[42] E.g., SAA 10, 104.

[43] E.g., SAA 10, 362+363.

[44] SAA 10, 23 (chief-scribe Issar-šumu-ēreš); SAA 10, 72 (Nabû-aḫḫē-erība); and SAA 10, 51 (Balasî). Issar-šumu-ēreš and Nabû-aḫḫē-erība had an argument about it (SAA 8, 83); cf. Parpola 1983: 14–15 (LAS 12).

[45] E.g., SAA 10, 42.

[46] SAA 10, 170; cf. Hunger 1992: XIX.

[47] Lambert 2007: 42–51.

[48] SAA 10, 33. The omen is probably quoted from a section — now lost — of the thirty-second tablet of *Šumma ālu* regarding mongoose omens; cf. Parpola 1983: 23 (LAS 15).

[49] SAA 13, 37, rev. 6 (LAS 317); cf. Nissinen 1998: 78–81.

BIBLIOGRAPHY

Ambos, Claus

2007 "Types of Ritual Failure and Mistakes in Ritual in Cuneiform Sources." In *When Rituals Go Wrong: Mistakes, Failure, and the Dynamics of Rituals*, edited by U. Hüsken, pp. 25–47. Studies in the History of Religions 115. Leiden and Boston: Brill.

Betz, Hans D., editor

1997 *The Greek Magical Papyri in Translation, Including the Demotic Spells*. Chicago: University of Chicago Press.

Butler, Sally A. L.

1998 *Mesopotamian Conceptions of Dreams and Dream Rituals*. Alter Orient und Altes Testament 258. Münster: Ugarit-Verlag.

Cole, Steven W., and Peter Machinist

1998 *Letters from Priests to the Kings Esarhaddon and Assurbanipal*. State Archives of Assyria 13. Helsinki: Helsinki University Press.

Elman, Yaakov

1975 "Authoritative Oral Tradition in Neo-Assyrian Scribal Circles." *Journal of the Ancient Near Eastern Society* 7: 19–32.

Hunger, Hermann

1992 *Astrological Reports to Assyrian Kings*. State Archives of Assyria 8. Helsinki: Helsinki University Press.

Jean, Cynthia

2006 *La magie néo-assyrienne en contexte: Recherches sur le métier d'exorciste et le concept d'ašiputu*. State Archives of Assyria Studies 17. Helsinki: The Neo-Assyrian Text Corpus Project.

Lambert, Wilfred G.

2007 *Babylonian Oracle Questions*. Mesopotamian Civilizations 13. Winona Lake: Eisenbrauns.

Nissinen, Martti

1998 *References to Prophecy in Neo-Assyrian Sources*. State Archives of Assyria Studies 7. Helsinki: The Neo-Assyrian Text Corpus Project.

Parpola, Simo

1983 *Letters from Assyrian Scholars to the Kings Esarhaddon and Assurbanipal*, Part 2: *Commentary and Appendices*. Alter Orient und Altes Testament 5/2. Kevelaer: Butzon & Bercker.

1993 *Letters from Assyrian and Babylonian Scholars*. State Archives of Assyria 10. Helsinki: Helsinki University Press.

1997 *Assyrian Prophecies*. State Archives of Assyria 9. Helsinki: Helsinki University Press.

Parpola, Simo, and Kazuko Watanabe

1988 *Neo-Assyrian Treaties and Loyalty Oaths*. State Archives of Assyria 2. Helsinki: Helsinki University Press.

Searle, John R.

1995 *The Construction of Social Reality*. New York: Free Press.

Starr, Ivan

1990 *Queries to the Sungod: Divination and Politics in Sargonid Assyria*. State Archives of Assyria 4. Helsinki: Helsinki University Press.

14

PROPHECY AS A FORM OF DIVINATION; DIVINATION AS A FORM OF PROPHECY*

JOANN SCURLOCK, ELMHURST COLLEGE

Two Akkadian texts from the late periods, namely the Uruk Prophecy and the Dynastic Prophecy, employ phraseology that positively invites comparison with the Book of Daniel.[1] This apparent similarity of format has given rise to heated debate on the relationship, if any, between Mesopotamian forms of communication with the gods on the one hand and biblical prophecy on the other.[2]

HISTORICAL OMENS

Both Mesopotamian Prophecies fall into a broader category of what one might term historical omens. Already in extispicy manuals from the Old Babylonian period, apodoses occasionally take the form: "omen of king so and so." These apodoses refer to real or imagined historical events that are alleged to have been predicted by various irregularities in the exta.

---

* This paper has materially benefited from comments by R. Beal, S. Holloway, J. Stackert, B. D. Thomas, and the two commentators for the conference, A. Guinan and M. Nissinen. Any mistakes which remain are, of course, my own.

[1] Both were also current in the Hellenistic period. An earlier set of prophetic texts was found in the library of Assurbanipal. Of these, the Marduk Prophecy is the closest in form to the Uruk and Dynastic Prophecies, and also uses the "king will arise" formula.

[2] For a summary discussion, see Ellis 1989. Pursuant to the Landsberger tradition of avoiding any contact between Assyriology and biblical studies, there is a strong tendency either to passively avoid using biblically charged terminology for Mesopotamia or even to invent a new terminology that is designed to distance biblical prophecy, covenants, and so forth from their Mesopotamian equivalents. Curiously, in the case of biblical comparisons, it is not unusual that the implications for the biblical comparanda are what is driving the desire to put Mesopotamian evidence on a side track. That a repositioning into their original Mesopotamian context might require a re-evaluation of theologically significant biblical texts is a reason to embrace, not to avoid, comparison. Even for the non-religious for whom the truth of the matter has no soteriological implications, declining to make helpful comparisons due to terminological walls may seriously impede understanding, introduce non-existent contradictions, and make the answering of certain questions essentially impossible. Therefore, Assyriological euphemisms for Mesopotamian prophetic texts will not be employed here. For similar arguments for the use of "prophet" for Mesopotamian practitioners of prophecy but with continuation of "Literary predictive texts" for the Uruk and Dynastic Prophecies, see Nissinen 2004 and 2003. It is understandable that Nissinen wishes to make a distinction between a message from God actually delivered directly from the mouth of a living person (also attested from ancient Mesopotamia) and something which makes predictions and recommends behavior but which was, from its inception, a written composition. Texts like the Uruk and Dynastic Prophecies were not, however, generated "by the book" — there was no manual for deciding what historical event was ominous in this particular way. Their composition required expertise (science), to be sure (a knowledge of history or at least access to historical texts), but they also required inspiration (art), making them closer to prophecy in the broadest sense than to divination. Why not simply create sub-categories within the designation "prophecy" to reflect the potentially significant differences between oral and written forms of the phenomenon?

For Mesopotamians, all sorts of everyday occurrences had potentially ominous significance, so it is hardly surprising that at some point significant historical events began to acquire predictive value in their own right, which brings us to the Uruk Prophecy.

In the Uruk Prophecy, a sequence of eleven kings appears, all but three of whom are specifically said to be bad. In every case, the kings in question are not named but simply described as "a king will arise." King 1 is described as being from the Sealand (that is, a Chaldean) and ruling in Babylon. Chaldean King 2 is supposed to have taxed Uruk to the point of utter ruin. His major crime, however, was that he stole a statue of a divinity described as the old protective goddess of Uruk and took her to Babylon. All was not well in the land until the goddess was finally returned by Good King 10. King 11 was the son of King 10 and the probable original directee of the prophecy. He will also be a good king, rule the four quarters, and produce a dynasty that lasts forever.

I have argued elsewhere that the goddess in question was Nanaya, who was "stolen" by kings of Babylon, carried off to Elam, and then "rescued" for Uruk by Assyrian king Assurbanipal, the Good King 10 of the prophecy (Scurlock 2006). Thus, the description of a series of historical events as if they were not past but about to happen in the future utilizing the formula: "a king will arise" served to "predict" the sequence Sennacherib, Esarhaddon, Assurbanipal by way of prophesying the return of the original statue of the goddess Nanaya to her home in Uruk.

Nabopolassar, a Chaldean tribesman based in Babylon,[3] allied with the Medes against Assyria and founded the Neo-Babylonian empire. In order to enlist Elamite help for this enterprise, he "returned" Nanaya to Elam, where she remained. At the point of composition, the statue of Nanaya was once again missing from Uruk, and the original referent of this prophecy will have been the ill-fated Sin-šar-iškun to whom the people of Uruk were dating their documents years after Nabopolassar had seized power in Babylon.

And yet the Uruk Prophecy was still being copied in the Persian or even the Seleucid period. The virtue of prophecies is that they do not actually say that Sin-šar-iškun is going to defeat Nabopolassar, which, when it does not happen automatically, unmasks them as false prophecy. What this one does say is that when a Chaldean steals a statue from Uruk, after some suitable interval of time, hopefully not too long, a king and his son will come along and make everything right again. If that king and his son were not Assurbanipal and Sin-šar-iškun, then why not Cyrus and Cambyses or Darius and Xerxes?

To note is that the author laid out a single sequence of events in the past in the hopes of happy repetition in the future. The situation with the Dynastic Prophecy[4] is a bit more complicated, and not solely due to the fragmentary nature of its preservation. In this Seleucid-period composition, the author seems to have laid out repeating sequences of events.

[3] M. Jursa would like to see Nabopolassar as the son of Kudurru, a "quisling" governor of Uruk for the Assyrians. However, Kudurru is a shortened version of a variety of possible longer names, including Elamite Kudur-Naḫḫunte and there were as many as thirty different persons by this name mentioned in the Assyrian corpus. Kudurru had a son, but his name is unknown (being lost in lacunae in the only text which mentions him). The dynasty lavished its attentions on Babylon, which suggests an origin in that vicinity.

[4] See Grayson 1975b: 24–36.

THE DYNASTIC PROPHECY

On the text of the Dynastic Prophecy, each column seems to contain one key pattern. Column i mentions Assyria and Babylon in the context of overthrowing and destroying, ending with someone bringing extensive booty into Babylon, decorating the Esagila and Ezida, and building a palace in Babylon. Besides ending the Assyrian empire, Nabopolassar also did extensive building on Babylon and the Esagila complex. It would seem, then, that column i describes the fall of Assyria to Nabopolassar (Grayson 1975b: 24).

Column ii has a rebel prince arise and establish a dynasty of Harran. This is a Bad King who neglects the New Years' *akītu* festival and generally plots evil against Akkad. Then, a king of Elam will arise who will depose the Harranian and settle him abroad. This is also a Bad King. This column is well-enough preserved to allow us to see that the pattern presented was of a "king of Harran" (in whom we may recognize Nabonidus) replaced by a "king of Elam" (whom we know to be Cyrus) (Grayson 1975b: 24–26). The description of the usurpation of Nabonidus and his interruption of the *akītu* festival is a good indication that Babylon is the source for this text, as is the characterization of Cyrus as an oppressive king who was "stronger than the land." It can only be Babylon, smarting under the forced return of statuary purloined by Nabonidus from the cult centers of Babylonia, like Mme de Boigne weeping bitter tears over the repatriation of Napolean's looted art treasures by Wellington, who would dare to refer to Cyrus as a "Bad King."

The characterization of Nabonidus as Harranian is a reflection of the king's devotion to Sîn of Harran, and Cyrus of Anshan was indeed an Elamite. What is interesting is that the last king of Assyria, Aššur-uballiṭ, was not in line for the throne and made his stand in Harran or, in other words, could easily have been described as a rebel king who established himself in Harran. Moreover, Nabopolassar was able to defeat him with the help of Elamites as key allies. This suggests that columns i–ii present a repeating pattern in which a monarch of questionable legitimacy, based in the west at Harran, was defeated by a monarch either based in the east in Elam or with substantial assistance from that quarter.

Column iii describes a king who is clearly marked as Darius III. The prophecy envisages a king who reigns two years, is done in by a eunuch, and is replaced by some prince or other who reigns five years. Arses reigned for two years and was assassinated by the eunuch-general Bagoas. Bagoas picked Darius, who was not in the direct line of succession. Darius III ruled for five years (Grayson 1975b: 26).

According to the prophecy, the king was attacked by an army of Haneans who defeated and plundered him. Afterwards, the king was able to rally his troops and, with the assistance of Enlil (that is, Ahuramazda), Shamash (that is, Mithra), and Marduk (that is, Persis), to defeat the Haneans, after which he rewarded Babylon with tax exemptions.

The first episode involving the "Haneans" can only be a reference to the Battle of Issus which pitted Alexander the Great against Darius III. So, the "Haneans" (apparently Alexander and his Greek troops) are initially successful, but then the king (Darius III) is able to mount a counteroffensive followed by gracious tax breaks for Babylon. This particular section of the text has occasioned much puzzlement since "everybody knows" that Alexander defeated Darius (Grayson 1975b: 26–27). What everybody does not know, however, is that between the Battle of Issus and the Battle of Gaugamela nearly two years elapsed during which Alexander puttered around in Egypt and Libya while the Persian satrap Ariwarat recovered Paphlagonia and Cappadocia, celebrating on his coins with the motif of a Simurg devouring a Greek stag, and Andromachus, Alexander's hapless satrap of Syria, was burned alive by the Samaritans (Olmstead 1948: 508, 513).

The source of the Dynastic Prophecy's (mis)information was probably a Babylonian inscription of Darius III boasting of victory and ascribing his success to the assistance of local gods by way of explaining tax exemptions or other largesse being showered on the population. In any case, the ultimate fate of Darius III is not of concern to this column of the text, which cares only that there is a pattern: Haneans win (the battle), Haneans lose (the war).

This is obviously a repeat of the pattern of columns i–ii of this text in which an earlier set of confrontations between east and west culminated in victories for the east, which raises an interesting question. Since it is Babylon's point of view that is reflected in the prophecy, we may assume that the object was to foresee a time when the fortunes of Babylon were in some sense restored, if not to their full glory at least to tax-exempt status, and to argue that bad treatment of Babylon was always a formula for disaster.

In this context, it is hard to imagine that there was no discussion of the events of the reigns of Darius and Xerxes in which Babylon was so centrally involved. This was not a good time for Babylon, since both Darius and Xerxes besieged the city and, even if the Esagila was not actually destroyed, there were certainly deaths and confiscations. The only redeeming feature was the fact that Xerxes was assassinated. The same could be said of Sennacherib, who unquestionably destroyed the Esagila, and whose assassination by his own sons could be understood as presaging the fall of Assyria. Putting this together, a discussion of the events at Babylon under the Persians in prophetic guise would have sent the clear message that any empire that tampered with the Esagila was doomed to fail.

So did they just assume you were supposed to know this or, alternatively, was the Dynastic Prophecy actually a six-column text?[5] In the latter case, there is room for two missing episodes, the first, the treatment of Babylon by Darius and Xerxes, and the second, another curious omission, if omission it be: the first major encounter between Greeks and Persians in Mesopotamia at the Battle of Cunaxa, in which Babylonian levies took part and in which east defeated west.

Here ended the revolt of Cyrus the younger with his Greek troops against Artaxerxes II (the reasonably decent Persian monarch who gets good press in the Book of Esther). Cyrus won the battle, but was killed in the process. In short, this is unproblematically a case of Haneans win (the battle), Haneans lose (the war). If this reconstruction is accurate, we have so far the following patterns.

col. i	Harran (Aššur-uballiṭ II) loses to Elam (Nabopolassar and Elamite allies)
col. ii	Harran (Nabonidus) loses to Elam (Cyrus)
col. iii	Darius, turbulence, Xerxes, assassination
col. iv	Haneans win (Battle of Cunaxa); Haneans lose (the war)
col. v	Haneans win (Battle of Issus); Haneans lose (the war)

[5] On this point, see also Lambert 1978: 12–13.

The fragmentary final column, which presumably contained the actual prophecy, has three sections:

> a king who did something, reigned and died
>
> ---
>
> a broken section
>
> ---
>
> somebody seizing the land. Whoever these last people are, they will be extinguished.

This fragmentary final column's three sections ostensibly refer to Alexander in Babylon and the installation of Seleucus as satrap, followed by the expulsion of Seleucus by Antigonus, and ending with the subsequent return of Seleucus I who would then be the somebody (singular) who is described as seizing the land.[6] We also know that Seleucus was eventually assassinated by Ptolemy Keraunos. Sherwin-White, to the contrary notwithstanding,[7] the somebodies who are being "extinguished" are presumably the Seleucids.

The Babylonians seem to have taken it rather hard that, whereas Nebuchadnezzar II made Babylon one of the greatest cities in the world, Seleucus I moved the capital to a new city of his own foundation, Seleucia, which, to add insult to injury was on the Tigris rather than the Euphrates. Fine words of propaganda commissioned from local historians (Berossos) need to be backed up by fine deeds if they are to have the desired effect, particularly with the people of Babylon who were not exactly famous for being easy to deal with, having, like cult centers everywhere, an attitude that generosity was simply their due as the "navel of the earth."

Indeed, it is striking how similar the rule of the Greeks at Babylon as summarized in this text was to that of the Persians before them. As presented in the Dynastic Prophecy, Alexander played the role of Darius, who conquered himself an empire and took Babylon. Seleucus I, the new Xerxes, was successful at Babylon and led his army in campaigns to the west, but ended up assassinated by Ptolemy Keraunos. Fragmentary as it is, it is clear from the prophecy that this set of events was to be followed in short order, depending on the reading of the text, either by the "extinguishing" of the Seleucids or the usurpation of the throne by some new group as had already happened to the Assyrians, Babylonians, and Persians before them.

col. i	Harran (Assur-uballiṭ) loses to Elam (Nabopolassar and Elamite allies)
col. ii	Harran (Nabonidus) loses to Elam (Cyrus)
col. iii	Darius, turbulence, Xerxes, assassination
col. iv	Haneans win (Battle of Cunaxa); Haneans lose (the war)

---

[6] See Grayson 1975b: 27.

[7] Sherwin-White (1987: 10–14) argues that the Dynastic Prophecy is a pro-Seleucid document predicting the (quasi-Messianic) return of Nebuchadnezzar II in the form of Seleucus I. The problem with this interpretation is that, although definitely pro-Nabopolassar, the text is also quite clearly pro-Darius III, which it really should not be by this understanding. On this point, see also Briant 2002: 863–64. The argument (p. 14) that "extinguished" can be read in middle voice(!) to mean "They will rule" is nonsense. Even if the verb is not the final-weak *balû* but the middle-weak *bêlu*, there is no reason to suppose that the subject is the Seleucids. Akkadian "to rule" refers to facts on the ground, and implies neither legitimacy nor a condition of long duration. If somebody else has recently "begun to rule" over Akkad, then whether the Seleucids were actually extinguished or not in the process, their rule is at an end, and that is the point of the prophecy.

col. v Haneans win (Battle of Issus); Haneans lose (the war)

col. vi Alexander, turbulence, Seleucus, assassination

Lining up these repeating sequences of events against one another by way of prophecy serves to demonstrate that the west and its gods have always been defeated by the east and its gods. As for the misadventures of Seleucus I, it is certain, for anyone who has eyes and can see, that the Seleucids will be "extinguished" or at the very least replaced by some future dynasty, a salutary warning to anyone who dares to tamper, in however trivial a way, with the privileged status of Babylon.

MESOPOTAMIAN HISTORICAL OMENS AS PROPHECY?

As may be seen from these examples, late Mesopotamian historical omens have a sort of quality of prayers for deliverance to them, where recitation(s) of negatively charged past events followed by positively charged resolution(s) of crisis, all of it projected into the future, become(s) a sort of complaint to the gods about the current political situation and a signaled desire for them to produce a king who will act as savior. Both the Uruk Prophecy and the Dynastic Prophecy were probably composed for the edification of the specific king who was meant to play this messianic role (in the former case Sîn-šar-iškun and the latter Arsaces I or Mithradates I).[8]

This is remembering always that the gods lay in wait to reward a king who succeeded or to punish one who failed to play the desired role, and that if one monarch proved unmoved, there were always other kings to whom one could apply. The Uruk Prophecy was still being copied in Hellenistic Uruk, long after the failure of the original prophecy to come to fruition. As for the Dynastic Prophecy, unless the Parthians were very nice to Babylon, it would be understood as predicting their demise at the hands of yet another conqueror.

It having been noted that the Mesopotamian "prophecies" refer to events that have, in fact, already occurred, it is tempting to regard them as some sort of prediction after the fact, at best false prophecy and at worst political propaganda. But is this fair? I would like to suggest a new approach to the problem of Mesopotamian "prophetic" texts by inverting the paradigm and asking not whether Mesopotamian divination can represent a form of prophecy, but whether biblical prophecy can represent a form of divination or, as Ionian Greek philosophers put it, prophecy involves not only the present and the future but also the past.

[8] Similarly, the Marduk Prophecy was probably directed to Assurbanipal. This apparently first-person narration by Marduk portrays this god as particularly fond of the city of Aššur, where he was a guest of Tukulti-Ninurta I. It also describes the rescue of the Marduk statue by Nebuchadnezzar I from Elam in such a way as to promise that, if any future king, say Assurbanipal, were to rebuild Babylon and the Esagila after terrible troubles, say the Šamaš-šum-ukin revolt, Marduk would reward him with total victory over Elam and, most importantly, extraordinary peace and prosperity in the land: "The grass of winter (will last) till summer. The grass of summer will last to winter. The harvest of the land will thrive. The marketplace will prosper ... Brother will love his brother. A son will fear his father as his god ... A man will regularly pay his taxes." See Longman 1997: 480–81, line 149.

BIBLICAL PROPHECY AS HISTORICAL OMENS?

In Mesopotamia, the assumption was that omens were the language of the gods which they used to communicate with mankind and that they constituted a warning which allowed humans to avoid the portended event. In the case of an unsolicited omen, the situation could be saved by the prompt performance of NAM.BÚR.BI.[9] In the case of a solicited omen, no harm would come from a negative response as long as you did not do what you had been told not to do and did not eat any of the "ill-omened" meat.

In Mesopotamia we are generally talking about messages written in the stars or on the liver, which require a whole science to decipher. This would all be *kesheph* in Israel but there was still room for using historical events themselves as a sort of omen. It is to be remembered that not all divinatory practices were rejected in Israelite religion (lot oracles were actually mandated) and, given the fact that God was believed to give signs in the form of specific outcomes to political events, there would be, in theory, no objection to using past historical events affecting the community to divine the will of God.

As with Mesopotamian solicited omens, no harm would come to any king who listened to the prophets and took their advice, assuming that God's anger was not too great. And even if it was great indeed, as with Mesopotamian solicited omens, there were procedures (modified mourning rites such as dressing in sackcloth and ashes) that could be used to avert God's wrath and the evil consequences that were sure to follow.

So, even though most other methods of divination were frowned upon in Israel, historical events could readily be seen as part of a code whereby Yahweh communicated with his people and could, therefore, be used to decode and validate other messages delivered by other means, as by direct vision. A similar relationship existed in ancient Mesopotamia between solicited and unsolicited omens — one could use a solicited omen to gain clarification (not just that the god is angry but why and how many sheep is this going to cost) but also to check the veracity of an unsolicited omen. From this perspective, the historical event is the more reliable form of divination that can be used to check the less reliable form of simply allowing people to claim to speak for God. As with the surrounding cultures, not all events would be ominous and those that were could come round again and again in no particular order and millennia after the first occurrence, and the point was still that Yahweh responds to human behavior in certain ways which make it possible to detect a coming crisis and avert it by prompt action (avoiding sanctioned behavior, mortification, and prayer) before it is too late.

We shall here examine two possible examples of biblical prophecies in which historical events that had already passed at the time of composition were either used to validate, or were actually the basis for, the prediction of what was going to happen in the future. One is Nahum, which has not infrequently been classified as false prophecy,[10] and the other is Isaiah 36–37 (= 2 Kings 18:13–19:37 — the alleged two sieges of Jerusalem by Sennacherib).

---

[9] A NAM.BÚR.BI is a ritual designed to dispel the evil consequences of a bad omen.

[10] "Because there is no call to repentance in the oracles but, on the contrary, a great exhultation over the fall of Nineveh, scholars have attributed a virulent nationalism to Nahum and have even alleged that he tends to exhibit the characteristics of false prophecy" (Cathcart 1992: 999).

NAHUM

Let us begin with Nahum. I have argued elsewhere that this prophet mentions some very striking and probably very accurate descriptions of the fall of Nineveh.[11] However, my object was never to convict Nahum as a false prophet. On the contrary, his is one of the only true prophecies in the corpus (if by true you mean that what was originally predicted actually happened in good time).

At one level, Nahum is just a description of what happened when the Babylonians (the warriors "clothed in crimson") took a rather tardy revenge for Sennacherib's treatment of Babylon. However, a recurring theme broached already in the opening psalm (Nahum 1:2–10)[12] is the universality of the application of God's vengeance. "*Who can stand before His wrath? Who can resist his fury?*" within which is embedded an ominous warning: "*Why will you plot against the Lord? He wreaks utter destruction: No adversary opposes him twice!*"[13]

Indeed, throughout, passages which describe the terrible things that have happened or are in the process of happening to Nineveh or Egypt[14] (marked as third-person forms with the exception of Nahum 3:16–19) alternate with clear addresses to Judah and dire warnings addressed to "you." Note in particular Nahum 1:11–14 and 2:1–2,[15] where the destruction of Judah's enemies is followed with terrifying suddenness by God's angry curse directed at "you": "*The base plotter who designed evil against the Lord has left you. ... The Lord has commanded concerning you ... I shall do away with the carved and graven images in the temples of your gods*" and "*Celebrate your festivals, O Judah, fulfill your vows. Never again shall the scoundrels invade you, they have totally vanished. A shatterer has come up against you.... Brace all your strength.*"

Nahum 2:3–14 begins with "*For the Lord has restored the Pride of Jacob*" and proceeds through a harrowing description of the destruction of Nineveh to end with: "*I am going to deal with you declares the Lord of Hosts: I will burn your thicket in fire ... the sound of your messengers will be heard no more.*" So also Nahum 3:1–5 which begins with "*Alas, bloody city ... Hosts of slain and heaps of corpses, dead bodies without number — they stumble over bodies*" to end with "*I am going to deal with you declares the Lord of Hosts: I will lift up your skirts over your face.*"

---

[11] Scurlock 1990: 382–84. For other articles that make similar arguments, see Huddlestun 2003: 104–08 (with previous bibliography). Babylonian revenge for Sennacherib's destruction of Babylon by water apparently took the form of manipulating the irrigation system which Sennacherib had built to water the gardens of Nineveh so as to produce an artificial flood.

[12] The famous acrostic, about which much ink has been spilt, lists the first fifteen letters of the Hebrew alphabet in correct order. Fifteen is the number of the goddess Ištar, a complex of the individual goddesses of many cities including, but by no means confined to, Nineveh.

[13] As pointed out in Coggins 1985: 27–29, these comments are primarily, if not exclusively, directed at the community itself.

[14] Once it is realized that Nahum is not predicting the fall of Assyria from the vantage point of the eighth or seventh century, but describing contemporary events as a sign from God, the most likely source for the reference to Thebes is Nebuchadnezzar's 601 B.C. campaign against Egypt, not, as is usually asserted, to some Assyrian campaign there, real or imagined. This does not affect the argument of Huddlestun (2003: 97–110) that the passage describing the destruction of Thebes is more about imagining cities destroyed by water than a careful depiction of actual events there.

[15] Nahum is here quoted more or less from Jewish Publication Society 1999.

The key to understanding this difficult prophecy is the realization that Nahum is a lament. Whole sections of Lamentations echo Nahum; compare also Ezekiel as follows:

Nahum 1:2	Lamentations 2:17
The Lord is a passionate, avenging God.	*The Lord has done what he purposed ... he has torn down without pity.*
Nahum 2:1–2	Lamentations 4:21
Celebrate your festivals, O Judah, fulfill your vows ... A shatterer has come up against you ... Brace all your strength!	*Rejoice and exult, Fair Edom, who dwell in the land of Uz. To you, too, the cup will pass, you shall get drunk and expose your nakedness.*
Nahum 2:8	Lamentations 2:10–11
Its mistress is led out and exiled ... her handmaidens ... beating their breasts	*The maidens of Jerusalem have bowed their heads to the ground. My eyes are spent with tears*
Nahum 3:1	Ezekiel 22:2–4
Ah, city of bloodshed, utterly treacherous	*Arraign the city of bloodshed ... defiled by the idols you have made.*
Nahum 3:5	Lamentations 1:8–9
I will lift up your skirts over your face and display your nakedness to the nations ... I will throw filth over you.	*All who admired her despise her, for they have seen her nakedness. ... Her filth clings to her skirt.*
Nahum 3:7	Lamentations 1:9
Who will console her?	*She has sunk appallingly, with none to comfort her.*
Nahum 3:11	Lamentations 2:12
You too shall drink of this till you faint away	*As they faint away like the wounded in the squares of the town.*
Nahum 3:13	Lamentations 2:9
The gates of your land have opened themselves ... Fire has consumed your bars.	*Her gates have sunk into the ground, he has smashed her bars to bits.*

Nahum 3:15 *There fire will devour you* *the sword will put an end* *to you.*	Lamentations 4:11 *The Lord vented all His fury ...* *He kindled a fire in Zion which* *consumed her foundations.*
Nahum 3:18 *Alas, how your shepherds* *slumber ... your people are* *scattered over the hills,* *with none to gather them.*	Lamentations 1:6 *Her leaders were like bucks* *that found no pasture;* *They could only walk feebly* *before the pursuer.*
Nahum 3:19 *There is no healing your hurt;* *your wound is mortal*	Lamentations 2:13 *For your ruin is vast as the sea;* *who can heal you?*
Nahum 3:19 *All who hear the news about* *you clap their hands over you.*	Lamentations 2:15–16 *All who pass your way clap their hands at* *you; they hiss and wag their head at Fair* *Jerusalem ... (They say): Ah, this is the day* *we hoped for; we have lived to see it!*

Ezekiel's "city of bloodshed" is Jerusalem, and the Lamentations passages that speak of sorrow and destruction are lamentations for Jerusalem's destruction by Nebuchadnezzar. Those invited to rejoice, as Judah is invited to rejoice in Nahum, are those, like Edom in Lamentations, upon whom God's judgment is about to, but has not yet fallen (Lamentations 4:21–22): *Rejoice and exult, Fair Edom, who dwell in the land of Uz. To you, too, the cup will pass, you shall get drunk and expose your nakedness. Your iniquity, Fair Zion is expiated ... Your iniquity, Fair Edom, He will note; he will uncover your sins.*

The juxtaposition strongly suggests that Nahum is lamenting the fall of Nineveh and the ruin of Egypt by way of predicting the fall of Jerusalem and Judah to Nebuchadnezzar.[16] In short: "*Your iniquity, Fair Nineveh is expiated ... Your iniquity, Fair Jerusalem, He will note; he will uncover your sins.*" This impression is confirmed by the Qumran Nahum commentary (4Q169)[17] in which Assyria and Egypt are taken to represent Ephraim and Manasseh, that is, the Samaritans whose city John Hyrcanus completely destroyed, including running rivers over it so that it would never be rebuilt (Josephus, *Antiquities* 13.10.3). As in the original, this total destruction by water was seen to predict, in its turn, the fall of Jerusalem and Judah

---

[16] To my way of thinking, comments such as: "Instead of grieving over the sin of Judah and striving with might and main to warn her of the error of her ways so that she might turn and live, Nahum was apparently content to lead her in a joyous celebration of the approaching death of Assyria" (Smith 1911: 281) or "Nahum was wrong. There was spiritual weakness here too. Nahum gives no conscious recognition of the fact that the sins of the Assyrians were also the sins of the Judeans" (Taylor and Cleland 1956: 957), as well as attempts to justify him by joining in with the alleged schadenfreude, display the most profound misunderstanding of Nahum's message. With Jeremias 1970, the warnings are for the community, and not its enemies. This is not, however, to accept a Hellenistic date for all or even part of Nahum.

[17] See Wise, Abegg, and Cook 1996: 215–20.

to a foreign conqueror. This conqueror was the Roman army, once again, a prophecy that was fulfilled in historical time.

As with the Uruk Prophecy, it is sufficient in Nahum to mention the ominous events by themselves without need for them to have been repeated for any significance to be drawn from them. The fall of one capital city predicts the fall of another capital city just as one return of Nanaya predicts another, future, return of Nanaya.

ISAIAH

Our second biblical example is Isaiah 36–37 (= 2 Kings 18:13–19:37). Although treated as a historical appendix by redactors, this is, as we shall see, actually a prophecy or rather two interwoven prophecies. In dealing with this passage, it is hard not to notice that, despite inclusion among historical materials in 2 Kings, it is by no means a simple and unedited account of Sennacherib's 701 B.C. campaign against Jerusalem.

> *The angel of the Lord went forth and struck down one hundred and eighty-five thousand in the Assyrian camp. Early the next morning, there they were, all the corpses of the dead* (Isaiah 37:36 = 2 Kings 19:35).

It has been argued by R. E. Clements (1984: 58–61, 91) that this passage is a Josianic addition to Isaiah 37 and a reflection of Zion Theology, by which is meant the idea that Jerusalem was impregnable.[18] Another set of lines, Isaiah 37:30–32 (= 2 Kings 19:29–31), speaks of survivors of the house of Judah and a remnant from Jerusalem and must be a post-Josianic addition to the text,[19] since, by the time these verses will have been added, the city was no longer impregnable, but had instead fallen to some foreign conqueror.

Even with these lines removed, however, there remain difficulties. As presented in 2 Kings 18:13–19:37, Sennacherib's behavior is little short of bizarre. Sennacherib invades Judah, sets up camp at Lachish, and negotiates a monetary settlement with Hezekiah (18:13–15). Afterwards(!), he sends envoys to Jerusalem, demanding surrender. Hezekiah is upset, but not a word is said about any tribute payment having been made and then ignored by evil Assyrians. Isaiah (18:16–19:9) reassures him that Sennacherib will hear a report and return home and Sennacherib does indeed hear a report. He does not, however, return home, but instead sends a letter thundering dire threats. Hezekiah is very upset, but reacts as if this was the first time he had ever received any message from Sennacherib. Isaiah reassures Hezekiah that all is well, again without any indication that this is the second time round, and prophesies that the king of Assyria will not shoot so much as an arrow against Jerusalem. Sennacherib does indeed go home, but there is nothing about any report; the proximate reason for the departure is the slaughter of Sennacherib's army by the Angel of the Lord (Isaiah 19:10–37).[20]

---

[18] Ironically, it is the failure of Sennacherib's annals to confirm this clearly exaggerated if not legendary event that has caused Assyrian annals to be branded as outright lies, an opinion which stills prevails in many quarters. See Mayer 2003: 169, 171.

[19] Clements (1984: 57) has this as a separate prophecy and the latest addition, but still Josianic. Others, among them Wildberger (2002: 430–32), assign a postexilic date to these lines. Gallagher (1999: 234–37) insists that this is a prophecy of the historical Isaiah referring to the events of 701 B.C.

[20] For a more elegant presentation of this argument, see Wildberger 2002: 364–66.

It has long been argued (by Stade, Levy, and others) that 2 Kings 18:14–16 (the tribute payment) is part of an excerpt from the royal annals of Judah dealing with Sennacherib's campaign (Text A), which is generally supposed to have been rather clumsily worked into the rest of the narrative.[21] Indeed, the tribute payment is clearly out of order and belongs among the reasons that Sennacherib in fact went home.[22] Even so, there are enough discrepancies to suggest either two separate sieges of Jerusalem by Sennacherib or two different accounts of the same siege of Jerusalem (Texts B_1 and B_2). So what are we to make of this?

Text Correspondences:

- Text A = 2 Kings 18:14–16 = 2 Kings A
- Text B_1 = $Isaiah_A$ = 2 Kings 18:17–19:9a, 36–37 = 2 Kings B_1
- Text B_2 = $Isaiah_B$ = 2 Kings 19:9b–28, 32–34 = 2 Kings B_2

Let us examine the Isaiah version of these events. Taken by itself, Isaiah 36–37 readily divides into two separate accounts. The first of these, which we shall term $Isaiah_A$, more or less corresponds to 2 Kings B_1. Taken as a whole, this gives a seamless account of Sennacherib's 701 B.C. siege of Jerusalem and its aftermath. In other words, Isaiah 36:1–37:9a (= 2 Kings 18:17–19:9a) tells a complete story that follows directly and without apparent disjunction into Isaiah 37:37–38 (= 2 Kings 19:36–37) as follows:

> *In the fourteenth year of King Hezekiah, Sennacherib, king of Assyria, went on an expedition against all the fortified cities of Jerusalem and captured them. ... Do not be frightened by the words you have heard, with which the servants of the king of Assyria have blasphemed me. I am about to put in him such a spirit that, when he hears a certain report, he will return to his own land, and there I will cause him to fall by the sword. ... The king of Assyria heard a report that Tirhakah, king of Ethiopia, had come out to fight against him* (Isaiah 36:1–37:9a). ... *So Sennacherib, the king of Assyria, broke camp and went back home to Nineveh. ... His sons Adram-melech and Sharezer slew him with the sword, and fled into the land of Ararat. His son Esarhaddon reigned in his stead.* (Isaiah 37:37–38)

Interposed in the middle, is a section (Isaiah 37:9b–29, 33–35 = 2 Kings 19:9b–28, 32–34) that seems to start all over again from the beginning with no better attempt to fit it into the rest of the story than the somewhat awkward transition: *Again, he sent envoys to Hezekiah with this message* (Isaiah 37:9b = 2 Kings 19:9b). We shall designate this intrusive text, which more or less corresponds to 2 Kings B_2, by the term $Isaiah_B$.

There are two ways of understanding this intrusion. Either there were two sieges of Jerusalem by Sennacherib, one in 701 B.C. and another later in his reign,[23] or $Isaiah_B$ (= 2 Kings B_2) is a later addition. We may safely ignore Becking's introduction of a mythical

[21] See Stade 1886: 172–86; Levy 1928: 156–58. See also Cogan and Tadmor 1988: 240–41. Even Gallagher (1999: 146–48) accepts this division. As Clements (1984: 12–13) points out, Text A and Sennacherib's annals are in more or less complete agreement as to what happened on the campaign. Cf. also Wildberger 2002: 363; Smelik 1986: 85. For a full reconstruction of this campaign, using Text A and Sennacherib's annals together, see Mayer 2003: 172–85.

[22] On this point, see also Wildberger 2002: 378.

[23] For the two-siege theory of Albright and others, see Cogan and Tadmor 1988: 246–51. Clements (1984: 22, 91–92) also offers arguments against this approach and Grabbe (2003) has declared it more or less dead.

campaign of Sargon II of Assyria against Judah in 715 B.C.[24] Since Isaiah$_B$ speaks of God as lord of all kingdoms and creator of heaven and earth (Isaiah 37:16)[25] and includes a polemic against gods other than Yahweh as the *work of human hands, wood and stone* (Isaiah 37:19 = 2 Kings 19:17),[26] many commentators have been inclined to see Isaiah$_B$ (= 2 Kings B$_2$) as a later addition to a completed text. How late is a matter of dispute, with Cogan and Tadmor opting for two or three generations after the prophet Isaiah,[27] Clements and Machinist for the reign of Josiah,[28] Wildberger suggesting Jehoiakim or Zedekiah,[29] and Na'aman arguing for the seventh century (late Neo-Babylonian) or sixth century (early Persian) B.C.[30] Of course, it could always be a Hellenistic embellishment, assuming, of course, that the text was not finalized until so late a date.

What is not a matter of dispute, among those who accept the multiple accounts theory and even for some who do not, is that Isaiah$_B$ (= 2 Kings B$_2$) is referring, however inaccurately, to Sennacherib's 701 B.C. campaign against Jerusalem. And inaccurate it certainly would be;[31] Wildberger is little short of calling Isaiah$_B$ a brazen lie, that is, "not interested in historical reality" and constructed "as a testimony to belief."[32] Na'aman is more charitable, arguing for a receding of memory: "Reading Account B$_1$, it is clear that the story was written when the memory of Assyria ... was still very much alive. In Account B$_2$, on the other hand, Assyria appears as an abstract power, representing more the concept of a strong military power than a concrete historical entity. The story remains the same if we replace the name Assyria with the name of another power (e.g., Babylonia, Persia)."[33] Inaccurate, that is, if we must believe that the reference is actually to Sennacherib's 701 B.C. campaign against Jerusalem.

---

[24] So Becking, who takes Text A to be referring to the events of 701 B.C. (Becking 2003: 67–69), whereas Text B, taken in its entirety, is referring to events which he purports to have taken place in 715 B.C. (Becking 2003: 69–70). This reconstruction is based on the difficult chronology of Hezekiah's reign, over which much ink has been spilt but which, by his chronology, yields a date of 715 B.C. for Hezekiah's fourteenth year (Becking 2003: 56). The fact that Assyrian annals make no mention of any campaign against Judah in that year is, of course, ignored as irrelevant as is the fact that 2 Kings 18:13 specifically mentions Sennacherib as the king of Assyria involved. Becking's reconstruction "corresponds" with what he is willing to accept as evidence and is "coherent" with his mental picture of Assyrian expansion, so whether or not it is historically true by any objective standard does not actually matter (Becking 2003: 60–61). Why argue?

[25] For a discussion, see Wildberger 2002: 420–23.

[26] For a probable Deuteronomistic (Josianic) or exilic date for Isaiah 37:18–19, see Cogan and Tadmor 1988: 235–36, ad lines 15–19.

[27] See Cogan and Tadmor 1988: 243–44.

[28] Clements 1984: 56–63, 68, 70–71, 91–95. This is for 2 Kings B$_2$; he places the rest of the Hezekiah narrative (2 Kings 20) somewhat later, in the reign of Zedekiah (Clements 1984: 103–04); cf. Machinist 2000: 155–56, 161–62.

[29] Wildberger (2002: 417, 425, 431) tentatively places it in the period of Babylonian threat to Jerusalem.

[30] Na'aman 2000: 394–400; Na'aman 2003: 212–13. Cf. Gonçalves 1986: 480.

[31] Gallagher (1999: 14–15, 146, 149–59) will accept no arguments for the division of the text into 2 Kings B$_1$ and B$_2$. In this he resembles minimalists such as Smelik (1986). Smelik's argumentation is based on literary analysis, which allows him to posit a Persian-period date for the combined account (Smelik 1986: 85) without having to worry about historical content (essentially nill). Literature is, by definition, literature and not history. Gallagher is, however, not a minimalist and is thus forced to defend the historical accuracy of the account of 2 Kings B$_2$ (1999: 40–41, 224–52) with the result that his "historical" reconstruction of Sennacherib's third campaign is seriously compromised.

[32] Wildberger 2002: 417, 425, 431.

[33] Na'aman 2000: 400. Ben Zvi (2003: 80–85) uses the 2 Kings B$_2$ material to paint a picture of an object lesson, directed at an exilic audience, about how to deal with imperial powers. In principle, once you have submitted, you need to stay that way, which seems obvious but is hard to argue when the example of Hezekiah springs immediately to mind. The "demonization" of Sennacherib, then, allowed the compiler to warn that Hezekiah's successful revolt against Assyria was not to be taken as a precedent for

Of course Isaiah$_B$ specifically mentions Sennacherib and kings of Assyria and cannot, therefore, by conventional wisdom, be referring to later events as, for example, Nebuchadnezzar's siege of Jerusalem. Indeed, negative references to Babylon are generally suspected of being updatings of original polemics against Assyria.[34] This would mean that even if the text actually said "Nebuchadnezzar" and "Babylon," as indeed some allegedly updated passages do, it could still be taken as a reference to Sargon II or Sennacherib and Assyria.

This argument has never made any sense. Sennacherib was not very cuddly, but he failed to take the city of Jerusalem, whereas Nebuchadnezzar destroyed the city and burned the temple after hacking to bits and removing everything of value in it. Are we really to believe that Jews were so outraged by **not** having Jerusalem harmed by Sennacherib that its depopulation and destruction by Nebuchadnezzar was a preferable alternative?

In any case, people do not update their hatreds in this way. If they are indeed for whatever reason fixated on an old enemy, they call the new enemy by the old name. Indeed, one of the Qumran Isaiah commentaries (4Q163) insists that a number of passages that explicitly say "Assyria" actually refer to Babylon.[35]

Yes, the more recent parts of the dialectic are packed with examples of diatribes that seem inappropriate for, and in some cases cannot possibly refer to, the ostensible victim of abuse. But many, if not all, of these are sub-rosa critiques, often by way of organizing rebellion, against thin-skinned conquerors who may be safely vilified under the cover of a **backdating** of hatreds to political entities no longer in any position to object. So, for example, the Whore of Babylon in Revelations is a Babylon of seven hills, obviously not the real Babylon at all (what hills?!), but either Rome or Constantinople.

All strongly negative references, particularly ones that appear to be out of consonance with historical reality and/or later additions to the text, need to be examined to make sure that they are not actually sub-rosa references to a later enemy cleverly camouflaged as an earlier one. "Babylon" may be a *Deckname* for Persians, Seleucids, or Romans; "Assyria" or "Edom" may be a *Deckname* for Babylonians, Persians, Seleucids, or Romans, and so forth.

In the more recent parts of the dialectic, references of this kind are the rule, but I would argue that sub-rosa vilification begins with the Babylonians at the latest. For example, Isaiah 33:1 is often taken as referring to Assyria, but Assyria can never be the *destroyer never destroyed*, despite the fact that Assyria is the only enemy which has been recently mentioned (31:8). Assyria may have been a destroyer, but they were certainly, and quite spectacularly, destroyed. The referent must be Babylon, which was indeed never destroyed[36] or perhaps, if

revolt against other imperial powers such as Babylon or Persia.

[34] Central to this debate is the insistence of many scholars, beginning with W. H. Cobb and among them Assyriologist H. Winckler, that Isaiah 14:3–23, despite explicit mention of Babylon, was originally a diatribe against some Assyrian king, usually Sargon II. Gallagher (1999: 87–90) sides with Sargon as the villain and does not even acknowledge the existence of contrary arguments. This thesis is not, however, universally accepted — for references, see Wildberger 1997: 47–77 and Blenkinsopp 2000: 286–87 — and it is almost certainly wrong. For ice water poured on Grimme's idea that Isaiah 13 was also originally (what else?) a diatribe specifically against Sargon II, see Wildberger 1997: 11–39.

[35] See in particular Frag. 6+7 ad Isaiah 10:17–19 and Frag. 25 ad Isaiah 30:30–32 (Wise et al. 1996: 212–13).

[36] The Babylonian empire fell to Cyrus but with minimal loss of life, and Babylon was not even severely damaged, let alone eradicated down to the last blade of grass as contemplated by the prophets. Babylon did not last for ever, of course, but, having survived major revolts against the Persians, it just sort of faded away over the course of the Hellenistic and Parthian periods. By contrast, archaeological evidence reveals that every major capital of the Assyrian empire was

the text is late enough, Rome.[37] Careful reading confirms that this impassioned and defiant cri du coeur is addressed to a *destroyer* who has destroyed the city of Jerusalem (32:9–15), again not the Assyrians but Babylon or Rome.

So if Isaiah$_B$ (= 2 Kings B_2) is not a fabrication, it needs to be considered whether it is a sub-rosa reference to some post-Sennacherib enemy disguised as an attack on the by then defunct Assyrians. Taking the second alternative, how long defunct will the Assyrians have been at the time of composition? Are the new enemy Romans? Greeks? Persians? Babylonians? And why bring up the real Sennacherib at all?

To find out, we must examine Isaiah$_B$, the alleged second account of the siege of Jerusalem by Sennacherib (Isaiah 37:9b–29, 33–36), to see whether we can find an actual post-Sennacherib enemy whose behavior matches that described. Isaiah$_B$ begins with a message from the Mesopotamian king.

> *Again, he sent envoys to Hezekiah with this message … Do not let your God on whom you rely deceive you by saying that Jerusalem will not be handed over to the king of Assyria. You yourself have heard what the kings of Assyria have done to all the countries: They doomed them! Will you, then, be saved? Did the gods of the nations whom my fathers destroyed save them? Gozen, Haran, Rezeph, and Edenites in Telassar? Where is the king of Hamath, the king of Arpad, or a king of the cities of Sepharvaim, Hena, or Ivvah?* (Isaiah 37:9b–13)

Despite specific mention of the king of Assyria, this passage cannot possibly (as argued already by Holloway and Na'aman) be the voice of Sennacherib referring to the campaigns of his real ancestors. In Sennacherib's time, Guzana, Harran, Raṣapa, and Bit-Adini were not still smoking ruins but thriving metropolises of the Assyrian empire. Harran was a second capital and major cult center. Sennacherib would have as likely boasted of the alleged complete and permanent destruction of these places as Queen Victoria would of leveling Cardiff and Edinburgh and sacking Canterbury.[38]

In any case, comparing the fate of Jerusalem to that of these other cities would not be much of a threat. They might have been quite wrecked at the time of Assyrian conquest centuries earlier, but, by the time Sennacherib was speaking, these cities were thriving, as the Judeans would have known very well. So what fate was Sennacherib supposed to be threatening them with — do what I want or I will make you third capital of the Assyrian empire and better off than you are now?!

so thoroughly destroyed as not to recover until the Persian or Hellenistic periods. Everywhere there was massive loss of life; at Kalḫu, the palace wells contained literally hundreds of bodies of shackled prisoners who had been thrown into them to drown. See Hussein 2008: 91; al-Fakhri 2008: 99.

[37] Wildberger (2002: 270–72) places this passage in the Persian period.

[38] On these points, see Holloway 1995. Gallagher (1999: 40–41, 224–52) defends the historical accuracy of the letter to Hezekiah and has the following comments on contrary evidence: "Holloway's article is useful and informative. … Nevertheless his conclusions on 2 Kings 19:12 are incautious. … The ninth century BC is too obscure for us to know exactly what happened to Harran at that time. It may have been omitted from Shamshi-Adad V's list of rebellious cities due to some political expediency." The reference in 2 Kings 19:11–13 is to total and permanent destruction, which cannot have occurred in the reign of Shamshi-Adad V or of any other Assyrian monarch. In any case, insisting that the lack of evidence for your position must be due to some unknown cause may be described in a number of ways, but "cautious" is not among them.

In sum, Harran was never slated for permanent destruction by Assyrians; it was, however, by Nebuchadnezzar, who specifically targeted the sanctuary, and the city was not rebuilt until the time of Nabonidus. Guzana, Raṣapa and Bit-Adini will also have been conquered in the course of Nabopolassar's conquest of Upper Mesopotamia in 612–610 B.C.; Hamath was added after Nebuchadnezzar defeated Egyptian troops in the Battle of Carchemish in 605.[39] All of this would seem to point to the Babylonians as the new enemy being targeted for sub-rosa vilification, and this impression is reinforced by the continuation:

> *Hezekiah took the letter ... he went up to the temple of the Lord, and spreading it out before him, he prayed: O Lord of hosts, God of Israel ... You alone are God over all the kingdoms of the earth. You have made the heavens and the earth. Incline your ear, O Lord and listen! ... Hear all the words of the letter that Sennacherib sent to taunt the living God. Truly O Lord, the kings of Assyria have laid waste all lands along with their (own) land,[40] and cast their gods into the fire; they destroyed them because they were not gods but the work of human hands, wood and stone. Therefore, O Lord, our God, save us from his hand, that all the kingdoms of the earth may know that you, O Lord, alone are God* (Isaiah 37:14–20).

Despite the specific references to Sennacherib and kings of Assyria, the religious policy expressed again marks the actual referent clearly as Nebuchadnezzar.[41] His argument: "My god is going to kill your god and there is nothing you can do about it." The case of Sîn of Harran is the best-known example of this policy, but we know, from a variety of sources including the inscriptions of Nabonidus and compositions used as part of the scribal curriculum,[42] that the Neo-Babylonian conquest specifically targeted cult centers in areas which resisted Babylonian rule, including Akkad (Babylonia) which was, as Isaiah 37:18 (= 2 Kings 19:17) notes, "their (own) land."

In the words of Nabonidus, describing the fall of Assyria at the hands of the Babylonians and their Medean allies:

> (Marduk) provided him (Nabopolassar) with helpers ... (And) he (the king of the Umman-manda) swept on like a flood storm ... avenging Babylon in retaliation. The king of the Umman-manda ... demolished the sanctuaries of all the gods of Subartu (Assyria). He also demolished the towns within the territory of Akkad (Babylonia) which were hostile to the king of Akkad and had not come to his assistance (in fighting Assyria). None of their cult centers did he omit, laying waste their towns worse than a flood storm."[43]

So much was destroying cult centers part of the "mystique" of Neo-Babylonian kings that, before he was allowed to resume his throne in the annual Babylonian New Year's Festival, he was made to swear not to destroy Babylon, command its overthrow, wreck the Esagila Temple, or smash Babylon's walls.[44]

---

[39] On these points, see Na'aman 2000: 394–98; 2003: 204–11.

[40] See Wildberger 2002: 408, 422.

[41] Xerxes does boast of burning devil worshippers in their temples, and the Romans also burned the temple in Jerusalem, but for scale and consistency of policy, it would be hard to find a better match among Judah's enemies than Nebuchadnezzar for this passage.

[42] For details, see Scurlock 2006a.

[43] The Ehulhul Inscription, apud Liverani 2001: 390.

[44] Sachs 1969: 334.

God's answer, allegedly delivered by Isaiah, to Nebuchadnezzar's imagined threats begins as follows:

> *Thus says the Lord, the God of Israel ... She despises you, laughs you to scorn, the virgin daughter Zion; Behind you she wags her head, daughter Jerusalem. ... You said: "With my many chariots I climbed the mountain heights, the recesses of Lebanon; I cut down its lofty cedars, its choice cypresses. I reached the remotest heights, its forest park. I dug wells and drank water in foreign lands; I dried up with the soles of my feet all the rivers of Egypt." ... Long ago I prepared it, from days of old I planned it, now I have brought it to pass; that you should reduce fortified cities into heaps of ruins*, etc. (Isaiah 37:21–27)

"*Long ago I prepared it, from days of old I planned it, now I have brought it to pass*" is a pretty clear reference to some terrible and complete disaster which has taken place in historical time. Elsewhere, the Hebrew Bible uses the allegory of the devastation of the forests of Lebanon[45] and of the drying up of the rivers of Egypt[46] to refer to the fall of Assyria and the terrible defeats inflicted on its ally Egypt by the Neo-Babylonian army. This sounds like wild exaggeration. However, the prosaic Babylonian Chronicle boasts of the Battle of Carchemish in 605 B.C. that "not a single man returned home," and more heavy losses followed during Nebuchadnezzar's abortive invasion of Egypt in 601 B.C.[47]

More poetically, Ezekiel 30:10–31:12:

> *Thus says the Lord God: I will put an end to the throngs of Egypt by the hand of Nebuchadnezzar, king of Babylon. He, and his people with him, the most ruthless of nations shall be brought in to devastate the land. They shall draw their swords against Egypt, and fill the land with the slain. I will turn the Niles into dry land ... Behold, Assyria was a cypress in Lebanon ... the envy of all Eden's trees in the garden of God. Therefore, thus says the Lord God: Because it became lofty in stature ... and because it became proud of heart ... I have handed it over ... Foreigners, the most ruthless of nations, cut it down and left it on the mountains.*

This poetic imagery reflects the fact that Nabopolassar engaged in a campaign of death and literally apocalyptic destruction against Assyria and its allies,[48] which was continued by

---

45 This is usually cited as Assyrians cutting timber for palaces (Gallagher 1999: 231–33). Normal harvesting is not what is being described. In any case, Neo-Babylonian kings are just as prone to boast about cutting cedars as Assyrian ones (as, for example, in the Wadi Brisa inscription, cited in Wildberger 1997: 58).

46 This is usually taken as referring to Assyria on the grounds that Assyrian kings occasionally mention exhausting wells. See, for example, Cogan and Tadmor 1988: 237 ad line 24. Exhausting a well in the desert is one thing; drying up a river, quite another. As the Ezekiel passage indicates, the reference is metaphorical, meaning the extinction of life as would, of course, result from a low, or absent, inundation. Once again, this points clearly to a Babylonian referent. Assyrian kings invaded Egypt with a view to turning it into a grateful tributary; Nebuchadnezzar was determined to see to it that he had no more trouble from this quarter. Different desired outcomes require different strategies.

47 Grayson 1975a: 99:1–10, 101: 5–7.

48 Modern scholars are too eager to be taken in by Babylonian spin doctoring, of which a classic example is the Wadi Brisa inscription (see Oppenheim 1969: 307), which describes the destruction of Assyria as a military campaign to eradicate the evil enemy of the scattered people of Lebanon and to allow them to lie in safe pastures. It was, of course, the Assyrians who made the people of Lebanon lie in safe pastures (i.e., pacification of the area preparatory to "ruling" them), and the Babylonians who scattered them. Otherwise it would not have been necessary to mount a military expedition in order to cut trees that "no other god requested and no other king had felled." It is also interesting that Lebanon's forest

his son Nebuchadnezzar. Commentators, historians, and archaeologists assume, pro forma, that it was Assyrian policy to leave a smoking ruin behind them wherever they went. On the contrary, whatever their proud boasts, Assyrian kings did as little damage as possible to areas they were planning to hold, since everything that got knocked down was going to have to be rebuilt, and at Assyrian taxpayers' expense.

Scorched earth was Neo-Babylonian policy, not because they were evil monsters, but to ensure that Assyria would never rise again. The campaigns of Nabopolassar and Nebuchadnezzar were a lethal mix of vengeance, fear, and realpolitik (cheating the Medes out of their share of the booty and the wealth and power which extensive and prosperous lands would have given them). Even so, Nebuchadnezzar was amazingly patient with Jerusalem, only burning the temple and the city after both Jehoiakim and Zedediah had revolted against him (2 Kings 24–25).

The Babylonian Chronicles describe these campaigns as "marching around victoriously." This harmless-sounding phrase refers, as we know from Assurbanipal's description of his Elamite campaign, to the depopulation of foreign regions, the destruction of their infrastructure, and the targeting of local cult centers. An even more terrifying phrase appears in the inscriptions of Nabopolassar, who says that the god Marduk unleashed Nergal on the Assyrians. The reference is to the Erra Epic and opening of the Gates of the Netherworld to allow a Great Flood of nomads to slaughter good and bad alike, again with cult centers as the prime targets.[49]

As imagined, this Euphrates flood is about to wash against the walls of Jerusalem and is stopped by a prophecy, allegedly from the mouth of Isaiah, which continues:

> *I am aware whether you stand or sit; I know whether you come and go ... Because of your rage against me ... I will put my hook in your nose and my bit in your mouth, and make you return the way you came. ... Therefore, thus says the Lord concerning the king of Assyria: He shall not reach this city, nor shoot an arrow at it, nor come before it with a shield, nor cast of siege works against it. He shall return by the same way he came, without entering the city, says the Lord. I will shield and save this city for my own sake, and for the sake of my servant David.* (Isaiah 37:28–29, 33–35)

Isaiah$_B$ is, then, readily recognizable as a description of Nabopolassar and Nebuchadnezzar's campaigns against Assyria and allies and of the religious policy that was used to justify them. In other words, Isaiah$_B$ originally looked forward to the eventual political and theological confrontation between Nebuchadnezzar and Jerusalem with the expectation that Jerusalem would emerge unscathed, classic Zion Theology. The phrasing of Isaiah 37:33–35 is eerily echoed in Lamentations 4:12: *The kings of the earth did not believe, nor any of the inhabitants of the world, that foe or adversary could enter the gates of Jerusalem.*

This prophecy was never delivered by the historical Isaiah,[50] nor indeed does it belong among the prophecies of Isaianic prophets, but instead among those whom Jeremiah refers

was the "forest of Marduk" which, of course, meant that Babylonians could not by definition be said to be "plundering" when vast quantities of cedars were hauled off (without payment) to Babylon.

[49] See Scurlock 2006a.

[50] On this point, see also Clements 1984: 28–51, 69–70, while not necessarily agreeing entirely with his arguments for the dating of specific passages. Most commentators concur with Clements that part or all of Isaiah 22 is pertinent to this issue (Clements 1984: 33–34; Wildberger 1997: 357–77). Clements' instinct is that Isaiah, like Jeremiah and Ezekiel, did not favor revolts against imperial powers. I would concur and add that none of these prophets had any kind words for those calling themselves prophets who encouraged such revolts (see below). Gallagher (1999: 218–20,

to as "peace prophets" and who prophesied relentlessly in favor of revolt against Babylon.[51] All this would seem to strongly support Wildberger's suggested date of Nebuchadnezzar's campaigns for the composition of 2 Kings B_2 (= $Isaiah_B$). Zedekiah, king of Judah, installed by Nebuchadnezzar (2 Kings 36:10), will very likely have had a Babylonian minder resident in the capital. If revolt were to be argued for in this context, a *Deckname* will have been in order. And who better than Babylon's archenemy Sennacherib to allow for plotting under the Babylonians' very noses?

But what about 2 Kings B_1 and its Isaianic equivalent, $Isaiah_A$? Is this also Nebuchadnezzar, as Hardmeier has argued?[52] It cannot, obviously, be any earlier than the death of Sennachrib in 681 B.C., to which it refers. This is not, however, long enough after the events of 701 B.C. for memory significantly to have faded.[53] But is it an accurate representation of that campaign? With $Isaiah_B$ = 2 Kings B_2 (the Nebuchadnezzar section) removed, the Assyrian campaign against Judah as described in $Isaiah_A$ (Isaiah 36:1–37:9a, 37–38) is remarkably non-violent — the cities are captured and plundered, but not destroyed, knocked to pieces, and burnt (as the stock phase in Assyrian annals would have it).

> *In the fourteenth year of King Hezekiah, Sennacherib, king of Assyria, went on an expedition against all the fortified cities of Judah and captured them* (Isaiah 36:1).

This cannot possibly refer, as we have seen, to Nebuchadnezzar's "marching around victoriously." It might not, at first blush, seem to fit Sennacherib either. This Assyrian king was not exactly famous for the gentleness of his treatment of adversaries, and his annals are not shy about claiming to have destroyed, knocked down, and burnt just about every city in the way of the Assyrian army. Nonetheless, we know from Sennacherib's annals and from the relief sculptures of his palace that, although he set up camp and sent out flying columns of cavalry into the Judean countryside, Judean cities were taken and plundered, but not burned, knocked down or destroyed apart from whatever damage was necessarily inflicted in the process of taking them.[54] By "plundering" was meant not disorganized looting but the acquisition of human resources. So, the citizens of Lachish, who surrendered, were not slaughtered, but a selection[55] of the population was collected together, along with their animals and moveable possessions, and carried off to Assyria.

229–39) has the historical Isaiah prophecying salvation and specifically underwriting Zion Theology. Most commentators, however, cautiously concur with Clements (see Wildberger 2002: 423–25, 433; Wildberger 1997: 376–77).

[51] See Clements 1984: 97–98.

[52] For arguments that the campaigns described in Isaiah 36–37 are references to those of Nebuchadnezzar based on a comparison with Jeremiah 37–40, see Hardmeier 1990: 392–408.

[53] For an approximate date for the "original narrative" of $Isaiah_A$ to shortly after Sennacherib's assassination in 681 B.C. but based on traditions going back to Sennacherib's campaign of 701 B.C., see Wildberger 2002: 385, 406.

[54] For the sources relating to this campaign (with previous bibliography), see Mayer 2003: 186–200. The Lachish reliefs show the city being taken and plundered. Assyrian representation of a city being burned, knocked down, and destroyed is quite distinctive and readily recognizable. The city is shown emptied of inhabitants with flames shooting up in all directions with or without Assyrian soldiers armed with pick-axes demolishing the walls. No such representation occurs in the reliefs depicting the Judean campaign. Archaeological evidence from Lachish often adduced to prove the total destruction of Judean cities by Sennacherib is by no means ironclad. There is no reason, apart from ideology and imagination, to assume that Level III was destroyed by Sennacherib rather than Nebuchadnezzar.

[55] Sennacherib is quite clear that he executed only upper-class types and did not carry everybody off (Mayer 2003: 187 iii 8–14).

Comparing this pacific passage with the rest of Sennacherib's annals, and indeed with Assyrian royal annals in general, it would be hard to argue that the reference was to anything but Sennacherib's 701 campaign against Judah.[56] In short, biblical archeologists to the contrary notwithstanding,[57] both biblical and Assyrian sources agree that Sennacherib's campaign was carried out with unusual restraint,[58] resulting in minimal damage to Judah's infrastructure. Nor is this all in Isaiah$_A$ that sounds very much like an actual Assyrian campaign.

> *From Lachish, the king of Assyria sent his commander with a great army to King Hezekiah in Jerusalem. ... The commander said to them ... Thus says the great king, the king of Assyria: On what do you base this confidence of yours? Do you think mere words substitute for strategy and might in war? On whom, then, do you rely, that you rebel against me? This Egypt, the staff on which you rely, is in fact a broken reed which pierces the hand of anyone who leans on it* (Isaiah 36:2–6).

The veracity of this passage has been challenged, but that the Assyrian commander made some sort of speech before the walls of Jerusalem is very probable. Parleys of the sort were standard practice in Assyria — they saved both time and money and brought territory in relatively undamaged and ready to yield profits in the form of taxes. Terms agreed to were always scrupulously honored, making parleys a very effective tool in the Assyrian arsenal of conquest.[59] Moreover, as Cohen has pointed out, the alleged Assyrian speech is, in fact, packed with Assyrianisms.[60]

> *Then the commander stepped forward and cried out in a loud voice in Judean ... Thus says the king ... Make peace with me and surrender! Then each of you will eat of his own vine and of his own fig tree, and drink the water of his own cistern, until I come to take you to a land like your own, a land of grain and wine, of bread and vineyards* (Isaiah 36:13–17).

There is nothing implausible in this passage. What the Assyrians are essentially saying is: "We plan to deport you." It is incredible,[61] but true, that this was an argument for surrender so powerful that the Judean authorities begged the *rab šaqê* to deliver his speech in Aramaic so that the "men sitting on the wall" would not understand him (Isaiah 36:11–12). Why? Because, conquered peoples carried off by Assyrians were settled in unwalled villages and turned into productive taxpayers and citizen-soldiers.[62] The Assyrian government also built aqueducts and dug wells to bring water to parched fields. What the riff-raff of Jerusalem was hearing was: "Green card and citizenship in five years." And, of course, the alternative was terrible death and destruction.

---

[56] For very similar arguments on the evidence from Assyrian presentation of captives on the Lachish reliefs, see Uehlinger 2003: 283–84.

[57] For a survey, see Grabbe 2003: 3–20. Archaeological levels are notoriously difficult to date, and much of the argument is by necessity circular: A site in Judah with *lmlk* jar handles was destroyed. It must have been destroyed by Sennacherib since he destroyed every city in Judah according to 2 Kings (sic). Therefore the *lmlk* jar handles must date no later than Hezekiah. Therefore any destroyed site with *lmlk* jar handles must have been destroyed by Sennacherib. Therefore Sennacherib destroyed every city in Judah.

[58] On this point, see also Mayer 2003: 184–85.

[59] On this point, see also Cogan and Tadmor 1988: 242–43; and Wildberger 2002: 380–81.

[60] Cohen 1979: 32–48. Gallagher (1999: 155–56, 164–216) regards the *rab šaqê*'s speeches as genuine.

[61] Indeed, Wildberger (2002: 379–80, 397–98) is highly skeptical that the real *rab šaqê* would have said any such thing.

[62] On this point, see also Cogan and Tadmor 1988: 233, line 32.

The contrast between Isaiah$_A$'s description of the concluding paragraphs of Sennacherib's speech (Isaiah 36:18–20 = 2 Kings 18:32–35) and Isaiah$_B$'s description of what is allegedly the same speech (Isaiah 37:9–13 = 2 Kings 19:10–13) and Hezekiah's summary of it (Isaiah 37:18–19 = 2 Kings 19:17–19), could not be more striking.[63]

Isaiah$_A$	Isaiah$_B$
Do not let Hezekiah seduce you by saying: "The Lord will save us." Has any of the gods of the nations ever rescued his land from the hand of the king of Assyria? Where are the gods of Hamath and Arpad? Where are the gods of Sepharvaim? Where are the gods of Samaria? Have they saved Samaria from my hand? Which of all the gods of these lands ever rescued his land from my hand? Will the Lord then save Jerusalem from my hand?	*Do not let your God on whom you rely deceive you by saying that Jerusalem will not be handed over to the king of Assyria. You yourself have heard what the kings of Assyria have done to all the countries: They doomed them! Will you, then, be saved? Did the gods of the nations whom my fathers destroyed save them? Guzana, Harran, Raṣapa, and Adini in Telassar? ... Truly, O Lord, the kings of Assyria have laid waste all the nations and their lands, and cast their gods into the fire.*

Samaria, which the Assyrians indeed take, is foregrounded in Sennacherib's speech in Isaiah$_A$, whereas what is actually Nebuchadnezzar's imagined speech in Isaiah$_B$ makes a similar fuss about Harran. The Nebuchadnezzar speech in Isaiah$_B$ has nothing to say about taking people away to "lands of grain and wine" but on the contrary talks about "dooming" people. The reference is to the custom of *herem*, in which cities dedicated to God were completely and permanently destroyed, and all those doomed within them, whether men, women, and children or animals, were slaughtered.[64]

The religious policy of the Assyrians in Sennacherib's speech in Isaiah$_A$ is also strikingly different from the alleged Assyrians (actually Babylonians) of the Nebuchadnezzar speech in Isaiah$_B$,[65] and in consonance with the real Sennacherib's theology. From Assyria's point of view, the gods were organized into a divine assembly which reflected the collective will. Foreign gods were potentially members and assumed to side with Assyria;[66] after a visit to Assyria proper, they returned home,[67] but continued to receive offerings in Assyria as part of the *takultu*.[68] No member of the divine assembly in good standing would dream of opposing the collective will represented by Aššur and would not have been able to do so successfully if he/she had tried.

[63] Gallagher (1999: 155–56) suggests that the 2 Kings B_2 version (19:10–13) is a modification by an Assyrian scribe working personally for Sennacherib and in any case is determined to see it as a "more accurate" description of Assyrian history than the 2 Kings B_1 version (18:32–35).

[64] It is hard to imagine how this struck Wildberger (2002: 365) as more "peaceable" than the *rab šaqê*'s speech.

[65] On this point, see also Cogan and Tadmor 1988: 236, line 18. Even Gallagher (1999: 206–07, 229) has to admit that throwing gods into the fire was not a typical Assyrian practice.

[66] On this point, see also Cogan and Tadmor 1988: 232, line 25; Wildberger 2002: 394–95.

[67] See Cogan 1974; Holloway 2002.

[68] See Frankena 1954.

This patterning of contrasts between Assyria and Babylon is consistent in the book of Isaiah in particular, and indeed in the prophets in general. If some foreign power is being criticized for greedy plundering or boasting followed by wimpish failure, it is the historical Assyrians who are being referred to and, if it says Sargon or Sennacherib (as Isaiah 36:1; 37:37), it means Sargon or Sennacherib. Horrific and unmeasured violence or its poetic allegorical equivalents — cutting down the trees of Lebanon or drying up the rivers of Egypt — mark the referent of the passage as Babylon at the earliest, whether it actually says "Babylon" (as Isaiah 14:1–23) or explicitly says "Assyria" (as Isaiah 37:21).

According to Isaiah$_A$, Hezekiah was perturbed by the *rab šaqê*'s speech (Isaiah 36:22–37:4), but Isaiah (37:5–6) prophesied that Sennacherib would return home in the face of Ethiopian intervention and die there by violence.

> *Do not be frightened by the words you have heard, with which the servants of the king of Assyria have blasphemed me. I am about to put in him such a spirit that, when he hears a certain report, he will return to his own land, and there I will cause him to fall by the sword. … The king of Assyria heard a report that Tirhakah, king of Ethiopia, had come out to fight against him. … So Sennacherib, the king of Assyria, broke camp and went back home to Nineveh. When he was worshiping in the shrine of the weapon of his god, his sons Adram-melech and Sharezer slew him with the sword, and fled into the land of Ararat. His son Esarhaddon reigned in his stead* (Isaiah 37:6–9, 37–38).

Again according to Sennacherib, the Ethiopians intervened; Sennacherib went home and Hezekiah kept his kingdom which, if we may trust the *rab šaqê*'s speech, was not Sennacherib's original intention.[69] We also know that Sennacherib was murdered and by the sons enumerated.[70] The only unverifiable detail is the location of the murder, which looks suspiciously like a prophetic addition. *The shrine of the weapon of his god* is usually rendered *the temple of his god Nisroch*, allegedly a Mesopotamian divinity. There is, however, no such god. The most probable suggestion is that this mysterious "Nisroch" is a deliberate deformation of Assyrian *maṣruhu* "(god's) weapon" using two other Hebrew roots which evoke concepts of hubris and nemesis.[71]

The assassination of Sennacherib is not just tacked onto Isaiah$_A$ as an afterthought. On the contrary, the patricide is directly prophesied by Isaiah (37:7), and the focus of the narrative is as much on this as on the deliverance of Jerusalem. Indeed, Jerusalem's salvation is an almost incidental by-product of the report which comes to send Sennacherib home where he can be murdered. Not only that, but in the biblical account the specific mention of Taharqa, who was not on the throne in 701 B.C. but would have been by 681 B.C.,[72] points to a date for the composition of Isaiah$_A$ shortly after the death of Sennacherib,[73] and not shortly after

[69] See Mayer 2003: 186–88 ii 73–iii 6, 37–49.

[70] Parpola 1980. On this section of the text, see also Cogan and Tadmor 1988: 239–40, line 37.

[71] See Scurlock 2009, "Nisroch."

[72] Taharqa ruled from 690 to 664 B.C. For a discussion of this problem, see Wildberger 2002: 382–83; Cogan and Tadmor 1988: 234, line 9.

[73] For a similar suggestion for the dating of Isaiah$_A$ on the basis of the mention of Taharqa, see Rofé 1988: 92; and Na'aman 2003: 213–17. Compare Gonçalves 1986: 441–42. Cogan and Tadmor (1988: 244) treat the notice of Sennacherib's assassination as a Neo-Babylonian addition to the text drawing on the Babylonian Chronicles. I suspect, however, that the annals of the kings of Judah kept very good records of matters of such immediate interest, and informants (Israelites in exile in Assyria who came to Jerusalem to celebrate Passover) would have been ready at hand.

his third campaign as might be expected if the deliverance of Jerusalem had been the original focus of the narrative.

We notice also a curious omission from Isaiah$_A$. Isaiah$_B$ lays out its prophecy against Nebuchadnezzar in two phases: Isaiah 37:22b–29, a poetic cri du coeur which represents the actual prophecy (the word of God via the mouth of the prophet) and Isaiah 37:33–36 which represents a sort of translation and directly predicts what is going to happen.[74] In Isaiah$_A$, the translation is present (Isaiah 37:6b–7) but the actual prophecy is missing. A search through the rest of the book of Isaiah readily allows the restoration of this missing passage in the form of what is now Isaiah 10:5–15 as follows:[75]

> *Woe to Assyria! My rod in anger, my staff in wrath. Against an impious nation I send him, and against a people under my wrath I order him to seize plunder, carry off loot, and tread them down like the mud of the streets. But this is not what he intends ... "Are not my commanders all kings?" he says, "Is not Calno like Carchemish, or Hamath like Arpad, or Samaria like Damascus? Just as my hand reached out to idolatrous kingdoms that had more images than Jerusalem and Samaria, just as I treated Samaria and her idols, shall I not do to Jerusalem and her graven images? ... By my own power I have done it, and by my wisdom, for I am shrewd. I have moved the boundaries of peoples, their treasures I have pillaged, and, like a giant, I have pulled down the enthroned. My hand has seized as in a nest the riches of nations; as one takes eggs left alone, so I took in all the earth." ... Will the axe boast against him who hews with it? Will the saw exalt itself above him who wields it? As if a rod could sway him who lifts it, or a staff him who is not wood!* (Isaiah 10:5–15)

This passage would appear[76] to be of a piece with Isaiah 36–37.[77] That it belongs specifically to Isaiah$_A$ and not Isaiah$_B$ should by now also be quite clear. Note that a great deal of fuss is made about conquest and plundering, but not a word about destruction, let alone dooming people and throwing gods into the fire. It also speaks prominently of Samaria, with nary a word about Harran, Guzana, etc. Most significantly, it takes as its motif the weapon before which Sennacherib was killed. These verses should, in my opinion, be reinserted (see Appendix) between Hezekiah's plea to Isaiah to pray for the community (Isaiah 37:1–4) and Isaiah's direct prediction of the future (Isaiah 37:6b–7).

So what was the point of Isaiah$_A$ (= 2 Kings B$_1$ + Isaiah 10:5–15) and why was it not composed until 681 B.C. rather than immediately after Sennacherib's failed siege of 701

---

[74] This relationship is missed by many scholars, who regard the actual prophecy as an "expansion" of its translation. See, for example, Cogan and Tadmor 1988: 236, lines 21–38; Wildberger 2002: 365, 415.

[75] Ben Zvi (1990: 89–91) comes the closest to arguing for a direct connection between Isaiah 10:5–15 and 2 Kings B$_1$. Clements (1984: 55–56) is also only a hair away, arguing that the author of 2 Kings B$_1$ had "knowledge" of Isaiah 10:5–15. So also Gallagher (1999: 75–87). Indeed, it is rare to find anyone who does not bring up Isaiah 10:5ff. in the context of Sennacherib's campaign against Judah and Jerusalem. For references, see Wildberger 1991: 415.

[76] Clements (1984: 36–39) and Wildberger (1991: 415–16) assign the passage to the reign of Sargon II. Nonetheless, they correctly note that verses 16ff. are later additions (Clements 1984: 37–39, 42–43; Wildberger 1991: 413).

[77] See, for example, Blenkinsopp 2000: 251–54. What has impeded recognition of this passage actually belonging in Isaiah$_A$ (as opposed to merely paralleling it in a general way) is the fact that many scholars incorrectly attach Isaiah 10:15 to the following, much later, addition (Blenkinsopp 2000: 254–56). As noted already by Gray (1912: 194, 199–200), verses 16ff. do not certainly belong to Isaiah 10:1–15 and are usually included with it for no better reason than "something like the substance of these verses is certainly required at this point."

B.C.? Theologically speaking, Isaiah 10:1–15 accepts Sennacherib's claim to be acting for God (Isaiah 36:10) but makes the rather subtle argument that Sennacherib does not know the God whose instrument he is if he thinks that the God of Jerusalem is on a par with the gods of Samaria. In other words, the question for Isaiah$_A$ is whether the divinity of Jerusalem, at whose altar Hezekiah is insisting that Judah offer exclusive worship, (Isaiah 36:7) is, in fact, Yahweh or just some local god, like the gods of Samaria or Damascus or Hamath or any other city in the area. Since Jerusalem was a Jebusite city when David made it his capital, this is an absolutely devastating argument.[78] Hezekiah is himself, as pointed out by Machinist (2000: 158), not altogether certain on this point, sending a delegation which includes the elders of the priests to beg Isaiah to pray for Hezekiah and his people to "your God" (Isaiah 37:1–4).[79] In sharp contrast when, in Isaiah$_B$, the issue is whether Marduk was going to kill Yahweh or the other way round, "Hezekiah" prays directly to "our God" (Isaiah 37:14–20).

Arguments of this power and cogency cannot be taken down by logic; they may be answered only by a sign from God. Isaiah$_A$ is, therefore, essentially a solicited omen in which a particular sign is designated as the answer to a question posed to God. This was not an uncommon practice in Israel as is attested to by Deuteronomy 13:2–4 in which it is argued that certain matters theological may not be settled in this way. Similarly, the story of Rabbi Eliezer[80] quoted by Winitzer in this volume.

In this case, the desired sign was not fire from heaven (Elijah and the prophets of Baʿal in 1 Kings 18), the premature death of a false prophet (Jeremiah and Hananiah in Jeremiah 28), a river flowing backwards, or a buckling wall (Rabbi Eliezer and Rabbi Joshua), but a historical event, namely (Isaiah 37:6b–7) that Sennacherib would hear a report, go home, and there be killed by his own sons. This is, of course, what happened (Isaiah 37:37–38), but with the added detail that Sennacherib was worshiping the weapon of Aššur when he died. Since, according to Isaiah 10:15, Sennacherib was himself the weapon of God, his death in that location was a sign from God that the god of whom Sennacherib was the weapon was the God of Jerusalem and of Mt. Zion and not even in the same league with the gods of Samaria.

Were the theological arguments about the identity of Yahweh and the legitimacy of the high places which Hezekiah removed (Isaiah 36:7) actually raised by Sennacherib or indeed by the historical Isaiah as opposed to his followers? Perhaps not,[81] but the point was that Sennacherib might conceivably have made such arguments,[82] and that Sennacherib's failure and death were a sign from God resolving these issues.

I say conceivably because it was possible for a few fortunate foreign gods to be accepted as syncretic equivalents to Aššur himself. Two of these syncretic equivalents, Sîn of Harran and Anu (= El) were also, separately, potential syncretic equivalents of Yahweh, which made

[78] Indeed, there are not a few biblical scholars who would wholeheartedly concur with this opinion, if rephrased as David having adopted Jebusite cultus and the Jebusite priesthood when he made Jerusalem his capital. So, for example, Rupprecht 1977 and Ahlström 1963.

[79] In view of 2 Samuel 7:12–16, this is a truly remarkable request.

[80] Baba Meṣiʿa 59b.

[81] Weinfeld (1964: 207–09) argues that the high places argument was the invention of an Isaianic source. Machinist (2000: 163–64) and Wildberger (2002: 379, 393) also place it in the context of an inter-Judean debate. Less plausibly, Ben Zvi (1990) argues that the entire speech of the *rab šaqê* was the invention of the Deuteronomist historian. Gallagher (1999: 193–200, 204–09) argues for the authenticity of these elements as Assyrian propaganda.

[82] On the importance of the plausibility of historical narratives, see Ben Zvi 2003: 96–103.

it at least plausible that Sennacherib would have seen Yahweh and Aššur as the same god. Since Aššur had only a single sanctuary but could be worshipped in any place that his weapon had been erected, it was also not implausible that Sennacherib would be a defender of Yahwist high places. What would have beggared belief, and indeed the contrary position is claimed for Sennacherib, is that the national god of Assyria was actually the *numen loci* of Jerusalem.

With Isaiah$_B$ removed, what is left in Isaiah$_A$ is a careful description of Sennacherib's campaign into Judah and its aftermath which was to lead to God's judgment on Sennacherib in the form of a failed campaign[83] and assassination, all of which actually happened in historical time.[84] Again, as with Babylonian religious policy in Isaiah$_B$, Assyrian religious policy is accurately described in Isaiah$_A$. In other words, Isaiah$_A$ was intended a prophecy against Sennacherib's alleged denial of the equation of Yahweh and the god of Jerusalem, with the annalistic account of Sennacherib's campaign and particularly its aftermath (Isaiah 36:1–3, 37:37–38) constituting the fulfillment of that prophecy. The accuracy of historical reporting in Isaiah$_A$ should come as no surprise to students of divination, since the impartiality of the diviner is an essential feature of the credibility of solicited omens. If the events described never happened or were not credibly described, manipulation of the oracle would be glaringly obvious.

With Clements,[85] the following passage will have been added to Isaiah$_A$ subsequently, when it was incorporated[86] into 2 Kings:

> *The angel of the Lord went forth and struck down one hundred and eighty-five thousand in the Assyrian camp. Early the next morning, there they were, all the corpses of the dead* (Isaiah 37:36 = 2 Kings 19:35).

The effect will have been to refocus Isaiah$_A$ on the salvation of Jerusalem and to have made the prophet Isaiah "predict" the fall of Assyria *by a sword not wielded by man* (Isaiah 31:8; cf. Hos. 1:7).[87] This will have been for the benefit of Josiah, who was counting on the

[83] If Sennacherib intended to incorporate Judah, then being forced to leave the local dynasty in place was essentially at some level a failure, even if tribute payments were resumed. On this point, see also Wildberger 2002: 394.

[84] On this point, see also Clements 1984: 52–56.

[85] Clements 1984: 57–61, 91, 94.

[86] Na'aman (2000: 400–02; 2003: 217–20) argues for a Deuteronomistic (by which he means Josianic) incorporation of 2 Kings B_1 (= Isaiah$_A$) into a combined narrative with 2 Kings A. That 2 Kings B_1 was actually composed for the occasion is essentially out of the question if, with Weinfeld (1964: 207–09), we see the authors intending this as a pro-high places and not, as Na'aman (2003) and Ben Zvi (1990: 91) assume, an anti-high places argument. Even with the addition of Isaiah 37:36 = 2 Kings 19:35 (the Angel of the Lord slaying the Assyrian army), this passage forces into the open some rather wide holes in Deuteronomistic logic, as, ironically, pointed out by Ben Zvi (1990: 86), "the inductive method of reasoning fails when someone thinks about Jerusalem") and, more forcefully, by Machinist (2000: 156–60). This in itself suggests an author having to live with a pre–existent text which caused him great grief, but which he could not safely ignore. Similar problems appear elsewhere in Kings as, for example, 2 Kings 14:23–29, where the thesis that it was the moral failure to deal with the high places that caused the military failures of the Northern Kingdom (2 Kings 17:7–23) runs aground on the apparently inescapable fact that Jeroboam II was able to achieve almost miraculous success against Damascus and Hamath despite the fact that *he did not desist from any of the sins which Jeroboam son of Nebat had caused Israel to commit.*

[87] On this point, see also Clements 1984: 92–95. To note, however, is that a careful reading reveals that both Judah and Jerusalem had escaped Sennacherib's 701 campaign with minimal damage, thus, ironically, strengthening Clements' point while disagreeing with him.

impregnability of Jerusalem when he sided with Babylon against Assyria and Egypt.[88] This, of course, presupposes that this passage belongs to a late version of Isaiah$_A$ and not to Isaiah$_B$, as is usually assumed. For what it is worth, Ben Sirah 48:18–21 quotes this line as part of what was apparently a separately circulating (or reconstructed) version of Isaiah$_A$:

> *During his (Hezekiah's) reign Sennacherib led an invasion, and sent his adjutant* (in Isaiah$_B$, the message is in the form of a letter) ... *The people's hearts melted within them, and they were in anguish like that of childbirth.* (= Isaiah 37:3) ... *God struck the camp of the Assyrians and routed them with a plague* (= Isaiah 37:36).

Subsequently, apparently in the reign of Zedekiah (see above), further changes were made.[89] Into the very midst of what was, with the possible exception of the more complex theological arguments and the Angel of the Lord addition, an accurate account of Sennacherib's failed attempt on Jerusalem and its aftermath (Isaiah$_A$), was inserted a second time and later, but again reasonably accurate, if somewhat poetic, account of Nebuchadnezzar's campaigns against Assyria and Egypt (Isaiah$_B$; see Appendix).

The purpose of the juxtaposition would appear to be to predict that Nebuchadnezzar's campaign against Jerusalem would end in the same way as Sennacherib's or, to put it another way, that Isaiah's prophecy against Sennacherib applied also to Nebuchadnezzar. Of course, any historian of the time could have reached the same conclusion by simple logical syllogism. Sennacherib failed to take Jerusalem but destroyed Babylon and "put his hooks in the nose" (Isaiah 37:29) of several of its kings. It hardly seemed conceivable that Nebuchadnezzar, who was not even properly Babylonian, but a Chaldean (2 Kings 25:10, 13), was going to be able to succeed where Sennacherib had failed.

But the kings of Judah were not in the habit of consulting historians. The imprimatur of prophecy ensured proper divination of the will of God. And Zedekiah, who had been made to swear by God (2 Kings 36:13; cf. Ezekiel 17:11–21) that he would remain loyal to Nebuchadnezzar, would not have dreamed of attempting revolt against the Babylonian juggernaut without one. His position was made particularly difficult by the fact the city had already fallen once to Nebuchadnezzar, who not only carried off Jehoiakim but "all Jerusalem" including "all seven thousand men of the army" so that: *None were left among the people of the land except the poor.* Not only that, but all the treasures of the temple of the Lord were plundered, including Solomon's gold utensils (2 Kings 24:10–17).

The peace prophets (Jeremiah 23:16–17) vilified by Jeremiah[90] insisted that these vessels would be recovered (Jeremiah 27:16–22, 28:3, 6) and that the revolt would be successful even

---

[88] Text A (the tribute payment) may also have been added at this time. As pointed out by Wildberger (2002: 363), the interest shown in 2 Kings 18:14–16 in the temple and its furnishings is characteristic of the Deuteronomistic historians. If so, the notice about the tribute would reinforce the theme, otherwise quite prominent in the Deuteronomistic history, of unfinished business (Moses and Joshua; David and Solomon; Elijah and Elishah, etc.) with, of course, Josiah as the completer and thus the culmination of human history up to that point. From this perspective, the fact that Hezekiah achieved deliverance from the Assyrians by buying them off, with temple funds and gold plate no less, and by admitting that Sennacherib was justified in attacking him, would leave it to Josiah to complete the liberation from foreign domination and the concomitant return to the days of Solomonic glory. As Ben Zvi (2003: 81 n. 23) points out, Hezekiah as presented is essentially admitting to sinning against God, certainly not a stamp of approval, whatever the source.

[89] On the possibility of a long period of redaction for the Deuteronomistic history (quite differently argued), see Clements 1984: 90–104.

[90] The peace prophets were equally unpopular with Ezekiel (13:1–16) and the Isaianic prophets (Isaiah 28:14–22).

to the point of return of the exiles (Jeremiah 28:1–4, 10–11). This prediction was breathtakingly counterintuitive and once again required a sign,[91] correspondingly provided as follows:[92]

> *This shall be a sign for you: this year you shall eat the aftergrowth, next year, what grows of itself; but in the third year, sow and reap, plant vineyards and eat their fruit! The remaining survivors of the house of Judah shall again strike root below and bear fruit above. For out of Jerusalem shall come a remnant, and from Mount Zion, survivors. The zeal of the Lord of hosts shall do this* (Isaiah 37:30–32).

The idea that this sign must refer to the Assyrians because they deliberately destroyed the economic base of places they conquered[93] is nonsense. The proverbially greedy Assyrians were after tax revenue, and it is as possible to tax a deserted waste as to get blood from a turnip. In any case, there is nothing in this verse about anybody targeting anybody's economic base. The reference is actually metaphorical. Judah and Jerusalem are like a field in which the harvest has been destroyed. Just as when, in such a case, one eats what is left in the first year, and the land lies fallow in the second, but in the third year one plants and enjoys an abundant harvest, so there is a remnant in Judah and survivors in Jerusalem, and the city will remain vacant for a time but then be repopulated and flourish as never before. If Isaiah 37:4b *Send up a prayer for the remnant that is here* in Hezekiah's address to Isaiah in account Isaiah_A is not simply hyperbole, it could also have been added at this point.[94]

The metaphorical three years have a historical referent, namely Jehoiakim's three-month reign in Jerusalem (2 Kings 24:8). The implication is, of course, that the punishment for previous sins (2 Kings 24:3–4) is over, and the prophecy will work as planned or, as Nahum says: *The enemy shall not rise a second time ... For, says the Lord, be they ever so many and vigorous, still they shall be mown down and disappear* (Nahum 1:9–12).

The same assertion is made in the account of Hezekiah's illness (2 Kings 20:1–10) which has:

> *In three days you shall go up to the Lord's temple; I will add fifteen years to your life. I will rescue you and the city from the hand of the king of Assyria; I will be a shield to this city for my own sake, and for the sake of my servant David.*[95]

In short, once the period of three (years, months, days) representing God's punishment for your sins is over, you are going to have peace and success. In this case, Jehoiakim has already done the three (months), and so there should, according to this peace prophet, be a green light for revolt.

---

[91] Cf. Wildberger 2002: 400. As Wildberger points out (2002: 415–16), the sign in question is in no way appropriate to Hezekiah.

[92] I am indebted to R. Beal for this suggestion.

[93] Gallagher 1999: 235–36.

[94] Wildberger (2002: 382, 385) is suspicious of Isaiah 37:3–4 because it contains this half line. On the other hand, see Wildberger 2002: 401.

[95] This would make the bulk, at any rate, of the Hezekiah's illness story an addition of Zedekiah's scribes, and the specific explanation given in 2 Kings 20:12–19 for the looting of the palace storehouses and making palace servants out of some of Hezekiah's descendants points in the same direction. As of Zedekiah, all that had happened was that the city had been looted, the population deported, and Jehoiakim taken captive (2 Kings 24:12–13,15). It is hard to imagine anyone worrying about such matters after Nebuchadnezzar had killed Zedekiah's sons before his eyes and blinded him, torn down the walls of Jerusalem, burned the city and the temple to the ground, broken up the bronze pillars and even the bronze sea, and executed sixty-seven prisoners in cold blood (2 Kings 25:6–21). On this point, see Clements 1984: 63–71, accepted in Cogan and Tadmor 1988: 260–63.

Using Sennacherib and Assyria for Nebuchadnezzar and Babylon in Isaiah_B would, in this context, have been far more than a *Deckname*. Calling Nebuchadnezzar Sennacherib made him Sennacherib and guaranteed that he, too, would fail. It also tempted God (Isaiah 7:10–12; Deuteronomy 6:16), in that the failure of the prophecy against Nebuchadnezzar would compromise the original sign that Jerusalem was indeed the home of Yahweh.

Far from expressing undying hatred, the continual harping on Assyria still quite apparent in the latest phases of the dialectic takes advantage of their well-known demise to wish, even to cause, the same fate to befall other, even more dangerous, enemies. Indeed, the *Targum of the Minor Prophets* interprets Nahum 1:8: "But in fierce anger and in great wrath he shall make an end of the nations which rose up and utterly destroyed the Sanctuary and he shall deliver his adversaries to Gehinnam."[96] The intent is, of course, not to pretend that Assyria destroyed the sanctuary, but to apply Nahum's prophecy against Babylon and Rome.

Isaiah 36–37 is, then, a real prophecy (and not just a historical appendix) that uses a past historical event (Sennacherib's failed siege of Jerusalem and his subsequent assassination) as its basis. As with Isaiah_A which treats historical events as signs from God, Isaiah_B relies for its credibility on the very historical accuracy which has caused Isaiah 36–37 not to be recognized as a prophecy. To note also is that, as with the Mesopotamian Dynastic Prophecy, predictive power is derived from the partial repetition of a sequence of events. Dynastic Prophecy: east defeated west; east defeated west; Persian king Xerxes was assassinated and the Persians lost out. East has again defeated west twice; Greek king Seleucus was assassinated. Therefore, the Greeks will lose out. Isaiah 36–37: Sennacherib made a campaign against Judah, besieged Jerusalem, and failed; Nebuchadnezzar has made or will make a campaign against Judah and Jerusalem; therefore, he will fail. Also interesting is that the association between an assassinated ruler and the fall of his kingdom is made in both Mesopotamian and biblical prophecies.

As for the use of past historical events as a basis for prophecy, 2 Kings 18:13–19:37 is not a lone example of this phenomenon. It is hard to think that the fuss made about the release of Jehoiakim in 2 Kings 25:27–30 is not a prophecy of the eventual release and restoration of the Israelite community[97] and, indeed, it is replaced in 2 Chronicles 36:22–23 by the decree of Cyrus the Great of Persia. Even closer to Isaiah 36–37 is the curious statement in 2 Chronicles 33:11 that Manasseh was taken in chains by Aššurbanipal to Babylon (and not Nineveh). It has been argued[98] that this passage is a disguised reference to the Babylonian exile. If so, backdating the exile to the period of Manasseh would serve to ensure that, like the original Manasseh, the community would repent and be returned to its kingdom in Jerusalem.

Unfortunately, the result of Nebuchadnezzar's campaign was not ignominious defeat and assassination, but the triumph of Babylon. Nebuchadnezzar crushed Egypt, Tyre, and the Arabs, burned the temple in Jerusalem, and deported most of the population of Judah to Babylonia. Swelled with booty and captives, Babylon became a megalopolis. In short, by the Deuteronomic test for a false prophet (Deuteronomy 18:21–22), the author of Isaiah_B, this, pseudo-Isaianic, prophecy was a false prophet.

Of course, the historical Isaiah was also potentially in the position of having originally predicted something (the fall of Jerusalem to Sennacherib) which never, in fact, occurred[99] raising another issue of interest to students of divination. In a sense, biblical prophecy as

[96] See Cathcart and Gordon 1989: 132–33.

[97] See von Rad 1953: 90–91.

[98] See Curtis 1910: 497–99.

[99] See Clements 1984: 29–36.

practiced by the kings of Israel and Judah was a system of solicited omens. In other words, the king determined a course of action and then consulted the prophets as to whether or not he should pursue it. The prophets then prophesied, giving the king his answer not, except in the method, significantly different from a Mesopotamian king asking his diviner to cut open a sheep. Indeed, the Hittite king Muršili in his Plague Prayers treats divination and prophecy as essentially the same: "Let the matter ... be established through divination or let me see it in a dream or let a prophet speak of it."[100]

We are, then, entitled to ask of biblical prophecy the same question that we routinely ask of divination. Why did the Israelites and Judeans question the veracity of individual prophets but never the institution of prophecy as such? The simple answer is that the predictions of true prophets came true, and spectacularly so. Another reason is that more reliable forms of divination were banned in Israel. I say more reliable because there was an inherent credibility problem built into the institution of prophecy which may account for its relative rarity in Mesopotamia, where the full range of divinatory practices was allowed.

What distinguishes prophecy from other forms of divination is that it is an art rather than a science. A diviner was an expert, who spent years of careful study before attempting to make any predictions. Like modern physicians who kill patients, an unsuccessful diviner could always fall back on having practiced his profession "by the book." No such luck for a prophet — even Moses had to go to spectacular lengths to have his claims of talking to God accepted by the Israelites (Exodus 19:9–20:22).

Inevitably, the prophetic credibility problem was unevenly distributed. The predictions of gloom-and-doom prophets all too often came true, since disaster was never far around the corner for a small country like Judah with nasty neighbors. It was thus the "peace" (victory and success) prophets who would have been regularly falsified and their testimony was, in consequence, particularly suspect.

To quote Jeremiah 28:8–9:

> *From of old, the prophets who were before you and me prophesied war, woe and pestilence against many lands and mighty kingdoms. But the prophet who prophesies peace is recognized as truly sent by the Lord only when his prophetic prediction is fulfilled.*

Indeed, spectacular examples of false prophets as, for example, Zekediah son of Chenanah who sent Ahab to his death at Ramoth-Gilead (1 Kings 22:11, 20–28) and Hananiah son of Azzur who persuaded Zedekiah to revolt against Babylon (Jeremiah 28:1–17) are always advocates of "peace" (victory and success).

That Isaiah originally prophesied a fall of Jerusalem to the Assyrians which did not, in fact, occur is, therefore, only problematic to the modern observer. This would not be the first or the last time that God relented and did not send the threatened punishment. As with Mesopotamian unsolicited omens, doom-and-gloom prophecies did not cause the events which they foretold, nor indeed were they certain and irreversible. On the contrary, the point was to warn the community so that prompt action in the form of repentance and a bit of pleading and sackcloth could avert the predicted disaster.

Isaiah's prophecy against Hezekiah, quoted in Isaiah 39:3–8 (= 2 Kings 20:12–19) was fulfilled, not because Isaiah prophesied it, but because Hezekiah accepted the omen which it

---

[100] Beckman 1997: 156–60.

represented (Isaiah 39:8 = 2 Kings 20:19). By contrast, as described in Jeremiah 26:18–19, the failure of Jerusalem to fall in the reign of Hezekiah as predicted by Micah of Moreseth was due to Hezekiah's entreaties which made the Lord *repent of the evil with which he had threatened them*. Micah is not, for this, being called a false prophet, but on the contrary one who spoke in the name of the Lord, and for the peoples' benefit.

"Peace" prophets had, then, a truly serious credibility problem even when their predictions were not, as in the case of the likely success of Zedekiah's revolt, breathtakingly counterintuitive. This provides yet another motive for the author of Isaiah_B to have grafted his prophecy onto an earlier, and fulfilled, prophecy of a known quantity (Isaiah) who was held in high renown and generally recognized as a true prophet.

Nonetheless, Isaiah_B remains a prophecy from a "peace" (victory and success) prophet, and it was not fulfilled. Not only that, but the author was a prophet (dare we suggest even Hananiah himself?) who, in advocating Zedekah's rebellion against Nebuchadnezzar, directly contradicted Jeremiah *who spoke the word of the Lord* (2 Kings 36:12). So why was this blatantly false prophecy preserved for us in 2 Kings and why, for that matter, does the Book of Isaiah as we have it include the falsely attributed Isaiah_B?

True vs. False Prophecy

The enduring popularity of the prophecies of Nostradamus rests not so much in their vaunted accuracy in predicting past events as in the perception that they are of continuing relevance for the future. When a prophecy relating to some specific king's specific war against a specific enemy was fulfilled in ancient Israel, this was doubtless appreciated, but why, come to think of it, would anyone other than the prophets' guild wish to keep a copy? In only two cases would there be any reason to retain its memory. One was that the prophecy managed not to come true without being actually falsified (Isaiah_B's prediction of disaster for Nebuchadnezzar). The other was that the prophecy came true but seemed nonetheless not completely to have been fulfilled (Nahum's prediction of disaster for Jerusalem). It is these, and these alone, that will have survived the centuries.

Thus, as with the Uruk Prophecy, biblical prophecies were not necessarily invalidated by failure to immediately come to fruition. So, for example, the prophet Haggai's exhortation to rebuild the temple as a recipient of God's glory was not dampened by disappointment at the results; the true fulfillment was simply deferred to some date in the hopefully near future (Haggai 1:1–2:9).

By the simple expedient of reinterpreting Isaiah 37:30–32 as referring to the fall of Jerusalem, it was possible to reapply what was allegedly Isaiah's prediction of disaster for Nebuchadnezzar qua Sennacherib, a.k.a. "Nebuchadnezzar, king of the Assyrians" to future Babylons such as the Persians, the Seleucids, and ultimately Rome. Prophecies such as Nahum and Isaiah 36–37 thus achieved the sort of status accorded in Mesopotamia to the omens in the diviners' manual, that is, they were pronouncements potentially valid not just for the situation to which they originally applied but at specific points scattered throughout the past, present, and future. What began as Sennacherib being proven wrong by a sign from God became a generalized omen of Assyria: "If a king attacks Jerusalem, he will fail to take the city and subsequently be assassinated." To which Josiah, or perhaps Zedekiah, added: "and his kingdom will fall."

CONCLUSION AND REFLECTIONS

In conclusion, the Uruk Prophecy and the Dynastic Prophecy qualify as prophetic texts in the biblical sense. However, it must be noted that there remains a significant difference — quite apart from a breathtaking beauty of language completely absent from either the Uruk or the Dynastic Prophecy, the biblical examples have a universal quality, whereas the Mesopotamian ones are typically zoned in on a particular little city-state of southern Mesopotamia (Uruk or Babylon) and involve matters which will not have resonated, or at least not positively resonated, outside of that zone. Elam cared about Nanay but certainly did not want her in Uruk. Other cities of Babylonia might have wanted Mesopotamia to return to the center of power, but not under Babylon's leadership, and both Uruk and Ur sided with Xerxes against Babylon. By contrast, in their endless "Jeremiads," the prophets are strikingly the voice of mankind crying out against the Babylonian, not for what he did to Judah, but for what he did to "us."

APPENDIX

STAGE 1: COMPOSITION OF ISAIAH$_A$ USING MATERIAL DRAWN FROM AN ANNALISTIC SOURCE AND A PROPHETIC SOURCE

Approximate Date: Shortly after the assassination of Sennacherib

Motive: To settle theological issues raised by Sennacherib's invasion of Judah

Text:

In the fourteenth year of King Hezekiah, Sennacherib, king of Assyria, went on an expedition against all the fortified cities of Judah and captured them. From Lachish, the king of Assyria sent his commander with a great army to King Hezekiah in Jerusalem. ... The commander said to them ... Thus says the great king, the king of Assyria: On what do you base this confidence of yours? Do you think mere words substitute for strategy and might in war? On whom, then, do you rely, that you rebel against me? This Egypt, the staff on which you rely, is in fact a broken reed which pierces the hand of anyone who leans on it. ... But if you say to me: "We rely on the Lord our God," is he not the one whose high places and altars Hezekiah removed, commanding Judah and Jerusalem to worship before this altar? ... Was it without the Lord's will that I have come up to destroy this land? The Lord said to me: "Go up and destroy that land!" ... Do not let Hezekiah seduce you by saying, "The Lord will save us." Has any of the gods of the nations ever rescued his land from the hand of the king of Assyria? Where are the gods of Hamath and Arpad? Where are the gods of Sepharvaim? Where are the gods of Samaria? Have they saved Samaria from my hand? Which of all the gods of these lands ever rescued his land from my hand? Will the Lord then save Jerusalem from my hand? (Isaiah 36:1–20)

The story continues with the mission to Hezekiah who sends a message to Isaiah (Isaiah 36:21–37:4)

When the servants of King Hezekiah had come to Isaiah, he said to them: "Tell this to your master." Thus says the Lord, the God of Israel: In answer to your prayer for help against Sennacherib, king of Assyria, this is the word the Lord has spoken concerning him. (Isaiah 37:5–6, 21–22)

Woe to Assyria! My rod in anger, my staff in wrath. Against an impious nation I send him, and against a people under my wrath I order him to seize plunder, carry off loot, and tread them down like the mud of the streets. But this is not what he intends ... "Are not my commanders all kings?" he says, "Is not Calno like Carchemish, or Hamath like Arpad, or Samaria like Damascus? Just as my hand reached out to idolatrous kingdoms that had more images than Jerusalem and Samaria, just as I treated Samaria and her idols, shall I not do to Jerusalem and her graven images? ... By my own power I have done it, and by my wisdom, for I am shrewd. I have moved the boundaries of peoples, their treasures I have pillaged, and, like a giant, I have pulled down the enthroned. My hand has seized as in a nest the riches of nations; as one takes eggs left alone, so I took in all the earth." ... Will the axe boast against him who hews with it? Will the saw exalt itself above him who wields it? As if a rod could sway him who lifts it, or a staff him who is not wood! (Isaiah 10:5–15)

Therefore, thus says the Lord concerning the king of Assyria: Do not be frightened by the words you have heard, with which the servants of the king of Assyria have blasphemed me. I am about to put in him such a spirit that, when he hears a certain report, he will return to his own land, and there I will cause him to fall by the sword. ... The king of Assyria heard a report that Tirhakah, king of Ethiopia, had come out to fight against him. ... So Sennacherib, the king of Assyria, broke camp and went back home to Nineveh. When he was worshiping in the shrine of the weapon of his god, his sons Adram-melech and Sharezer slew him with the sword, and fled into the land of Ararat. His son Esarhaddon reigned in his stead. (Isaiah 37:33, 6–9, 37–38)

STAGE 2: INCORPORATION OF ISAIAH$_A$ INTO AN EARLY VERSION OF 2 KINGS WITH ADDITIONS

Approximate Date: Before the death of Josiah at Megiddo

Motive: To underwrite Josiah's mission

Text:

The angel of the Lord went forth and struck down one hundred and eighty-five thousand in the Assyrian camp. Early the next morning, there they were, all the corpses of the dead. (Isaiah 37:36 = 2 Kings 19:35)

Hezekiah, king of Judah sent this message to the king of Assyria at Lachish: "I have done wrong. Leave me, and I will pay whatever tribute you impose on me." The king of Assyria exacted three hundred talents of silver and thirty talents of gold from Hezekiah, king of Judah. Hezekiah paid him all the funds there were in the temple of the Lord and in the palace treasuries. He broke up the door panels and the uprights of the temple of the Lord which he himself had ordered to be overlaid with gold, and gave the gold to the king of Assyria. (2 Kings 18:14–15)

The effect of 2 Kings 19:35 was to make Isaiah$_A$ (and the assassination of Sennacherib) predict the fall of Assyria. This will have served to underwrite Josiah's policy of siding against Assyria in the conflict and to make the historical Isaiah predict that no harm would come to Jerusalem in the process. The tribute payment narrative in 2 Kings 18:14–15 cut Hezekiah down to size, and left the role of savior to Josiah.

STAGE 3: COMPOSITION OF ISAIAH$_B$ AND INTEGRATION INTO A MODIFIED ISAIAH$_A$

Approximate Date: Preparatory to Zedekiah's revolt against Nebuchadnezzar

Motive: To inspire the faithful for that revolt

Text:

Thus shall you say to Hezekiah, king of Judah: "Do not let your God on whom you rely deceive you by saying that Jerusalem will not be handed over to the king of Assyria. You yourself have heard what the kings of Assyria have done to all the countries: They doomed them! Will you, then, be saved? Did the gods of the nations whom my fathers destroyed save them? Gozen, Haran, Rezeph, and Edenites in Telassar? Where is the king of Hamath, the king of Arpad, or a king of the cities of Sepharvaim, Hena or Ivvah?" (Isaiah 37:9b–13)

> *Hezekiah took the letter … he went up to the temple of the Lord, and spreading it out before him, he prayed: O Lord of hosts, God of Israel … You alone are God over all the kingdoms of the earth. You have made the heavens and the earth. Incline your ear, O Lord and listen! … Hear all the words of the letter that Sennacherib sent to taunt the living God. Truly O Lord, the kings of Assyria have laid waste all the nations and their lands, and cast their gods into the fire; they destroyed them because they were not gods but the work of human hands, wood and stone. Therefore, O Lord, our God, save us from his hand, that all the kingdoms of the earth may know that you, O Lord, alone are God.* (Isaiah 37:14–20)

> *She despises you, laughs you to scorn, the virgin daughter Zion; Behind you she wags her head, daughter Jerusalem. … You said: "With my many chariots I climbed the mountain heights, the recesses of Lebanon; I cut down its lofty cedars, its choice cypresses. I reached the remotest heights, its forest park. I dug wells and drank water in foreign lands; I dried up with the soles of my feet all the rivers of Egypt." … Long ago I prepared it, from days of old I planned it, now I have brought it to pass; that you should reduce fortified cities into heaps of ruins … I am aware whether you stand or sit; I know whether you come and go … Because of your rage against me … I will put my hook in your nose and my bit in your mouth, and make you return the way you came.* (Isaiah 37:22b–29)

> *This shall be a sign for you: this year you shall eat the aftergrowth, next year, what grows of itself; but in the third year, sow and reap, plant vineyards and eat their fruit! The remaining survivors of the house of Judah shall again strike root below and bear fruit above. For out of Jerusalem shall come a remnant, and from Mount Zion, survivors. The zeal of the Lord of hosts shall do this.* (Isaiah 37:30–32)

> *He shall not reach this city, nor shoot an arrow at it, nor come before it with a shield, nor cast of siege works against it. He shall return by the same way he came, without entering the city, says the Lord. I will shield and save this city for my own sake, and for the sake of my servant David. (The angel of the Lord went forth and struck down one hundred and eighty-five thousand in the Assyrian camp. Early the next morning, there they were, all the corpses of the dead.)* (Isaiah 37:33–36)

Method:

1. To Isaiah 37:6, right after *Tell this to your master*, the insertion of *Thus says the Lord* allowed current Isaiah 37:6b–9a to follow directly. Current Isaiah 10:5–15 was removed from this passage to make room for a new prophecy allegedly against Sennacherib but actually against Nebuchadnezzar.
2. The addition of *Again he sent envoys to Hezekiah with this message:* allowed the author to incorporate an account of an imagined confrontation between Nebuchadnezzar and Jerusalem complete with commander's speech and responding prayer by Hezekiah (Isaiah 37:9b–20).
3. The addition of *Then Isaiah, son of Amoz, sent this message to Hezekiah:* allowed what was originally the introduction to the poetic prophetic answer of Isaiah to Sennacherib's boast to take its current position as Isaiah 37:21b–22 and to become the introduction to the poetic prophetic answer of a peace prophet to Nebuchadnezzar (Isaiah 37:22b–29).

4. Isaiah 37:30–32 looks intrusive, and may be (see below), but more probably was part of the original Isaiah$_B$ giving a sign confirming the validity of the prophecy. As such, it replaced the sign originally given in Isaiah$_A$ (Isaiah 10:5, 15; 37:38).
5. What is now Isaiah 37:33a was originally the introduction to what is now Isaiah 37:6b–7, the prosaic translation of the poetic prophecy of Isaiah against Sennacherib. Here, it serves as the introduction to the prosaic translation of the "peace" prophet's poetic prophecy against Nebuchadnezzar, which follows directly (Isaiah 33b–35).
6. Isaiah 37:36 (the angel of the Lord slaughtering Assyrians) was either retained from the Josianic rewrite or, less probably, added at this point.
7. The rest of Isaiah$_A$, namely the part in which the prophecy was fulfilled by the return home of Sennacherib and his assassination, plus the account of Hezekiah's illness and the mission of Merodach-Baladan, rounded out the passage (Isaiah 37:37–38 plus 38:1–39:8).

Less probably, Stage 4: Addition of the last verses

Approximate Date: Exilic or postexilic period

Motive: To inspire the faithful for a revolt against a new master

Text:

> *This shall be a sign for you: this year you shall eat the aftergrowth, next year, what grows of itself; but in the third year, sow and reap, plant vineyards and eat their fruit! The remaining survivors of the house of Judah shall again strike root below and bear fruit above. For out of Jerusalem shall come a remnant, and from Mount Zion, survivors. The zeal of the Lord of hosts shall do this.* (Isaiah 37:30–32)

Whether or not it was an exilic or postexilic addition, Isaiah 37:30–32 was crucial to the continuing validity of Zion Theology. With its help, impregnability could be redefined to mean that, even after its total destruction by Nebuchadnezzar, the city of Jerusalem would be rebuilt and in good time just as, even when crops fail completely, there is a plentiful harvest again in the third year.

To note is that the dialogue on this subject is taken up at some point by the Book of Jonah which adds that even after three days in the whale (the proverbial three years of punishment of 2 Kings 19:29–31 = Isaiah 37:30–31 which are also Hezekiah's three days of illness in 2 Kings 20:5–6 = Isaiah 38:4–6), the sinful must change their evil ways in order to avoid further punishment, and that God's mercy consists not in sparing the rod but in granting an opportunity to repent before it is too late.

BIBLIOGRAPHY

Ahlström, Gösta W.

1963 *Aspects of Syncretism in Israelite Religion*. Horae Soederblomianae 5. Lund: Gleerup.

Becking, B.

2003 "Chronology: A Skeleton without Flesh? Sennacherib's Campaign against Judah as a Case-Study." In *"Like a Bird in a Cage": The Invasion of Sennacherib in 701 BCE,* edited by L. L. Grabbe, pp. 46–72. Journal for the Study of the Old Testament, Supplement Series 363. Sheffield: Sheffield Academic Press.

Beckman, G.

1997 "Plague Prayers of Muršili II." In *The Context of Scripture*, Volume 1: *Canonical Compositions from the Biblical World*, edited by W. W. Hallo, pp. 156–60. Leiden and New York: Brill.

Ben Zvi, Ehud

1990 "Who Wrote the Speech of Rabshakeh and When?" *Journal of Biblical Literature* 109: 79–92.

2003 "Malleability and Its Limits: Sennacherib's Campaign against Judah as a Case-Study." In *"Like a Bird in a Cage": The Invasion of Sennacherib in 701 BCE,* edited by L. L. Grabbe, pp. 73–105. Journal for the Study of the Old Testament, Supplement Series 363. Sheffield: Sheffield Academic Press.

Blenkinsopp, Joseph

2000 *Isaiah 1–39: A New Translation with Introduction and Commentary*. New York: Doubleday.

Briant, Pierre

2002 *From Cyrus to Alexander: A History of the Persian Empire*. Translated by P. T. Daniels. Winona Lake: Eisenbrauns.

Cathcart, K. J.

1992 "The Book of Nahum." In *Anchor Bible Dictionary*, Volume 4: K–N, edited by D. N. Freedman, pp. 998–1000. New York: Doubleday.

Cathcart, Kevin J., and R. P. Gordon

1989 *The Targum of the Minor Prophets*. The Aramaic Bible 14. Wilmington: Michael Glazier.

Clements, R. E.

1984 *Isaiah and the Deliverance of Jerusalem: A Study of the Interpretation of Prophecy in the Old Testament*. Journal for the Study of the Old Testament, Supplement Series 13. Sheffield: Journal for the Study of the Old Testament Press.

Cogan, Mordechai

1974 *Imperialism and Religion: Assyria, Judah, and Israel in the Eighth and Seventh Centuries B.C.E.* Society of Biblical Literature, Monograph Series 19. Missoula: Scholars Press.

Cogan, Mordechai, and Hayim Tadmor

1988 *II Kings: A New Translation with Introduction and Commentary*. The Anchor Bible 11. Garden City: Doubleday.

Coggins, Richard J.

1985 *Israel among the Nations: A Commentary on the Books of Nahum and Obadiah*. Grand Rapids: Eerdmans.

Cohen, C.
1979 "Neo-Assyrian Elements in the First Speech of the Biblical Rab-Šaqê." *Israel Oriental Studies* 9: 32–48.

Curtis, Edward Lewis
1910 *The Books of Chronicles.* The International Critical Commentary. New York: Scribners.

Ellis, Maria de Jong
1989 "Observations on Mesopotamian Oracles and Prophetic Texts: Literary and Historical Considerations." *Journal of Cuneiform Studies* 41: 127–86.

al-Fakhri, J.
2008 "Excavation of the Well in Court 80." In *New Light on Nimrud*, edited by J. E. Curtis et al., pp. 99–100. London: British Institute for the Study of Iraq.

Frankena, R.
1954 *Takultu: De sacrale maaltijd in het Assyrische ritueel, met een overzicht over de in Assur vereerde goden.* Leiden: Brill.

Gallagher, William R.
1999 *Sennacherib's Campaign to Judah: New Studes.* Studies in the History and Culture of the Ancient Near East 18. Leiden and Boston: Brill.

Gonçalves, Francolino J.
1986 *L'expédition de Sennachérib en Palestine dans la littérature hébraïque ancienne.* Publications de l'Institut orientaliste de Louvain 34. Louvain la-Neuve: Université catholique de Louvain, Institut orientaliste.

Grabbe, Lester L., editor
2003 *"Like a Bird in a Cage": The Invasion of Sennacherib in 701 BCE.* Journal for the Study of the Old Testament, Supplement Series 363. Sheffield: Sheffield Academic Press.

Gray, G. B.
1912 *The Book of Isaiah* 1 *(I–XXVII).* The International Critical Commentary. New York: Charles Scribner.

Grayson, A. Kirk
1975a *Assyrian and Babylonian Chronicles.* Texts from Cuneiform Sources 5. Locust Valley: J. J. Augustin.
1975b *Babylonian Historical-Literary Texts.* Toronto: University of Toronto Press.

Hardmeier, Christof
1990 *Prophetie im Streit vor dem Untergang Judas: Erzählkommunikative Studien zur Entsehungssituation der Jesaya- und Jeremiaerzählungen in II Reg 18–20 und Jer 37–40.* Beihefte zur Zeitschrift für die Alttestmentliche Wissenschaft 187. Berlin: Walter de Gruyter.

Holloway, Steven W.
1995 "Harran: Cultic Geography in the Neo-Assyrian Empire and Its Implications for Sennacherib's 'Letter to Hezekiah' in 2 Kings." In *The Pitcher is Broken: Memorial Essays for Gösta W. Ahlström*, edited by S. W. Holloway and L. K. Handy, pp. 276–314. Journal for the Study of the Old Testament, Supplement Series 190. Sheffield: Sheffield Academic Press.
2002 *Aššur is King! Aššur is King! Religion and the Exercise of Power in the Neo-Assyrian Empire.* Culture and History of the Ancient Near East 10. Leiden: Brill.

Huddlestun, J. R.
2003 "Nahum, Nineveh, and the Nile: The Description of Thebes in Nahum 3:8–9." *Journal of Near Eastern Studies* 62: 97–110.

Hussein, M. M.

2008 "Recent Excavations in Nimrud." In *New Light on Nimrud*, edited by J. E. Curtis et al., pp. 83–98. London: British Institute for the Study of Iraq.

Jeremias, Jörg

1970 *Kultprophetie und Gerichtsverkündigung in der späten Königszeit Israels*. Wissenschaftliche Monographien zum Alten und Neuen Testament 35. Neukirchen-Vluyn: Neukirchener Verlag.

Jewish Publication Society

1999 *The Traditional Hebrew Text and the New Jewish Publication Society Translation*. 2nd edition. Philadelphia: The Jewish Publication Society.

Lambert, Wilfried G.

1978 *The Background of Jewish Apocalyptic*. London: Athlone Press of the University of London.

Levy, J.

1928 "Sanherib und Hizkia." *Orientalistische Literaturzeitung* 31: 156–58.

Liverani, Mario

2001 "The Fall of the Assyrian Empire: Ancient and Modern Interpretations." In *Empires: Perspectives from Archaeology and History*, edited by S. E. Alcock et al., pp. 374–91. Cambridge: Cambridge University Press.

Longman, Tremper

1997 "The Marduk Prophesy." In *The Context of Scripture*, Volume 1: *Canonical Compositions from the Biblical World*, edited by W. W. Hallo, pp. 480–81. Leiden and New York: Brill.

Machinist, Peter

2000 "The *Rab Šāqeh* at the Wall of Jerusalem: Israelite Identity in the Face of the Assyrian 'Other.'" *Hebrew Studies* 41: 151–68.

Mayer, Walter

2003 "Sennacherib's Campaign of 701 BCE" In *"Like a Bird in a Cage": The Invasion of Sennacherib in 701 BCE,* edited by L. L. Grabbe, pp. 168–200. Journal for the Study of the Old Testament, Supplement Series 363. Sheffield: Sheffield Academic Press.

Na'aman, Nadav

2000 "New Light on Hezekiah's Second Prophetic Story (2 Kgs 19,9b–35)." *Biblica* 81: 39–402.

2003 "Updating the Messages: Hezekiah's Second Prophetic Story (2 Kgs 19,9–35) and the Community of Babylonian Deportees." In *"Like a Bird in a Cage": The Invasion of Sennacherib in 701 BCE*, edited by L. L. Grabbe, pp. 201–20. Journal for the Study of the Old Testament, Supplement Series 363. Sheffield: Sheffield Academic Press.

Nissinen, Martti

2003 "Neither Prophesies nor Apocalypses: The Akkadian Literary Predictive Texts." In *Knowing the Ending from the Beginning: The Prophetic, the Apocalyptic and Their Relationship*, edited by L. L. Grabbe and R. D. Haak, pp. 134–48. London: T&T Clark.

2004 "What is Prophesy? An Ancient Near Eastern Perspective." In *Inspired Speech: Prophecy in the Ancient Near East; Essays in Honor of Herbert B. Huffmon*, edited by J. Kaltner and L. Stulman, pp. 17–37. Journal for the Study of the Old Testament, Supplement Series. London: T&T Clark.

Olmstead, A. T.

1948 *History of the Persian Empire*. Chicago: University of Chicago Press.

Oppenheim, A. Leo

1969 "Babylonian and Assyrian Historical Texts." In *Ancient Near Eastern Texts Relating to the Old Testament*, edited by J. B. Pritchard, p. 307. 3rd edition. Princeton: Princeton University Press.

Parpola, Simo

1980 "The Murderer of Sennacherib." In *Death in Mesopotamia: Papers Read at the XXVIe Rencontre Assyriologique Internationale*, edited by B. Alster, pp. 171–82. Copenhagen: Akademisk Forlag.

Pritchard, James B., editor

1969 *Ancient Near Eastern Texts Relating to the Old Testament*. 3rd edition. Princeton: Princeton University Press.

von Rad, Gerhard

1953 *Studies in Deuteronomy*. Translated by D. Stalker. Studies in Biblical Theology 9. Chicago: Henry Regnery.

Rofé, Alexander

1988 *The Prophetical Stories: The Narratives about Prophets in the Hebrew Bible, Their Literary Types and History*. Jerusalem: Magnes Press.

Rupprecht, Konrad

1977 *Der Tempel von Jerusalem*. Beihefte zur Zeitschrift für die alttestamentliche Wissenschaft 144. Berlin: Walter de Gruyter.

Sachs, A.

1969 "Temple Program for the New Year's Festival in Babylon." In *Ancient Near Eastern Texts Relating to the Old Testament*, edited by J. B. Pritchard, p. 334. 3rd edition. Princeton: Princeton University Press.

Scurlock, JoAnn

1990 "The Euphrates Flood and the Ashes of Nineveh (Diod. II.27.1–28.7)." *Historia* 39: 382–84.

2006a "Josiah: The View from Mesopotamia." *Biblical Research* 51: 9–24.

2006b "Whose Truth and Whose Justice?: The Uruk Prophecy Revisited." In *Orientalism, Assyriology and the Bible*, edited by S. W. Holloway, pp. 449–67. Hebrew Bible Monographs 10. Sheffield: Sheffield Phoenix.

2009 "Nisroch." In *The New Interpreter's Dictionary of the Bible*, vol. N, p. 277. Nashville: Abingdon Press.

Sherwin-White, Susan

1987 "Seleucid Babylonia: A Case Study for the Installation and Development of Greek Rule." In *Hellenism in the East: The Interaction of Greek and non-Greek Civilizations from Syria to Central Asia after Alexander*, edited by A. Kuhrt and S. Sherwin-White, pp. 1–31. Hellenistic Culture and Society 2. Berkeley: University of California Press.

Smelik, K. A. D.

1986 "Distortion of Old Testament Prophesy" In *Crises and Perspectives: Studies in Ancient Near Eastern Polytheism, Biblical Theology, Palestinian Archaeology, and Intertestamental Literature; Papers Read at the Joint British-Dutch Old Testament Conference, Held at Cambridge, U.K., 1985*, edited by J. C. de Moor, pp. 70–93. Oudtestamentische Studiën 24. Leiden: Brill.

Smith, John M. P.

1911 *A Critical and Exegetical Commentary on the Books of Micah, Zephaniah and Nahum*. The International Critical Commentary 15. New York: Scribners.

Stade, B.

1886 "Miscellen. 16. Anmerkungen zu 2 Kö 15–21. Zu 18,13–19,37." *Zeitschrift für die alttestamentliche Wissenschaft* 4: 172–86.

Taylor, C. L., and J. T. Cleland

1956 "The Book of Nahum." In *The Interpreter's Bible* 6. New York: Abingdon.

Uehlinger, Christoph

2003 "Clio in a World of Pictures: Another Look at the Lachish Reliefs from Sennacherib's Southwest Palace at Nineveh." In *"Like a Bird in a Cage": The Invasion of Sennacherib in 701 BCE*, edited by L. L. Grabbe, pp. 221–307. Journal for the Study of the Old Testament, Supplement Series 363. Sheffield: Sheffield Academic Press.

Weinfeld, Moshe

1964 "Cult Centralization in Israel in the Light of a Neo-Babylonian Analogy." *Journal of Near Eastern Studies* 23: 202–12.

Wildberger, Hans

1991 *Isaiah 1–12: A Continental Commentary*. Translated by T. H. Trapp. Minneapolis: Fortress.

1997 *Isaiah 13–27: A Continental Commentary*. Translated by T. H. Trapp. Minneapolis: Fortress.

2002 *Isaiah 28–39: A Continental Commentary*. Translated by T. H. Trapp. Minneapolis: Fortress.

Wise, Michael O.; Martin G. Abegg, Jr.; and Edward M. Cook

1996 *Dead Sea Scrolls: A New Translation*. San Francisco: Harper.

15

TRACES OF THE OMEN SERIES *ŠUMMA IZBU* IN CICERO, *DE DIVINATIONE*[*]

JOHN JACOBS, LOYOLA UNIVERSITY MARYLAND

Divination played a central role not only in the cultures of the ancient Near East, but also in those of the ancient Mediterranean. Recent years have witnessed a welcome resurgence of interest in the subject — divination between theory and practice, divination between belief and skepticism, divination between religion and science.[1] In particular, scholars have focused on the central role that divination played in the social, religious, and political life of the fall of the Roman Republic, during the century beginning with the Gracchan revolution (133–121 B.C.) and ending with Octavian's victory over Antony and Cleopatra at the battle of Actium (31 B.C.).[2] One of the key figures during this tumultuous period of transition from Republic to Empire was the orator and statesman Marcus Tullius Cicero (106–43 B.C.). Like many, if not most, of his contemporaries, Cicero held complex, and often conflicting, views about the role of divination both in the life of the individual and in the life of the state.[3] In a series of three treatises composed around the time of Caesar's assassination on the Ides of March in 44 B.C. — *De natura deorum* (*On the Nature of the Gods*), *De divinatione* (*On Divination*), and *De fato* (*On Fate*) — Cicero examines how the major contemporary schools of philosophy address the many difficult and challenging questions concerning the relationship between the worlds of god and man. While scholars have long studied divination in the ancient Near East and in the ancient Mediterranean in isolation, few have undertaken any substantial comparative analysis of the available material. In this paper, I attempt to begin to bridge this divide: in particular, I attempt to discover traces of the omen series *Šumma izbu* in the *De divinatione* and to explain how that omen series may have been transmitted, along with others, from east to west.

In the two-book *De divinatione*, as elsewhere in his extensive corpus of rhetorical and philosophical works, Cicero explores his chosen subject through a fictional dialogue. On this occasion, he converses with his younger brother, Quintus — as literary characters, and not as

* I would like to thank Amar Annus for organizing the University of Chicago Oriental Institute Seminar "Science and Superstition: Interpretation of Signs in the Ancient World" and for inviting me to present an earlier version of this paper on that occasion. (An even earlier version was presented at the 218th annual meeting of the American Oriental Society, also in Chicago, in March 2008.)

1 For the ancient Near East, see Maul 1993; Rochberg 2004; and Heeßel 2007. For the ancient Mediterranean, see Wildfang and Isager 2000; Johnston and Struck 2005; and Kany-Turpin 2005. Standard literature on divination in the ancient Mediterranean includes Bouché-Leclercq 1879–82 (Greek, Etruscan, and Roman divination); Wülker 1903 (Roman); Luterbacher 1904 (Roman); Thulin 1905–09 (Etruscan); Halliday 1913 (Greek); and Bloch 1963 (Greek, Etruscan, and Roman). See also Johnston 2008 for a brief introduction to certain aspects of Greek divination.

2 See MacBain 1982; Rosenberger 1998; Rasmussen 2003; and Engels 2007. For divination in Imperial Rome, see Vigourt 2001. The most important ancient sources include, besides Cicero, the omen reports in, among others, Livy, Tacitus, and Suetonius, as well as the interesting collection of prodigies later compiled by Julius Obsequens.

3 For Cicero's views on divination, see Guillaumont 1984 and 2006; as well as Linderski 1986.

historical figures speaking *in propria persona* — during a visit to his estate at Tusculum (cf. Cicero, *De divinatione* 1.5.8–6.11).[4] The dramatic date of the conversation may have been some time late in 45 or early in 44 B.C.; in all likelihood, Cicero substantially completed the *De divinatione* before Caesar's assassination, but revised it and (only then) published it shortly after the Ides of March.[5] In book 1, Quintus presents the traditional Stoic and Peripatetic arguments in favor of the view that divination is a means by which man can (potentially) discern the will of the gods; in book 2, Marcus furnishes a typically Academic deconstruction of these arguments.[6] For more than a century, scholars concentrated most of their efforts on the study of Cicero's sources, including, most notably, the Peripatetic Cratippus of Pergamum (ca. first century B.C.) and the Stoic Posidonius (ca. 135–ca. 51 B.C.).[7] During the past twenty-five years, however, scholars have rediscovered the *De divinatione* as an erudite and sophisticated treatment of an important cultural phenomenon, something much different from and, accordingly, something much more than a straightforward expression of Cicero's (or, rather, Quintus' and Marcus') personal views.[8] Nevertheless, the *De divinatione* also remains an important source for information about the *Realien* of divination in the ancient Mediterranean (Greek, Etruscan, and Roman), as well as in the ancient Near East.

Conversely, the omen series of the ancient Near East remain a largely unexplored, but potentially quite significant, source of information about the *Realien* of divination not only in the ancient Near East, but also in the ancient Mediterranean. These series, now extant only in fragments for the most part, cover virtually every type of divinatory practice, from terrestrial and celestial omens to teratological, physiognomic, and oneiromantic (or oneirological) omens, from lecanomancy (oil divination) to libanomancy (smoke divination). Of particular importance for the comparative study of divination in the ancient Near East and the ancient Mediterranean are the twenty-four tablets of the teratological series known by the incipit *Šumma izbu* ("If the malformed birth").[9] Each of the entries in this omen series appears in the form of a conditional statement, consisting of a protasis and an apodosis (or, in some cases,

[4] Giomini 1975 provides the standard critical edition, while the standard commentaries in English are Pease 1920–23 (books 1 and 2) and Wardle 2006 (only book 1). Both commentators also offer good overviews of the place of the dialogue in Republican Rome and in Cicero's oeuvre: see Pease 1920–23: 9–13; and Wardle 2006: 1–8.

[5] For these dates, see Pease 1920–23: 13–15; and Wardle 2006: 37–43, as well as, for further discussion of the manifold problems surrounding this chronology, Durand 1903; Falconer 1923 (*contra* Durand); and Giomini 1971.

[6] For an overview of the structure and themes of the work, see Pease 1920–23: 15–18; and Wardle 2006: 20–28 (although Wardle unfortunately appears to overlook Goar 1968, a brief but interesting reading of the dialogue). For the sake of clarity and simplicity, I use the *cognomen* "Cicero" when I wish to refer to the author of the work, but the *praenomina* "Quintus" and "Marcus" when I wish to refer to the two participants in the dialogue.

[7] For a summary of the major results of this extensive *Quellenforschung*, see Pease 1920–23: 18–29; and Wardle 2006: 28–36 (although Wardle unfortunately appears to overlook Hartfelder 1878, a short but important study).

[8] For a balanced discussion about the central issues addressed by this recent work, see Wardle 2006: 8–28. The scholarship essentially divides into two camps: the "traditional" reading (e.g., Linderski 1982; Momigliano 1984; and Troiani 1984) and the newer "Cambridge" reading (e.g., Denyer 1985; Beard 1986; and Schofield 1986; cf. Timpanaro 1994 and Repici 1995 *per contra*). See most recently Krostenko 2000, a lengthy and largely successful attempt at harmonizing these two readings. See also Pease 1920–23: 29–37, for the *Nachleben* of the work.

[9] Leichty (1970) provides the standard critical edition, building on the texts in Fossey 1912 and Dennefeld 1914: see also now Heeßel 2007. Leichty (1970: 1–2) provides an indispensable summary of the key scholarship on the omen series, including Jastrow 1914 and Fossey 1921–22; see also now the editions of the Ugaritic and Hittite material.

multiple apodoses). The protases, themselves organized according to certain fixed patterns (e.g., from head to toe, from right to left to both), determine the arrangement of the series: tablets 1–4 ("omens derived from human births"); tablet 5 ("omens derived from sheep"); tablets 6–17 ("omens derived from the birth of an *izbu*"); and tablets 18–24 ("omens derived from specific animals"). The apodoses, in contrast, concern both public and private affairs, including "stock" and "historical" apodoses.[10] In addition to the evidence offered by the tablets themselves, scholars have also collected other materials attesting to the importance of birth divination in the daily life of the ancient Near East and, later, in the daily life of the ancient Mediterranean, especially among the Etruscans and the Romans.[11] Toward the end of the introduction to his edition, Leichty catalogs the extant tablets for the series *Šumma izbu*, as well as the extant excerpt and commentary tablets — materials in Akkadian, Ugaritic, Hittite, and Hurrian which come from sites all across the ancient Near East and which span a range of some fifteen hundred years, from the Old Babylonian period to the Seleucid era.[12] Furthermore, in his proposed timeline for the transmission of this omen series through these various channels, Leichty explicitly supports the notion that knowledge of these teratological omens may have spread from the ancient Near East to the ancient Mediterranean.[13]

Thus far, however, no Classicist seems to have taken note of this idea and considered the possible influence of the omen series *Šumma izbu* on Etruscan and Roman divination. This is all the more surprising since Cicero himself evinces, at the very least, a good general grasp of the sheer variety of divinatory practices throughout both the ancient Mediterranean and the ancient Near East (cf. Cicero, *De divinatione,* 1.1.1–4.7 and 1.41.90–42.94, especially 1.42.93, on the peculiar Etruscan interest in teratology).[14] In this paper, I present the initial results of a broader inquiry into the relationship between the ancient Near East and the ancient Mediterranean in the realm of divination. While there are certainly many omen series which appear to have left at least some traces in Greek and Latin literature (and, especially, in the *De divinatione*), the omen series *Šumma izbu* appears to have left some of the clearest and

[10] See Leichty 1970: 2–7, whose terminology I adopt. For the so-called "historical" omens, see also Nougayrol 1944–45; and Goetze 1947a (especially 253 n. 1 and the *Šumma izbu* omens numbered 2, 15, 18, 24, and 37).

[11] See Leichty 1970: 7–16; cf. Hunger 1909 (on animal omens in the related series *Šumma ālu* ["When the City"]). For birth divination among the Greeks, see Schatz 1901; and Steiner 1909; cf. Leichty 1970: 14.

[12] See Leichty 1970: 20–30, in which is discussed not only "the sources" and the "text history," but also several of the technical issues surrounding the "language and writing system" of the tablets. For the two Old Babylonian tablets, see Leichty 1970: 201–07; as well as Goetze 1947b: 9–11, 13, and pl. 10 (= YOS 10 12), and 11, 15, and pls. 117–18 (= YOS 10 56). For the Ugaritic tablets, see now Dietrich and Loretz 1990; and Pardee 2000. For the Hittite tablets, see now Riemschneider 1970 and 2004. In his review of Leichty 1970, Heimpel (1973: 586–87), argues (*contra* Leichty 1970: 21) that STT 2 307 can be placed and that it can be used for a fuller reconstruction of the text at the beginning of tablet 19 (especially the historical omen numbered 25 [for Narām-Sin]).

[13] See Leichty 1970: 21, with a timetable and a chart illustrating this transmission; under the entry in the timetable for ca. 1350 B.C., he notes, "Still later, the tradition, if not the texts, may pass to the Etruscans and then to Rome."

[14] For Cicero, *De divinatione* 1.1.1–4.7, see Pease 1920–23: 39–65 *ad* 1.1–7; Badalì 1976; and Wardle 2006: 90–118 *ad* 1.1–7. For Cicero, *De divinatione* 1.41.90–42.94, see Pease 1920–23: 254–64 *ad* 1.90–94; and Wardle 2006: 321–31 *ad* 1.90–94. In their comments on the key passage (1.42.93), Pease (1920–23: 262–63 *ad* 1.93) at least mentions the omen series *Šumma izbu*, while Wardle (2006: 329 *ad* 1.93), faced with one of Pease's many overwhelming lists of primary and secondary sources, drops all references to the ancient Near Eastern material in his condensed version of the note.

most interesting of these traces. Accordingly, in what follows, I first review the evidence for abnormal human births in the *De divinatione*. Then, I discuss one of these abnormal births in detail (the lion birth omen recorded in Cicero, *De divinatione* 1.53.121) and connect it with the legend surrounding the birth of Pericles, recorded first by Herodotus in his *Historiae* (6.131.2) and then, later, by Plutarch in his biography *Pericles* (3). Finally, I will review the evidence for abnormal human births and, in particular, the evidence for other lion birth omens in the series *Šumma izbu* (especially the lion birth omen recorded in *Šumma izbu* 1.5). By the end of the paper, we will see how, in all likelihood, not just the tradition, but even the text, passed to the Etruscans and then to Rome.

ABNORMAL HUMAN BIRTHS IN CICERO, *DE DIVINATIONE*

Quintus mentions a number of abnormal births and, especially, abnormal human births in his argument in favor of divination in book 1. In an early list of prodigies, he includes the example of a mule which had recently foaled: *quid, qui inridetur partus hic mulae nonne, quia fetus extitit in sterilitate naturae, praedictus est ab haruspicibus incredibilis partus malorum?* ("Why? Should the recent parturition of a mule (a creature which is naturally sterile), which was predicted by [the] *haruspices* as an incredible progeny of evils, be ridiculed?" 1.18.36).[15] In a later list, Quintus mentions the example of the birth of an hermaphrodite: *quid, cum Cumis Apollo sudavit Capuae Victoria, quid, ortus androgyni nonne fatale quoddam monstrum fuit?* ("When Apollo sweated at Cumae and Victory at Capua, when men-women were born, was it not a portent of disaster?" 1.43.98).[16] In a final list (to which we will return shortly), he even reports the birth of a two-headed child: *et si puella nata biceps esset, seditionem in populo fore, corruptelam et adulterium domi* ("If a girl were born with two heads[,] there would be popular revolt[,] and seduction and adultery in the home" 1.53.121).[17] In general, then, Cicero displays a profound knowledge of the various traditions related to birth divination in both the

[15] Unless otherwise stated, all translations of *De divinatione* 1 are from Wardle 2006, while all translations of *De divinatione* 2 are my own. Pease (1920–23: 153–55 *ad* 1.36) catalogs other instances of the foaling of mules and also notes the likely paronomasia between *partus ... mulae* and *partus ... malorum*, while Wardle (2006: 199 *ad* 1.36) identifies the omen with an event either in 50 (Obsequens, *Liber prodigiorum* 65) or 49 B.C. (Appian, *Bella civilia* 2.5.36, not 2.144, as given in Wardle 2005; cf. 1.9.83, in 83). Cf. also Pliny the Elder, *Historia naturalis* 8.73.173. In his response to Quintus, Marcus addresses this prodigy in 2.22.49–50 (see Pease 1920–23: 434–35 *ad* 2.49–50) and 2.28.61 (see Pease 1920–23: 451–52 *ad* 2.61).

[16] Pease (1920–23: 272–73 *ad* 1.98) again catalogs other instances of the prodigy, while Wardle (2006: 340–41 *ad* 1.98) adds to this inventory and again notes the historical context of many of the omens. Cf. also Pliny the Elder, *Historia naturalis* 7.11.33. (Wardle incorrectly renders *ortus androgyni* in the plural: *androgyni* is a genitive with *ortus*, not a nominative.)

[17] Pease (1920–23: 313–14 *ad* 1.121) once more catalogs other instances of the prodigy (cf. Cicero, *De divinatione* 2.58.120, and especially, Lucan, *Bellum civile* 1.616–38), while Wardle (2006: 399 *ad* 1.121) once more adds to the inventory and notes the historical context of many of the omens. At the end of his note on the passage, Wardle also observes how "the interpretation reveals the Etruscan distinction between public and private significance (Thulin 1909: 116 n. 1)": as we have seen, however, this distinction between public (*seditionem* ***in populo*** *fore*) and private (*corruptelam et adulterium* **domi** [*fore*]) affairs is a feature which dates back to the origins of the tradition in the ancient Near East.

ancient Mediterranean and the ancient Near East.[18] In what follows, I consider several other omen reports in the *De divinatione*, all of which concern not just abnormal human births, but even, more specifically, dreams had about abnormal human births by pregnant mothers and the eventual fulfillment of those dreams in the nature and character of the child when he is born.

Dreams, of course, play a major role in both books of the *De divinatione*, with Quintus first arguing for their potential validity in 1.20.39–30.65, and then Marcus arguing against that position in 2.58.119–72.150.[19] Dreams had by pregnant mothers about abnormal human births constitute an interesting and important category of this phenomenon — something of a mixture between "artificial" divination (i.e., teratology) and "natural" divination (i.e., oneirology).[20] At one end of the spectrum, Quintus introduces perhaps the most famous of these abnormal-birth dream omens during his treatment of dreams in book 1: the story that Hecuba, the wife of King Priam of Troy, first dreamed that she gave birth to a burning torch and then actually gave birth to Paris (or Alexander), whose rape of Helen caused the outbreak of the Trojan War and, thus, the fall of Troy (1.21.42, including a quotation from Ennius' *Alexander*).[21] At the other end of the spectrum, Marcus introduces a general report about another of these abnormal-birth dream omens during his treatment of the subject later in book 2: the story that an unnamed woman, unsure whether or not she was pregnant, first dreamed that her womb had been sealed and then consulted two separate dream interpreters, only to receive the conflicting explanations that her dream might or might not signify that she was, in fact, with child (2.70.145).[22] In each of these passages, Cicero divides the narrative into two major sections: first, the dream itself (*parere ... / visa est*, 1.21.42 ~ *parere ... visa est*, 2.70.145) and, then, the interpretation(s) of the dream.

[18] Leichty (1970: 14–16) briefly discusses some of this material, but mentions only a few of the examples cited here. Other famous examples include the woman who gave birth to a serpent in 83 B.C. (Pliny the Elder, *Historia naturalis* 7.11.34; Obsequens, *Liber prodigiorum* 57; and Appian, *Bella civilia* 1.9.83 — Wardle [2006: 329 *ad* 1.93] somewhat misleadingly uses the plural "women with children of different species" when he cites these three passages) and the woman who gave birth to a boy with an elephant's head at Sinuessa in 209 B.C. (Livy, *Ab urbe condita* 27.11.5), as well as the two pigs born with human heads, again at Sinuessa(!), in 200 and 198 B.C. (Livy, *Ab urbe condita* 31.12.7 and 32.9.3). Cf. also the vague *biformes hominum partus* in Tacitus, *Annales* 12.64.1.

[19] For dreams elsewhere in the work, see 1.2.4, 3.5–7, 6.10–12, 32.70–71, 44.99, 50.114–51.117, 53.121, 55.124–58.132; 2.5.12–6.17, 11.26–27, 48.100, 49.101, and 52.107–53.109 (with Pease and Wardle). Recent literature on dreams in the ancient Mediterranean includes Walde 2001; Holowchak 2002; and Harris 2003.

[20] Lanzoni 1927 provides the only full-length study of the subject. I will not include the dream had by the mother of Phalaris (1.23.46 and 2.66.136) in this discussion, since Cicero does not explicitly say that she was pregnant at the time: nevertheless, the content and the language of the passage strongly suggest that she was (cf. especially 1.20.39, which I discuss in detail below). For Cicero, *De divinatione* 1.23.46, see Pease 1920–23: 173–74 *ad* 1.46; and Wardle 2006: 222–23 *ad* 1.46. For Cicero, *De divinatione* 2.66.136, see Pease 1920–23: 566 *ad* 2.136.

[21] For the birth of Paris (or Alexander) and the fall of Troy, see also 1.31.66–67 (including another quotation from Ennius' *Alexander*), 1.39.84–40.89, and 2.55.112–113 (with Pease and Wardle). For a similar connection between Catiline and the near fall of Rome in 63 B.C. (through a conspiracy hatched by Catiline and quashed by Cicero), see 1.11.17–13.22 and 2.20.45–21.47; cf. the link between the destruction of the temple of Artemis at Ephesus and the birth of another Alexander, Alexander the Great, in 356 B.C., in 1.23.47 (again, with Pease and Wardle).

[22] See Pease 1920–23: 575–76 *ad* 2.145.

At the beginning of his argument in favor of the potential validity of dreams, Quintus introduces an example of an abnormal-birth dream omen drawn not from mythology or popular folklore, but from history — the birth of Dionysius I (ca. 430–367 B.C.), tyrant of Syracuse:

> Sed omittamus oracula, veniamus ad somnia. de quibus disputans Chrysippus multis et minutis somniis colligendis facit idem quod Antipater ea conquirens, quae Antiphontis interpretatione explicata declarant illa quidem acumen interpretis, sed exemplis grandioribus decuit uti. Dionysi mater eius qui Syracosiorum tyrannus fuit, ut scriptum apud Philistum est et doctum hominem et diligentem et aequalem temporum illorum, cum praegnans hunc ipsum Dionysium alvo contineret, somniavit se peperisse satyriscum. huic interpretes portentorum, qui Galeotae tum in Sicilia nominabantur, responderunt, ut ait Philistus, eum quem illa peperisset clarissimum Graeciae diuturna cum fortuna fore.
>
> But let's leave oracles and let's come on to dreams. In his discussion of these Chrysippus, by collecting many trivial dreams, does what Antipater does, searching out those dreams which, when explained according to the interpretation of Antiphon, demonstrate the intelligence of the interpreter, but he ought to have used more weighty examples. As it is written in Philistus, a learned and careful man, a contemporary of the times, the mother of the Dionysius who was the tyrant of Syracuse, when pregnant and carrying this Dionysius in her womb, dreamt that she had given birth to a small satyr. The interpreters of portents, who at that time in Sicily were called Galeotae, replied to her, so Philistus says, that the son to whom she gave birth would be the most famous in Greece enjoying long-lasting good fortune.
>
> — Cicero, *De divinatione* 1.20.39[23]

In this omen report, Cicero again divides the narrative into two major sections. First, he repeats the dream itself: *Dionysi mater eius ..., cum praegnans hunc ipsum Dionysium alvo contineret, somniavit se peperisse satyriscum*. Then, he recounts the interpretation of the dream: *huic interpretes portentorum, ..., responderunt, ..., eum quem illa peperisset clarissimum Graeciae diuturna cum fortuna fore*. Several features mark the derivative nature of this report. On the one hand, Cicero inserts parenthetical expansions in order to explain, for example, which Dionysius he is speaking about (*Dionysi mater eius* ***qui Syracosiorum tyrannus fuit***) and who the Galeotae are (*huic interpretes portentorum,* ***qui Galeotae tum in Sicilia nominabantur***). On the other hand, these parenthetical expansions necessitate resumptive and, therefore, repetitive phraseology like *cum praegnans hunc ipsum Dionysium alvo contineret* and *quem illa peperisset*. Most of all, of course, Cicero cites Philistus (ca. 430–356 B.C.) not once but twice as his authority for the story, thereby disclaiming any responsibility for its veracity or falsity (*ut scriptum apud Philistum est* and *ut ait Philistus*). In an effort at further supporting the authority of his source, Cicero offers yet another parenthetical expansion, on Philistus' credibility (*et doctum hominem et diligentem et aequalem temporum illorum*). In moving from

[23] See Pease 1920–23: 161–64 *ad* 1.39; and Wardle 2006: 208–12 *ad* 1.39. In his response to Quintus, Marcus addresses this dream in 2.66.136 (see Pease 1920–23: 566 *ad* 2.136). Cf. also a second prodigy pertaining to the tyrant cited by Cicero from Philistus, mentioned by Quintus in 1.33.73 (see Pease 1920–23: 219–21 *ad* 1.73; and Wardle 2006: 284–86 *ad* 1.73) and by Marcus in 2.31.67 (see Pease 1920–23: 460 *ad* 2.67).

mythology and popular folklore to history, Cicero exercises more caution in his handling of *exempla*.[24]

This review of abnormal births and, especially, abnormal-birth dream omens, brings us to perhaps the most intriguing and most important of these reports: the lion birth omen related by Quintus in 1.53.121. Before we proceed with the analysis of that passage, however, I would like to pause for a moment in order to address a point of lexicography. Even though translators and commentators alike universally understand *videor* (the passive of *video* "to see") in the sense of "to dream" in 1.21.42, 2.70.145, and 1.20.39 (as well as in 1.23.46), neither of the two major Latin dictionaries registers this meaning among its many entries for the verb.[25] While this presents no major obstacle, since lexica rarely provide an accounting for every instance of every word, it is nevertheless reassuring to discover incontrovertible evidence for the equation *videri* = *somniare* in Valerius Maximus' version of the dream in Cicero, *De divinatione* 1.20.39:

> Tutioris somni mater eiusdem Dionysi. quae cum eum conceptum utero haberet, parere visa est Satyriscum, consultoque prodigiorum interprete clarissimum ac potentissimum Graii sanguinis futurum certo cum eventu cognovit.
>
> The mother of the same Dionysius had a dream that was safer for her. While she bore Dionysius in her womb, she dreamt that she gave birth to a little satyr. She consulted an interpreter of prodigies, and he realized that her son would be the most famous and powerful man of the Greek race, and that is exactly what happened.
>
> — Valerius Maximus, *Facta et dicta memorabilia* 1.7.ext.7[26]

Now, where Cicero has the reflexive construction *somniavit se peperisse satyriscum*, Valerius has the passive construction *parere visa est Satyriscum* — the same passive construction which also occurs several times in Cicero (*parere ... / visa est*, 1.21.42 and *parere ... visa est*, 2.70.145, as well as *visam esse videre*, 1.23.46).[27] As we will see momentarily, Cicero also uses *videor* in precisely this sense in 1.53.121. Accordingly, there is no reason not to interpret that omen, like those in 1.21.42, 2.70.145, and 1.20.39 (and 1.23.46, too?) as an abnormal-birth dream omen.[28]

---

[24] The dream of the mother of Phalaris (1.23.46; cf. 2.66.136) exhibits all the same features as the dream of the mother of Dionysius, including not just the dream and its interpretation, but also the careful citation of a respected authority, in this case, Heraclides Ponticus (fourth century B.C.); cf. ***doctus*** *vir*, 1.23.46 ~ ***doctum*** *hominem*, 1.20.39.

[25] See C. T. Lewis and C. Short, *A Latin Dictionary* (Oxford, 1879), s.v. *vĭdĕo* 7; and P. G. W. Glare, ed., *Oxford Latin Dictionary* (Oxford and New York, 1982), s.v. *uideō* 20–24. The *Thesaurus Linguae Latinae* has not yet reached this letter and likely will not for some time to come.

[26] The translation is from Walker 2004. (The subject of *cognovit*, however, is not the interpreter but the mother.)

[27] In general, Valerius Maximus, *Facta et dicta memorabilia* 1.7.ext.7 virtually repeats Cicero, *De divinatione* 1.20.39 verbatim: *mater eiusdem Dionysi* ~ *Dionysi mater eius*; *quae cum eum conceptum utero haberet* ~ *cum praegnans hunc ipsum Dionysium alvo contineret*; *parere visa est Satyriscum* ~ *somniavit se peperisse satyriscum*; *consultoque prodigiorum interprete* ~ *huic interpretes portentorum, ..., responderunt*; and *clarissimum ac potentissimum Graii sanguinis futurum certo cum eventu cognovit* ~ *eum quem illa peperisset clarissimum Graeciae diuturna cum fortuna fore*.

[28] There are, however, several complexities of usage which remain to be examined in greater detail. For example, when Cicero uses *videor* in the sense of "to dream" he (or, in the case of 1.21.42, Ennius) often adds some other indication that the verb is to be understood in this sense, especially through the addition of a prepositional phrase (cf. *in somnis*, 1.21.42 and *in quiete*, 2.70.145, as well as *in somnis*, 1.23.46). The collocation *videor, ..., somniare* in 2.68.142 presents another problem — perhaps *somniare* should be

CICERO, *DE DIVINATIONE* 1.53.121

Toward the end of his lengthy exposition of the Stoic and Peripatetic arguments in favor of the validity of divination in book 1, Quintus restates his case for both natural and artificial divination, relying heavily on the authority of Posidonius (1.49.109–57.131: note the explicit mention of Posidonius in 55.125 and 57.130; cf. 1.3.6, 30.64; 2.15.35, 21.47).[29] In the midst of this restatement of his case, he dwells at some length on the possibility of rational explanation(s) for divination, and he marshals together several historical *exempla* as evidence:

> Idemque mittit et signa nobis eius generis, qualia permulta historia tradidit, quale scriptum illud videmus: si luna paulo ante solis ortum defecisset in signo Leonis, fore ut armis Dareus et Persae ab Alexandro et Macedonibus [proelio] vincerentur Dareusque moreretur; et si puella nata biceps esset, seditionem in populo fore, corruptelam et adulterium domi; **et si mulier leonem peperisse visa esset, fore ut ab exteris gentibus vinceretur ea res publica in qua id contigisset**.
>
> And it is the same god who sends signs to us of the kind that history has handed down to us in very great number, such as we see recorded here: if an eclipse of the moon occurred a little before sunrise in the sign Leo, Darius and the Persians would be defeated militarily by Alexander and the Macedonians [in battle] and Darius would die; if a girl were born with two heads there would be popular revolt and seduction and adultery in the home; **and if a woman dreamt that she gave birth to a lion, the country in which this had happened would be overcome by foreign nations.**
>
> — Cicero, *De divinatione* 1.53.121[30]

In this important passage, Quintus mentions three distinct omens as the type of *exempla* to be found throughout Greek and Latin historiography. Interestingly, all three omens appear in the form of a conditional statement, with a protasis in the pluperfect subjunctive (*defecisset, nata ... esset*, and *visa esset*) and an apodosis either in the future infinitive or in the equivalent *fore ut* construction (*fore ut ... vincerentur ... moreretur, fore,* and *fore ut ... vinceretur*) — that is, what is known as a future most vivid conditional statement in indirect discourse (i.e., *oratio obliqua*) in secondary sequence. Beyond this morphosyntactical similarity, Cicero also links the first and third omens via paronomasia between the proper noun (i.e., constellation) *Leo* (*in signo Leonis*) in the protasis of the celestial omen and the common noun *leo* (*leonem*) in the protasis of the teratological / oneirological omen.[31] He then cements this connection between the two omens via the repetition of the verb *vinco*, describing the defeat of Darius and the Persians in the first omen (*vincerentur*; cf. *moreretur*) and the defeat of the city in which the woman has the dream about giving birth to the lion in the third (*vinceretur*). In

deleted as an explanatory gloss? Regardless of these difficulties, however, the equation *videri* = *somniare* is secure, and I would also like to note that δοκέω, the corresponding verb in Greek, bears the meaning "to dream" from Aeschylus (τεκεῖν δράκοντ' ἔδοξεν *Choephori* 527) to Artemidorus (throughout his *Oneirocritica*) and beyond: see H. G. Liddell, R. Scott, and H. S. Jones, *A Greek-English Lexicon* (9th edition; Oxford and New York), s.v. δοκέω I. 1.

[29] For the distribution of the material in Cicero, *De divinatione* 1.49.109–57.131 between Cratippus and Posidonius, see Pease 1920–23: 20–24, especially 22 n. 100 (on pp. 22–23); and Wardle 2006: 30–31, 32–36, and 370–71 *ad* 1.109–31.

[30] See Pease 1920–23: 313–14 *ad* 1.121; and Wardle 2006: 398–99 *ad* 1.121.

[31] For lions in general in the ancient Mediterranean, see Steier 1926; and Usener 1994.

what follows, I focus on this third omen, the lion birth omen, although I return to the first and second in the final section.

Surprisingly, neither Pease nor Wardle offers much in the way of commentary on this third omen.[32] Pease connects the dream in 1.53.121 with that had by the mother of Dionysius I in 1.20.39, and then he connects it with the legend surrounding the birth of Pericles: Wardle, in turn, simply repeats this information.[33] In connecting the omen with the dream had by Agariste while she was pregnant with Pericles, however, neither Pease nor Wardle adequately addresses the essential *Quellenfrage*: did Cicero derive his information from Herodotus directly or, rather, indirectly through Posidonius?[34] While nothing stands in the way of Cicero taking this material from Posidonius, nothing also stands in the way of his taking it from Herodotus — or his taking it from Posidonius in the full knowledge that it ultimately went back to Herodotus. Given the fact that Cicero explicitly attributes the very next *exemplum* to Herodotus by name, I incline toward the opinion that Cicero not only knew that Herodotus was the ultimate source, but also used him directly.[35] However one chooses to approach this question, all agree that the omen in 1.53.121 ultimately goes back, in some way, to the legend surrounding the birth of Pericles:

> τούτων δὲ συνοικησάντων γίνεται Κλεισθένης τε ὁ τὰς φυλὰς καὶ τὴν δημοκρατίαν Ἀθηναίοισι καταστήσας, ἔχων τὸ οὔνομα ἀπὸ τοῦ μητροπάτορος τοῦ Σικυωνίου· οὗτος τε δὴ γίνεται Μεγακλέϊ καὶ Ἱπποκράτης, ἐκ δὲ Ἱπποκράτεος Μεγακλέης τε ἄλλος καὶ Ἀγαρίστη ἄλλη, ἀπὸ τῆς Κλεισθένεος Ἀγαρίστης ἔχουσα τὸ οὔνομα. **ἣ συνοικήσασά τε Ξανθίππῳ τῷ Ἀρίφρονος καὶ ἔγκυος ἐοῦσα εἶδε ὄψιν ἐν τῷ ὕπνῳ, ἐδόκεε δὲ λέοντα τεκεῖν· καὶ μετ᾽ ὀλίγας ἡμέρας τίκτει Περικλέα Ξανθίππῳ.**
>
> The marriage of Megacles and Agariste produced the Cleisthenes who fixed the tribes and established democracy at Athens. He was named after his mother's father, the tyrant of Sicyon. As well as Cleisthenes, Megacles also had a son called Hippocrates, who became the father of another Megacles and another Agariste, named after Cleisthenes' daughter. **This Agariste, the daughter of Hippocrates, married Xanthippus the son of Ariphron. When she was pregnant she dreamt she gave birth to a lion, and then a few days later she bore Xanthippus a son, Pericles.**
>
> — Herodotus, *Historiae* 6.131.2[36]

[32] See Pease 1920–23: 314 *ad* 1.121; and Wardle 2006: 399 *ad* 1.121.

[33] Compare "The mother of Pericles had this dream (Herodotus, *Historiae* 6, 131; Plutarch, *Pericles* 3)" (Pease) with "Pericles' mother Agariste had this dream (Herodotus, *Historiae* 6.131.2; Plutarch, *Pericles* 3.3)" (Wardle).

[34] Note the difference between 1.53.121, where Cicero refers generally to *permulta historia*, and the other historical *exempla* discussed above, where he refers specifically to Philistus (1.20.39) and Heraclides Ponticus (1.23.46).

[35] The passage reads thus: *eiusdem generis etiam illud est, **quod scribit Herodotus**, Croesi filium cum esset infans locutum; quo ostento regnum patris et domum funditus concidisse* ("Of the same kind is the following example, **which Herodotus has written**: Croesus' son spoke although he was a mute; following this portent his father's kingdom and house were utterly wiped out" 1.53.121 ~ Herodotus, *Historiae* 1.85). See Pease 1920–23: 314–15 *ad* 1.121; and Wardle 2006: 400 *ad* 1.121; as well as Pease 1920, although Wardle wrongly claims that this is "the only citation of Herodotus as a source in [the] *De divinatione*" (cf. 2.56.115–116 ~ Herodotus, *Historiae* 1.53–54 and 91, with Pease 1920–23: 535–41 *ad* 2.115–16). Cicero also explicitly refers to Herodotus (and Philistus), for example, in Cicero, *De oratore* 2.13.55–57.

[36] The translation is from Waterfield 1998.

In this passage, Herodotus offers a partial genealogy for one of the most famous and powerful families of ancient Athens, the Alcmaeonids, whose ranks included, among others, Cleisthenes, the father of Athenian democracy, and, more importantly for our purposes, Pericles (ca. 495–429 B.C.). In particular, Herodotus relates that Pericles' mother, Agariste, while pregnant by her husband, Xanthippus, had a dream in which she gave birth to a lion and that, after a few days, she gave birth to her son, a son who would later come to dominate Athenian politics for over three decades, from his initial ascent to power in 461 until his death from the plague in 429.[37]

Scholars have long debated the significance of the omen in Herodotus — whether the dream suggests that Pericles will be a blessing or a curse for Athens — but little attention seems to have been paid to the importance of the omen in Cicero for this discussion.[38] More recently, Wardle has ventured his own fresh assessment of the question, although the contrast he draws between an originally positive and a later negative interpretation of the omen is restricted rather too narrowly within the confines of Greek history and historiography (and overlooks the relevant Near Eastern evidence; see below).[39] Regardless, it is clear that the omen report in Herodotus is the ultimate source for the omen report in Cicero, even despite the shift from the narrative statement in the Greek to the conditional statement in the Latin (through Posidonius?). In particular, it is clear that *leonem peperisse visa esset* (Cicero, *De divinatione* 1.53.121) represents a close translation of ἐδόκεε δὲ λέοντα τεκεῖν (Herodotus, *Historiae* 6.131.2).[40] Where Herodotus connects the dream with the actual birth of Pericles, Cicero connects it more generally with the defeat of the city in which the woman has the dream about giving birth to the lion. Perhaps Posidonius provided the link here between the narrative and the conditional, between the legend surrounding the birth of Pericles and the lion birth dream omen, in an exegesis of the Herodotus passage somewhere in his περὶ μαντικῆς (*On Divination*). Whatever the exact circumstances of transmission, the lion birth dream omen in Cicero (*De divinatione* 1.53.121) ultimately goes back to Herodotus (*Historiae* 6.131.2).

Beyond Herodotus and Cicero, the legend surrounding the birth of Pericles also appears later in the opening chapters of the biography of the Athenian general and statesman written by the Greek philosopher and biographer Plutarch (born before A.D. 50–died after A.D. 120):

---

[37] There is abundant evidence for other lion birth omens in Greek literature, for example, Herodotus, *Historiae* 1.84.3 (cf. Pease 1920–23: 314 *ad* 1.121, and Leichty 1970: 14) and 5.92β.3, as well as Aristophanes, *Equites* 1036–44, *Thesmophoriazusae* 502–16, and *Ranae* 1417–36, along with Valerius Maximus, *Facta et dicta memorabilia* 7.2.ext.7. For other lion dream omens, see Artemidorus, *Oneirocritica* 1.24, 37; 2.12, 37; 3.66; and 4.56.

[38] For the interpretation of the dream as positive in nature, see, for example, How and Wells 1912: 2.119–20 *ad* 6.131.2; Dyson 1929; and Harvey 1966: 254 and 255 (*contra* Strasburger 1955: 16–17). For the interpretation of the dream as rather more ambiguous, see, for example, Focke 1927: 28–29; Fornara 1971: 53–54; and Scott 2005: 430–31 *ad* 6.131.2.

[39] Wardle 2006: 400 *ad* 1.121: "The potential ambiguity of her dream has been emphasized, in that the lion could symbolize great courage or regal qualities[,] or something wild and destructive (e.g., Fornara 1971: 53–54). A predominantly positive interpretation would seem probable in the original context (cf. Aristophanes, *Thesmophoriazusae* 514; see Dyson 1929: 186–94; Harvey 1966: 255; Artemidorus, *Oneirocritica* 2.12). The negative interpretation arises from the defeat of Athens in the Peloponnesian War, for which Pericles retrospectively was considered responsible."

[40] More literally, the pleonasm in εἶδε ὄψιν ἐν τῷ ὕπνῳ ἐδόκεε δὲ λέοντα τεκεῖν should be translated as "She saw a vision in her sleep, and she dreamed that she gave birth to a lion" (Herodotus, *Historiae* 6.131.2, with ἐν τῷ ὕπνῳ ~ *in somnis*, Cicero, *De divinatione* 1.21.42 and 23.46, and *in quiete*, 2.70.145, indicating that the verb δοκέω is to be understood in the sense of "to dream," just as *videor* is to be understood in the same sense in 1.21.42, 23.46; and 2.70.145).

1. Περικλῆς γὰρ ἦν τῶν μὲν φυλῶν Ἀκαμαντίδης, τῶν δὲ δήμων Χολαργεύς, οἴκου δὲ καὶ γένους τοῦ πρώτου κατ' ἀμφοτέρους. 2. Ξάνθιππος γὰρ ὁ νικήσας ἐν Μυκάλῃ τοὺς βασιλέως στρατηγοὺς ἔγημεν Ἀγαρίστην Κλεισθένους ἔγγονον, ὃς ἐξήλασε Πεισιστρατίδας καὶ κατέλυσε τὴν τυραννίδα γενναίως καὶ νόμους ἔθετο καὶ πολιτείαν ἄριστα κεκραγμένην πρὸς ὁμόνοιαν καὶ σωτηρίαν κατέστησεν. 3. **αὕτη κατὰ τοὺς ὕπνους ἔδοξε τεκεῖν λέοντα, καὶ μεθ' ἡμέρας ὀλίγας ἔτεκε Περικλέα**, τὰ μὲν ἄλλα τὴν ἰδέαν τοῦ σώματος ἄμεμπτον, προμηκη δὲ τῇ κεφαλῇ καὶ ἀσύμμετρον. 4. ὅθεν αἱ μὲν εἰκόνες αὐτοῦ σχεδὸν ἅπασαι κράνεσι περιέχονται, μὴ βουλομένων, ὡς ἔοικε, τῶν τεχνιτῶν ἐξονειδίζειν. οἱ δ' Ἀττικοὶ ποιηταὶ σχινοκέφαλον αὐτὸν ἐκάλουν· τὴν γὰρ σκίλλαν ἔστιν ὅτε καὶ σχῖνον ὀνομάζουσι.

1. Pericles belonged to the tribe of Acamantis and the deme of Cholargus, and he was descended on both sides from the noblest lineage in Athens. 2. His father was Xanthippus, who defeated the Persian generals at Mycale. His mother, Agariste, was the niece of that Cleisthenes who not only performed the noble exploit of driving out the Pisistratids and destroying their tyranny, but went on to establish laws and a constitution that was admirably balanced so as to promote harmony between the citizens and security for the whole state. 3. **Agariste once had a dream that she had given birth to a lion, and a few days later she was delivered of Pericles.** His physical features were almost perfect, the only exception being his head, which was rather long and out of proportion. 4. For this reason almost all his portraits show him wearing a helmet, since the artists apparently did not wish to taunt him with his deformity. However, the comic poets of Athens nicknamed him "*schinocephalus*" or "squill-head."

— Plutarch, *Pericles* 3.1–4[41]

In this passage, Plutarch unabashedly offers little more than a loose paraphrase of the material in Herodotus — solid evidence that he was still being closely read and directly used as a source long after Cicero.[42] With due allowance for the inevitable changes in the language during the half millennium which separates the two, αὕτη κατὰ τοὺς ὕπνους ἔδοξε τεκεῖν λέοντα, καὶ μεθ' ἡμέρας ὀλίγας ἔτεκε Περικλέα (Plutarch, *Pericles* 3.3) virtually repeats ἣ συνοικήσασά τε Ξανθίππῳ τῷ Ἀρίφρονος καὶ ἔγκυος ἐοῦσα εἶδε ὄψιν ἐν τῷ ὕπνῳ, ἐδόκεε δὲ λέοντα τεκεῖν· καὶ μετ' ὀλίγας ἡμέρας τίκτει Περικλέα Ξανθίππῳ (Herodotus, *Historiae* 6.131.2) verbatim.[43] In the lines immediately following this passage, Plutarch discusses the disproportionate shape of Pericles' head (Plutarch, *Pericles* 3.3) and cites several humorous jabs from Old Comedy in order to show how the Attic poets "capitalized" on this physical deformity (Plutarch, *Pericles* 3.4–7).[44] With due caution, I would like to suggest that Plutarch here intends a connection between Agariste's dream about Pericles' lion birth and

[41] The translation is from Scott-Kilvert 1960. See Stadter 1989: 62–66 *ad* 3.1–4.

[42] Stadter (1989: 64–65 *ad* 3.3) mentions both Herodotus, *Historiae* 6.131.2, and the controversy surrounding the interpretation of the dream of Agariste, but, like the commentators on Herodotus, he does not mention Cicero, *De divinatione* 1.53.121.

[43] Note the difference between the compressed phraseology of αὕτη κατὰ τοὺς ὕπνους ἔδοξε τεκεῖν λέοντα (Plutarch) and the expanded phraseology of ἣ ... εἶδε ὄψιν ἐν τῷ ὕπνῳ ἐδόκεε δὲ λέοντα τεκεῖν (Herodotus); cf. the treatment of Cicero, *De divinatione* 1.20.39 by Valerius Maximus, *Facta et dicta memorabilia* 1.7.ext.7 in light of Cicero, *De divinatione* 1.21.42, 23.46; and 2.70.145.

[44] Stadter (1989: 65 *ad* 3.3) notes that "P[lutarch] and the authors he quotes here are our only evidence for anything unusual in Pericles' appearance." See also Schwarze 1971; Podlecki 1987: 81–88; and Stadter 1989: lxiii–lxix.

his "leonine" appearance. The key to cementing this connection lies in Plutarch's description of Pericles' head: προμήκη δὲ τῇ κεφαλῇ καὶ ἀσύμμετρον (Plutarch, *Pericles* 3.3). On the one hand, this description accords well with ancient descriptions of a medical condition known as λεοντίασις, which is defined as an early stage of the more widely known condition ἐλεφαντίασις (Rufus apud Oribasius 45.28.2 and Pseudo-Galen, *Introductio seu medicus* 14.757.6 and 11–12 K; cf. λεόντιον, Aretaeus, *De causis et signis diuturnorum morborum* 2.13.8, as well as the related verb λεοντιάω).[45] On the other hand, Greek possesses two compound adjectives which well describe this condition, λεοντοκέφαλος ("having the head of a lion") and λεοντοπρόσωπος ("having the face of a lion"), and Lucian indeed uses the former of these adjectives in his *Hermotimus* in order to deride the Egyptians as "dog-headed and lion-headed men" (κυνοκεφάλους καὶ λεοντοκεφάλους ἀνθρώπους, 44). In short, Plutarch appears to claim that the link between Agariste's dream about giving birth to a lion and Pericles' birth a few days later lies in the physical resemblance between Pericles and the lion from the dream. If this argument stands, then Plutarch evidently interprets this dream and its relation to the subsequent birth somewhat differently from Herodotus and Cicero.

Thus far, I have limited the discussion to Cicero's *De divinatione* and a select few other passages from elsewhere in Greek and Latin literature. In the course of this discussion, I have reviewed the evidence in the dialogue for both abnormal human births (1.18.36, 1.43.98, and 1.53.121) and dreams about abnormal human births (1.21.42 and 2.70.145, as well as 1.23.46). I have devoted particular attention to the dream had by the mother of Dionysius I (1.20.39), as well as to that had by Agariste, the mother of Pericles (1.53.121). By examining the lion birth omen in 1.53.121 in light of the related omens in Herodotus' *Historiae* (6.131.2) and Plutarch's *Pericles* (3), I have sought to elucidate the meaning of this omen for each of these three writers, as well as to venture a tentative reconstruction of the circumstances of its transmission. At this point, accordingly, I will broaden the scope of inquiry in order to include not only the ancient Mediterranean, but also the ancient Near East.

ABNORMAL HUMAN BIRTHS IN THE OMEN SERIES *ŠUMMA IZBU*

Interestingly, all three of the omens recorded in *De divinatione* 1.53.121 resemble omens from one or more of the major omen series from the ancient Near East. Thus, the celestial omen reads like an entry from the series *Enūma Anu Enlil* ("When Anu and Enlil"): *si luna paulo ante solis ortum defecisset in signo Leonis, fore ut armis Dareus et Persae ab Alexandro et Macedonibus* [*proelio*] *vincerentur Dareusque moreretur* ("If an eclipse of the moon occurred a little before sunrise in the sign Leo, Darius and the Persians would be defeated militarily by Alexander and the Macedonians [in battle] and Darius would die").[46] Likewise, the terrestrial / teratological omen reads like an entry from either the series *Šumma ālu* or the

[45] Modern medicine recognizes two related conditions: leontiasis ossea and facies leonina. In addition to a series of articles published in the *British Journal of Surgery* during the middle decades of the twentieth century, see most recently Lee et al. 1996; and Maramattom 2006 (both with images of patients).

[46] Pease (1920–23: 313 *ad* 1.121) connects this omen with one in John Lydus, *De ostentis* 9 W, while Wardle (2006: 398 *ad* 1.121) also connects it with one in BM 36746 (so Wardle; more correctly, BM 36746 + 36842 + 37173), that in obv. 5′–7′ (see Rochberg-Halton 1984, especially 134 and 136 for the text and translation, respectively, of obv. 5′–7′).

series *Šumma izbu*: *et si puella nata biceps esset, seditionem in populo fore, corruptelam et adulterium domi* ("If a girl were born with two heads[,] there would be popular revolt[,] and seduction and adultery in the home").[47] Finally, the teratological / oneirological omen reads like an entry from either the series *Šumma izbu* or a Mesopotamian dream-book: *et si mulier leonem peperisse visa esset, fore ut ab exteris gentibus vinceretur ea res publica in qua id contigisset* ("If a woman dreamt that she gave birth to a lion, the country in which this had happened would be overcome by foreign nations").[48] As even this brief review of the evidence in 1.53.121 well illustrates, much of the material in the *De divinatione* reflects Cicero's knowledge about the art and the science of divination not only in the ancient Mediterranean, but also in the ancient Near East. In what follows, I again focus on the third of these three omens, the lion birth omen: in particular, I trace the history of this omen back to its origins in the lion birth omens of *Šumma izbu*.

Tablets 1–4 of the series *Šumma izbu* contain the "omens derived from human births," that is, omens derived from the birth of a child (or, in some cases, children) with any number of serious physical abnormalities.[49] This catalog of prodigies includes several lion birth omens, not only in the tablets of the "canonical" series, but also in those of the Old Babylonian version and in those of the Hittite translation of *Šumma izbu* (thence to Greece, Etruria, and Rome?):[50]

> BE MUNUS UR.MAḪ Ù.TU URU.BI DAB-*bat* **LUGAL.BI LAL-*mu***
>
> If a woman gives birth to a lion — that city will be seized; its king will be put in fetters.
>
> — *Šumma izbu* 1.5[51]

[47] Indeed, several strikingly similar omens appear in *Šumma izbu*: DIŠ *iz-bu-um* 2 SAG.DU-*šu ša la a-wa-as-sú-ú* | GIŠ.GU.ZA *i-ṣa-ab-ba-at* ("If an anomaly has two heads — a person with no right to the throne | will seize it" YOS 10 56 ii 8–9 [= omen 23]; cf. YOS 10 56 ii 11–13 [= omen 25], 35–39 [= omen 34]; and iii 21–23 [= omen 46]), as well as BE MUNUS Ù.TU-*ma* 2 SAG.DU.MEŠ-*šú* ZI *dan-nu ana* KUR ZI-*ma* LUGAL *ina* AŠ.TE-*šú* ZI-*bi* ("If a woman gives birth, and (the child) has two heads — there will be a fierce attack against the land and the king will give up his throne" *Šumma izbu* 2.20; cf. 1.48 and 74). (All translations of *Šumma izbu* are from Leichty 1970.)

[48] For dreams and dream-books in the ancient Near East, see Oppenheim 1956. In the course of his discussion about "dreams and their interpretation in the ancient Near East," Oppenheim discusses a number of dreams from Cicero's *De divinatione* (1956: 197, 208–09, and 210, cf. 206), as well as from Herodotus' *Historiae* (252), and Plutarch's *Alexander* (209) and *De Iside* (187 and 252), but he does not discuss the dream in Cicero, *De divinatione* 1.53.121.

[49] Leichty (1970: 25) identifies these tablets as an originally separate series, known by the incipit *Šumma sinništu arātma* ("If a woman is pregnant"); cf. ***mater gravida*** (Cicero, *De divinatione* 1.21.42), ***matrona*** *cupiens dubitans, essetne* **praegnans** (2.70.145), and *Dionysi mater eius ..., cum praegnans hunc ipsum Dionysium alvo contineret* (1.20.39), as well as ***matrem*** *Phalaridis* (1.23.46) and ***mulier*** (1.53.121), both of which, however, do not explicitly mention pregnancy.

[50] Fossey 1921–22: 14–17, especially 15: "Le lion est l'animal qui apparaît le plus souvent." For lions in general in the ancient Near East, see Cassin 1981; Heimpel, Ünal, and Braun-Holzinger 1987–90; and Strawn 2005.

[51] Cf. *Šumma izbu* 1.6–18. The commentary on 1.5 (1.4–6; Leichty 1970: 211) offers the following interpretation: LUGAL.BI LAL-*mu* | LAL // *ka-mu-u* ("its king will be put in fetters" | LAL // *kamû* "to put in fetters" 1.4), *ka-mu-u* | *ṣa-ba-tú* ("to put in fetters" | "to seize" 1.5), and *ka-mu-u* | *da-a-ku* ("to put in fetters" | "to kill" 1.6).

BE MUNUS Ù.TU-*ma* SAG.DU UR.MAḪ GAR **LUGAL** *dan-nu ina* KUR GÁL-*ši*

If a woman gives birth, and (the child) has a lion's head — there will be a harsh king in the land.

— *Šumma izbu* 2.1[52]

BE MUNUS Ù.TU-*ma* IGI.MEŠ-*šú* GIM IGI UR.MAḪ [...]

If a woman gives birth, and (the child's) eyes are like the eye(s) of a lion — [...].

— *Šumma izbu* 2.44′[53]

BE MUNUS Ù.TU-*ma* GEŠTU UR.MAḪ GAR LUGAL KALAG.GA *ina* KUR GÁL-*ši*

If a woman gives birth, and (the child) has the ear of a lion — there will be a harsh king in the land.

— *Šumma izbu* 3.1[54]

BE MUNUS.LUGAL Ù.TU-*ma* IGI UR.MAḪ GAR LUGAL GABA.RI NU TUK

If a woman of the palace gives birth, and (the child) has the face of a lion — the king will have no opponent.

— *Šumma izbu* 4.56[55]

DIŠ *iz-bu-um pa-ni* UR.MAḪ *ša-ki-in* LUGAL [*da*]-*an-nu-um* | *ib-ba-aš-ši-ma ma-tam ša-ti ú-na-aš*

If an anomaly has the face of a lion — there will be a harsh king, and he will weaken that land.

— YOS 10 56 i 26–27 (= omen 11)[56]

DIŠ *iz-bu-um ki-ma* UR.MAḪ *a-mu-ut* ᵐ*Na-ra-am*-ᵈEN.ZU | *ša ki-ša-tam i-bé-lu-ú*

If an anomaly is like a lion — omen of Narām-Sin who ruled the world.

— YOS 10 56 iii 8–9 (= omen 40)[57]

[52] Cf. *Šumma izbu* 2.2–8. The commentary on 2.1 (2.77; Leichty 1970: 214) offers the following interpretation: LUG[AL] | [...] ("king" | "[...]"); cf. the commentary on 1.5.

[53] Cf. *Šumma izbu* 2.45′.

[54] Cf. *Šumma izbu* 3.2–23.

[55] Cf. *Šumma izbu* 4.47–55 and 57–61.

[56] Cf. YOS 10 56 i 28–30 (= omen 12), iii 3–5 (= 38), and iii 30 (= 49). (I thank Francesca Rochberg for calling my attention to the lion birth omen in YOS 10 56 i 26–27, *per litteras electronicas*).

[57] Cf. YOS 10 56 i 6–7 (= omen 3), ii 38–39 (= 16), ii 42–43 (= 18), iii 10–11 (= 41), iii 12–13 (= 42), iii 14–15 (= 43), iii 33–34 (= 51), and iii 36–37 (= 53). Other lion omens appear in iii 26–29 (= 48) and iii 31–32 (= 50).

ták-ku SAL-[*za ḫ*]*a-a-ši* | *nu-u*[*š-ši* SAG.D]U-*SÚ ŠA* UR.MAḪ | [*ki-ša* o-o-] x -*aš* LUGAL-*uš* | [*ud-ni-i*? *an-da*?] *ki-ša*.

If a woman gives birth, | and his/her (i.e., the child's) head [is] that of a lion, | then a king of ... | will be [in? the land?].

— KBo 6.25 + KBo 13.35 vs. III 8′–11′[58]

In addition to these examples from tablets 1–4, the remaining tablets of the series *Šumma izbu* offer no fewer than 140 other lion birth omens.[59] Even a cursory examination of these entries in the series not only demonstrates the central importance of the lion birth omen in the divinatory practices of the ancient Near East, but also strengthens the probability that a knowledge of the lion birth omen eventually spread from the ancient Near East to the ancient Mediterranean. On the one hand, the protases of the omens cited above mention not only the birth of a child with the general appearance of a lion (*Šumma izbu* 1.5 and YOS 10 56 iii 8–9 [= omen 40]), but also the birth of a child with a specific leonine feature, whether it be the head (*Šumma izbu* 2.1 and KBo 6.25 + KBo 13.35 vs. III 8′–11′), the eyes (*Šumma izbu* 2.44′), the ear (*Šumma izbu* 3.1), or the face (*Šumma izbu* 4.56 and YOS 10 56 i 26–27 [=

---

[58] KBo 6.25 + KBo 13.35 = *CTH* 538–540: see Riemschneider 1970 and 2004. (The translation is my own.)

[59] The following catalog of lion birth omens covers tablets 5–24, as well as the other materials in Leichty 1970:

Tablet 5: ewe gives birth to lion (1–89, especially 51, ewe gives birth to lion with human face).

Tablet 6: ewe gives birth to lamb with face of lion (53; cf. 46–52 and 54–58).

Tablet 7: *izbu* has head of lion (1–7; cf. 8–23); *izbu* has head(s) of two lions (24; cf. 25, as well as 26–30); cheek of *izbu* has face of lion (63′–64′); izbu has teeth of lion (66′; cf. 65′ and 68′); and *izbu* has whiskers(?) of lion (67′).

Tablets 8 and 9*:* no lion birth omens.

Tablet 10: *izbu* has eyes of lion (39′; cf. 38′); eyelid of *izbu* is like eyelid of lion (40′–41′); and hair on one of the two heads of *izbu* is like hair (i.e., mane) of lion (76′–78′; cf. 79′).

Tablet 11: ear of *izbu* is like ear of lion(?) (39′, cf. 1–37, 38′, and 40′–41′) and *izbu* has hair of lion (87′).

Tablet 12: *izbu* has nose of lion (35; cf. 9–10, 15, 36, and 38).

Tablet 13: *izbu* has *sapnu* of lion (1; cf. Leichty 1970: 151–52 and CAD s.v. *sapnu*).

Tablet 14: legs of *izbu* are like paws of lion (47; cf. 41–46 and 48–54, as well as 55 and 56′–69′).

Tablets 15 and 16: no lion birth omens.

Tablet 17: *izbu* has hair of lion (59′; cf. 60′–66β) and womb of *izbu* has head of lion (76′; cf. 72′–75′ and 77′).

Tablet 18: goat gives birth to lion (16′; cf. 15′ and 17′–28′, as well as 29′ and 33′).

Tablet 19: cow gives birth to calf with paw(s) of lion (13′–16′), calf with head of lion (18′), and calf (which is?) the likeness of a lion (24′–27′, as well as 28′). Cf. also Gurney and Hulin 1964: 307 omens 30–31: see Heimpel 1973: 586–87.

Tablet 20: mare gives birth to twins with hair of lion (4′; cf. 1 and 2′), twins with paw(s?) of lion (6′; cf. 5′), twins with head of lion (10′; cf. 9′ and 11′–13′, as well as 7′–8′), and twins which are like a lion (15′; cf. 16′–17′); and mare gives birth to lion (20′; cf. 21′–25′, as well as 26′–32′).

Tablet 21: mare gives birth to *izbu* with hair of lion (6–7 and 9; cf. 8) and *izbu* with paws of lion (10–11; cf. 12–13); *izbu* of mare has paw(s?) and head of lion, and paw(s?), mouth, and head of lion (38′–39′; cf. 26–33, 34′–35′, and 36′–37′); *izbu* of mare has face of lion and tail of dog, and face of dog and tail of lion (43′–44′; cf. 45′–46′); and *izbu* of mare has paw(s?) of lion (50′; cf. 51′–52′, as well as 53′–55′).

Tablets 22, 23, and 24*:* no lion birth omens.

Cf. K. 6816 4 (Leichty 1970: 196); K. 9837 (CT 28 15) 7 (1970: 196–97); K. 8823 18 (1970: 198); K. 6743 (CT 28 13) + K. 14527 2 (1970: 198); and *aḫû* (cf. 1970: 22) 9; cf. 2–8 and 10–19 (1970: 199–200). Unfortunately, however, there are no lion birth omens in the Ugaritic translation of *Šumma izbu* (RS 24.247+ = *KTU* 1.103 + 1.145 and RS 24.302 = *KTU* 1.140); see Dietrich and Loretz 1990; and Pardee 2000.

omen 11]). On the other hand, the apodoses, all public in nature, include both "stock" (*Šumma izbu* 1.5, 2.1, 3.1, and 4.56; YOS 10 56 i 26–27; and KBo 6.25 + KBo 13.35 vs. III 8′–11′) and "historical" (YOS 10 56 iii 8–9) predictions.[60] Most of all, these omens bring us back to Cicero, Herodotus, and Plutarch.

In particular, I would like to suggest that, beyond its affinity with the famous legend surrounding the birth of Pericles, the lion birth omen reported by Cicero in *De divinatione* 1.53.121 also reflects a knowledge of the omen recorded in *Šumma izbu* 1.5: *et si mulier leonem peperisse visa esset, fore ut ab exteris gentibus vinceretur ea res publica in qua id contigisset* ~ BE MUNUS UR.MAḪ Ù.TU URU.BI DAB-*bat* **LUGAL.BI LAL-*mu***. Indeed, even a superficial comparison between the two omens reveals the stunning correspondences between them in both protasis and apodosis.[61] I am not the first, however, to bring these two passages together. In fact, nearly a century ago, Jastrow briefly remarked on the evident link between the two omens in a study of the birth omens which seems not to have attracted the attention of later scholars.[62] By and large, Jastrow correctly assesses the relationship between the two omens, from their close similarities in content and language to their "agreement" in "the exceptional character of the interpretation" of the omen not in a positive, but in a negative light. Jastrow, however, does incorrectly claim that "even the form of the omen, stating that the woman actually gave birth to a lion[,] is the same in both." While Ù.TU certainly does indicate that she actually gave birth, we have seen that *peperisse visa esset* indicates that she only dreamed that she had given birth, and not that she had actually done so.[63] The reason for

[60] Leichty (1970: 6–7) briefly discusses the relationship between protasis and apodosis in *Šumma izbu* 3.1. Later in the introduction, in the section on the "probability of natural incidence" (1970: 16–20), he analyzes the omens of tablet 3 (19–20) and concludes that 3.1 "must be interpreted metaphorically" (19): perhaps, but we have also seen that the Greeks later recognized "looking like a lion" as a valid medical condition (i.e., leontiasis), and so we may at least consider the possibility that a similar medical condition was recognized in the ancient Near East.

[61] Cf. BE MUNUS UR.MAḪ Ù.TU ~ *et si mulier leonem peperisse visa esset* (with BE ~ *si*, MUNUS ~ *mulier*, UR.MAḪ ~ *leonem*, and Ù.TU ~ *peperisse visa esset*) and URU.BI DAB-*bat* **LUGAL.BI LAL-*mu*** ~ *fore ut ab exteris gentibus vinceretur ea res publica in qua id contigisset*. If we transfer the future most vivid condition in Cicero, *De divinatione* 1.53.121, from indirect discourse in secondary sequence into direct discourse, the correspondence becomes even clearer: *si mulier leonem peperisse visa erit, ab exteris gentibus vincetur ea res publica in qua id contigerit*.

[62] Jastrow 1914: 53–54: "So, e.g., Cicero preserves the wording of such a birth-omen which presents a perfect parallel to what we find in the collections of the Babylonian-Assyrian bârû priests, to wit, that if a woman gives birth to a lion, it is an indication that the state will be vanquished by an enemy. If we compare with this a statement in a Babylonian-Assyrian text dealing with birth-omens, viz.: 'If a woman gives birth to a lion, that city will be taken, the king will be imprisoned', it will be admitted that the coincidence is too close to be accidental. The phraseology, resting upon the resemblance between man and animals, is identical. The comparison of an infant to a lion, as of a new-born lamb to a lion[,] is characteristic of the Babylonian-Assyrian divination texts and even the form of the omen, stating that the woman actually gave birth to a lion[,] is the same in both[,] while the basis of interpretation — the lion pointing to an exercise of strength — is likewise identical. Ordinarily the resemblance of the feature of an infant to a lion points to increased power on the part of the king of the country, but in the [*sic*] specific case, the omen is unfavorable also in the Babylonian text. It is the enemy who will develop power, so that the agreement between the Babylonian and Etruscan [*sic*] omen extends even to the exceptional character of the interpretation in this particular instance." For more on Cicero, see also Jastrow 1914: 54, 57, and 74.

[63] This is an important point, because Jastrow does not mention either Herodotus, *Historiae* 6.131.2 or Plutarch, *Pericles* 3. (Elsewhere, he also misinterprets the paragraph numbers in the margins of Rossbach's edition of Julius Obsequens for year-dates [these are given in the margin in AUC / B.C., beginning with 564 / 190] and, consequently, reassigns the omens to "the years 55 to 132 A.D." [1914: 51].) Conversely, neither Pease (1920–23: 314 *ad* 1.121) nor Wardle (2006: 399 *ad* 1.121) mentions Jastrow or *Šumma*

this shift from an actual birth to a dream about a birth may lie in the desire to rationalize the omen and avoid the challenge of explaining how a woman could give birth to an animal of a different species. Otherwise, the nature of the relationship between the omens in *Šumma izbu* 1.5 and Cicero, *De divinatione* 1.53.121 well illustrates how such material, in some ways, changed and, in other ways, remained the same during its transmission from east to west. On the one hand, the protasis remains essentially the same; on the other, the apodosis undergoes a substantial alteration: where the omen in *Šumma izbu* 1.5 refers to the capture of both the city and the king, the omen in *De divinatione* 1.53.121 refers only to the fall of the *res publica* (i.e., Rome). In essence, while the phenomena themselves remain the same, what they portend is continually adapted to meet the needs and expectations of each individual culture.

Until the (unlikely) discovery of a Greek, Latin, or even Etruscan translation, there is no way to prove that the texts of the major omen series traveled from the ancient Near East to the ancient Mediterranean. Nonetheless, given the existence of *Šumma izbu* materials not only in Akkadian, but also in Ugaritic, Hittite, and Hurrian, and given the extensive contacts between Greece and, later, Rome, and the areas where these languages were spoken and these texts were read, there is every reason to suppose that the omen series did make the journey along one of the many streams of tradition flowing from east to west.[64] In particular, I have sought to trace the lion birth omen recorded by Cicero in *De divinatione* 1.53.121 back to Herodotus' *Historiae* (6.131.2) and, beyond that, back to the lion birth omens recorded in *Šumma izbu* (especially 1.5). There are, no doubt, many traces of that omen series and others in *De divinatione*, as well as elsewhere in Greek and Latin literature, some already found and some still awaiting discovery.

ABBREVIATIONS

CAD	A. Leo Oppenheim et al., editors, *The Assyrian Dictionary of the Oriental Institute of the University of Chicago*
CT	Cuneiform Texts from Babylonian Tablets in the British Museum
CTH	E. Laroche, *Catalogue des textes hittites* (Paris, 1966)
KBo	Keilschrifttexte aus Boghazköi
KTU	M. Dietrich, O. Loretz, and J. Sanmartín, eds., *Die keilalphabetischen Texte aus Ugarit* (Kevelaer & Neukirchen-Vluyn, 1976)
RS	Museum siglum of the Louvre and Damascus (Ras Shamra)
STT 2	Gurney and Hulin 1964
YOS 10	Goetze 1947b

izbu 1.5. This is all the more surprising in the case of Pease, because he cites Jastrow 1914 elsewhere in his commentary (e.g., 1920–23: 314–15 *ad* 1.121; cf. Pease 1920: 201–02).

64 The very existence of the so-called Graeco-Babyloniaca further testifies to the extent of this cultural interaction; see most recently Westenholz 2007, especially 278–80 (citing Leichty 1970: 200–01, lines 11–13 of BM 41548) on the difficulties surrounding the interpretation of the evidence for the transmission of *Šumma izbu* on parchment.

BIBLIOGRAPHY

Badalì, R.

1976 "Il proemio del *De divinatione*." *Rivista di cultura classica e medioevale* 18: 27–47.

Beard, Mary

1986 "Cicero and Divination: The Formation of a Latin Discourse." *The Journal of Roman Studies* 76: 33–46.

Bloch, Raymond

1963 *Les prodiges dans l'Antiquité classique (Grèce, Étrurie et Rome)*. Mythes et religions. Paris: Presses Universitaires de France.

Bouché-Leclercq, A.

1879–82 *Histoire de la divination dans l'antiquité*. 4 volumes. Paris: Ernest Leroux. Reprint, Brussels: Culture Civilisation, 1963. Reprint, with a preface by Stella Georgoud, Collection Horos, Grenoble: J. Millon, 2003.

Cassin, Elena

1981 "Le roi et le lion." *Revue de l'histoire des religions* 198: 355–401.

Dennefeld, Ludwig, editor

1914 *Babylonisch-assyrische Geburts-Omina, zugleich ein Beitrag zur Geschichte der Medizin*. Assyriologische Bibliothek 22. Leipzig: J. C. Hinrichs.

Denyer, Nicholas

1985 "The Case against Divination: An Examination of Cicero's *De divinatione*." *Proceedings of the Cambridge Philological Society* 211 = n.s. 31: 1–10.

Dietrich, Manfred, and Oswald Loretz

1990 *Mantik in Ugarit: Keilalphabetische Texte der Opferschau, Omensammlungen, Nekromantie*. Abhandlungen zur Literatur Alt-Syrien-Palästinas 3. Münster: Ugarit-Verlag.

Durand, René

1903 "La date du 'De divinatione.'" In *Mélanges Boissier: Recueil de mémoires concernant la littérature et les antiquités romaines dédié à Gaston Boissier à l'occasion de son 80ᵉ anniversaire*, edited by A. Fontemoing, pp. 173–83. Paris: A. Fontemoing.

Dyson, G. W.

1929 "LEONTA TEKEIN." *The Classical Quarterly* 23: 186–95.

Engels, David

2007 *Das römische Vorzeichenwesen (753–27 v. Chr.): Quellen, Terminologie, Kommentar, historische Entwicklung*. Stuttgart: Franz Steiner.

Falconer, William A.

1923 Review of *La date du* "De divinatione," by M. Durand. *Classical Philology* 18: 310–27.

Focke, Friedrich

1927 *Herodot als Historiker*. Tübinger Beiträge zur Altertumswissenschaft, Heft 1. Stuttgart: W. Kohlhammer.

Fornara, Charles W.

1971 *Herodotus: An Interpretative Essay*. Oxford: Clarendon Press.

Fossey, Charles, editor

1912 *Présages assyriens tirés des naissance: Transcription, traduction, tables et commentaire*. Babyloniaca: Études de philologie assyro-babylonienne 5. Paris: Paul Geuthner.

Fossey, Charles

1921–22 *Deux principes de la divination assyro-babylonienne d'après le traité* šumma izbu. Paris: École pratique des hautes études, Section des sciences religieuses 1921–22: 1–18.

Giomini, Remo

1971 *Problemi cronologici e compositivi del* De divinatione *ciceroniano*. Rome: A. Signorelli.

1975 *M. Tulli Ciceronis scripta quae manserunt omnia*, Fasc. 46; De divinatione, De fato, Timaeus. Bibliotheca scriptorum Graecorum et Romanorum Teubneriana. Leipzig: B. G. Teubner.

Goar, Robert J.

1968 "The Purpose of *De divinatione*." *Transactions of the American Philological Association* 99: 241–48.

Goetze, Albrecht

1947a "Historical Allusions in Old Babylonian Omen Texts." *Journal of Cuneiform Studies* 1: 253–65.

1947b *Old Babylonian Omen Texts*. Yale Oriental Series 10. New Haven: Yale University Press; London: Geoffrey Cumberlege; Oxford University Press.

Guillaumont, François

1984 *Philosophe et augure: Recherches sur la théorie cicéronienne de la divination*. Collection Latomus 184. Brussels: Éditions Latomus.

2006 *Le* De divinatione *de Cicéron et les théories antiques de la divination*. Collection Latomus 298. Brussels: Éditions Latomus.

Gurney, O. R., and P. Hulin, editors

1964 *The Sultantepe Tablets*, Volume 2. Occasional Publications of the British Institute of Archaeology at Ankara 7. London: British Institute of Archaeology at Ankara.

Halliday, W. R.

1913 *Greek Divination: A Study of Its Methods and Principles*. London: Macmillan.

Harris, W. V.

2003 "Roman Opinions about the Truthfulness of Dreams." *The Journal of Roman Studies* 93: 18–34.

Hartfelder, K.

1878 *Die Quellen von Ciceros zwei Büchern* De divinatione. Beilage zum *Programm des Grossherzoglichen Gymnasiums zu Freiburg*; Programm 487. Freiburg: Universitäts-Buchdruckerei von Chr. Lehmann.

Harvey, F. D.

1966 "The Political Sympathies of Herodotus." *Historia* 15: 254–55.

Heeßel, Nils P., editor

2007 *Divinatorische Texte* I: *Terrestrische, teratologische, physiognomische und oneiromantische Omina*. Ausgrabungen der Deutschen Orient-Gesellschaft in Assur, Inschriften 9. Keilschrifttexte aus Assur literarischen Inhalts 1. Wissenschaftliche Veröffentlichung der Deutschen Orient-Gesellschaft 116. Wiesbaden: Otto Harrassowitz.

Heimpel, Wolfgang

1973 Review of *The Omen Series* šumma izbu, by Erle Leichty. *Journal of the American Oriental Society* 93: 585–87.

Heimpel, W.; A. Ünal; and E. A. Braun-Holzinger

1987–90 "Löwe." *Reallexikon der Assyriologie* 7: 80–94.

Holowchak, Mark

2002 *Ancient Science and Dreams: Oneirology in Greco-Roman Antiquity*. Lanham: University Press of America.

How, H. H., and J. Wells

1912 *A Commentary on Herodotus*. 2 volumes. Oxford: Clarendon Press.

Hunger, Johannes

1909 *Babylonische Tieromina nebst griechisch-römischen Parallelen*. Mitteilungen der Vorderasiatischen Gesellschaft 14.3. Berlin: Wolf Peiser.

Jastrow, Morris, Jr.

1914 *Babylonian-Assyrian Birth-Omens and Their Cultural Significance*. Religionsgeschichtliche Versuche und Vorarbeiten 14.5. Gießen: Verlag von Alfred Töpelmann (vormals J. Ricker).

Johnston, Sarah Iles

2008 *Ancient Greek Divination*. Blackwell Ancient Religions. Malden and Oxford: Wiley-Blackwell.

Johnston, Sarah Iles, and Peter T. Struck, editors

2005 Mantikê: *Studies in Ancient Divination*. Religions in the Graeco-Roman World 155. Leiden and Boston: Brill.

Kany-Turpin, José, editor

2005 *Signe et prédiction dans l'Antiquité. Actes du colloque international interdisciplinaire de Créteil et de Paris, 22–24 mai 2003*. Saint-Etienne: Publications de l'Université de Saint-Etienne.

Krostenko, Brian A.

2000 "Beyond (Dis)belief: Rhetorical Form and Religious Symbol in Cicero's *De divinatione*." *Transactions of the American Philological Association* 130: 353–91.

Lanzoni, Francesco

1927 "Il sogno presago della madre incinta nella letteratura medievale e antica." *Analecta Bollandiana* 45: 225–61.

Lee, Vivian S.; Michael S. Webb, Jr.; Salutario Martinez; Charles P. McKay; and George S. Leight, Jr.

1996 "Uremic leontiasis ossea: 'Bighead' Disease in Humans? Radiologic, Clinical, and Pathologic Features." *Radiology* 199.1: 233–40.

Leichty, Erle

1970 *The Omen Series* šumma izbu. Texts from Cuneiform Sources 4. Locust Valley: J. J. Augustin.

Linderski, Jerzy

1982 "Cicero and Roman Divination." *La parola del passato* 37: 12–38.

1986 "Watching the Birds: Cicero the Augur and the Augural *templa*." *Classical Philology* 81: 330–40.

Luterbacher, Franz

1904 *Der Prodigienglaube und Prodigienstil der Römer*. Eine historisch-philologische Abhandlung in neuer Bearbeitung. Beilage zum *Jahresbericht über das Gymnasium in Burgdorf*. Burgdorf: Buchdruckerei P. Eggenweiler, in Kommission bei C. Langlois et Cie.

MacBain, Bruce

1982 *Prodigy and Expiation: A Study in Religion and Politics in Republican Rome*. Collection Latomus 177. Brussels: Éditions Latomus.

Maramattom, Boby Varkey

2006 "Leontiasis ossea and Post Traumatic Cervical Cord Contusion in Polyostotic Fibrous Dysplasia." *Head and Face Medicine* 2: 24.

Maul, Stefan M.

2003 "Omina und Orakel." *Reallexikon der Assyriologie* 10: 45–88.

Momigliano, Arnaldo

1984 "The Theological Efforts of the Roman Upper Classes in the First Century B.C." *Classical Philology* 79: 199–211.

Nougayrol, Jean

1944–45 "Note sur la place des présages historiques dans l'extispicine babylonienne." *Annuaire de l'École pratique des hautes études, Section des sciences religieuses* 1944–45: 5–41.

Oppenheim, A. Leo

1956 "The Interpretation of Dreams in the Ancient Near East, with a Translation of an Assyrian Dream-book." *Transactions of the American Philosophical Society,* n.s., 46.3: 179–373.

Pardee, Dennis

2000 *Les textes rituels.* 2 volumes. Ras Shamra-Ougarit 12. Paris: Éditions Recherche sur les civilisations.

Pease, Arthur Stanley

1920 "The Son of Croesus." *Classical Philology* 15: 201–02.

1920–23 *M. Tulli Ciceronis* De divinatione. University of Illinois Studies in Language and Literature 6.2–3: 159–326 and 327–500, and 8.2–3: 153–276 and 277–474. Reprint, Darmstadt: Wissenschaftliche Buchgesellschaft, 1963 and 1973.

Podlecki, A. J.

1987 *Plutarch:* Life of Pericles. *A Companion to the Penguin Translation from* The Rise and Fall of Athens, *Translated by Ian Scott-Kilvert, published in the Penguin Classics.* London: Gerald Duckworth; Bristol Classical Press.

Rasmussen, Susanne William

2003 *Public Portents in Republican Rome. Analecta Romana Instituti Danici* Supplementa 34. Rome: 'L'Erma' di Bretschneider.

Repici, Luciana

1995 "Gli stoici e la divinazione secondo Cicerone." *Hermes* 123: 175–92.

Riemschneider, Kaspar Klaus

1970 *Babylonische Geburtsomina in hethitischer Übersetzung.* Studien zu den Boğazköy-Texten 9. Wiesbaden: Otto Harrassowitz.

2004 *Die akkadischen und hethitischen Omentexte aus Boğazköy.* Dresdner Beiträge zu Hethitologie 12. Dresden: Verlag der Technische Universität (TU) Dresden.

Rochberg-Halton, Francesca

1984 "New Evidence for the History of Astrology." *Journal of Near Eastern Studies* 43: 115–40.

2004 *The Heavenly Writing: Divination, Horoscopy, and Astronomy in Mesopotamian Culture.* Cambridge and New York: Cambridge University Press.

Rosenberger, Veit

1998 *Gezähmte Götter: Das Prodigienwesen der römischen Republik.* Stuttgart: Franz Steiner.

Schatz, Friedrich

1901 *Die griechischen Götter und die menschlichen Missgeburten.* Wiesbaden: J. F. Bergmann.

Schofield, Malcolm

1986 "Cicero for and against Divination." *The Journal of Roman Studies* 76: 47–65.

Schwarze, Joachim

1971 *Die Beurteilung des Perikles durch die attische Komödie und ihre historische und historiographische Bedeutung*. Zetemata: Monographien zur klassischen Altertumswissenschaft, Heft 51. Munich: C. H. Beck.

Scott, Lionel

2005 *Historical Commentary on Herodotus, Book 6*. *Mnemosyne* Supplementum 268. Leiden and Boston: Brill.

Scott-Kilver, Ian, translator

1960 *Plutarch: The Rise and Fall of Athens;* Theseus, Solon, Themistocles, Aristides, Cimon, Pericles, Nicias, Alcibiades, Lysander. Penguin Classics. New York: Penguin Books.

Stadter, Philip A.

1989 *A Commentary on Plutarch's* Pericles. Chapel Hill and London: University of North Carolina Press.

Steier, August

1926 "Löwe." *Paulys Realencyclopädie der klassischen Altertumswissenschaft* 13.1: 968–90.

Steiner, Paulus

1909 *Teras*. Dissertatio inauguralis. Marpurgi Cattorum.

Strasburger, Hermann

1955 "Herodot und das perikleische Athen." *Historia* 4: 1–25.

Strawn, Brent A.

2005 *What Is Stronger than a Lion? Leonine Image and Metaphor in the Hebrew Bible and the Ancient Near East*. Orbis Biblicus et Orientalis 212. Fribourg: Academic Press; Göttingen: Vandenhoeck & Ruprecht.

Thulin, C. O.

1905–09 *Die etruskische Disciplin*. 3 Parts. *Göteborgs Högskolas Årsskrift* 11 (1905); 12 (1906); and 15 (1909). Göteborg: Wettergren och Kerber.

Timpanaro, Sebastiano

1994 "Alcuni fraintendimenti del *De divinatione*." In *Nuovi contributi di filologia e storia della lingua latina*, pp. 241–64. Testi e manuali per l'insegnamento universitario del latino 38. Bologna: Pàtron.

Troiani, Lucio

1984 "La religione e Cicerone." *Rivista storica italiana* 96: 920–52.

Usener, Knut

1994 "Zur Existenz des Löwen im Griechenland der Antike: Eine Überprüfung auf dem Hintergrund biologischer Erkenntnisse." *Symbolae Osloenses* 69: 5–33.

Vigourt, Annie

2001 *Les présages impériaux d'Auguste à Domitien*. Études d'archéologie et d'histoire ancienne. Paris: De Boccard.

Walde, Christine

2001 *Antike Traumdeutung und moderne Traumforschung*. Düsseldorf: Artemis & Winkler.

Walker, Henry John, translator

2004 *Valerius Maximus:* Memorable Deeds and Sayings: *One Thousand Tales from Ancient Rome*. Indianapolis and Cambridge: Hackett.

Wardle, David, translator

2006 *Cicero:* On divination / De divinatione *Book 1*. Clarendon Ancient History Series. Oxford: Clarendon Press; New York: Oxford University Press.

Waterfield, Robin, translator

1998 *Herodotus:* The Histories. Oxford World's Classics. Oxford and New York: Oxford University Press. With an introduction and notes by Carolyn Dewald.

Westenholz, Aage

2007 "The Graeco-Babyloniaca Once Again." *Zeitschrift für Assyriologie* 97: 262–313.

Wildfang, Robin Lorsch, and Jacob Isager, editors

2000 *Divination and Portents in the Roman World*. Odense: Odense University Press.

Wülker, Ludwig

1903 *Die geschichtliche Entwicklung des Prodigienswesens bei den Römern: Studien zur Geschichte und Überlieferung der Staatsprodigien*. Inaugural-Dissertation. Leipzig: Emil Glausch.

16

PROPHECY AND OMEN DIVINATION: TWO SIDES OF THE SAME COIN

MARTTI NISSINEN, UNIVERSITY OF HELSINKI

Divination is a system of knowledge and belief that serves the purpose of the maintenance of the symbolic universe[1] in a society sharing the conviction that things happening on earth are not coincidental but managed by superhuman agents, reflecting decisions made in the world of gods or spirits. The phenomenon of divination is known from all over the world, including the ancient eastern Mediterranean cultures where it had a fundamental socioreligious significance. "For most Greeks there was no such thing as 'coincidence,'"[2] and the same can be said of ancient Mesopotamians and the Levantine peoples, whose divinatory practices are well documented.[3]

The need for divination is triggered by uncertainty, and its purpose is to become conversant with superhuman knowledge in order to "elicit answers (that is, oracles) to questions beyond the range of ordinary human understanding."[4] Divination tends to be future-oriented, not necessarily in the sense of foretelling future events, but as a method of tackling the anxiety about the insecurity of life and coping with the risk brought about by human ignorance.[5] The rationale behind divination is the belief that a necessary amount of superhuman knowledge is available to humans, especially to those acknowledged by the society as diviners by virtue of their background, education, or behavior. The role of the diviner is essentially that of an intermediary between the human and superhuman worlds.

When mapping different methods of divination, it is customary to break them down into two categories: (1) inductive methods that involve systematization of signs and omens by observing physical objects (extispicy, astrology, bird divination, etc.); and (2) non-inductive or intuitive ones, such as dreams, visions, and prophecy. In the first category, the emphasis is on the cognitive process, while inspiration or possession are seen as typical of the second category.

The distinction between technical and non-technical divination is often traced back to Plato's *Phaedrus* (244a–245a), where Socrates makes the difference between the divinely inspired knowledge based on *mania* "madness" and the divinatory *tekhnē* based on observation and calculation, strongly in favor of the former as a source of divine knowledge: according to

---

[1] For the concepts of "symbolic universe" and "universe-maintenance," see Berger and Luckmann 1989: 109–12.

[2] Flower 2008: 108.

[3] For recent discussion on divination, in addition to the contributions in the present volume, see Heintz 1997 (eastern Mediterranean world); Koch-Westenholz 1995; Pongratz-Leisten 1999; Guinan 2002; Cancik-Kirschbaum 2003; Rochberg 2004; (Mesopotamia); Eidinow 2007; Flower 2008; Johnston 2008 (Greece); Dietrich and Loretz 1990 (Ugarit); Cryer 1994; Jeffers 1996 (Hebrew Bible); and Aune 2007 (early Christianity).

[4] Tedlock 2001: 189.

[5] For the concept of "risk," see Eidinow 2007: 13–25.

his reasoning, *mania* is divinely inspired and therefore superior to a sane mind (*sōphrosynē*), which is only of human origin. As we learn from John Jacobs's article in this book, Plato's discussion on divination is known by Cicero (*De divinatione* 1.1.1–3) who addresses its significance for philosophical inquiry into the relationship of divine and human worlds, and thus can be considered another harbinger of the modern concept of divination.

Moreover, and perhaps even more fundamentally, the dichotomy of prophecy and divination goes back to the Hebrew Bible, where prophecy is the privileged way of God's communication with humans, while other forms of divination are generally condemned (e.g., Leviticus 20:6; Deuteronomy 18:9–14; Isaiah 8:19). To be sure, divination is not censured altogether: dreams, for instance, do not seem to be denounced, and the divinatory apparatus called urim and thummim is part of the high priest's sacred breastplate (Exodus 28:30; Leviticus 8:8). The elevated status of prophecy is not challenged anywhere in the biblical and early Jewish tradition, however, despite the fact that, for example, the use of Mesopotamian astrology is abundantly evidenced by the Dead Sea Scrolls and the Talmud.[6]

Plato's alleged value judgments and, especially, the outspoken antagonism toward divination in the Jewish and Christian Bible are probably the main reason why the rather depreciating word "superstition" is often used of omen divination, seldom of prophecy. Today, however, many biblical, ancient Near Eastern, and Classical scholars (and I find myself certainly among them) would agree that prophecy should not be contrapositioned with divination but should be seen as one form of it.[7] In my language, the word "prophecy" basically stands for the transmission of allegedly divine knowledge by non-technical means.[8] This definition, based on the technical/non-technical divide, works quite well with regard to biblical and ancient Near Eastern texts, but fluctuates somewhat when applied to Greek sources, as it seems that the Greek seers or prophets could sometimes divine in both ways.[9]

As a scholarly concept, "prophecy" does not cover exactly the semantic field of any divinatory vocabulary in ancient sources, where an exact counterpart to it cannot be found. In Greek, for example, the titles *prophētēs*, *mantis,* and *promantis* are used of practitioners of divination of both types,[10] which suggests that the Greeks, Socrates notwithstanding, did not necessarily classify divination according to the technical/non-technical divide. Ancient texts were not written with our definitions in mind, and applying our terminology to ancient cultures and source materials often requires certain terminological flexibility. Anthropological evidence of divination points to the same direction: inductive, intuitive, and interpretative techniques easily overlap.[11] Nevertheless, the difference between divinatory techniques remains, leaving the boundaries between prophecy (as defined above) and omen divination as represented by ancient eastern Mediterranean sources worth exploring.

I would like to approach the issue of prophecy and divination with the help of two claims of which the papers included in this volume have made me increasingly convinced of: (1) that prophecy and omen divination are not the same thing, and (2) that they nevertheless belong firmly to the same symbolic universe, that is, to a shared conceptual, intellectual, and ideological world.

---

[6] See, for example, Albani 1999; Ben-Dov and Horowitz 2005; Geller 2006.

[7] Cf. Grabbe 1995: 139–41; Kitz 2003; Cancik-Kirschbaum 2003.

[8] Nissinen 2004: 20–25.

[9] Cf. Flower 2008: 84–91.

[10] See Flower 2008: 217–18.

[11] As, for example, the Zulu diviner described by Tedlock (2001: 193), who divined through the spirits (intuitive divination), with bones (inductive divination), and with the head (interpretation).

WHY A DISTINCTION SHOULD BE MADE BETWEEN PROPHECY AND OMEN DIVINATION

To put it simply, the distinction between prophecy and omen divination should be made because most prophets probably had nothing to do with livers of sacrificial animals or with the observation of the movements of stars; to all appearances, prophecy was not a "science" by any definition. There are no traces of features that Seth Richardson found characteristic of extispicy: systematic organization of phenomena, causal association to other repeatable phenomena, creation of extensible theoretical categories, and empirical method in the employment of observation.[12] The prophets were not versed in secret lore in written form, most of them were probably illiterate,[13] and their education and initiation (of which our knowledge is virtually nonexistent[14]) must have been of totally different kind than that of the practitioners of extispicy, astrology, or exorcism.

This is not to say that the prophets were not familiar with the religious language of their communities, or that they had no techniques of accomplishing their divinatory task. Prophetic oracles were predominantly verbal messages that were believed to be of divine origin, and the language used in them indicates a thorough knowledge of the oral/aural repertoire of the religious communities within which they were produced. The specific techniques of the prophets probably had to do with achieving the altered state of consciousness that enabled them to act as mouthpieces of the divine; heuristic examples of how such techniques of mediation between human and superhuman worlds could have worked are provided by shamanistic rites.[15] The prophetic messages were more often than not accompanied by a characteristic behavior that served as their identity-marker and a cultural signifier that made it possible for the audience to acknowledge their performances as prophetic.[16] Such behavior was evidently not expected of haruspices or astrologers.

Another feature that sets the prophets apart from the diviners of the scholarly type is their social location. While the prophets regularly communicate with kings in our sources, whether Mesopotamian, West Semitic, biblical, or Greek, they usually seem not to have belonged to the innermost circle of the kings who mostly were informed of their sayings through go-betweens. Prophets were clearly not part of the *ummānūtu*. This is not to say that the prophets represented a marginalized group or that their political agency was insignificant; however, the communication between the kings and the prophets is clearly not as intensive as that between kings and the scholars who maintained a regular correspondence with each other both at Mari and in Assyria.[17] As a matter of fact, it is the Hebrew Bible where the prophets and kings get together more often than anywhere else, the recurrent problems in their mutual appreciation notwithstanding.

---

[12] Richardson, this volume.

[13] An illustrative example of this is the letter from Mari (ARM 26 414), in which a prophet has a scribe write down a message to the king; the letter in question has been preserved (ARM 26 194); see Charpin 2002: 14–15, 29–31.

[14] The biblical "call narratives" hide rather than reveal the process of becoming a prophet in ancient Israel and Judah.

[15] See Siikala 1992. For the interface of shamanism and prophecy, see Huffmon 2004.

[16] For a stereotypical prophetic behavior, see Wilson 1980: 33–42; Grabbe 1995: 108–12; Nelson 2004.

[17] Cf. Sasson 1994 and, with the assumption of a more intensive contact between the prophets and the king, Charpin 2001, 34–37.

Moreover, prophets seem to come from different backgrounds. There were probably persons whose role as a *mahhû*, *raggimu*, *nābîʾ*, *ḥōzê*, *prophētēs*, or *promantis* was more or less permanent, but we also encounter slave girls uttering prophecies,[18] as well as gender-neutral persons called *assinnu*, who feature as prophets several times.[19] The typical venue for prophetic performances is the temple, which suggests that the persons who assumed the prophetic role were more or less closely affiliated with temples, either as members of their personnel or otherwise belonging to the worshipping community. The temples of Annunitum at Mari and Dagan at Terqa, those of Ištar in Arbela and Aššur in Assur, temples of Apollo at Delphi and Didyma, and the temple of Jerusalem are well-known centers of prophetic activity, and the image of a prophet, whether biblical, Near Eastern, or Greek, virtually always shows a temple as the backdrop. This is something that cannot be said of practitioners of extispicy, at least when it comes to the second millennium and later.[20]

In Assyria in particular, prophecy was deeply rooted in the worship of Ištar, and it is probable that the Assyrian prophets were mainly recruited from her devotees.[21] This may, at least in part, explain an intriguing difference in the gestalt of the prophets in contrast with Mesopotamian omen diviners: the prophetic role was open to all sexes: women, men, and the genderless *assinnu*s. In Greece, however, the gender distinction was less strict, since there were female seers who also practised technical divination.[22]

A final difference between prophecy and omen divination is that prophecy is basically an oral performance that neither presupposed written texts nor necessarily ever took a written form. This becomes quite evident when we compare the scanty number of written prophetic oracles available to us with the cornucopia of omen compendia and other divinatory texts. But the very fact that prophecy actually *was* written down, however exceptional this might have been, is the point where the difference between prophecy and omen divination begins to reduce. Namely, when prophecy was written down, it became a document available to scholarly application; for example, the Assyrian scribes could use the prophecies in the archives of Nineveh as sources of their scribal works.[23] The Hebrew Bible, again, reflects a process of the written prophecy becoming literary prophecy through centuries of scribal exegesis especially in Second Temple Judaism.[24] The literary conglomerate of biblical prophecy can, therefore, not be straightforwardly equated with ancient Israelite or Judahite prophecy.

The literarization of prophecy resulted in an authoritative set of texts that were acknowledged as prophecy and used as a basis for further exegesis; this development begins already within the Hebrew Bible and continues in later Second Temple Judaism as demonstrated, for example by the literary phenomenon of the "rewritten Bible,"[25] and by the Dead Sea Scrolls.[26] It is here that the power of the text with an "esoteric inner coherence"[27] brings prophecy very close to the realm of omen divination. By way of their textuality, even historical events could

---

[18] E.g., ARM 26 214; SAA 16 59.

[19] ARM 26 197; 212; 213; cf. the Assyrian prophets whose gender is ambiguous in SAA 9 1.1; 1.4; 1.5. For the *assinnu* and other Mesopotamian gender-neutral persons, see Huffmon 2004; Teppo 2008; Gabbay 2008.

[20] Cf. Richardson, this volume.

[21] Parpola 1997: XLVII–XLVIII.

[22] Flower 2008: 211–15.

[23] The best example of this is Esarhaddon's Nin A inscription, which demonstrably draws on the prophecies uttered on occasion of Esarhaddon's enthronement; see Nissinen 1998: 31.

[24] See, for example, Floyd 2006.

[25] See the contributions in Laato and van Ruiten 2008.

[26] See Jassen 2008a and 2008b.

[27] Frahm, this volume.

be interpreted as signs.[28] Especially in the Qumran Pesharim, quotations from the prophetic books are used in a way reminiscent of the interpretation of omens.[29]

When prophecy once was written down, it enabled, in Scott Noegel's words, "the exegetical process as an act of performative power that legitimates and promotes the cosmological and ideological systems upon which divination is based."[30] This leads us to my second point:

WHY PROPHECY AND OMEN DIVINATION BELONG TO THE SAME SYMBOLIC UNIVERSE

All differences notwithstanding, it would be wrong to separate prophecy from omen divination in a way that suggests a fundamental disparity in their conceptual, intellectual, and ideological basis. On the contrary, I would like to argue that prophecy and omen divination represent different ways of attaining the same goal, that is, becoming conversant with the divine knowledge and judgment. According to Avi Winitzer, "extispicy, or divination in general, is nothing less than a source of revelation; its product is tantamount to the divinely revealed word";[31] without doubt, the same is true for prophecy. Just as extispicy reports are not to be seen as predictions in the first place but rather as divine judgments,[32] prophecy is not primarily foretelling the future (even though it can be predictive) but proclaiming the divine will at each particular moment, either to an individual or, as is more often than not the case, to the king and through him the whole kingdom.

From a cognitive point of view, represented in this volume by Ulla Koch,[33] prophecy, like any other form of divination, can be seen as a system of making sense of the world, dealing with social or cognitive uncertainty, obtaining otherwise inaccessible information and "to get things done, to make things right and to keep them that way." Koch's criteria for a successful divination, that is, the appropriate signs, the strategic social information, and the credibility of the process including the neutrality of the diviner and an acknowledged superhuman agent, are well applicable to the prophetic process of communication; the prophetic process, as such, is usually not *based* on signs, but signs are nevertheless mentioned in prophecies.[34]

Especially in the royal context, divination was the medium through which the king was kept informed of his location within the divinely sanctioned order of the divine favors and obligations and the origin and legitimacy of his rule; this is what Beate Pongratz-Leisten aptly calls *Herrschaftswissen*.[35] It is through divination that the king is revealed "the secrets of the gods," that is, the decisions of the divine council usually proclaimed by the goddess Ištar, such as in the oracle from Ešnunna:

> O king Ibalpiel, thus says Kititum: The secrets of the gods (*niṣrētum ša ili*) are placed before me. Because you constantly pronounce my name with your mouth, I constantly disclose the secrets of the gods to you.[36]

---

[28] Scurlock, this volume.

[29] Cf. Nissinen, forthcoming.

[30] Noegel, this volume.

[31] Winitzer, this volume; cf. Lange 2003.

[32] Rochberg, this volume.

[33] Cf. the cognitive approach to the biblical polemic against divination in Levy, forthcoming.

[34] ARM 26 207:4; 212: 1′; 237:5; 240:4; Isa. 7:11; 8:18; 19:20; 38:7, 22; Jer. 44:29; Ezek. 4:3; 20:12, 20.

[35] Pongratz-Leisten 1999.

[36] FLP 1674: 3–8; Ellis 1987: 240.

This text, among many others, demonstrates that the prophets and other diviners function as intermediaries and channels of communication for the divine knowledge necessary for the king and country to live in safety and receive divine advice in times of crisis and uncertainty. Cynthia Jean provides us in this volume with several illuminating cases of the royal use of divination, and the examples could be multiplied.[37] The entire divinatory apparatus was at the king's disposal, and from his point of view it did not matter whether the divine word came from the mouth of the prophet or an *ummānu,* provided, of course, that these persons were proved to be of accredited background.[38]

The communicative aspect of divination is highlighted by several articles of this volume. The human intermediary, the diviner or the prophet, was indeed seen as a member in the imagined chain of divine-human communication, who was there to transmit the divine knowledge. Whatever intellectual capacity was required of the diviner, it was not the diviner's knowledge and wisdom that was handed over to the people but the "secrets of gods" entrusted to him. The mouth of the diviner or prophet was speaking, not words of his or her own but of divine origin.

The role of the diviners as mediators is indicated by the Akkadian phrase *ša pî* "from the mouth": the oral tradition of scholars is referred to as *ša pî ummānī*,[39] the colophons of Assyrian prophecies indicate the speaker with the phrase "*ša pî* man/woman NN from the city X."[40] In a similar vein, the Pythia was the spokesperson (*prophētis*) of Apollo[41] who, in turn, was the *prophētēs* of his father, Zeus;[42] and in the Hebrew Bible, a standard phrase is that the word (*dābar*) of YHWH "came" to the prophet. Hence, the diviner or the prophet was literally a mouthpiece, whose personality, in theory, did not affect the knowledge to be transmitted: "Your great divinity, Šamaš, knows, I, your slave, a diviner, do not know."[43]

Such a "neutral" transmission of messages of superhuman origin was unthinkable without being influenced or inspired, even possessed, by the divine. Prophets, as we saw, were recognized by their characteristic behavior indicating the altered state of consciousness required of anyone speaking divine words; but even in extispicy, the aspect of divine presence is significant, as demonstrated in this volume by Avi Winitzer. In the words of Alan Lenzi: "the diviner experienced the presence of the divine assembly itself, which had gathered around the victim to write their judgments in the organs of the animal."[44] While the diviners hardly performed extispicy in an altered state of consciousness comparable to that of the prophets, the credibility of the process required them to be neutral agents inspired by the superhuman agent.[45]

In final analysis, even Plato, whose distinction between inspired and technical divination has been so influential in dividing diviners into technical and inspired ones, recognizes the divine inspiration of the "technical" diviners. In his dialogue with Ion, Socrates juxtaposes

[37] Jean, this volume; cf. the thorough documentation of the royal-divine communication in Pongratz-Leisten 1999 and 2003.

[38] This may be one of the reasons why the prophet's name and domicile are mentioned in the colophons of the Neo-Assyrian oracles. Even in the letters from Mari, the origin of the prophecy, if not necessarily the name of the prophet, is usually indicated.

[39] See Jean, this volume, and cf. SAA 10 8.

[40] See Parpola 1997, LXIII.

[41] Thus Plato, *Phaedrus* 244b; Euripides, *Ion* 321, 1322.

[42] Thus Aeschylus, *Eumenides* 17–19; cf. Johnston 2008: 51; Flower 2008: 86.

[43] Lambert 2007: 18:18 and passim.

[44] Lenzi 2008: 55, quoted in Noegel, this volume.

[45] Flower 2008: 91.

the diviners with the poets inspired by the Muses while arguing for the divine origin of poetry (*Ion* 534c–d):

> For not by art does the poet sing, but by power divine; had he learned by rules of art, he would have known how to speak not of one theme only, but of all; and therefore God takes away reason from poets, and uses them as his ministers, as he also uses the pronouncers of oracles and holy prophets (*khrēsmōdois kai tois mantesi tois theiois*), in order that we who hear them may know them to be speaking not of themselves, who utter these priceless words while bereft of reason (*nous mē parestin*), but that God himself is the speaker, and that through them he is addressing us.

ABBREVIATIONS

ARM 26	Durand 1988
FLP	Registration number of tablets in the collection of the Free Library of Philadelphia
SAA 9	Parpola 1997
SAA 10	Parpola 1993
SAA 16	Luukko and Van Buylaere 2002

BIBLIOGRAPHY

Albani, Matthias

1999 "Horoscopes in the Qumran Scrolls." In *The Dead Sea Scrolls after Fifty Years: A Comprehensive Assessment*, Vol. 2, edited by P. W. Flint and J. C. VanderKam, pp. 279–330. Leiden: Brill.

Aune, David E.

2007 "'Magic' in Early Christianity and Its Ancient Mediterranean Context: A Survey of Some Recent Scholarship." In *Ancient Christianity and "Magic"/Il cristianesimo antico e la "magia,"* edited by T. Nicklas and T. J. Kraus, pp. 229–94. Annali di storia dell'esegesi 24/2. Bologna: Edizioni Dehoniane.

Ben-Dov, Jonathan, and Wayne Horowitz

2005 "The Babylonian Lunar Three in Calendrical Scrolls from Qumran," *Zeitschrift für Assyriologie* 95: 104–20.

Berger, Peter L., and Thomas Luckmann

1989 *The Social Construction of Reality: A Treatise in Sociology of Knowledge*. New York: Anchor Books. Reprint, 1967.

Cancik-Kirschbaum, Eva

2003 "Prophetismus und Divination: Ein Blick auf die keilschriftlichen Quellen." In *Propheten in Mari, Assyria und Israel*, edited by M. Köckert and M. Nissinen, pp. 33–53. Forschungen zur Religion und Literatur des Alten und Neuen Testaments 201. Göttingen: Vandenhoeck & Ruprecht.

Charpin, Dominique

2001 "Prophètes et rois dans le Proche-Orient amorrite." In *Prophètes et rois: Bible et Proche-Orient*, edited by A. Lemaire, pp. 21–53. Paris: Cerf.

2002 "Prophètes et rois dans le Proche-Orient amorrite: Nouvelles données, nouvelles perspectives." In *Florilegium marianum 6: Recueil d'études à la mémoire d'André Parrot*, edited by D. Charpin and J.-M. Durand, pp. 7–38. Mémoires de Nouvelles Assyriologiques Brèves et Utilitaires 7. Paris: SEPOA.

Cryer, Frederick H.

1994 *Divination in Ancient Israel and Its Near Eastern Environment: A Socio-Historical Investigation*. Journal for the Study of the Old Testament, Supplement Series 142. Sheffield: Journal for the Study of the Old Testament Press.

Dietrich, Manfried, and Oswald Loretz

1990 *Mantik in Ugarit: Keilalphabetische Texte der Opferschau, Omensammlungen, Nekromantie*. Abhandlungen zur Literatur Alt-Syrien-Palästinas 3. Münster: Ugarit-Verlag.

Durand, Jean-Marie

1988 *Archives épistolaires de Mari* I/1. Archives Royales de Mari 26/1. Paris: Éditions recherche sur les civilisations.

Eidinow, Esther

2007 *Oracles, Curses, and Risk among the Ancient Greeks*. Oxford: Oxford University Press.

Ellis, Maria de Jong

1987 "The Goddess Kititum Speaks to King Ibalpiel: Oracle Texts from Ishchali." *MARI* 5: 235–66.

Flower, Michael Attyah

2008 *The Seer in Ancient Greece*. Berkeley: University of California Press.

Floyd, Michael H.

2006 "The Production of Prophetic Books in the Early Second Temple Period." In *Prophets, Prophecy, and Prophetic Texts in Second Temple Judaism*, edited by M. H. Floyd and R. D. Haak, pp. 276–97. Library of Hebrew Bible/Old Testament Studies 427. London: T & T Clark.

Gabbay, Uri

2008 "The Akkadian Word for 'Third Gender': The *kalû* (gala) Once Again." In *Proceedings of the 51st Rencontre Assyriologique Internationale Held at the Oriental Institute of the University of Chicago, July 18–22, 2005*, edited by R. D. Biggs, J. Myers, and M. T. Roth, pp. 49–56. Studies in Ancient Oriental Civilizations 62. Chicago: The Oriental Institute.

Geller, M. J.

2006 "Deconstructing Talmudic Magic." In *Magic and the Classical Tradition*, edited by C. Burnett and W. F. Ryan, pp. 1–18. Warburg Institute Colloquia 7. London: The Warburg Institute.

Grabbe, Lester L.

1995 *Priests, Prophets, Diviners, Sages: A Socio-Historical Study of Religious Specialists in Ancient Israel.* Valley Forge: Trinity Press International.

Guinan, Ann

2002 "A Severed Head Laughed: Stories of Divinatory Interpretation." In *Magic and Divination in the Ancient World*, edited by L. Ciraolo and J. Seidel, pp. 7–40. Ancient Magic and Divination 2. Groningen: Styx.

Heintz, Jean-Georges, editor

1997 *Oracles et prophéties dans l'antiquité. Actes du Colloque de Strasbourg, 15–17 Juin 1995.* Université des sciences humaines de Strasbourg, Travaux du Centre de recherche sur le Proche-Orient et la Grèce antiques 15. Paris: de Boccard.

Huffmon, Herbert B.

2004 "The *assinnum* as Prophet: Shamans at Mari?" In *Nomades et sédentaires dans le Proche-Orient ancien*, edited by C. Nicolle, pp. 241–47. Amurru 3. Paris: Éditions Recherche sur les Civilisations.

Jassen, Alex P.

2008a "The Presentation of Ancient Prophets as Lawgivers at Qumran." *Journal of Biblical Literature* 127: 307–37.

2008b "Prophets and Prophecy in the Qumran Community." *AJS Review* 37: 299–334.

Jeffers, Ann

1996 *Magic and Divination in Ancient Palestine and Syria.* Studies in the History and Culture of the Ancient Near East 8. Leiden: Brill.

Johnston, Sarah Iles

2008 *Ancient Greek Divination.* Blackwell Ancient Religions. Chichester: Wiley-Blackwell.

Kitz, Anne Marie

2003 "Prophecy as Divination." *Catholic Biblical Quarterly* 65: 22–42.

Koch-Westenholz, Ulla

1995 *Mesopotamian Astrology: An Introduction to Babylonian and Assyrian Celestial Divination.* CNI Publications 19. Copenhagen: Museum Tusculanum Press.

Laato, Antti, and Jacques van Ruiten, editors

2008 *Rewritten Bible Reconsidered: Proceedings of the Conference in Karkku, Finland, August 24–26, 2006.* Studies in Rewritten Bible 1. Turku: Åbo Akademi Press; Winona Lake: Eisenbrauns.

Lambert, W. G.

2007 *Babylonian Oracle Questions*. Winona Lake: Eisenbrauns.

Lange, Armin

2003 "Interpretation als Offenbarung: Zum Verhältnis von Schriftauslegung und Offenbarung." In *Wisdom and Apocalypticism in the Dead Sea Scrolls and in the Biblical Tradition*, edited by F. García Martínez, pp. 17–33. Bibliotheca Ephemeridum theologicarum Lovaniensium 168. Leuven: Peeters.

Lenzi, Alan

2008 *Secrecy and the Gods: Secret Knowledge in Ancient Mesopotamia and Biblical Israel*. State Archives of Assyria Studies 19. Helsinki: Neo-Assyrian Text Corpus Project.

Levy, Gabriel

Forthcoming "The Biblical Polemic against Divination in Light of the Domestication of Folk Psychology." In *Unveiling the Hidden: Interdisciplinary Perspectives on Divination*, edited by A. Lisdorf and K. Munk. Berlin: Walter De Gruyter. Available at www.csr-arc.com/view.php?arc=6

Luukko, Mikko, and Greta Van Buylaere

2002 *The Political Correspondence of Esarhaddon*. State Archives of Assyria 16. Helsinki: Helsinki University Press.

Nelson, Richard D.

2004 "Priestly Purity and Prophetic Lunacy: Hosea 1:2–3 and 9:7." In *The Priests in the Prophets: The Portrayal of Priests, Prophets, and Other Religious Specialists in the Latter Prophets*, edited by L. L. Grabbe and A. Ogden Bellis, pp. 115–33. Journal for the Study of the Old Testament, Supplement Series 408. London: T & T Clark.

Nissinen, Martti

1998 *References to Prophecy in Neo-Assyrian Sources*. State Archives of Assyria Studies 7. Helsinki: Neo-Assyrian Text Corpus Project.

2004 "What Is Prophecy? An Ancient Near Eastern Perspective." In *Inspired Speech: Prophecy in the Ancient Near East, Essays in Honor of Herbert B. Huffmon*, edited by J. Kaltner and L. Stulman, pp. 17–37. Journal for the Study of the Old Testament, Supplement Series 378. London: T & T Clark.

Forthcoming "Pesharim as Divination: Qumran Exegesis, Omen Interpretation and Literary Prophecy." In *On Prophecy in the Dead Sea Scrolls and in the Hebrew Bible*, edited by K. de Troyer and A. Lange. Leuven: Peeters.

Parpola, Simo

1993 *Letters from Assyrian and Babylonian Scholars*. State Archives of Assyria 10. Helsinki: Helsinki University Press.

1997 *Assyrian Prophecies*. State Archives of Assyria 9. Helsinki: Helsinki University Press.

Pongratz-Leisten, Beate

1999 *Herrschaftswissen in Mesopotamien: Formen der Kommunikation zwischen Gott und König im 2. und 1. Jahrtausend v. Chr*. State Archives of Assyria Studies 10. Helsinki: Neo-Assyrian Text Corpus Project.

2003 "When Gods Are Speaking: Toward Defining the Interface between Polytheism and Monotheism." In *Propheten in Mari, Assyria und Israel*, edited by M. Köckert and M. Nissinen, pp. 132–68. Forschungen zur Religion und Literatur des Alten und Neuen Testaments 201. Göttingen: Vandenhoeck & Ruprecht.

Rochberg, Francesca

2004 *The Heavenly Writing: Divination, Horoscopy, and Astronomy in Mesopotamian Culture*. Cambridge: Cambridge University Press.

Sasson, Jack M.

1994 "The Posting of Letters with Divine Messages." In *Florilegium Marianum 2: Recueil d'études à la mémoire de Maurice Birot,* edited by D. Charpin and J.-M. Durand, pp. 299–316. Mémoires de Nouvelles Assyriologiques Brèves et Utilitaires 3. Paris: SEPOA.

Siikala, Anna-Leena

1992 "The Siberian Shaman's Technique of Ecstasy." In *Studies on Shamanism*, edited by A.-L. Siikala and M. Hoppál, pp. 26–40. Ethnologica Uralica 2. Helsinki: Finnish Anthropological Society; Budapest: Akadémiai Kiadó.

Tedlock, Barbara

2001 "Divination as a Way of Knowing: Embodiment, Visualisation, Narrative, and Interpretation." *Folklore* 112: 189–97.

Teppo, Saana

2008 "Sacred Marriage and the Devotees of Ištar." In *Sacred Marriages: The Divine-Human Sexual Metaphor from Sumer to Early Christianity*, edited by M. Nissinen and R. Uro, pp. 75–92. Winona Lake: Eisenbrauns.

Wilson, Robert R.

1980 *Prophecy and Society in Ancient Israel.* Philadelphia: Fortress Press.